メガ
me

⑥

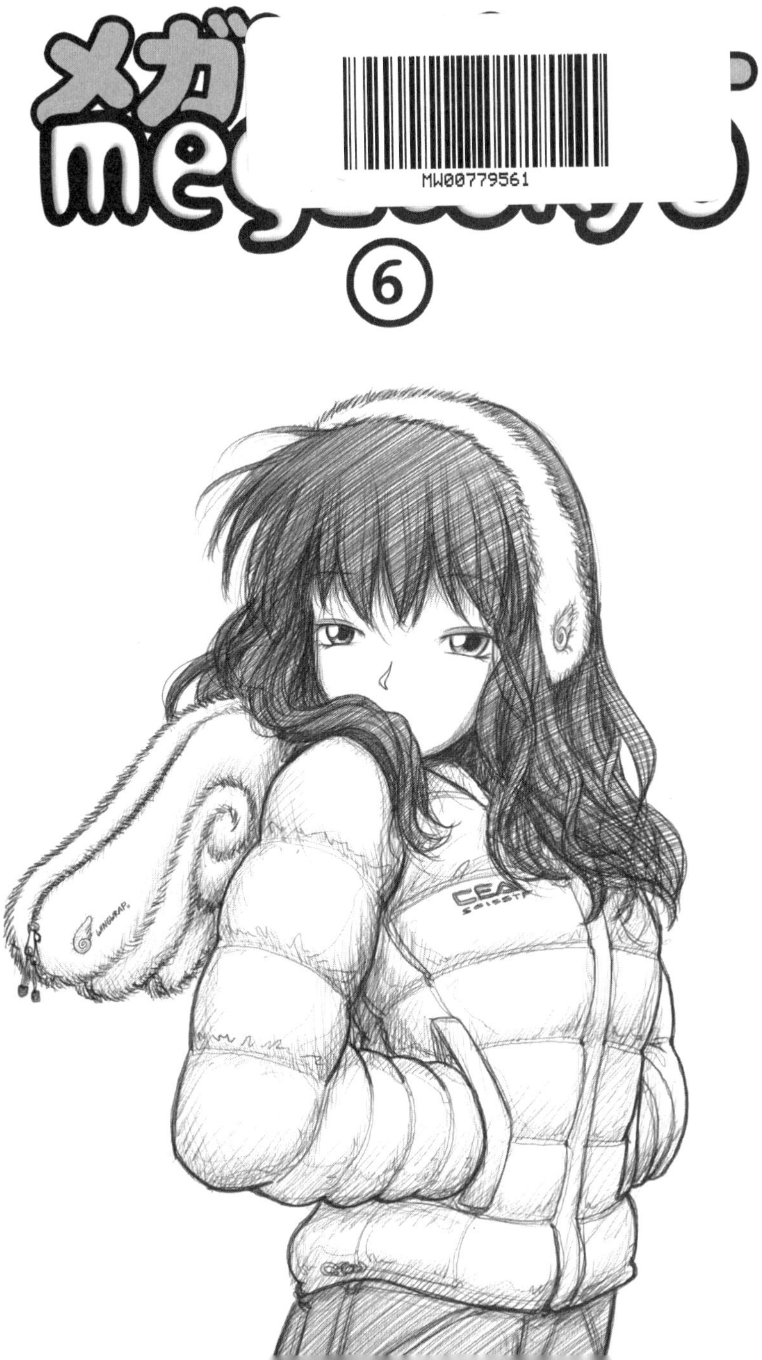

Fred Gallagher & Larry Berry
Design
Chynna Clugston Flores
Assistant Editor
Jim Chadwick
Editor

Diane Nelson
President
Dan DiDio and Jim Lee
Co-Publishers
Geoff Johns
Chief Creative Officer
John Rood
Executive Vice President–Sales,
Marketing and Business Development
Patrick Caldon
Executive Vice President–Finance
and Administration
Amy Genkins
Senior VP–Business and Legal Affairs
Steve Rotterdam
Senior VP–Sales and Marketing
John Cunningham
VP–Marketing
Terri Cunningham
VP–Managing Editor
Alison Gill
VP–Manufacturing
David Hyde
VP–Publicity
Hank Kanalz
VP–General Manager, WildStorm
Sue Pohja
VP–Book Trade Sales
Alysse Soll
VP–Advertising and Custom Publishing
Bob Wayne
VP–Sales
Mark Chiarello
Art Director

ISBN: 978-1-4012-2481-3

SUSTAINABLE FORESTRY INITIATIVE — Certified Fiber Sourcing — www.sfiprogram.org

メガトーキョー
megatokyo
6

RAWR!! RAWR! RAWR! RAWR! RAWR! R4WR! RAWR! RAWR! R4WR! RAWR! RAWR! RRRAR! R4WR! RAWR! RAWR! R4WR! RAWR!

story & art

FRED GALLAGHER

www.megatokyo.com

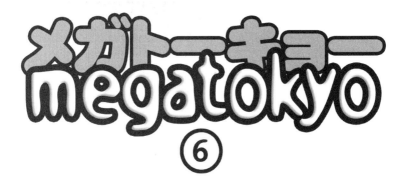

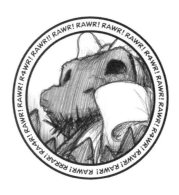

For Jack, who arrived somewhere
in the middle of Chapter 9 -
This is what your Dad was always working on :)

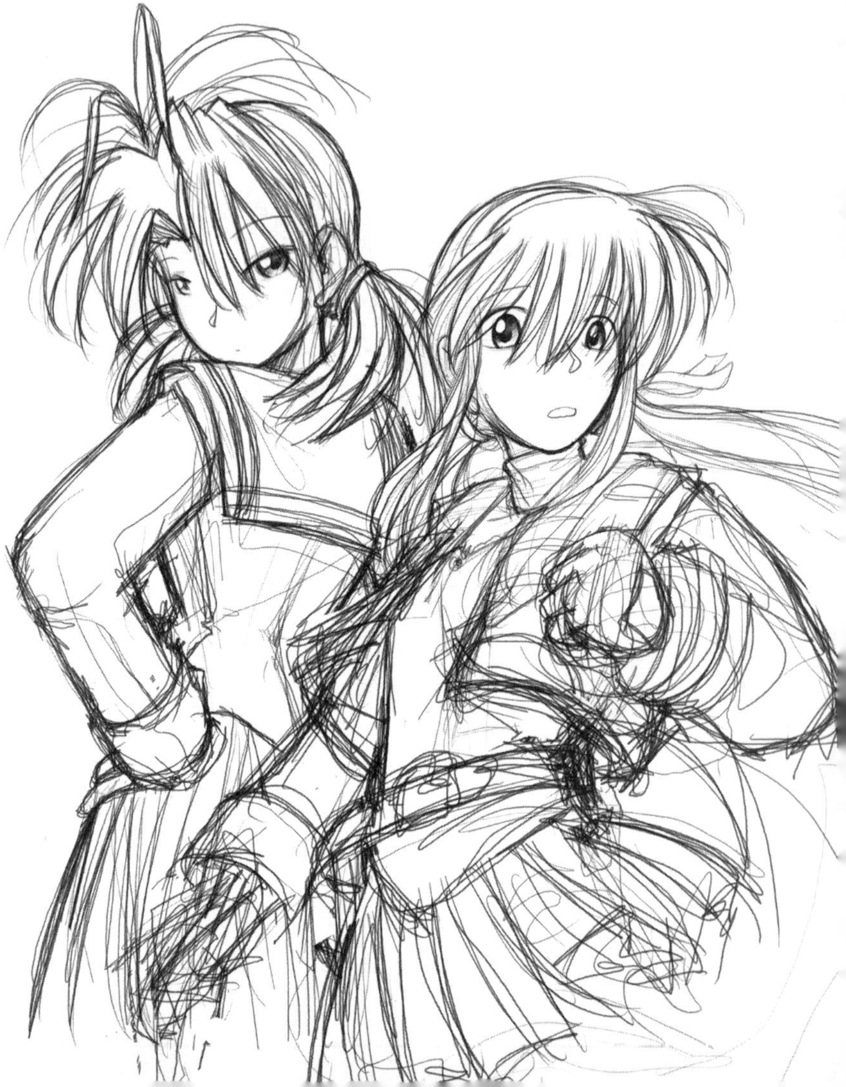

CONTENTS

freetalk-10years_of_MT.txt

It was 10 years ago in August 2000 that Rodney and I posted the very first Megatokyo comic. After a link and some kind words from Penny Arcade, we soon found ourselves flooded with readers and I've been trying to catch up ever since.

A lot has happened in those 10 years. Rodney and I parted ways and I continued doing MT on my own. MT was published across five volumes (now six) and became one of the best selling Original English Language (OEL) manga titles. We opened our own online store, Megagear. My art improved somewhat. MT became the first OEL manga published in Japan by Kodansha... It's all far more than I can cover with just one Fr33Talk page.

Why only one page of Fr33Talk at the beginning of this volume? Well, it's been about three years since Volume 5 came out and I soon realized I was quickly running out of pages: Two *very* long chapters, *two* omake episodes AND a series of 4-panel comics drawn by my friend Hawk... Thankfully, we were able to add more pages, resulting in the biggest MT volume yet.

A lot has happened in the 3 years since Volume 5, including a most substantial event - around page 71 to be exact. This had a slight impact on my posting schedule and it was a small factor in why many comics were originally posted in various unfinished states. It took a lot of work, but I managed to finish and fix up all those comics for this book.

A lot happens in the two days (9 days apart) covered in the two chapters in this book. If you've been reading online or you have been waiting for this book to read these chapters, I hope you enjoy them. It took three of the 10 years I've been working on Megatokyo to cover these two days. Hopefully, it was worth the wait.

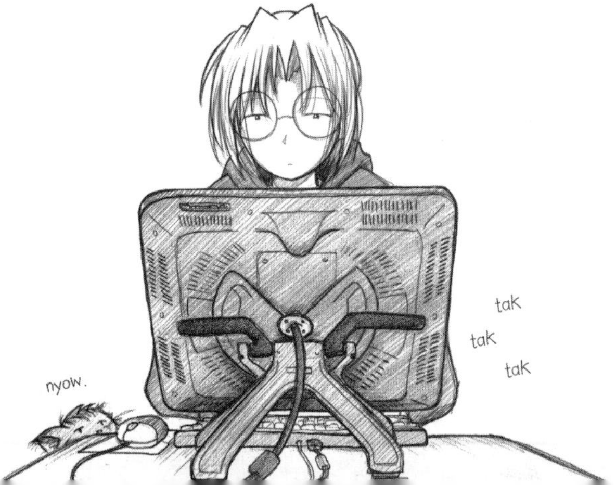
tak
tak
tak
nyow.

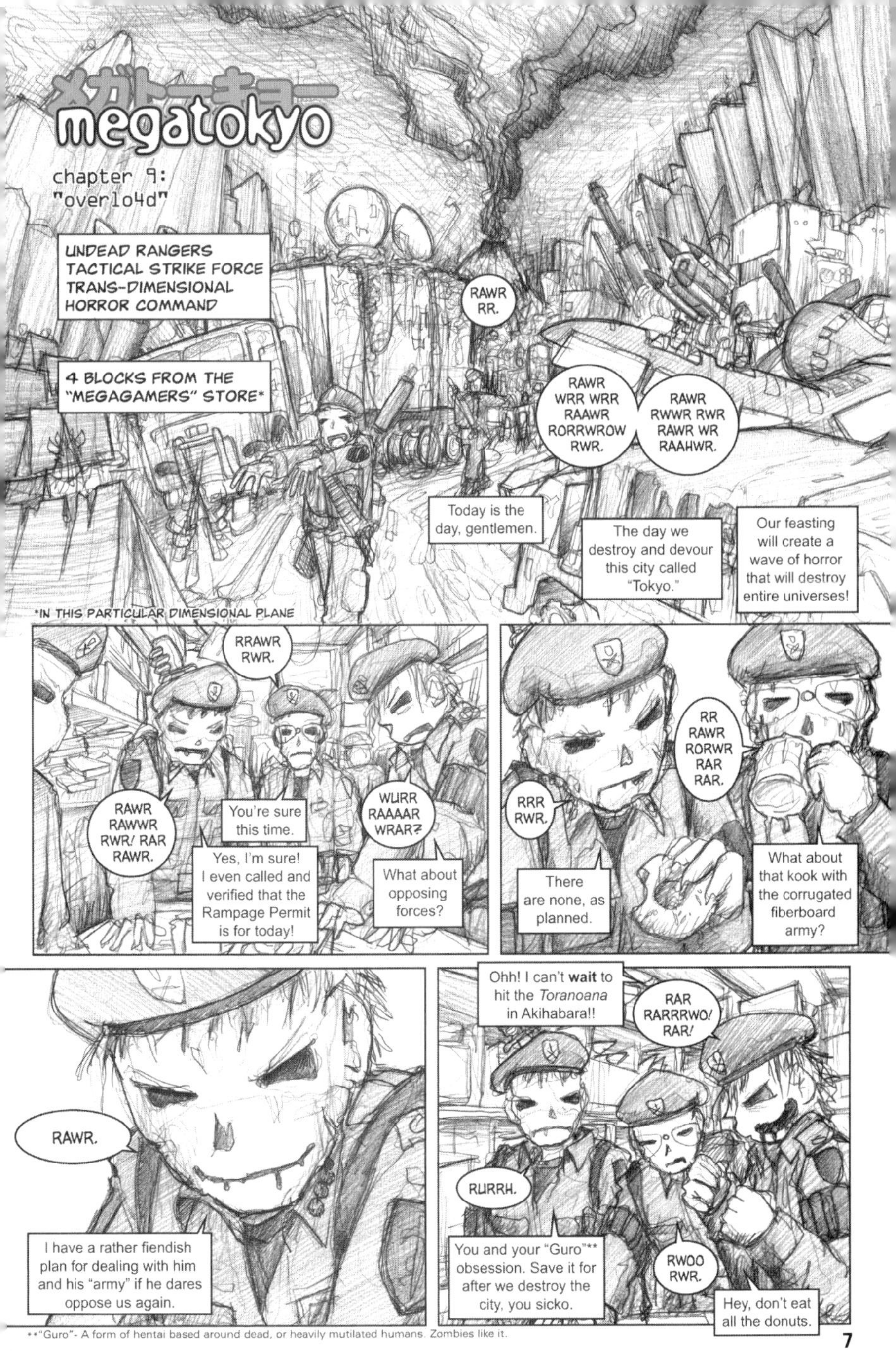

メガトーキョー
megatokyo
chapter 9: "overlo4d"
UNDEAD RANGERS TACTICAL STRIKE FORCE TRANS-DIMENSIONAL HORROR COMMAND
4 BLOCKS FROM THE "MEGAGAMERS" STORE*
RAWR RR.
RAWR WRR WRR RAAWR RORRWROW RWR.
RAWR RWWR RWR RAWR WR RAAHWR.
Today is the day, gentlemen.
The day we destroy and devour this city called "Tokyo."
Our feasting will create a wave of horror that will destroy entire universes!
*IN THIS PARTICULAR DIMENSIONAL PLANE
RRAWR RWR.
RAWR RAWWR RWR! RAR RAWR.
You're sure this time.
Yes, I'm sure! I even called and verified that the Rampage Permit is for today!
WURR RAAAAR WRAR?
What about opposing forces?
RR RAWR RORWR RAR RAR.
RRR RWR.
There are none, as planned.
What about that kook with the corrugated fiberboard army?
RAWR.
I have a rather fiendish plan for dealing with him and his "army" if he dares oppose us again.
Ohh! I can't **wait** to hit the *Toranoana* in Akihabara!!
RAR RARRRWO! RAR!
RURRH.
You and your "Guro"** obsession. Save it for after we destroy the city, you sicko.
RWOO RWR.
Hey, don't eat all the donuts.

**"Guro"- A form of hentai based around dead, or heavily mutilated humans. Zombies like it.

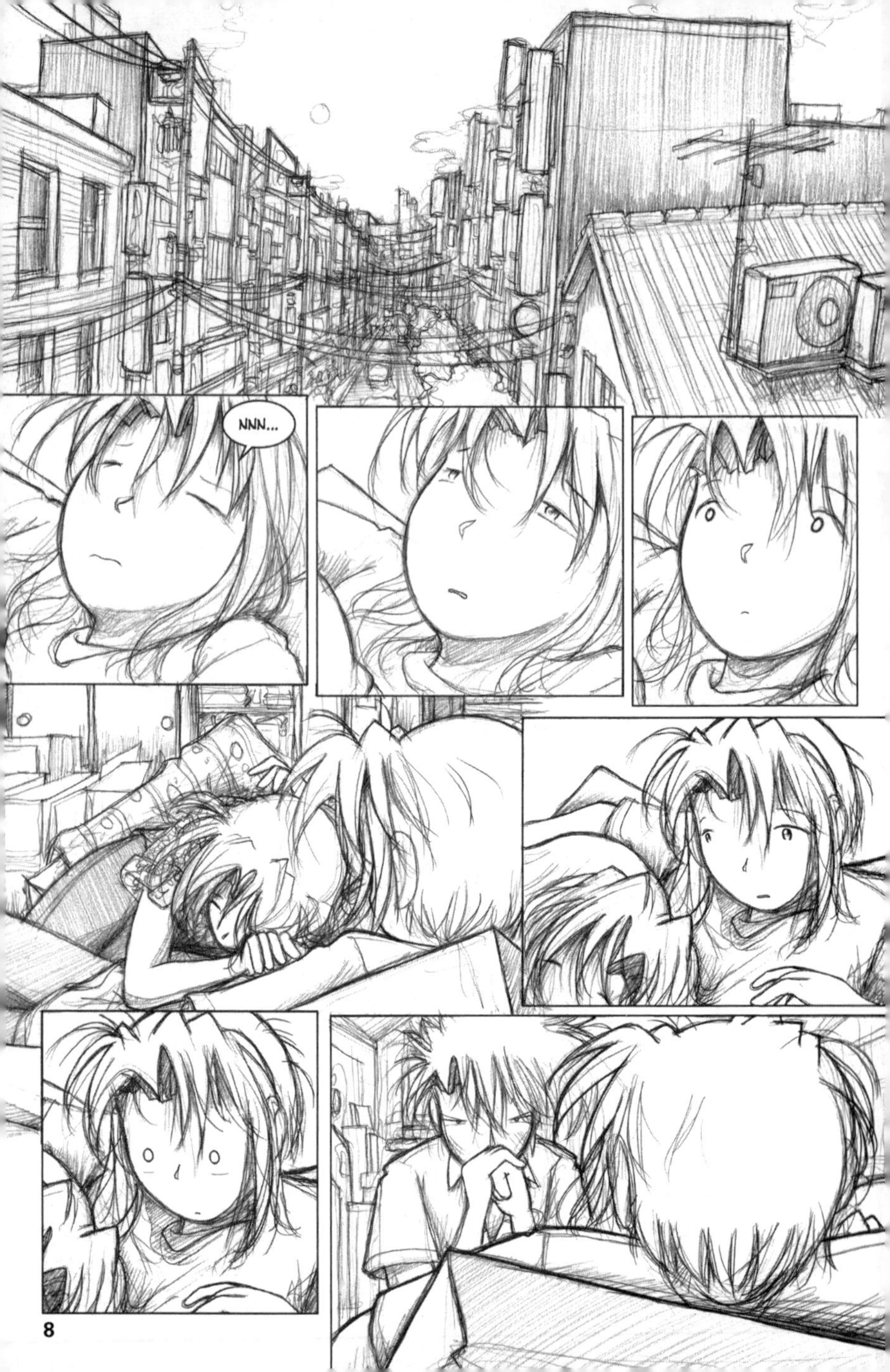
NNN...

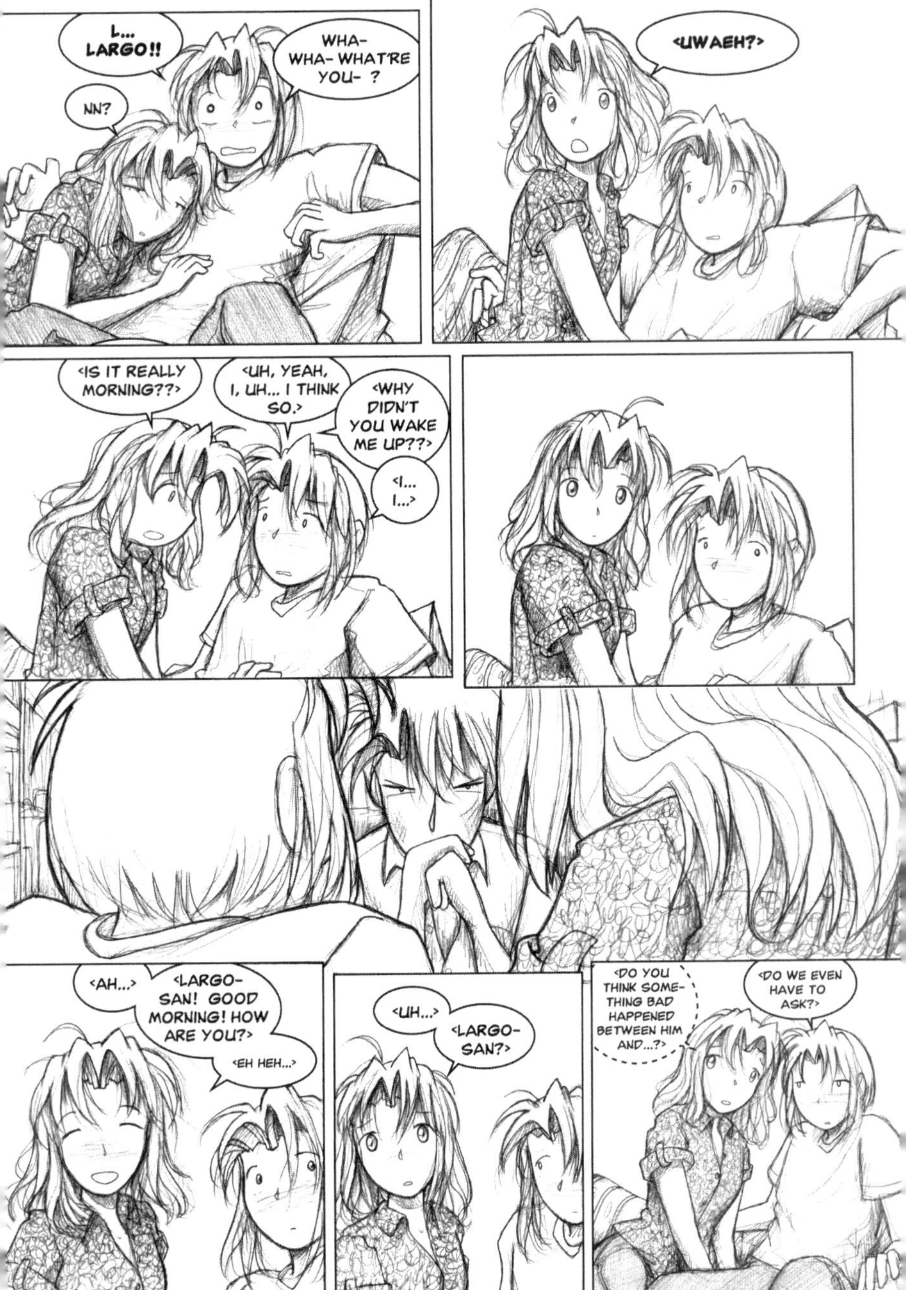
L... LARGO!!
WHA- WHA- WHAT'RE YOU- ?
NN?
<UWAEH?>
<IS IT REALLY MORNING??>
<UH, YEAH, I, UH... I THINK SO.>
<WHY DIDN'T YOU WAKE ME UP??>
<I... I...>
<AH...>
<LARGO-SAN! GOOD MORNING! HOW ARE YOU?>
<EH HEH...>
<UH...>
<LARGO-SAN?>
<DO YOU THINK SOME-THING BAD HAPPENED BETWEEN HIM AND...?>
<DO WE EVEN HAVE TO ASK?>

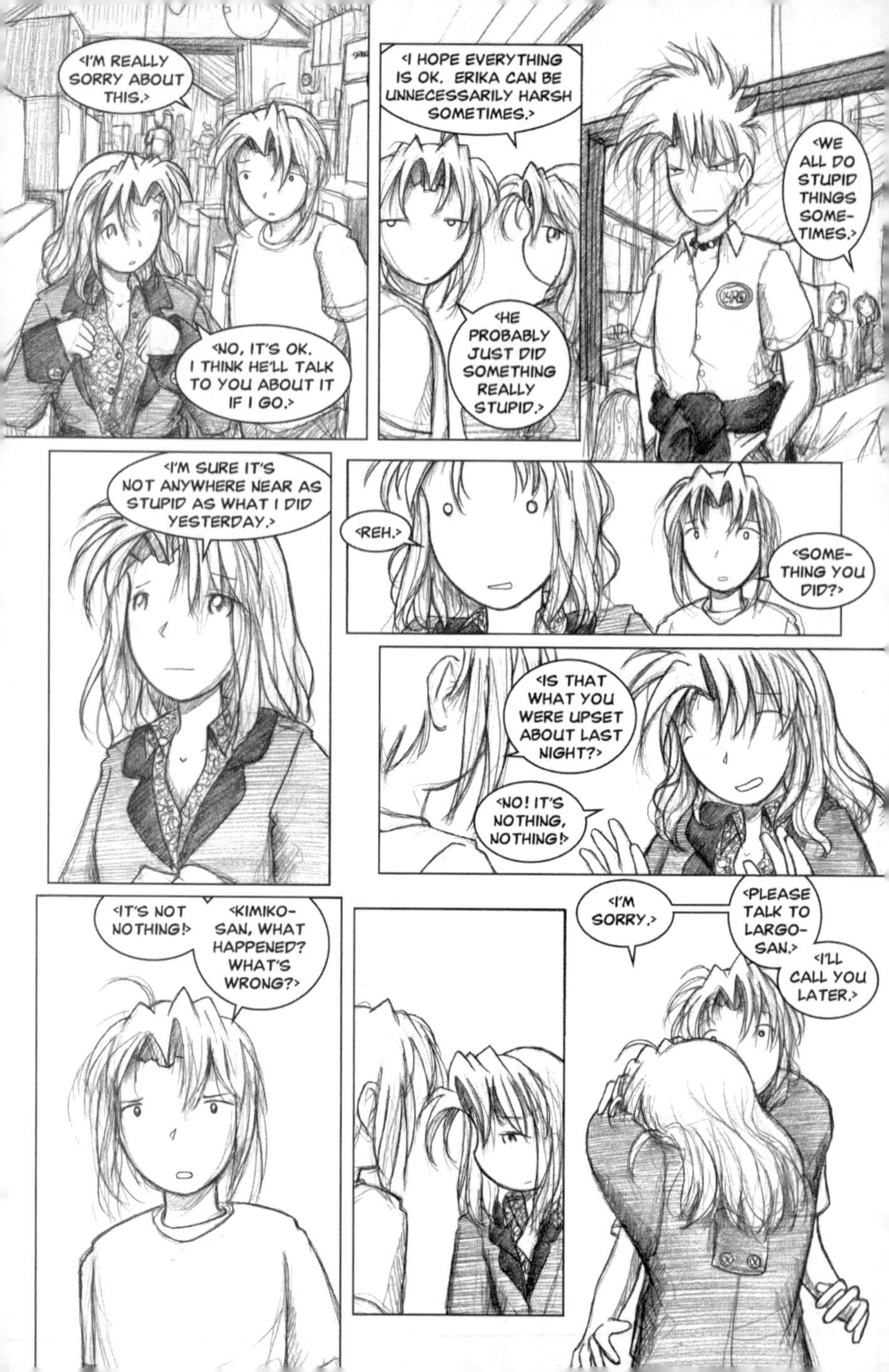

<I'M REALLY SORRY ABOUT THIS.>
<NO, IT'S OK. I THINK HE'LL TALK TO YOU ABOUT IT IF I GO.>
<I HOPE EVERYTHING IS OK. ERIKA CAN BE UNNECESSARILY HARSH SOMETIMES.>
<HE PROBABLY JUST DID SOMETHING REALLY STUPID.>
<WE ALL DO STUPID THINGS SOME-TIMES.>
<I'M SURE IT'S NOT ANYWHERE NEAR AS STUPID AS WHAT I DID YESTERDAY.>
<REH.>
<SOME-THING YOU DID?>
<IS THAT WHAT YOU WERE UPSET ABOUT LAST NIGHT?>
<NO! IT'S NOTHING, NOTHING!>
<IT'S NOT NOTHING!>
<KIMIKO-SAN, WHAT HAPPENED? WHAT'S WRONG?>
<I'M SORRY.>
<PLEASE TALK TO LARGO-SAN.>
<I'LL CALL YOU LATER.>

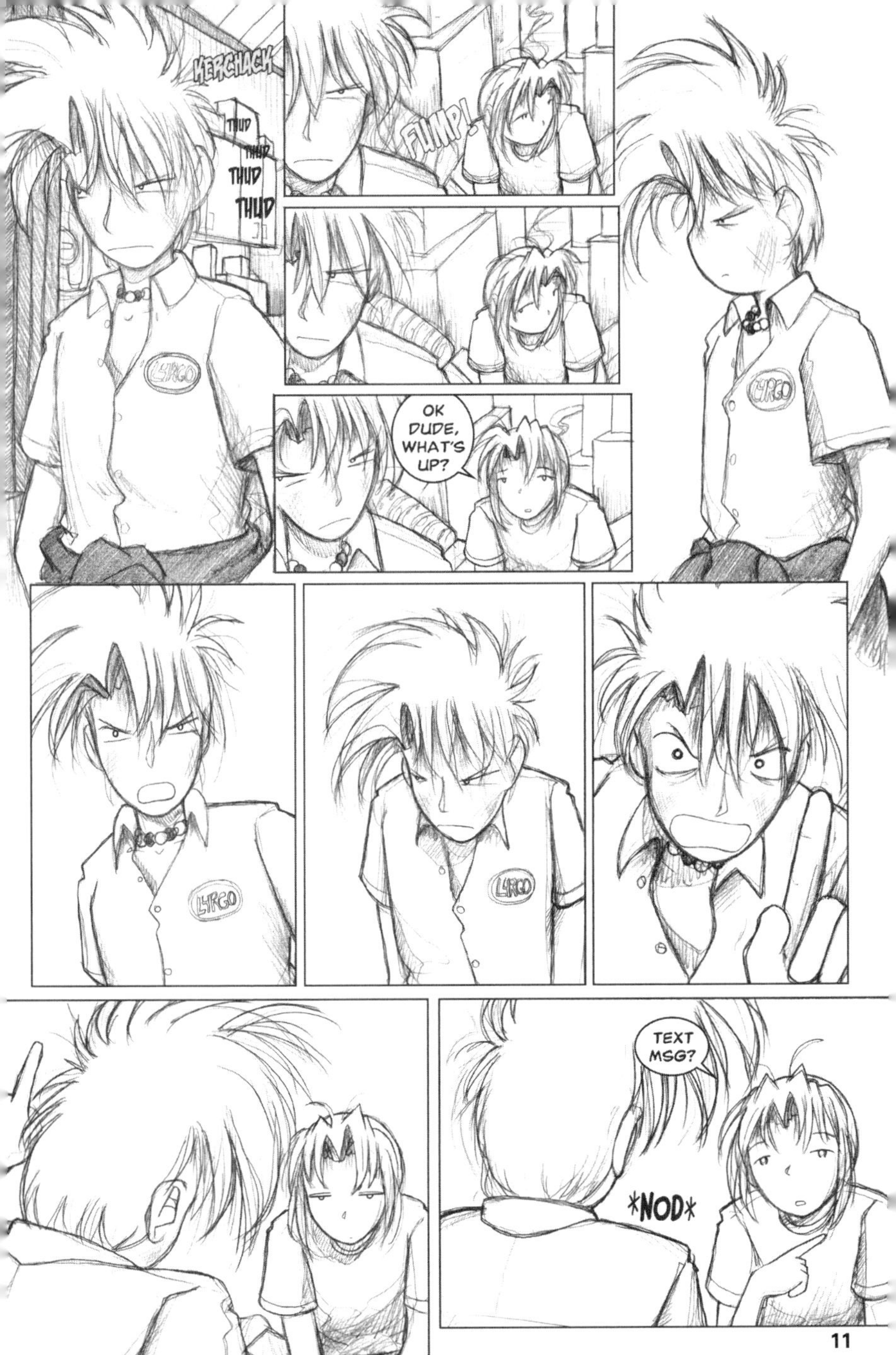
KERCHACK
THUD
THUD
THUD
THUD
FUMP!
OK DUDE, WHAT'S UP?
TEXT MSG?
NOD

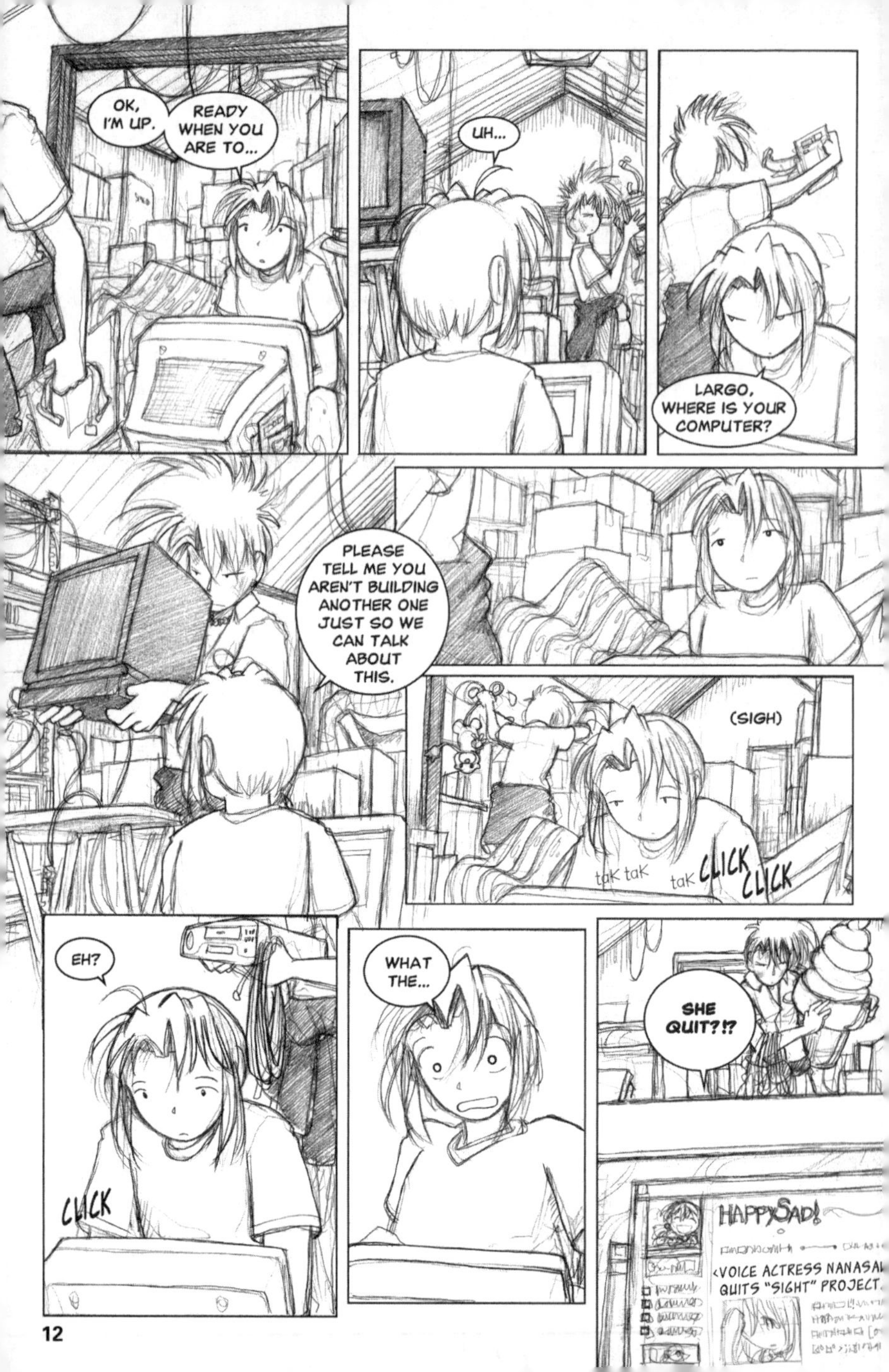
OK, I'M UP.
READY WHEN YOU ARE TO...
UH...
LARGO, WHERE IS YOUR COMPUTER?
PLEASE TELL ME YOU AREN'T BUILDING ANOTHER ONE JUST SO WE CAN TALK ABOUT THIS.
(SIGH)
tak tak tak CLICK CLICK
EH?
CLICK
WHAT THE...
SHE QUIT?!?
HAPPYxSAD!
<VOICE ACTRESS NANASA
QUITS "SIGHT" PROJECT.

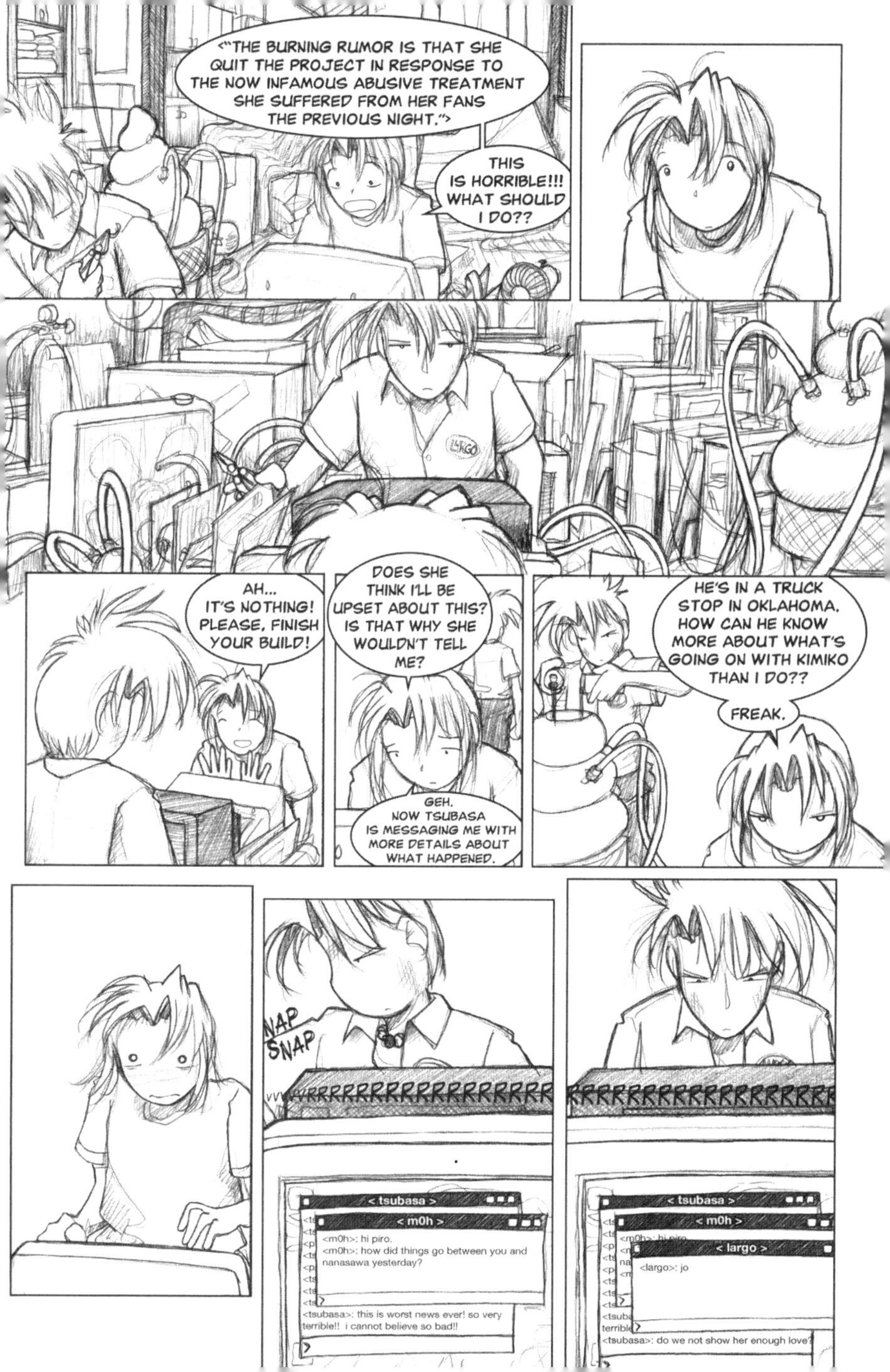
<"THE BURNING RUMOR IS THAT SHE QUIT THE PROJECT IN RESPONSE TO THE NOW INFAMOUS ABUSIVE TREATMENT SHE SUFFERED FROM HER FANS THE PREVIOUS NIGHT.">
THIS IS HORRIBLE!!! WHAT SHOULD I DO??
AH... IT'S NOTHING! PLEASE, FINISH YOUR BUILD!
DOES SHE THINK I'LL BE UPSET ABOUT THIS? IS THAT WHY SHE WOULDN'T TELL ME?
GEH. NOW TSUBASA IS MESSAGING ME WITH MORE DETAILS ABOUT WHAT HAPPENED.
HE'S IN A TRUCK STOP IN OKLAHOMA. HOW CAN HE KNOW MORE ABOUT WHAT'S GOING ON WITH KIMIKO THAN I DO??
FREAK.
NAP
SNAP
VVVVRRRRRRRRRRRRRRRRRR
< tsubasa >
< m0h >
<m0h>: hi piro.
<m0h>: how did things go between you and nanasawa yesterday?
<tsubasa>: this is worst news ever! so very terrible!! i cannot believe so bad!!
RRRRRRRRRRRRRRRRRRR
< tsubasa >
< m0h >
< largo >
<largo>: jo
<tsubasa>: do we not show her enough love?

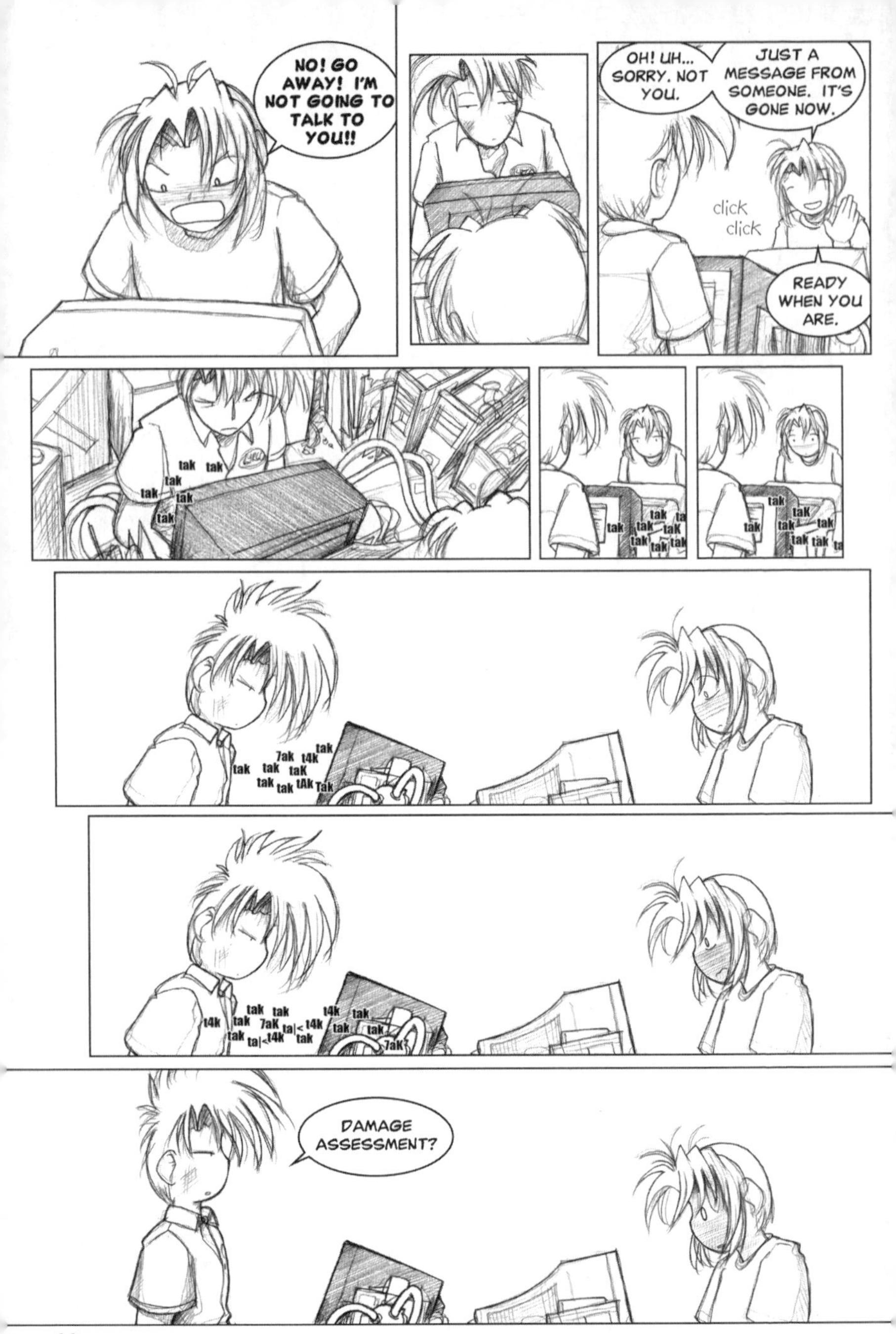
NO! GO AWAY! I'M NOT GOING TO TALK TO YOU!!
OH! UH... SORRY. NOT YOU.
JUST A MESSAGE FROM SOMEONE. IT'S GONE NOW.
click click
READY WHEN YOU ARE.
tak tak tak tak tak tak
tak tak tak tak tak tak tak
tak tak tak tak tak tak tak
tak 7ak t4k tak tak tak taK tak tak tAk Tak
t4k tak tak tak 7aK ta|< t4k tak t4k tak tak ta|< tak 7aK
DAMAGE ASSESSMENT?

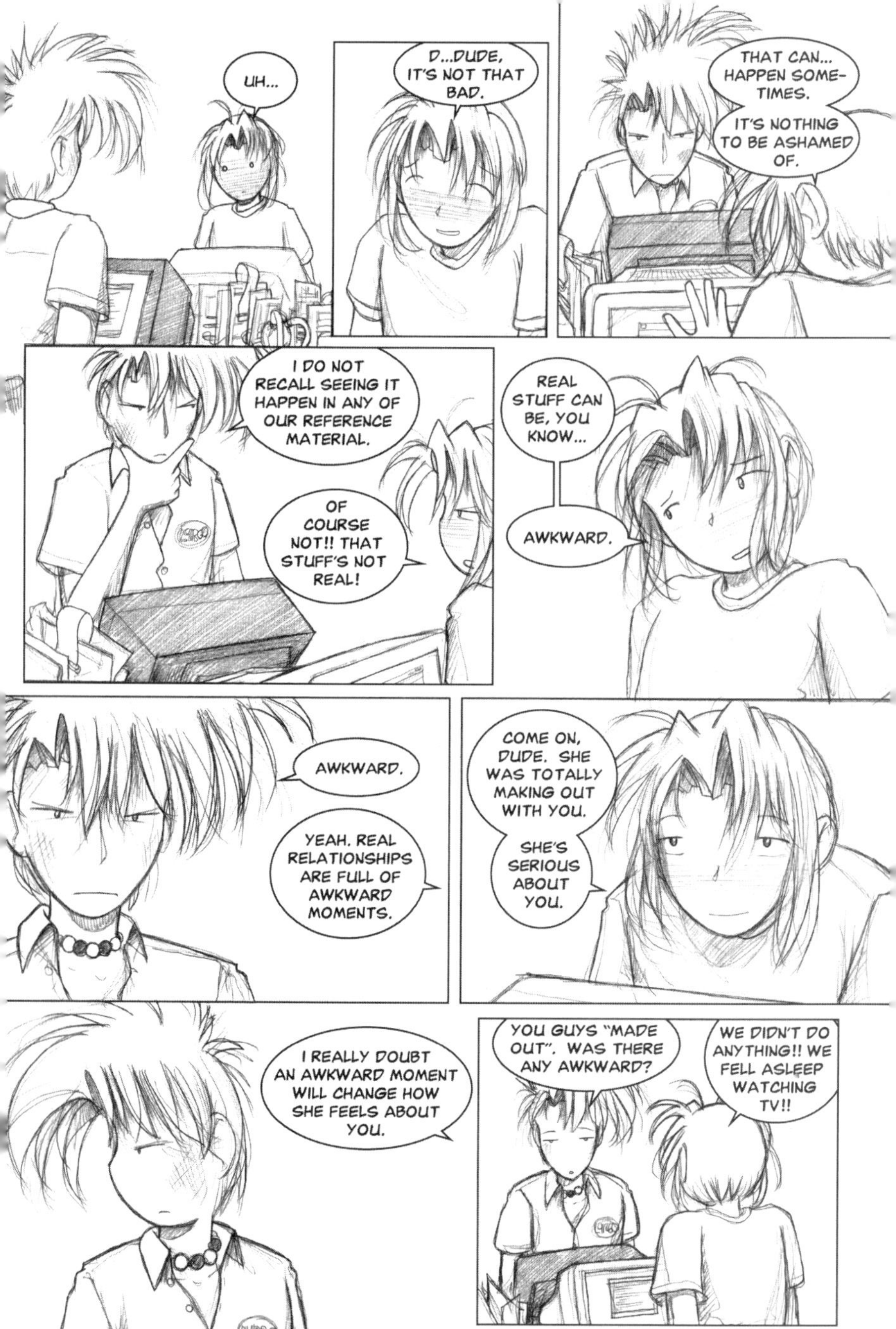
UH...
D...DUDE, IT'S NOT THAT BAD.
THAT CAN... HAPPEN SOME-TIMES.
IT'S NOTHING TO BE ASHAMED OF.
I DO NOT RECALL SEEING IT HAPPEN IN ANY OF OUR REFERENCE MATERIAL.
OF COURSE NOT!! THAT STUFF'S NOT REAL!
REAL STUFF CAN BE, YOU KNOW...
AWKWARD.
AWKWARD.
YEAH. REAL RELATIONSHIPS ARE FULL OF AWKWARD MOMENTS.
COME ON, DUDE. SHE WAS TOTALLY MAKING OUT WITH YOU.
SHE'S SERIOUS ABOUT YOU.
I REALLY DOUBT AN AWKWARD MOMENT WILL CHANGE HOW SHE FEELS ABOUT YOU.
YOU GUYS "MADE OUT". WAS THERE ANY AWKWARD?
WE DIDN'T DO ANYTHING!! WE FELL ASLEEP WATCHING TV!!

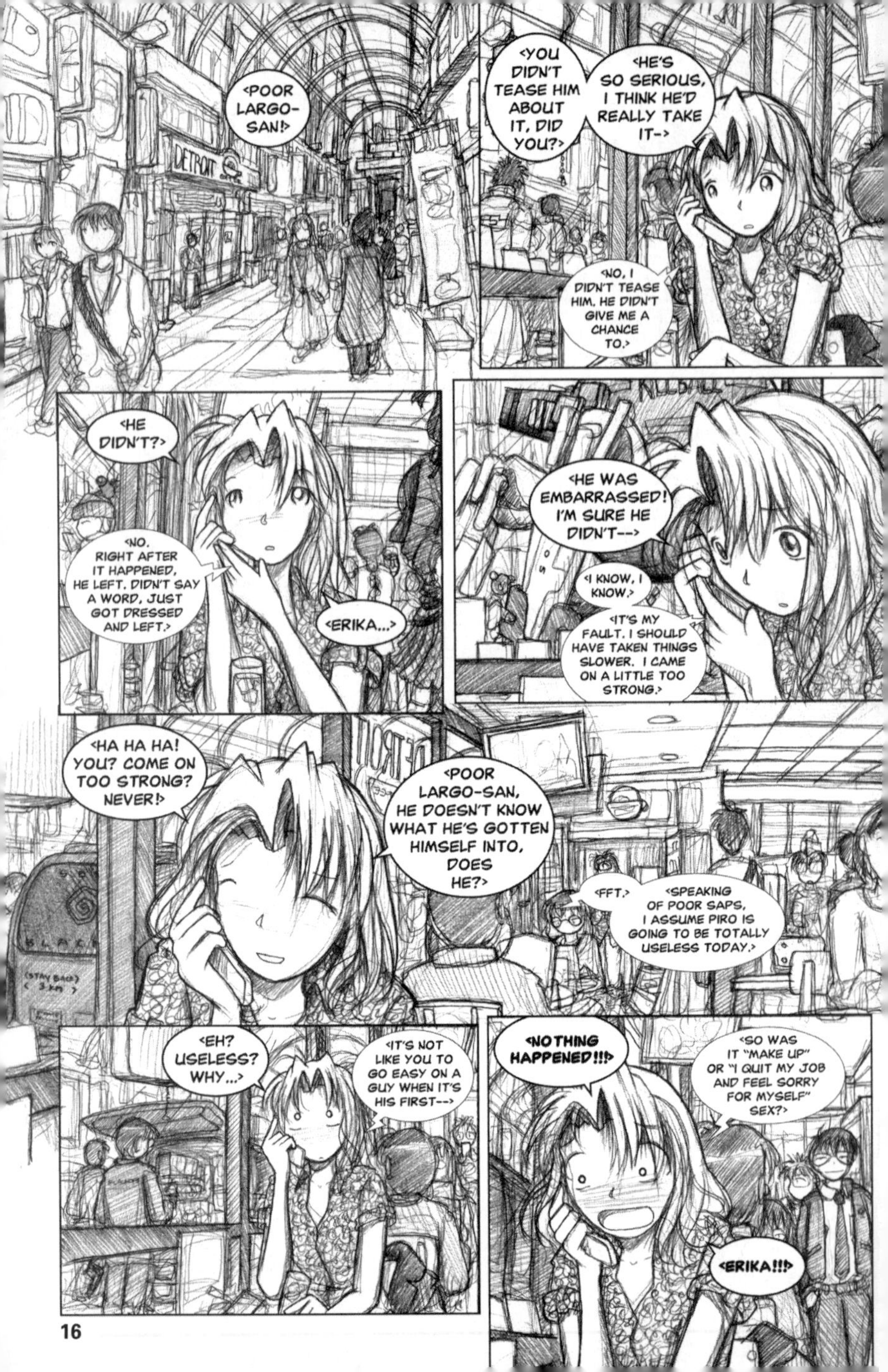
<POOR LARGO-SAN!>
<YOU DIDN'T TEASE HIM ABOUT IT, DID YOU?>
<HE'S SO SERIOUS, I THINK HE'D REALLY TAKE IT->
<NO, I DIDN'T TEASE HIM. HE DIDN'T GIVE ME A CHANCE TO.>
<HE DIDN'T?>
<NO. RIGHT AFTER IT HAPPENED, HE LEFT. DIDN'T SAY A WORD, JUST GOT DRESSED AND LEFT.>
<ERIKA...>
<HE WAS EMBARRASSED! I'M SURE HE DIDN'T-->
<I KNOW, I KNOW.>
<IT'S MY FAULT. I SHOULD HAVE TAKEN THINGS SLOWER. I CAME ON A LITTLE TOO STRONG.>
<HA HA HA! YOU? COME ON TOO STRONG? NEVER!>
<POOR LARGO-SAN, HE DOESN'T KNOW WHAT HE'S GOTTEN HIMSELF INTO, DOES HE?>
<FFT.>
<SPEAKING OF POOR SAPS, I ASSUME PIRO IS GOING TO BE TOTALLY USELESS TODAY.>
<EH? USELESS? WHY...>
<IT'S NOT LIKE YOU TO GO EASY ON A GUY WHEN IT'S HIS FIRST-->
<NOTHING HAPPENED!!!>
<SO WAS IT "MAKE UP" OR "I QUIT MY JOB AND FEEL SORRY FOR MYSELF" SEX?>
<ERIKA!!!>

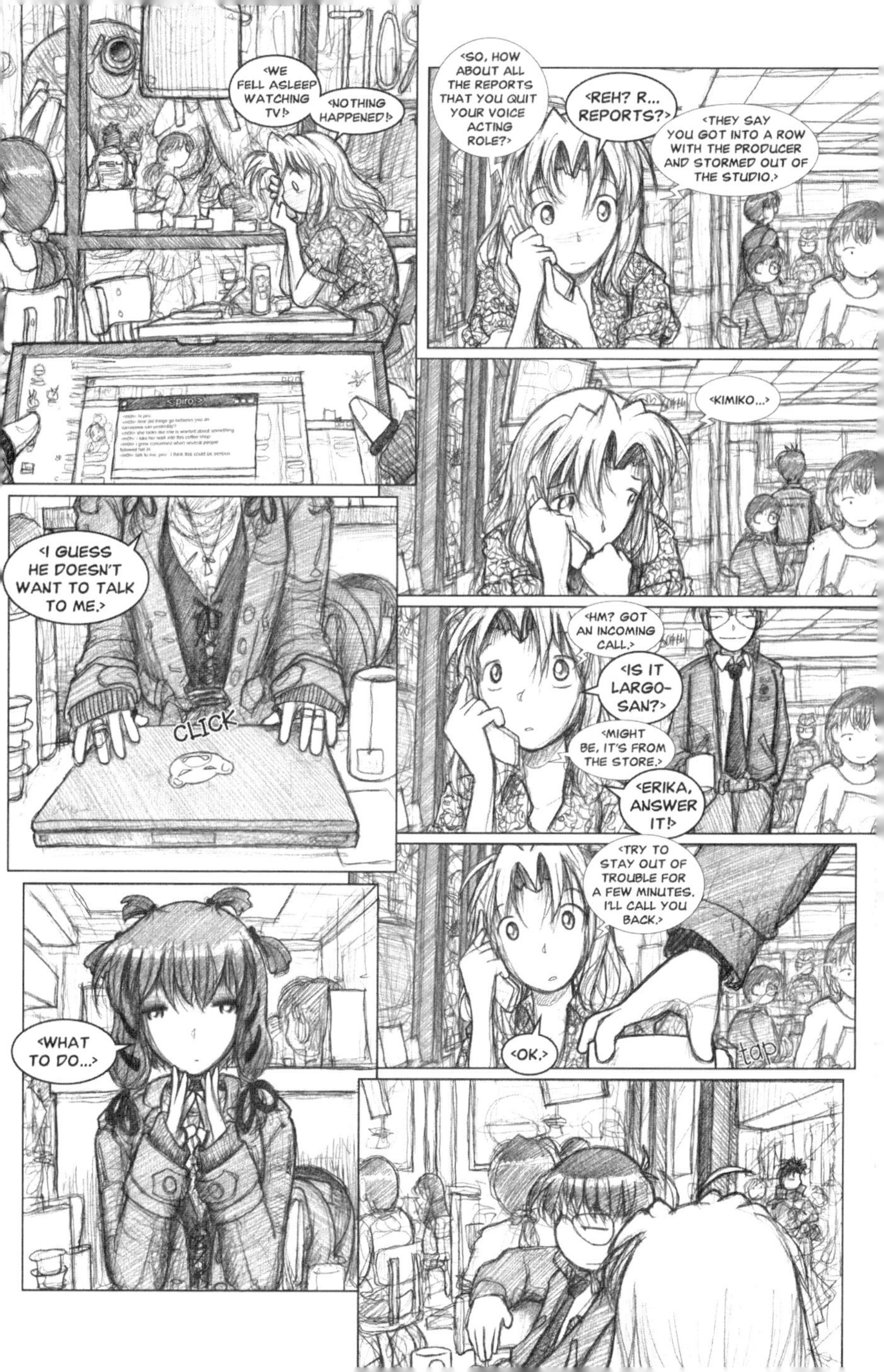
<WE FELL ASLEEP WATCHING TV!>
<NOTHING HAPPENED!>
< piro >
<SO, HOW ABOUT ALL THE REPORTS THAT YOU QUIT YOUR VOICE ACTING ROLE?>
<REH? R... REPORTS?>
<THEY SAY YOU GOT INTO A ROW WITH THE PRODUCER AND STORMED OUT OF THE STUDIO.>
<KIMIKO...>
<I GUESS HE DOESN'T WANT TO TALK TO ME.>
CLICK
<HM? GOT AN INCOMING CALL.>
<IS IT LARGO-SAN?>
<MIGHT BE, IT'S FROM THE STORE.>
<ERIKA, ANSWER IT!>
<TRY TO STAY OUT OF TROUBLE FOR A FEW MINUTES. I'LL CALL YOU BACK.>
<OK.>
tap
<WHAT TO DO...>

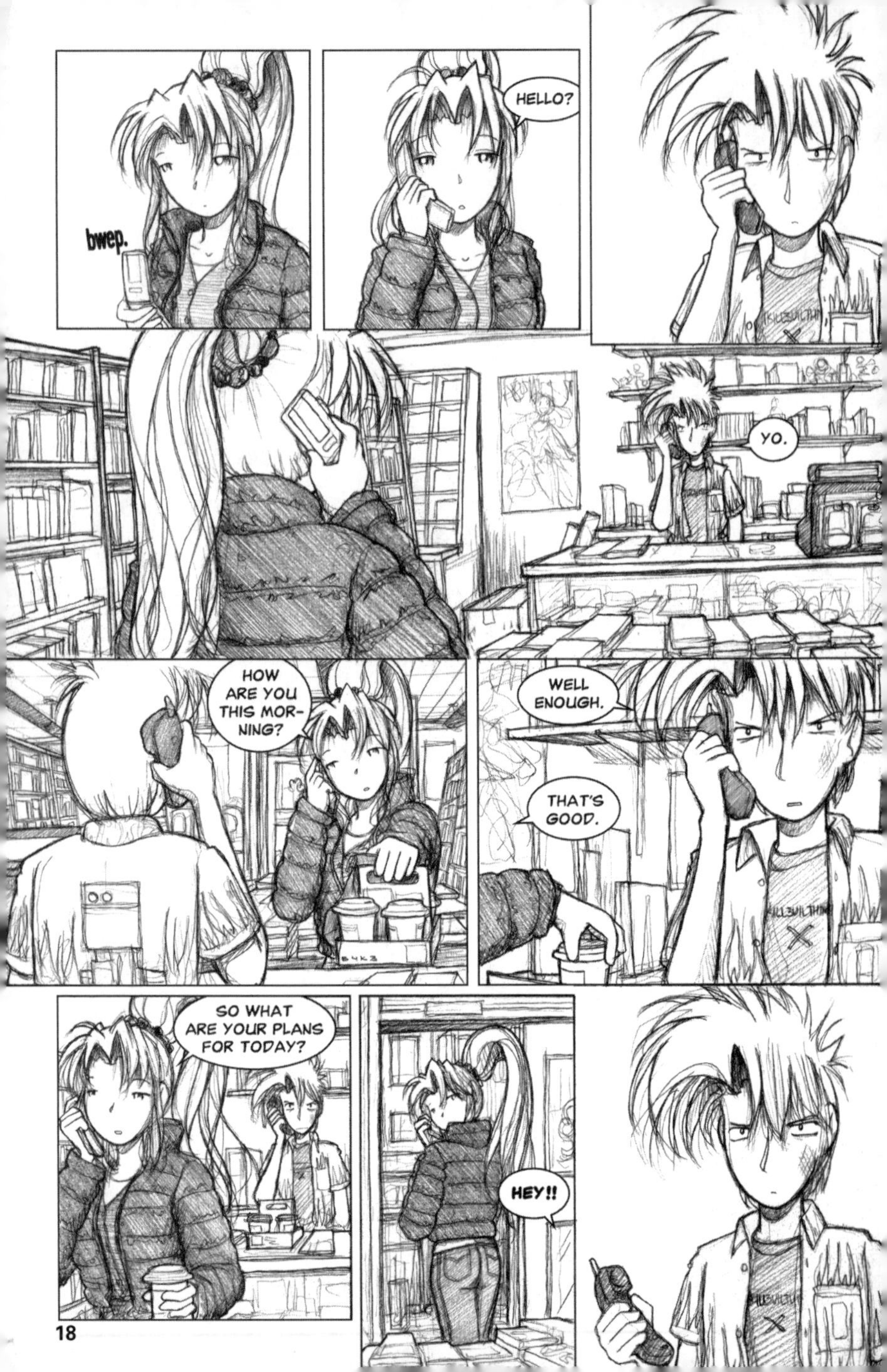
bwep.
HELLO?
YO.
HOW ARE YOU THIS MOR-NING?
WELL ENOUGH.
THAT'S GOOD.
SO WHAT ARE YOUR PLANS FOR TODAY?
HEY!!

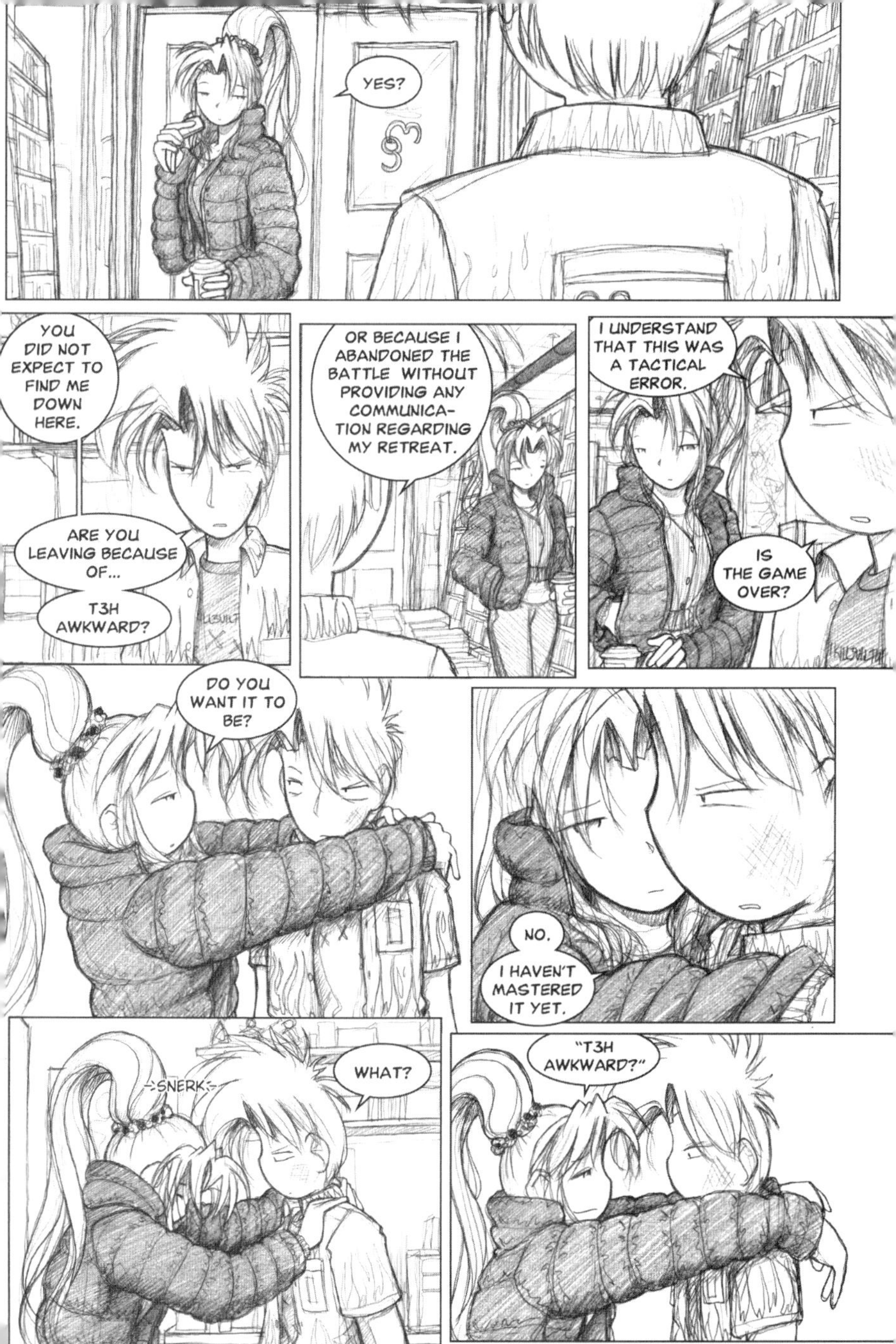
YES?
YOU DID NOT EXPECT TO FIND ME DOWN HERE.
ARE YOU LEAVING BECAUSE OF...
T3H AWKWARD?
OR BECAUSE I ABANDONED THE BATTLE WITHOUT PROVIDING ANY COMMUNICATION REGARDING MY RETREAT.
I UNDERSTAND THAT THIS WAS A TACTICAL ERROR.
IS THE GAME OVER?
DO YOU WANT IT TO BE?
NO.
I HAVEN'T MASTERED IT YET.
SNERK
WHAT?
"T3H AWKWARD?"

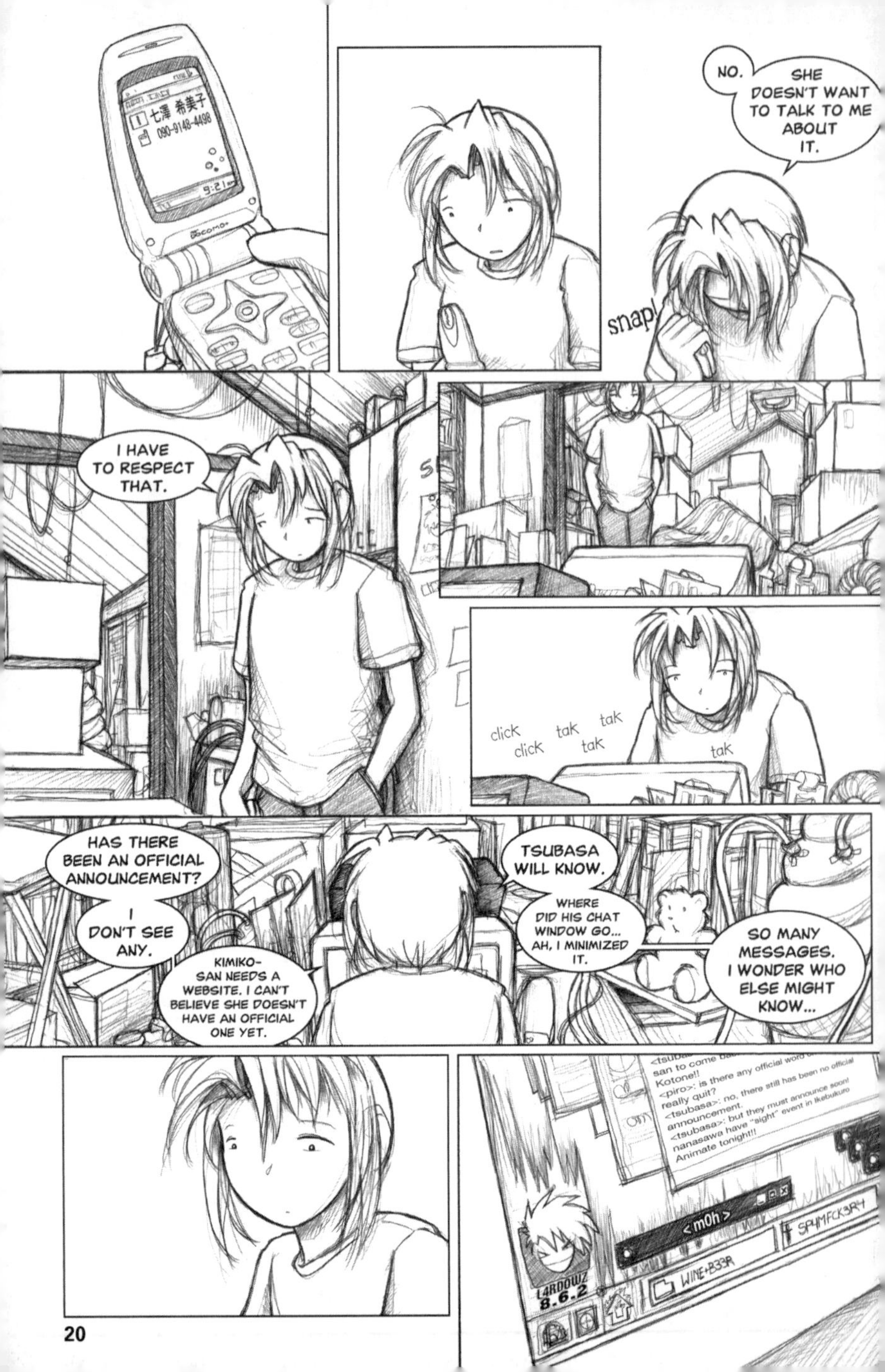

七澤 希美子
090-9148-4498
9:21
NO.
SHE DOESN'T WANT TO TALK TO ME ABOUT IT.
snap!
I HAVE TO RESPECT THAT.
click click
tak tak tak
tak
HAS THERE BEEN AN OFFICIAL ANNOUNCEMENT?
I DON'T SEE ANY.
KIMIKO-SAN NEEDS A WEBSITE. I CAN'T BELIEVE SHE DOESN'T HAVE AN OFFICIAL ONE YET.
TSUBASA WILL KNOW.
WHERE DID HIS CHAT WINDOW GO... AH, I MINIMIZED IT.
SO MANY MESSAGES. I WONDER WHO ELSE MIGHT KNOW...
san to come
Kotone!!
<piro>: is there any official word
really quit?
<tsubasa>: no, there still has been no official
announcement.
<tsubasa>: but they must announce soon!
nanasawa have "sight" event in Ikebukuro
Animate tonight!!
< m0h >
SP4MFCK3R4
WINE+B33R
L4RDOWZ
8.6.2

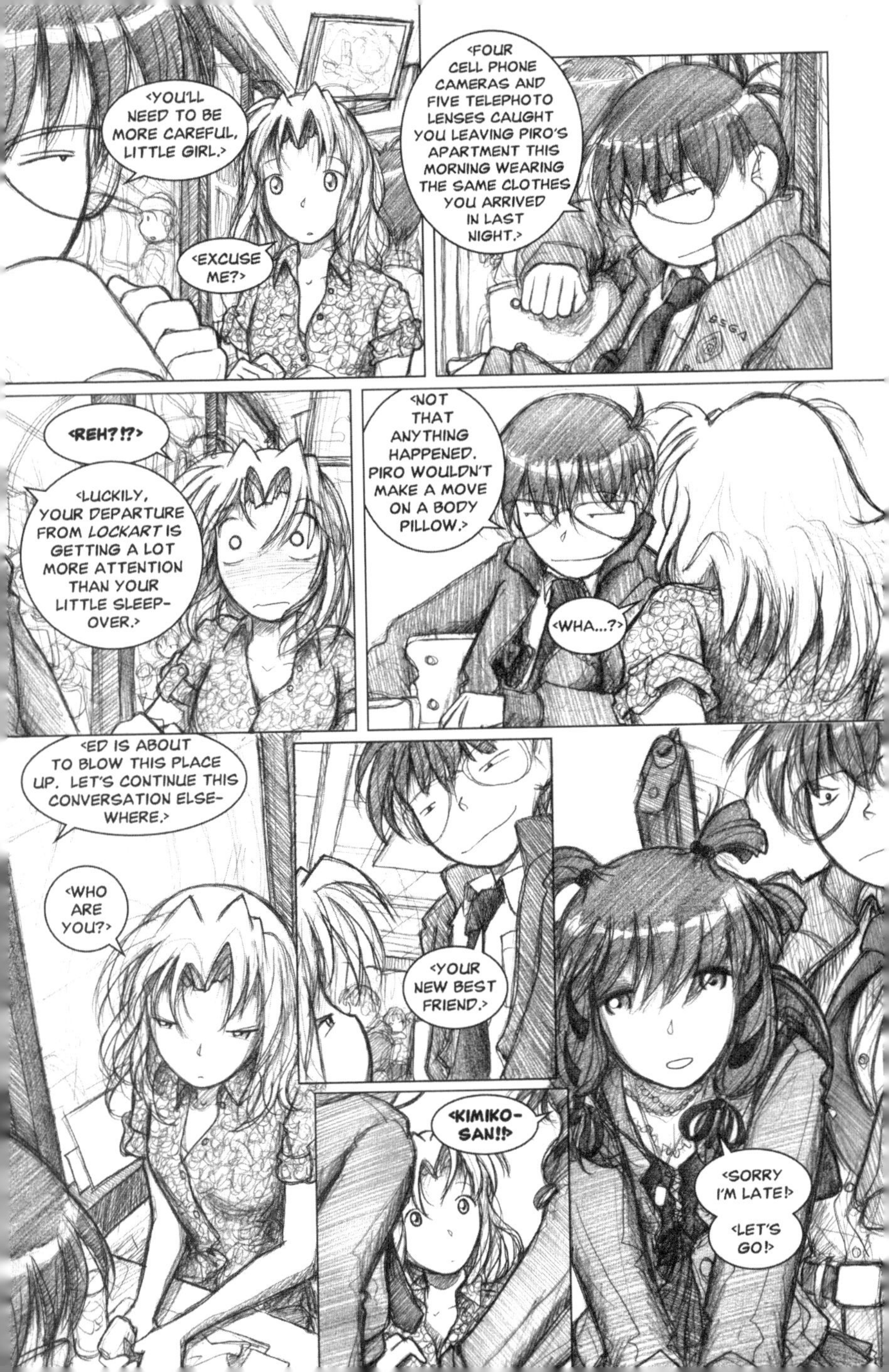
<YOU'LL NEED TO BE MORE CAREFUL, LITTLE GIRL.>
<EXCUSE ME?>
<FOUR CELL PHONE CAMERAS AND FIVE TELEPHOTO LENSES CAUGHT YOU LEAVING PIRO'S APARTMENT THIS MORNING WEARING THE SAME CLOTHES YOU ARRIVED IN LAST NIGHT.>
<REH?!?>
<LUCKILY, YOUR DEPARTURE FROM *LOCKART* IS GETTING A LOT MORE ATTENTION THAN YOUR LITTLE SLEEP-OVER.>
<NOT THAT ANYTHING HAPPENED. PIRO WOULDN'T MAKE A MOVE ON A BODY PILLOW.>
<WHA...?>
<ED IS ABOUT TO BLOW THIS PLACE UP. LET'S CONTINUE THIS CONVERSATION ELSE-WHERE.>
<WHO ARE YOU?>
<YOUR NEW BEST FRIEND.>
<KIMIKO-SAN!!>
<SORRY I'M LATE!>
<LET'S GO!>

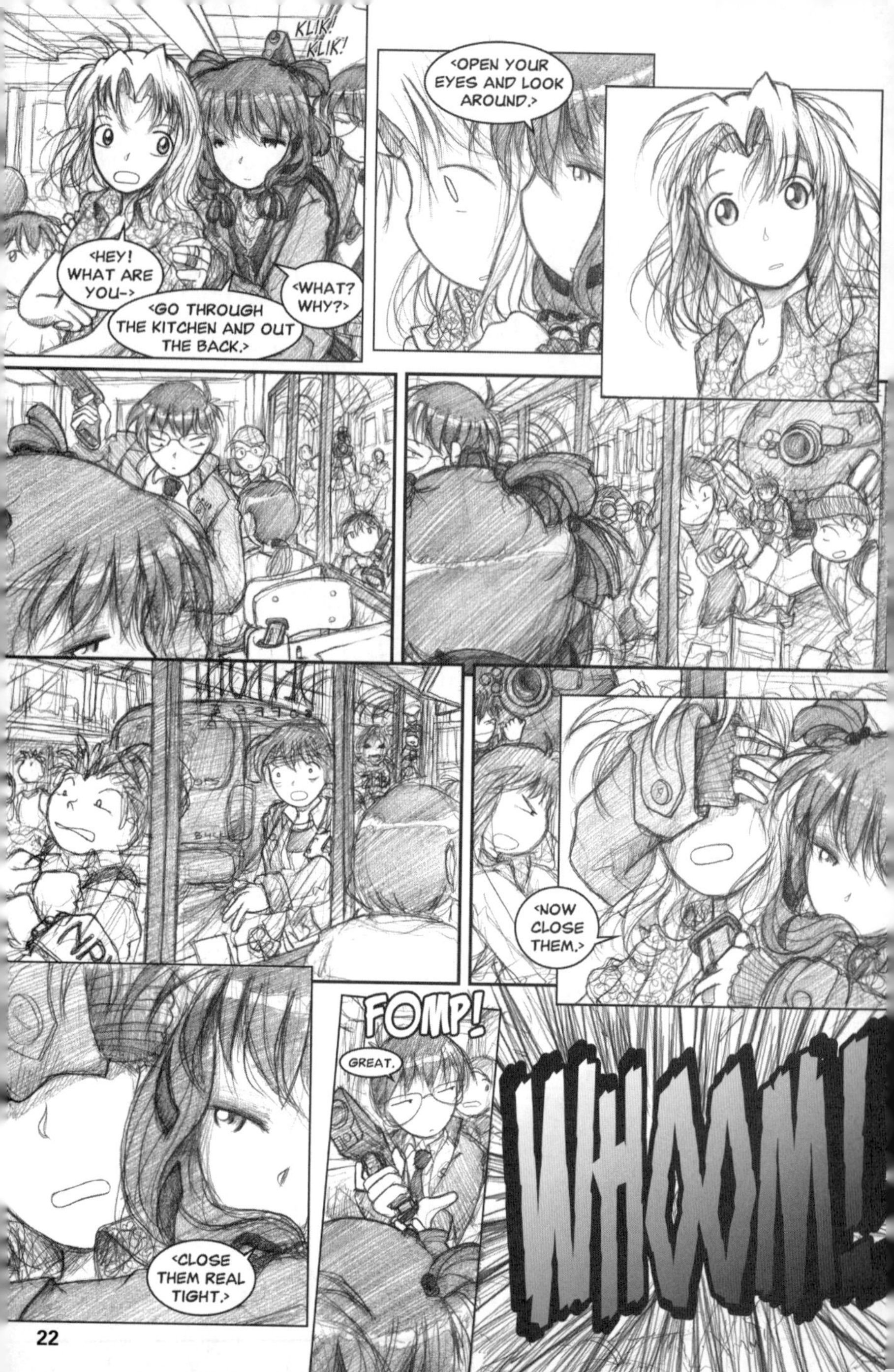
KLIK! KLIK!
<HEY! WHAT ARE YOU->
<GO THROUGH THE KITCHEN AND OUT THE BACK.>
<WHAT? WHY?>
<OPEN YOUR EYES AND LOOK AROUND.>
<NOW CLOSE THEM.>
<CLOSE THEM REAL TIGHT.>
FOMP!
GREAT.
WHOOM!

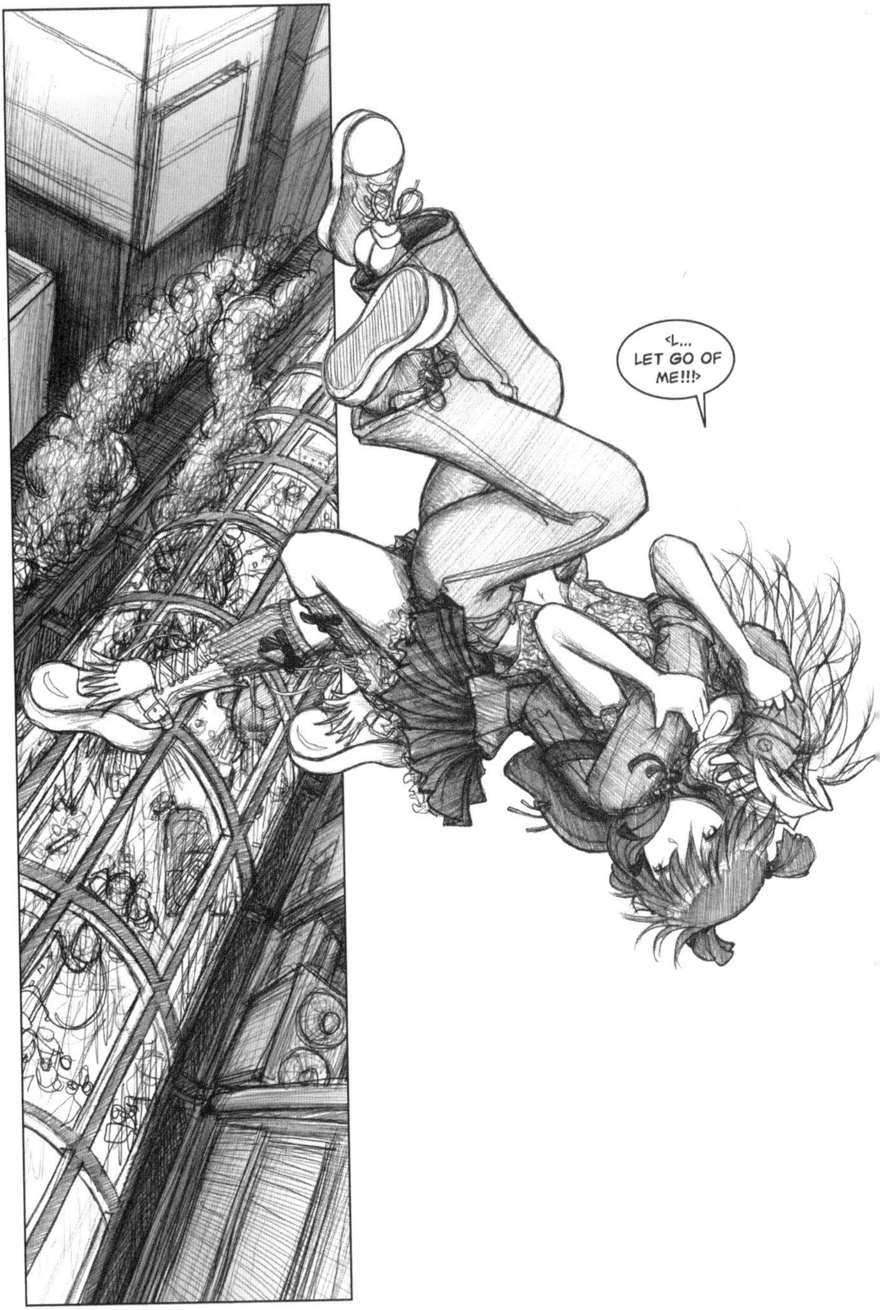
<L... LET GO OF ME!!!>

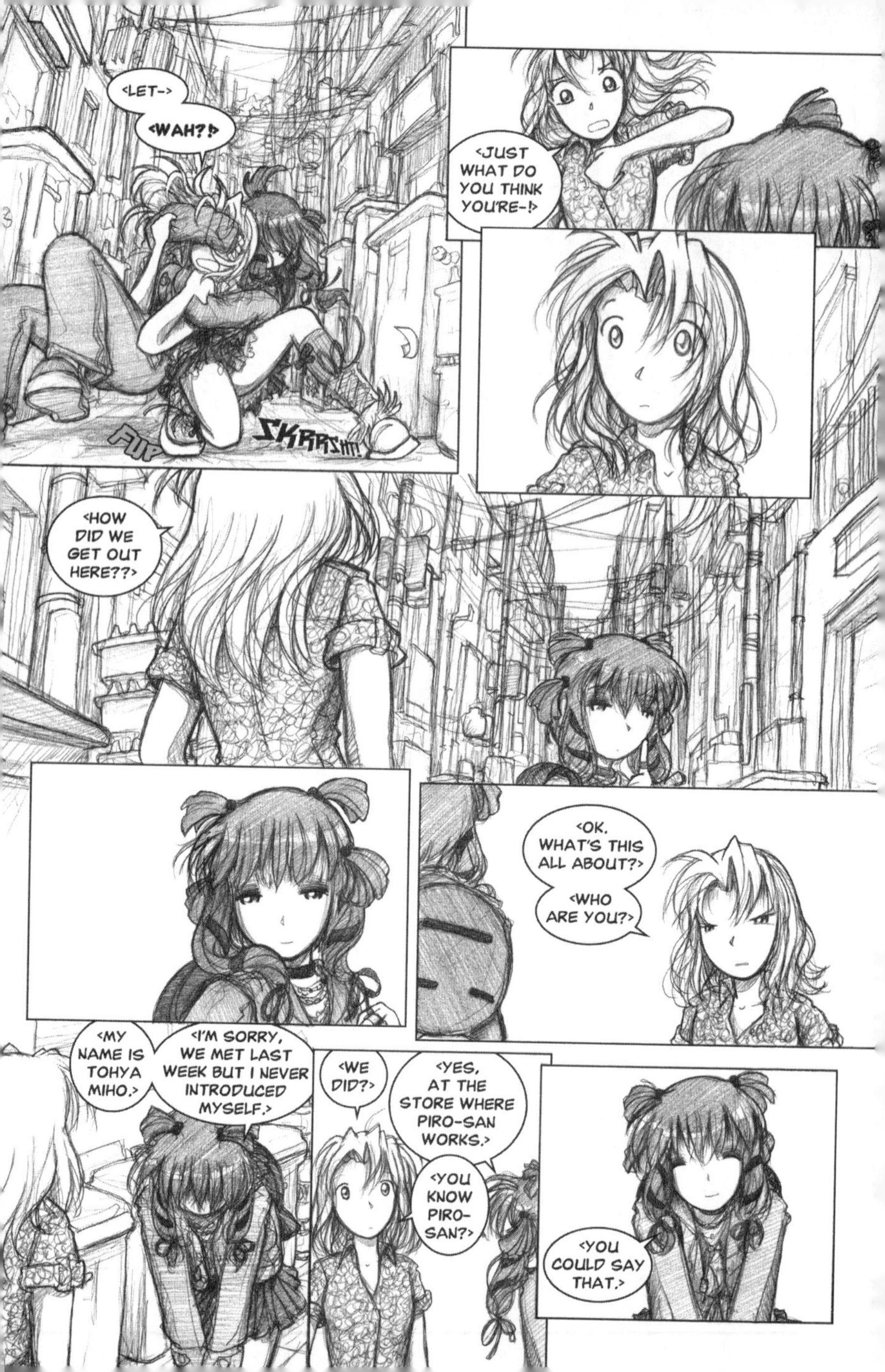
<LET->
<WAH?!>
FUP
SKRRSH!!
<JUST WHAT DO YOU THINK YOU'RE-!>
<HOW DID WE GET OUT HERE??>
<OK. WHAT'S THIS ALL ABOUT?>
<WHO ARE YOU?>
<MY NAME IS TOHYA MIHO.>
<I'M SORRY, WE MET LAST WEEK BUT I NEVER INTRODUCED MYSELF.>
<WE DID?>
<YES, AT THE STORE WHERE PIRO-SAN WORKS.>
<YOU KNOW PIRO-SAN?>
<YOU COULD SAY THAT.>

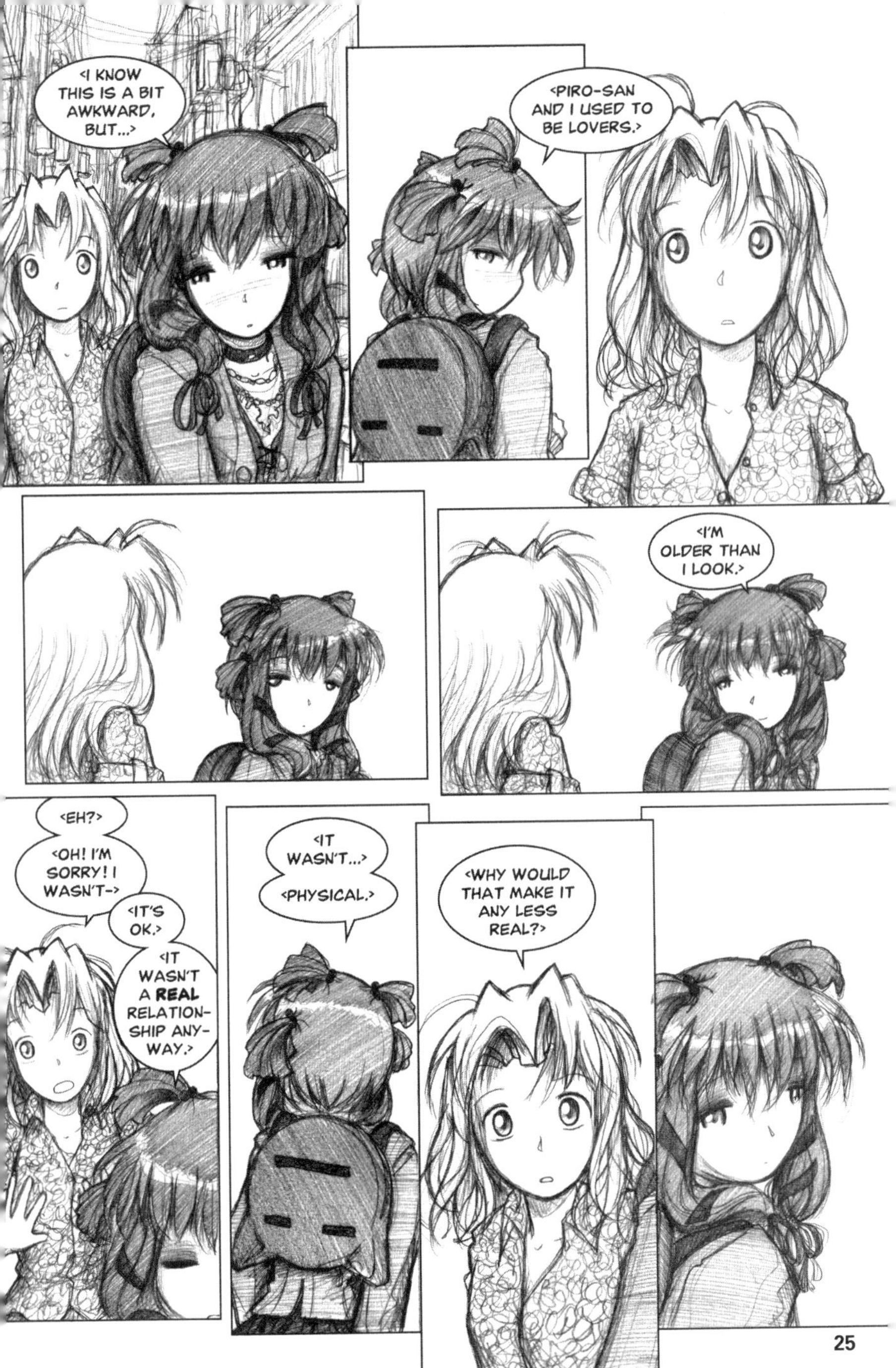
<I KNOW THIS IS A BIT AWKWARD, BUT...>
<PIRO-SAN AND I USED TO BE LOVERS.>
<I'M OLDER THAN I LOOK.>
<EH?>
<OH! I'M SORRY! I WASN'T->
<IT'S OK.>
<IT WASN'T A **REAL** RELATIONSHIP ANYWAY.>
<IT WASN'T...>
<PHYSICAL.>
<WHY WOULD THAT MAKE IT ANY LESS REAL?>

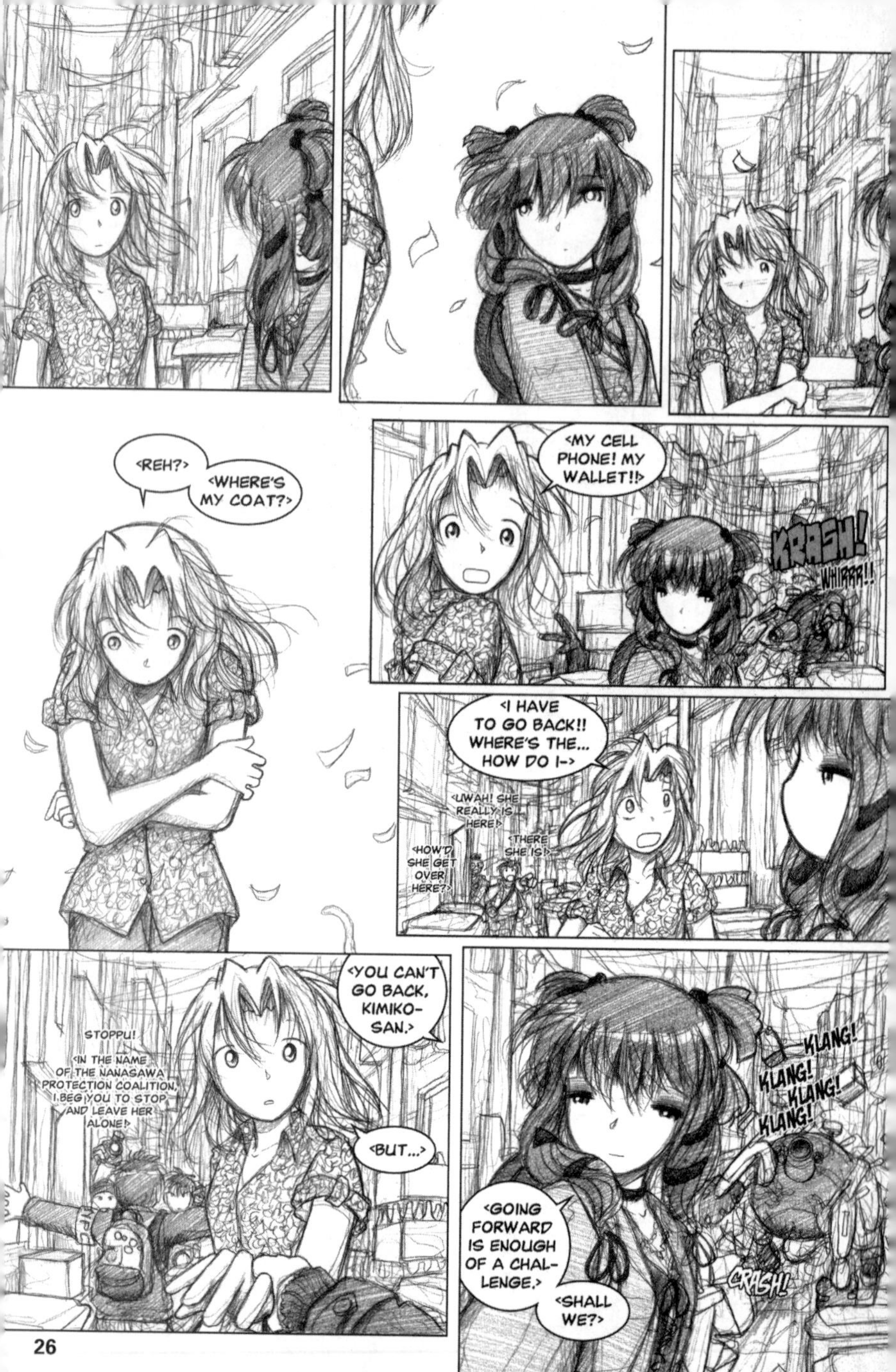
<REH?>
<WHERE'S MY COAT?>
<MY CELL PHONE! MY WALLET!!>
KRASH!
WHIRRR!!
<I HAVE TO GO BACK!! WHERE'S THE... HOW DO I->
<UWAH! SHE REALLY IS HERE!>
<THERE SHE IS!>
<HOW'D SHE GET OVER HERE?>
<YOU CAN'T GO BACK, KIMIKO-SAN.>
STOPPU!
<IN THE NAME OF THE NANASAWA PROTECTION COALITION, I BEG YOU TO STOP AND LEAVE HER ALONE!>
<BUT...>
KLANG!
KLANG!
KLANG!
KLANG!
<GOING FORWARD IS ENOUGH OF A CHAL-LENGE.>
CRASH!
<SHALL WE?>

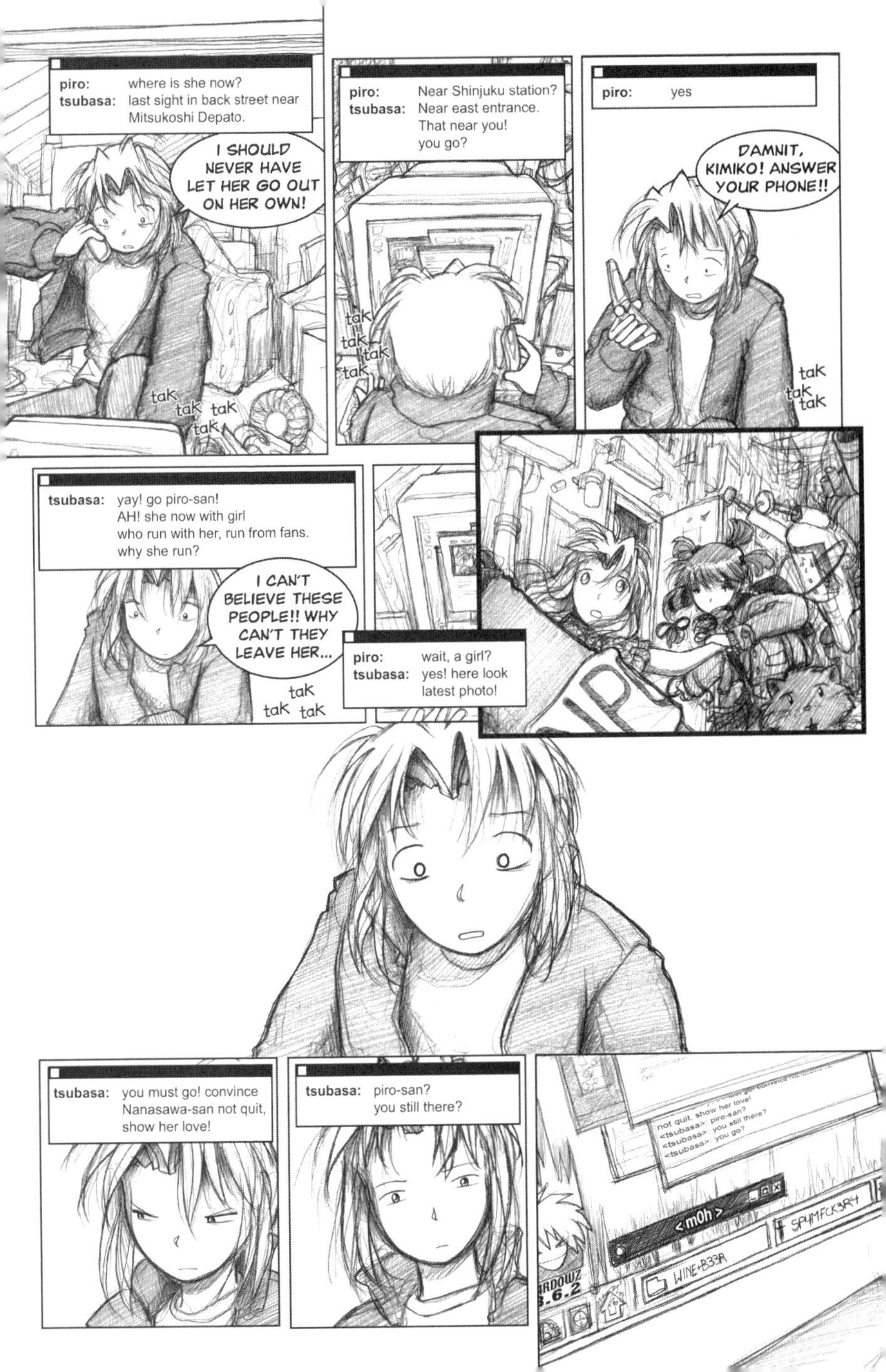

piro: where is she now?
tsubasa: last sight in back street near Mitsukoshi Depato.
I SHOULD NEVER HAVE LET HER GO OUT ON HER OWN!
tak tak tak tak
piro: Near Shinjuku station?
tsubasa: Near east entrance. That near you! you go?
tak tak tak tak
piro: yes
DAMNIT, KIMIKO! ANSWER YOUR PHONE!!
tak tak tak
tsubasa: yay! go piro-san! AH! she now with girl who run with her, run from fans. why she run?
I CAN'T BELIEVE THESE PEOPLE!! WHY CAN'T THEY LEAVE HER...
tak tak tak
piro: wait, a girl?
tsubasa: yes! here look latest photo!
tsubasa: you must go! convince Nanasawa-san not quit, show her love!
tsubasa: piro-san? you still there?
not quit, show her love!
<tsubasa>: piro-san?
<tsubasa>: you still there?
<tsubasa>: you go?
<m0h>
SP4MFCK3R4
WINE+B33R
RDOWZ
3.6.2

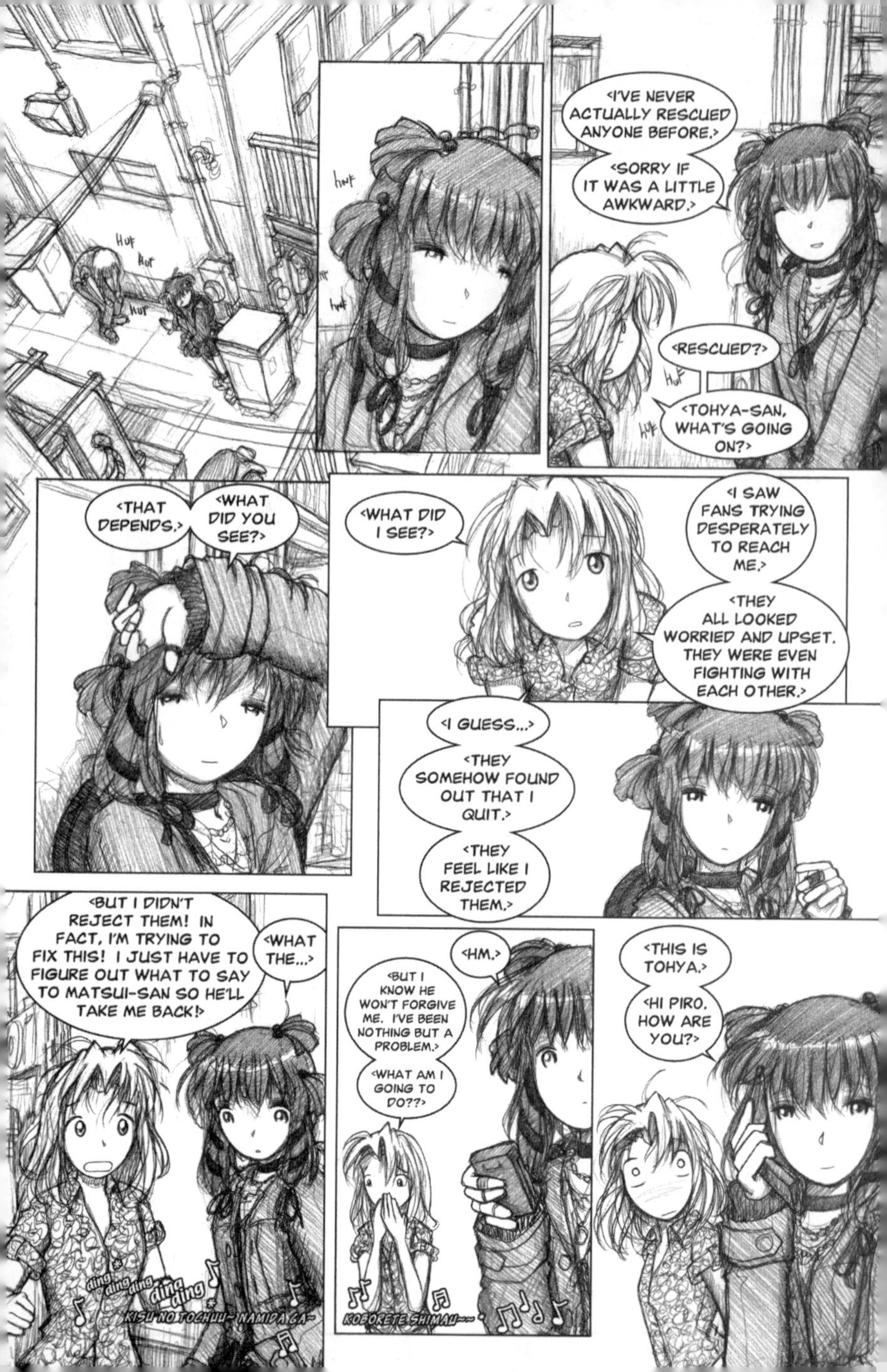
HUF
HUF
HUF
HUF
HUF
<I'VE NEVER ACTUALLY RESCUED ANYONE BEFORE.>
<SORRY IF IT WAS A LITTLE AWKWARD.>
<RESCUED?>
<TOHYA-SAN, WHAT'S GOING ON?>
<THAT DEPENDS.>
<WHAT DID YOU SEE?>
<WHAT DID I SEE?>
<I SAW FANS TRYING DESPERATELY TO REACH ME.>
<THEY ALL LOOKED WORRIED AND UPSET. THEY WERE EVEN FIGHTING WITH EACH OTHER.>
<I GUESS...>
<THEY SOMEHOW FOUND OUT THAT I QUIT.>
<THEY FEEL LIKE I REJECTED THEM.>
<BUT I DIDN'T REJECT THEM! IN FACT, I'M TRYING TO FIX THIS! I JUST HAVE TO FIGURE OUT WHAT TO SAY TO MATSUI-SAN SO HE'LL TAKE ME BACK!>
<WHAT THE...>
ding ding ding ding ding
KISU NO TOCHUU~ NAMIDA GA~
<HM.>
<BUT I KNOW HE WON'T FORGIVE ME. I'VE BEEN NOTHING BUT A PROBLEM.>
<WHAT AM I GOING TO DO??>
KOBORETE SHIMAU~~~
<THIS IS TOHYA.>
<HI PIRO. HOW ARE YOU?>

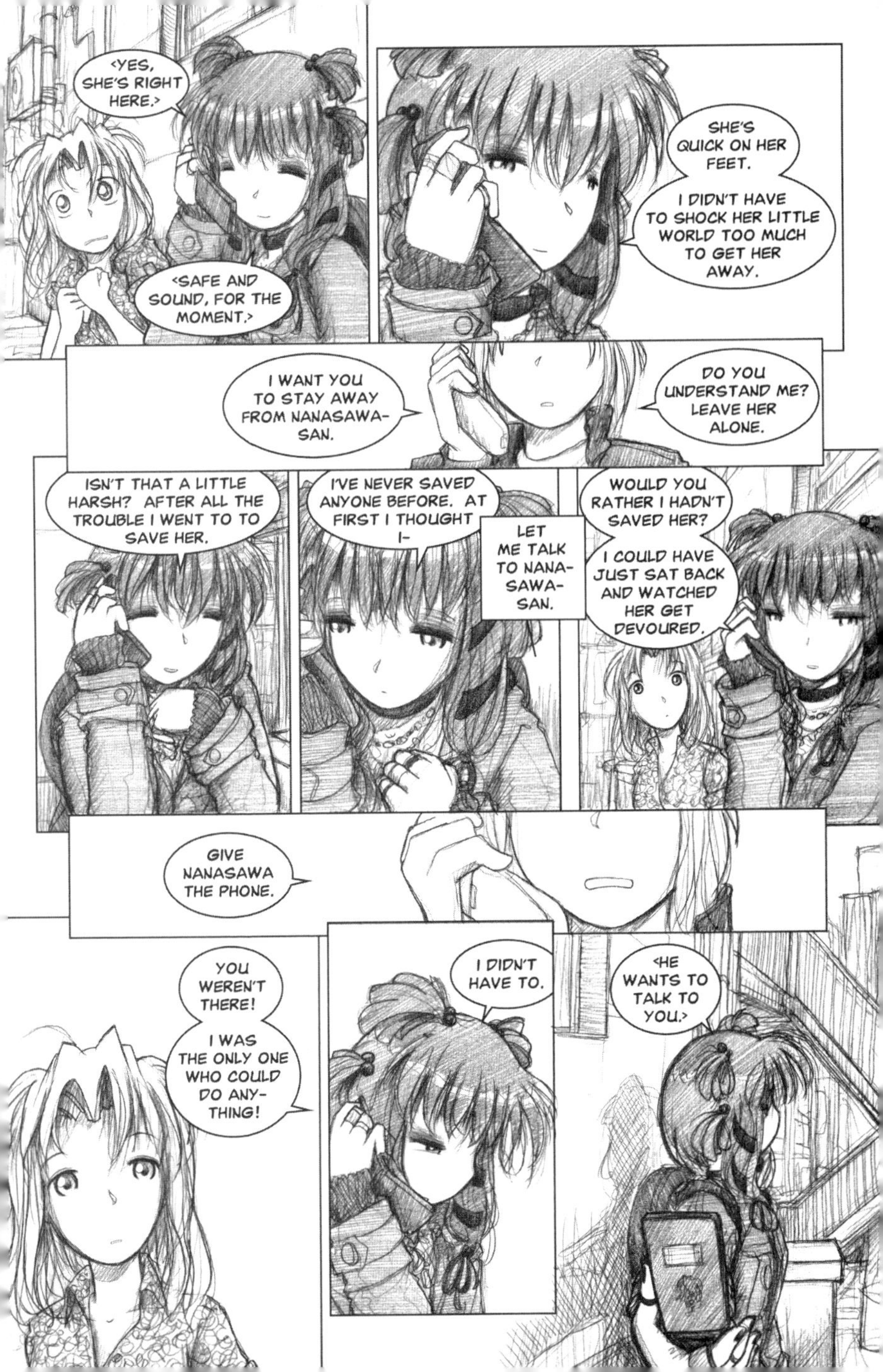
<YES, SHE'S RIGHT HERE.>
<SAFE AND SOUND, FOR THE MOMENT.>
SHE'S QUICK ON HER FEET.
I DIDN'T HAVE TO SHOCK HER LITTLE WORLD TOO MUCH TO GET HER AWAY.
I WANT YOU TO STAY AWAY FROM NANASAWA-SAN.
DO YOU UNDERSTAND ME? LEAVE HER ALONE.
ISN'T THAT A LITTLE HARSH? AFTER ALL THE TROUBLE I WENT TO TO SAVE HER.
I'VE NEVER SAVED ANYONE BEFORE. AT FIRST I THOUGHT I-
LET ME TALK TO NANA-SAWA-SAN.
WOULD YOU RATHER I HADN'T SAVED HER?
I COULD HAVE JUST SAT BACK AND WATCHED HER GET DEVOURED.
GIVE NANASAWA THE PHONE.
YOU WEREN'T THERE!
I WAS THE ONLY ONE WHO COULD DO ANY-THING!
I DIDN'T HAVE TO.
<HE WANTS TO TALK TO YOU.>

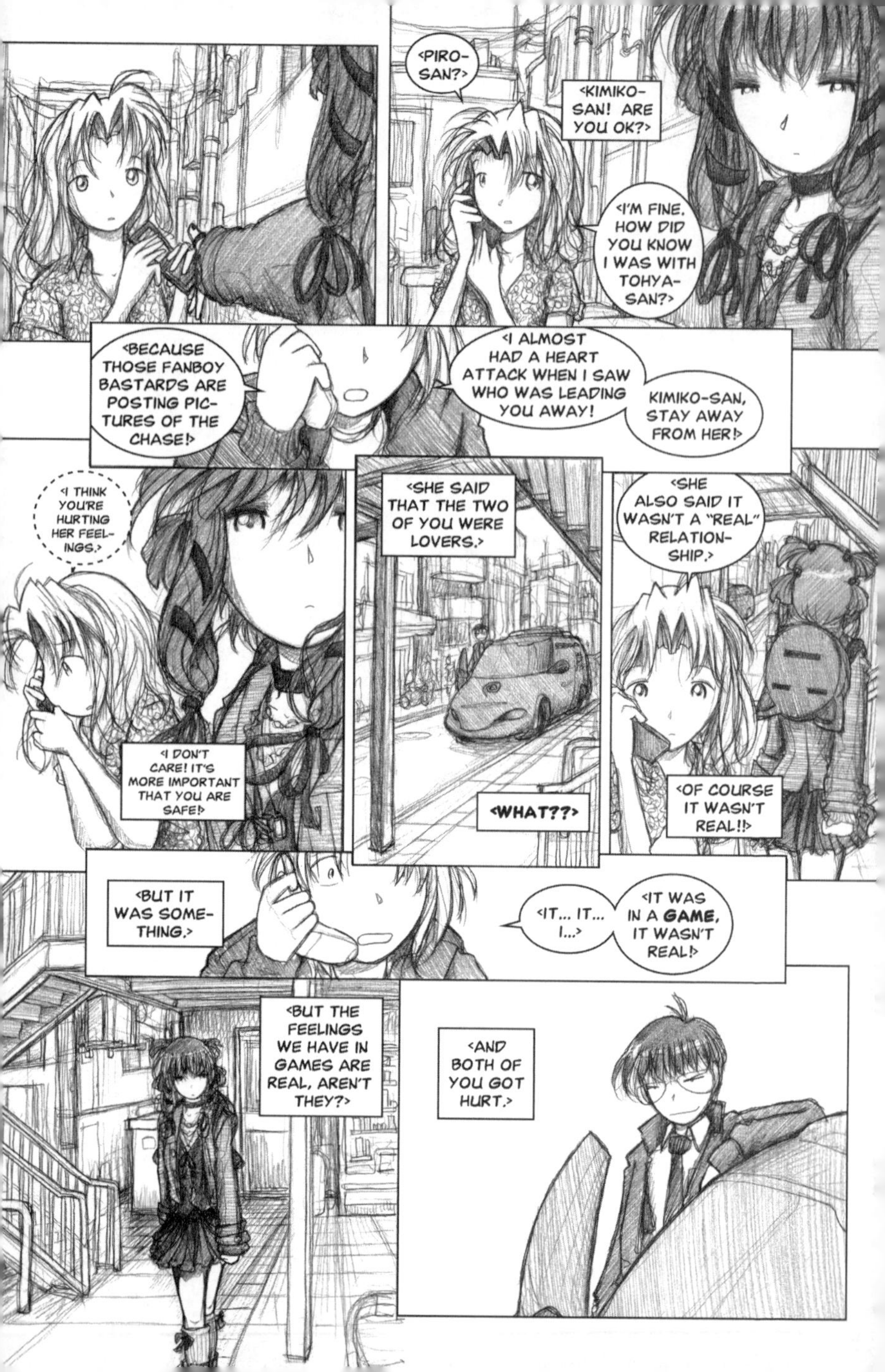
<PIRO-SAN?>
<KIMIKO-SAN! ARE YOU OK?>
<I'M FINE. HOW DID YOU KNOW I WAS WITH TOHYA-SAN?>
<BECAUSE THOSE FANBOY BASTARDS ARE POSTING PICTURES OF THE CHASE!>
<I ALMOST HAD A HEART ATTACK WHEN I SAW WHO WAS LEADING YOU AWAY!
KIMIKO-SAN, STAY AWAY FROM HER!>
<I THINK YOU'RE HURTING HER FEELINGS.>
<I DON'T CARE! IT'S MORE IMPORTANT THAT YOU ARE SAFE!>
<SHE SAID THAT THE TWO OF YOU WERE LOVERS.>
<WHAT??>
<SHE ALSO SAID IT WASN'T A "REAL" RELATIONSHIP.>
<OF COURSE IT WASN'T REAL!!>
<BUT IT WAS SOMETHING.>
<IT... IT... I...>
<IT WAS IN A **GAME**, IT WASN'T REAL!>
<BUT THE FEELINGS WE HAVE IN GAMES ARE REAL, AREN'T THEY?>
<AND BOTH OF YOU GOT HURT.>

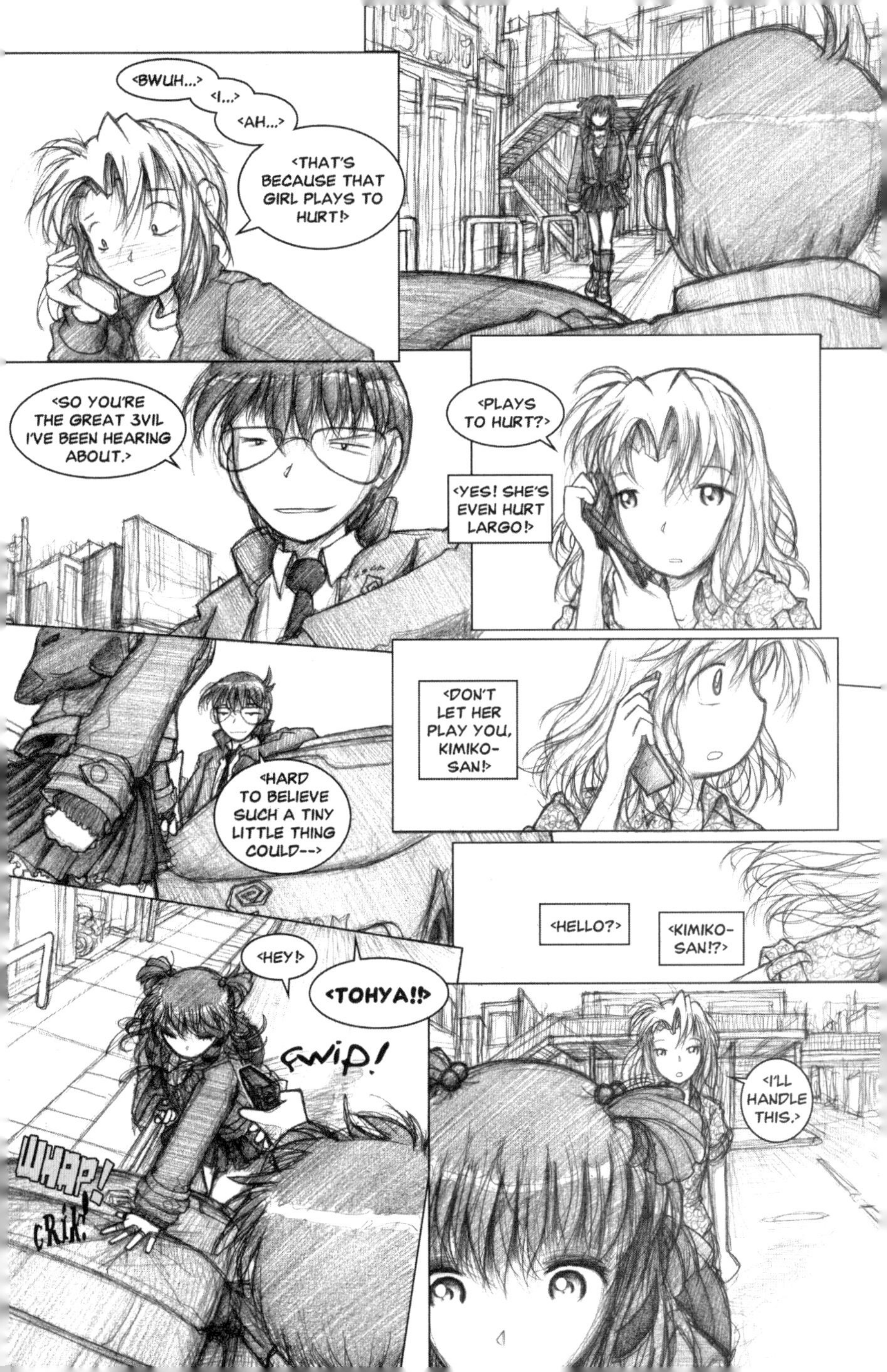

<BWUH...>
<I...>
<AH...>
<THAT'S BECAUSE THAT GIRL PLAYS TO HURT!>
<SO YOU'RE THE GREAT 3VIL I'VE BEEN HEARING ABOUT.>
<PLAYS TO HURT?>
<YES! SHE'S EVEN HURT LARGO!>
<HARD TO BELIEVE SUCH A TINY LITTLE THING COULD-->
<DON'T LET HER PLAY YOU, KIMIKO-SAN!>
<HELLO?>
<KIMIKO-SAN!?>
<HEY!>
<TOHYA!!>
FWIP!
WHAP!
CRIK!
<I'LL HANDLE THIS.>

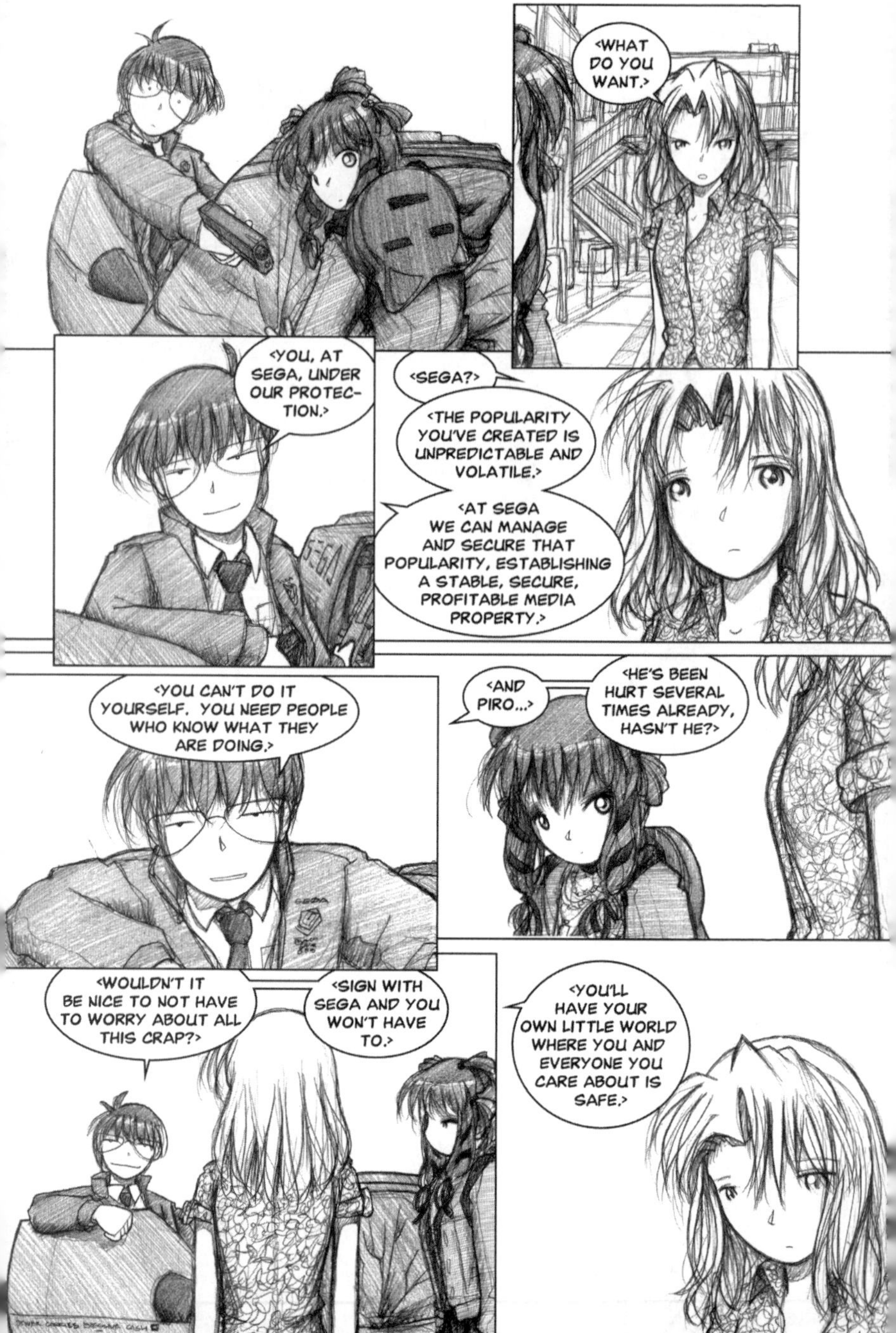
<WHAT DO YOU WANT.>
<YOU, AT SEGA, UNDER OUR PROTECTION.>
<SEGA?>
<THE POPULARITY YOU'VE CREATED IS UNPREDICTABLE AND VOLATILE.>
<AT SEGA WE CAN MANAGE AND SECURE THAT POPULARITY, ESTABLISHING A STABLE, SECURE, PROFITABLE MEDIA PROPERTY.>
<YOU CAN'T DO IT YOURSELF. YOU NEED PEOPLE WHO KNOW WHAT THEY ARE DOING.>
<AND PIRO...>
<HE'S BEEN HURT SEVERAL TIMES ALREADY, HASN'T HE?>
<WOULDN'T IT BE NICE TO NOT HAVE TO WORRY ABOUT ALL THIS CRAP?>
<SIGN WITH SEGA AND YOU WON'T HAVE TO.>
<YOU'LL HAVE YOUR OWN LITTLE WORLD WHERE YOU AND EVERYONE YOU CARE ABOUT IS SAFE.>

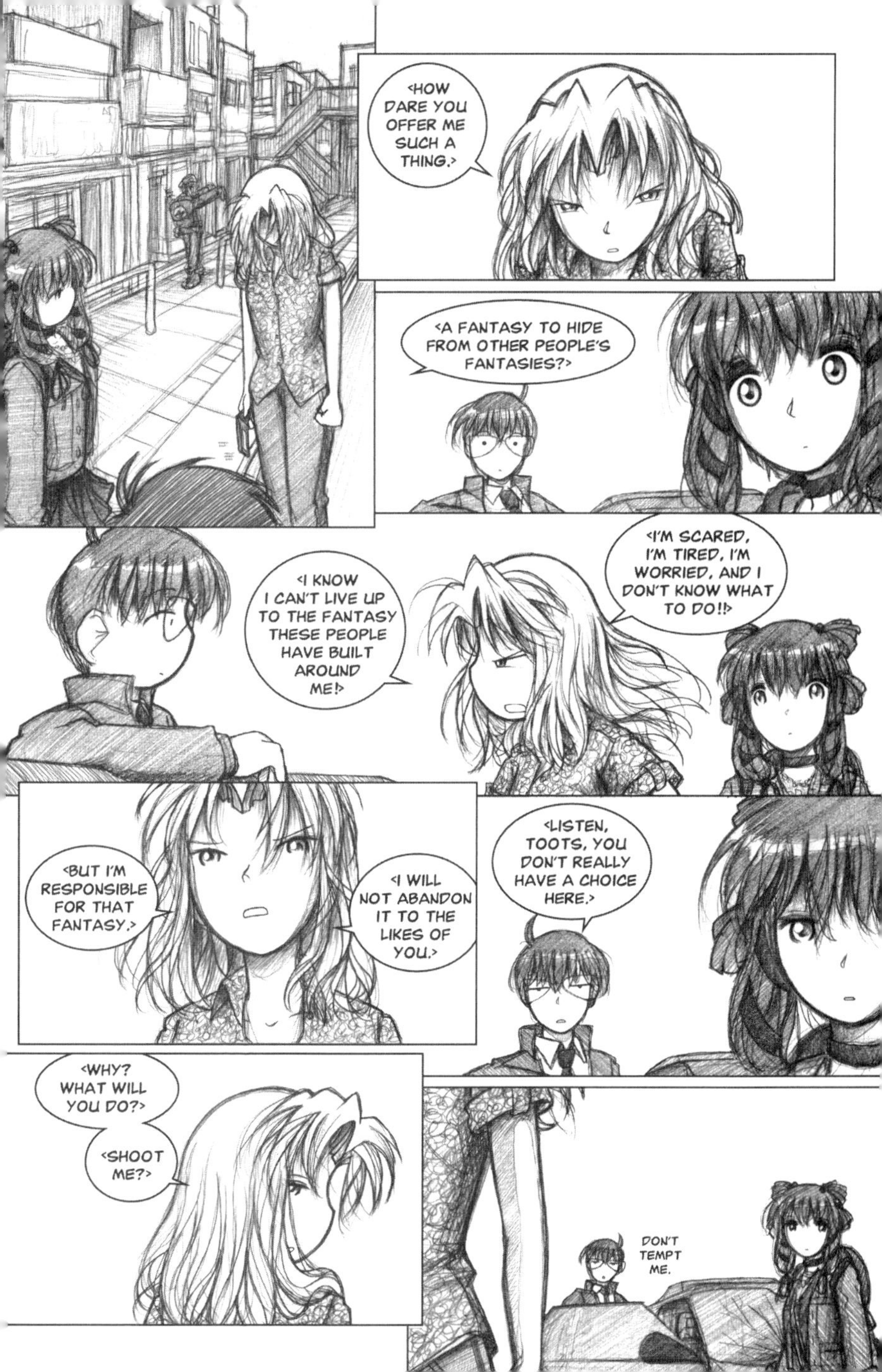
<HOW DARE YOU OFFER ME SUCH A THING.>
<A FANTASY TO HIDE FROM OTHER PEOPLE'S FANTASIES?>
<I KNOW I CAN'T LIVE UP TO THE FANTASY THESE PEOPLE HAVE BUILT AROUND ME!>
<I'M SCARED, I'M TIRED, I'M WORRIED, AND I DON'T KNOW WHAT TO DO!!>
<BUT I'M RESPONSIBLE FOR THAT FANTASY.>
<I WILL NOT ABANDON IT TO THE LIKES OF YOU.>
<LISTEN, TOOTS, YOU DON'T REALLY HAVE A CHOICE HERE.>
<WHY? WHAT WILL YOU DO?>
<SHOOT ME?>
DON'T TEMPT ME.

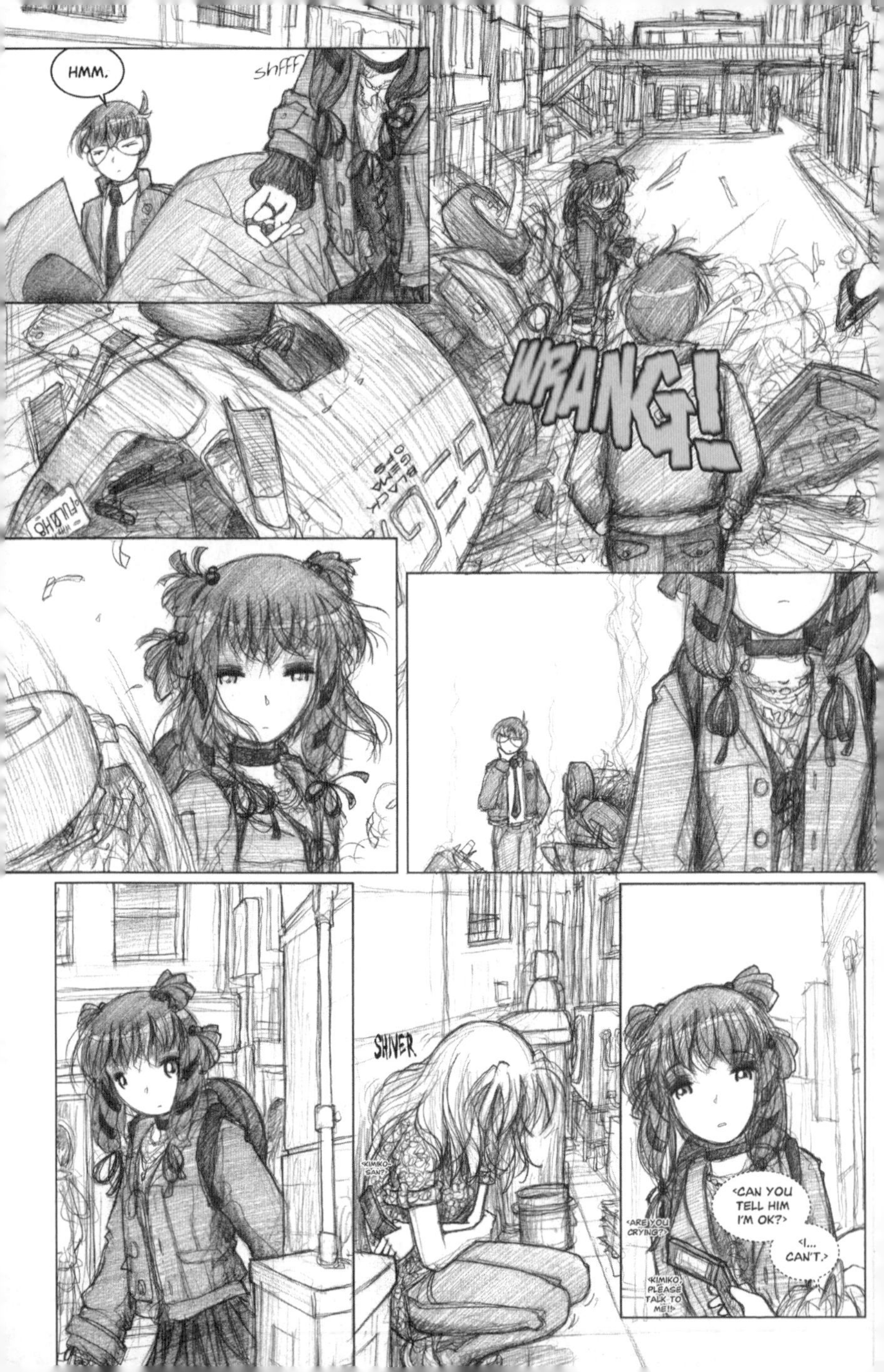
HMM.
shfff
WRANG!
SHIVER
<KIMIKO-SAN?>
<ARE YOU CRYING?>
<KIMIKO, PLEASE TALK TO ME!!>
<CAN YOU TELL HIM I'M OK?>
<I... CAN'T.>

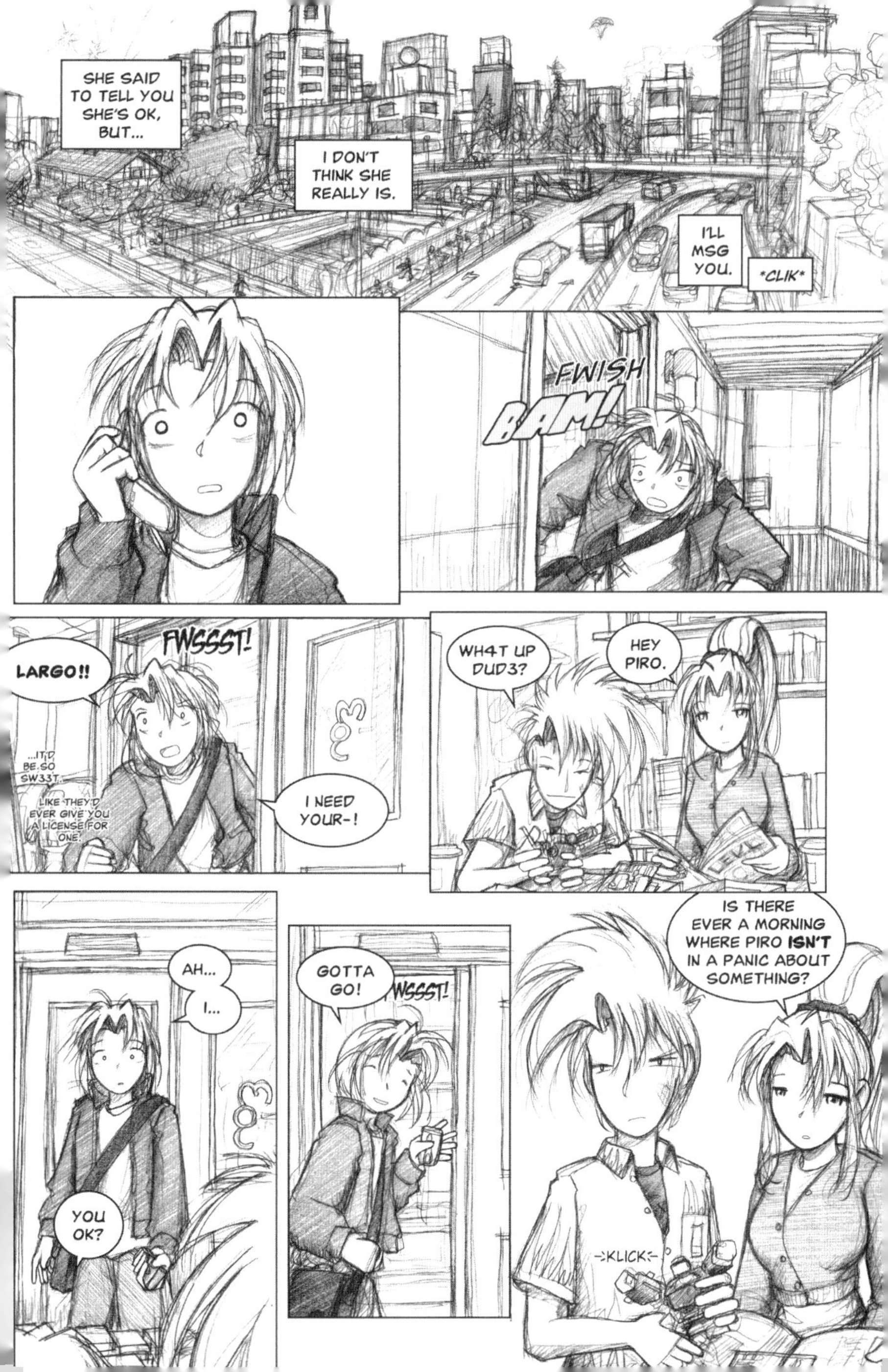
SHE SAID TO TELL YOU SHE'S OK, BUT...
I DON'T THINK SHE REALLY IS.
I'LL MSG YOU.
CLIK
FWISH
BAM!
LARGO!!
FWSSST!
...IT'D BE SO SW33T.
LIKE THEY'D EVER GIVE YOU A LICENSE FOR ONE.
I NEED YOUR-!
WH4T UP DUD3?
HEY PIRO.
AH...
I...
YOU OK?
GOTTA GO!
WSSST!
IS THERE EVER A MORNING WHERE PIRO ISN'T IN A PANIC ABOUT SOMETHING?
-KLICK-

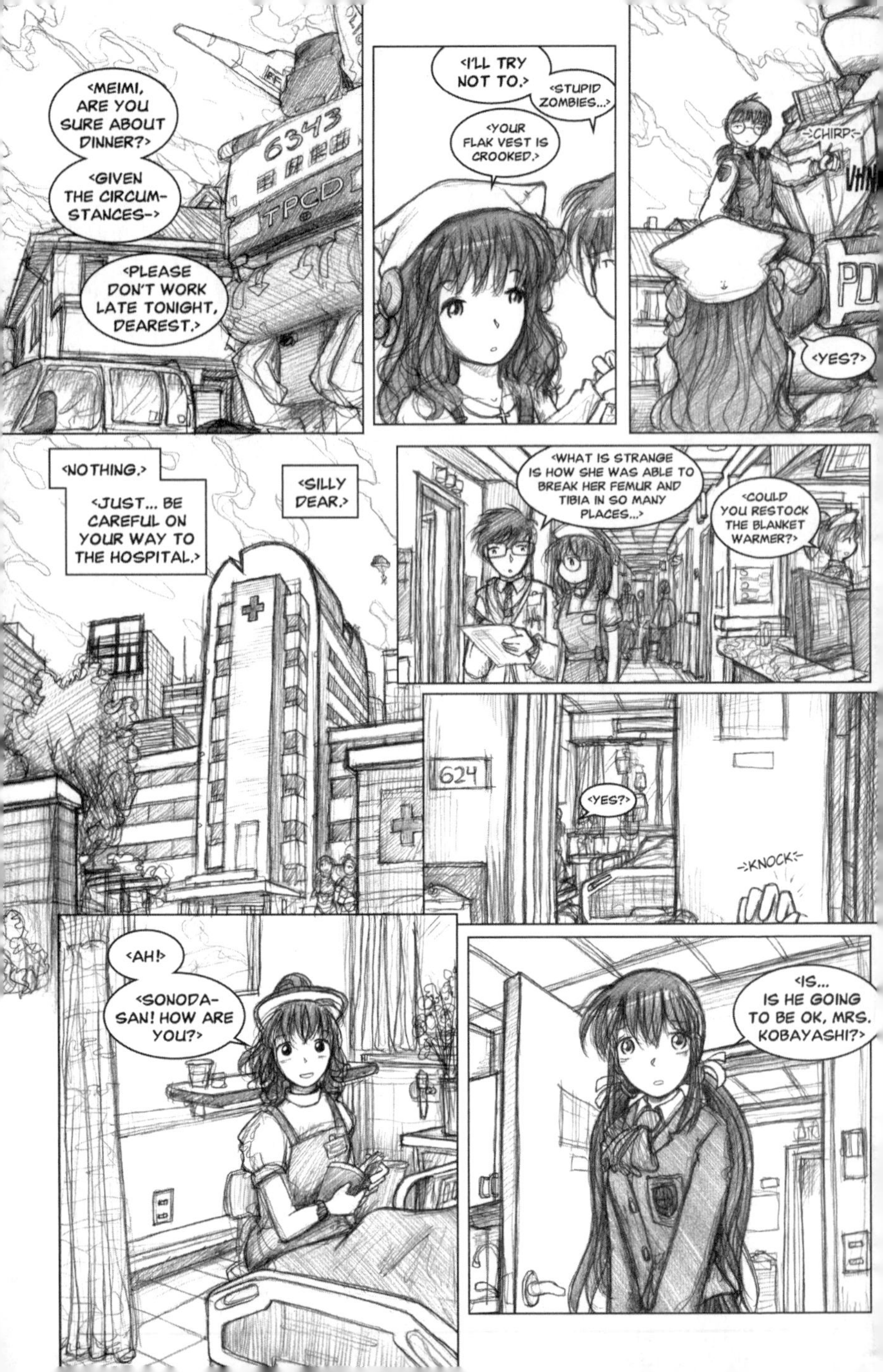
6343
TPCD
<MEIMI, ARE YOU SURE ABOUT DINNER?>
<GIVEN THE CIRCUM-STANCES–>
<PLEASE DON'T WORK LATE TONIGHT, DEAREST.>
<I'LL TRY NOT TO.>
<STUPID ZOMBIES...>
<YOUR FLAK VEST IS CROOKED.>
CHIRP
<YES?>
<NOTHING.>
<JUST... BE CAREFUL ON YOUR WAY TO THE HOSPITAL.>
<SILLY DEAR.>
<WHAT IS STRANGE IS HOW SHE WAS ABLE TO BREAK HER FEMUR AND TIBIA IN SO MANY PLACES...>
<COULD YOU RESTOCK THE BLANKET WARMER?>
624
<YES?>
KNOCK
<AH!>
<SONODA-SAN! HOW ARE YOU?>
<IS... IS HE GOING TO BE OK, MRS. KOBAYASHI?>

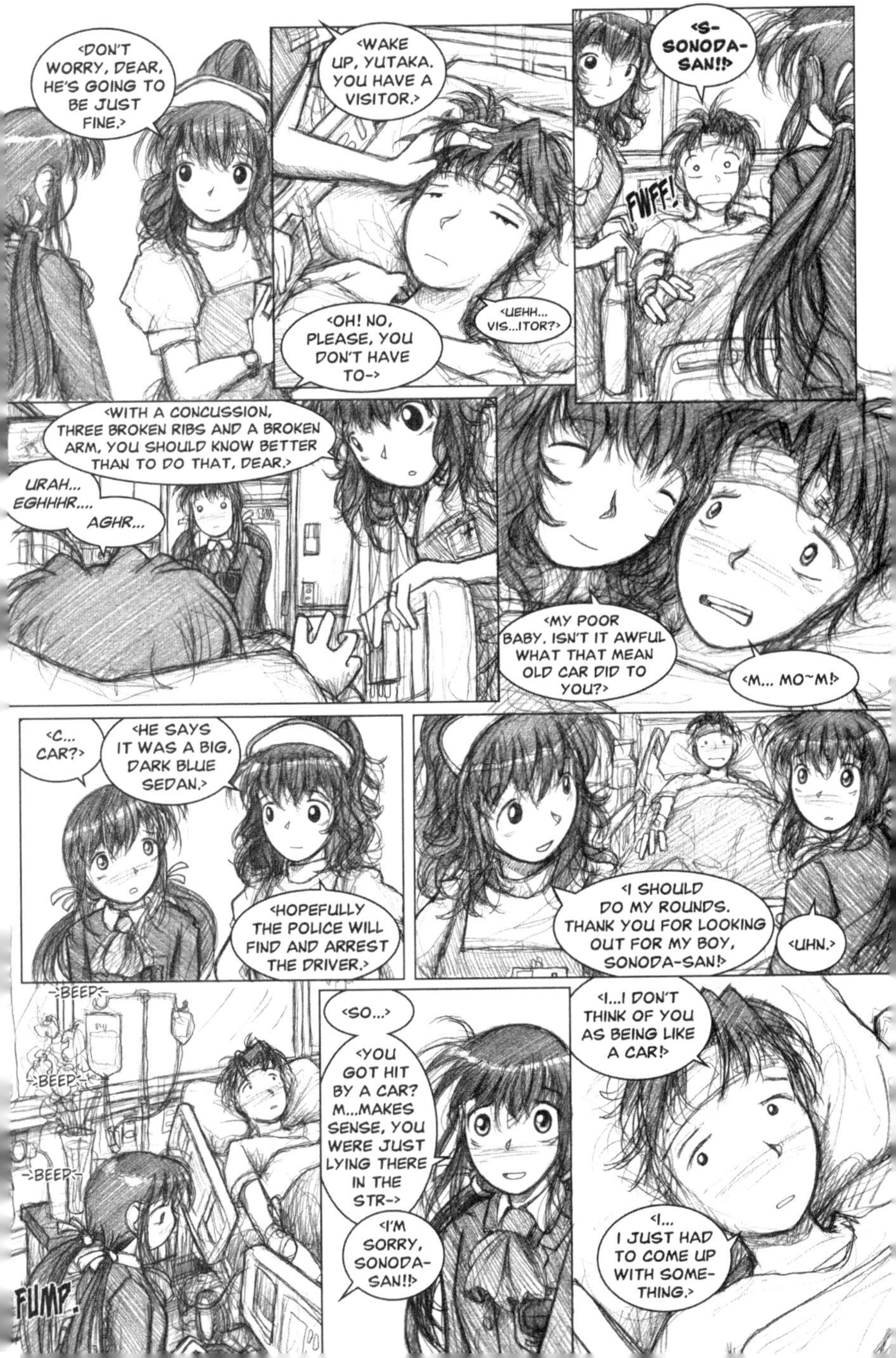
<DON'T WORRY, DEAR, HE'S GOING TO BE JUST FINE.>
<WAKE UP, YUTAKA. YOU HAVE A VISITOR.>
<UEHH... VIS...ITOR?>
<OH! NO, PLEASE, YOU DON'T HAVE TO–>
<S-SONODA-SAN!!>
FWFF!
<WITH A CONCUSSION, THREE BROKEN RIBS AND A BROKEN ARM, YOU SHOULD KNOW BETTER THAN TO DO THAT, DEAR.>
URAH... EGHHHR.... AGHR...
<MY POOR BABY. ISN'T IT AWFUL WHAT THAT MEAN OLD CAR DID TO YOU?>
<M... MO~M!>
<C... CAR?>
<HE SAYS IT WAS A BIG, DARK BLUE SEDAN.>
<HOPEFULLY THE POLICE WILL FIND AND ARREST THE DRIVER.>
<I SHOULD DO MY ROUNDS. THANK YOU FOR LOOKING OUT FOR MY BOY, SONODA-SAN!>
<UHN.>
BEEP
BEEP
BEEP
FUMP.
<SO...>
<YOU GOT HIT BY A CAR? M...MAKES SENSE, YOU WERE JUST LYING THERE IN THE STR–>
<I'M SORRY, SONODA-SAN!!>
<I...I DON'T THINK OF YOU AS BEING LIKE A CAR!>
<I... I JUST HAD TO COME UP WITH SOME-THING.>

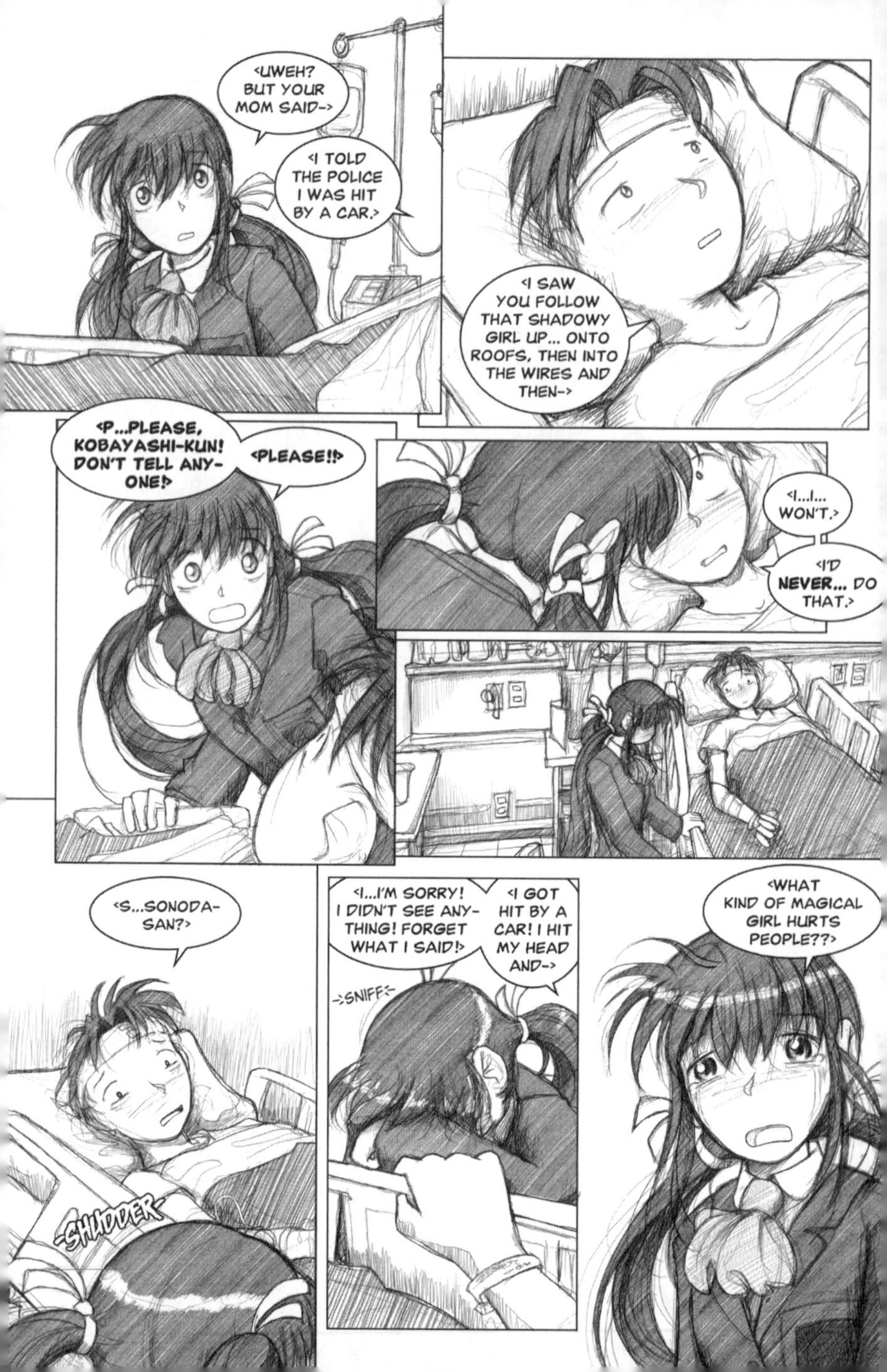
<UWEH? BUT YOUR MOM SAID->
<I TOLD THE POLICE I WAS HIT BY A CAR.>
<I SAW YOU FOLLOW THAT SHADOWY GIRL UP... ONTO ROOFS, THEN INTO THE WIRES AND THEN->
<P...PLEASE, KOBAYASHI-KUN! DON'T TELL ANY-ONE!>
<PLEASE!!>
<I...I... WON'T.>
<I'D **NEVER...** DO THAT.>
<S...SONODA-SAN?>
SHUDDER
<I...I'M SORRY! I DIDN'T SEE ANY-THING! FORGET WHAT I SAID!>
<I GOT HIT BY A CAR! I HIT MY HEAD AND->
SNIFF
<WHAT KIND OF MAGICAL GIRL HURTS PEOPLE??>

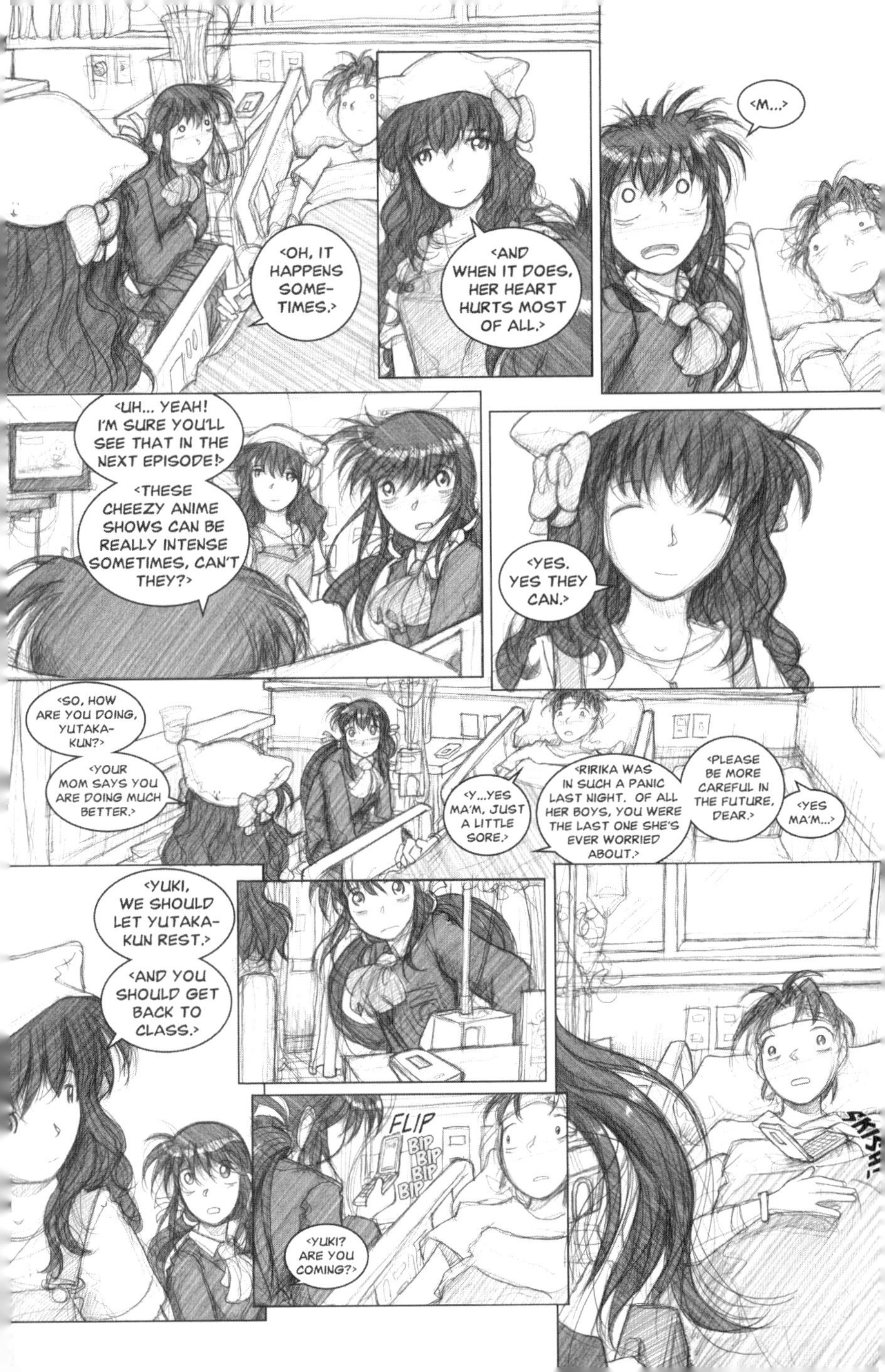
<OH, IT HAPPENS SOME-TIMES.>
<AND WHEN IT DOES, HER HEART HURTS MOST OF ALL.>
<M...>
<UH... YEAH! I'M SURE YOU'LL SEE THAT IN THE NEXT EPISODE!>
<THESE CHEEZY ANIME SHOWS CAN BE REALLY INTENSE SOMETIMES, CAN'T THEY?>
<YES. YES THEY CAN.>
<SO, HOW ARE YOU DOING, YUTAKA-KUN?>
<YOUR MOM SAYS YOU ARE DOING MUCH BETTER.>
<Y...YES MA'M, JUST A LITTLE SORE.>
<RIRIKA WAS IN SUCH A PANIC LAST NIGHT. OF ALL HER BOYS, YOU WERE THE LAST ONE SHE'S EVER WORRIED ABOUT.>
<PLEASE BE MORE CAREFUL IN THE FUTURE, DEAR.>
<YES MA'M...>
<YUKI, WE SHOULD LET YUTAKA-KUN REST.>
<AND YOU SHOULD GET BACK TO CLASS.>
FLIP
BIP BIP BIP BIP
<YUKI? ARE YOU COMING?>
SKISH!

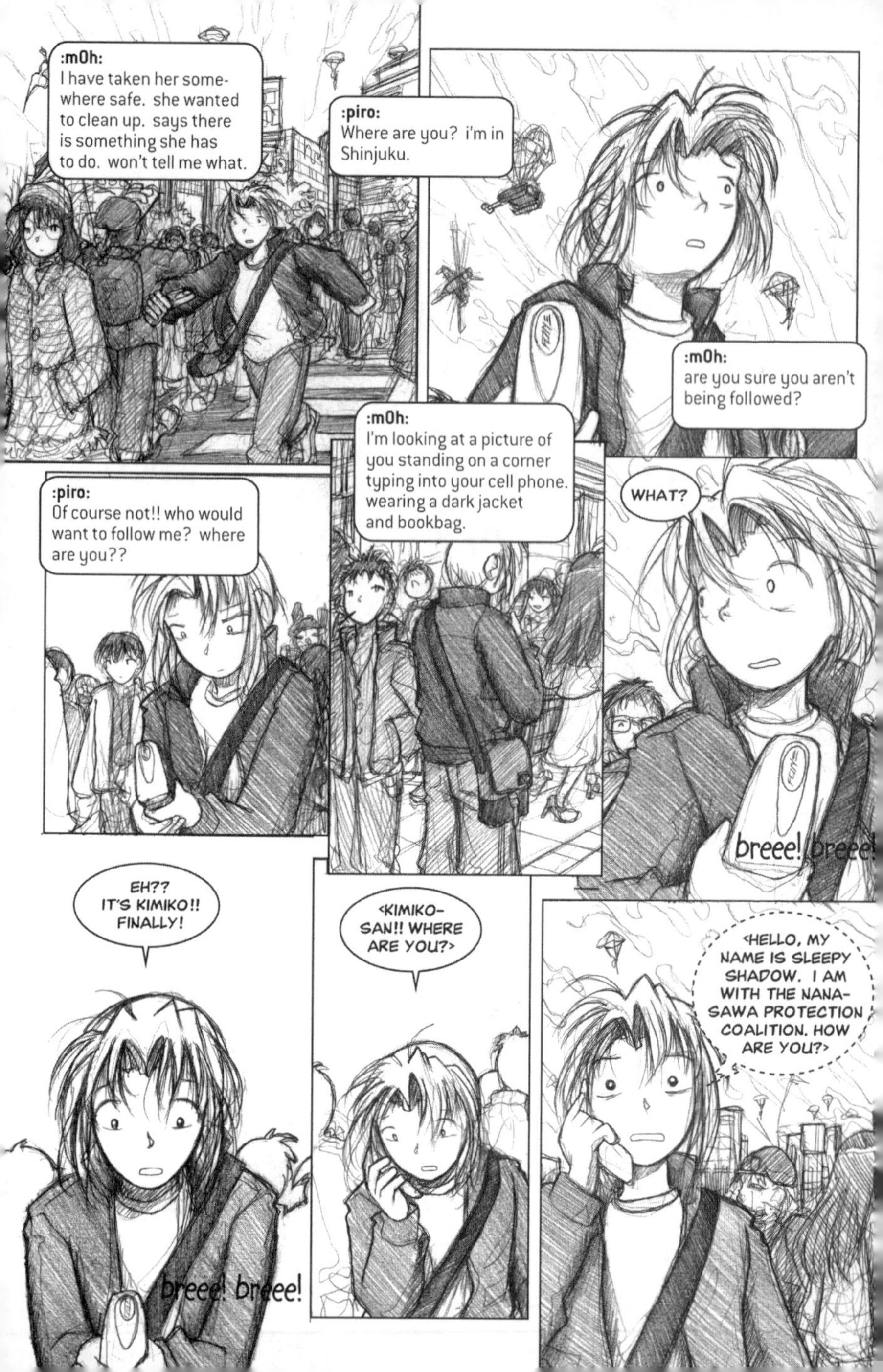
:m0h:
I have taken her some-where safe. she wanted to clean up. says there is something she has to do. won't tell me what.
:piro:
Where are you? i'm in Shinjuku.
:m0h:
are you sure you aren't being followed?
:piro:
Of course not!! who would want to follow me? where are you??
:m0h:
I'm looking at a picture of you standing on a corner typing into your cell phone. wearing a dark jacket and bookbag.
WHAT?
breee! breee!
EH?? IT'S KIMIKO!! FINALLY!
breee! breee!
<KIMIKO-SAN!! WHERE ARE YOU?>
<HELLO, MY NAME IS SLEEPY SHADOW. I AM WITH THE NANA-SAWA PROTECTION COALITION. HOW ARE YOU?>

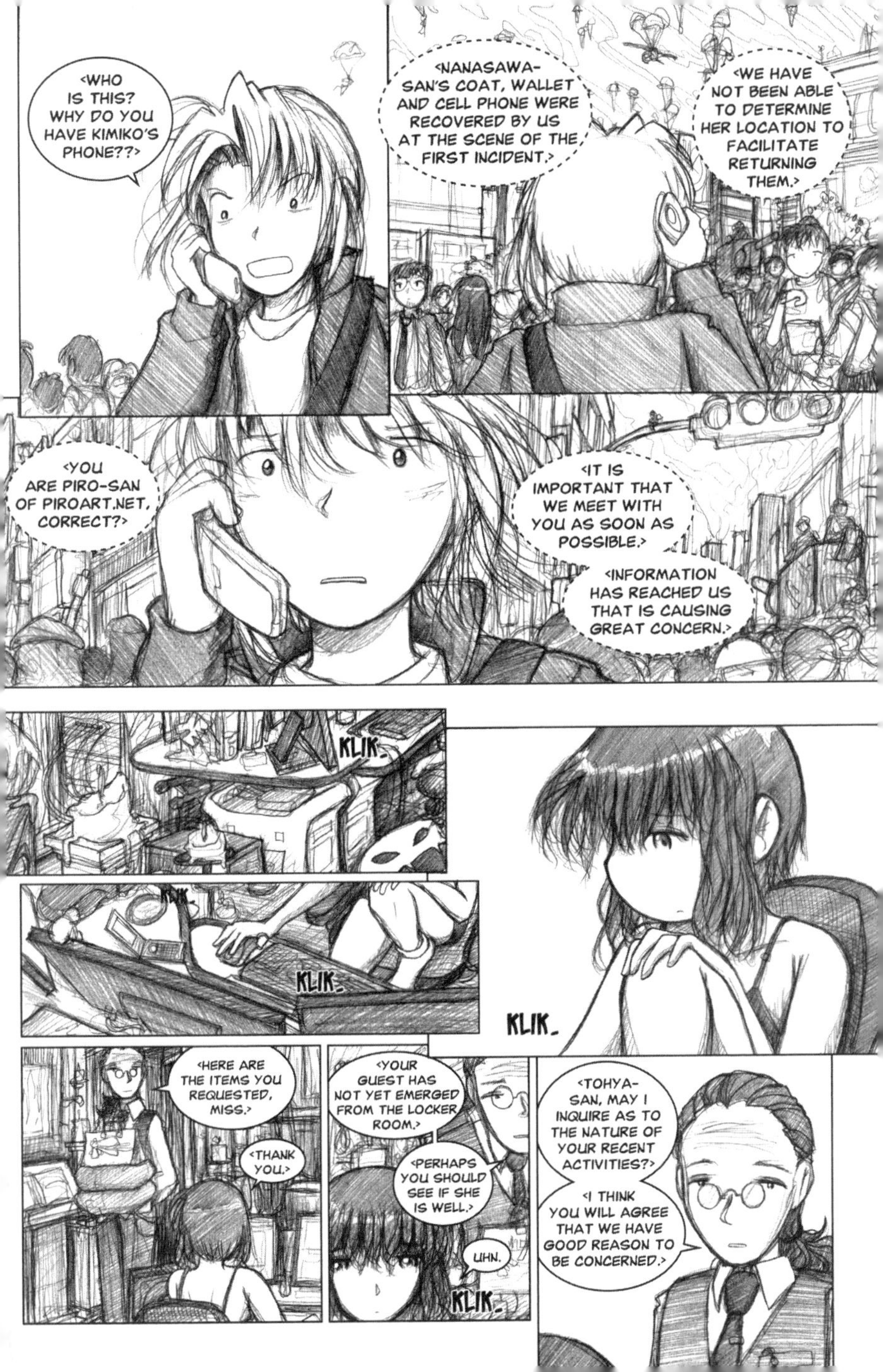
<WHO IS THIS? WHY DO YOU HAVE KIMIKO'S PHONE??>
<NANASAWA-SAN'S COAT, WALLET AND CELL PHONE WERE RECOVERED BY US AT THE SCENE OF THE FIRST INCIDENT.>
<WE HAVE NOT BEEN ABLE TO DETERMINE HER LOCATION TO FACILITATE RETURNING THEM.>
<YOU ARE PIRO-SAN OF PIROART.NET, CORRECT?>
<IT IS IMPORTANT THAT WE MEET WITH YOU AS SOON AS POSSIBLE.>
<INFORMATION HAS REACHED US THAT IS CAUSING GREAT CONCERN.>
KLIK.
KLIK.
KLIK.
<HERE ARE THE ITEMS YOU REQUESTED, MISS.>
<THANK YOU.>
<YOUR GUEST HAS NOT YET EMERGED FROM THE LOCKER ROOM.>
<PERHAPS YOU SHOULD SEE IF SHE IS WELL.>
UHN.
KLIK.
<TOHYA-SAN, MAY I INQUIRE AS TO THE NATURE OF YOUR RECENT ACTIVITIES?>
<I THINK YOU WILL AGREE THAT WE HAVE GOOD REASON TO BE CONCERNED.>

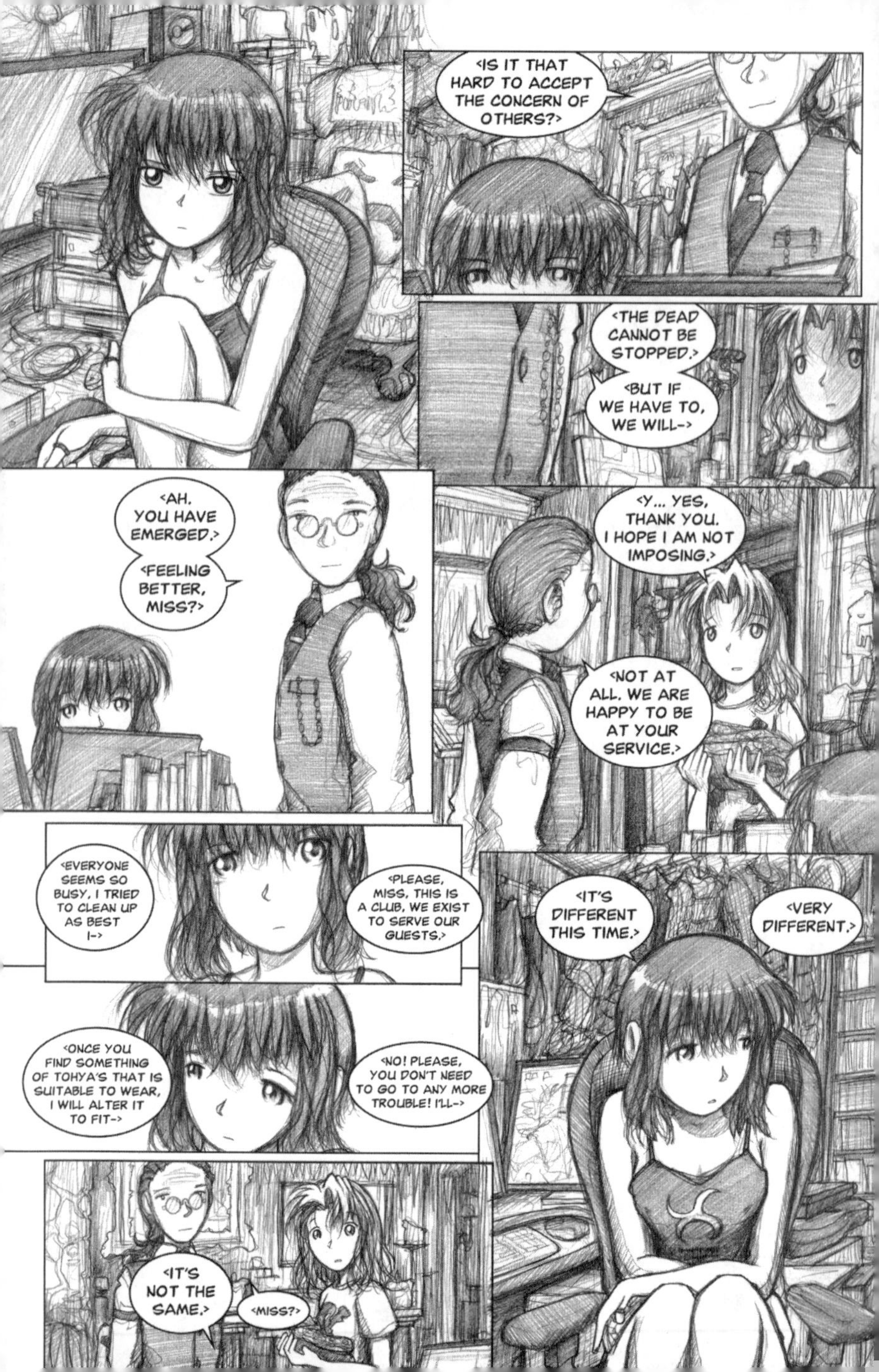
<IS IT THAT HARD TO ACCEPT THE CONCERN OF OTHERS?>
<THE DEAD CANNOT BE STOPPED.>
<BUT IF WE HAVE TO, WE WILL->
<AH. YOU HAVE EMERGED.>
<FEELING BETTER, MISS?>
<Y... YES, THANK YOU. I HOPE I AM NOT IMPOSING.>
<NOT AT ALL. WE ARE HAPPY TO BE AT YOUR SERVICE.>
<EVERYONE SEEMS SO BUSY, I TRIED TO CLEAN UP AS BEST I->
<PLEASE, MISS, THIS IS A CLUB, WE EXIST TO SERVE OUR GUESTS.>
<ONCE YOU FIND SOMETHING OF TOHYA'S THAT IS SUITABLE TO WEAR, I WILL ALTER IT TO FIT->
<NO! PLEASE, YOU DON'T NEED TO GO TO ANY MORE TROUBLE! I'LL->
<IT'S NOT THE SAME.>
<MISS?>
<IT'S DIFFERENT THIS TIME.>
<VERY DIFFERENT.>

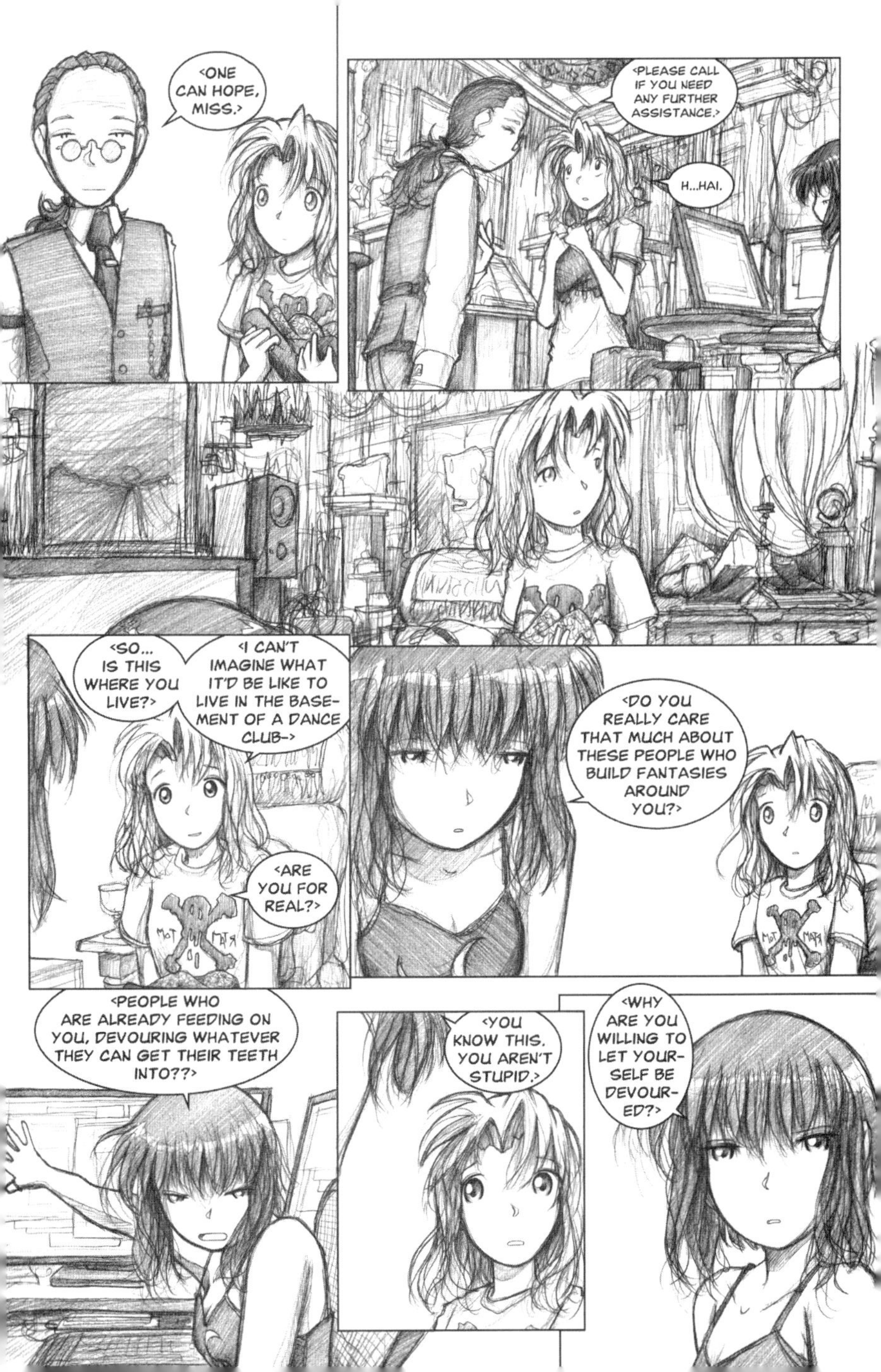
<ONE CAN HOPE, MISS.>
<PLEASE CALL IF YOU NEED ANY FURTHER ASSISTANCE.>
H...HAI.
<SO... IS THIS WHERE YOU LIVE?>
<I CAN'T IMAGINE WHAT IT'D BE LIKE TO LIVE IN THE BASE-MENT OF A DANCE CLUB–>
<ARE YOU FOR REAL?>
<DO YOU REALLY CARE THAT MUCH ABOUT THESE PEOPLE WHO BUILD FANTASIES AROUND YOU?>
<PEOPLE WHO ARE ALREADY FEEDING ON YOU, DEVOURING WHATEVER THEY CAN GET THEIR TEETH INTO??>
<YOU KNOW THIS. YOU AREN'T STUPID.>
<WHY ARE YOU WILLING TO LET YOUR-SELF BE DEVOUR-ED?>

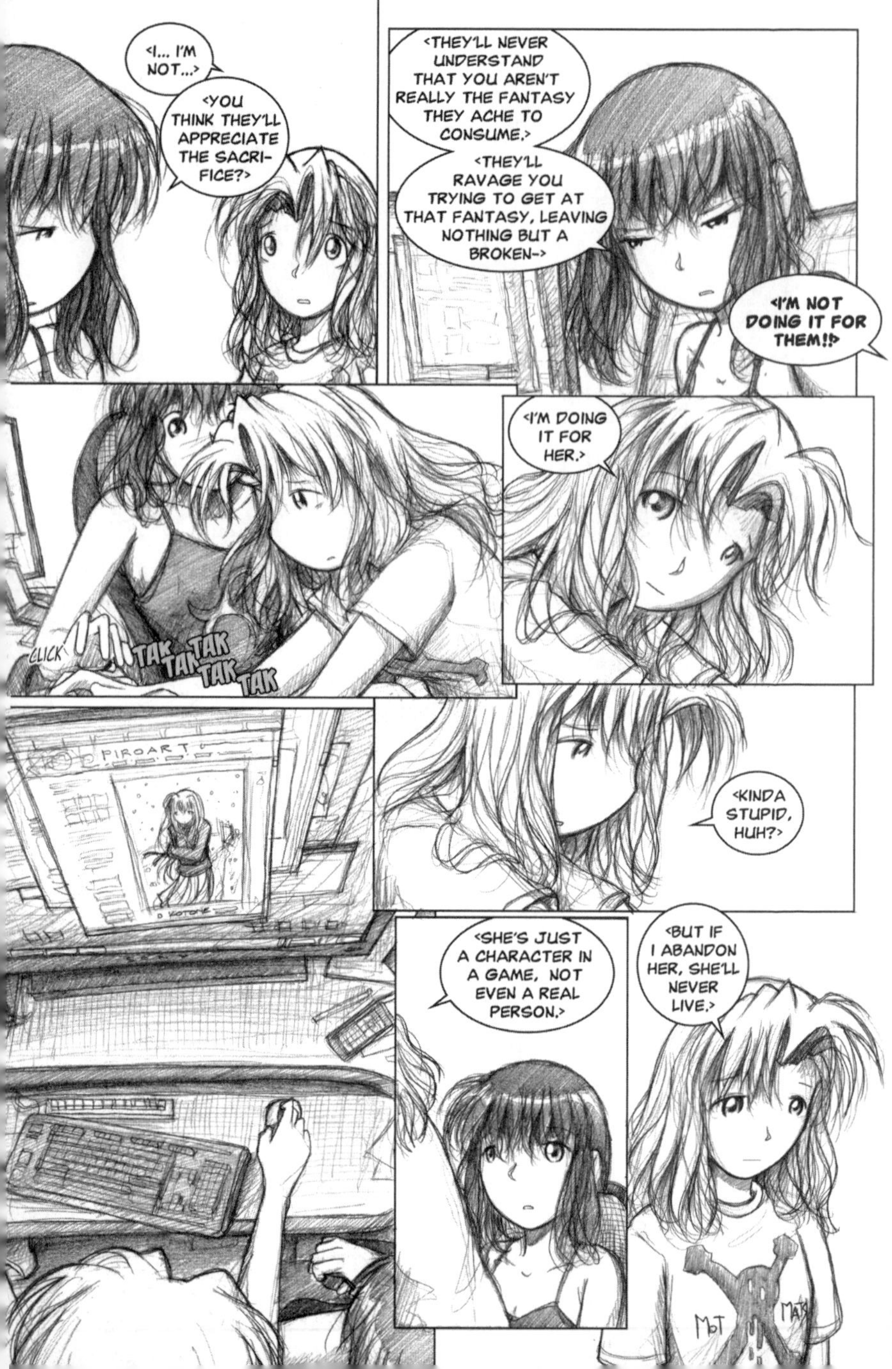
<I... I'M NOT...>
<YOU THINK THEY'LL APPRECIATE THE SACRI-FICE?>
<THEY'LL NEVER UNDERSTAND THAT YOU AREN'T REALLY THE FANTASY THEY ACHE TO CONSUME.>
<THEY'LL RAVAGE YOU TRYING TO GET AT THAT FANTASY, LEAVING NOTHING BUT A BROKEN-->
<I'M NOT DOING IT FOR THEM!!>
CLICK
TAK TAK TAK TAK TAK
<I'M DOING IT FOR HER.>
PIROART
<KINDA STUPID, HUH?>
<SHE'S JUST A CHARACTER IN A GAME, NOT EVEN A REAL PERSON.>
<BUT IF I ABANDON HER, SHE'LL NEVER LIVE.>

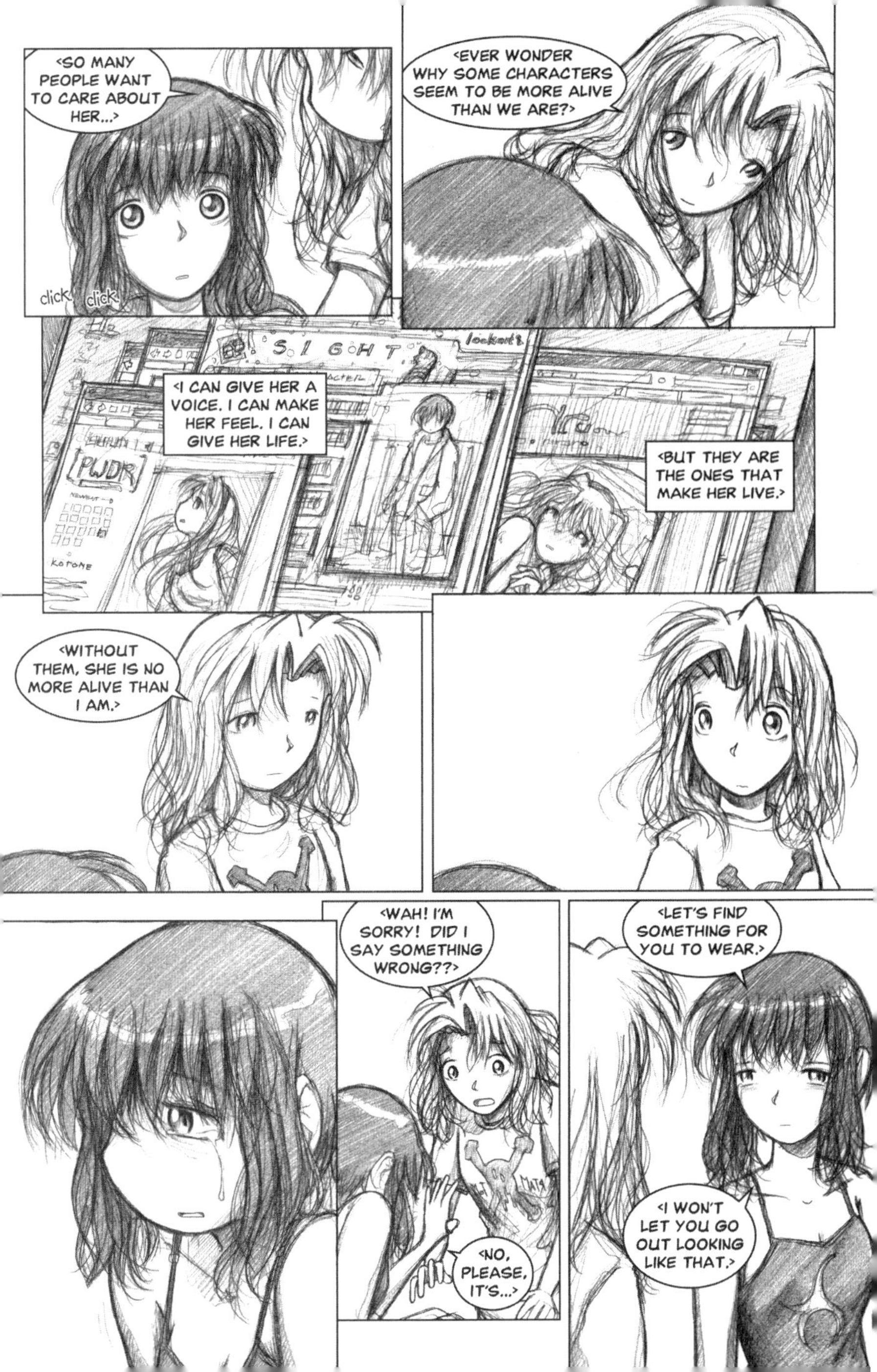
<SO MANY PEOPLE WANT TO CARE ABOUT HER...>
click click
<EVER WONDER WHY SOME CHARACTERS SEEM TO BE MORE ALIVE THAN WE ARE?>
<I CAN GIVE HER A VOICE. I CAN MAKE HER FEEL. I CAN GIVE HER LIFE.>
<BUT THEY ARE THE ONES THAT MAKE HER LIVE.>
<WITHOUT THEM, SHE IS NO MORE ALIVE THAN I AM.>
<WAH! I'M SORRY! DID I SAY SOMETHING WRONG??>
<NO, PLEASE, IT'S...>
<LET'S FIND SOMETHING FOR YOU TO WEAR.>
<I WON'T LET YOU GO OUT LOOKING LIKE THAT.>

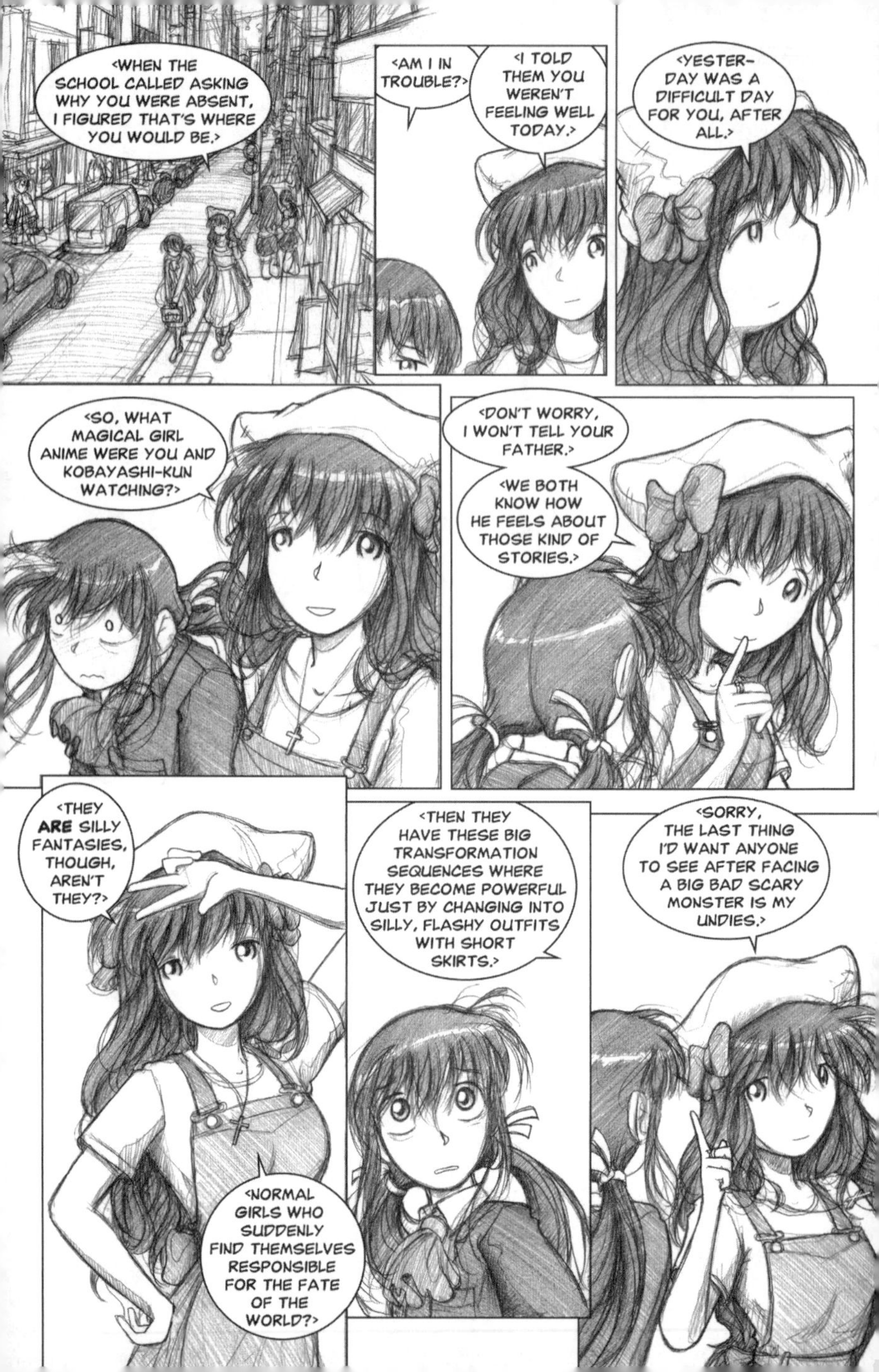

<WHEN THE SCHOOL CALLED ASKING WHY YOU WERE ABSENT, I FIGURED THAT'S WHERE YOU WOULD BE.>
<AM I IN TROUBLE?>
<I TOLD THEM YOU WEREN'T FEELING WELL TODAY.>
<YESTER-DAY WAS A DIFFICULT DAY FOR YOU, AFTER ALL.>
<SO, WHAT MAGICAL GIRL ANIME WERE YOU AND KOBAYASHI-KUN WATCHING?>
<DON'T WORRY, I WON'T TELL YOUR FATHER.>
<WE BOTH KNOW HOW HE FEELS ABOUT THOSE KIND OF STORIES.>
<THEY **ARE** SILLY FANTASIES, THOUGH, AREN'T THEY?>
<NORMAL GIRLS WHO SUDDENLY FIND THEMSELVES RESPONSIBLE FOR THE FATE OF THE WORLD?>
<THEN THEY HAVE THESE BIG TRANSFORMATION SEQUENCES WHERE THEY BECOME POWERFUL JUST BY CHANGING INTO SILLY, FLASHY OUTFITS WITH SHORT SKIRTS.>
<SORRY, THE LAST THING I'D WANT ANYONE TO SEE AFTER FACING A BIG BAD SCARY MONSTER IS MY UNDIES.>

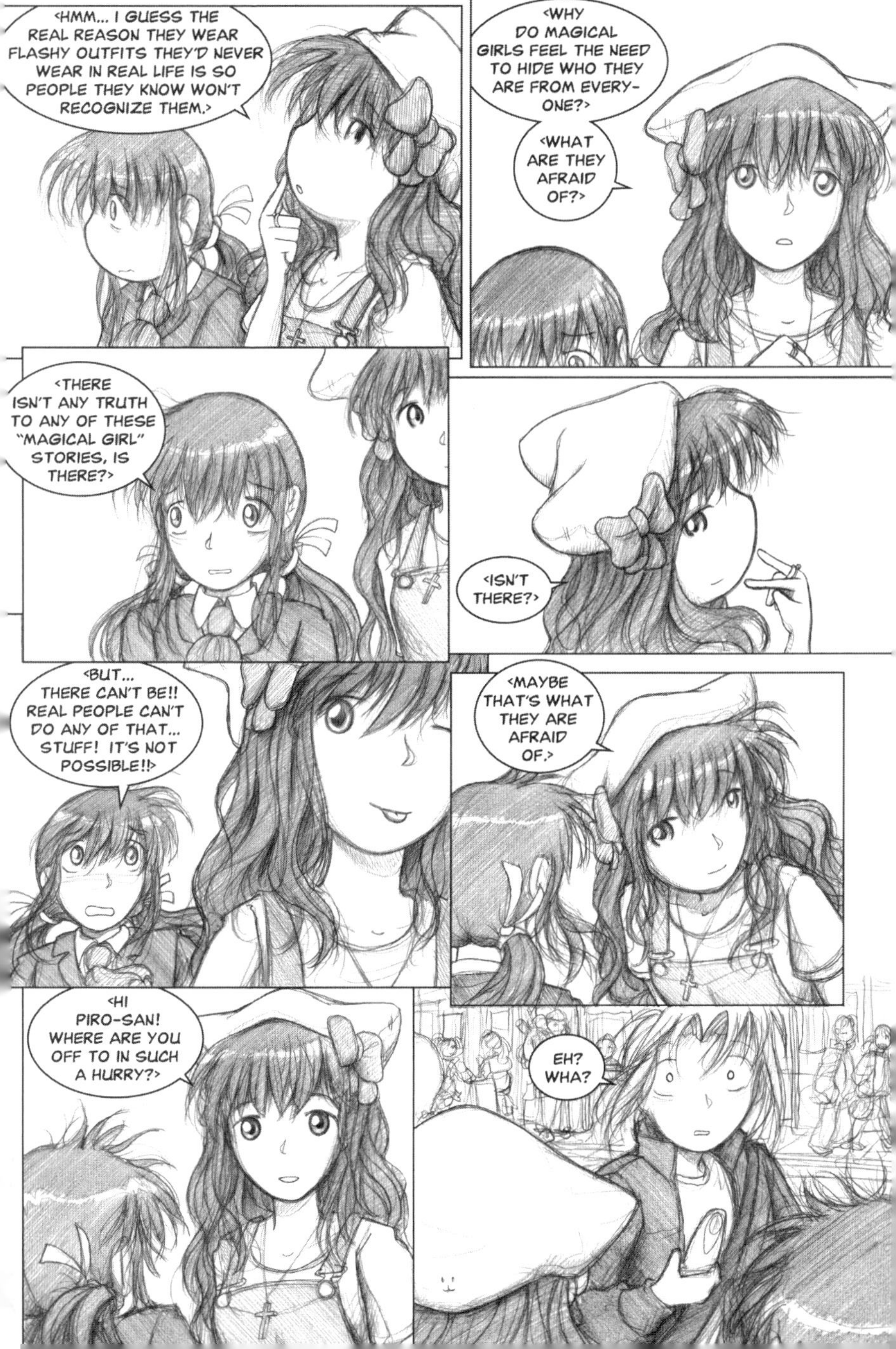
<HMM... I GUESS THE REAL REASON THEY WEAR FLASHY OUTFITS THEY'D NEVER WEAR IN REAL LIFE IS SO PEOPLE THEY KNOW WON'T RECOGNIZE THEM.>
<WHY DO MAGICAL GIRLS FEEL THE NEED TO HIDE WHO THEY ARE FROM EVERY-ONE?>
<WHAT ARE THEY AFRAID OF?>
<THERE ISN'T ANY TRUTH TO ANY OF THESE "MAGICAL GIRL" STORIES, IS THERE?>
<ISN'T THERE?>
<BUT... THERE CAN'T BE!! REAL PEOPLE CAN'T DO ANY OF THAT... STUFF! IT'S NOT POSSIBLE!!>
<MAYBE THAT'S WHAT THEY ARE AFRAID OF.>
<HI PIRO-SAN! WHERE ARE YOU OFF TO IN SUCH A HURRY?>
EH? WHA?

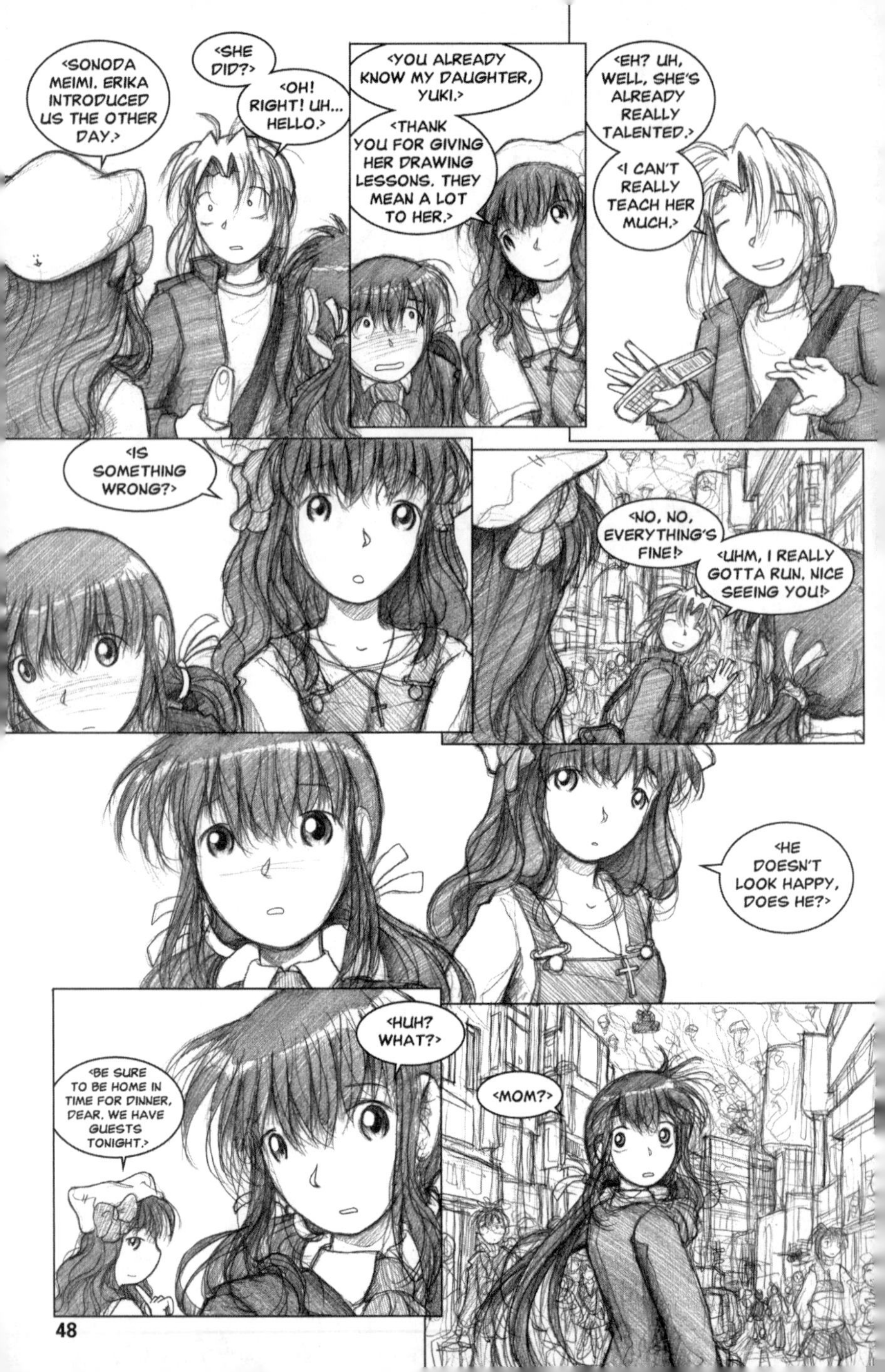
<SONODA MEIMI. ERIKA INTRODUCED US THE OTHER DAY.>
<SHE DID?>
<OH! RIGHT! UH... HELLO.>
<YOU ALREADY KNOW MY DAUGHTER, YUKI.>
<THANK YOU FOR GIVING HER DRAWING LESSONS. THEY MEAN A LOT TO HER.>
<EH? UH, WELL, SHE'S ALREADY REALLY TALENTED.>
<I CAN'T REALLY TEACH HER MUCH.>
<IS SOMETHING WRONG?>
<NO, NO, EVERYTHING'S FINE!>
<UHM, I REALLY GOTTA RUN. NICE SEEING YOU!>
<HE DOESN'T LOOK HAPPY, DOES HE?>
<BE SURE TO BE HOME IN TIME FOR DINNER, DEAR. WE HAVE GUESTS TONIGHT.>
<HUH? WHAT?>
<MOM?>

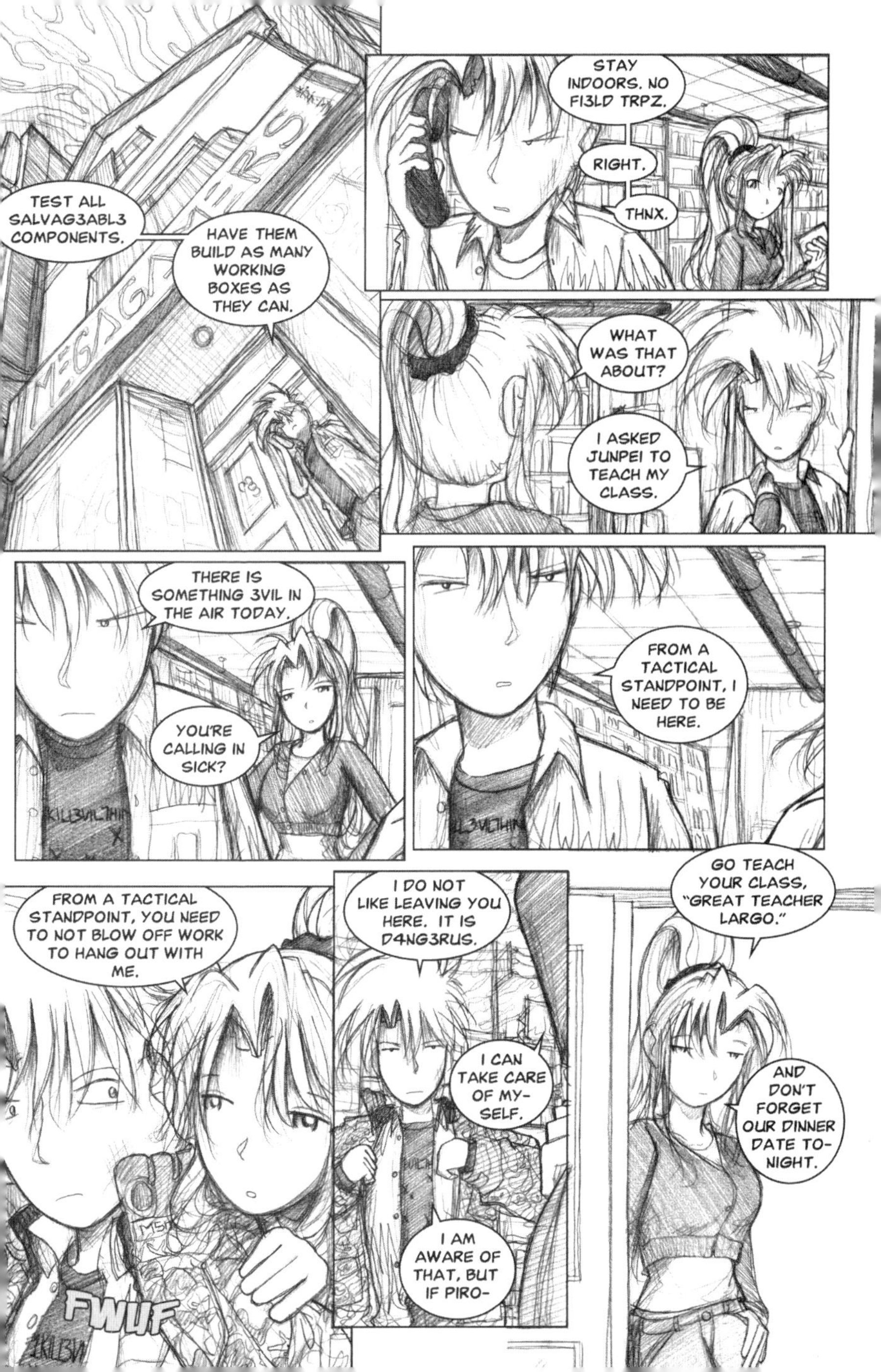
TEST ALL SALVAG3ABL3 COMPONENTS.
HAVE THEM BUILD AS MANY WORKING BOXES AS THEY CAN.
MEGAGAMERS
STAY INDOORS. NO FI3LD TRPZ.
RIGHT.
THNX.
WHAT WAS THAT ABOUT?
I ASKED JUNPEI TO TEACH MY CLASS.
THERE IS SOMETHING 3VIL IN THE AIR TODAY.
YOU'RE CALLING IN SICK?
FROM A TACTICAL STANDPOINT, I NEED TO BE HERE.
FROM A TACTICAL STANDPOINT, YOU NEED TO NOT BLOW OFF WORK TO HANG OUT WITH ME.
FWUF
I DO NOT LIKE LEAVING YOU HERE. IT IS D4NG3RUS.
I CAN TAKE CARE OF MY-SELF.
I AM AWARE OF THAT, BUT IF PIRO-
GO TEACH YOUR CLASS, "GREAT TEACHER LARGO."
AND DON'T FORGET OUR DINNER DATE TO-NIGHT.

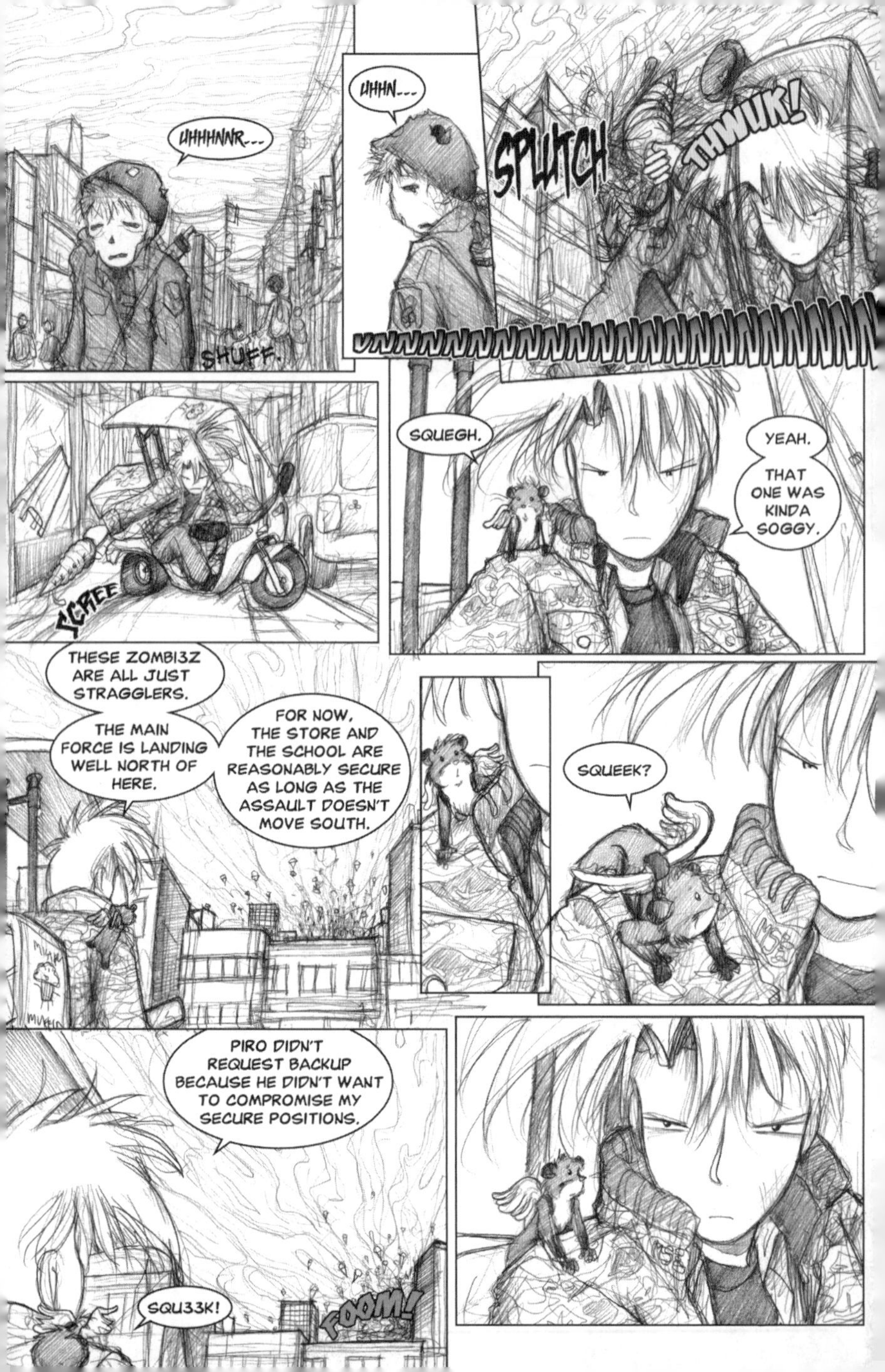
UHHHNNR...
SHUFF.
UHHN...
SPLUTCH
THWUK!
VNNNNNNNNNNNNNNNNNNNNNNNNNN
SCREE
SQUEGH.
YEAH.
THAT ONE WAS KINDA SOGGY.
THESE ZOMBI3Z ARE ALL JUST STRAGGLERS.
THE MAIN FORCE IS LANDING WELL NORTH OF HERE.
FOR NOW, THE STORE AND THE SCHOOL ARE REASONABLY SECURE AS LONG AS THE ASSAULT DOESN'T MOVE SOUTH.
SQUEEK?
PIRO DIDN'T REQUEST BACKUP BECAUSE HE DIDN'T WANT TO COMPROMISE MY SECURE POSITIONS.
SQU33K!
FOOM!

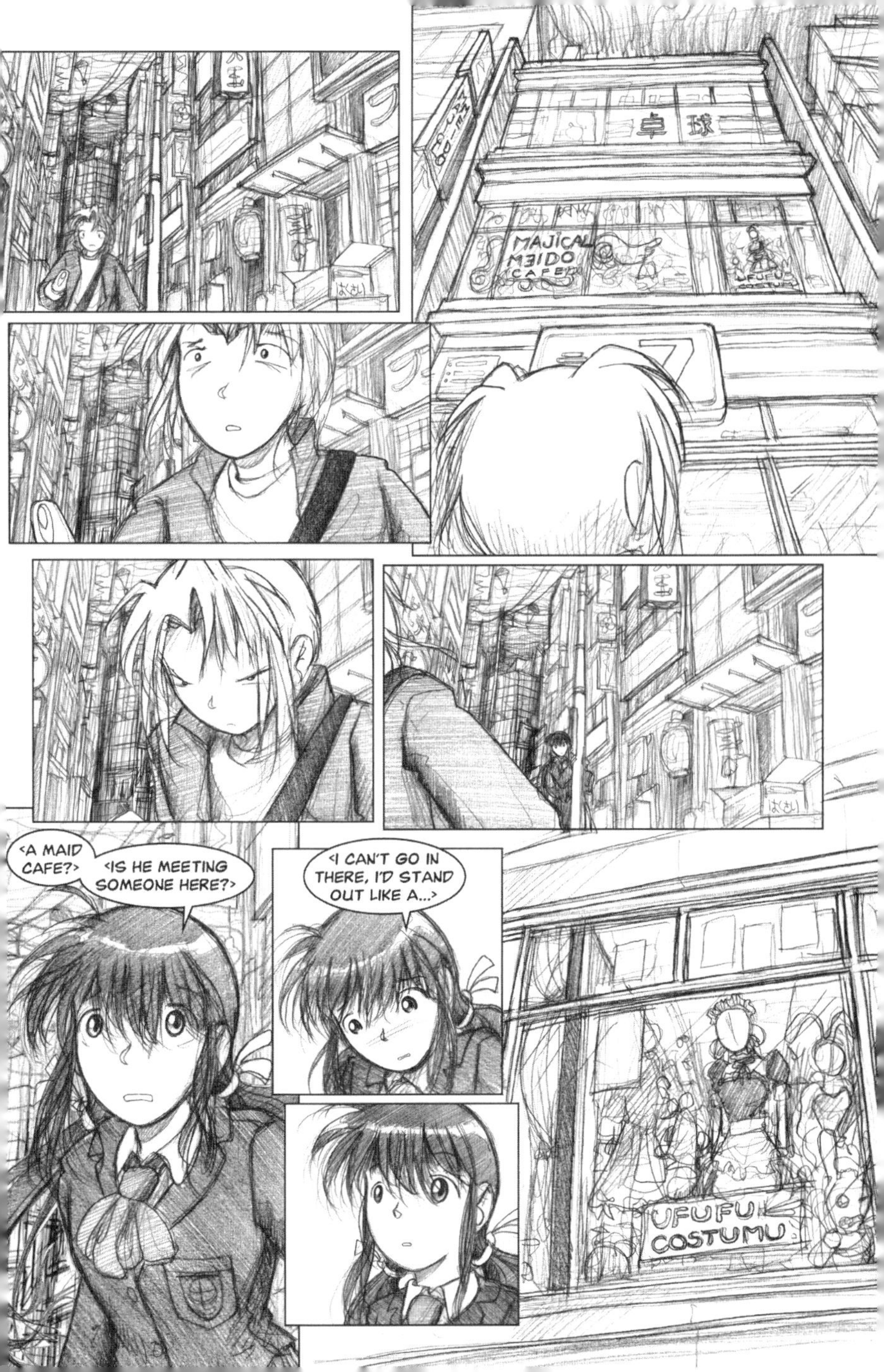

卓球
MAJICAL MEIDO CAFE
UFUFU COSTUMU
<A MAID CAFE?>
<IS HE MEETING SOMEONE HERE?>
<I CAN'T GO IN THERE, I'D STAND OUT LIKE A...>
UFUFU COSTUMU

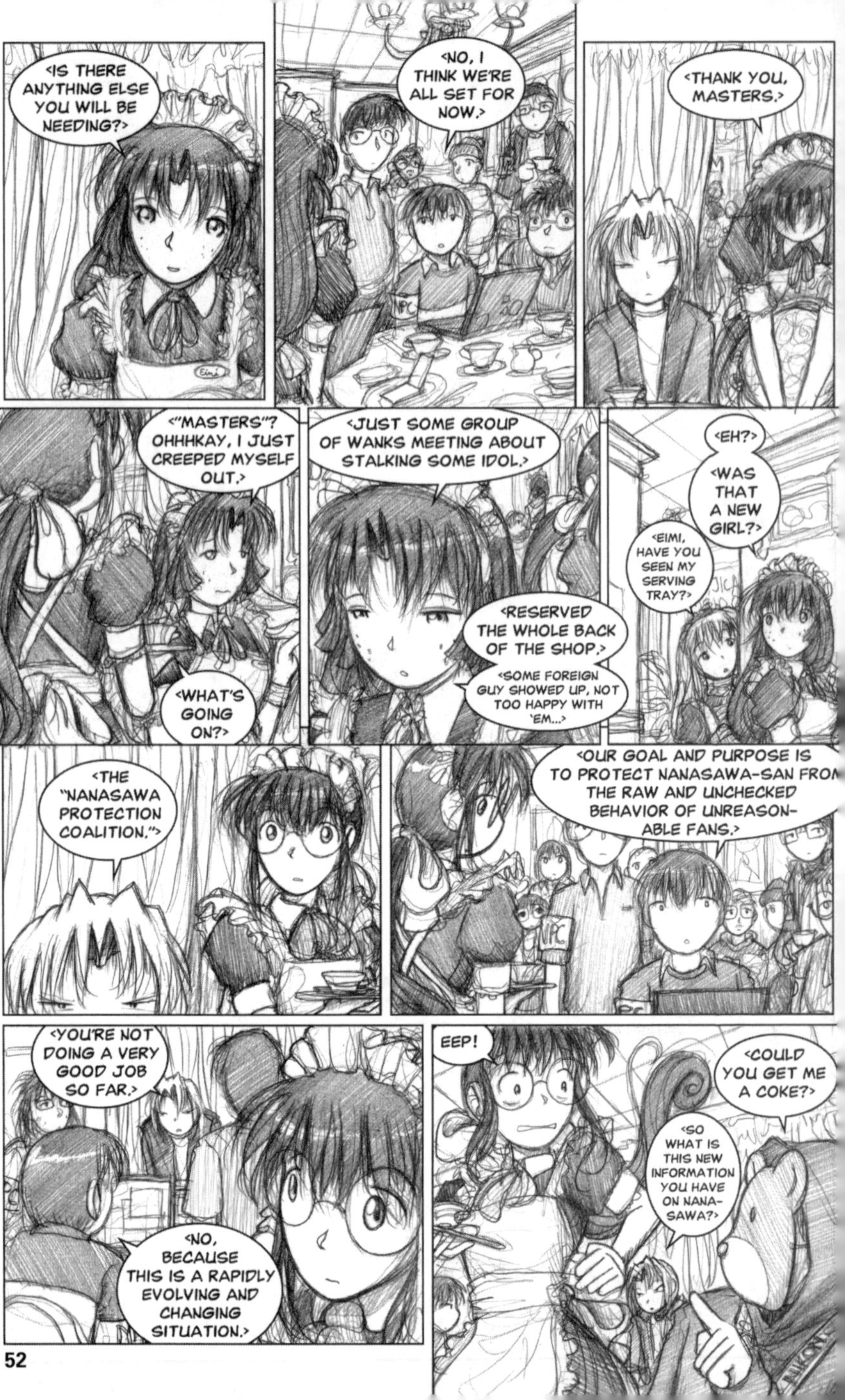

<IS THERE ANYTHING ELSE YOU WILL BE NEEDING?>
<NO, I THINK WE'RE ALL SET FOR NOW.>
<THANK YOU, MASTERS.>
<"MASTERS"? OHHHKAY, I JUST CREEPED MYSELF OUT.>
<WHAT'S GOING ON?>
<JUST SOME GROUP OF WANKS MEETING ABOUT STALKING SOME IDOL.>
<RESERVED THE WHOLE BACK OF THE SHOP.>
<SOME FOREIGN GUY SHOWED UP, NOT TOO HAPPY WITH 'EM...>
<EH?>
<WAS THAT A NEW GIRL?>
<EIMI, HAVE YOU SEEN MY SERVING TRAY?>
<THE "NANASAWA PROTECTION COALITION.">
<OUR GOAL AND PURPOSE IS TO PROTECT NANASAWA-SAN FROM THE RAW AND UNCHECKED BEHAVIOR OF UNREASON-ABLE FANS.>
<YOU'RE NOT DOING A VERY GOOD JOB SO FAR.>
<NO, BECAUSE THIS IS A RAPIDLY EVOLVING AND CHANGING SITUATION.>
EEP!
<COULD YOU GET ME A COKE?>
<SO WHAT IS THIS NEW INFORMATION YOU HAVE ON NANA-SAWA?>

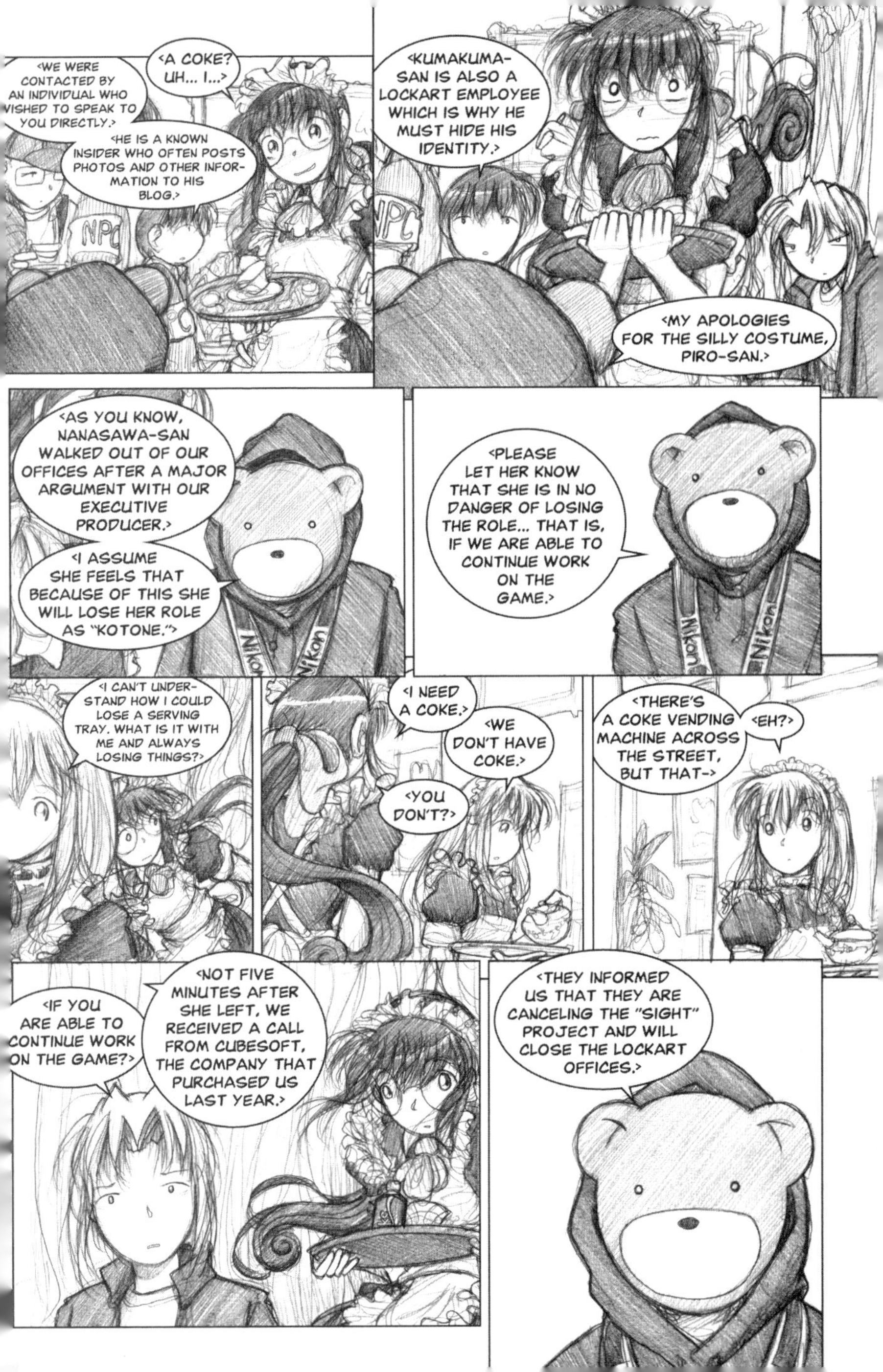
<WE WERE CONTACTED BY AN INDIVIDUAL WHO WISHED TO SPEAK TO YOU DIRECTLY.>
<A COKE? UH... I...>
<HE IS A KNOWN INSIDER WHO OFTEN POSTS PHOTOS AND OTHER INFORMATION TO HIS BLOG.>
NPC
<KUMAKUMA-SAN IS ALSO A LOCKART EMPLOYEE WHICH IS WHY HE MUST HIDE HIS IDENTITY.>
NPC
<MY APOLOGIES FOR THE SILLY COSTUME, PIRO-SAN.>
<AS YOU KNOW, NANASAWA-SAN WALKED OUT OF OUR OFFICES AFTER A MAJOR ARGUMENT WITH OUR EXECUTIVE PRODUCER.>
<I ASSUME SHE FEELS THAT BECAUSE OF THIS SHE WILL LOSE HER ROLE AS "KOTONE.">
Nikon
<PLEASE LET HER KNOW THAT SHE IS IN NO DANGER OF LOSING THE ROLE... THAT IS, IF WE ARE ABLE TO CONTINUE WORK ON THE GAME.>
Nikon
<I CAN'T UNDERSTAND HOW I COULD LOSE A SERVING TRAY. WHAT IS IT WITH ME AND ALWAYS LOSING THINGS?>
<I NEED A COKE.>
<WE DON'T HAVE COKE.>
<YOU DON'T?>
<THERE'S A COKE VENDING MACHINE ACROSS THE STREET, BUT THAT->
<EH?>
<IF YOU ARE ABLE TO CONTINUE WORK ON THE GAME?>
<NOT FIVE MINUTES AFTER SHE LEFT, WE RECEIVED A CALL FROM CUBESOFT, THE COMPANY THAT PURCHASED US LAST YEAR.>
<THEY INFORMED US THAT THEY ARE CANCELING THE "SIGHT" PROJECT AND WILL CLOSE THE LOCKART OFFICES.>

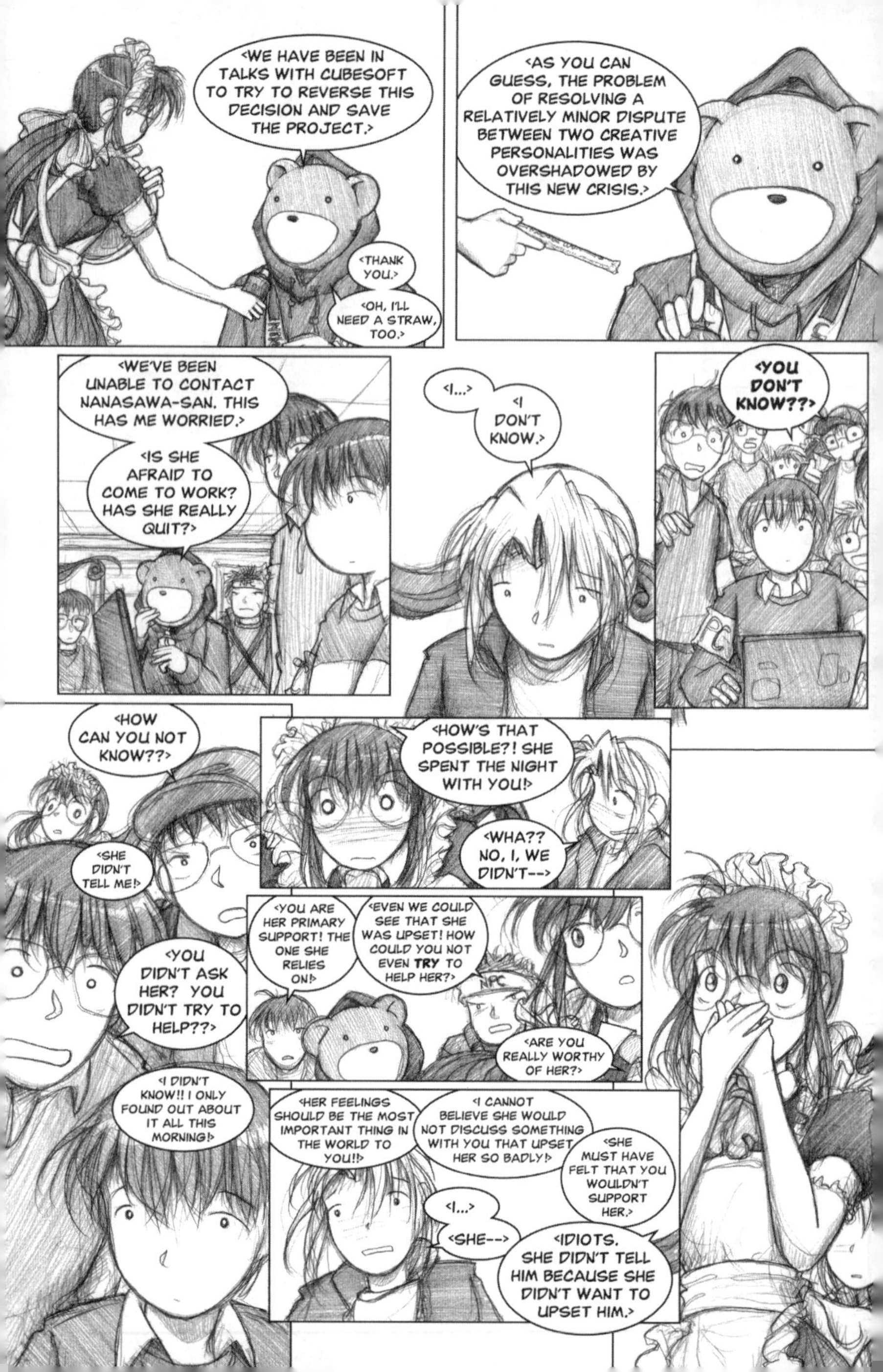
<WE HAVE BEEN IN TALKS WITH CUBESOFT TO TRY TO REVERSE THIS DECISION AND SAVE THE PROJECT.>
<THANK YOU.>
<OH, I'LL NEED A STRAW, TOO.>
<AS YOU CAN GUESS, THE PROBLEM OF RESOLVING A RELATIVELY MINOR DISPUTE BETWEEN TWO CREATIVE PERSONALITIES WAS OVERSHADOWED BY THIS NEW CRISIS.>
<WE'VE BEEN UNABLE TO CONTACT NANASAWA-SAN. THIS HAS ME WORRIED.>
<IS SHE AFRAID TO COME TO WORK? HAS SHE REALLY QUIT?>
<I...>
<I DON'T KNOW.>
<YOU DON'T KNOW??>
<HOW CAN YOU NOT KNOW??>
<SHE DIDN'T TELL ME!>
<YOU DIDN'T ASK HER? YOU DIDN'T TRY TO HELP??>
<I DIDN'T KNOW!! I ONLY FOUND OUT ABOUT IT ALL THIS MORNING!>
<HOW'S THAT POSSIBLE?! SHE SPENT THE NIGHT WITH YOU!>
<WHA?? NO, I, WE DIDN'T-->
<YOU ARE HER PRIMARY SUPPORT! THE ONE SHE RELIES ON!>
<EVEN WE COULD SEE THAT SHE WAS UPSET! HOW COULD YOU NOT EVEN TRY TO HELP HER?>
<ARE YOU REALLY WORTHY OF HER?>
<HER FEELINGS SHOULD BE THE MOST IMPORTANT THING IN THE WORLD TO YOU!!>
<I CANNOT BELIEVE SHE WOULD NOT DISCUSS SOMETHING WITH YOU THAT UPSET HER SO BADLY!>
<SHE MUST HAVE FELT THAT YOU WOULDN'T SUPPORT HER.>
<I...>
<SHE-->
<IDIOTS. SHE DIDN'T TELL HIM BECAUSE SHE DIDN'T WANT TO UPSET HIM.>

‹SHE IS RIGHT, OF COURSE.›

‹WHICH IS PART OF WHY I AM HERE.›

‹NO, I HAVEN'T HIRED ANY NEW GIRLS RECENTLY. WHY DO YOU ASK?›

‹NANASAWA'S CONCERN FOR OTHERS IS SUCH THAT SHE BURIES HER OWN FEELINGS DEEP INSIDE HERSELF.›

‹SO DEEP THAT SHE DOESN'T EVEN CONSIDER THEM "REAL."›

‹HER ONLY ESCAPE IS TO PLAY CHARACTERS THAT CAN FEEL WHAT SHE WON'T ALLOW HERSELF TO FEEL.›

‹UWEH??›

‹BECAUSE I DON'T REMEMBER SEEING THAT ONE BEFORE.›

URUDABEEP!! BURUDABEEP!!

‹WHICH DOES LITTLE TO RESOLVE HER REAL EMOTIONAL BURDENS.›

‹KOBAYASHI-KUN?? NO, NOT NOW!!›

‹HEY!›

‹I AM TERRIBLY WORRIED THAT NANASAWA WILL FEEL RESPONSIBLE FOR THE CANCELLATION OF THE "SIGHT" PROJECT AND THE CONSEQUENCES OF ITS DEMISE.›

‹I WISH TO PREVENT THIS AT ALL COSTS.›

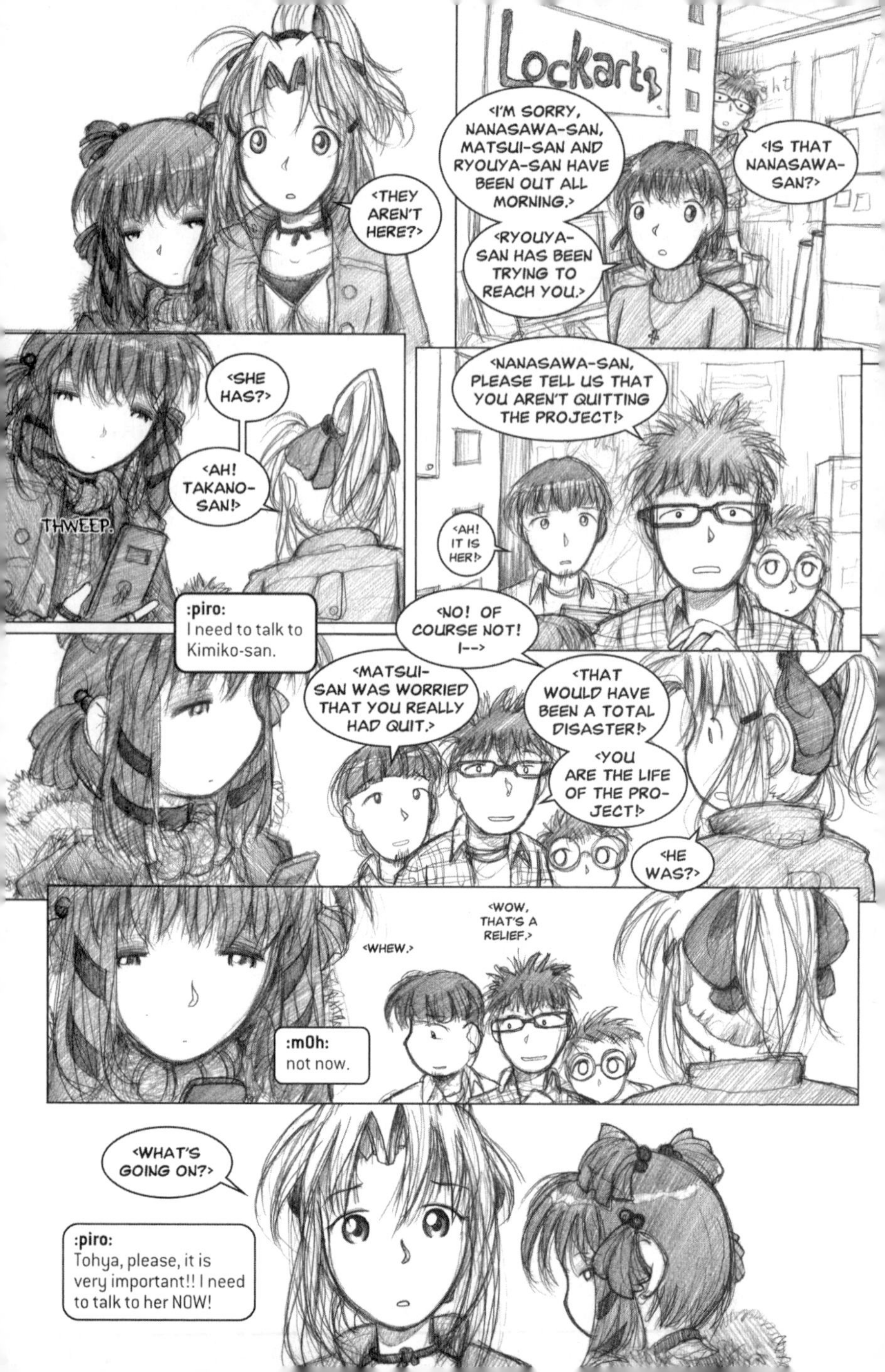

<THEY AREN'T HERE?>
Lockart
<I'M SORRY, NANASAWA-SAN, MATSUI-SAN AND RYOUYA-SAN HAVE BEEN OUT ALL MORNING.>
<RYOUYA-SAN HAS BEEN TRYING TO REACH YOU.>
<IS THAT NANASAWA-SAN?>
<SHE HAS?>
<AH! TAKANO-SAN!>
THWEEP.
:piro:
I need to talk to Kimiko-san.
<NANASAWA-SAN, PLEASE TELL US THAT YOU AREN'T QUITTING THE PROJECT!>
<AH! IT IS HER!>
<NO! OF COURSE NOT! I-->
<MATSUI-SAN WAS WORRIED THAT YOU REALLY HAD QUIT.>
<THAT WOULD HAVE BEEN A TOTAL DISASTER!>
<YOU ARE THE LIFE OF THE PROJECT!>
<HE WAS?>
:mOh:
not now.
<WHEW.>
<WOW, THAT'S A RELIEF.>
<WHAT'S GOING ON?>
:piro:
Tohya, please, it is very important!! I need to talk to her NOW!

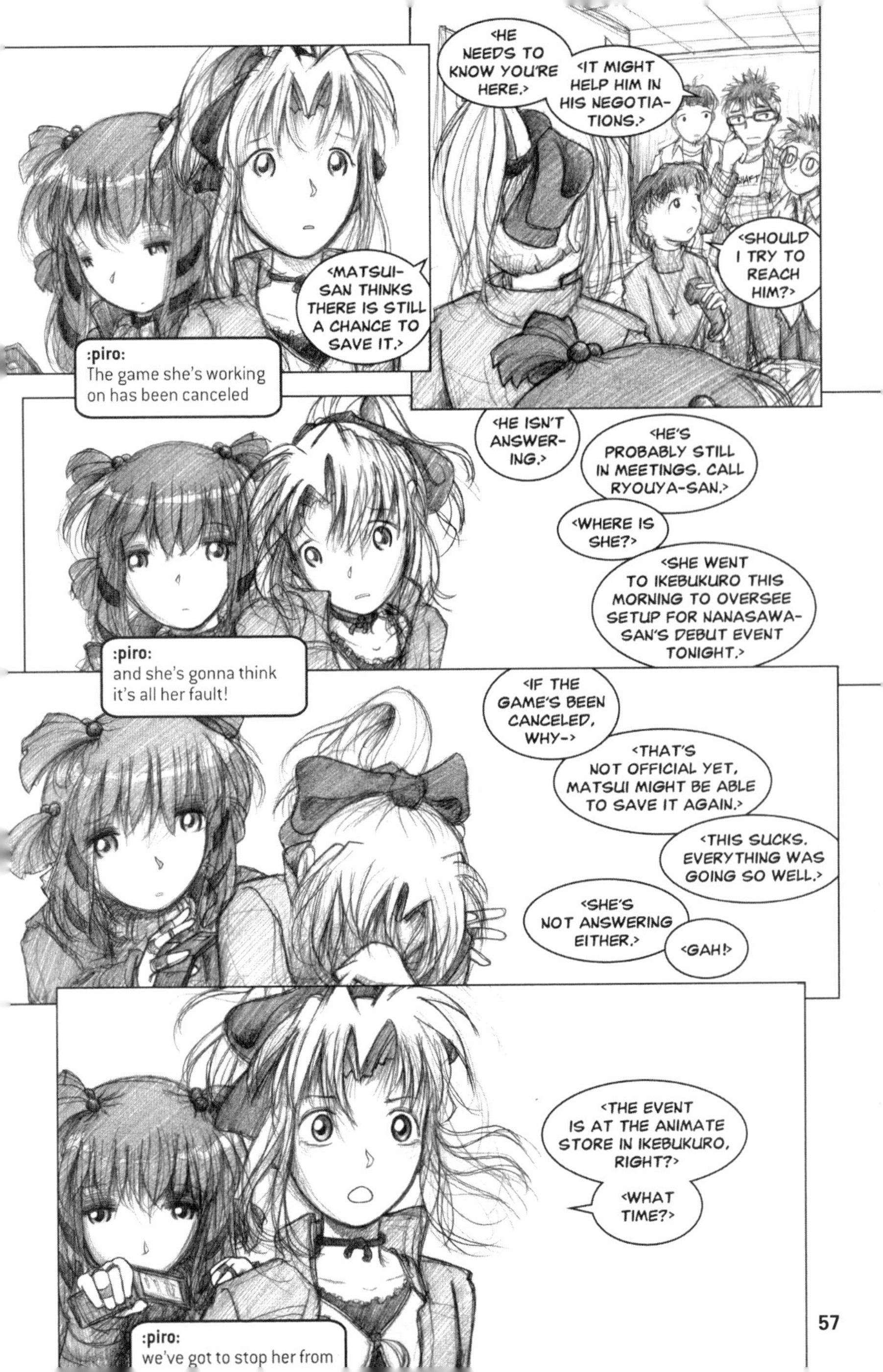

:piro:
The game she's working on has been canceled
‹MATSUI-SAN THINKS THERE IS STILL A CHANCE TO SAVE IT.›
‹HE NEEDS TO KNOW YOU'RE HERE.›
‹IT MIGHT HELP HIM IN HIS NEGOTIATIONS.›
‹SHOULD I TRY TO REACH HIM?›
‹HE ISN'T ANSWERING.›
‹HE'S PROBABLY STILL IN MEETINGS. CALL RYOUYA-SAN.›
‹WHERE IS SHE?›
‹SHE WENT TO IKEBUKURO THIS MORNING TO OVERSEE SETUP FOR NANASAWA-SAN'S DEBUT EVENT TONIGHT.›
:piro:
and she's gonna think it's all her fault!
‹IF THE GAME'S BEEN CANCELED, WHY-›
‹THAT'S NOT OFFICIAL YET, MATSUI MIGHT BE ABLE TO SAVE IT AGAIN.›
‹THIS SUCKS. EVERYTHING WAS GOING SO WELL.›
‹SHE'S NOT ANSWERING EITHER.›
‹GAH!›
‹THE EVENT IS AT THE ANIMATE STORE IN IKEBUKURO, RIGHT?›
‹WHAT TIME?›
:piro:
we've got to stop her from

DAMMIT, TOHYA, ANSWER ME!!

:yukis0211:
<I can't talk right now.>

<IS EVERYTHING OK? IS SHE GOING TO HELP US PROTECT NANASAWA-SAN?>

<DID YOU FIND OUT WHERE SHE IS?>

<ARE THEY IN A SAFE PLACE?>

:kobayashi_y:
<I'm sorry! I thought it might be OK to msg you between classes. Sorry! Sorry!>

<I DON'T KNOW.>

<SHE SAID NANA-SAWA-SAN IS GOING TO HER EVENT TONIGHT.>

<THAT'S ALL SHE WOULD TELL ME.>

:yukis0211:
<No! that's not it. I'm not at school.>

<YOU MEAN HER DEBUT EVENT AT THE ANIMATE IN IKEBUKURO?>

<IS SHE REALLY GOING?>

<EVERYONE ASSUMES THAT IT'S BEEN CANCELED!>

<YES. EVEN IF THEY CANCEL IT, SHE'LL DO IT. THAT'S HOW SHE IS.>

:kobayashi_y:
<you're not?>

TAK TAK TAK

TAP TAP TAP TAP

TAK TAK TAK TAK TAK

TIP TIP TIP TIP TIP TIP

TAP TAP TAP

PAK PAK PAK PAK PAK

:kobayashi_y:
<where are you?>

<WHAT ARE YOU DOING?!?!>

<EIMI, I DON'T THINK SHE'S--->

<AH...>

<SORRY.>

KYA--!!

WHUMP! KRASH!

:kobayashi_y:
<if you're busy we can talk later.>

59

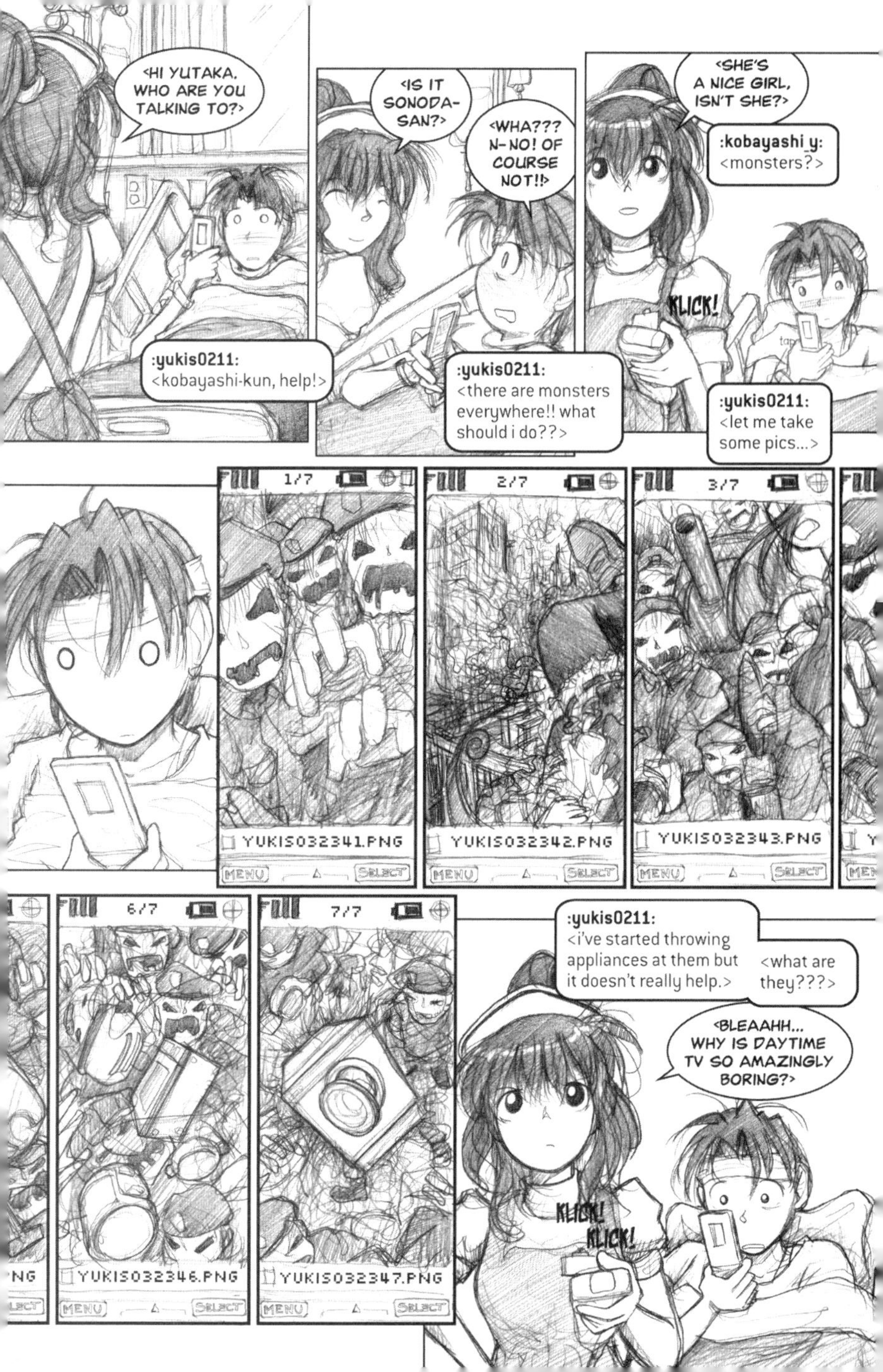

<HI YUTAKA, WHO ARE YOU TALKING TO?>
:yukis0211: <kobayashi-kun, help!>
<IS IT SONODA-SAN?>
<WHA??? N-NO! OF COURSE NOT!!>
:yukis0211: <there are monsters everywhere!! what should i do??>
<SHE'S A NICE GIRL, ISN'T SHE?>
:kobayashi_y: <monsters?>
KLICK!
tap
:yukis0211: <let me take some pics...>
1/7
YUKIS032341.PNG
MENU
SELECT
2/7
YUKIS032342.PNG
MENU
SELECT
3/7
YUKIS032343.PNG
MENU
SELECT
6/7
YUKIS032346.PNG
MENU
SELECT
7/7
YUKIS032347.PNG
MENU
SELECT
:yukis0211: <i've started throwing appliances at them but it doesn't really help.>
<what are they???>
<BLEAAHH... WHY IS DAYTIME TV SO AMAZINGLY BORING?>
KLICK!
KLICK!

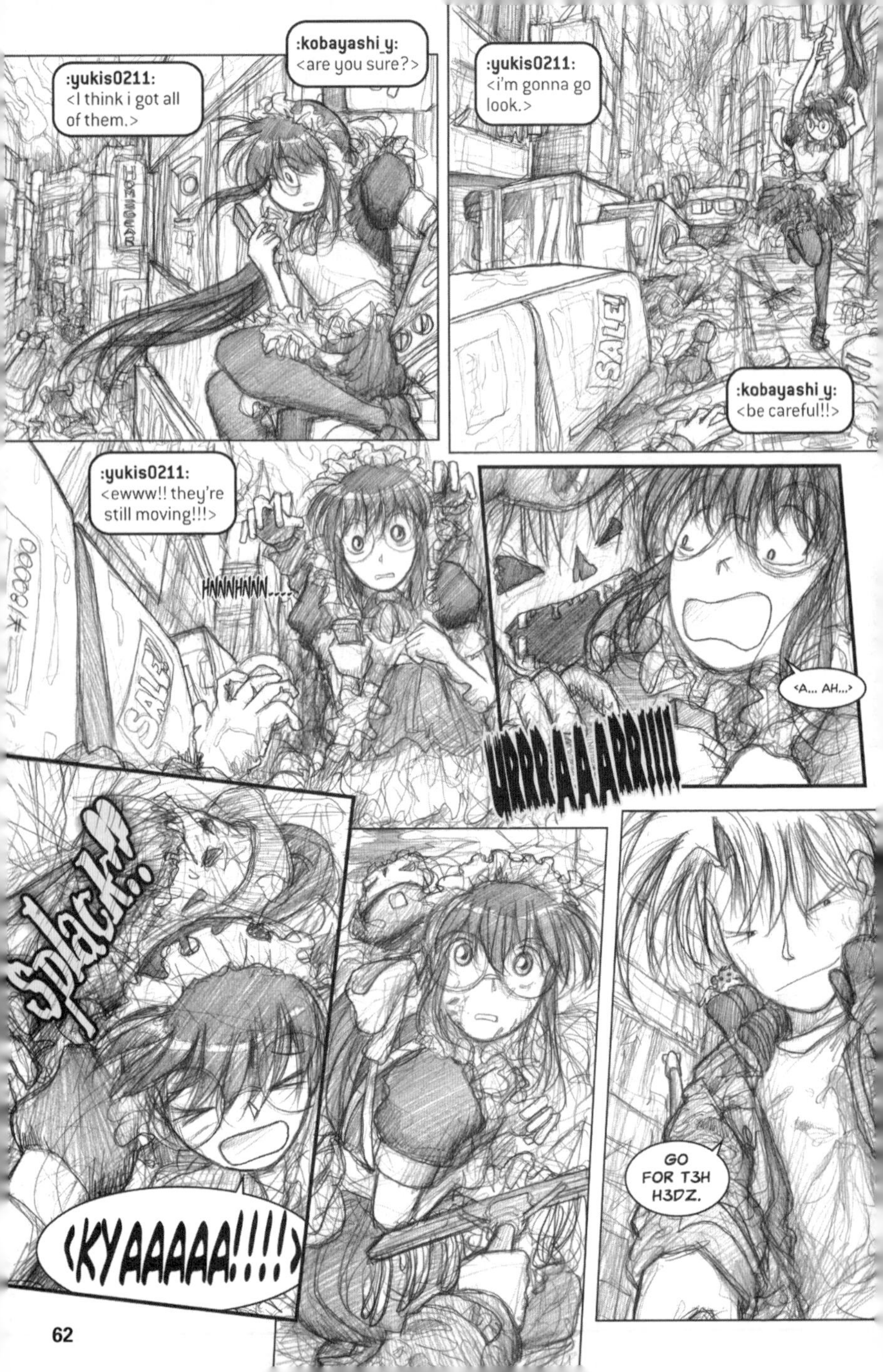
:yukis0211: <I think i got all of them.>
:kobayashi_y: <are you sure?>
:yukis0211: <i'm gonna go look.>
SALE!
:kobayashi_y: <be careful!!>
:yukis0211: <ewww!! they're still moving!!!>
HNNNHNNN....
<A... AH...>
URRRAAARR!!!!!
Splack!!
<KYAAAAA!!!!>
GO FOR T3H H3DZ.

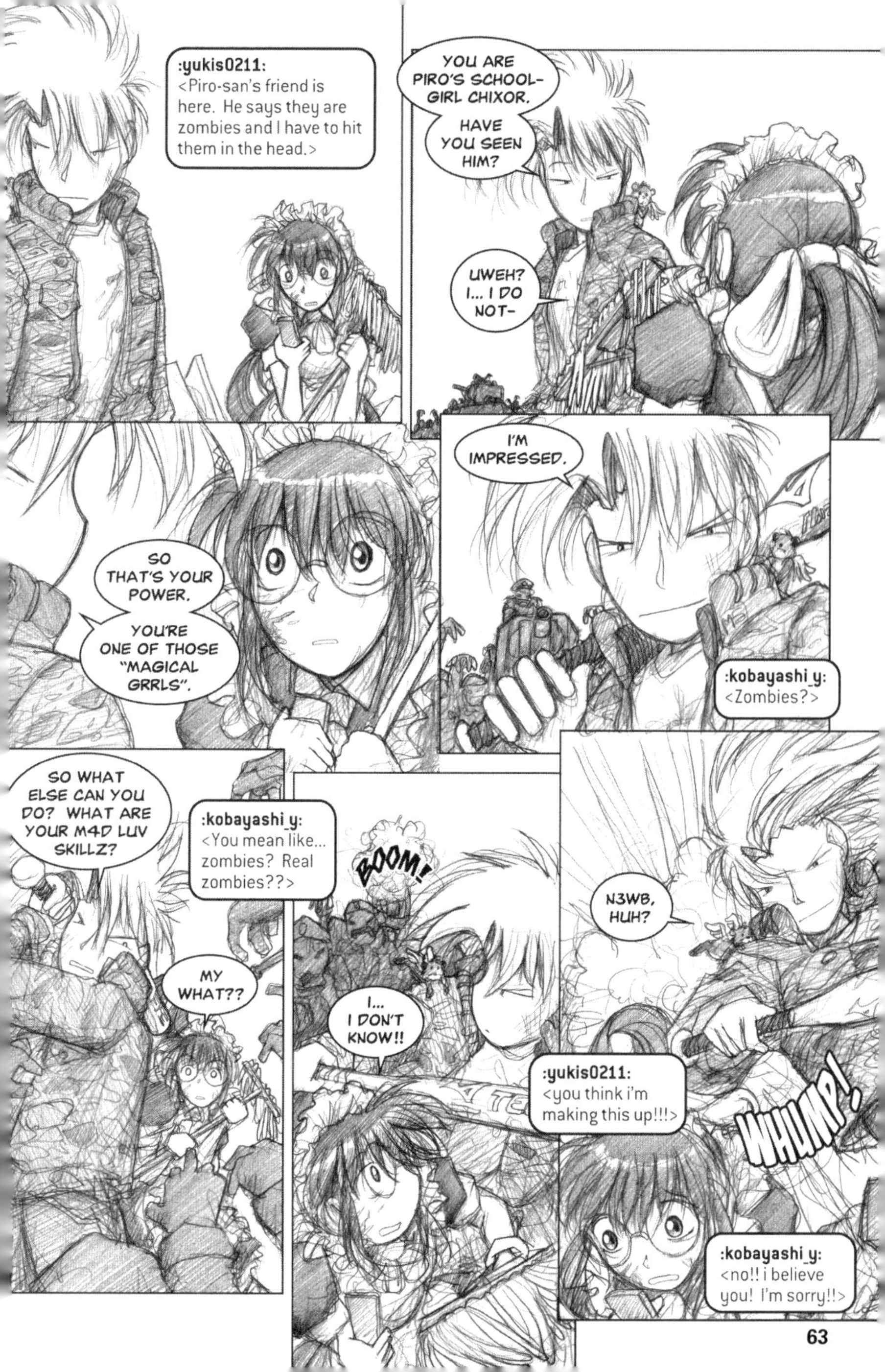

:yukis0211:
<Piro-san's friend is here. He says they are zombies and I have to hit them in the head.>
YOU ARE PIRO'S SCHOOL-GIRL CHIXOR.
HAVE YOU SEEN HIM?
UWEH? I... I DO NOT-
SO THAT'S YOUR POWER.
YOU'RE ONE OF THOSE "MAGICAL GRRLS".
I'M IMPRESSED.
:kobayashi_y:
<Zombies?>
SO WHAT ELSE CAN YOU DO? WHAT ARE YOUR M4D LUV SKILLZ?
:kobayashi_y:
<You mean like... zombies? Real zombies??>
MY WHAT??
BOOM!
I... I DON'T KNOW!!
N3WB, HUH?
:yukis0211:
<you think i'm making this up!!!>
WHUMP!
:kobayashi_y:
<no!! i believe you! I'm sorry!!>

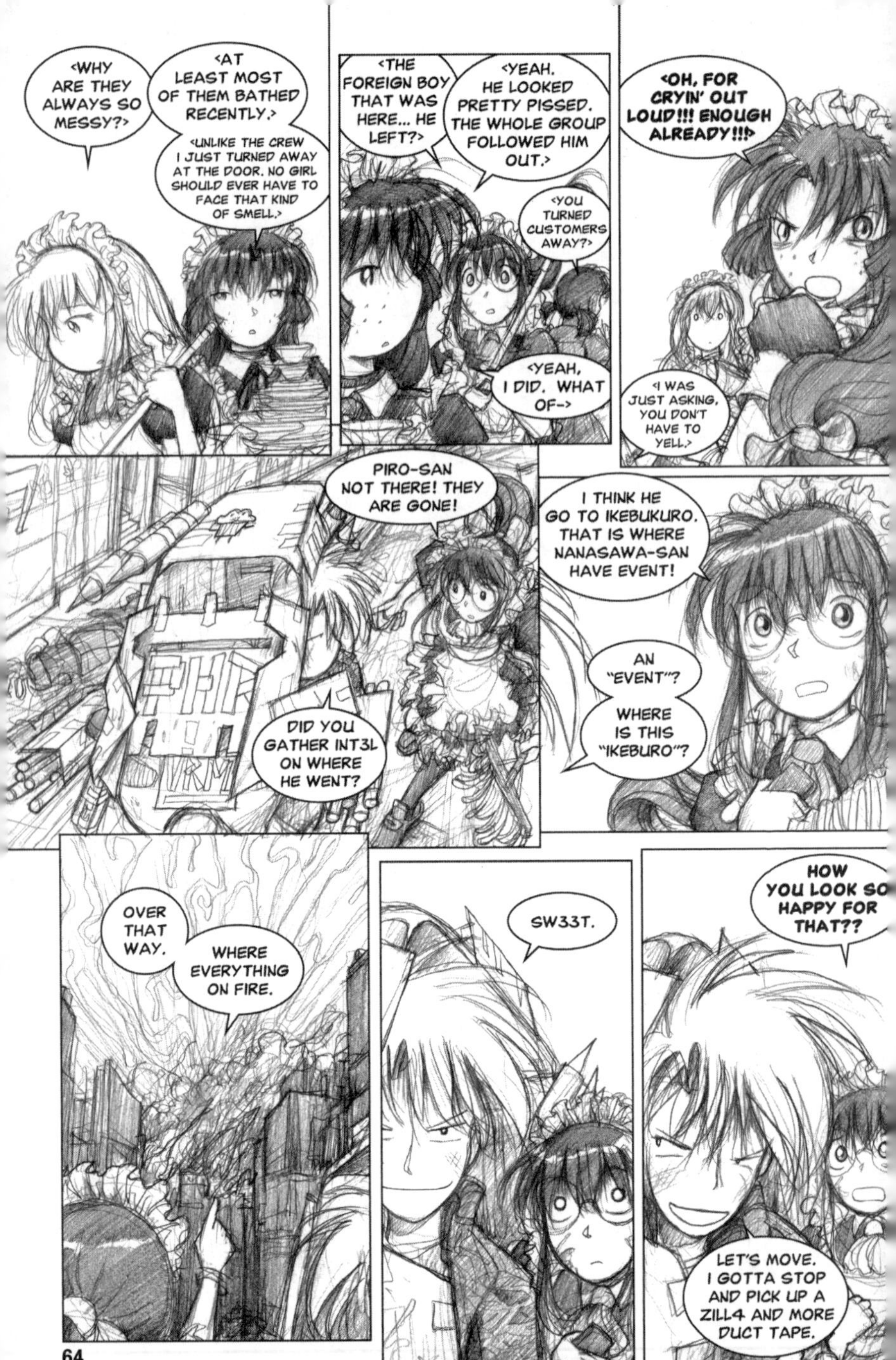
<WHY ARE THEY ALWAYS SO MESSY?>
<AT LEAST MOST OF THEM BATHED RECENTLY.>
<UNLIKE THE CREW I JUST TURNED AWAY AT THE DOOR. NO GIRL SHOULD EVER HAVE TO FACE THAT KIND OF SMELL.>
<THE FOREIGN BOY THAT WAS HERE... HE LEFT?>
<YEAH. HE LOOKED PRETTY PISSED. THE WHOLE GROUP FOLLOWED HIM OUT.>
<YOU TURNED CUSTOMERS AWAY?>
<YEAH, I DID. WHAT OF->
<OH, FOR CRYIN' OUT LOUD!!! ENOUGH ALREADY!!!>
<I WAS JUST ASKING, YOU DON'T HAVE TO YELL.>
PIRO-SAN NOT THERE! THEY ARE GONE!
DID YOU GATHER INT3L ON WHERE HE WENT?
I THINK HE GO TO IKEBUKURO. THAT IS WHERE NANASAWA-SAN HAVE EVENT!
AN "EVENT"?
WHERE IS THIS "IKEBURO"?
OVER THAT WAY.
WHERE EVERYTHING ON FIRE.
SW33T.
HOW YOU LOOK SO HAPPY FOR THAT??
LET'S MOVE. I GOTTA STOP AND PICK UP A ZILL4 AND MORE DUCT TAPE.

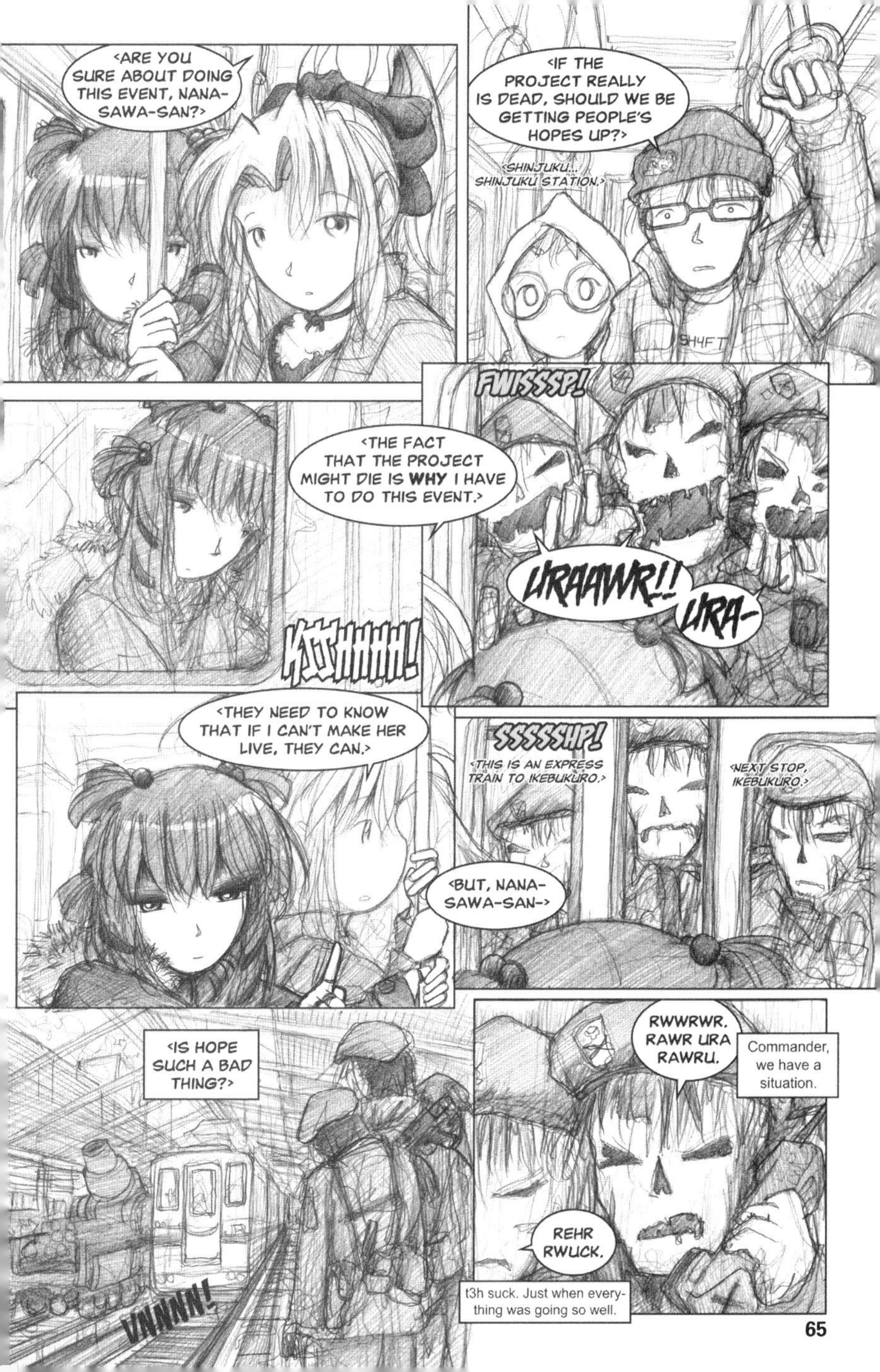

<ARE YOU SURE ABOUT DOING THIS EVENT, NANA-SAWA-SAN?>
<IF THE PROJECT REALLY IS DEAD, SHOULD WE BE GETTING PEOPLE'S HOPES UP?>
<SHINJUKU... SHINJUKU STATION.>
<THE FACT THAT THE PROJECT MIGHT DIE IS **WHY** I HAVE TO DO THIS EVENT.>
KTCHHHH!
FWISSSP!
URAAWR!!
URA-
<THEY NEED TO KNOW THAT IF I CAN'T MAKE HER LIVE, THEY CAN.>
<BUT, NANA-SAWA-SAN->
SSSSSHP!
<THIS IS AN EXPRESS TRAIN TO IKEBUKURO.>
<NEXT STOP, IKEBUKURO.>
<IS HOPE SUCH A BAD THING?>
VNNNN!
RWWRWR. RAWR URA RAWRU.
Commander, we have a situation.
REHR RWUCK.
t3h suck. Just when everything was going so well.

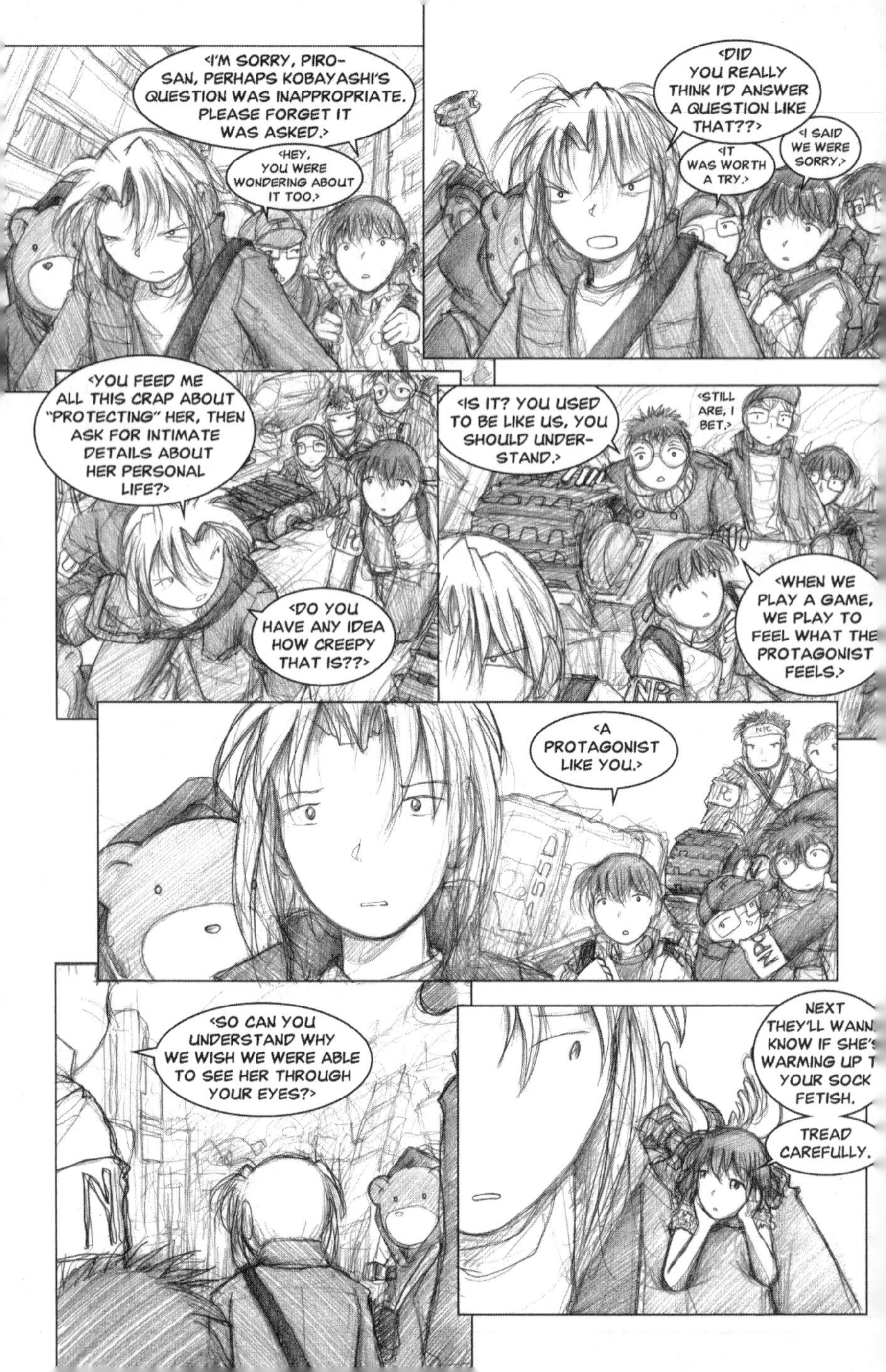
<I'M SORRY, PIRO-SAN, PERHAPS KOBAYASHI'S QUESTION WAS INAPPROPRIATE. PLEASE FORGET IT WAS ASKED.>
<HEY, YOU WERE WONDERING ABOUT IT TOO.>
<DID YOU REALLY THINK I'D ANSWER A QUESTION LIKE THAT??>
<IT WAS WORTH A TRY.>
<I SAID WE WERE SORRY.>
<YOU FEED ME ALL THIS CRAP ABOUT "PROTECTING" HER, THEN ASK FOR INTIMATE DETAILS ABOUT HER PERSONAL LIFE?>
<DO YOU HAVE ANY IDEA HOW CREEPY THAT IS??>
<IS IT? YOU USED TO BE LIKE US, YOU SHOULD UNDER-STAND.>
<STILL ARE, I BET.>
<WHEN WE PLAY A GAME, WE PLAY TO FEEL WHAT THE PROTAGONIST FEELS.>
<A PROTAGONIST LIKE YOU.>
<SO CAN YOU UNDERSTAND WHY WE WISH WE WERE ABLE TO SEE HER THROUGH YOUR EYES?>
NEXT THEY'LL WANN KNOW IF SHE'S WARMING UP T YOUR SOCK FETISH.
TREAD CAREFULLY.

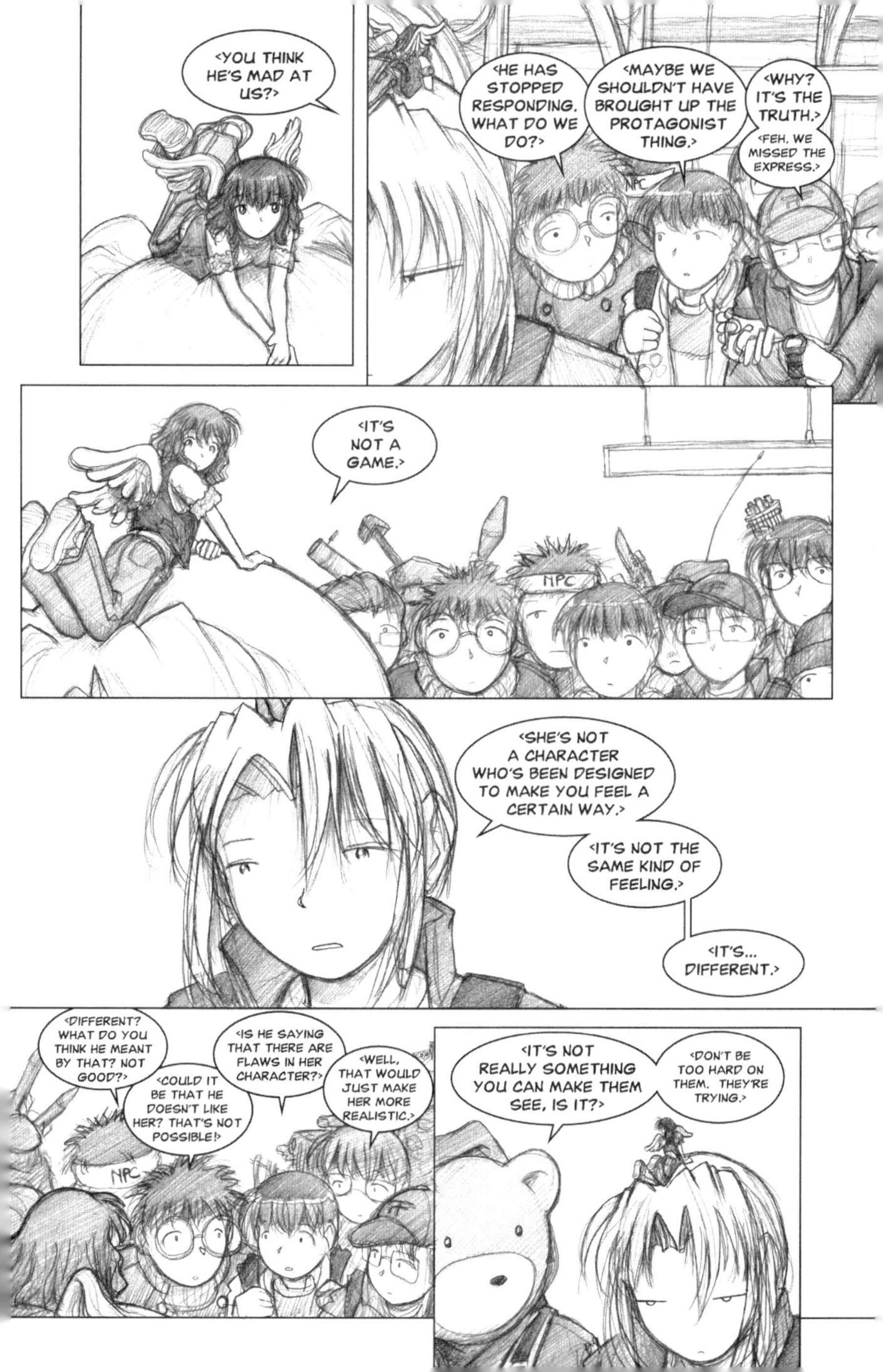
<YOU THINK HE'S MAD AT US?>
<HE HAS STOPPED RESPONDING. WHAT DO WE DO?>
<MAYBE WE SHOULDN'T HAVE BROUGHT UP THE PROTAGONIST THING.>
<WHY? IT'S THE TRUTH.>
<FEH. WE MISSED THE EXPRESS.>
NPC
<IT'S NOT A GAME.>
NPC
<SHE'S NOT A CHARACTER WHO'S BEEN DESIGNED TO MAKE YOU FEEL A CERTAIN WAY.>
<IT'S NOT THE SAME KIND OF FEELING.>
<IT'S... DIFFERENT.>
<DIFFERENT? WHAT DO YOU THINK HE MEANT BY THAT? NOT GOOD?>
<COULD IT BE THAT HE DOESN'T LIKE HER? THAT'S NOT POSSIBLE!>
<IS HE SAYING THAT THERE ARE FLAWS IN HER CHARACTER?>
<WELL, THAT WOULD JUST MAKE HER MORE REALISTIC.>
NPC
<IT'S NOT REALLY SOMETHING YOU CAN MAKE THEM SEE, IS IT?>
<DON'T BE TOO HARD ON THEM. THEY'RE TRYING.>

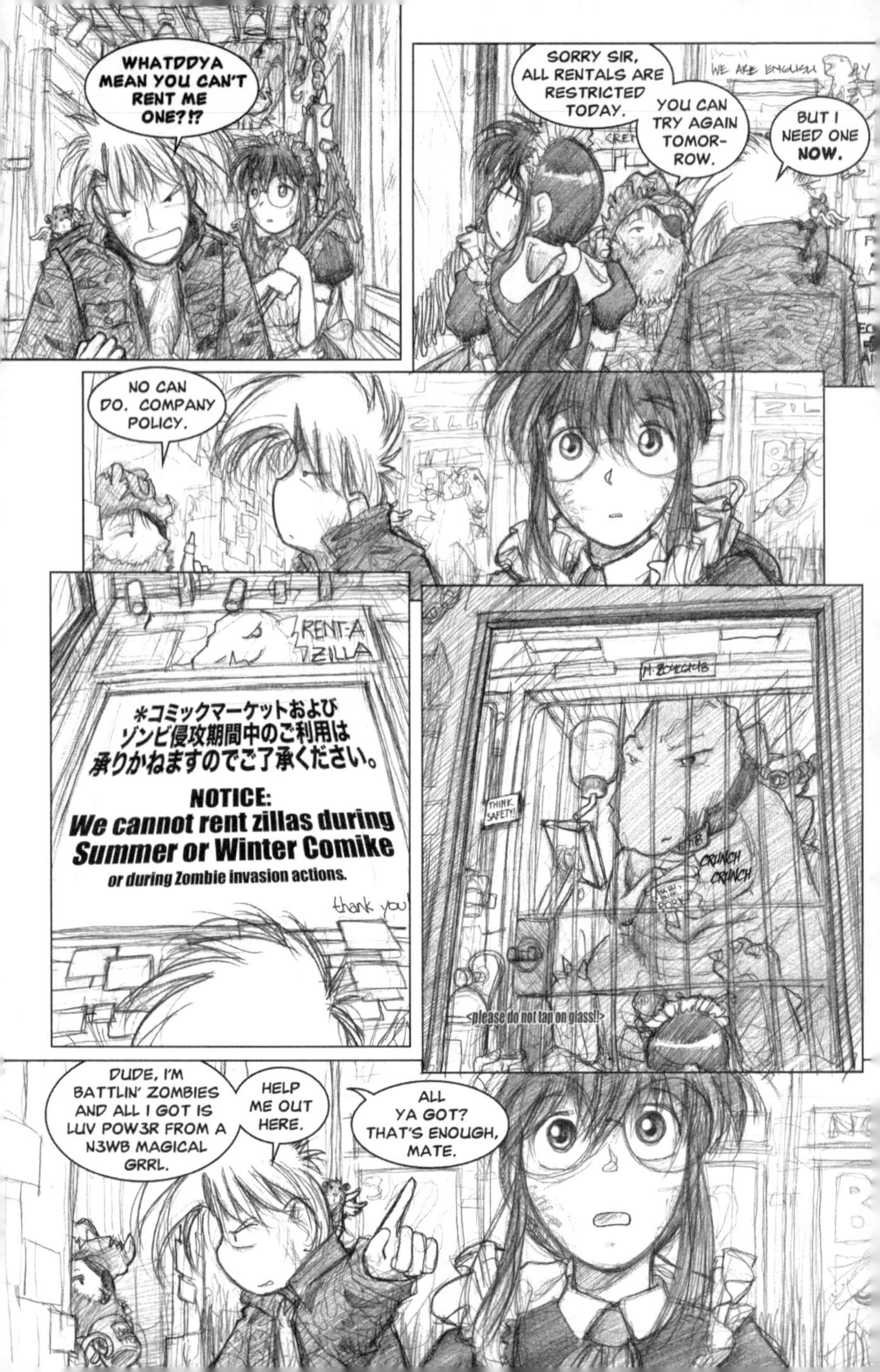
WHATDDYA MEAN YOU CAN'T RENT ME ONE?!?
SORRY SIR, ALL RENTALS ARE RESTRICTED TODAY.
YOU CAN TRY AGAIN TOMOR-ROW.
WE ARE ENGLISH
BUT I NEED ONE **NOW.**
NO CAN DO. COMPANY POLICY.
RENT-A ZILLA
＊コミックマーケットおよび
ゾンビ侵攻期間中のご利用は
承りかねますのでご了承ください。
NOTICE:
We cannot rent zillas during
Summer or Winter Comike
or during Zombie invasion actions.
thank you!
THINK SAFETY!
CRUNCH
CRUNCH
<please do not tap on glass!!>
DUDE, I'M BATTLIN' ZOMBIES AND ALL I GOT IS LUV POW3R FROM A N3WB MAGICAL GRRL.
HELP ME OUT HERE.
ALL YA GOT? THAT'S ENOUGH, MATE.

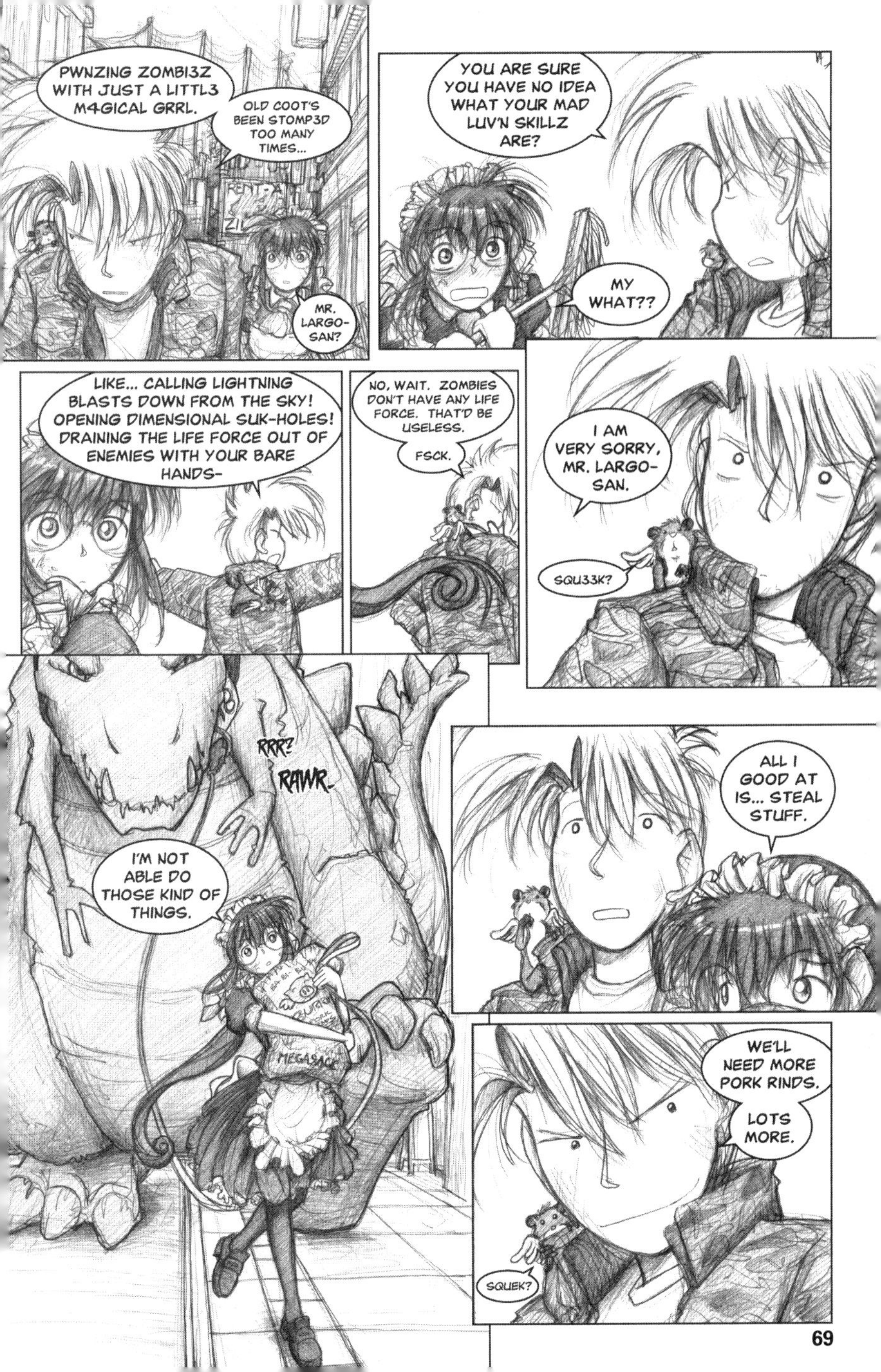
PWNZING ZOMBI3Z WITH JUST A LITTL3 M4GICAL GRRL.
OLD COOT'S BEEN STOMP3D TOO MANY TIMES...
RENT-A
ZI
MR. LARGO-SAN?
YOU ARE SURE YOU HAVE NO IDEA WHAT YOUR MAD LUV'N SKILLZ ARE?
MY WHAT??
LIKE... CALLING LIGHTNING BLASTS DOWN FROM THE SKY! OPENING DIMENSIONAL SUK-HOLES! DRAINING THE LIFE FORCE OUT OF ENEMIES WITH YOUR BARE HANDS-
NO, WAIT. ZOMBIES DON'T HAVE ANY LIFE FORCE. THAT'D BE USELESS.
FSCK.
I AM VERY SORRY, MR. LARGO-SAN.
SQU33K?
RRR?
RAWR.
I'M NOT ABLE DO THOSE KIND OF THINGS.
MEGASACK
ALL I GOOD AT IS... STEAL STUFF.
WE'LL NEED MORE PORK RINDS.
LOTS MORE.
SQUEK?

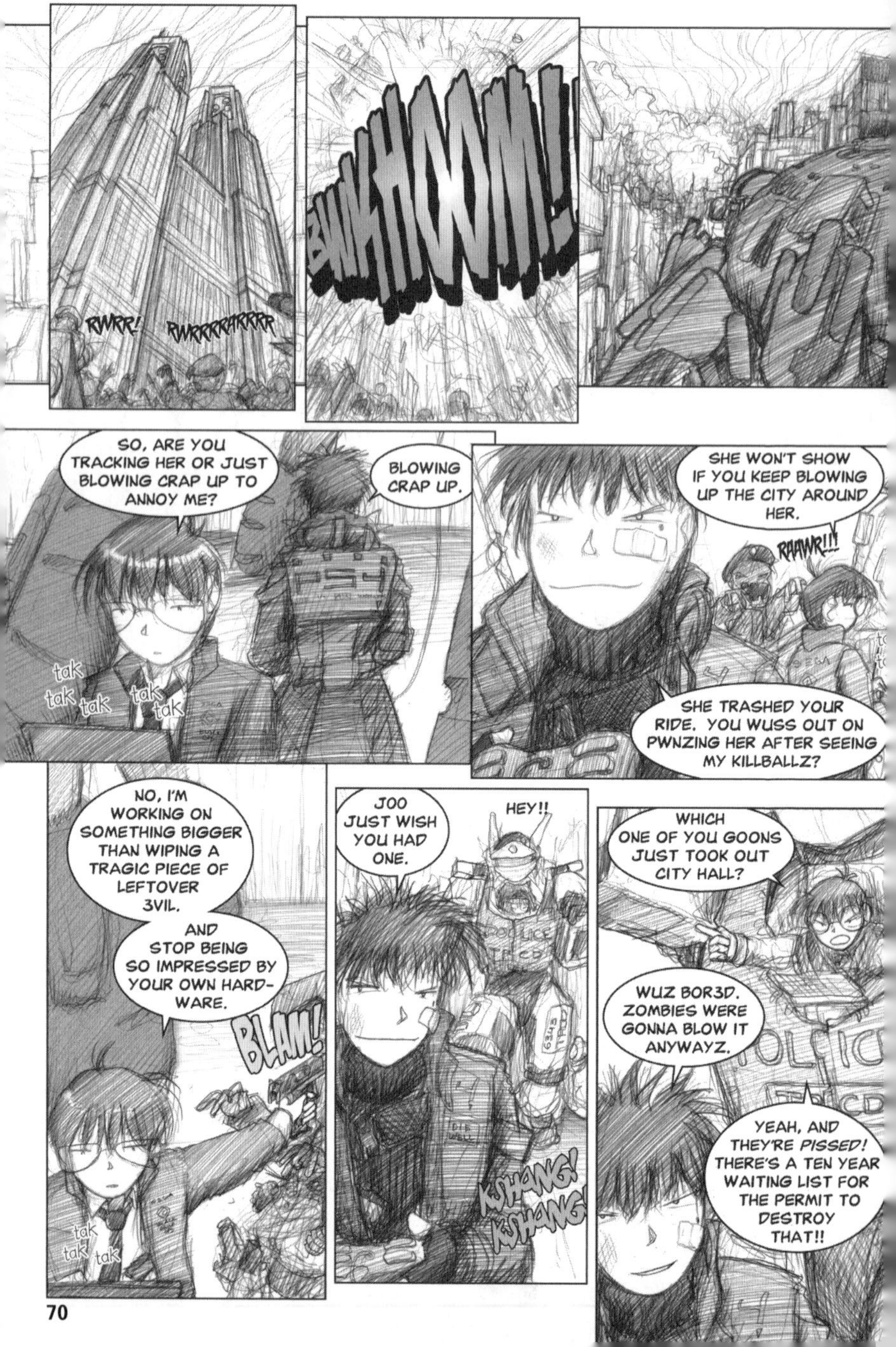
RWRR!
RWRRRRAHRRRR
BWUHOOM!!
SO, ARE YOU TRACKING HER OR JUST BLOWING CRAP UP TO ANNOY ME?
BLOWING CRAP UP.
tak tak tak tak tak
SHE WON'T SHOW IF YOU KEEP BLOWING UP THE CITY AROUND HER.
RAAWR!!!
SHE TRASHED YOUR RIDE. YOU WUSS OUT ON PWNZING HER AFTER SEEING MY KILLBALLZ?
NO, I'M WORKING ON SOMETHING BIGGER THAN WIPING A TRAGIC PIECE OF LEFTOVER 3VIL.
AND STOP BEING SO IMPRESSED BY YOUR OWN HARD-WARE.
BLAM!
tak tak tak
JOO JUST WISH YOU HAD ONE.
HEY!!
KSHANG! KSHANG!
WHICH ONE OF YOU GOONS JUST TOOK OUT CITY HALL?
WUZ BOR3D. ZOMBIES WERE GONNA BLOW IT ANYWAYZ.
YEAH, AND THEY'RE *PISSED!* THERE'S A TEN YEAR WAITING LIST FOR THE PERMIT TO DESTROY THAT!!

freetalk-2007.11.09.txt

It was at this point in Chapter 9 that real life for Seraphim and me got a *little* more complicated and a whole lot more *awesome* - Our son, Jack Obadiah Gallagher, was born (November 9th 2007).

As any new parent can attest, the first few weeks after the arrival of a little one can be more than a little hectic. It wasn't long before I realized there was no pause button for all this. It was about two weeks before I was finally able to get a new comic posted - the unMod Recap episode on the next page.

That was about two and a half years ago. Jack has grown into a vivacious, mischievous, entertaining, energetic, thoughtful and thoroughly awesome kid who gleefully scribbled over the comic on page 250 while I was working on it and somehow crashed Photoshop. His 133t sk1llz are becoming formidable. I wish I could say I was surprised when, while flipping through a printout of Chapter 10, the first character he pointed to was Largo Wasasdgaeiwarsdf
jnkziuiujio;aj'iopew'pjoas;lz uhagouherpad;oif Dkksd'klAsdA
Sd Asdfaefas Asdgaklsd; lasf;a aoiejrsgha;jbdf;aiwnbas
mxahiorawphiawijo;swjiSijlRSjkdfgzjklGSjklDjodfijGRSJKLNhds
japhwibjuefhhobjnAWdknszvfm.gks
retlz/xcv.rstjˆØ˜aiosdfhjpuioawhreuoahdphapsiuhapu
woe4hfpaiuhsxbnfahop-
so[aghawoihaophinasvojnaso[awnoaowpEOPASDNANOAWENAPWNOASNAWEFI
ONAWOEIOIA;WEAIOUWUEH[0834TU]0294TJHA'ZDXK
]as;opl]
Tuk'56dfg545643684
64838453544868456seropgkjpoiw4p[woks,l;gfl
powjjioajprgjp'ijagrijop'aegrijopargijpraegij'hstjipgjgijopegi
jpararghjgtijlghjjo[Gipbbjaego
[y35o
-]y35pu9-hps'ijoop
]gqhio'bgio;hnjop'ehstpio'jehtsiou;srthijlbgjlknaghr;oiuhaegou
;agrho;bdfjleqwjlhejknzm,nxdcnv
jk.l;fgnijl/aehho;abebno;bdh;oiu5o8aethi;djkflzh;oa

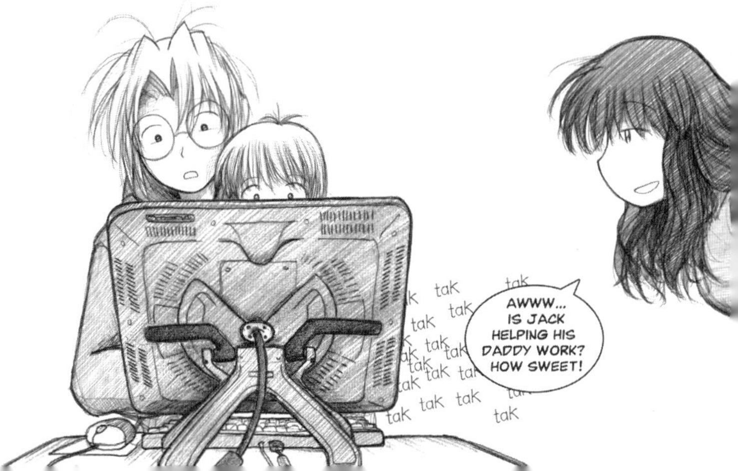
tak tak tak tak tak tak tak tak tak tak tak tak tak tak tak
AWWW... IS JACK HELPING HIS DADDY WORK? HOW SWEET!

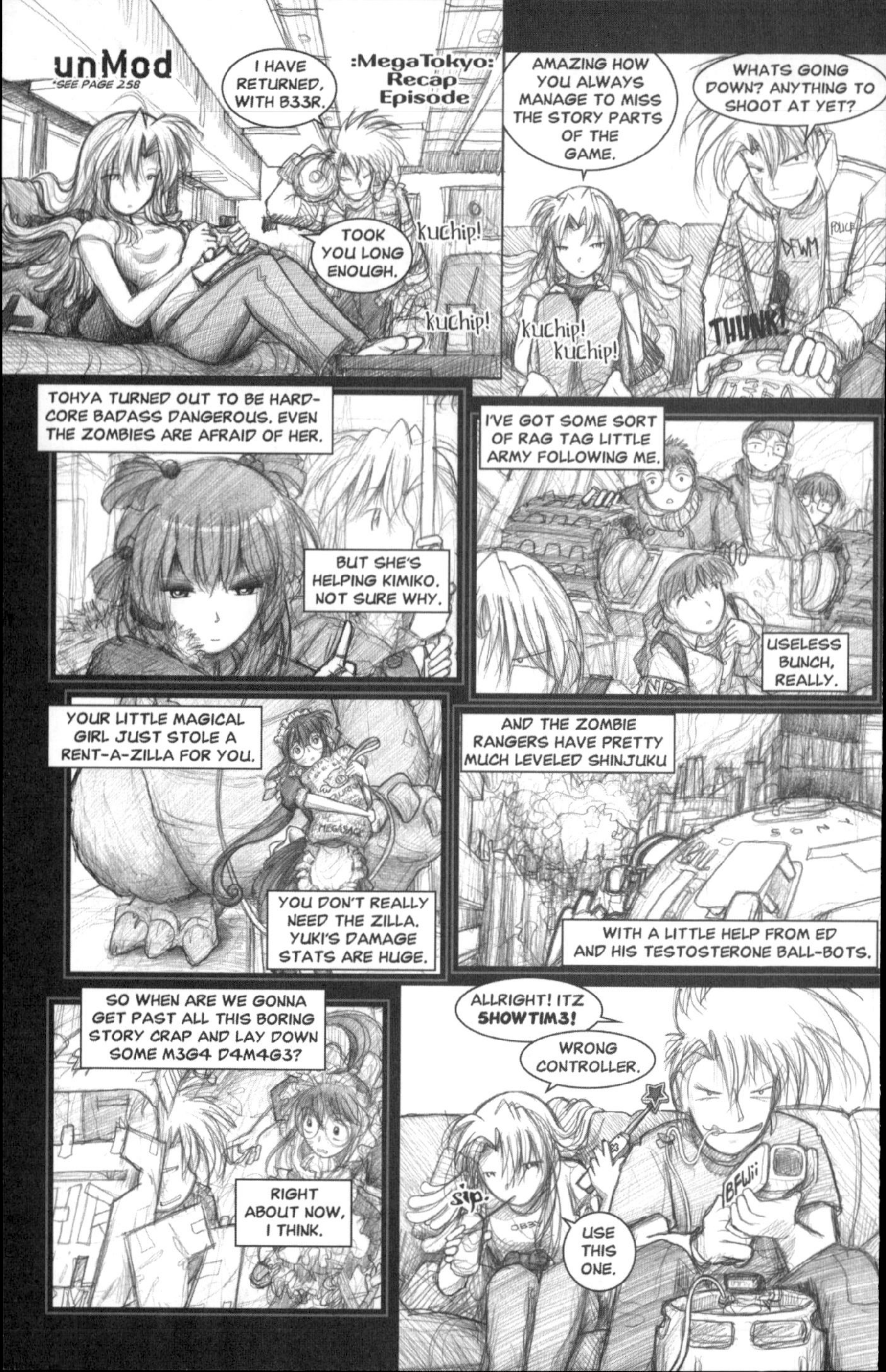
unMod
*SEE PAGE 258
I HAVE RETURNED, WITH B33R.
:MegaTokyo: Recap Episode
TOOK YOU LONG ENOUGH.
kuchip!
kuchip!
AMAZING HOW YOU ALWAYS MANAGE TO MISS THE STORY PARTS OF THE GAME.
WHATS GOING DOWN? ANYTHING TO SHOOT AT YET?
kuchip! kuchip!
THUNK!
TOHYA TURNED OUT TO BE HARD-CORE BADASS DANGEROUS. EVEN THE ZOMBIES ARE AFRAID OF HER.
BUT SHE'S HELPING KIMIKO. NOT SURE WHY.
I'VE GOT SOME SORT OF RAG TAG LITTLE ARMY FOLLOWING ME.
USELESS BUNCH, REALLY.
YOUR LITTLE MAGICAL GIRL JUST STOLE A RENT-A-ZILLA FOR YOU.
MEGASACK
YOU DON'T REALLY NEED THE ZILLA. YUKI'S DAMAGE STATS ARE HUGE.
AND THE ZOMBIE RANGERS HAVE PRETTY MUCH LEVELED SHINJUKU
WITH A LITTLE HELP FROM ED AND HIS TESTOSTERONE BALL-BOTS.
SO WHEN ARE WE GONNA GET PAST ALL THIS BORING STORY CRAP AND LAY DOWN SOME M3G4 D4M4G3?
RIGHT ABOUT NOW, I THINK.
ALLRIGHT! ITZ SHOWTIM3!
WRONG CONTROLLER.
sip.
BFWii
USE THIS ONE.

‹ZOMBIE FORCES ARE MASSING NORTH OF SHINJUKU STATION. FOUR MINUTE DELAY REPORTED ON THE YAMANOTE LINE.›

‹PROCEEDING WITH CLEAN-UP, SECTOR B6. REQUEST STATUS OF DETERGENT TANKER.›

‹SECTOR C8 IS STILL A LITTLE HOT. CAUTION ADVISED FOR UNITS IN THAT AREA.›

JETVAC

WET DRY
4464
PCD

VRRNNNNNN!!!

FSSSHH!

KSHT!

KSHT!

‹COLOR CHANGE REQUESTED BY BUILDING OWNER ON RE-BUILD. PINK. PLEASE ADVISE.›

‹I NEED TO CHECK ON A 24 HR UNRESTRICTED EXCESSIVE FORCE ERADICATION PERMIT, NUMBER UEFEP000014.›

‹ONE MOMENT, SIR.›

‹PERMIT WAS SECURED BY THE SONY ENFORCEMENT DIVISION YESTERDAY AT 22:34:29.›

‹REASON CITED: "ELIMINATION OF THREAT TO THE OPERATIONAL SECURITY OF INTELLECTUAL PROPERTIES."›

(SIGH) ‹THAT'S WHAT I THOUGHT.›

‹Y'KNOW, THERE ARE TIMES WHEN I REALLY DON'T LIKE THE WAY THIS ALL WORKS.›

‹YES SIR.›

‹OH, SIR, THE ZOMBIE FORCES HAVE PUT IN A REQUEST TO EXTEND THE CATA-CLYSM ZONE TO INCLUDE THE IKE-BUKURO AREA.›

‹IKEBUKURO? WHAT FOR?›

‹NO IDEA. MAYBE THEY ARE STILL HUNGRY, SIR.›

73

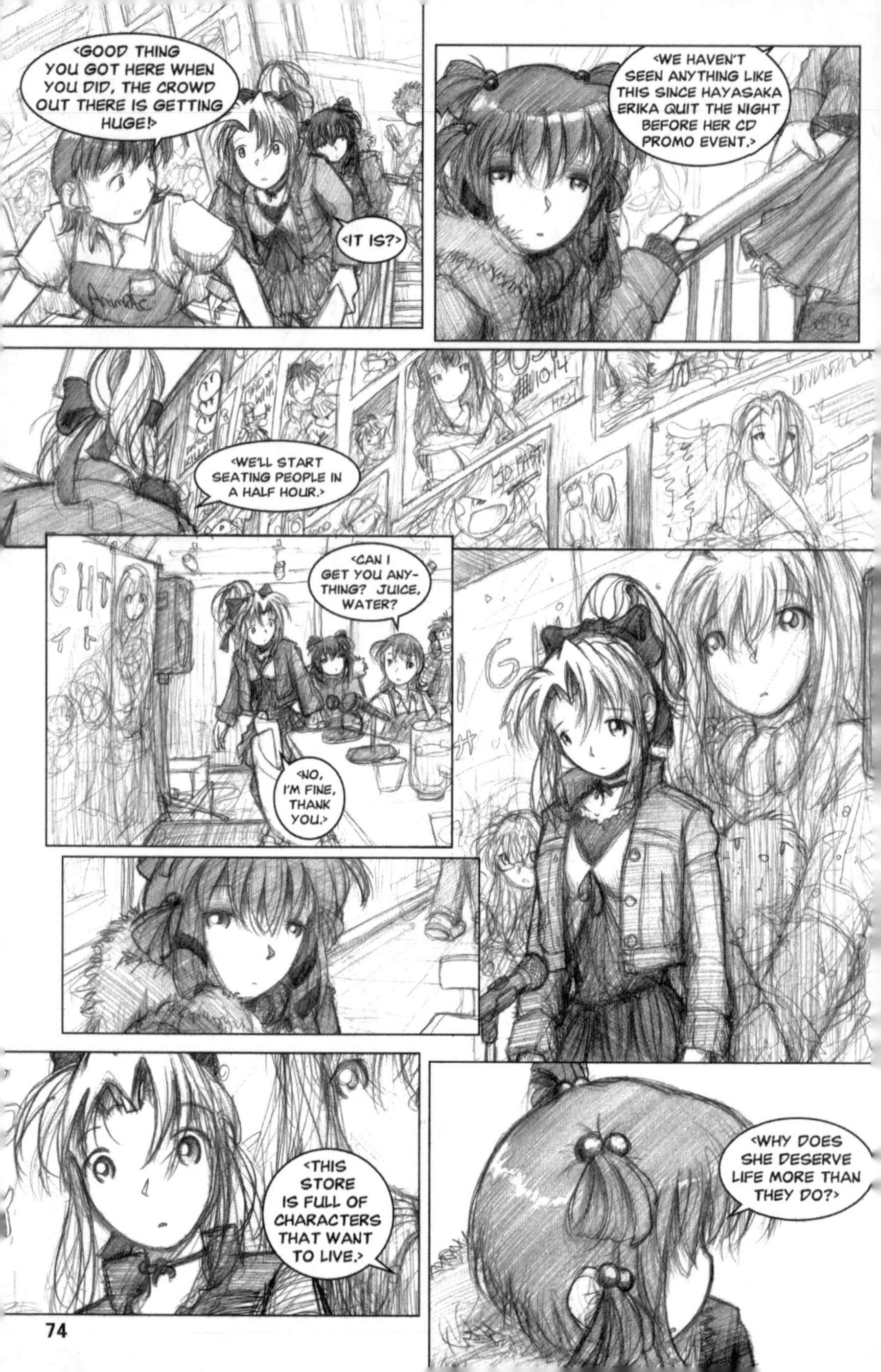
<GOOD THING YOU GOT HERE WHEN YOU DID, THE CROWD OUT THERE IS GETTING HUGE!>
<IT IS?>
<WE HAVEN'T SEEN ANYTHING LIKE THIS SINCE HAYASAKA ERIKA QUIT THE NIGHT BEFORE HER CD PROMO EVENT.>
<WE'LL START SEATING PEOPLE IN A HALF HOUR.>
<CAN I GET YOU ANY-THING? JUICE, WATER?>
<NO, I'M FINE, THANK YOU.>
<THIS STORE IS FULL OF CHARACTERS THAT WANT TO LIVE.>
<WHY DOES SHE DESERVE LIFE MORE THAN THEY DO?>

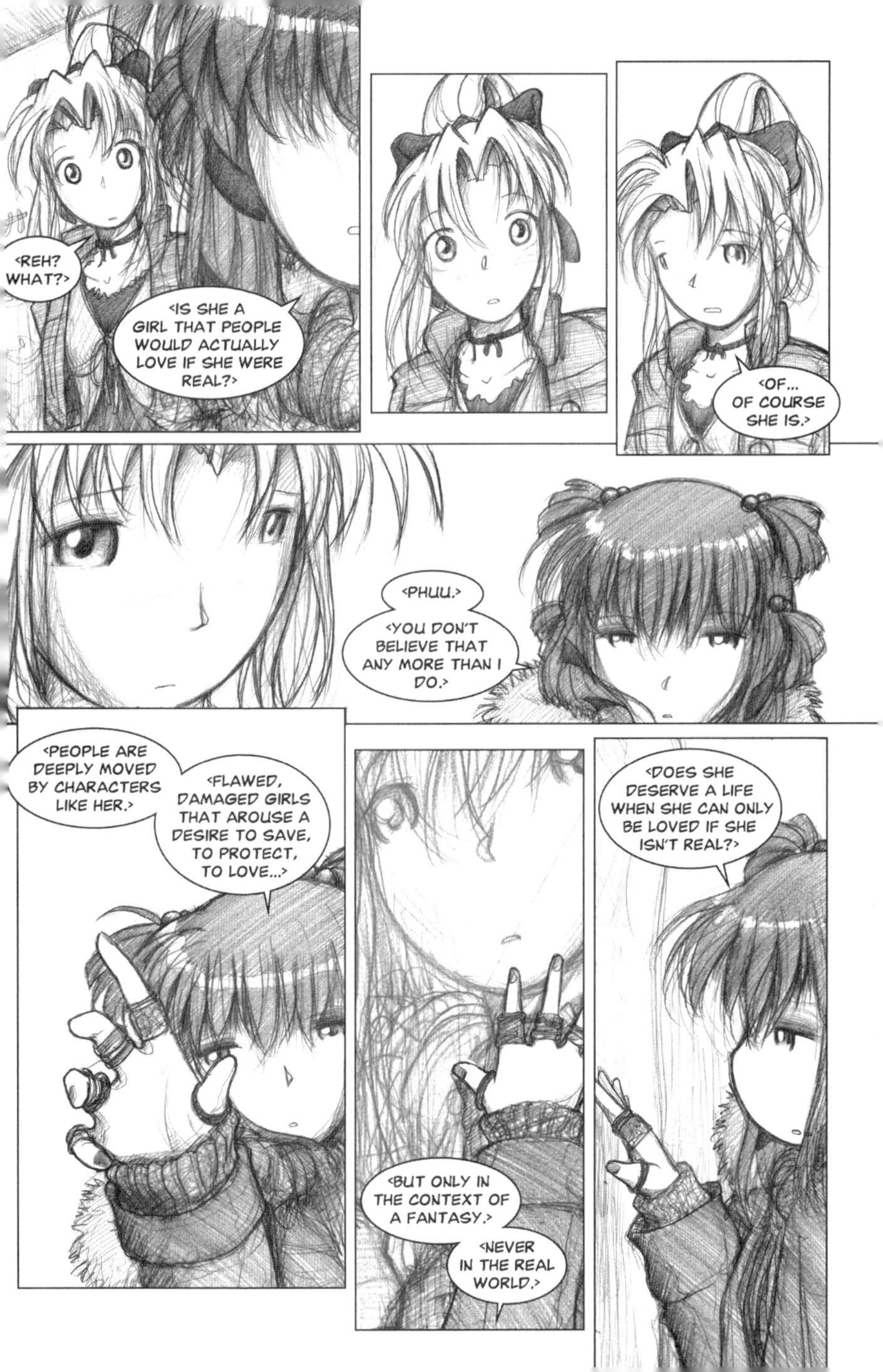

<REH? WHAT?>
<IS SHE A GIRL THAT PEOPLE WOULD ACTUALLY LOVE IF SHE WERE REAL?>
<OF... OF COURSE SHE IS.>
<PHUU.>
<YOU DON'T BELIEVE THAT ANY MORE THAN I DO.>
<PEOPLE ARE DEEPLY MOVED BY CHARACTERS LIKE HER.>
<FLAWED, DAMAGED GIRLS THAT AROUSE A DESIRE TO SAVE, TO PROTECT, TO LOVE...>
<BUT ONLY IN THE CONTEXT OF A FANTASY.>
<NEVER IN THE REAL WORLD.>
<DOES SHE DESERVE A LIFE WHEN SHE CAN ONLY BE LOVED IF SHE ISN'T REAL?>

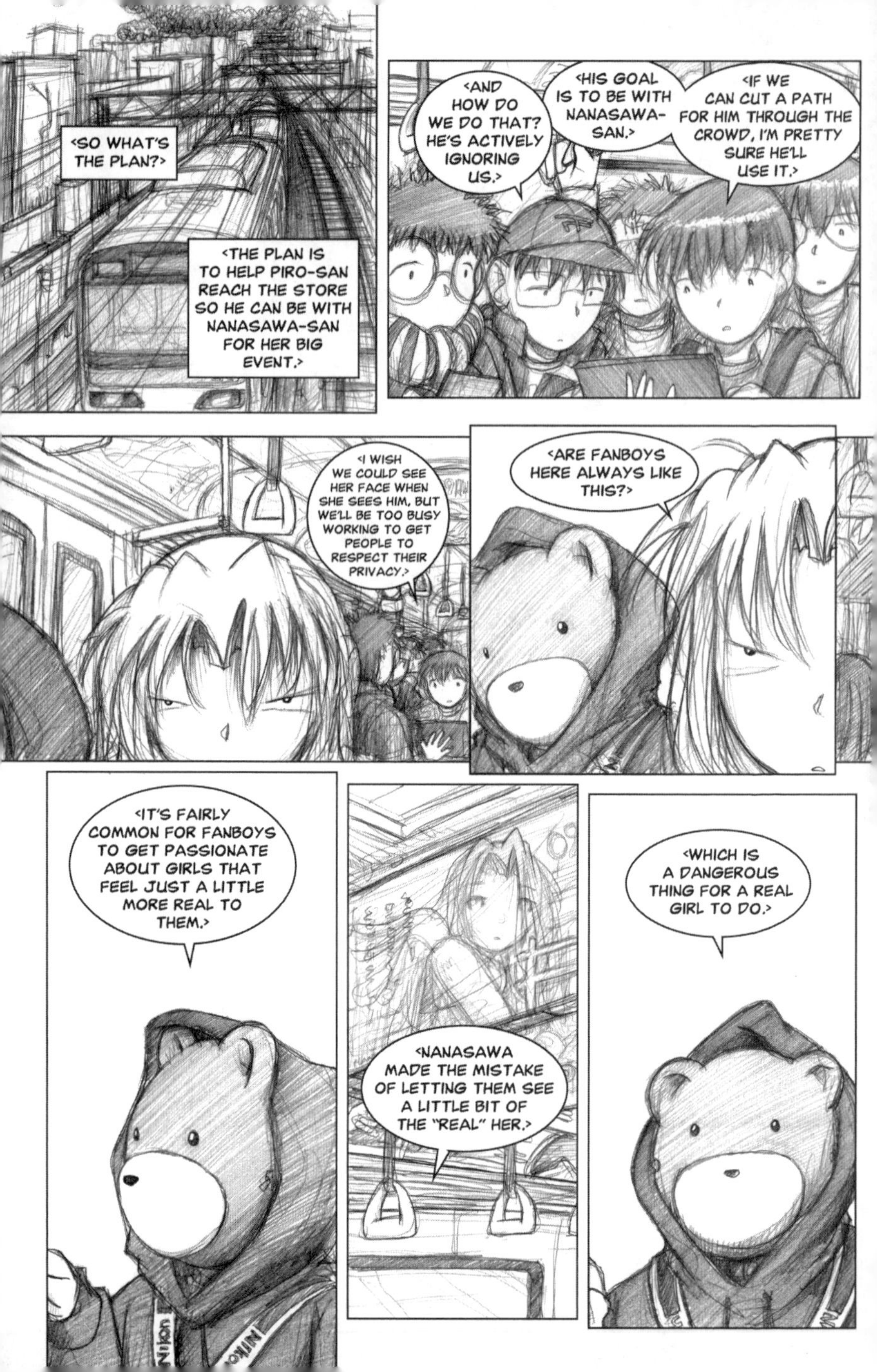
<SO WHAT'S THE PLAN?>
<THE PLAN IS TO HELP PIRO-SAN REACH THE STORE SO HE CAN BE WITH NANASAWA-SAN FOR HER BIG EVENT.>
<AND HOW DO WE DO THAT? HE'S ACTIVELY IGNORING US.>
<HIS GOAL IS TO BE WITH NANASAWA-SAN.>
<IF WE CAN CUT A PATH FOR HIM THROUGH THE CROWD, I'M PRETTY SURE HE'LL USE IT.>
<I WISH WE COULD SEE HER FACE WHEN SHE SEES HIM, BUT WE'LL BE TOO BUSY WORKING TO GET PEOPLE TO RESPECT THEIR PRIVACY.>
<ARE FANBOYS HERE ALWAYS LIKE THIS?>
<IT'S FAIRLY COMMON FOR FANBOYS TO GET PASSIONATE ABOUT GIRLS THAT FEEL JUST A LITTLE MORE REAL TO THEM.>
<NANASAWA MADE THE MISTAKE OF LETTING THEM SEE A LITTLE BIT OF THE "REAL" HER.>
<WHICH IS A DANGEROUS THING FOR A REAL GIRL TO DO.>

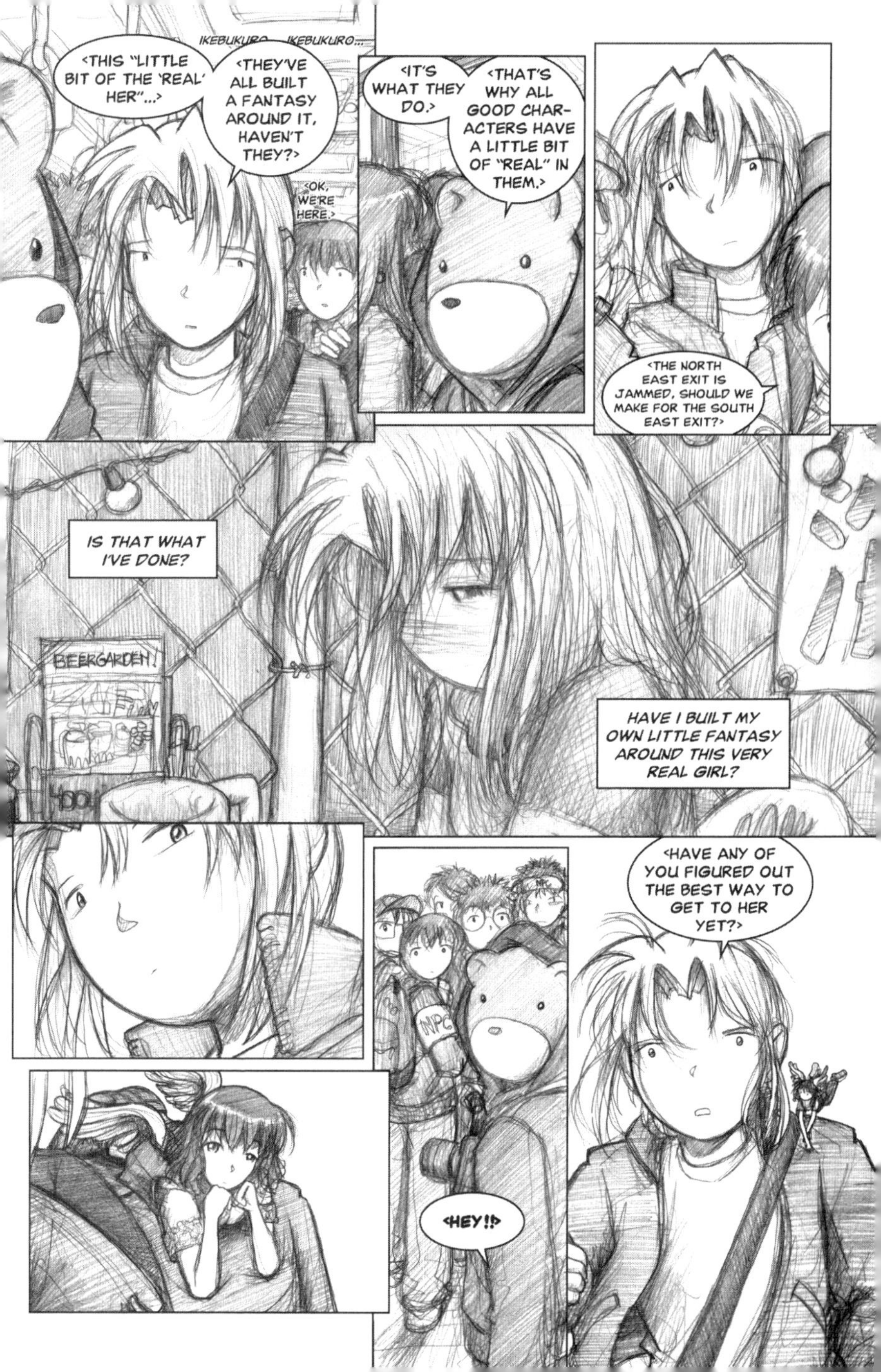
IKEBUKURO... IKEBUKURO...
<THIS "LITTLE BIT OF THE 'REAL' HER"...>
<THEY'VE ALL BUILT A FANTASY AROUND IT, HAVEN'T THEY?>
<OK, WE'RE HERE.>
<IT'S WHAT THEY DO.>
<THAT'S WHY ALL GOOD CHARACTERS HAVE A LITTLE BIT OF "REAL" IN THEM.>
<THE NORTH EAST EXIT IS JAMMED, SHOULD WE MAKE FOR THE SOUTH EAST EXIT?>
IS THAT WHAT I'VE DONE?
BEERGARDEN!
HAVE I BUILT MY OWN LITTLE FANTASY AROUND THIS VERY REAL GIRL?
NPC
NPC
<HEY!!>
<HAVE ANY OF YOU FIGURED OUT THE BEST WAY TO GET TO HER YET?>

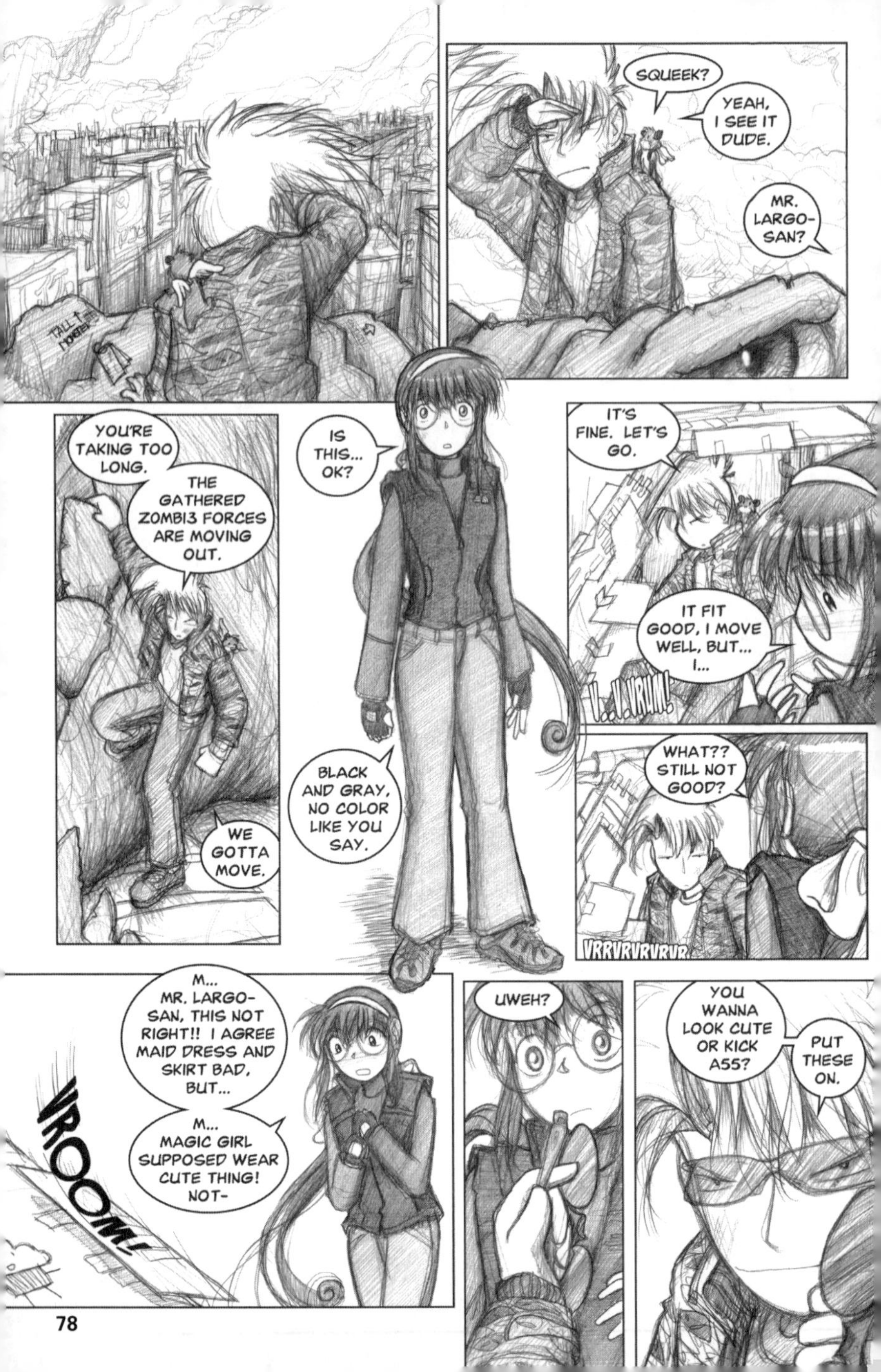
SQUEEK?
YEAH, I SEE IT DUDE.
MR. LARGO-SAN?
YOU'RE TAKING TOO LONG.
THE GATHERED ZOMBI3 FORCES ARE MOVING OUT.
WE GOTTA MOVE.
IS THIS... OK?
BLACK AND GRAY, NO COLOR LIKE YOU SAY.
IT'S FINE. LET'S GO.
IT FIT GOOD, I MOVE WELL, BUT... I...
V..V..VRUM!
WHAT?? STILL NOT GOOD?
VRRVRVRVRVR
M... MR. LARGO-SAN, THIS NOT RIGHT!! I AGREE MAID DRESS AND SKIRT BAD, BUT...
M... MAGIC GIRL SUPPOSED WEAR CUTE THING! NOT-
VROOM!
UWEH?
YOU WANNA LOOK CUTE OR KICK ASS?
PUT THESE ON.

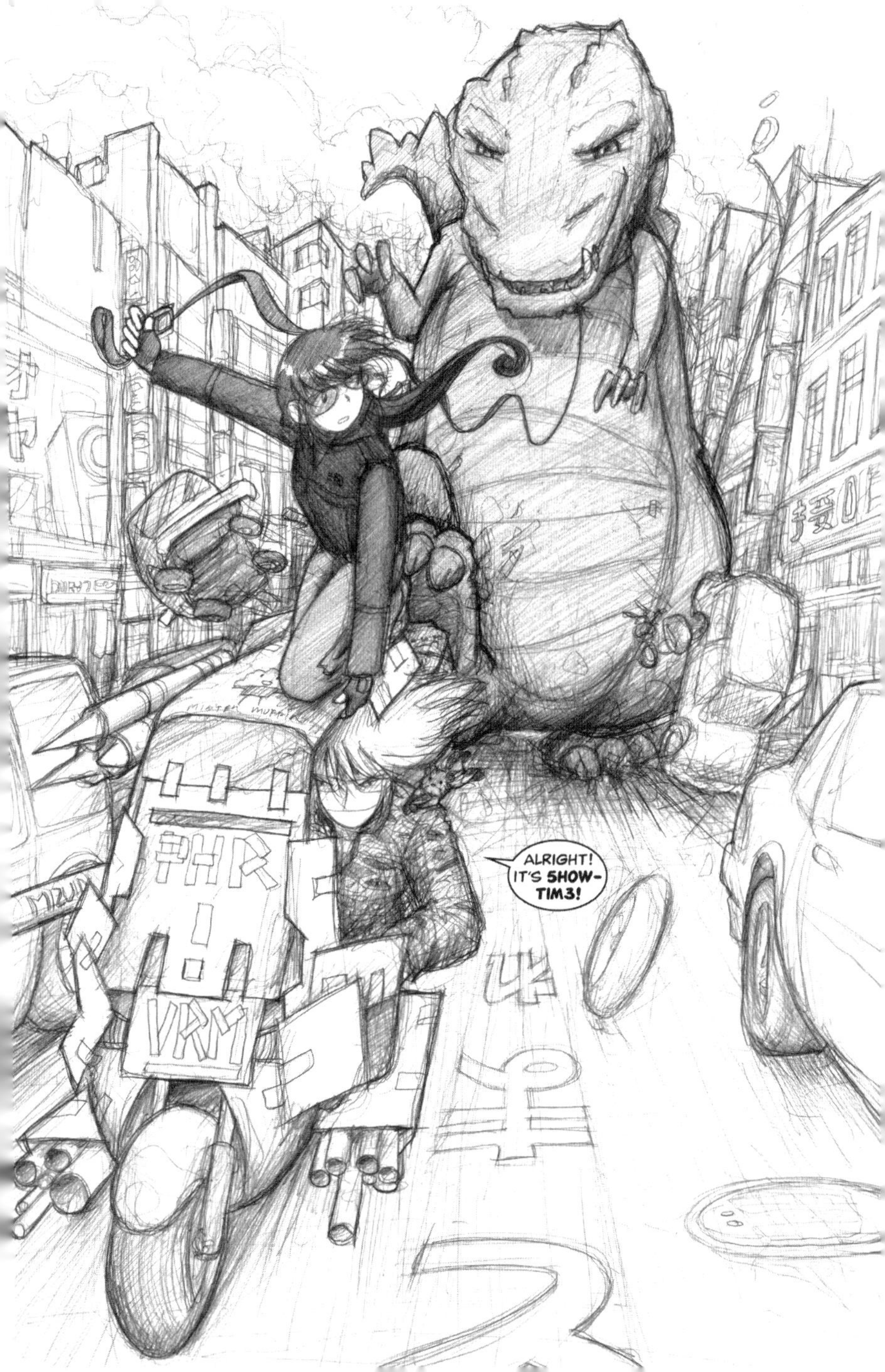
ALRIGHT! IT'S SHOW-TIM3!

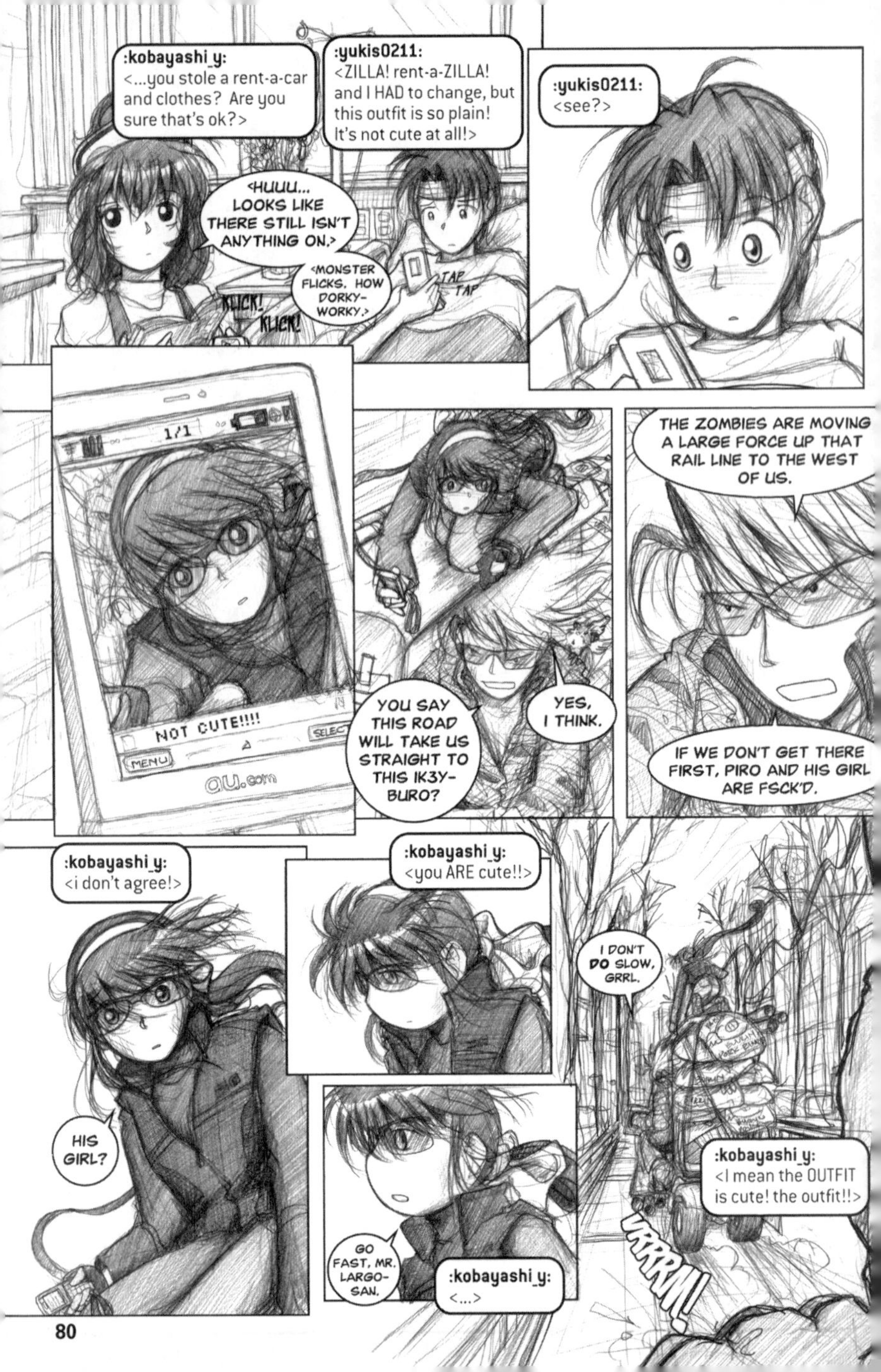

:kobayashi_y:
<...you stole a rent-a-car and clothes? Are you sure that's ok?>
:yukis0211:
<ZILLA! rent-a-ZILLA! and I HAD to change, but this outfit is so plain! It's not cute at all!>
<HUUU... LOOKS LIKE THERE STILL ISN'T ANYTHING ON.>
<MONSTER FLICKS. HOW DORKY-WORKY.>
KLICK! KLICK!
TAP TAP
:yukis0211:
<see?>
1/1
NOT CUTE!!!!
MENU
au.com
YOU SAY THIS ROAD WILL TAKE US STRAIGHT TO THIS IK3Y-BURO?
YES, I THINK.
THE ZOMBIES ARE MOVING A LARGE FORCE UP THAT RAIL LINE TO THE WEST OF US.
IF WE DON'T GET THERE FIRST, PIRO AND HIS GIRL ARE FSCK'D.
:kobayashi_y:
<i don't agree!>
HIS GIRL?
:kobayashi_y:
<you ARE cute!!>
GO FAST, MR. LARGO-SAN.
:kobayashi_y:
<...>
I DON'T DO SLOW, GRRL.
:kobayashi_y:
<I mean the OUTFIT is cute! the outfit!!>

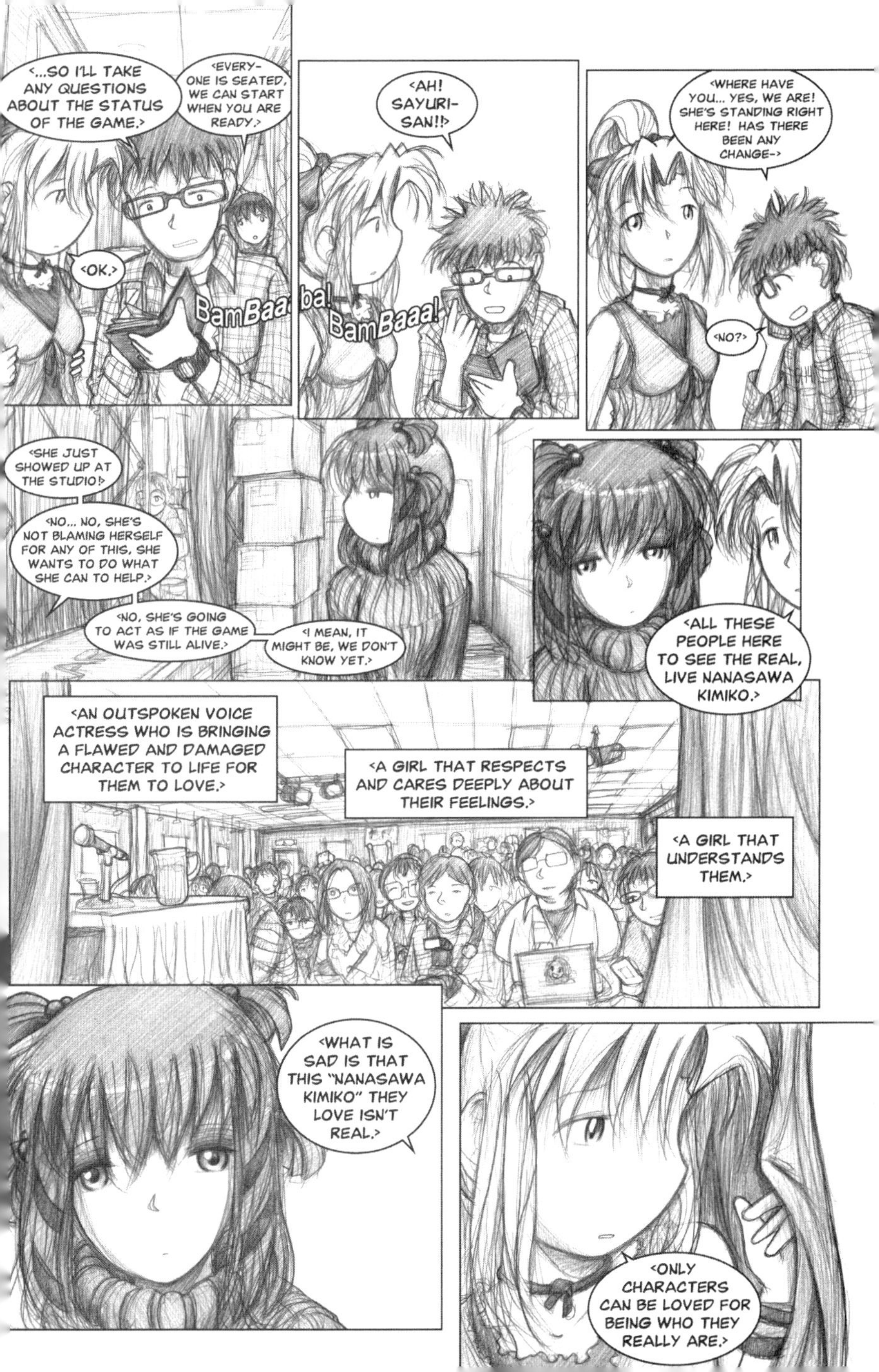
<...SO I'LL TAKE ANY QUESTIONS ABOUT THE STATUS OF THE GAME.>
<EVERY-ONE IS SEATED, WE CAN START WHEN YOU ARE READY.>
<OK.>
BamBaaaba!
<AH! SAYURI-SAN!!>
BamBaaa!
<WHERE HAVE YOU... YES, WE ARE! SHE'S STANDING RIGHT HERE! HAS THERE BEEN ANY CHANGE->
<NO?>
<SHE JUST SHOWED UP AT THE STUDIO!>
<NO... NO, SHE'S NOT BLAMING HERSELF FOR ANY OF THIS, SHE WANTS TO DO WHAT SHE CAN TO HELP.>
<NO, SHE'S GOING TO ACT AS IF THE GAME WAS STILL ALIVE.>
<I MEAN, IT MIGHT BE, WE DON'T KNOW YET.>
<ALL THESE PEOPLE HERE TO SEE THE REAL, LIVE NANASAWA KIMIKO.>
<AN OUTSPOKEN VOICE ACTRESS WHO IS BRINGING A FLAWED AND DAMAGED CHARACTER TO LIFE FOR THEM TO LOVE.>
<A GIRL THAT RESPECTS AND CARES DEEPLY ABOUT THEIR FEELINGS.>
<A GIRL THAT UNDERSTANDS THEM.>
<WHAT IS SAD IS THAT THIS "NANASAWA KIMIKO" THEY LOVE ISN'T REAL.>
<ONLY CHARACTERS CAN BE LOVED FOR BEING WHO THEY REALLY ARE.>

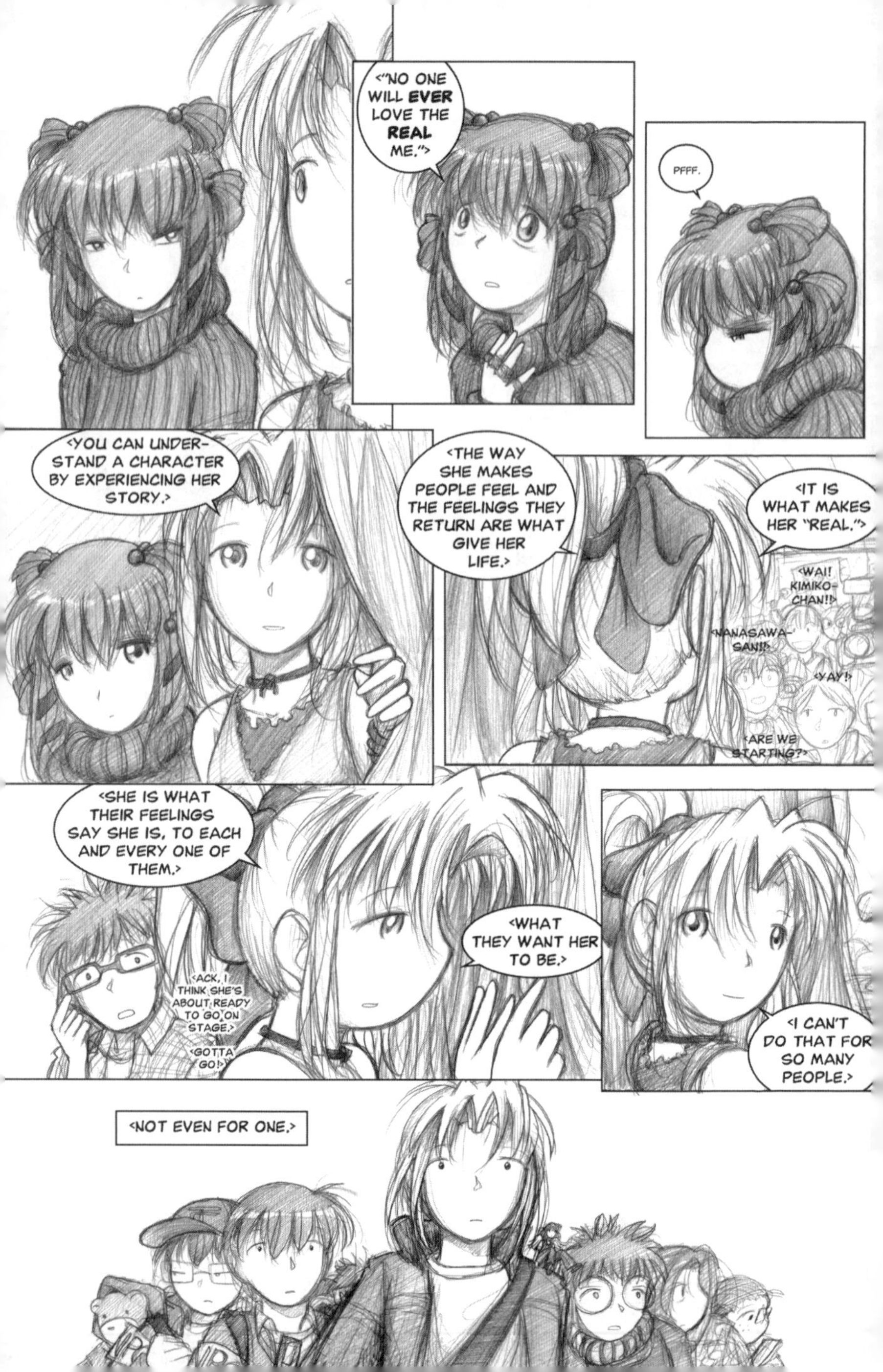
<"NO ONE WILL **EVER** LOVE THE **REAL** ME.">
PFFF.
<YOU CAN UNDER-STAND A CHARACTER BY EXPERIENCING HER STORY.>
<THE WAY SHE MAKES PEOPLE FEEL AND THE FEELINGS THEY RETURN ARE WHAT GIVE HER LIFE.>
<IT IS WHAT MAKES HER "REAL.">
<WAI! KIMIKO-CHAN!!>
<NANASAWA-SAN!!>
<YAY!>
<ARE WE STARTING?>
<SHE IS WHAT THEIR FEELINGS SAY SHE IS, TO EACH AND EVERY ONE OF THEM.>
<ACK, I THINK SHE'S ABOUT READY TO GO ON STAGE.>
<GOTTA GO!>
<WHAT THEY WANT HER TO BE.>
<I CAN'T DO THAT FOR SO MANY PEOPLE.>
<NOT EVEN FOR ONE.>

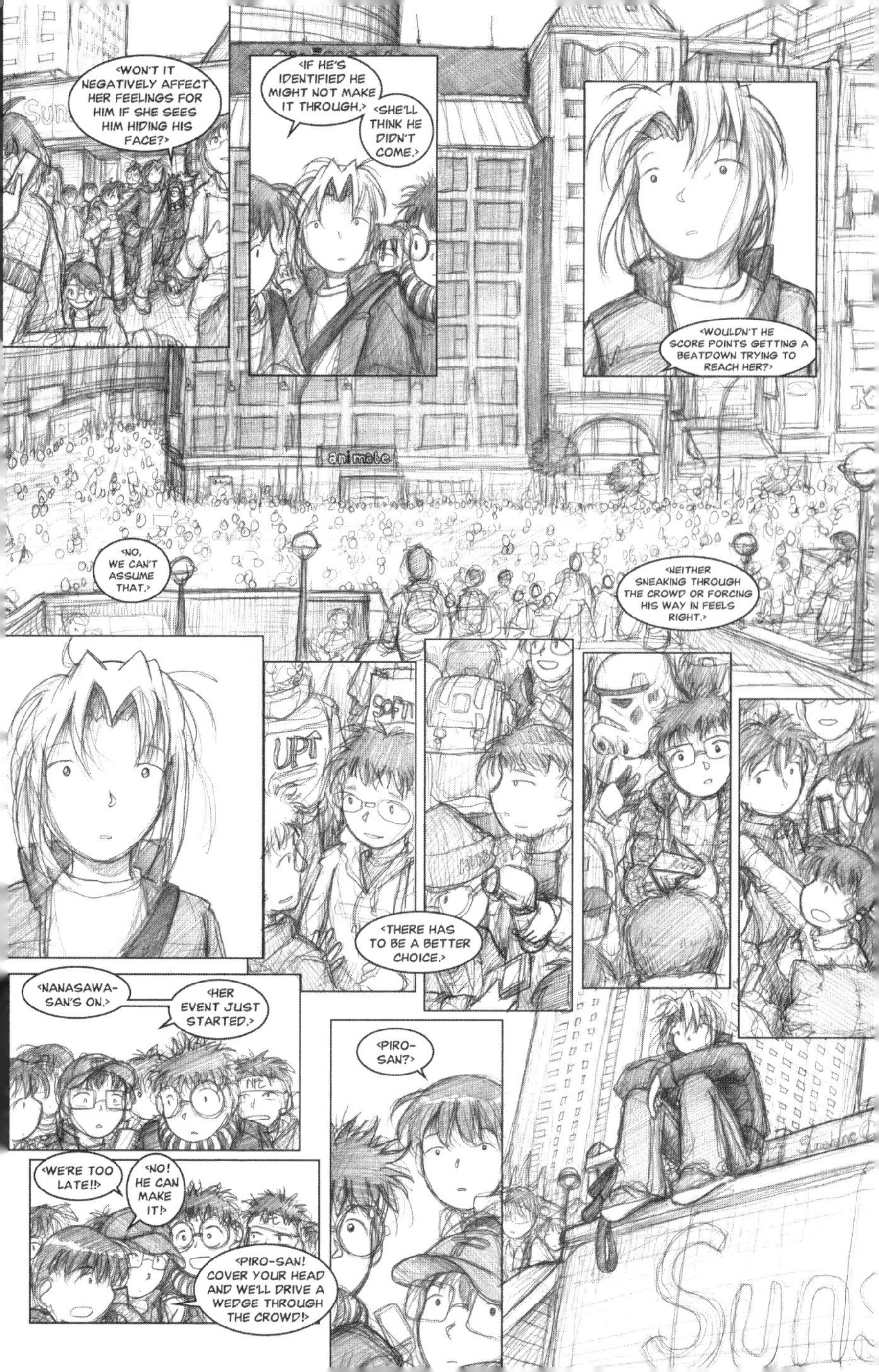

<WON'T IT NEGATIVELY AFFECT HER FEELINGS FOR HIM IF SHE SEES HIM HIDING HIS FACE?>
<IF HE'S IDENTIFIED HE MIGHT NOT MAKE IT THROUGH.>
<SHE'LL THINK HE DIDN'T COME.>
<WOULDN'T HE SCORE POINTS GETTING A BEATDOWN TRYING TO REACH HER?>
animate
<NO, WE CAN'T ASSUME THAT.>
<NEITHER SNEAKING THROUGH THE CROWD OR FORCING HIS WAY IN FEELS RIGHT.>
<THERE HAS TO BE A BETTER CHOICE.>
<NANASAWA-SAN'S ON.>
<HER EVENT JUST STARTED.>
<WE'RE TOO LATE!!>
<NO! HE CAN MAKE IT!>
<PIRO-SAN! COVER YOUR HEAD AND WE'LL DRIVE A WEDGE THROUGH THE CROWD!>
<PIRO-SAN?>

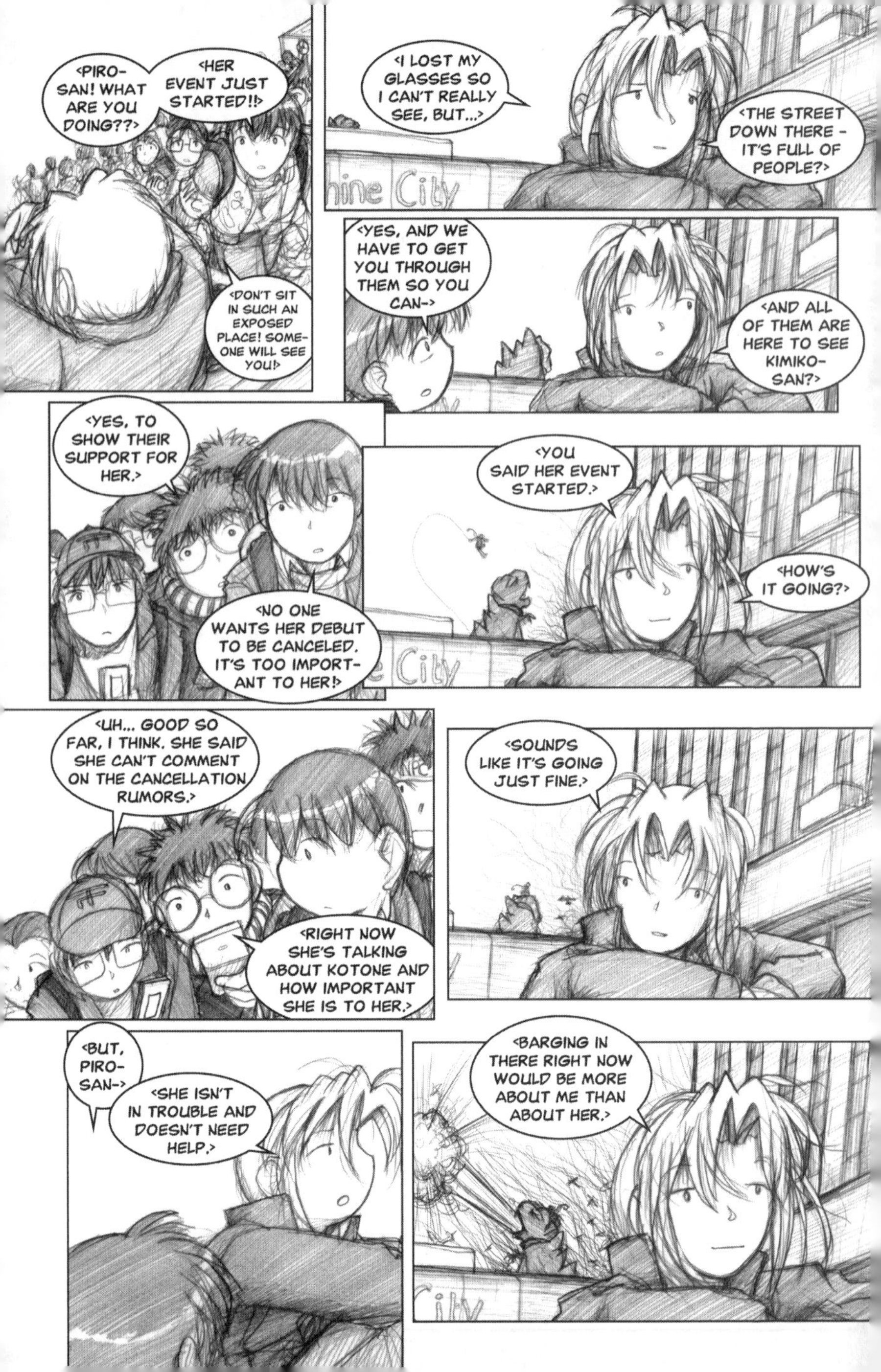
<PIRO-SAN! WHAT ARE YOU DOING??>
<HER EVENT JUST STARTED!!>
<DON'T SIT IN SUCH AN EXPOSED PLACE! SOME-ONE WILL SEE YOU!>
<I LOST MY GLASSES SO I CAN'T REALLY SEE, BUT...>
<THE STREET DOWN THERE - IT'S FULL OF PEOPLE?>
<YES, AND WE HAVE TO GET YOU THROUGH THEM SO YOU CAN->
<AND ALL OF THEM ARE HERE TO SEE KIMIKO-SAN?>
<YES, TO SHOW THEIR SUPPORT FOR HER.>
<NO ONE WANTS HER DEBUT TO BE CANCELED. IT'S TOO IMPORT-ANT TO HER!>
<YOU SAID HER EVENT STARTED.>
<HOW'S IT GOING?>
<UH... GOOD SO FAR, I THINK. SHE SAID SHE CAN'T COMMENT ON THE CANCELLATION RUMORS.>
<RIGHT NOW SHE'S TALKING ABOUT KOTONE AND HOW IMPORTANT SHE IS TO HER.>
<SOUNDS LIKE IT'S GOING JUST FINE.>
<BUT, PIRO-SAN->
<SHE ISN'T IN TROUBLE AND DOESN'T NEED HELP.>
<BARGING IN THERE RIGHT NOW WOULD BE MORE ABOUT ME THAN ABOUT HER.>

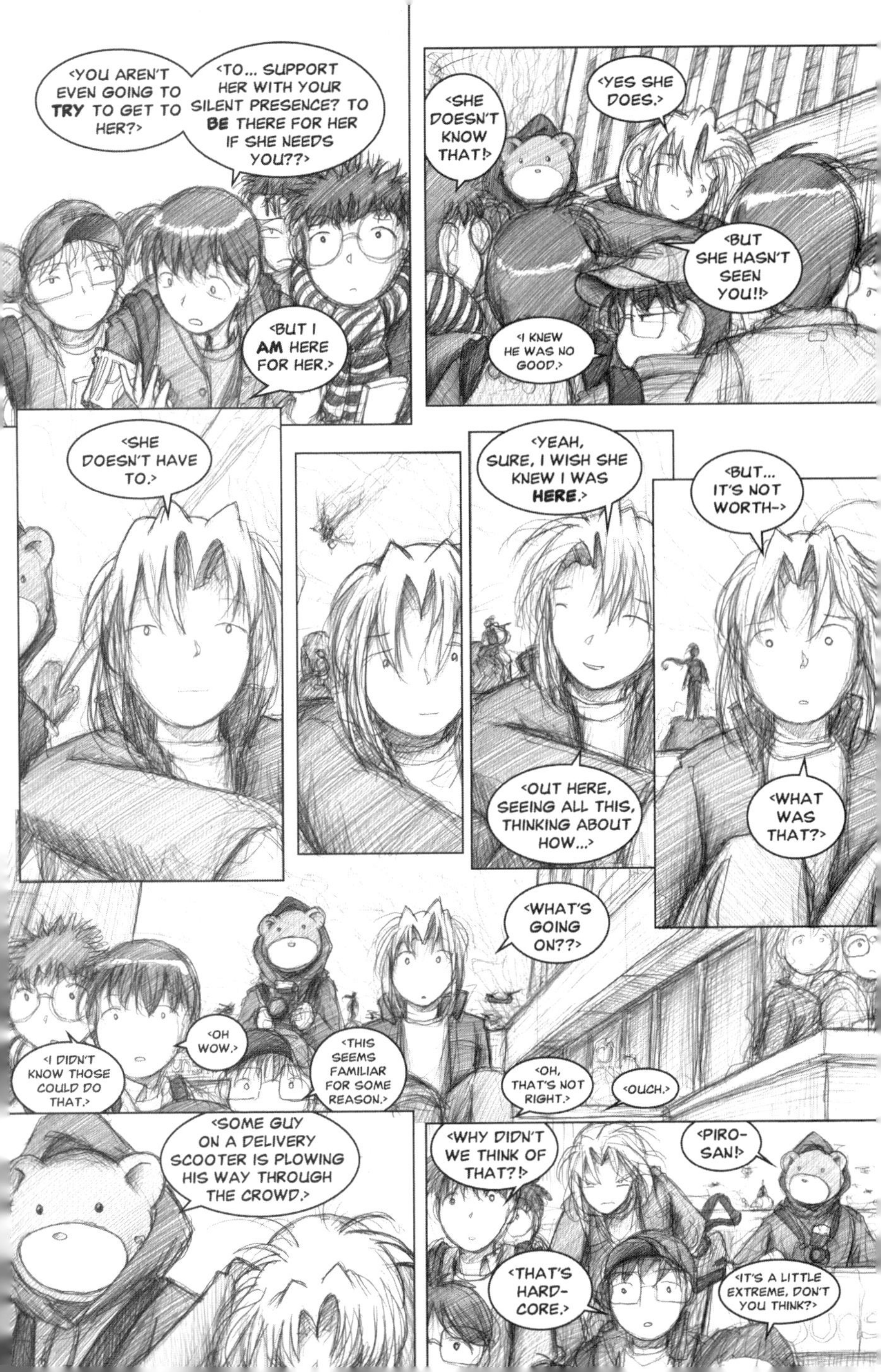
<YOU AREN'T EVEN GOING TO **TRY** TO GET TO HER?>
<TO... SUPPORT HER WITH YOUR SILENT PRESENCE? TO **BE** THERE FOR HER IF SHE NEEDS YOU??>
<BUT I **AM** HERE FOR HER.>
<SHE DOESN'T KNOW THAT!>
<YES SHE DOES.>
<BUT SHE HASN'T SEEN YOU!!>
<I KNEW HE WAS NO GOOD.>
<SHE DOESN'T HAVE TO.>
<YEAH, SURE, I WISH SHE KNEW I WAS **HERE**.>
<OUT HERE, SEEING ALL THIS, THINKING ABOUT HOW...>
<BUT... IT'S NOT WORTH–>
<WHAT WAS THAT?>
<I DIDN'T KNOW THOSE COULD DO THAT.>
<OH WOW.>
<THIS SEEMS FAMILIAR FOR SOME REASON.>
<WHAT'S GOING ON??>
<OH, THAT'S NOT RIGHT.>
<OUCH.>
<SOME GUY ON A DELIVERY SCOOTER IS PLOWING HIS WAY THROUGH THE CROWD.>
<WHY DIDN'T WE THINK OF THAT?!>
<PIRO-SAN!>
<THAT'S HARD-CORE.>
<IT'S A LITTLE EXTREME, DON'T YOU THINK?>

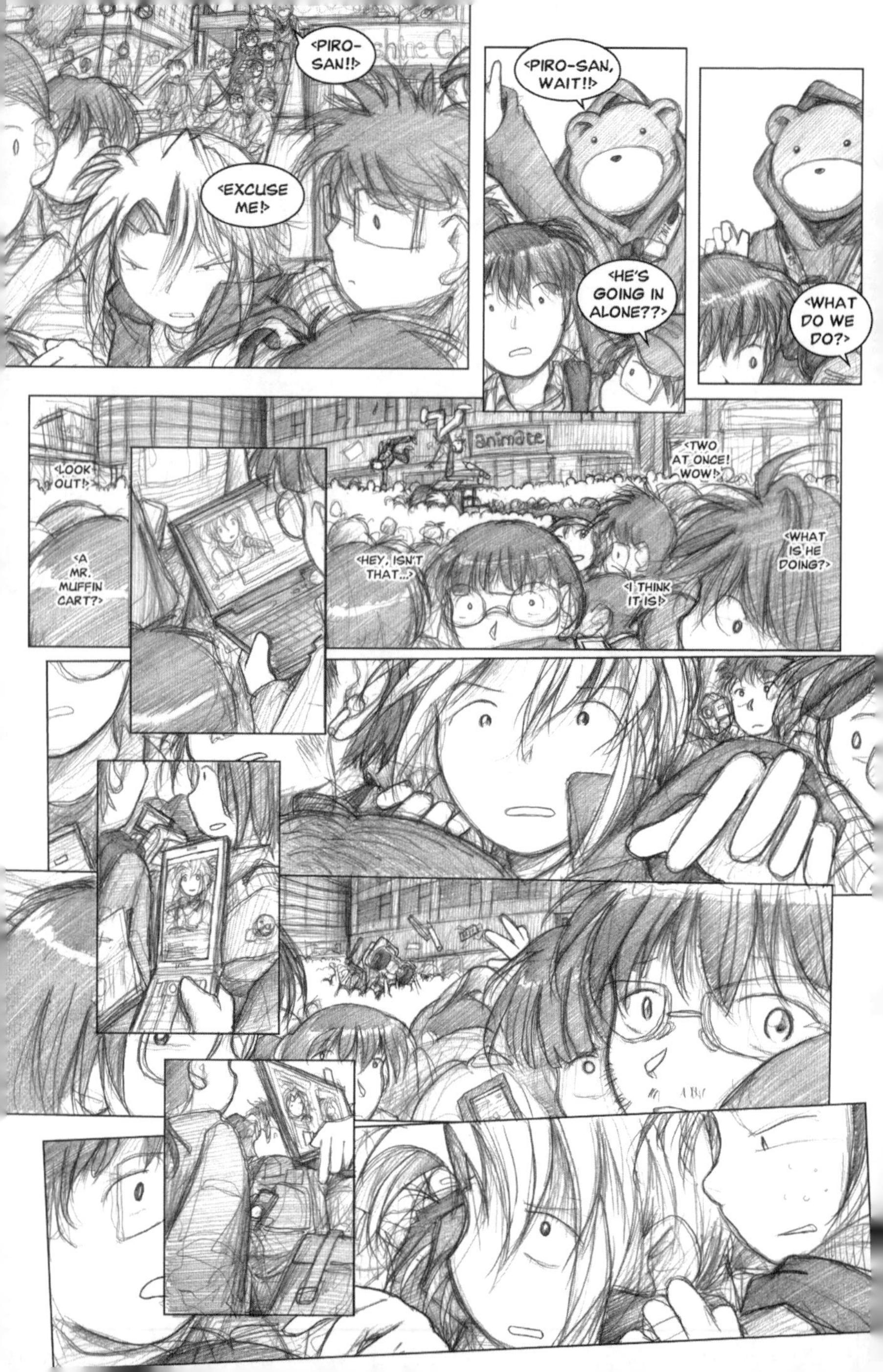

<PIRO-SAN!!>
<EXCUSE ME!>
<PIRO-SAN, WAIT!!>
<HE'S GOING IN ALONE??>
<WHAT DO WE DO?>
<LOOK OUT!>
<A MR. MUFFIN CART?>
<HEY, ISN'T THAT...>
<I THINK IT IS!>
<TWO AT ONCE! WOW!>
<WHAT IS HE DOING?>

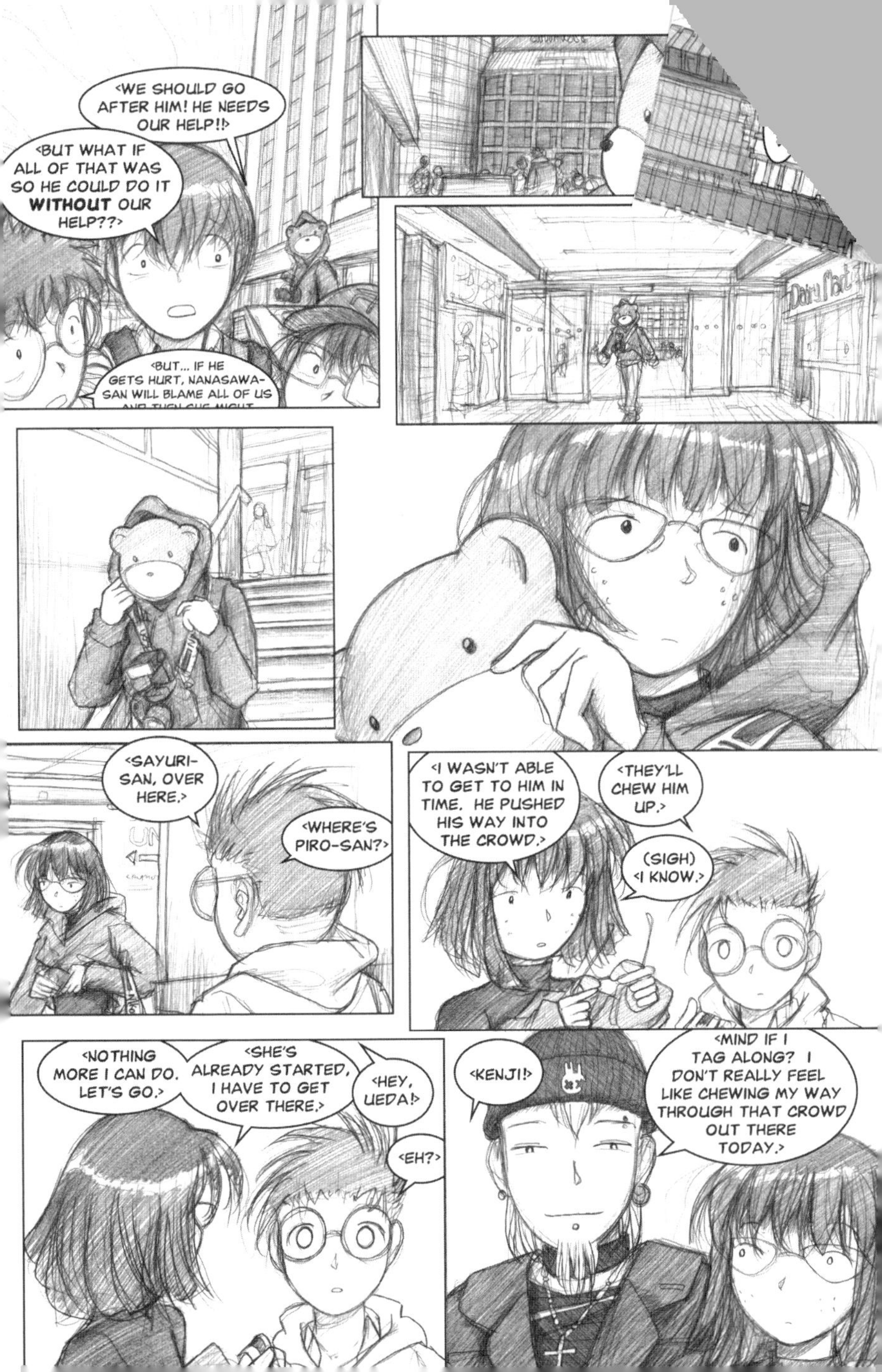
<WE SHOULD GO AFTER HIM! HE NEEDS OUR HELP!!>
<BUT WHAT IF ALL OF THAT WAS SO HE COULD DO IT **WITHOUT** OUR HELP??>
<BUT... IF HE GETS HURT, NANASAWA-SAN WILL BLAME ALL OF US
Dairy Mart
<SAYURI-SAN, OVER HERE.>
<WHERE'S PIRO-SAN?>
<I WASN'T ABLE TO GET TO HIM IN TIME. HE PUSHED HIS WAY INTO THE CROWD.>
<THEY'LL CHEW HIM UP.>
(SIGH) <I KNOW.>
<NOTHING MORE I CAN DO. LET'S GO.>
<SHE'S ALREADY STARTED, I HAVE TO GET OVER THERE.>
<HEY, UEDA!>
<EH?>
<KENJI!>
<MIND IF I TAG ALONG? I DON'T REALLY FEEL LIKE CHEWING MY WAY THROUGH THAT CROWD OUT THERE TODAY.>

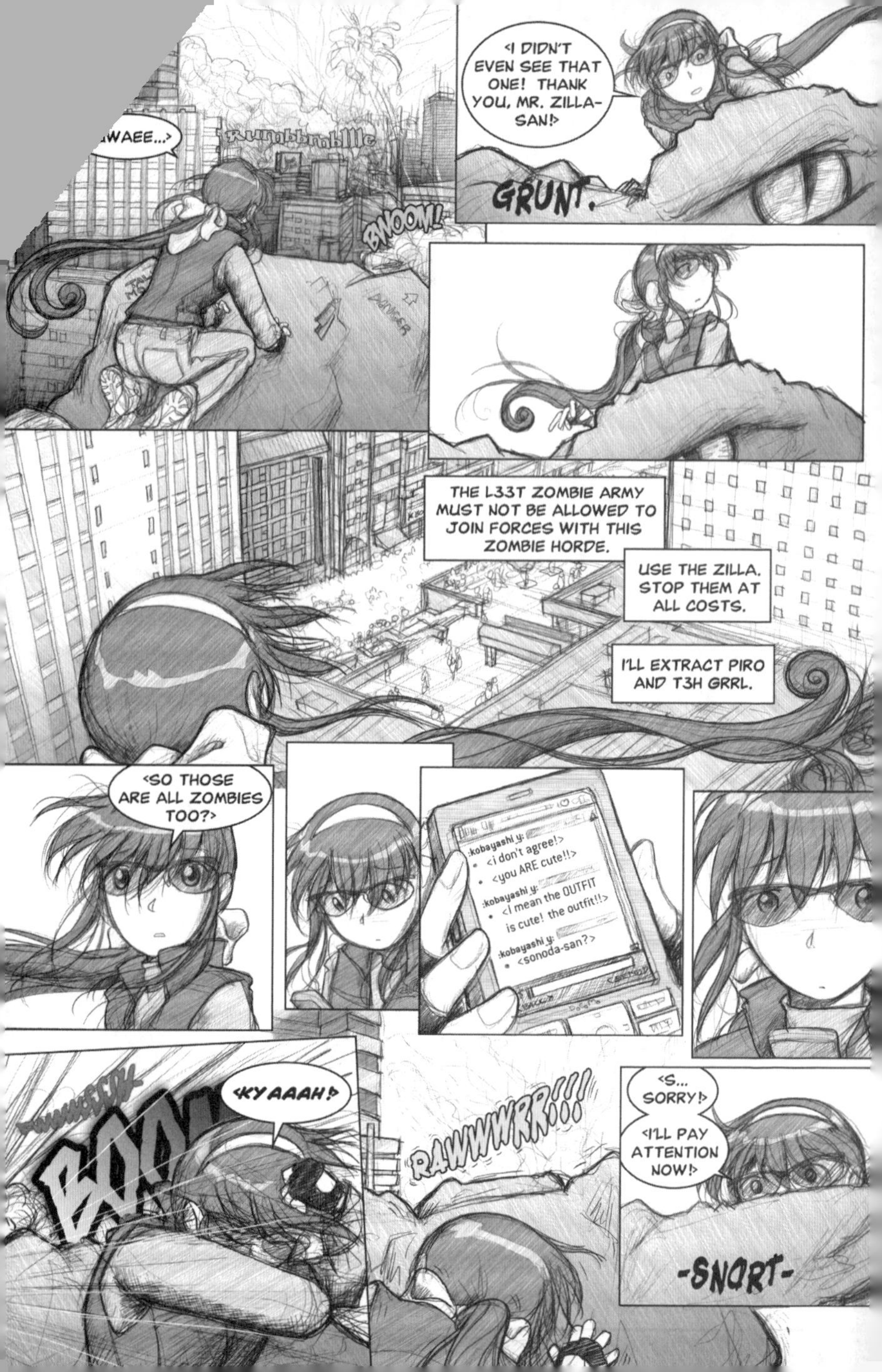

AWAEE...>
Rumbbmblllle
BWOOM!
<I DIDN'T EVEN SEE THAT ONE! THANK YOU, MR. ZILLA-SAN!>
GRUNT.
THE L33T ZOMBIE ARMY MUST NOT BE ALLOWED TO JOIN FORCES WITH THIS ZOMBIE HORDE.
USE THE ZILLA. STOP THEM AT ALL COSTS.
I'LL EXTRACT PIRO AND T3H GRRL.
<SO THOSE ARE ALL ZOMBIES TOO?>
:kobayashi_y:
<i don't agree!>
<you ARE cute!!>
:kobayashi_y:
<I mean the OUTFIT is cute! the outfit!!>
:kobayashi_y:
<sonoda-san?>
<KYAAAH!>
RAWWWRR!!!
<S... SORRY!>
<I'LL PAY ATTENTION NOW!>
-SNORT-

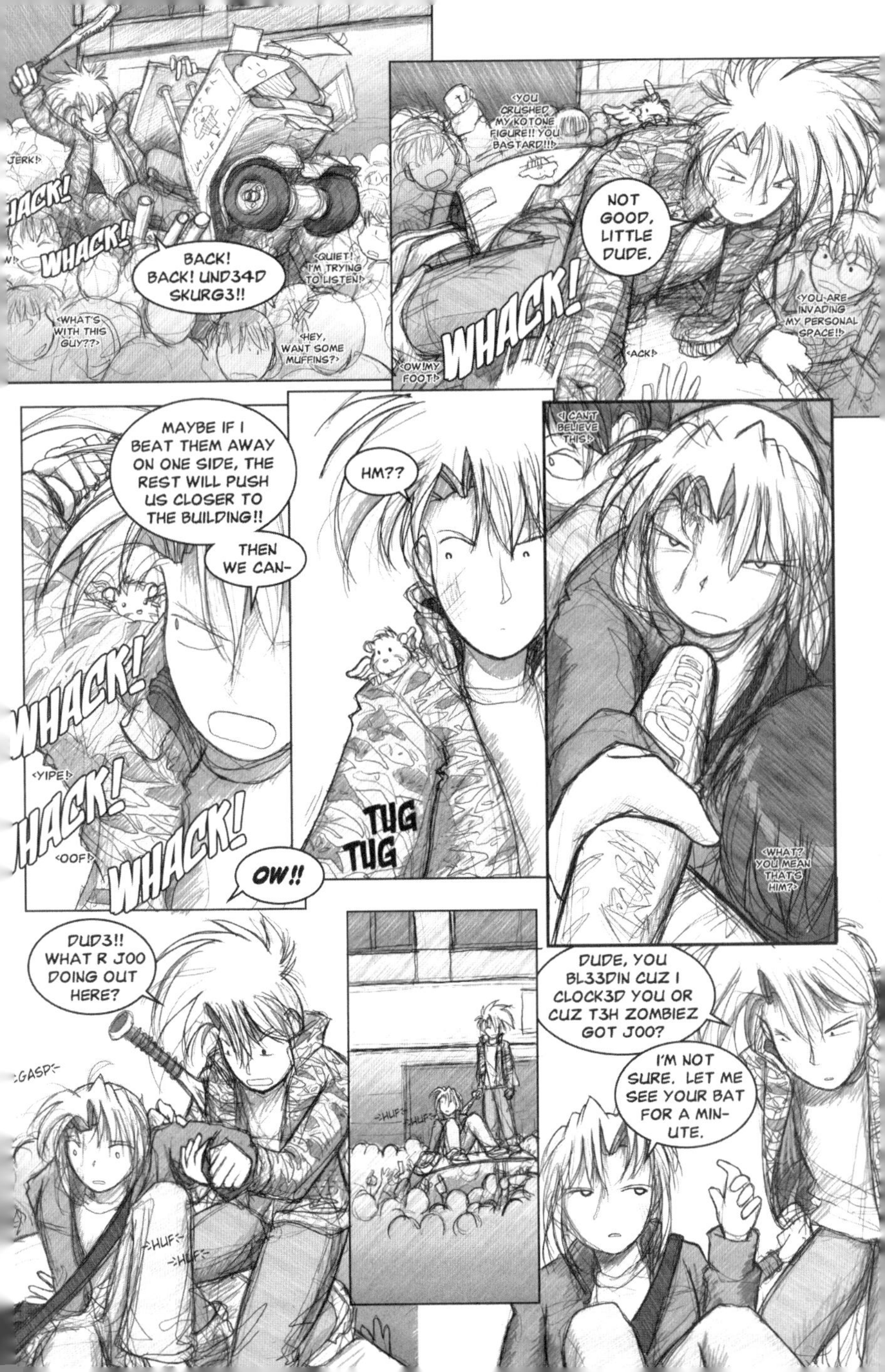
JERK!>
HACK!
WHACK!
BACK! BACK! UND34D SKURG3!!
<QUIET! I'M TRYING TO LISTEN!>
<WHAT'S WITH THIS GUY??>
<HEY, WANT SOME MUFFINS?>
<YOU CRUSHED MY KOTONE FIGURE!! YOU BASTARD!!!>
NOT GOOD, LITTLE DUDE.
WHACK!
<YOU ARE INVADING MY PERSONAL SPACE!!>
<OW! MY FOOT!>
<ACK!>
MAYBE IF I BEAT THEM AWAY ON ONE SIDE, THE REST WILL PUSH US CLOSER TO THE BUILDING!!
THEN WE CAN-
WHACK!
<YIPE!>
HACK!
<OOF!>
WHACK!
OW!!
HM??
TUG TUG
<I CAN'T BELIEVE THIS!>
<WHAT? YOU MEAN THAT'S HIM?>
DUD3!! WHAT R JOO DOING OUT HERE?
GASP
HUF HUF
HUF HUF
DUDE, YOU BL33DIN CUZ I CLOCK3D YOU OR CUZ T3H ZOMBIEZ GOT JOO?
I'M NOT SURE. LET ME SEE YOUR BAT FOR A MIN-UTE.

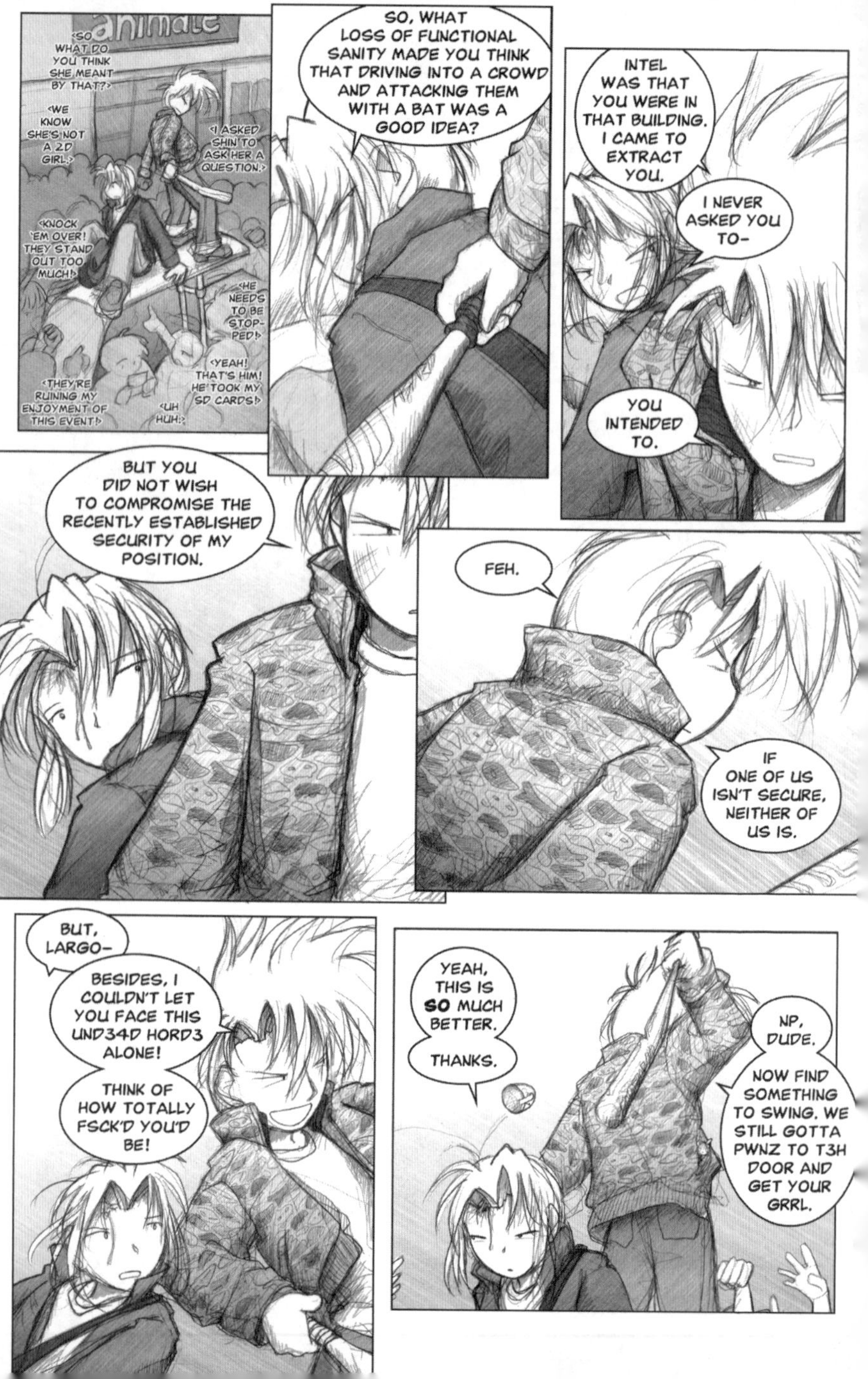
animate
<SO WHAT DO YOU THINK SHE MEANT BY THAT?>
<WE KNOW SHE'S NOT A 2D GIRL.>
<I ASKED SHIN TO ASK HER A QUESTION.>
<KNOCK 'EM OVER! THEY STAND OUT TOO MUCH!>
<HE NEEDS TO BE STOP-PED!>
<YEAH! THAT'S HIM! HE TOOK MY SD CARDS!>
<THEY'RE RUINING MY ENJOYMENT OF THIS EVENT!>
<UH HUH.>
SO, WHAT LOSS OF FUNCTIONAL SANITY MADE YOU THINK THAT DRIVING INTO A CROWD AND ATTACKING THEM WITH A BAT WAS A GOOD IDEA?
INTEL WAS THAT YOU WERE IN THAT BUILDING. I CAME TO EXTRACT YOU.
I NEVER ASKED YOU TO-
YOU INTENDED TO.
BUT YOU DID NOT WISH TO COMPROMISE THE RECENTLY ESTABLISHED SECURITY OF MY POSITION.
FEH.
IF ONE OF US ISN'T SECURE, NEITHER OF US IS.
BUT, LARGO-
BESIDES, I COULDN'T LET YOU FACE THIS UND34D HORD3 ALONE!
THINK OF HOW TOTALLY FSCK'D YOU'D BE!
YEAH, THIS IS **SO** MUCH BETTER.
THANKS.
NP, DUDE.
NOW FIND SOMETHING TO SWING. WE STILL GOTTA PWNZ TO T3H DOOR AND GET YOUR GRRL.

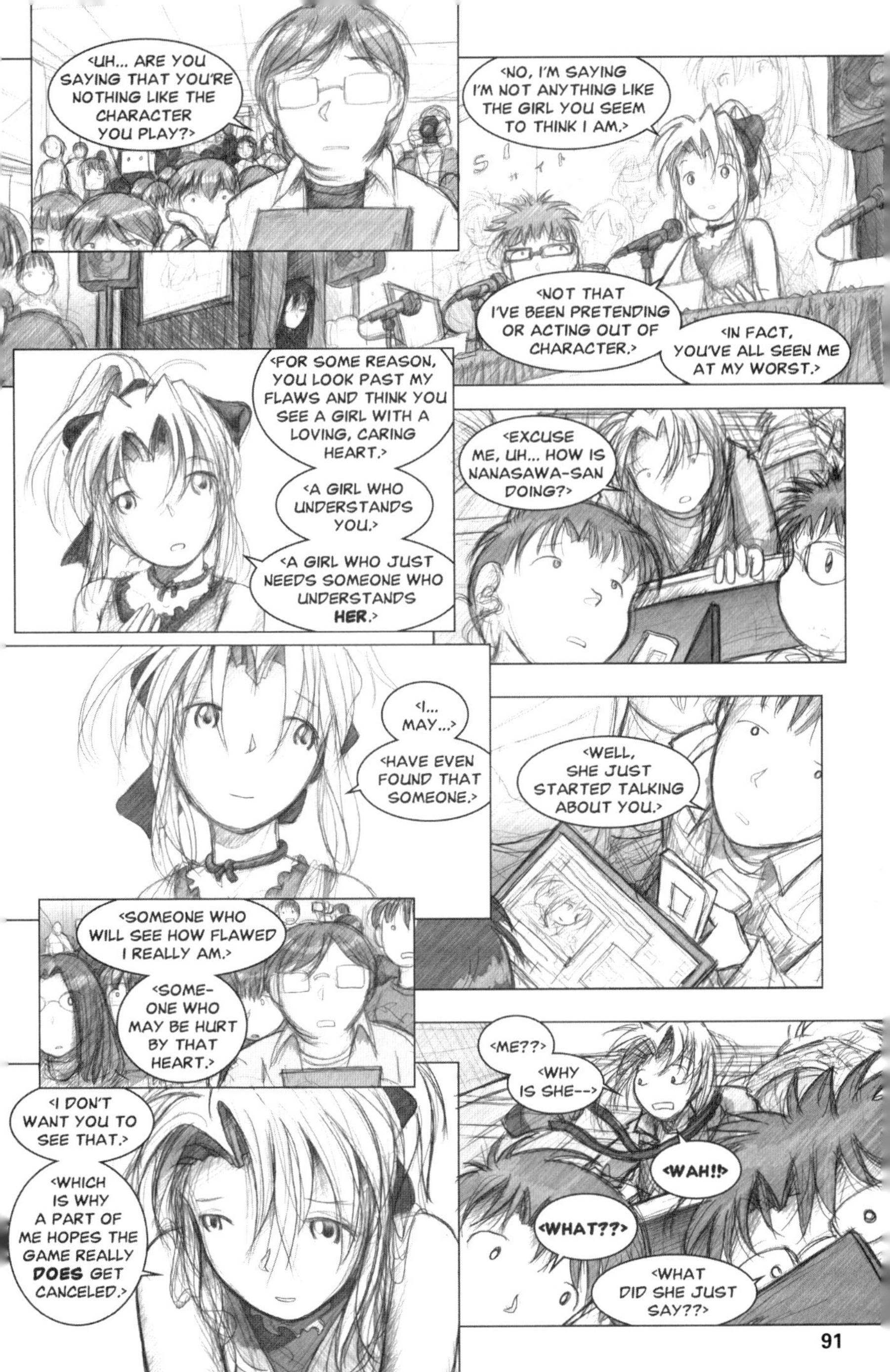
<UH... ARE YOU SAYING THAT YOU'RE NOTHING LIKE THE CHARACTER YOU PLAY?>
<NO, I'M SAYING I'M NOT ANYTHING LIKE THE GIRL YOU SEEM TO THINK I AM.>
<NOT THAT I'VE BEEN PRETENDING OR ACTING OUT OF CHARACTER.>
<IN FACT, YOU'VE ALL SEEN ME AT MY WORST.>
<FOR SOME REASON, YOU LOOK PAST MY FLAWS AND THINK YOU SEE A GIRL WITH A LOVING, CARING HEART.>
<A GIRL WHO UNDERSTANDS YOU.>
<A GIRL WHO JUST NEEDS SOMEONE WHO UNDERSTANDS **HER**.>
<EXCUSE ME, UH... HOW IS NANASAWA-SAN DOING?>
<I... MAY...>
<HAVE EVEN FOUND THAT SOMEONE.>
<WELL, SHE JUST STARTED TALKING ABOUT YOU.>
<SOMEONE WHO WILL SEE HOW FLAWED I REALLY AM.>
<SOME-ONE WHO MAY BE HURT BY THAT HEART.>
<I DON'T WANT YOU TO SEE THAT.>
<WHICH IS WHY A PART OF ME HOPES THE GAME REALLY **DOES** GET CANCELED.>
<ME??>
<WHY IS SHE-->
<WAH!!>
<WHAT??>
<WHAT DID SHE JUST SAY??>

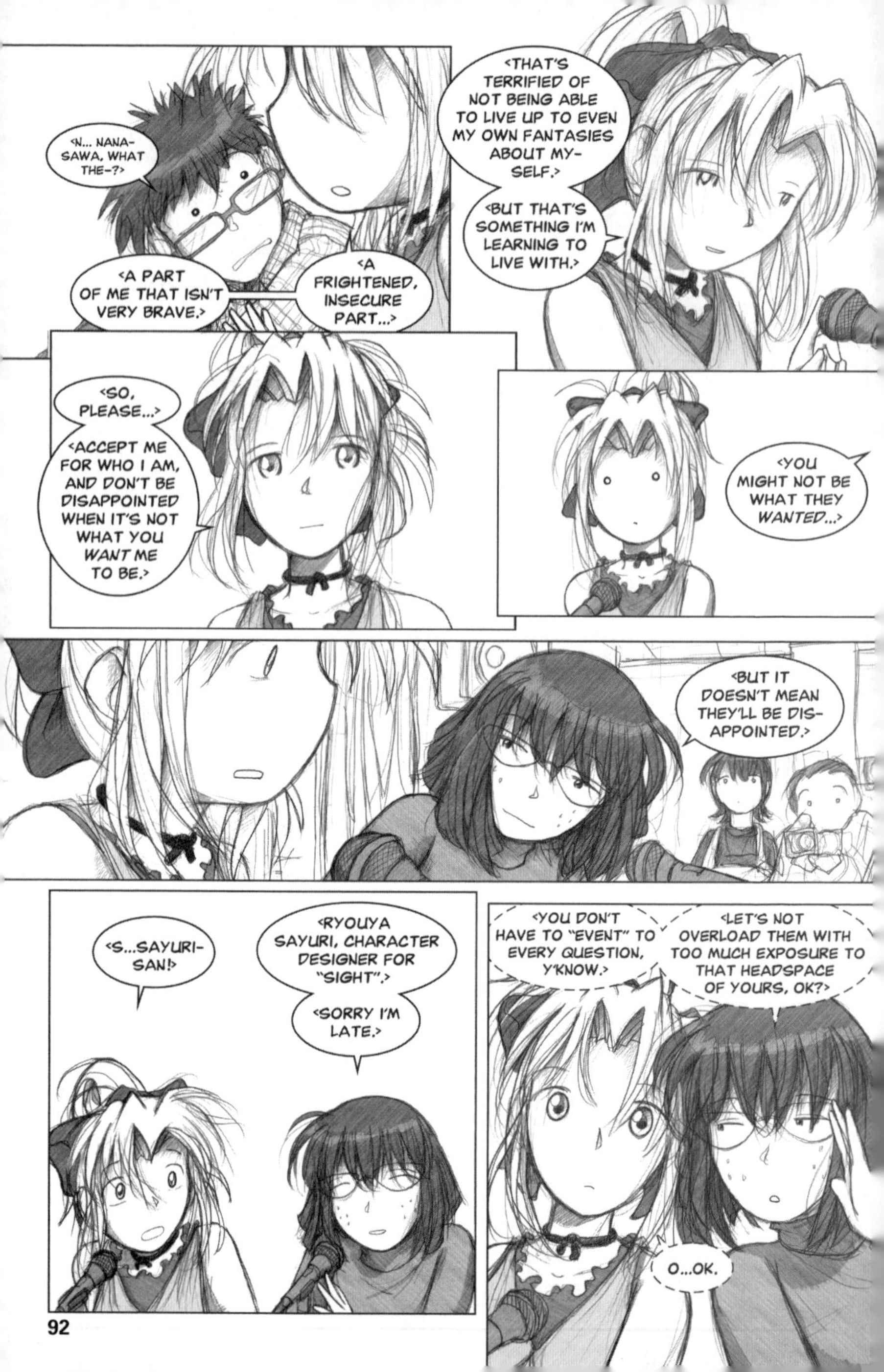

<N... NANA-SAWA, WHAT THE-?>
<A PART OF ME THAT ISN'T VERY BRAVE.>
<A FRIGHTENED, INSECURE PART...>
<THAT'S TERRIFIED OF NOT BEING ABLE TO LIVE UP TO EVEN MY OWN FANTASIES ABOUT MY-SELF.>
<BUT THAT'S SOMETHING I'M LEARNING TO LIVE WITH.>
<SO, PLEASE...>
<ACCEPT ME FOR WHO I AM, AND DON'T BE DISAPPOINTED WHEN IT'S NOT WHAT YOU *WANT* ME TO BE.>
<YOU MIGHT NOT BE WHAT THEY *WANTED*...>
<BUT IT DOESN'T MEAN THEY'LL BE DIS-APPOINTED.>
<S...SAYURI-SAN!>
<RYOUYA SAYURI, CHARACTER DESIGNER FOR "SIGHT".>
<SORRY I'M LATE.>
<YOU DON'T HAVE TO "EVENT" TO EVERY QUESTION, Y'KNOW.>
<LET'S NOT OVERLOAD THEM WITH TOO MUCH EXPOSURE TO THAT HEADSPACE OF YOURS, OK?>
O...OK.

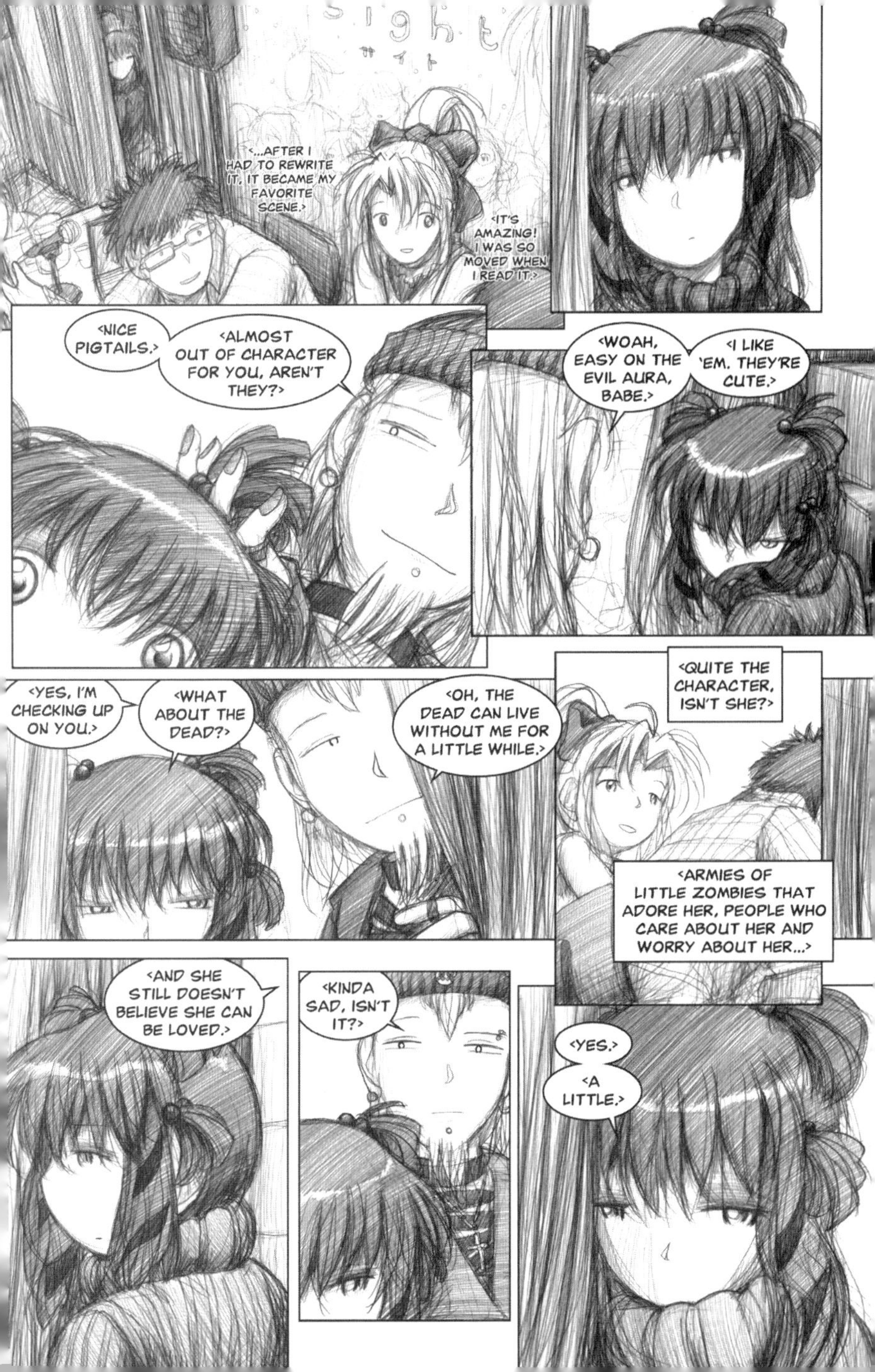
sight
サイト
<...AFTER I HAD TO REWRITE IT, IT BECAME MY FAVORITE SCENE.>
<IT'S AMAZING! I WAS SO MOVED WHEN I READ IT.>
<NICE PIGTAILS.>
<ALMOST OUT OF CHARACTER FOR YOU, AREN'T THEY?>
<WOAH, EASY ON THE EVIL AURA, BABE.>
<I LIKE 'EM. THEY'RE CUTE.>
<YES, I'M CHECKING UP ON YOU.>
<WHAT ABOUT THE DEAD?>
<OH, THE DEAD CAN LIVE WITHOUT ME FOR A LITTLE WHILE.>
<QUITE THE CHARACTER, ISN'T SHE?>
<ARMIES OF LITTLE ZOMBIES THAT ADORE HER, PEOPLE WHO CARE ABOUT HER AND WORRY ABOUT HER...>
<AND SHE STILL DOESN'T BELIEVE SHE CAN BE LOVED.>
<KINDA SAD, ISN'T IT?>
<YES.>
<A LITTLE.>

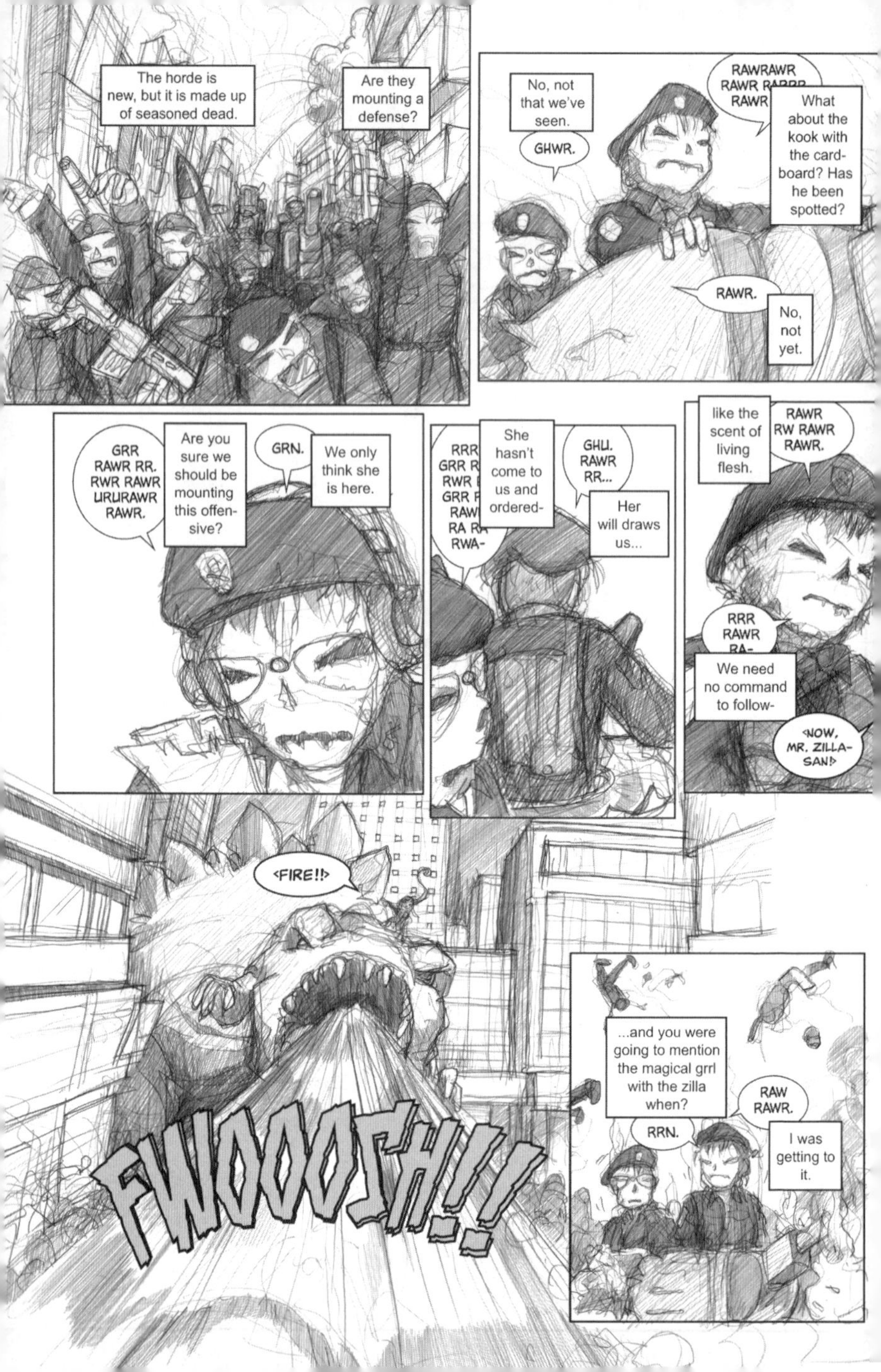

The horde is new, but it is made up of seasoned dead.
Are they mounting a defense?
No, not that we've seen.
GHWR.
RAWRAWR RAWR RAWR
What about the kook with the card-board? Has he been spotted?
RAWR.
No, not yet.
GRR RAWR RR. RWR RAWR URURAWR RAWR.
Are you sure we should be mounting this offen-sive?
GRN.
We only think she is here.
RRR GRR R RWR R GRR R RAW RA RA RWA-
She hasn't come to us and ordered-
GHU. RAWR RR...
Her will draws us...
like the scent of living flesh.
RAWR RW RAWR RAWR.
RRR RAWR RA-
We need no command to follow-
<NOW, MR. ZILLA-SAN!>
<FIRE!!>
FWOOOSH!!!
...and you were going to mention the magical grrl with the zilla when?
RAW RAWR.
RRN.
I was getting to it.

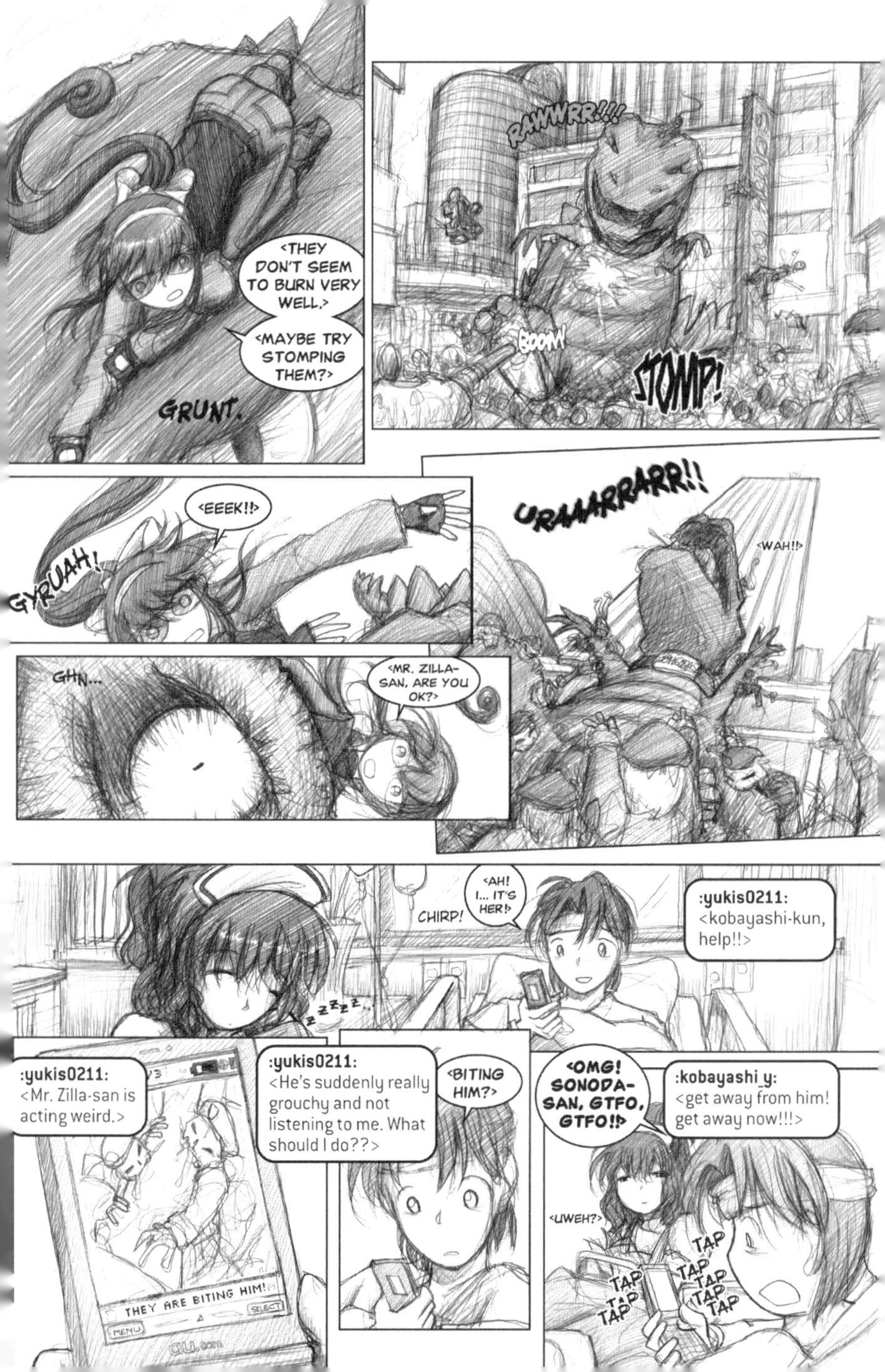
<THEY DON'T SEEM TO BURN VERY WELL.>
<MAYBE TRY STOMPING THEM?>
GRUNT.
RAWWRR!!!
BOOM!
STOMP!
<EEEK!!>
GYRUAH!
GHN...
<MR. ZILLA-SAN, ARE YOU OK?>
URAAARRARR!!
<WAH!!>
CHIRP!
<AH! I... IT'S HER!>
:yukis0211:
<kobayashi-kun, help!!>
ZZZZZ..
:yukis0211:
<Mr. Zilla-san is acting weird.>
THEY ARE BITING HIM!
SELECT
MENU
:yukis0211:
<He's suddenly really grouchy and not listening to me. What should I do??>
<BITING HIM?>
<OMG! SONODA-SAN, GTFO, GTFO!!>
:kobayashi_y:
<get away from him! get away now!!!>
<UWEH?>
TAP TAP TAP TAP TAP TAP TAP TAP

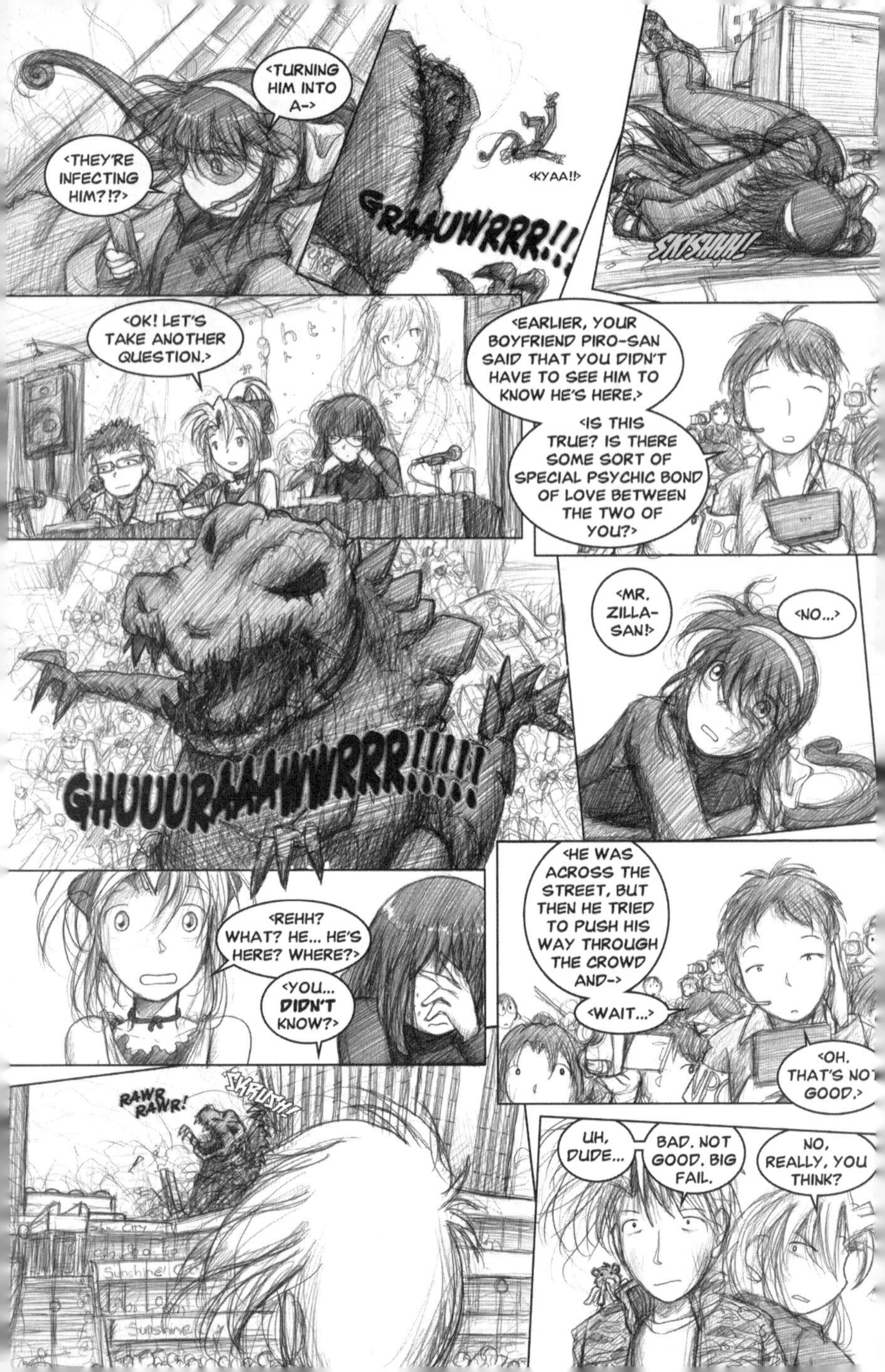
<TURNING HIM INTO A->
<THEY'RE INFECTING HIM?!?>
GRAAUWRRR!!!
<KYAA!!>
SKISHHH!
<OK! LET'S TAKE ANOTHER QUESTION.>
<EARLIER, YOUR BOYFRIEND PIRO-SAN SAID THAT YOU DIDN'T HAVE TO SEE HIM TO KNOW HE'S HERE.>
<IS THIS TRUE? IS THERE SOME SORT OF SPECIAL PSYCHIC BOND OF LOVE BETWEEN THE TWO OF YOU?>
GHUUURAAAWWRRR!!!!!!
<MR. ZILLA-SAN!>
<NO...>
<REHH? WHAT? HE... HE'S HERE? WHERE?>
<YOU... **DIDN'T** KNOW?>
<HE WAS ACROSS THE STREET, BUT THEN HE TRIED TO PUSH HIS WAY THROUGH THE CROWD AND->
<WAIT...>
<OH. THAT'S NOT GOOD.>
RAWR RAWR!
SKRUSH!
Sunshine
Sunshine
UH, DUDE...
BAD. NOT GOOD. BIG FAIL.
NO, REALLY, YOU THINK?

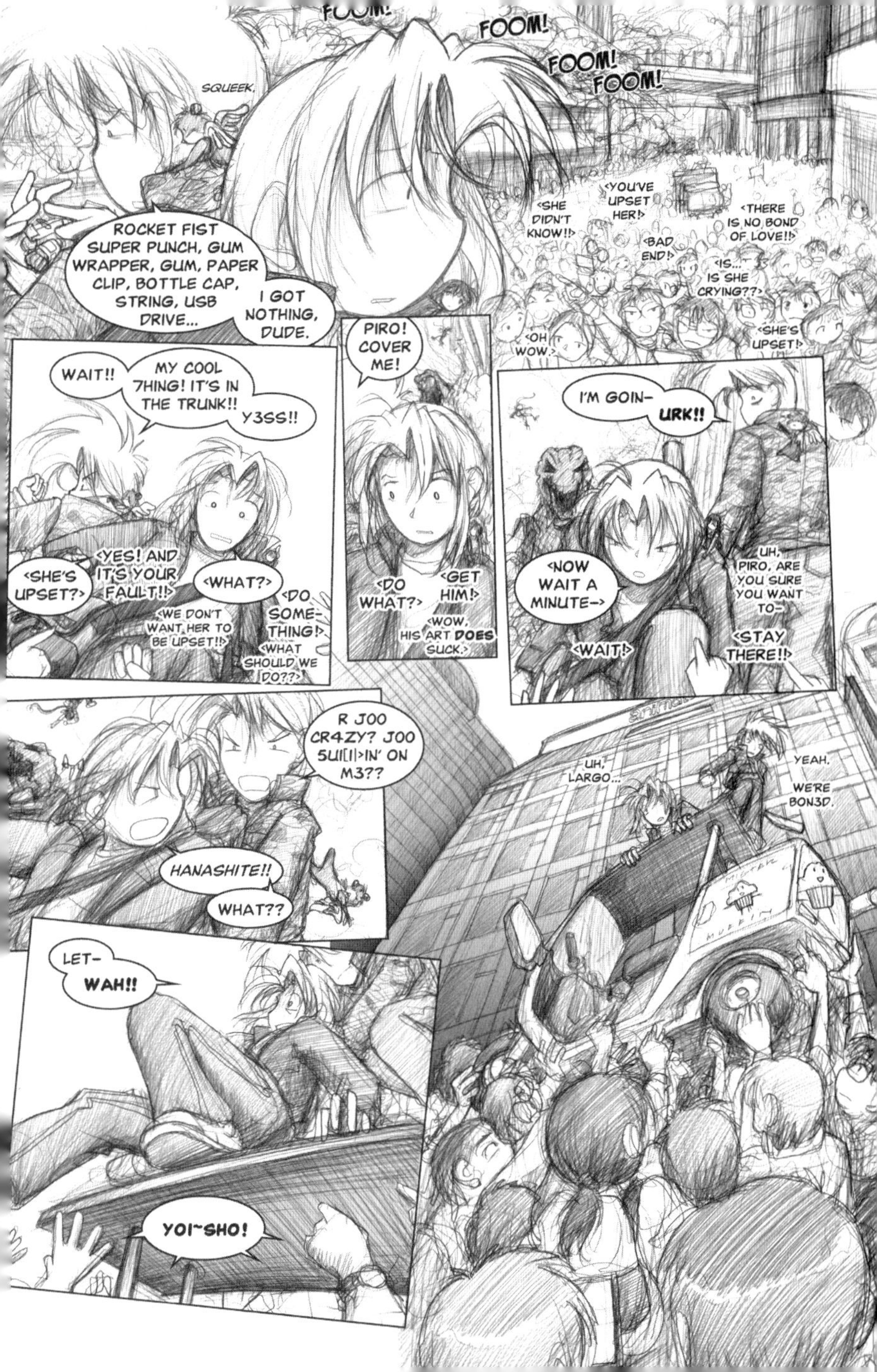
FOOM!
FOOM!
FOOM!
FOOM!
SQUEEK.
ROCKET FIST SUPER PUNCH, GUM WRAPPER, GUM, PAPER CLIP, BOTTLE CAP, STRING, USB DRIVE...
I GOT NOTHING, DUDE.
<SHE DIDN'T KNOW!!>
<YOU'VE UPSET HER!>
<THERE IS NO BOND OF LOVE!!>
<BAD END!>
<IS... IS SHE CRYING??>
<OH WOW.>
<SHE'S UPSET!>
WAIT!!
MY COOL 7HING! IT'S IN THE TRUNK!!
Y3SS!!
<SHE'S UPSET?>
<YES! AND IT'S YOUR FAULT!!>
<WHAT?>
<WE DON'T WANT HER TO BE UPSET!!>
<DO SOMETHING!>
<WHAT SHOULD WE DO??>
PIRO! COVER ME!
<DO WHAT?>
<GET HIM!>
<WOW, HIS ART **DOES** SUCK.>
I'M GOIN- **URK!!**
<NOW WAIT A MINUTE->
UH, PIRO, ARE YOU SURE YOU WANT TO-
<STAY THERE!!>
<WAIT!>
R JOO CR4ZY? JOO 5UI[|]>IN' ON M3??
HANASHITE!!
WHAT??
LET- **WAH!!**
YOI~SHO!
UH, LARGO...
YEAH.
WE'RE BON3D.

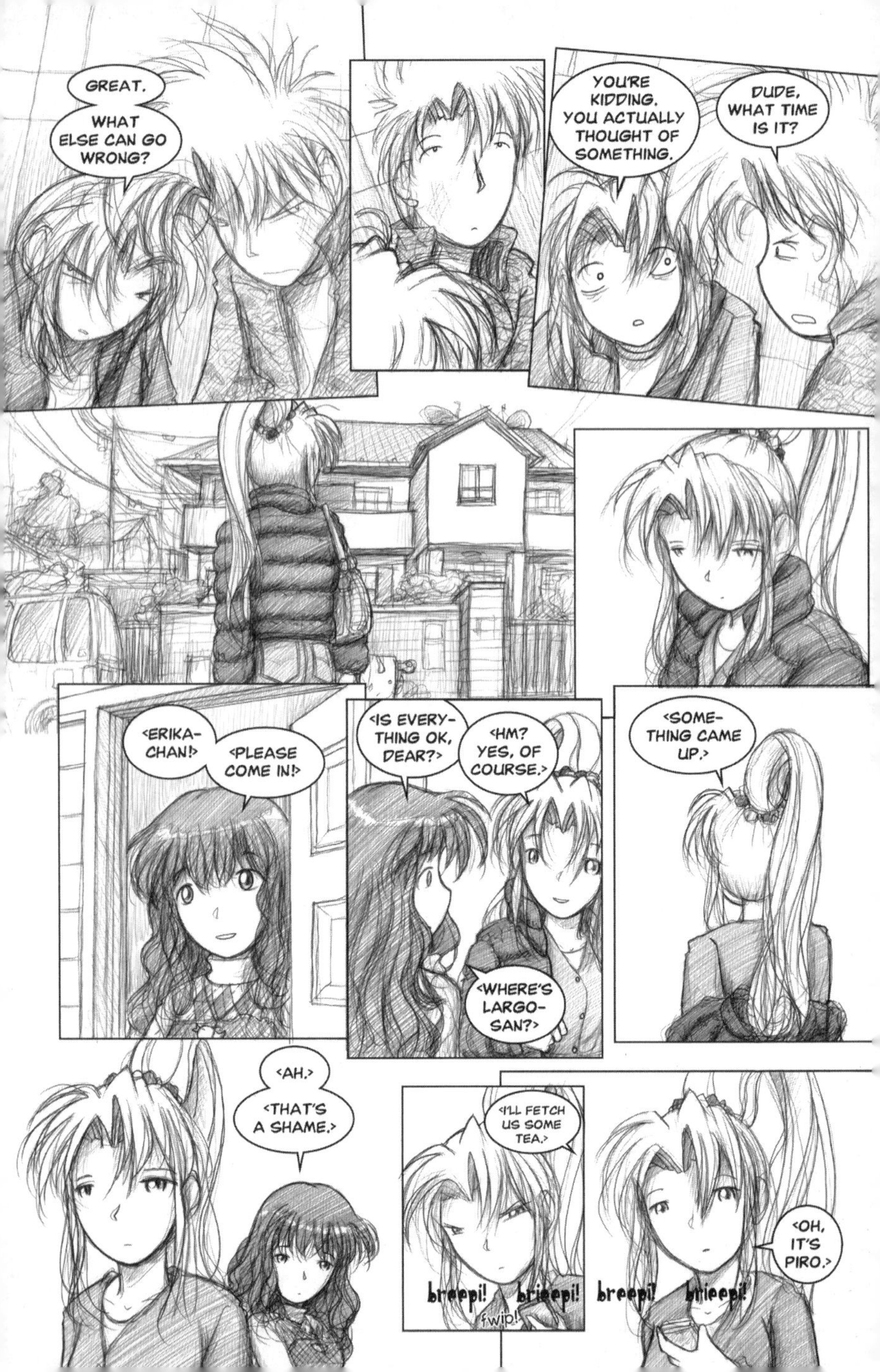
GREAT.
WHAT ELSE CAN GO WRONG?
YOU'RE KIDDING. YOU ACTUALLY THOUGHT OF SOMETHING.
DUDE, WHAT TIME IS IT?
<ERIKA-CHAN!>
<PLEASE COME IN!>
<IS EVERY-THING OK, DEAR?>
<HM? YES, OF COURSE.>
<WHERE'S LARGO-SAN?>
<SOME-THING CAME UP.>
<AH.>
<THAT'S A SHAME.>
<I'LL FETCH US SOME TEA.>
breepi!
brieepi!
fwip!
breepi!
brieepi!
<OH, IT'S PIRO.>

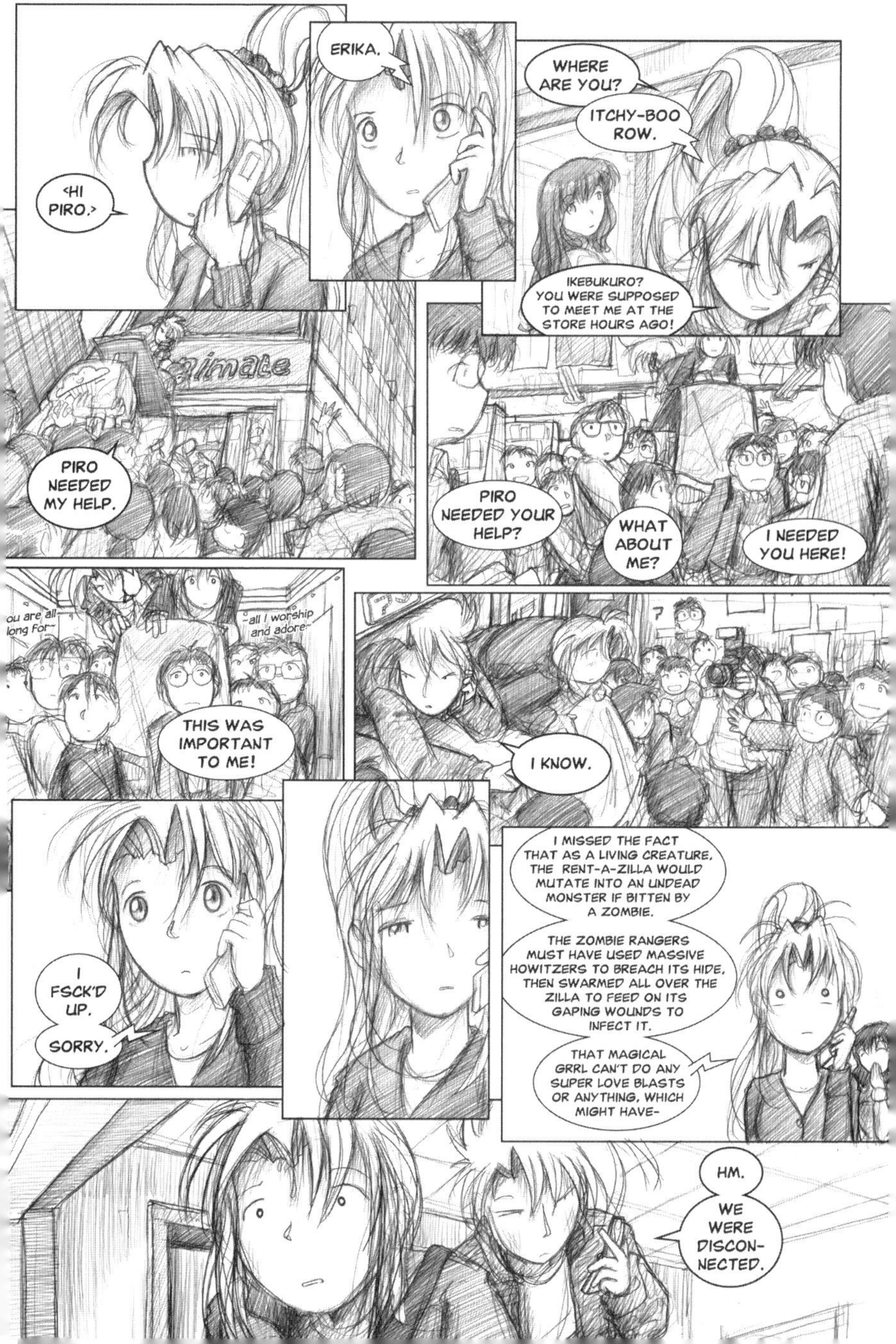
<HI PIRO.>
ERIKA.
WHERE ARE YOU?
ITCHY-BOO ROW.
IKEBUKURO? YOU WERE SUPPOSED TO MEET ME AT THE STORE HOURS AGO!
PIRO NEEDED MY HELP.
PIRO NEEDED YOUR HELP?
WHAT ABOUT ME?
I NEEDED YOU HERE!
ou are all long for~
~all I worship and adore~
THIS WAS IMPORTANT TO ME!
I KNOW.
I FSCK'D UP.
SORRY.
I MISSED THE FACT THAT AS A LIVING CREATURE, THE RENT-A-ZILLA WOULD MUTATE INTO AN UNDEAD MONSTER IF BITTEN BY A ZOMBIE.
THE ZOMBIE RANGERS MUST HAVE USED MASSIVE HOWITZERS TO BREACH ITS HIDE, THEN SWARMED ALL OVER THE ZILLA TO FEED ON ITS GAPING WOUNDS TO INFECT IT.
THAT MAGICAL GRRL CAN'T DO ANY SUPER LOVE BLASTS OR ANYTHING, WHICH MIGHT HAVE-
HM.
WE WERE DISCON-NECTED.

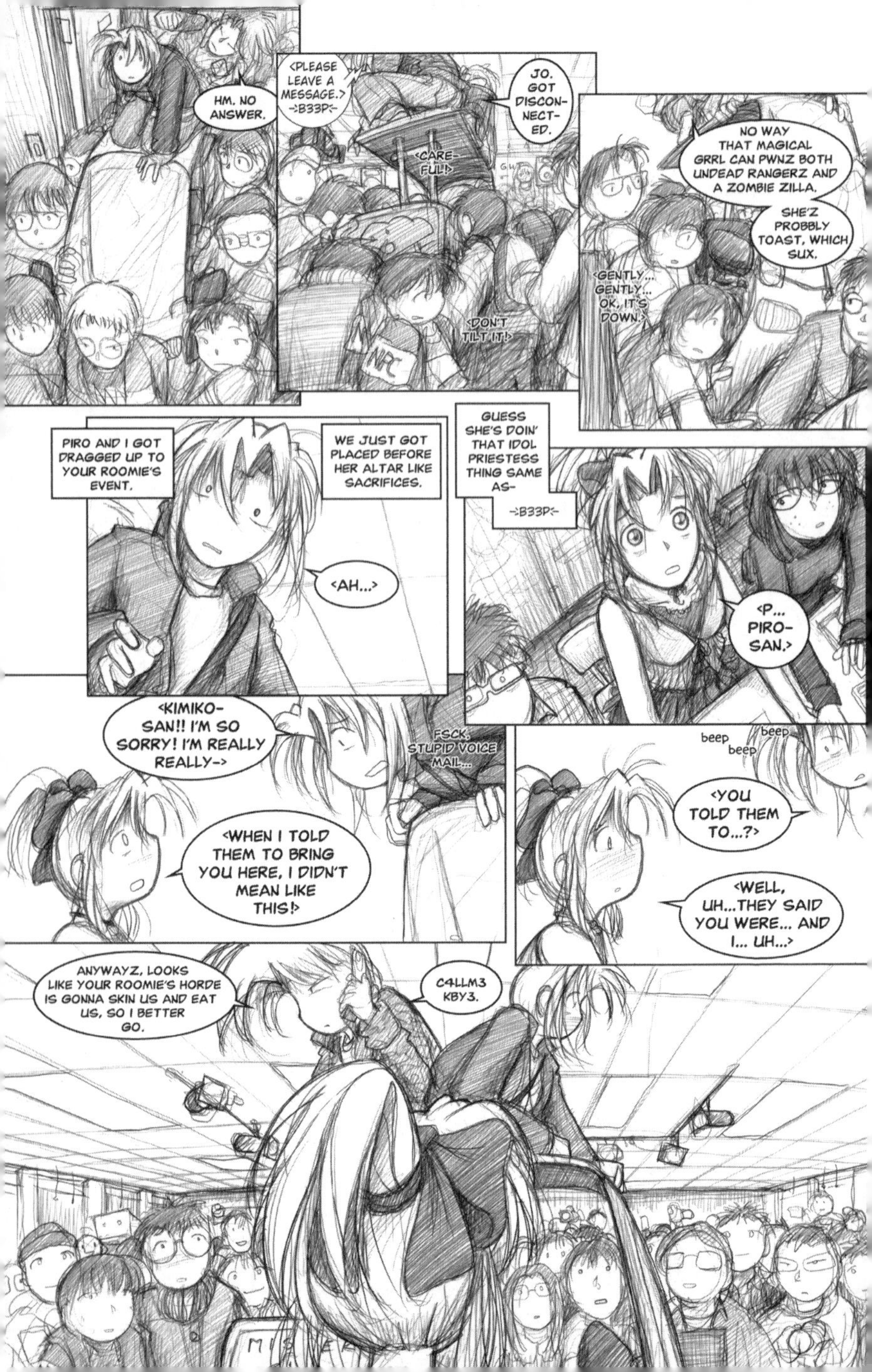
HM. NO ANSWER.
<PLEASE LEAVE A MESSAGE.>
-}B33P{-
JO. GOT DISCONNECTED.
<CAREFUL!>
<DON'T TILT IT!>
NO WAY THAT MAGICAL GRRL CAN PWNZ BOTH UNDEAD RANGERZ AND A ZOMBIE ZILLA.
SHE'Z PROBBLY TOAST, WHICH SUX.
<GENTLY... GENTLY... OK, IT'S DOWN.>
PIRO AND I GOT DRAGGED UP TO YOUR ROOMIE'S EVENT.
WE JUST GOT PLACED BEFORE HER ALTAR LIKE SACRIFICES.
<AH...>
GUESS SHE'S DOIN' THAT IDOL PRIESTESS THING SAME AS-
-}B33P{-
<P... PIRO-SAN.>
<KIMIKO-SAN!! I'M SO SORRY! I'M REALLY REALLY->
FSCK. STUPID VOICE MAIL...
<WHEN I TOLD THEM TO BRING YOU HERE, I DIDN'T MEAN LIKE THIS!>
beep beep beep
<YOU TOLD THEM TO...?>
<WELL, UH...THEY SAID YOU WERE... AND I... UH...>
ANYWAYZ, LOOKS LIKE YOUR ROOMIE'S HORDE IS GONNA SKIN US AND EAT US, SO I BETTER GO.
C4LLM3 KBY3.

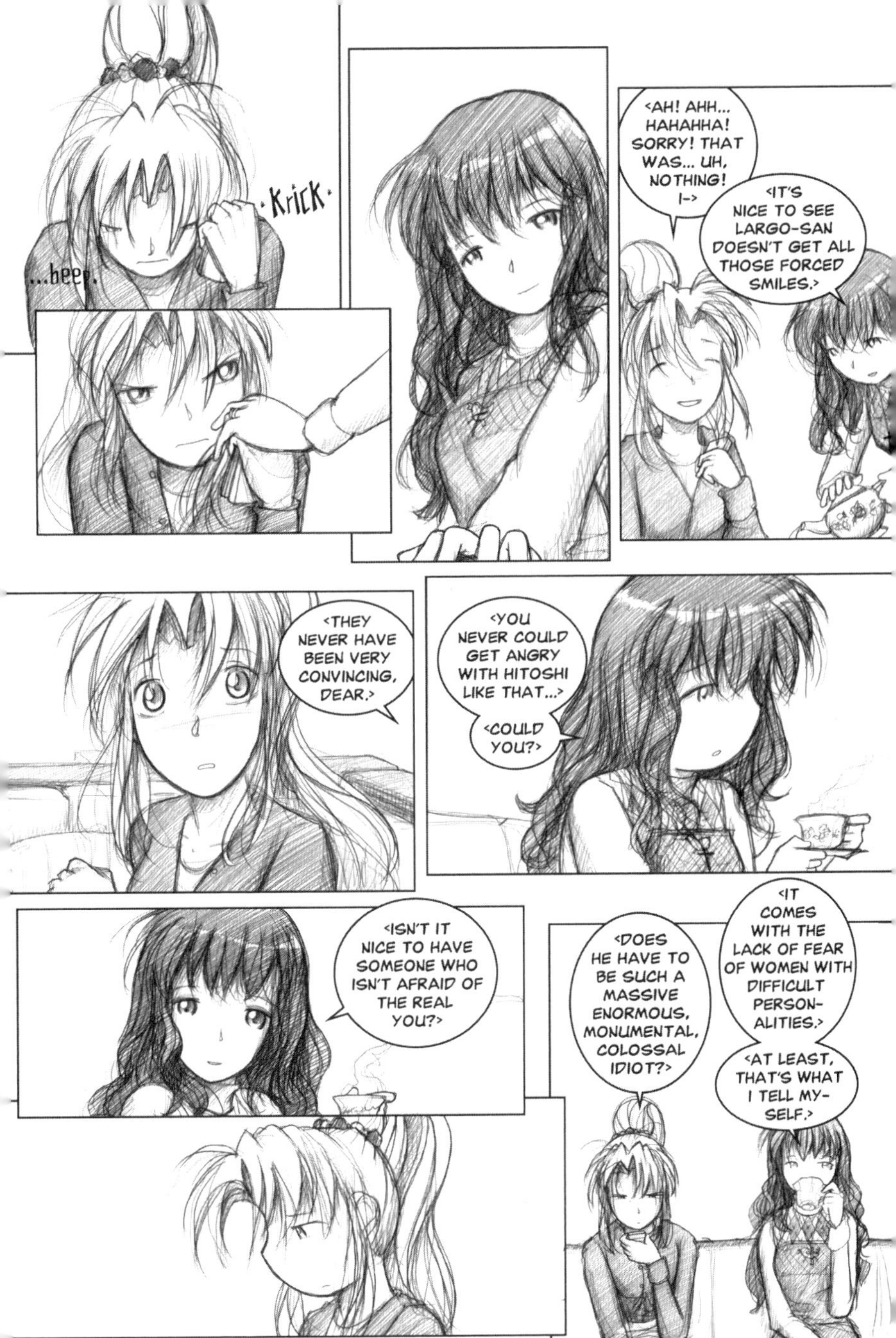
·Krick·
...beep.
<AH! AHH... HAHAHHA! SORRY! THAT WAS... UH, NOTHING! I->
<IT'S NICE TO SEE LARGO-SAN DOESN'T GET ALL THOSE FORCED SMILES.>
<THEY NEVER HAVE BEEN VERY CONVINCING, DEAR.>
<YOU NEVER COULD GET ANGRY WITH HITOSHI LIKE THAT...>
<COULD YOU?>
<ISN'T IT NICE TO HAVE SOMEONE WHO ISN'T AFRAID OF THE REAL YOU?>
<DOES HE HAVE TO BE SUCH A MASSIVE ENORMOUS, MONUMENTAL, COLOSSAL IDIOT?>
<IT COMES WITH THE LACK OF FEAR OF WOMEN WITH DIFFICULT PERSON-ALITIES.>
<AT LEAST, THAT'S WHAT I TELL MY-SELF.>

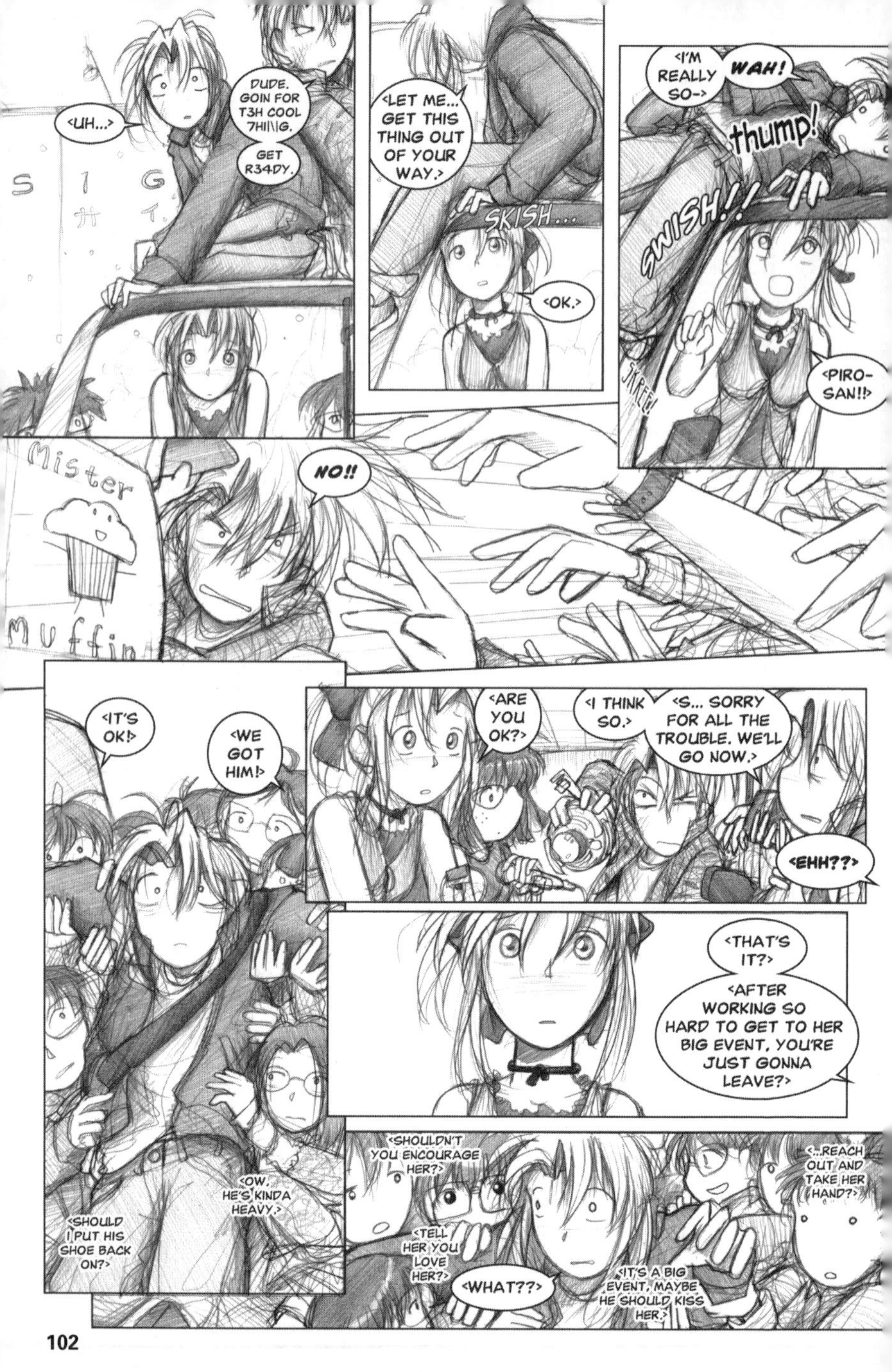
S I G
ガ イ
<UH...>
DUDE. GOIN FOR T3H COOL 7HI|\|G.
GET R34DY.
<LET ME... GET THIS THING OUT OF YOUR WAY.>
SKISH...
<OK.>
<I'M REALLY SO->
WAH!
thump!
SWISH!!
JKREE!
<PIRO-SAN!!>
Mister Muffin
NO!!
<IT'S OK!>
<WE GOT HIM!>
<OW, HE'S KINDA HEAVY.>
<SHOULD I PUT HIS SHOE BACK ON?>
<ARE YOU OK?>
<I THINK SO.>
<S... SORRY FOR ALL THE TROUBLE. WE'LL GO NOW.>
<EHH??>
<THAT'S IT?>
<AFTER WORKING SO HARD TO GET TO HER BIG EVENT, YOU'RE JUST GONNA LEAVE?>
<SHOULDN'T YOU ENCOURAGE HER?>
<TELL HER YOU LOVE HER?>
<WHAT??>
<IT'S A BIG EVENT, MAYBE HE SHOULD KISS HER.>
<...REACH OUT AND TAKE HER HAND?>

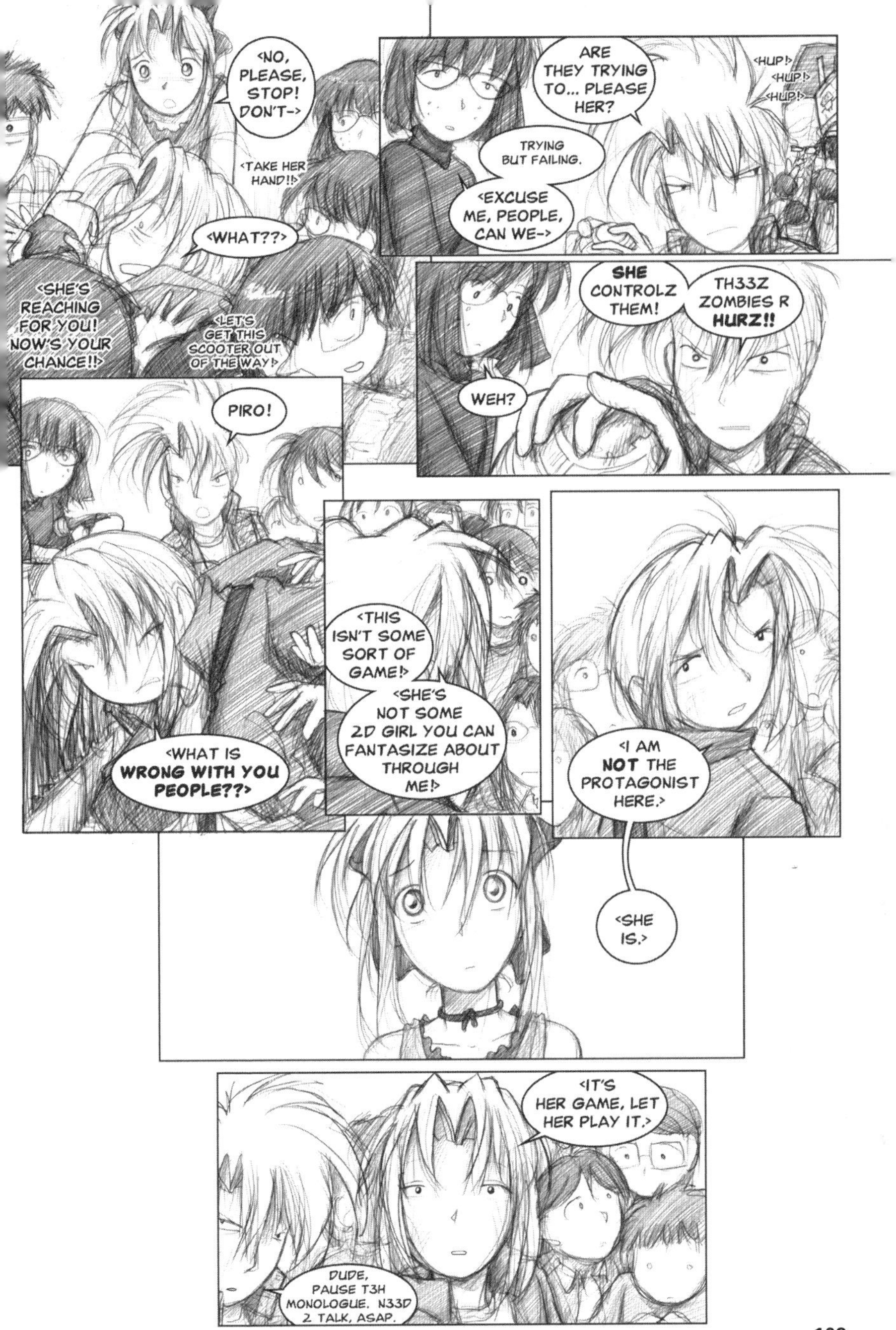
<NO, PLEASE, STOP! DON'T->
<TAKE HER HAND!!>
<WHAT??>
<SHE'S REACHING FOR YOU! NOW'S YOUR CHANCE!!>
<LET'S GET THIS SCOOTER OUT OF THE WAY!>
ARE THEY TRYING TO... PLEASE HER?
<HUP!>
<HUP!>
<HUP!>
TRYING BUT FAILING.
<EXCUSE ME, PEOPLE, CAN WE->
SHE CONTROLZ THEM!
TH33Z ZOMBIES R HURZ!!
WEH?
PIRO!
<WHAT IS WRONG WITH YOU PEOPLE??>
<THIS ISN'T SOME SORT OF GAME!>
<SHE'S NOT SOME 2D GIRL YOU CAN FANTASIZE ABOUT THROUGH ME!>
<I AM NOT THE PROTAGONIST HERE.>
<SHE IS.>
<IT'S HER GAME, LET HER PLAY IT.>
DUDE, PAUSE T3H MONOLOGUE. N33D 2 TALK, ASAP.

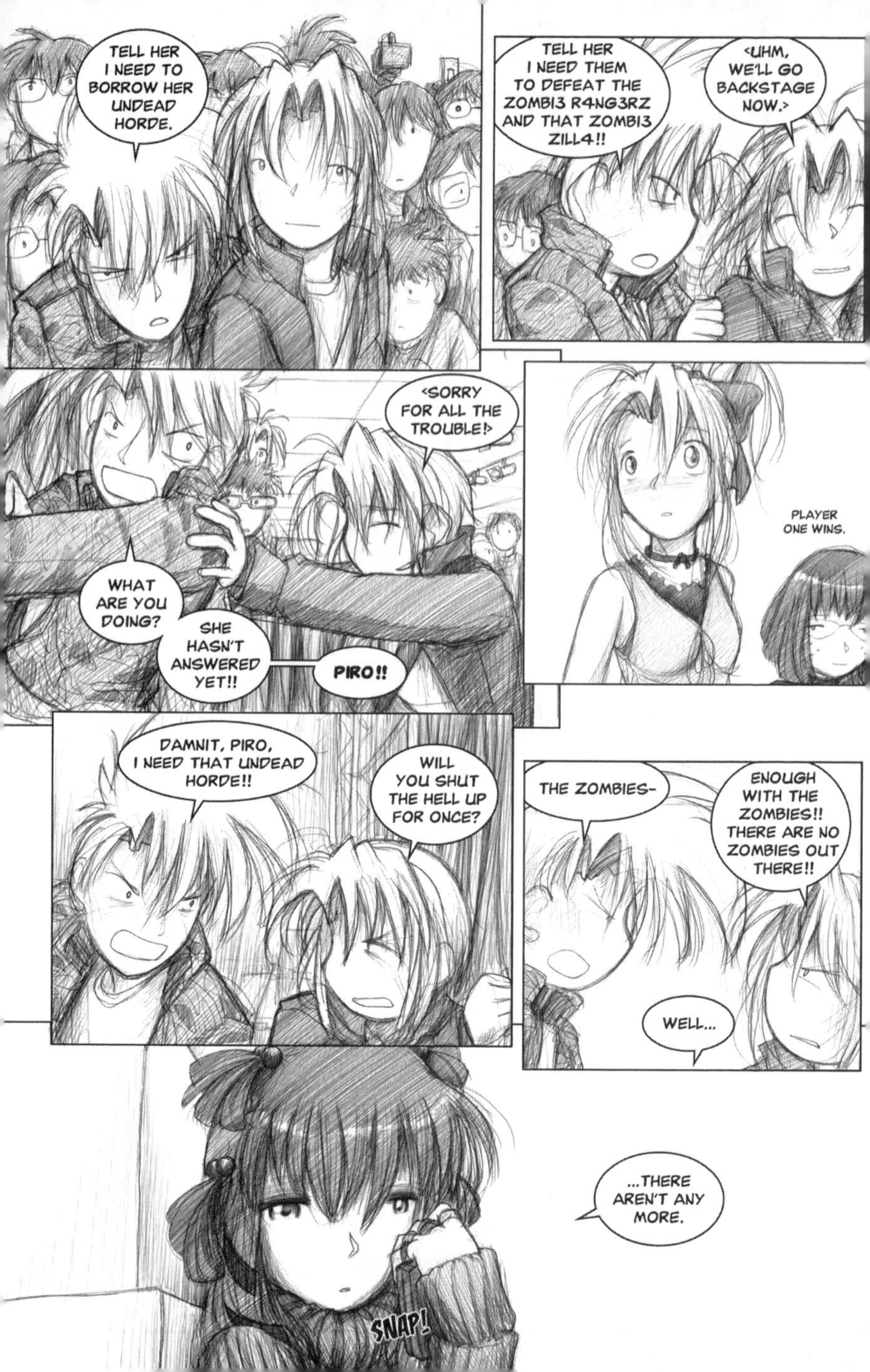
TELL HER I NEED TO BORROW HER UNDEAD HORDE.
TELL HER I NEED THEM TO DEFEAT THE ZOMBI3 R4NG3RZ AND THAT ZOMBI3 ZILL4!!
<UHM, WE'LL GO BACKSTAGE NOW.>
<SORRY FOR ALL THE TROUBLE!>
WHAT ARE YOU DOING?
SHE HASN'T ANSWERED YET!!
PIRO!!
PLAYER ONE WINS.
DAMNIT, PIRO, I NEED THAT UNDEAD HORDE!!
WILL YOU SHUT THE HELL UP FOR ONCE?
THE ZOMBIES-
ENOUGH WITH THE ZOMBIES!! THERE ARE NO ZOMBIES OUT THERE!!
WELL...
...THERE AREN'T ANY MORE.
SNAP!

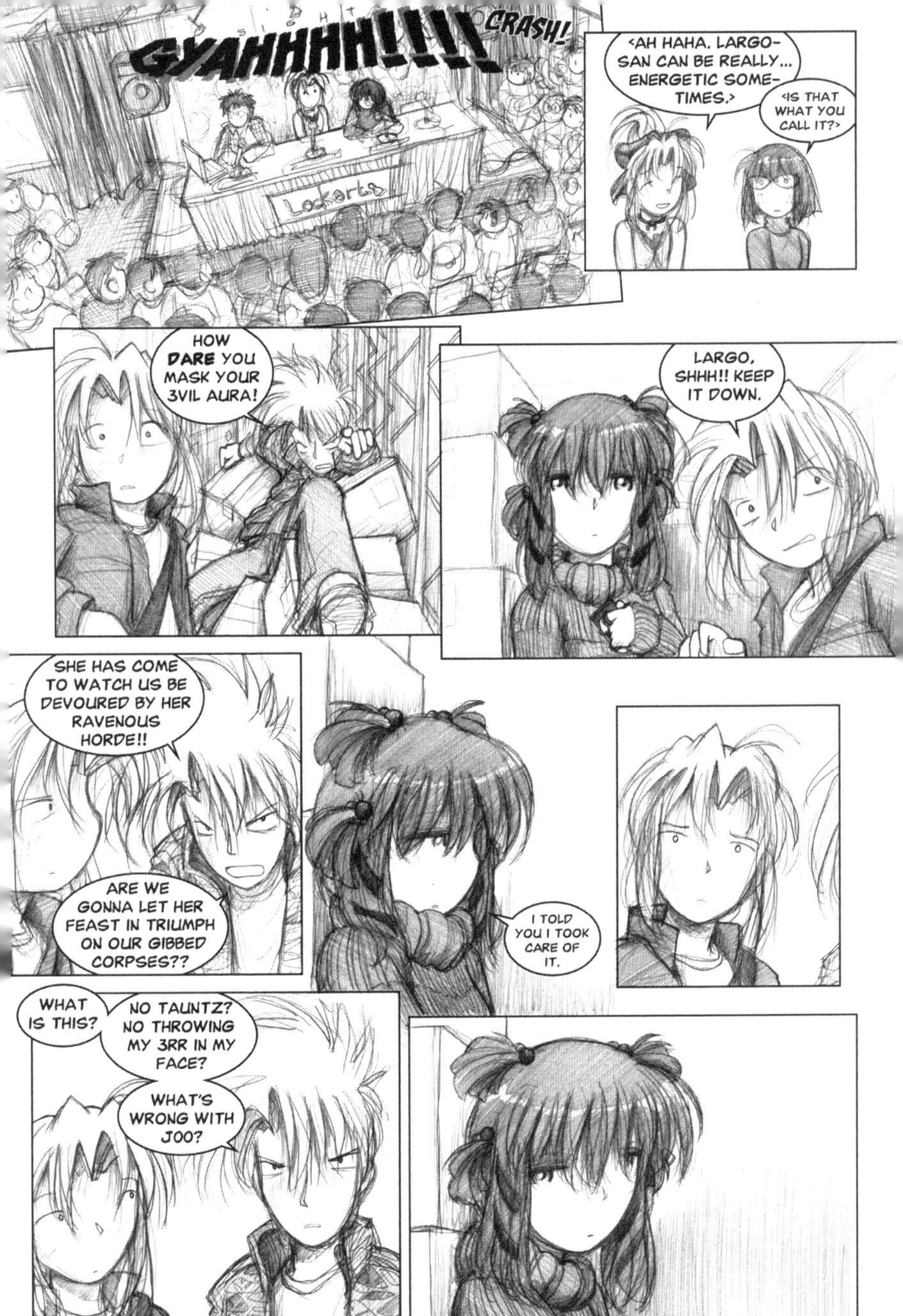
GYAHHHH!!!!
CRASH!
<AH HAHA. LARGO-SAN CAN BE REALLY... ENERGETIC SOME-TIMES.>
<IS THAT WHAT YOU CALL IT?>
HOW **DARE** YOU MASK YOUR 3VIL AURA!
LARGO, SHHH!! KEEP IT DOWN.
SHE HAS COME TO WATCH US BE DEVOURED BY HER RAVENOUS HORDE!!
ARE WE GONNA LET HER FEAST IN TRIUMPH ON OUR GIBBED CORPSES??
I TOLD YOU I TOOK CARE OF IT.
WHAT IS THIS?
NO TAUNTZ? NO THROWING MY 3RR IN MY FACE?
WHAT'S WRONG WITH JOO?

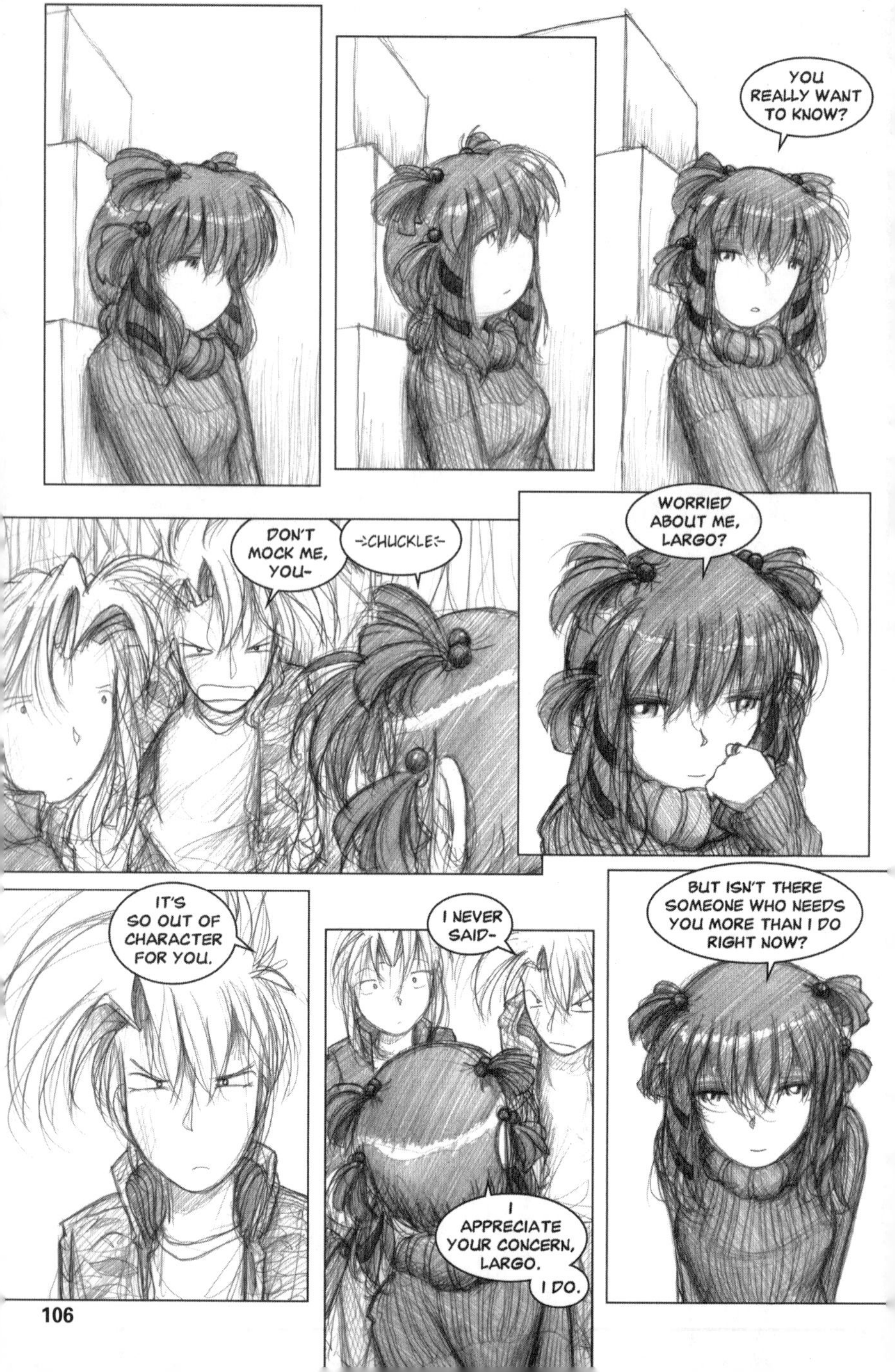
YOU REALLY WANT TO KNOW?
DON'T MOCK ME, YOU-
CHUCKLE
WORRIED ABOUT ME, LARGO?
IT'S SO OUT OF CHARACTER FOR YOU.
I NEVER SAID-
I APPRECIATE YOUR CONCERN, LARGO.
I DO.
BUT ISN'T THERE SOMEONE WHO NEEDS YOU MORE THAN I DO RIGHT NOW?

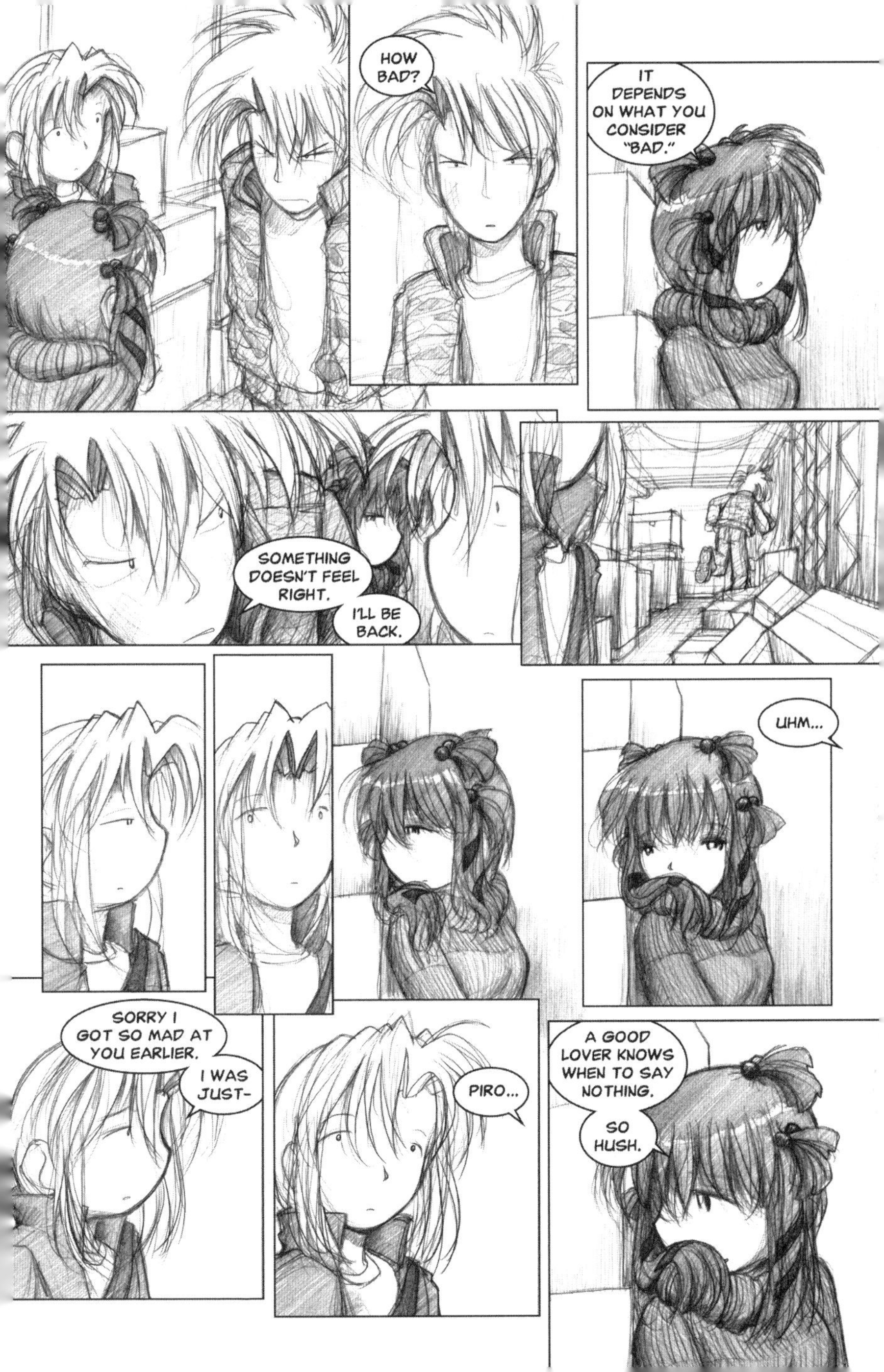
HOW BAD?
IT DEPENDS ON WHAT YOU CONSIDER "BAD."
SOMETHING DOESN'T FEEL RIGHT.
I'LL BE BACK.
UHM...
SORRY I GOT SO MAD AT YOU EARLIER.
I WAS JUST-
PIRO...
A GOOD LOVER KNOWS WHEN TO SAY NOTHING.
SO HUSH.

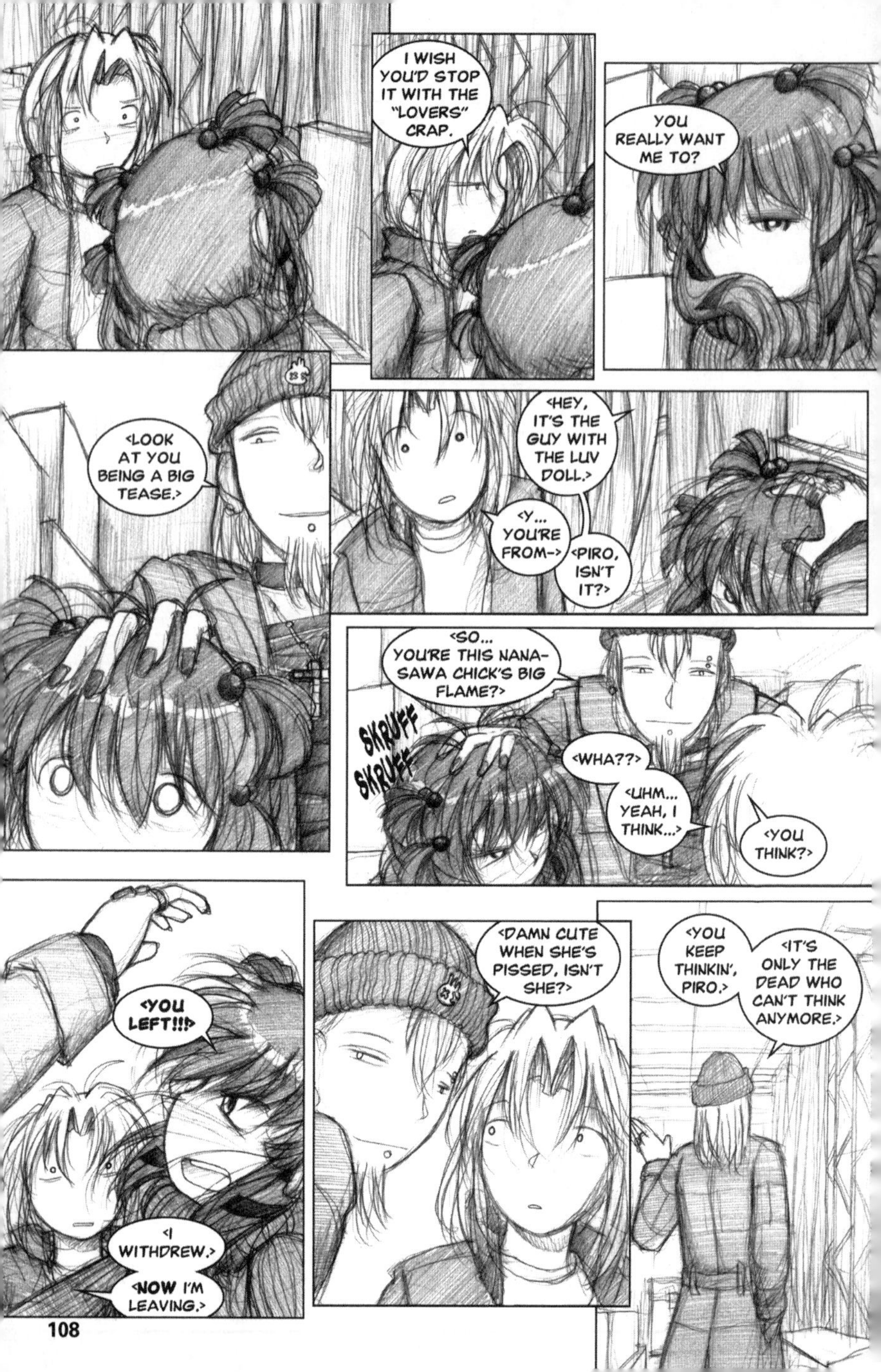

I WISH YOU'D STOP IT WITH THE "LOVERS" CRAP.
YOU REALLY WANT ME TO?
<LOOK AT YOU BEING A BIG TEASE.>
<HEY, IT'S THE GUY WITH THE LUV DOLL.>
<Y... YOU'RE FROM->
<PIRO, ISN'T IT?>
<SO... YOU'RE THIS NANA-SAWA CHICK'S BIG FLAME?>
SKRUFF SKRUFF
<WHA??>
<UHM... YEAH, I THINK...>
<YOU THINK?>
<YOU LEFT!!!>
<I WITHDREW.>
<**NOW** I'M LEAVING.>
<DAMN CUTE WHEN SHE'S PISSED, ISN'T SHE?>
<YOU KEEP THINKIN', PIRO.>
<IT'S ONLY THE DEAD WHO CAN'T THINK ANYMORE.>

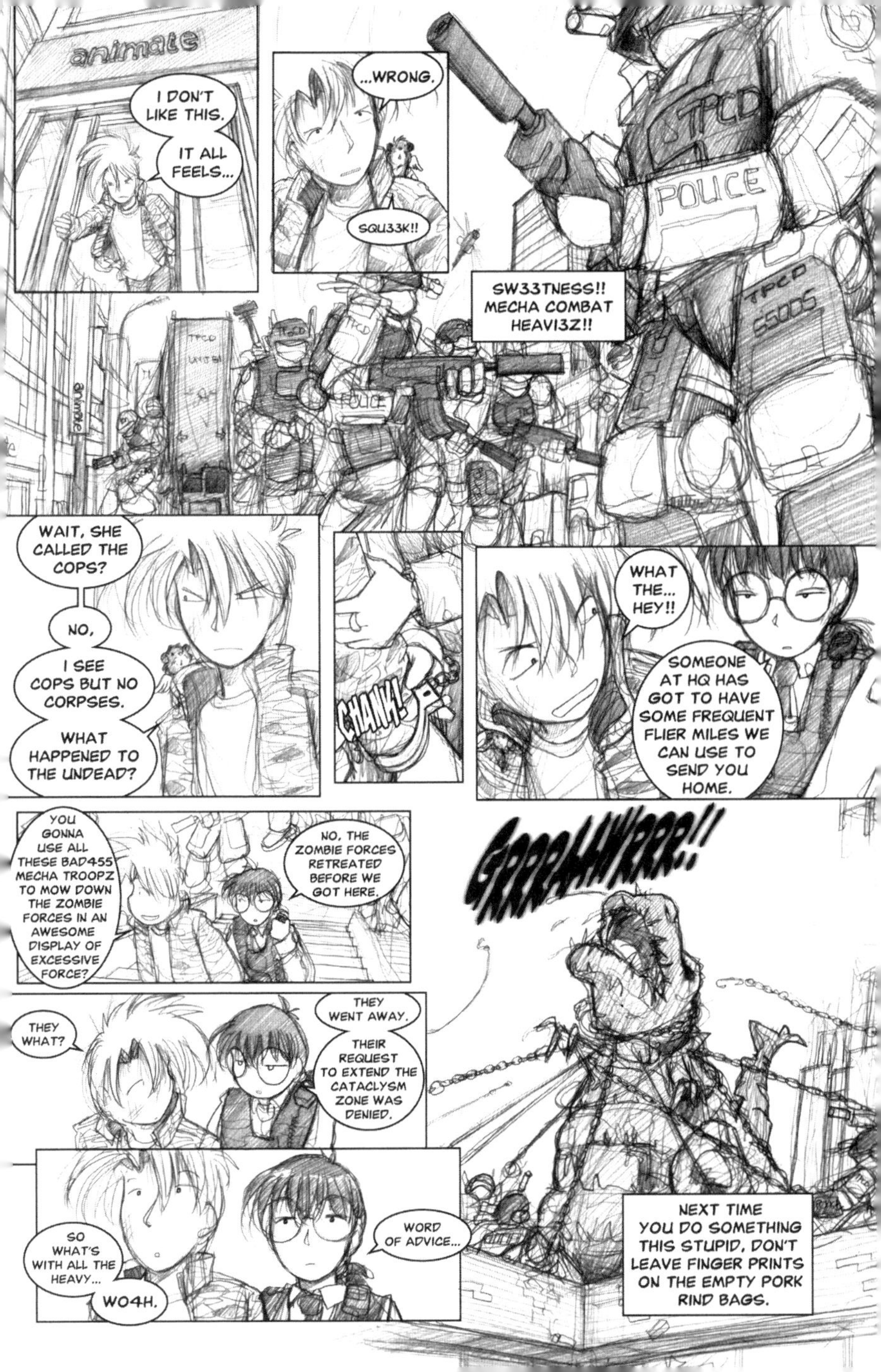
animate
I DON'T LIKE THIS.
IT ALL FEELS...
...WRONG.
SQU33K!!
SW33TNESS!! MECHA COMBAT HEAVI3Z!!
WAIT, SHE CALLED THE COPS?
NO,
I SEE COPS BUT NO CORPSES.
WHAT HAPPENED TO THE UNDEAD?
CHANK!
WHAT THE... HEY!!
SOMEONE AT HQ HAS GOT TO HAVE SOME FREQUENT FLIER MILES WE CAN USE TO SEND YOU HOME.
YOU GONNA USE ALL THESE BAD455 MECHA TROOPZ TO MOW DOWN THE ZOMBIE FORCES IN AN AWESOME DISPLAY OF EXCESSIVE FORCE?
NO, THE ZOMBIE FORCES RETREATED BEFORE WE GOT HERE.
THEY WHAT?
THEY WENT AWAY.
THEIR REQUEST TO EXTEND THE CATACLYSM ZONE WAS DENIED.
SO WHAT'S WITH ALL THE HEAVY...
WO4H.
WORD OF ADVICE...
GRRRAAWRRR!!
NEXT TIME YOU DO SOMETHING THIS STUPID, DON'T LEAVE FINGER PRINTS ON THE EMPTY PORK RIND BAGS.

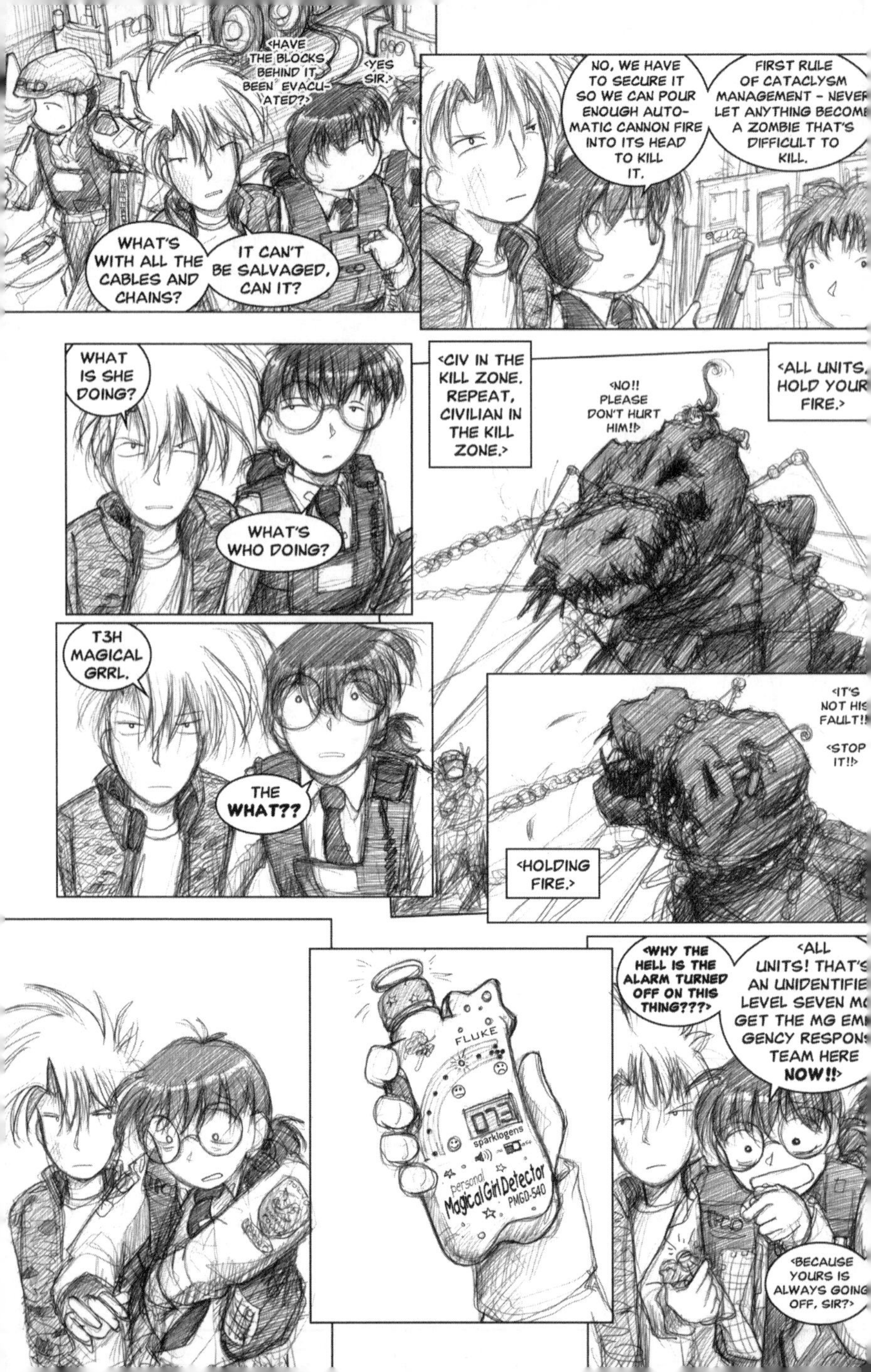
<HAVE THE BLOCKS BEHIND IT BEEN EVACU-ATED?>
<YES SIR.>
WHAT'S WITH ALL THE CABLES AND CHAINS?
IT CAN'T BE SALVAGED, CAN IT?
NO, WE HAVE TO SECURE IT SO WE CAN POUR ENOUGH AUTO-MATIC CANNON FIRE INTO ITS HEAD TO KILL IT.
FIRST RULE OF CATACLYSM MANAGEMENT - NEVER LET ANYTHING BECOME A ZOMBIE THAT'S DIFFICULT TO KILL.
WHAT IS SHE DOING?
WHAT'S WHO DOING?
T3H MAGICAL GRRL.
THE **WHAT??**
<CIV IN THE KILL ZONE. REPEAT, CIVILIAN IN THE KILL ZONE.>
<NO!! PLEASE DON'T HURT HIM!!>
<ALL UNITS, HOLD YOUR FIRE.>
<IT'S NOT HIS FAULT!!
<STOP IT!!>
<HOLDING FIRE.>
FLUKE
073
sparklogens
personal Magical Girl Detector
PMGD-540
<WHY THE HELL IS THE ALARM TURNED OFF ON THIS THING???>
<ALL UNITS! THAT'S AN UNIDENTIFIE LEVEL SEVEN M GET THE MG EME GENCY RESPONS TEAM HERE **NOW!!**>
<BECAUSE YOURS IS ALWAYS GOING OFF, SIR?>

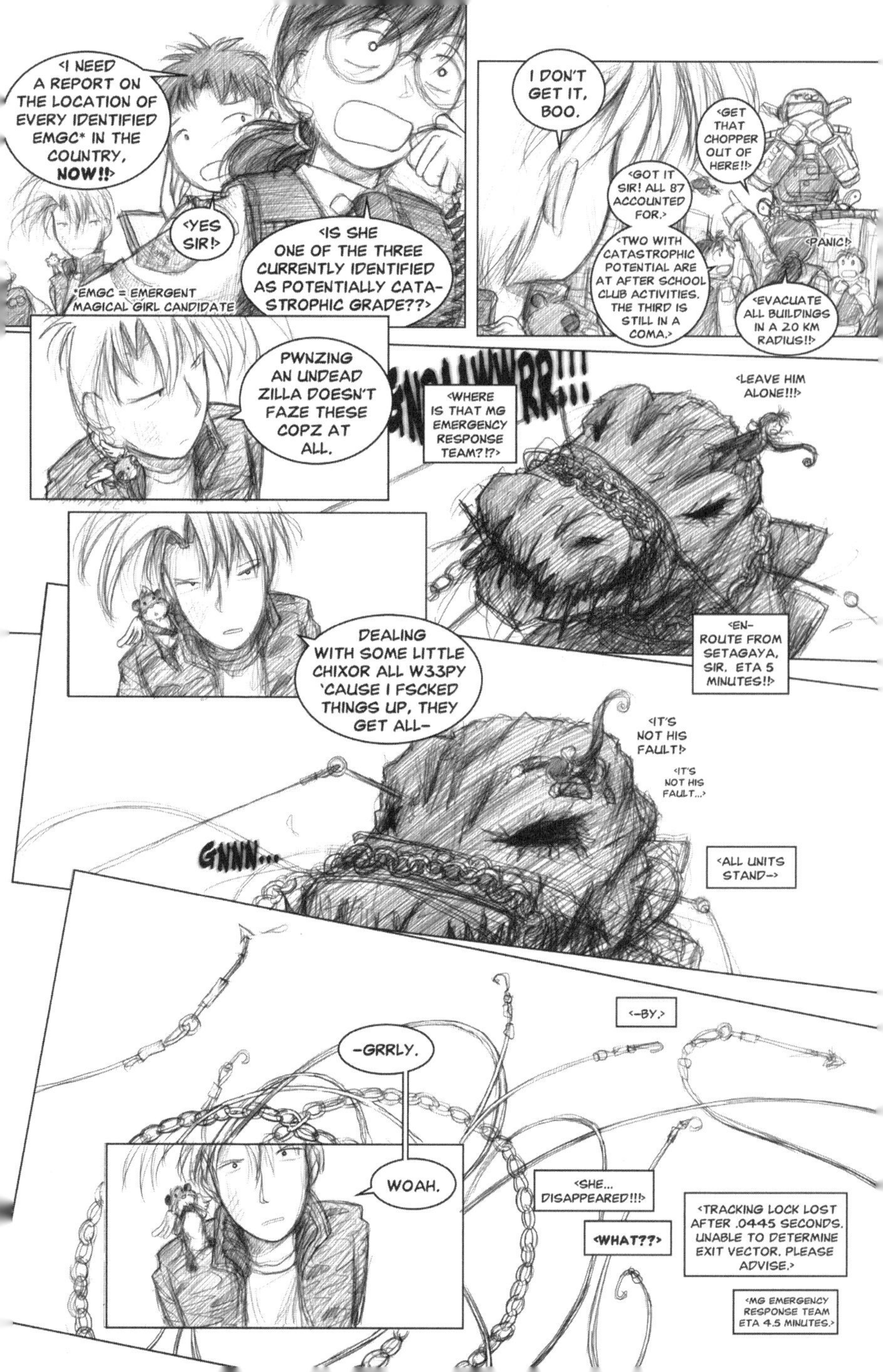
<I NEED A REPORT ON THE LOCATION OF EVERY IDENTIFIED EMGC* IN THE COUNTRY, **NOW!!**>
<YES SIR!>
<IS SHE ONE OF THE THREE CURRENTLY IDENTIFIED AS POTENTIALLY CATA-STROPHIC GRADE??>
*EMGC = EMERGENT MAGICAL GIRL CANDIDATE
I DON'T GET IT, BOO.
<GET THAT CHOPPER OUT OF HERE!!>
<GOT IT SIR! ALL 87 ACCOUNTED FOR.>
<TWO WITH CATASTROPHIC POTENTIAL ARE AT AFTER SCHOOL CLUB ACTIVITIES. THE THIRD IS STILL IN A COMA.>
<PANIC!>
<EVACUATE ALL BUILDINGS IN A 20 KM RADIUS!!>
PWNZING AN UNDEAD ZILLA DOESN'T FAZE THESE COPZ AT ALL.
GNOLLWWRR!!!
<WHERE IS THAT MG EMERGENCY RESPONSE TEAM?!?>
<LEAVE HIM ALONE!!!>
DEALING WITH SOME LITTLE CHIXOR ALL W33PY 'CAUSE I FSCKED THINGS UP, THEY GET ALL-
<EN-ROUTE FROM SETAGAYA, SIR. ETA 5 MINUTES!!>
<IT'S NOT HIS FAULT!>
<IT'S NOT HIS FAULT...>
GNNN...
<ALL UNITS STAND->
<-BY.>
-GRRLY.
WOAH.
<SHE... DISAPPEARED!!!>
<WHAT??>
<TRACKING LOCK LOST AFTER .0445 SECONDS. UNABLE TO DETERMINE EXIT VECTOR. PLEASE ADVISE.>
<MG EMERGENCY RESPONSE TEAM ETA 4.5 MINUTES.>

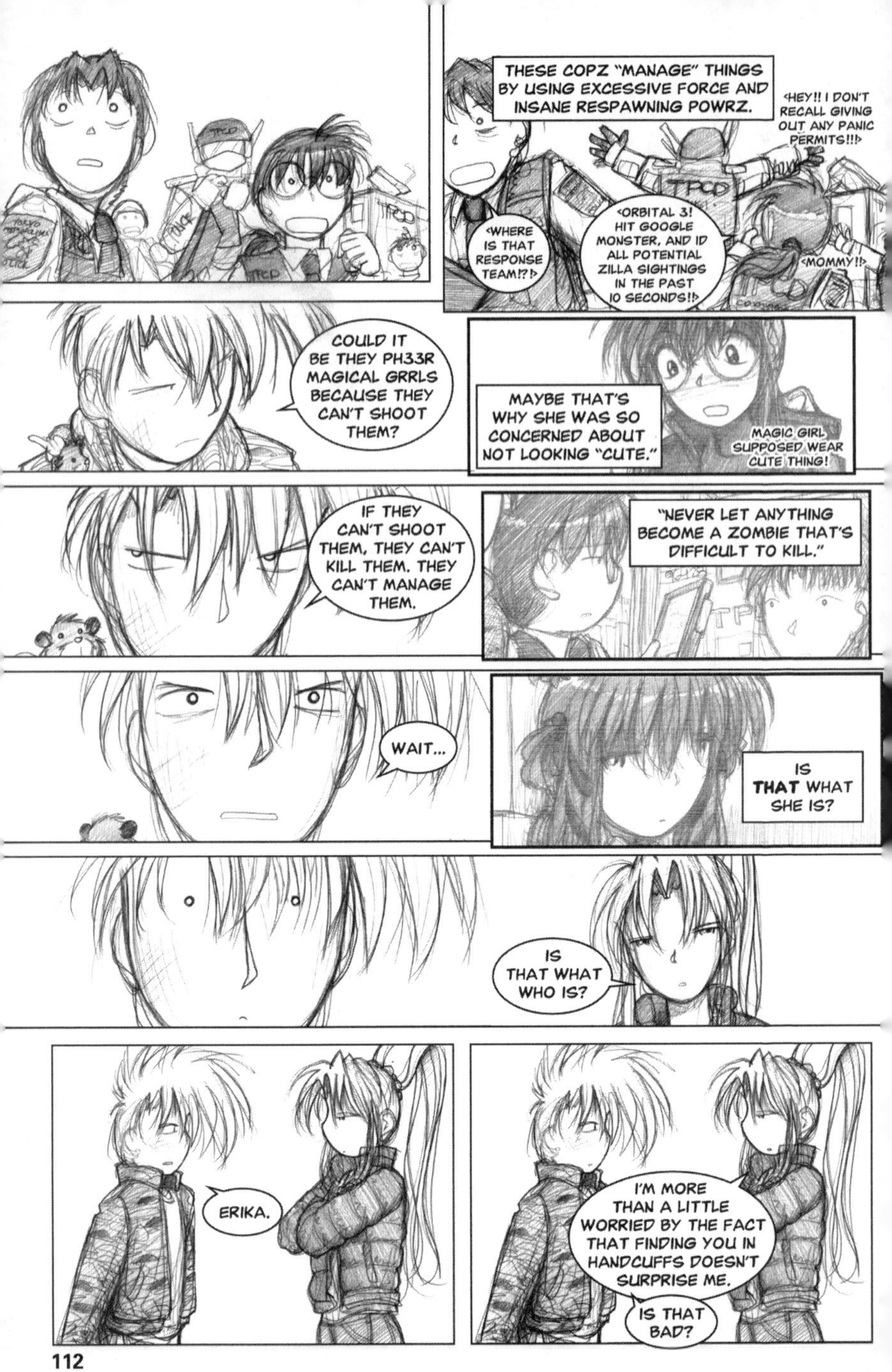
THESE COPZ "MANAGE" THINGS BY USING EXCESSIVE FORCE AND INSANE RESPAWNING POWRZ.
<HEY!! I DON'T RECALL GIVING OUT ANY PANIC PERMITS!!>
<WHERE IS THAT RESPONSE TEAM!?!>
<ORBITAL 3! HIT GOOGLE MONSTER, AND ID ALL POTENTIAL ZILLA SIGHTINGS IN THE PAST 10 SECONDS!!>
<MOMMY!!>
COULD IT BE THEY PH33R MAGICAL GRRLS BECAUSE THEY CAN'T SHOOT THEM?
MAYBE THAT'S WHY SHE WAS SO CONCERNED ABOUT NOT LOOKING "CUTE."
MAGIC GIRL SUPPOSED WEAR CUTE THING!
IF THEY CAN'T SHOOT THEM, THEY CAN'T KILL THEM. THEY CAN'T MANAGE THEM.
"NEVER LET ANYTHING BECOME A ZOMBIE THAT'S DIFFICULT TO KILL."
WAIT...
IS **THAT** WHAT SHE IS?
IS THAT WHAT WHO IS?
ERIKA.
I'M MORE THAN A LITTLE WORRIED BY THE FACT THAT FINDING YOU IN HANDCUFFS DOESN'T SURPRISE ME.
IS THAT BAD?

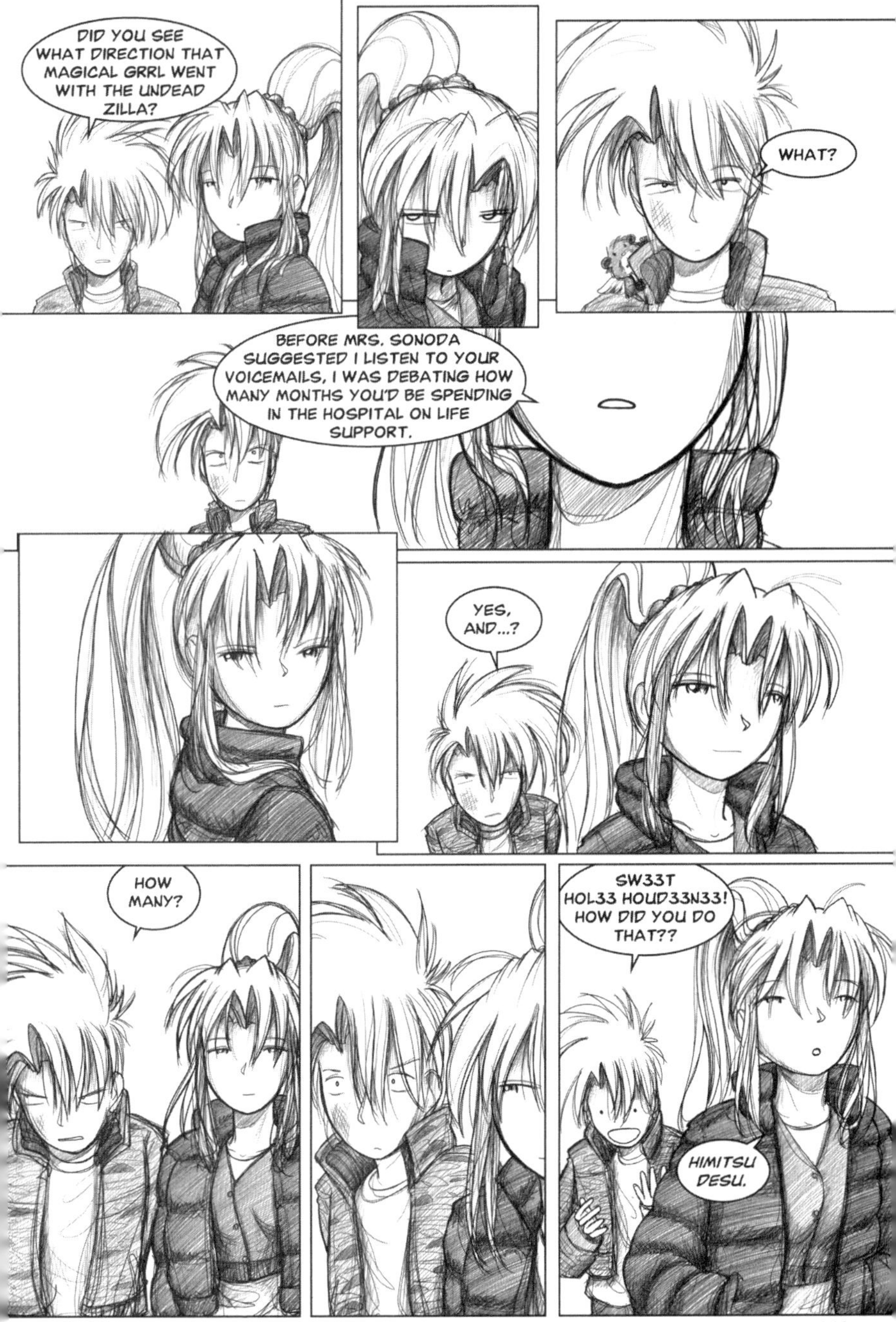
DID YOU SEE WHAT DIRECTION THAT MAGICAL GRRL WENT WITH THE UNDEAD ZILLA?
WHAT?
BEFORE MRS. SONODA SUGGESTED I LISTEN TO YOUR VOICEMAILS, I WAS DEBATING HOW MANY MONTHS YOU'D BE SPENDING IN THE HOSPITAL ON LIFE SUPPORT.
YES, AND...?
HOW MANY?
SW33T HOL33 HOUD33N33! HOW DID YOU DO THAT??
HIMITSU DESU.

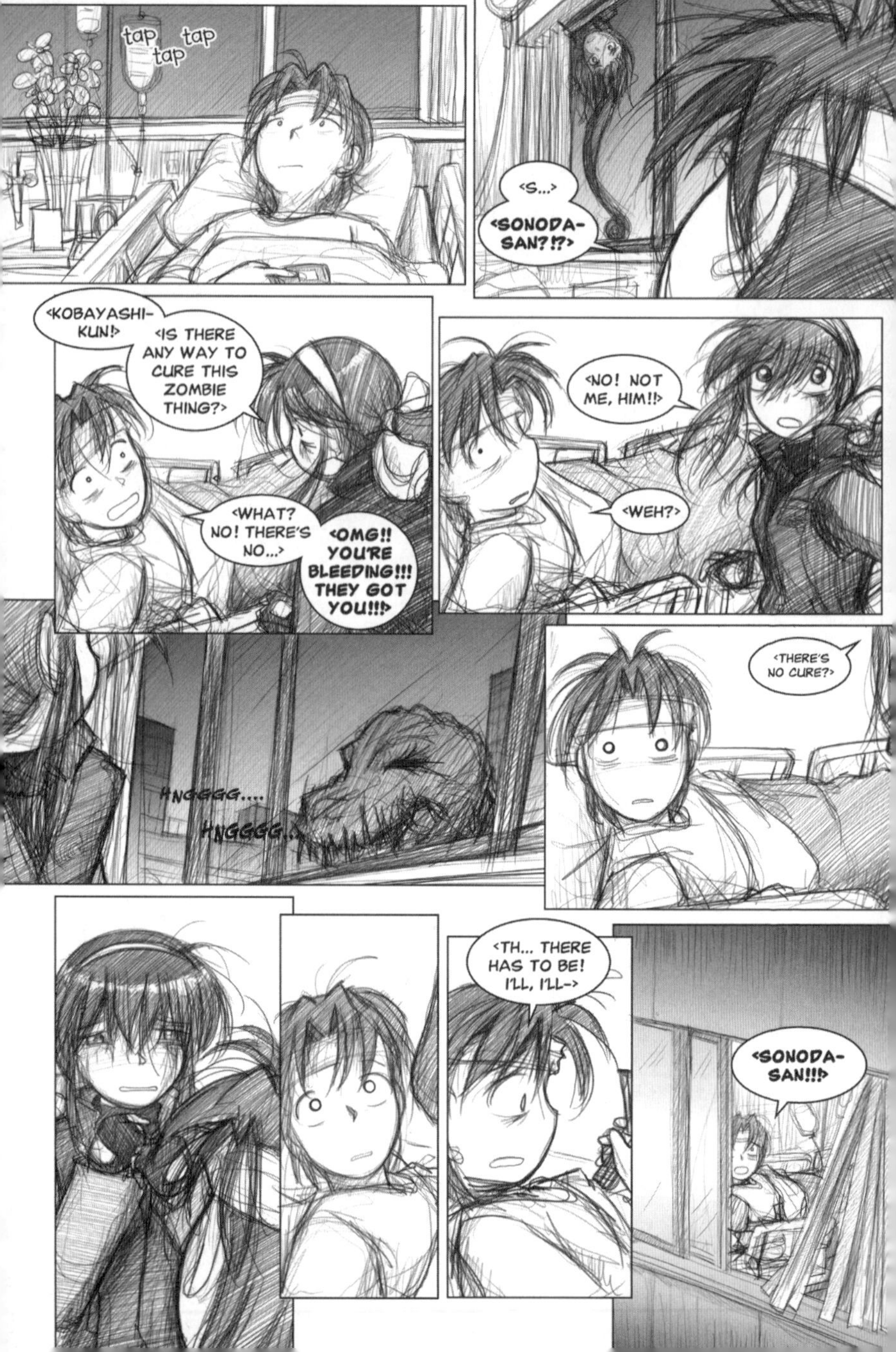
tap tap tap
<S...>
<SONODA-SAN?!?>
<KOBAYASHI-KUN!>
<IS THERE ANY WAY TO CURE THIS ZOMBIE THING?>
<WHAT? NO! THERE'S NO...>
<OMG!! YOU'RE BLEEDING!!! THEY GOT YOU!!!>
<NO! NOT ME, HIM!!>
<WEH?>
HNGGGG....
HNGGGG...
<THERE'S NO CURE?>
<TH... THERE HAS TO BE! I'LL, I'LL->
<SONODA-SAN!!!>

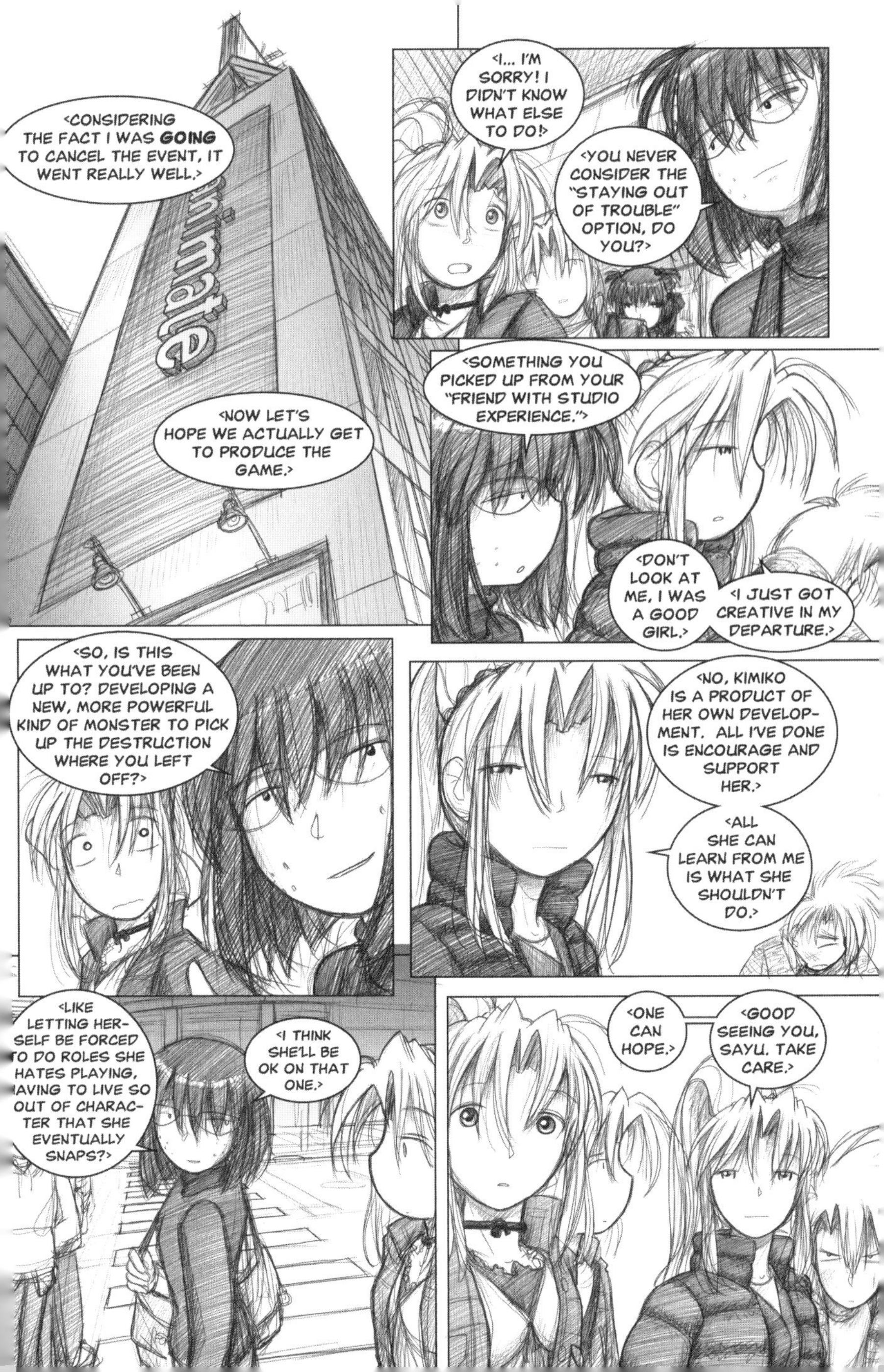

<CONSIDERING THE FACT I WAS **GOING** TO CANCEL THE EVENT, IT WENT REALLY WELL.>
animate
<NOW LET'S HOPE WE ACTUALLY GET TO PRODUCE THE GAME.>
<I... I'M SORRY! I DIDN'T KNOW WHAT ELSE TO DO!>
<YOU NEVER CONSIDER THE "STAYING OUT OF TROUBLE" OPTION, DO YOU?>
<SOMETHING YOU PICKED UP FROM YOUR "FRIEND WITH STUDIO EXPERIENCE.">
<DON'T LOOK AT ME, I WAS A GOOD GIRL.>
<I JUST GOT CREATIVE IN MY DEPARTURE.>
<SO, IS THIS WHAT YOU'VE BEEN UP TO? DEVELOPING A NEW, MORE POWERFUL KIND OF MONSTER TO PICK UP THE DESTRUCTION WHERE YOU LEFT OFF?>
<NO, KIMIKO IS A PRODUCT OF HER OWN DEVELOP-MENT. ALL I'VE DONE IS ENCOURAGE AND SUPPORT HER.>
<ALL SHE CAN LEARN FROM ME IS WHAT SHE SHOULDN'T DO.>
<LIKE LETTING HER-SELF BE FORCED TO DO ROLES SHE HATES PLAYING, HAVING TO LIVE SO OUT OF CHARAC-TER THAT SHE EVENTUALLY SNAPS?>
<I THINK SHE'LL BE OK ON THAT ONE.>
<ONE CAN HOPE.>
<GOOD SEEING YOU, SAYU. TAKE CARE.>

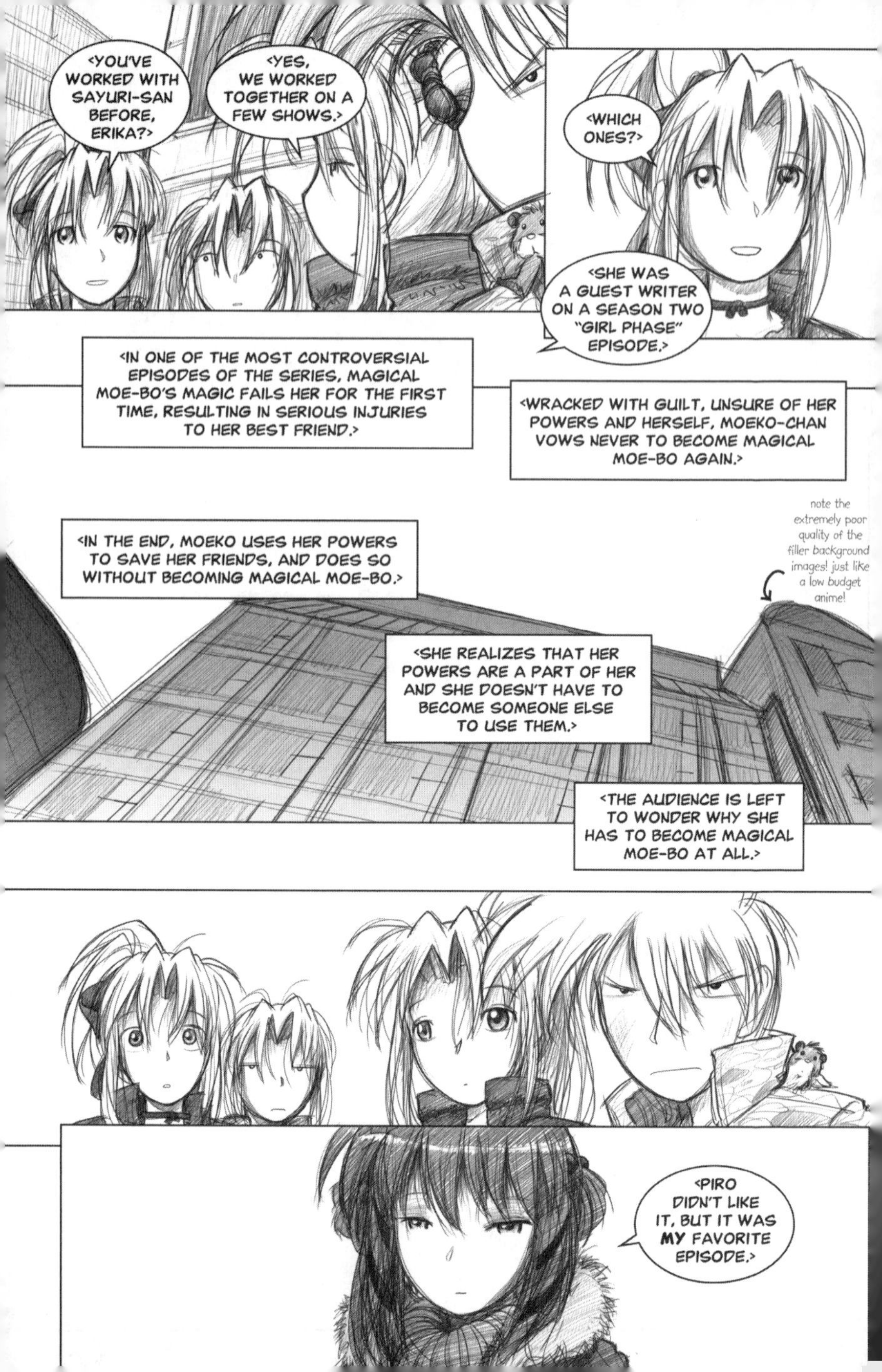

<YOU'VE WORKED WITH SAYURI-SAN BEFORE, ERIKA?>
<YES, WE WORKED TOGETHER ON A FEW SHOWS.>
<WHICH ONES?>
<SHE WAS A GUEST WRITER ON A SEASON TWO "GIRL PHASE" EPISODE.>
<IN ONE OF THE MOST CONTROVERSIAL EPISODES OF THE SERIES, MAGICAL MOE-BO'S MAGIC FAILS HER FOR THE FIRST TIME, RESULTING IN SERIOUS INJURIES TO HER BEST FRIEND.>
<WRACKED WITH GUILT, UNSURE OF HER POWERS AND HERSELF, MOEKO-CHAN VOWS NEVER TO BECOME MAGICAL MOE-BO AGAIN.>
<IN THE END, MOEKO USES HER POWERS TO SAVE HER FRIENDS, AND DOES SO WITHOUT BECOMING MAGICAL MOE-BO.>
note the extremely poor quality of the filler background images! just like a low budget anime!
<SHE REALIZES THAT HER POWERS ARE A PART OF HER AND SHE DOESN'T HAVE TO BECOME SOMEONE ELSE TO USE THEM.>
<THE AUDIENCE IS LEFT TO WONDER WHY SHE HAS TO BECOME MAGICAL MOE-BO AT ALL.>
<PIRO DIDN'T LIKE IT, BUT IT WAS **MY** FAVORITE EPISODE.>

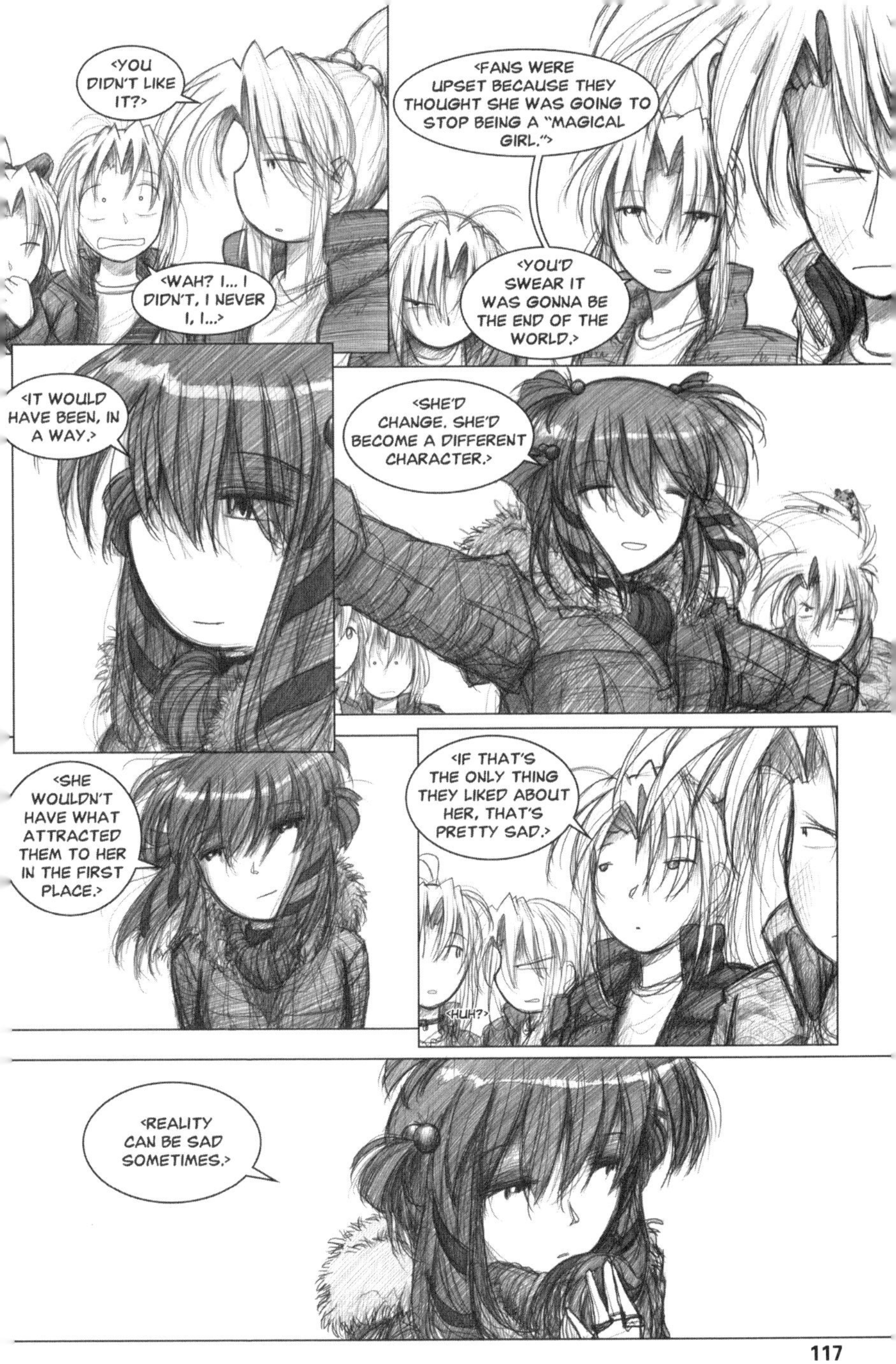
<YOU DIDN'T LIKE IT?>
<WAH? I... I DIDN'T, I NEVER I, I...>
<FANS WERE UPSET BECAUSE THEY THOUGHT SHE WAS GOING TO STOP BEING A "MAGICAL GIRL.">
<YOU'D SWEAR IT WAS GONNA BE THE END OF THE WORLD.>
<IT WOULD HAVE BEEN, IN A WAY.>
<SHE'D CHANGE. SHE'D BECOME A DIFFERENT CHARACTER.>
<SHE WOULDN'T HAVE WHAT ATTRACTED THEM TO HER IN THE FIRST PLACE.>
<IF THAT'S THE ONLY THING THEY LIKED ABOUT HER, THAT'S PRETTY SAD.>
<HUH?>
<REALITY CAN BE SAD SOMETIMES.>

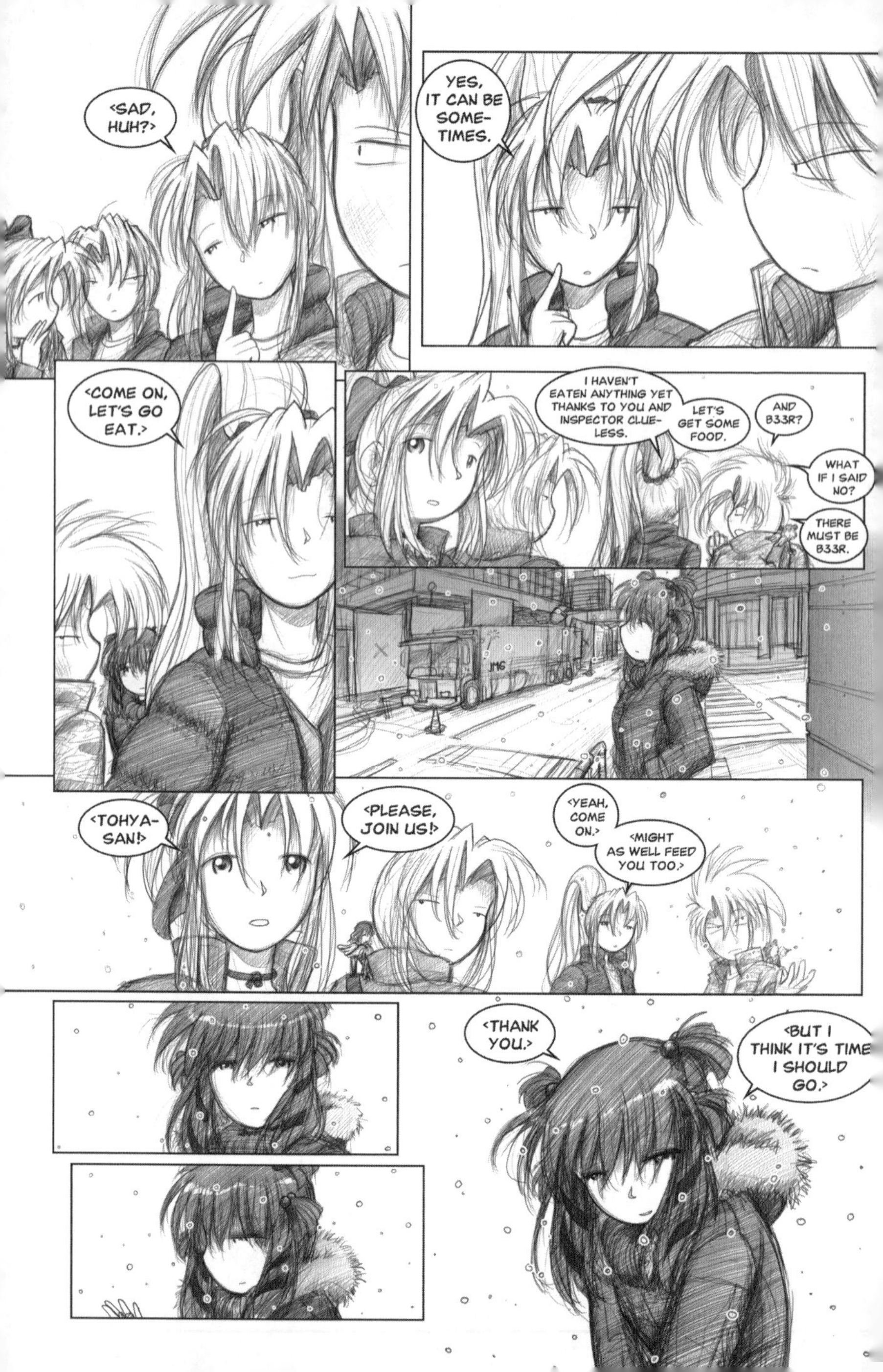
<SAD, HUH?>
YES, IT CAN BE SOME-TIMES.
<COME ON, LET'S GO EAT.>
I HAVEN'T EATEN ANYTHING YET THANKS TO YOU AND INSPECTOR CLUE-LESS.
LET'S GET SOME FOOD.
AND B33R?
WHAT IF I SAID NO?
THERE MUST BE B33R.
<TOHYA-SAN!>
<PLEASE, JOIN US!>
<YEAH, COME ON.>
<MIGHT AS WELL FEED YOU TOO.>
<THANK YOU.>
<BUT I THINK IT'S TIME I SHOULD GO.>

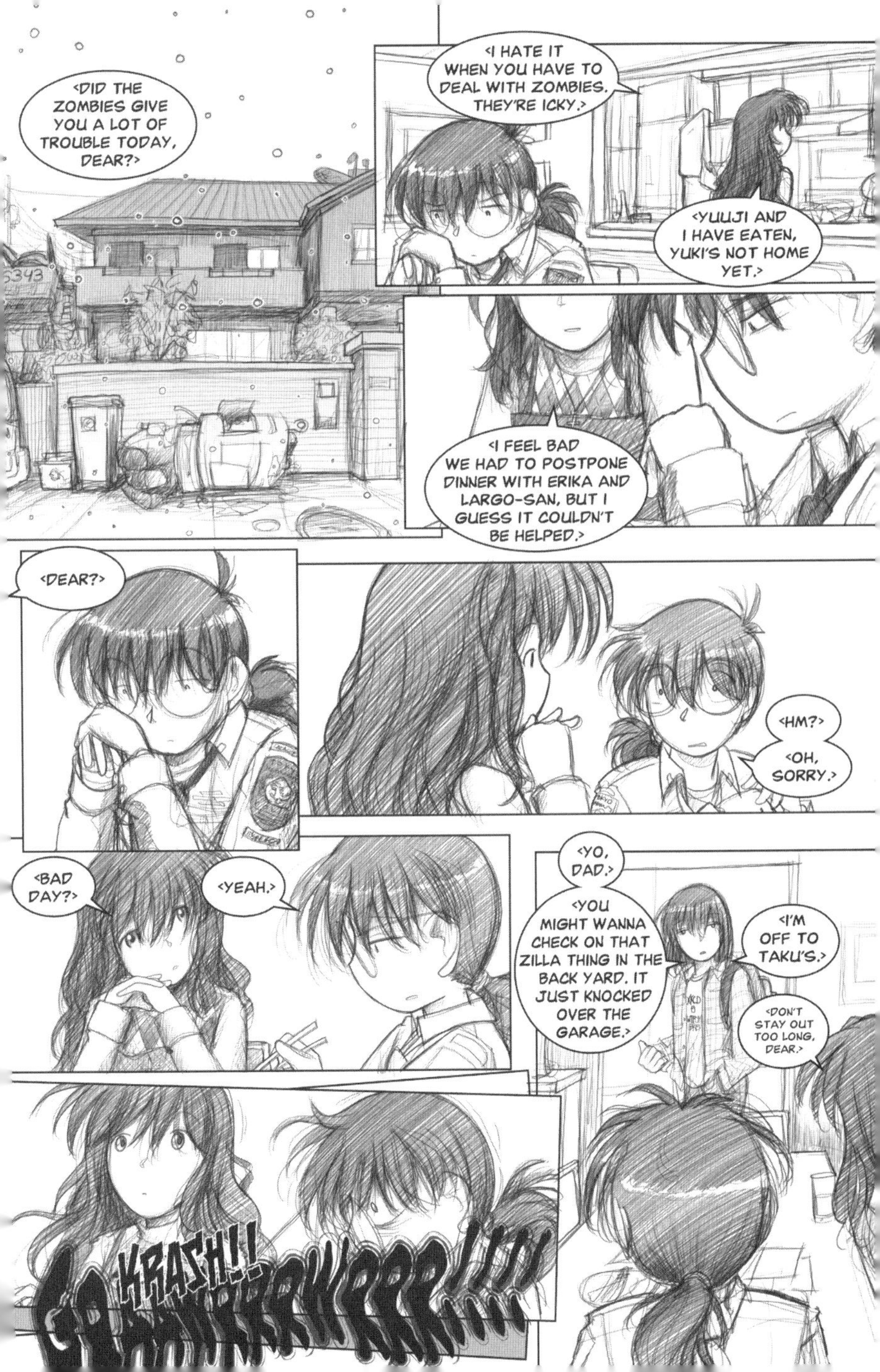
<DID THE ZOMBIES GIVE YOU A LOT OF TROUBLE TODAY, DEAR?>
<I HATE IT WHEN YOU HAVE TO DEAL WITH ZOMBIES. THEY'RE ICKY.>
<YUUJI AND I HAVE EATEN, YUKI'S NOT HOME YET.>
<I FEEL BAD WE HAD TO POSTPONE DINNER WITH ERIKA AND LARGO-SAN, BUT I GUESS IT COULDN'T BE HELPED.>
<DEAR?>
<HM?>
<OH, SORRY.>
<BAD DAY?>
<YEAH.>
<YO, DAD.>
<YOU MIGHT WANNA CHECK ON THAT ZILLA THING IN THE BACK YARD. IT JUST KNOCKED OVER THE GARAGE.>
<I'M OFF TO TAKU'S.>
<DON'T STAY OUT TOO LONG, DEAR.>
KRASH!!

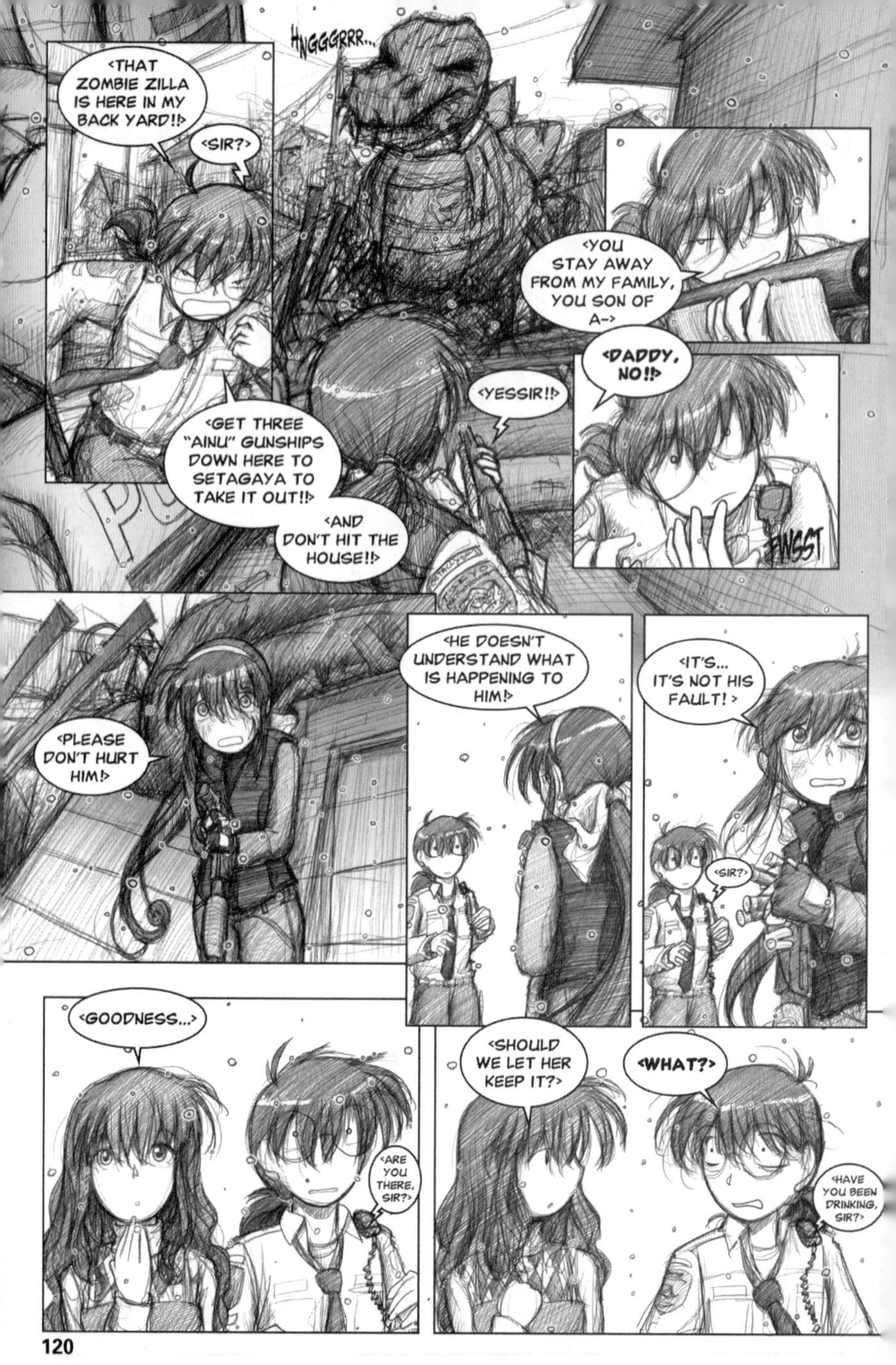
HNGGGRRR...
<THAT ZOMBIE ZILLA IS HERE IN MY BACK YARD!!>
<SIR?>
<GET THREE "AINU" GUNSHIPS DOWN HERE TO SETAGAYA TO TAKE IT OUT!!>
<YESSIR!!>
<AND DON'T HIT THE HOUSE!!>
<YOU STAY AWAY FROM MY FAMILY, YOU SON OF A–>
<DADDY, NO!!>
FWSST
<PLEASE DON'T HURT HIM!>
<HE DOESN'T UNDERSTAND WHAT IS HAPPENING TO HIM!>
<IT'S... IT'S NOT HIS FAULT! >
<SIR?>
<GOODNESS...>
<ARE YOU THERE, SIR?>
<SHOULD WE LET HER KEEP IT?>
<WHAT?>
<HAVE YOU BEEN DRINKING, SIR?>

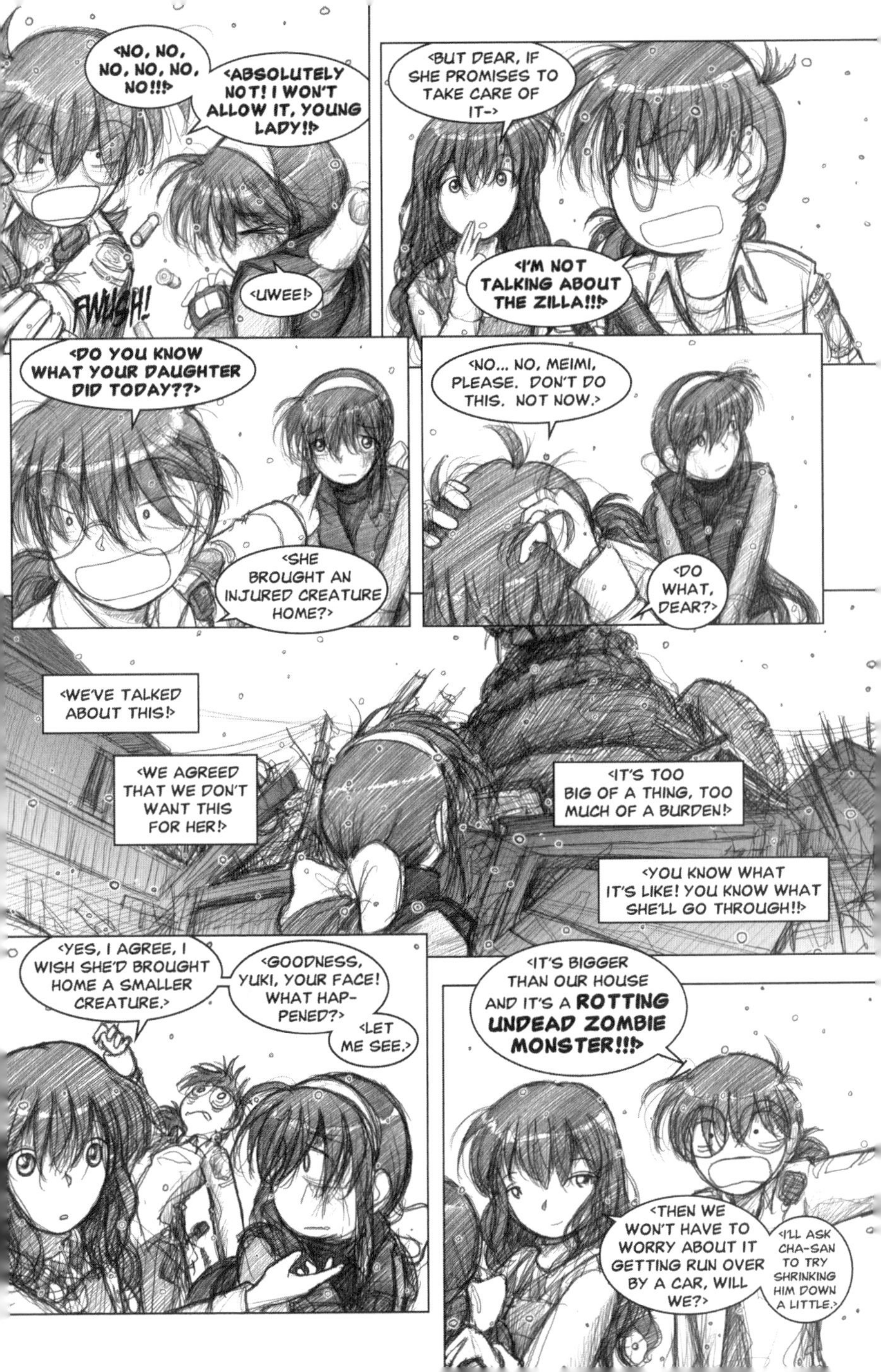
<NO, NO, NO, NO, NO, NO!!!>
<ABSOLUTELY NOT! I WON'T ALLOW IT, YOUNG LADY!!>
FWUSH!
<UWEE!>
<BUT DEAR, IF SHE PROMISES TO TAKE CARE OF IT->
<I'M NOT TALKING ABOUT THE ZILLA!!!>
<DO YOU KNOW WHAT YOUR DAUGHTER DID TODAY??>
<SHE BROUGHT AN INJURED CREATURE HOME?>
<NO... NO, MEIMI, PLEASE. DON'T DO THIS. NOT NOW.>
<DO WHAT, DEAR?>
<WE'VE TALKED ABOUT THIS!>
<WE AGREED THAT WE DON'T WANT THIS FOR HER!>
<IT'S TOO BIG OF A THING, TOO MUCH OF A BURDEN!>
<YOU KNOW WHAT IT'S LIKE! YOU KNOW WHAT SHE'LL GO THROUGH!!>
<YES, I AGREE, I WISH SHE'D BROUGHT HOME A SMALLER CREATURE.>
<GOODNESS, YUKI, YOUR FACE! WHAT HAP-PENED?>
<LET ME SEE.>
<IT'S BIGGER THAN OUR HOUSE AND IT'S A ROTTING UNDEAD ZOMBIE MONSTER!!!>
<THEN WE WON'T HAVE TO WORRY ABOUT IT GETTING RUN OVER BY A CAR, WILL WE?>
<I'LL ASK CHA-SAN TO TRY SHRINKING HIM DOWN A LITTLE.>

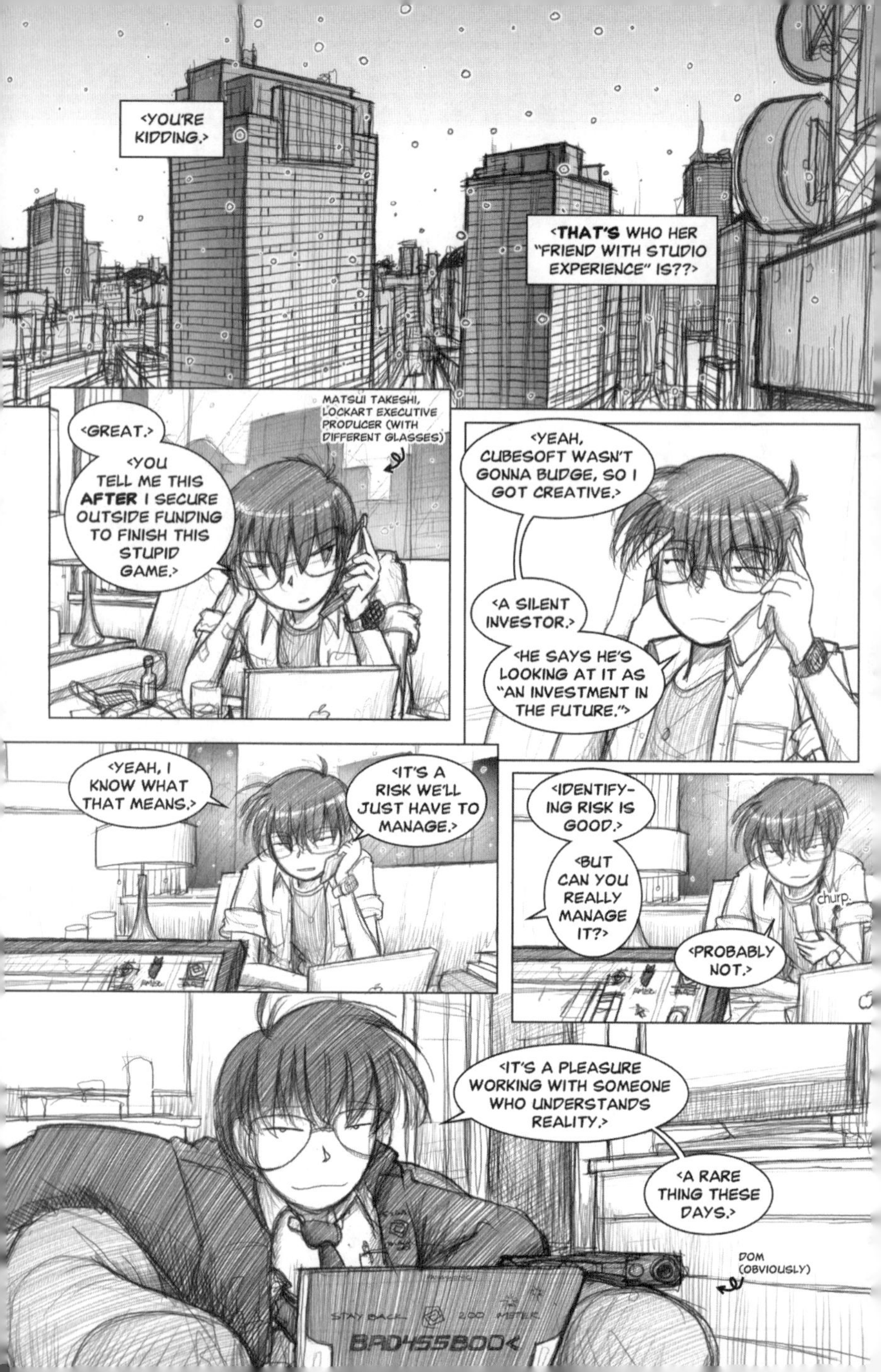
<YOU'RE KIDDING.>
<THAT'S WHO HER "FRIEND WITH STUDIO EXPERIENCE" IS??>
<GREAT.>
<YOU TELL ME THIS AFTER I SECURE OUTSIDE FUNDING TO FINISH THIS STUPID GAME.>
MATSUI TAKESHI, LOCKART EXECUTIVE PRODUCER (WITH DIFFERENT GLASSES)
<YEAH, CUBESOFT WASN'T GONNA BUDGE, SO I GOT CREATIVE.>
<A SILENT INVESTOR.>
<HE SAYS HE'S LOOKING AT IT AS "AN INVESTMENT IN THE FUTURE.">
<YEAH, I KNOW WHAT THAT MEANS.>
<IT'S A RISK WE'LL JUST HAVE TO MANAGE.>
<IDENTIFYING RISK IS GOOD.>
<BUT CAN YOU REALLY MANAGE IT?>
churp.
<PROBABLY NOT.>
<IT'S A PLEASURE WORKING WITH SOMEONE WHO UNDERSTANDS REALITY.>
<A RARE THING THESE DAYS.>
DOM (OBVIOUSLY)
STAY BACK 200 METER

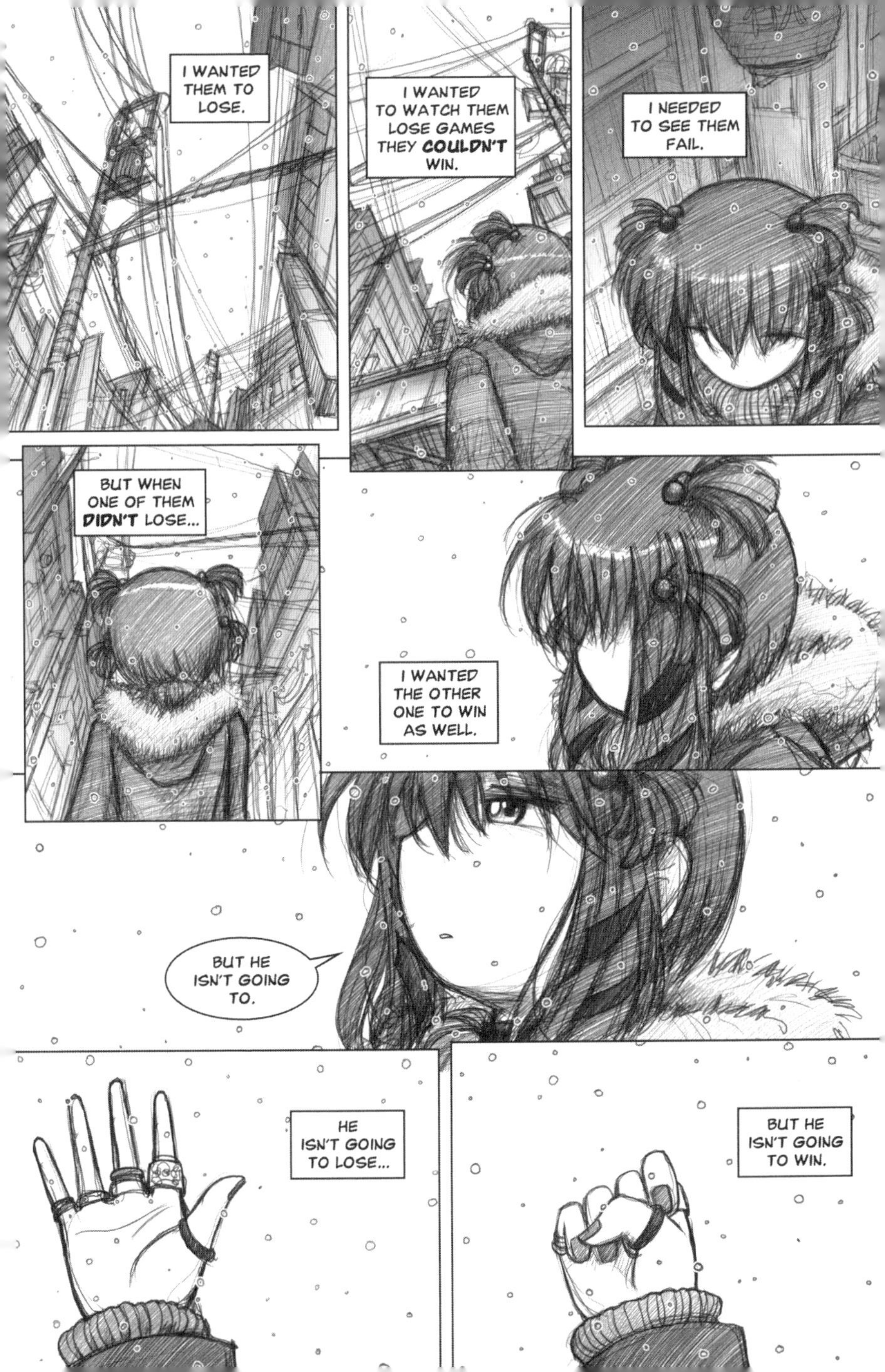
I WANTED THEM TO LOSE.
I WANTED TO WATCH THEM LOSE GAMES THEY **COULDN'T** WIN.
I NEEDED TO SEE THEM FAIL.
BUT WHEN ONE OF THEM **DIDN'T** LOSE...
I WANTED THE OTHER ONE TO WIN AS WELL.
BUT HE ISN'T GOING TO.
HE ISN'T GOING TO LOSE...
BUT HE ISN'T GOING TO WIN.

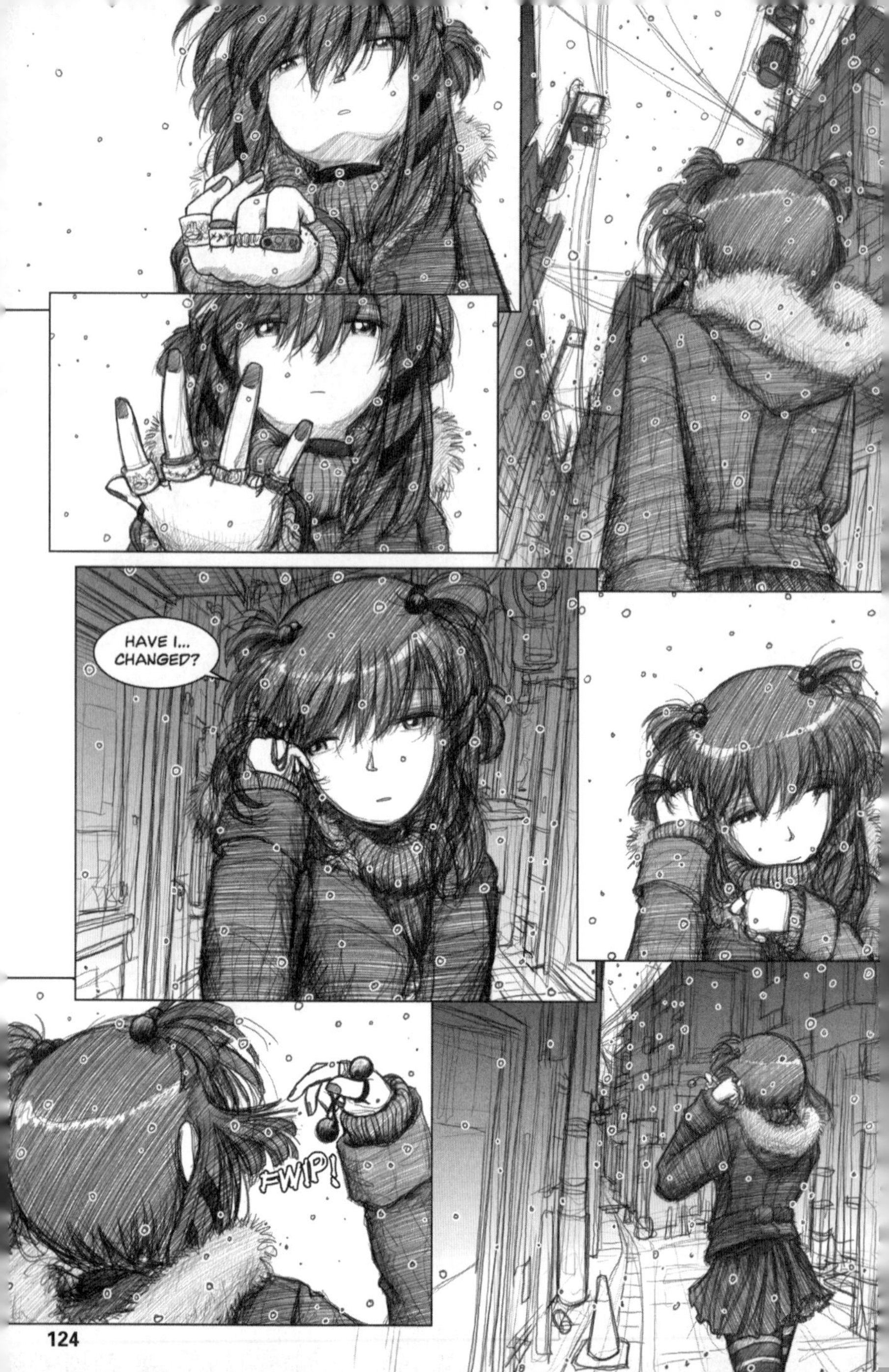
HAVE I... CHANGED?
FWIP!

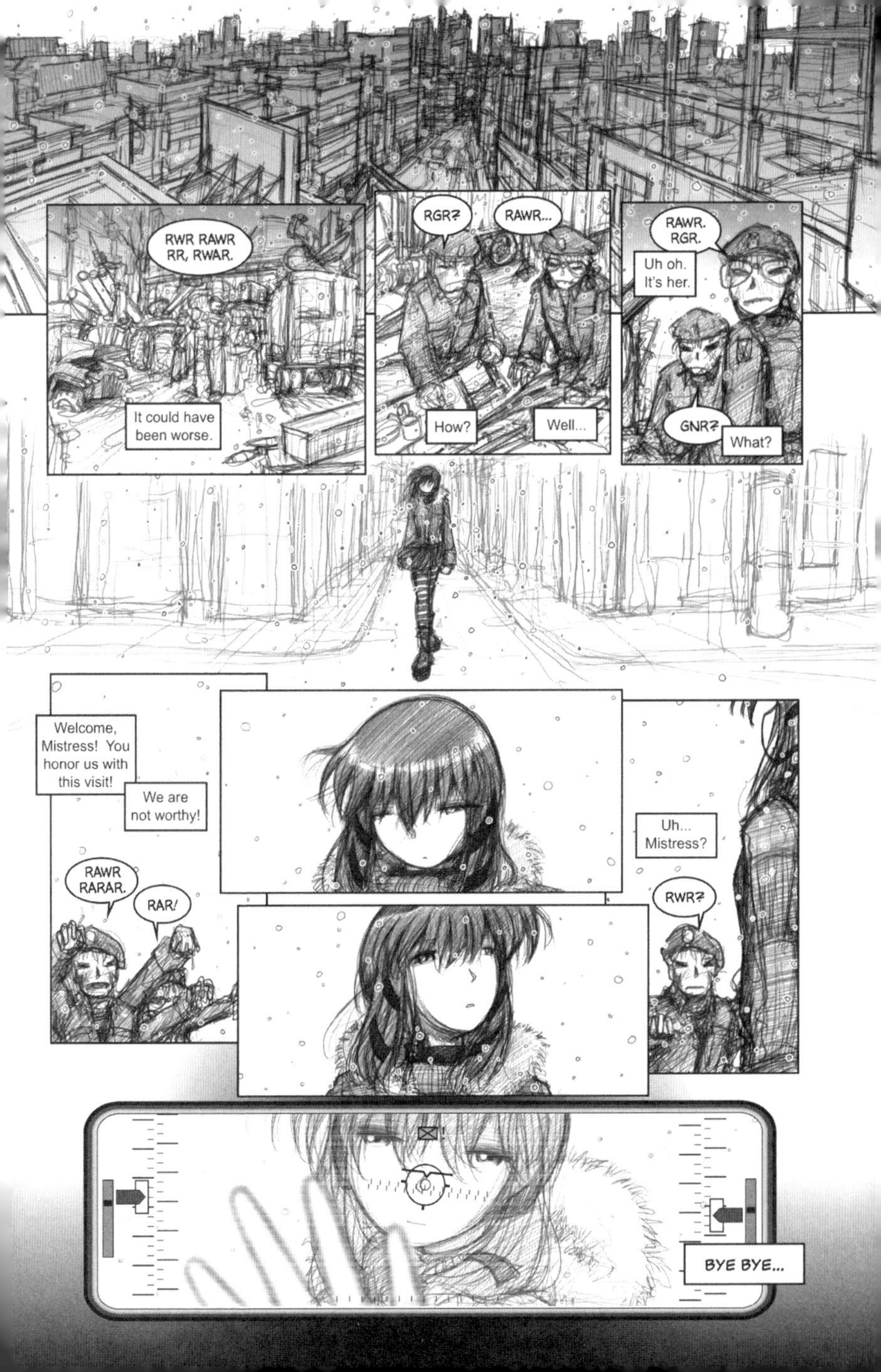
RWR RAWR RR, RWAR.
It could have been worse.
RGR?
RAWR...
How?
Well...
RAWR. RGR.
Uh oh. It's her.
GNR?
What?
Welcome, Mistress! You honor us with this visit!
We are not worthy!
RAWR RARAR.
RAR!
Uh... Mistress?
RWR?
BYE BYE...

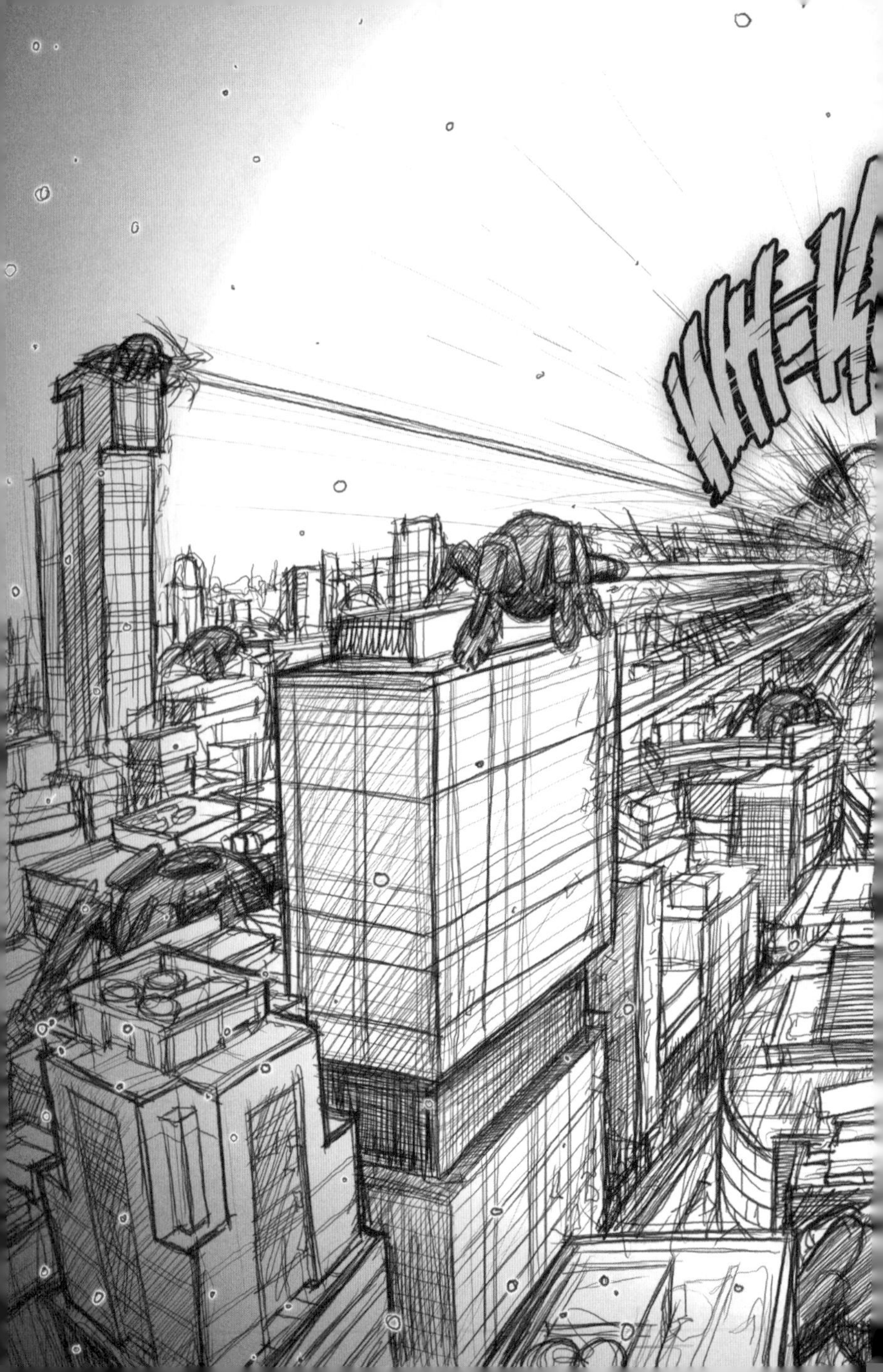
WH-K

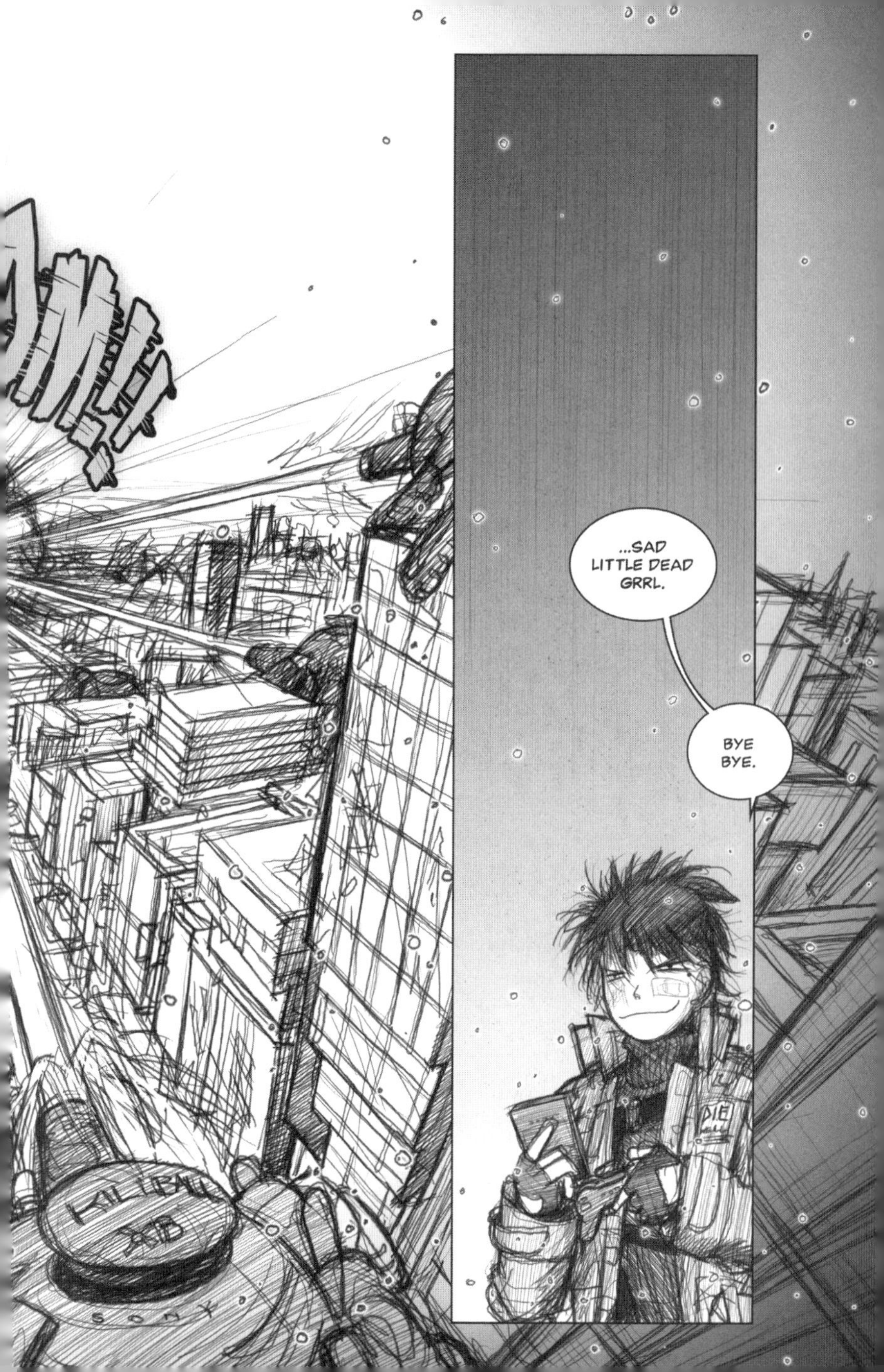
...SAD LITTLE DEAD GRRL.
BYE BYE.

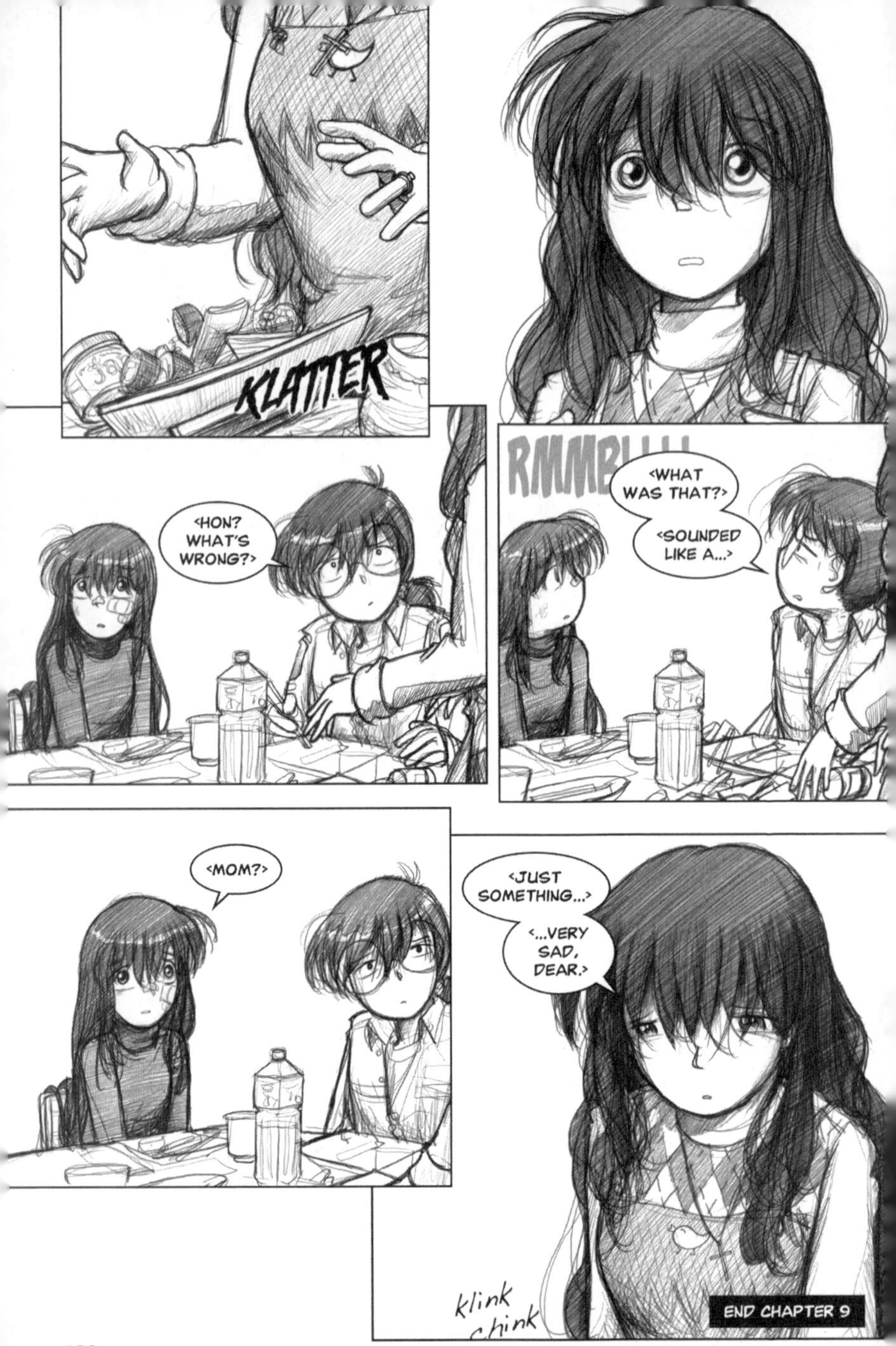
KLATTER
RMMBLLL
<HON? WHAT'S WRONG?>
<WHAT WAS THAT?>
<SOUNDED LIKE A...>
<MOM?>
<JUST SOMETHING...>
<...VERY SAD, DEAR.>
klink chink
END CHAPTER 9

あいだに

meanwhile...

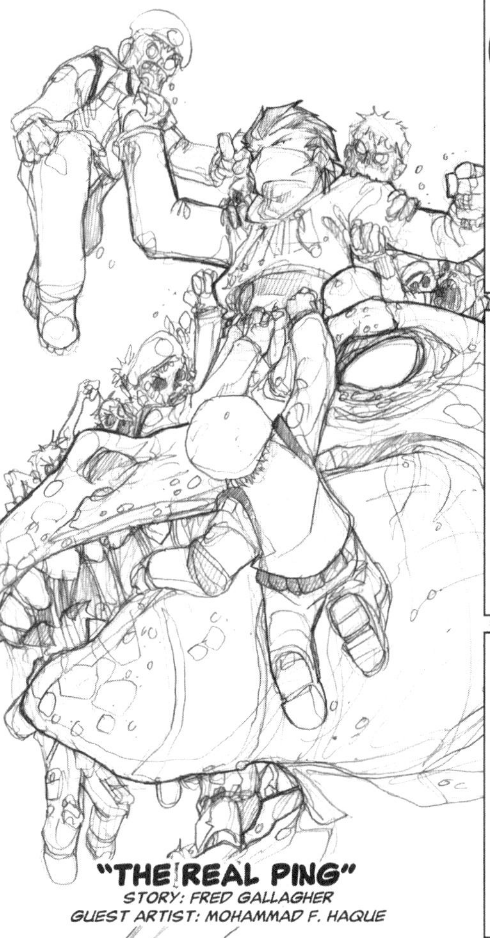

"THE REAL PING"

STORY: FRED GALLAGHER
GUEST ARTIST: MOHAMMAD F. HAQUE

"I FEEL SO FAKE"

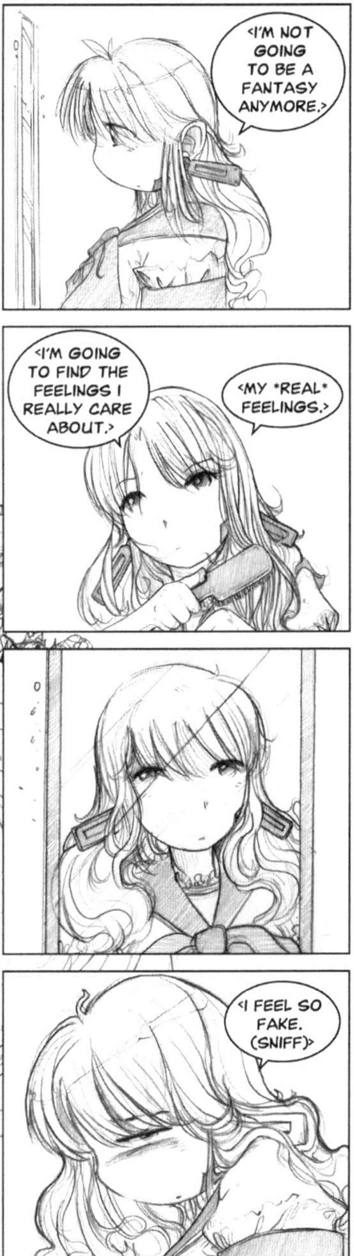
‹I'M NOT GOING TO BE A FANTASY ANYMORE.›
‹I'M GOING TO FIND THE FEELINGS I REALLY CARE ABOUT.›
‹MY *REAL* FEELINGS.›
‹I FEEL SO FAKE. (SNIFF)›

"NOT WORKING"

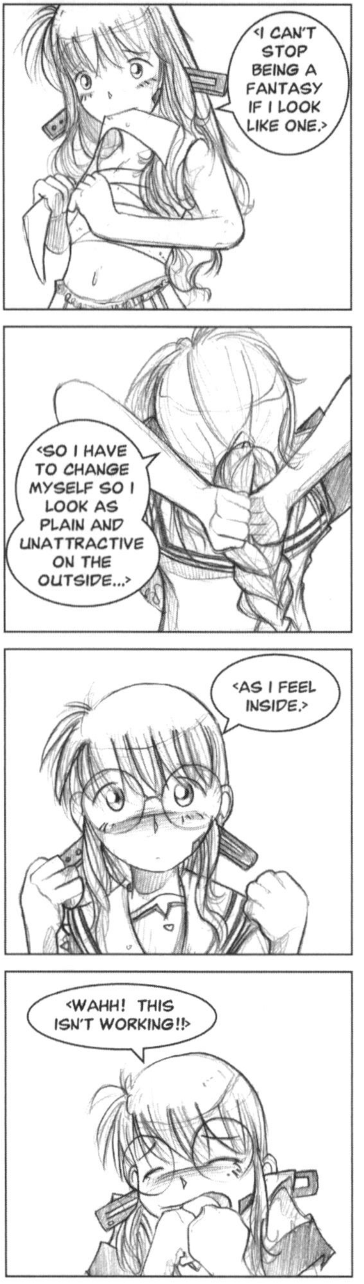
<I CAN'T STOP BEING A FANTASY IF I LOOK LIKE ONE.>
<SO I HAVE TO CHANGE MYSELF SO I LOOK AS PLAIN AND UNATTRACTIVE ON THE OUTSIDE...>
<AS I FEEL INSIDE.>
<WAHH! THIS ISN'T WORKING!!>

"NOT WORKING AT ALL"

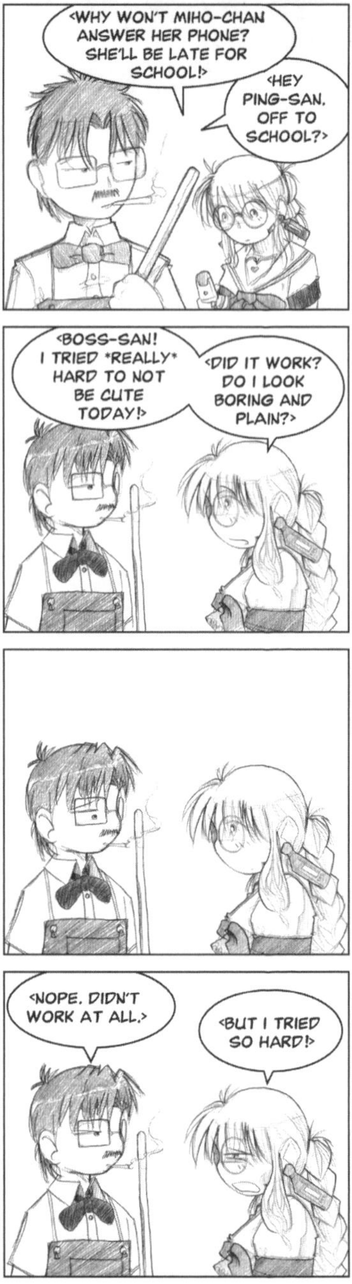
<WHY WON'T MIHO-CHAN ANSWER HER PHONE? SHE'LL BE LATE FOR SCHOOL!>
<HEY PING-SAN, OFF TO SCHOOL?>
<BOSS-SAN! I TRIED *REALLY* HARD TO NOT BE CUTE TODAY!>
<DID IT WORK? DO I LOOK BORING AND PLAIN?>
<NOPE. DIDN'T WORK AT ALL.>
<BUT I TRIED SO HARD!>

"AFRAID"

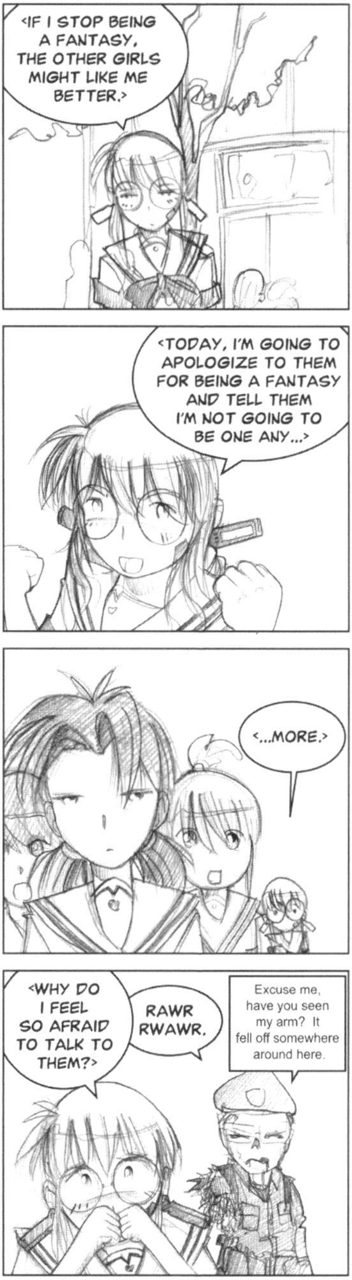
<IF I STOP BEING A FANTASY, THE OTHER GIRLS MIGHT LIKE ME BETTER.>
<TODAY, I'M GOING TO APOLOGIZE TO THEM FOR BEING A FANTASY AND TELL THEM I'M NOT GOING TO BE ONE ANY...>
<...MORE.>
<WHY DO I FEEL SO AFRAID TO TALK TO THEM?>
RAWR RWAWR.
Excuse me, have you seen my arm? It fell off somewhere around here.

"IS THAT BAD?"

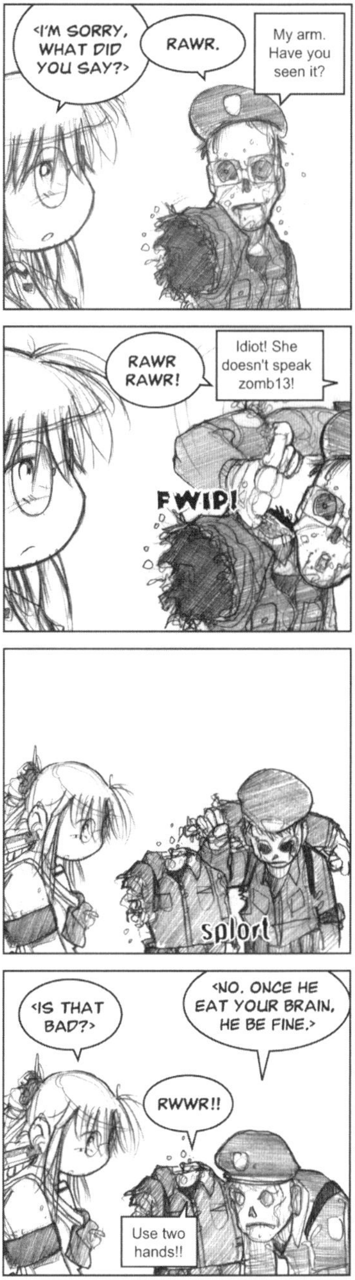
<I'M SORRY, WHAT DID YOU SAY?>
RAWR.
My arm. Have you seen it?
RAWR RAWR!
Idiot! She doesn't speak zomb13!
FWIP!
splort
<IS THAT BAD?>
<NO. ONCE HE EAT YOUR BRAIN, HE BE FINE.>
RWWR!!
Use two hands!!

"REAL BRAINS"

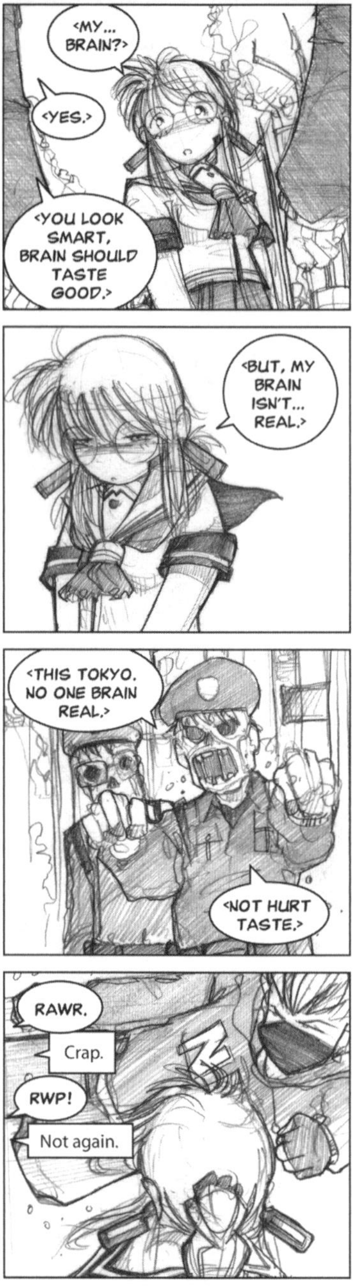
<MY... BRAIN?>
<YES.>
<YOU LOOK SMART, BRAIN SHOULD TASTE GOOD.>
<BUT, MY BRAIN ISN'T... REAL.>
<THIS TOKYO. NO ONE BRAIN REAL.>
<NOT HURT TASTE.>
RAWR.
Crap.
RWP!
Not again.

"IT REAL"

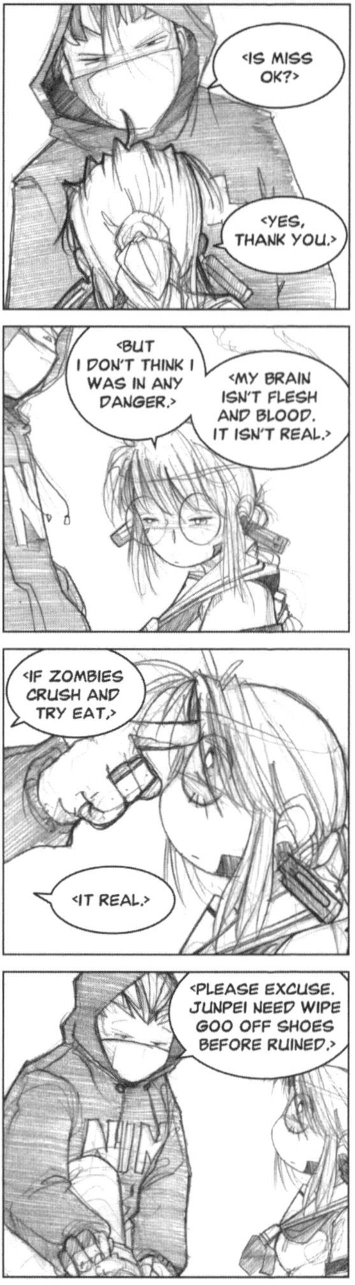
<IS MISS OK?>
<YES, THANK YOU.>
<BUT I DON'T THINK I WAS IN ANY DANGER.>
<MY BRAIN ISN'T FLESH AND BLOOD. IT ISN'T REAL.>
<IF ZOMBIES CRUSH AND TRY EAT,>
<IT REAL.>
<PLEASE EXCUSE. JUNPEI NEED WIPE GOO OFF SHOES BEFORE RUINED.>

"REALLY REAL"

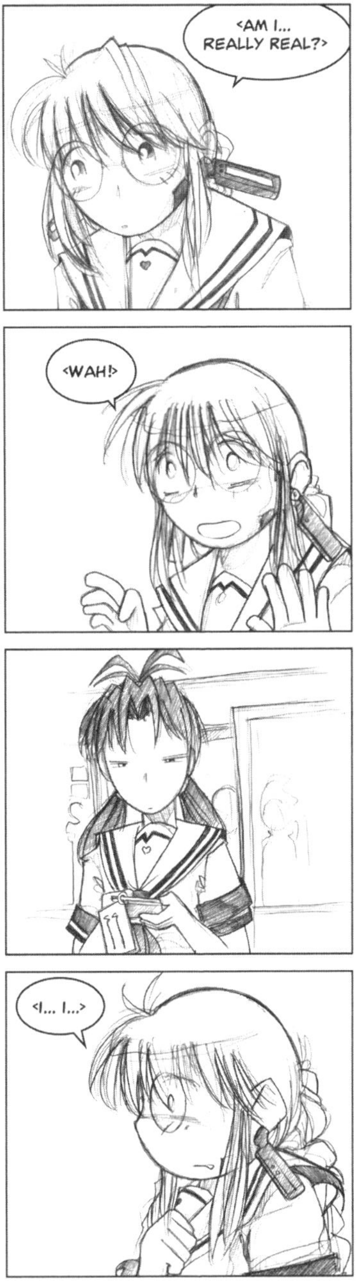
<AM I... REALLY REAL?>
<WAH!>
<I... I...>

"OVERDOING IT"

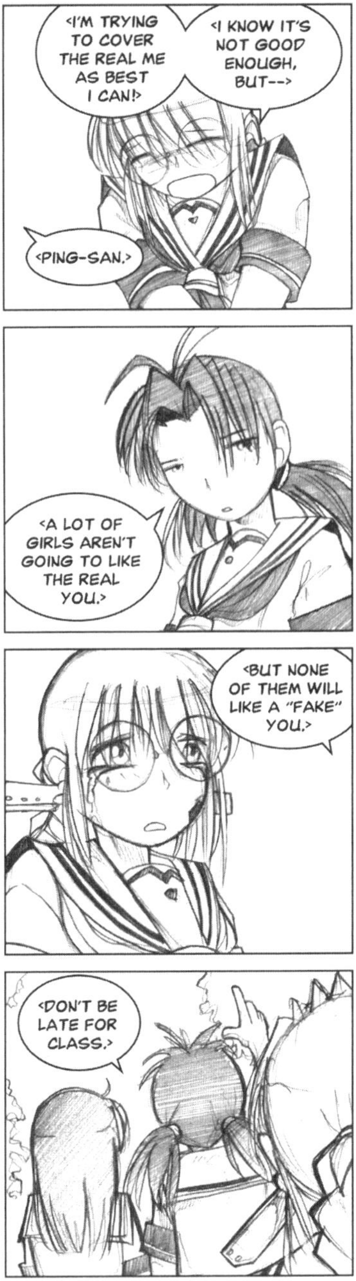
<I'M TRYING TO COVER THE REAL ME AS BEST I CAN!>
<I KNOW IT'S NOT GOOD ENOUGH, BUT-->
<PING-SAN.>
<A LOT OF GIRLS AREN'T GOING TO LIKE THE REAL YOU.>
<BUT NONE OF THEM WILL LIKE A "FAKE" YOU.>
<DON'T BE LATE FOR CLASS.>

DEAD DOM DAY: "THE THINKER"

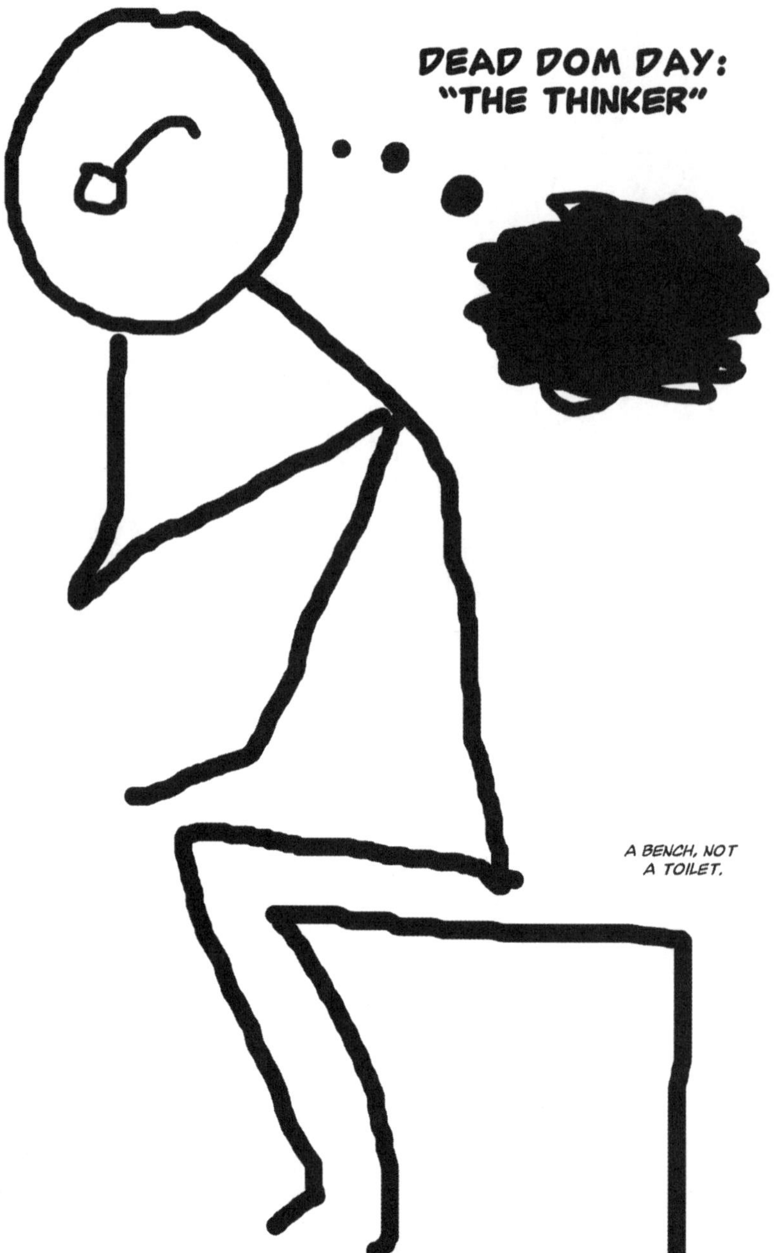
A BENCH, NOT
A TOILET.

MEGATOKYO OMAKE THEATER PRESENTS:

FULL
MEGATOKYO
PANIC!

CLAN'D WAR3Z

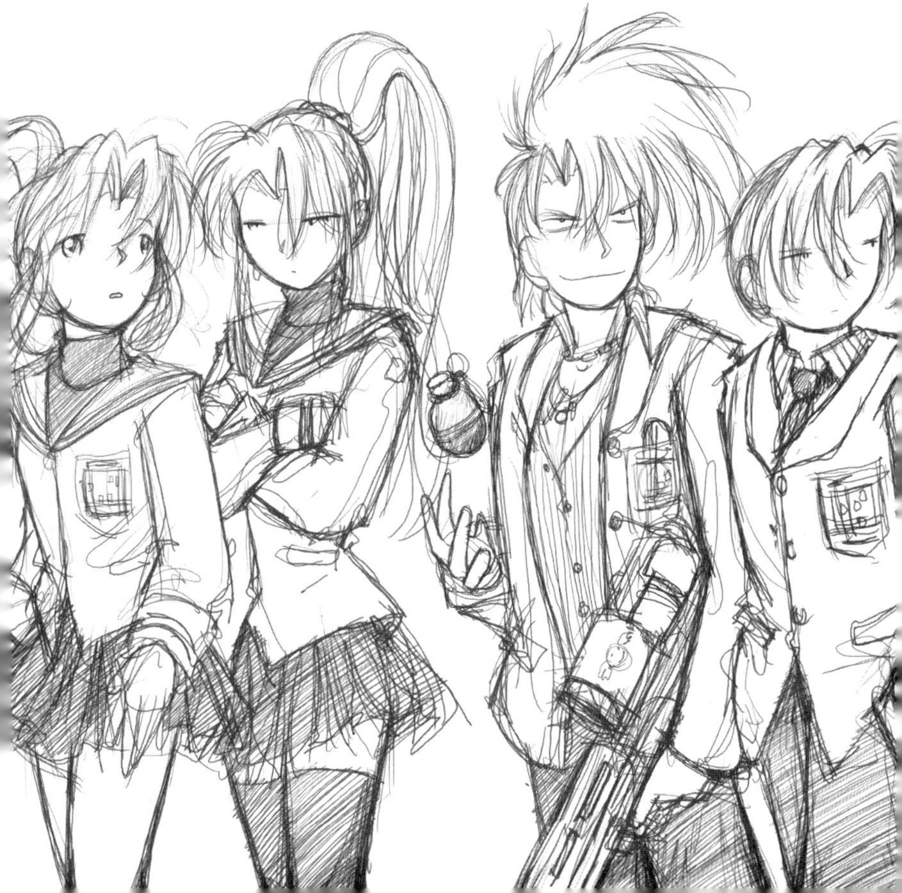

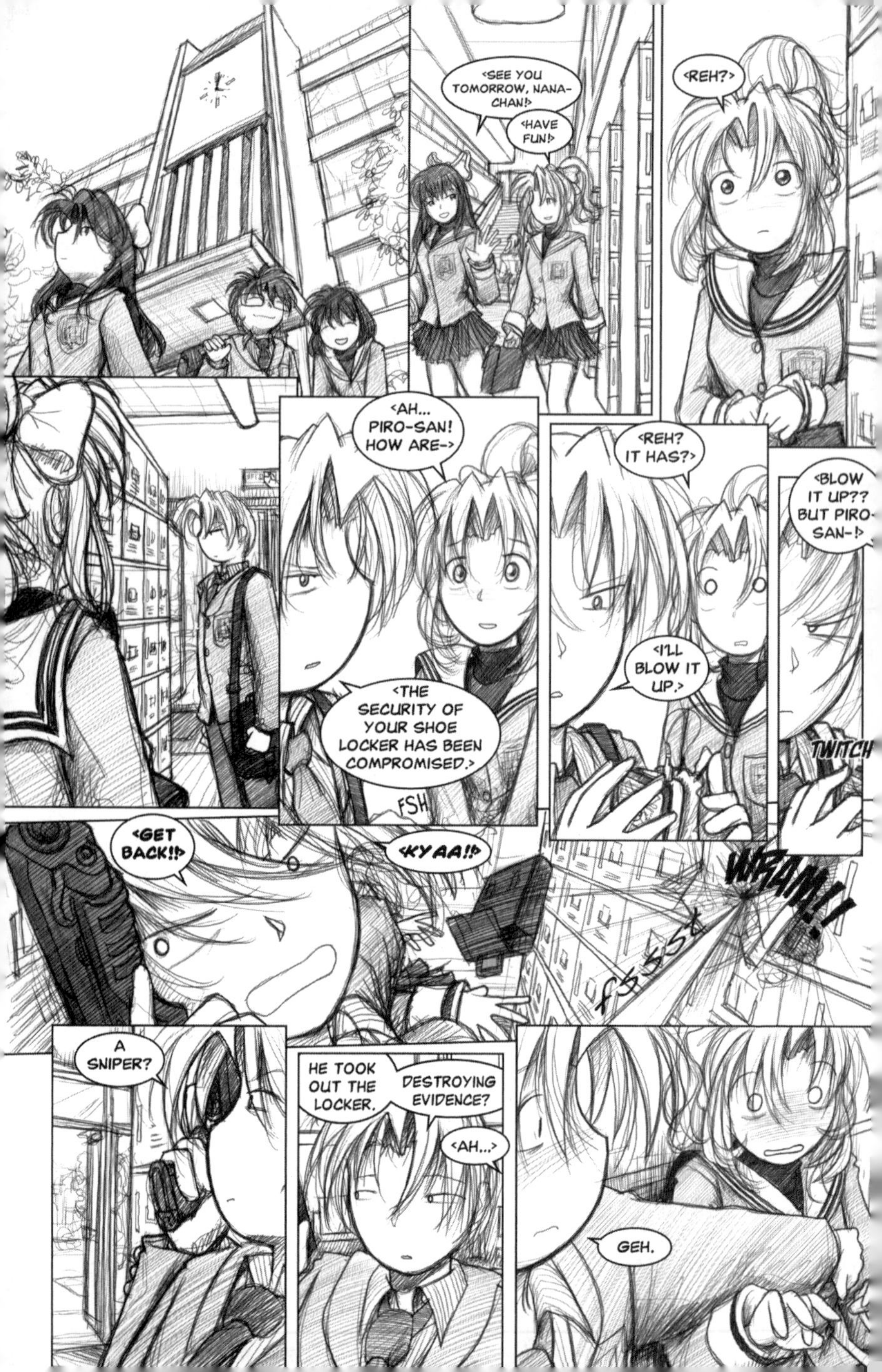
<SEE YOU TOMORROW, NANA-CHAN!>
<HAVE FUN!>
<REH?>
<AH... PIRO-SAN! HOW ARE->
<THE SECURITY OF YOUR SHOE LOCKER HAS BEEN COMPROMISED.>
FSH
<REH? IT HAS?>
<I'LL BLOW IT UP.>
<BLOW IT UP?? BUT PIRO-SAN-!>
TWITCH
<GET BACK!!>
<KYAA!!>
WRAM!!
A SNIPER?
HE TOOK OUT THE LOCKER.
DESTROYING EVIDENCE?
<AH...>
GEH.

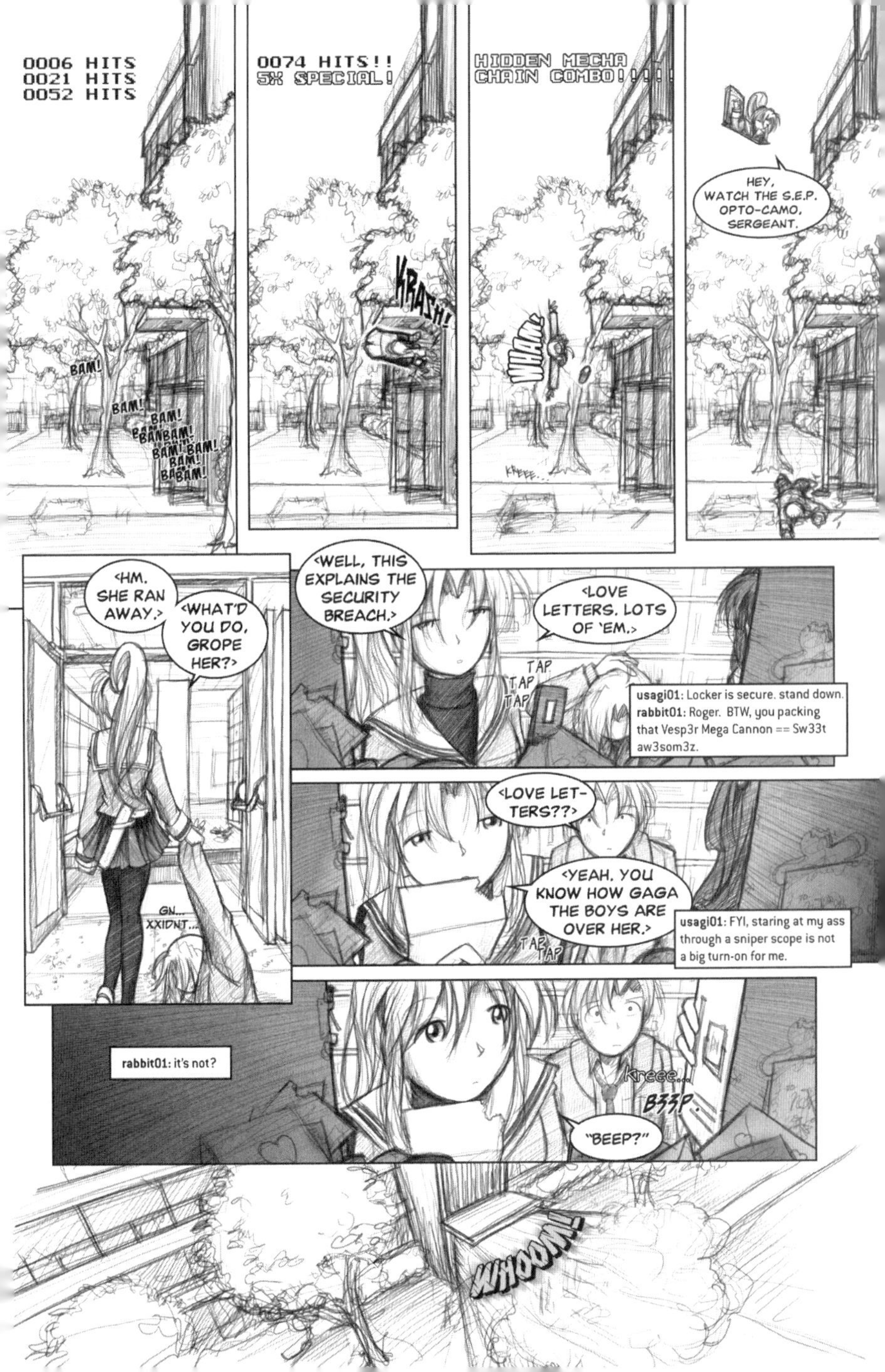
0006 HITS
0021 HITS
0052 HITS
BAM!
BAM!
BAM!
BANBAM!
BAM! BAM!
BAM!
BABAM!
0074 HITS!!
5X SPECIAL!
KRASH!
HIDDEN MECHA
CHAIN COMBO!!!!!
WHAM!
KREEEE...
HEY, WATCH THE S.E.P. OPTO-CAMO, SERGEANT.
<HM. SHE RAN AWAY.>
<WHAT'D YOU DO, GROPE HER?>
GN... XXIDNT...
<WELL, THIS EXPLAINS THE SECURITY BREACH.>
<LOVE LETTERS. LOTS OF 'EM.>
TAP TAP TAP
usagi01: Locker is secure. stand down.
rabbit01: Roger. BTW, you packing that Vesp3r Mega Cannon == Sw33t aw3som3z.
<LOVE LETTERS??>
<YEAH. YOU KNOW HOW GAGA THE BOYS ARE OVER HER.>
TAP TAP
usagi01: FYI, staring at my ass through a sniper scope is not a big turn-on for me.
rabbit01: it's not?
Kreee...
B33P.
"BEEP?"
WHOOM!

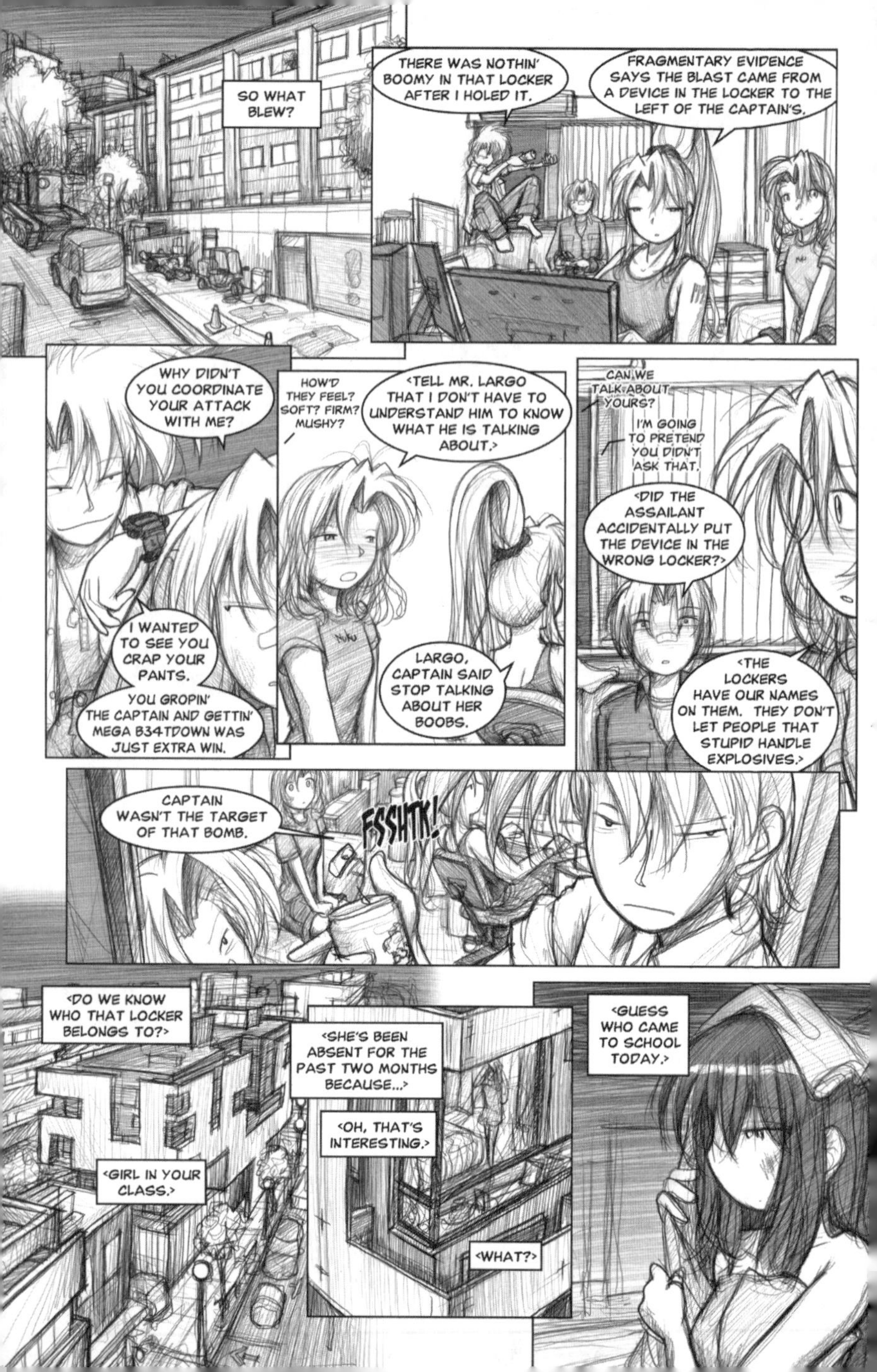
SO WHAT BLEW?
THERE WAS NOTHIN' BOOMY IN THAT LOCKER AFTER I HOLED IT.
FRAGMENTARY EVIDENCE SAYS THE BLAST CAME FROM A DEVICE IN THE LOCKER TO THE LEFT OF THE CAPTAIN'S.
WHY DIDN'T YOU COORDINATE YOUR ATTACK WITH ME?
I WANTED TO SEE YOU CRAP YOUR PANTS.
YOU GROPIN' THE CAPTAIN AND GETTIN' MEGA B34TDOWN WAS JUST EXTRA WIN.
HOW'D THEY FEEL? SOFT? FIRM? MUSHY?
<TELL MR. LARGO THAT I DON'T HAVE TO UNDERSTAND HIM TO KNOW WHAT HE IS TALKING ABOUT.>
LARGO, CAPTAIN SAID STOP TALKING ABOUT HER BOOBS.
CAN WE TALK ABOUT YOURS?
I'M GOING TO PRETEND YOU DIDN'T ASK THAT.
<DID THE ASSAILANT ACCIDENTALLY PUT THE DEVICE IN THE WRONG LOCKER?>
<THE LOCKERS HAVE OUR NAMES ON THEM. THEY DON'T LET PEOPLE THAT STUPID HANDLE EXPLOSIVES.>
CAPTAIN WASN'T THE TARGET OF THAT BOMB.
FSSHTK!
<DO WE KNOW WHO THAT LOCKER BELONGS TO?>
<GIRL IN YOUR CLASS.>
<SHE'S BEEN ABSENT FOR THE PAST TWO MONTHS BECAUSE...>
<OH, THAT'S INTERESTING.>
<WHAT?>
<GUESS WHO CAME TO SCHOOL TODAY.>

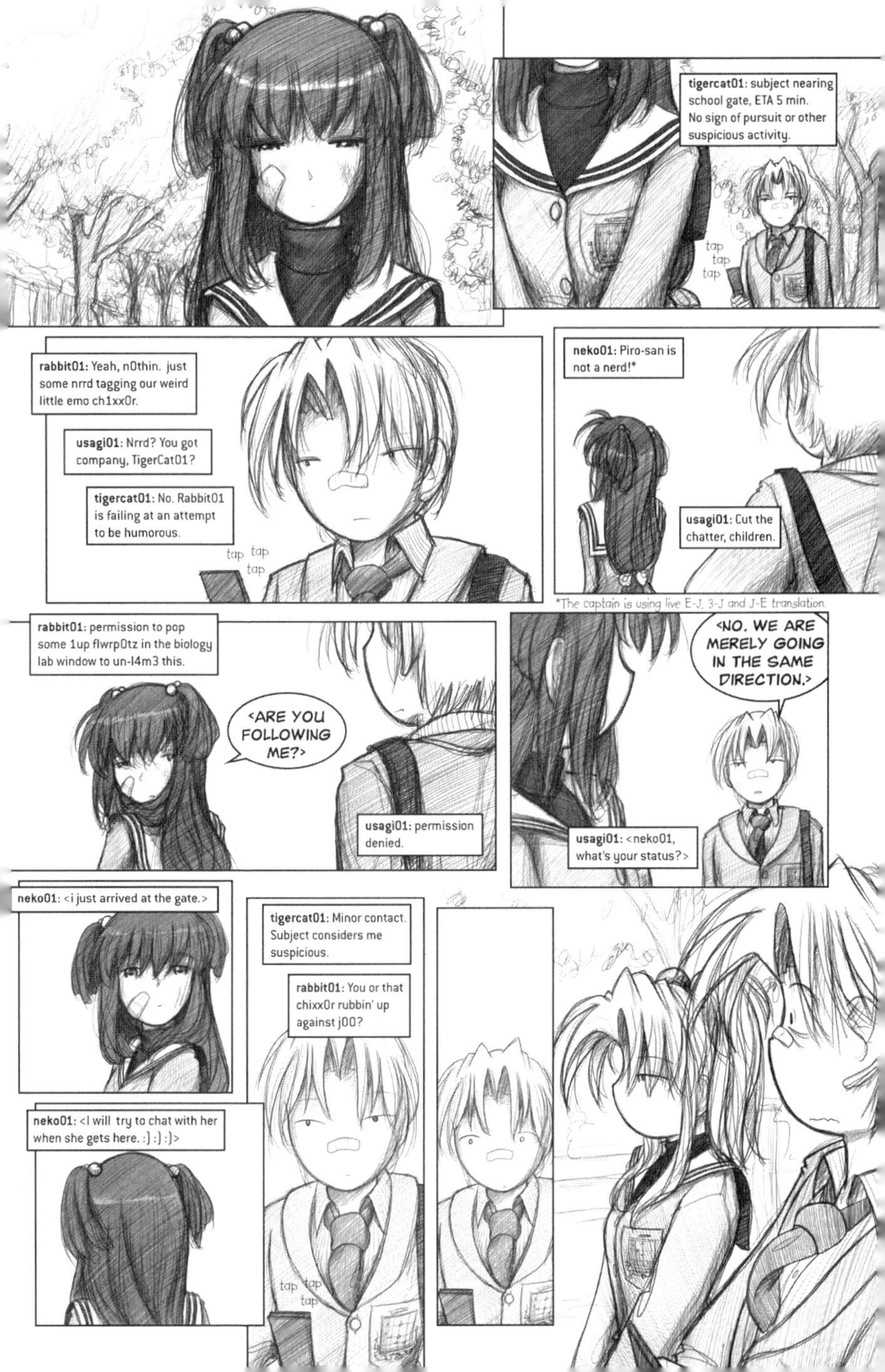
tigercat01: subject nearing school gate, ETA 5 min. No sign of pursuit or other suspicious activity.
tap tap tap
rabbit01: Yeah, n0thin. just some nrrd tagging our weird little emo ch1xx0r.
usagi01: Nrrd? You got company, TigerCat01?
tigercat01: No. Rabbit01 is failing at an attempt to be humorous.
tap tap tap
neko01: Piro-san is not a nerd!*
usagi01: Cut the chatter, children.
*The captain is using live E-J, J-J and J-E translation.
rabbit01: permission to pop some 1up flwrp0tz in the biology lab window to un-l4m3 this.
<ARE YOU FOLLOWING ME?>
usagi01: permission denied.
<NO. WE ARE MERELY GOING IN THE SAME DIRECTION.>
usagi01: <neko01, what's your status?>
neko01: <i just arrived at the gate.>
neko01: <I will try to chat with her when she gets here. :) :) :)>
tigercat01: Minor contact. Subject considers me suspicious.
rabbit01: You or that chixx0r rubbin' up against j00?
tap tap tap

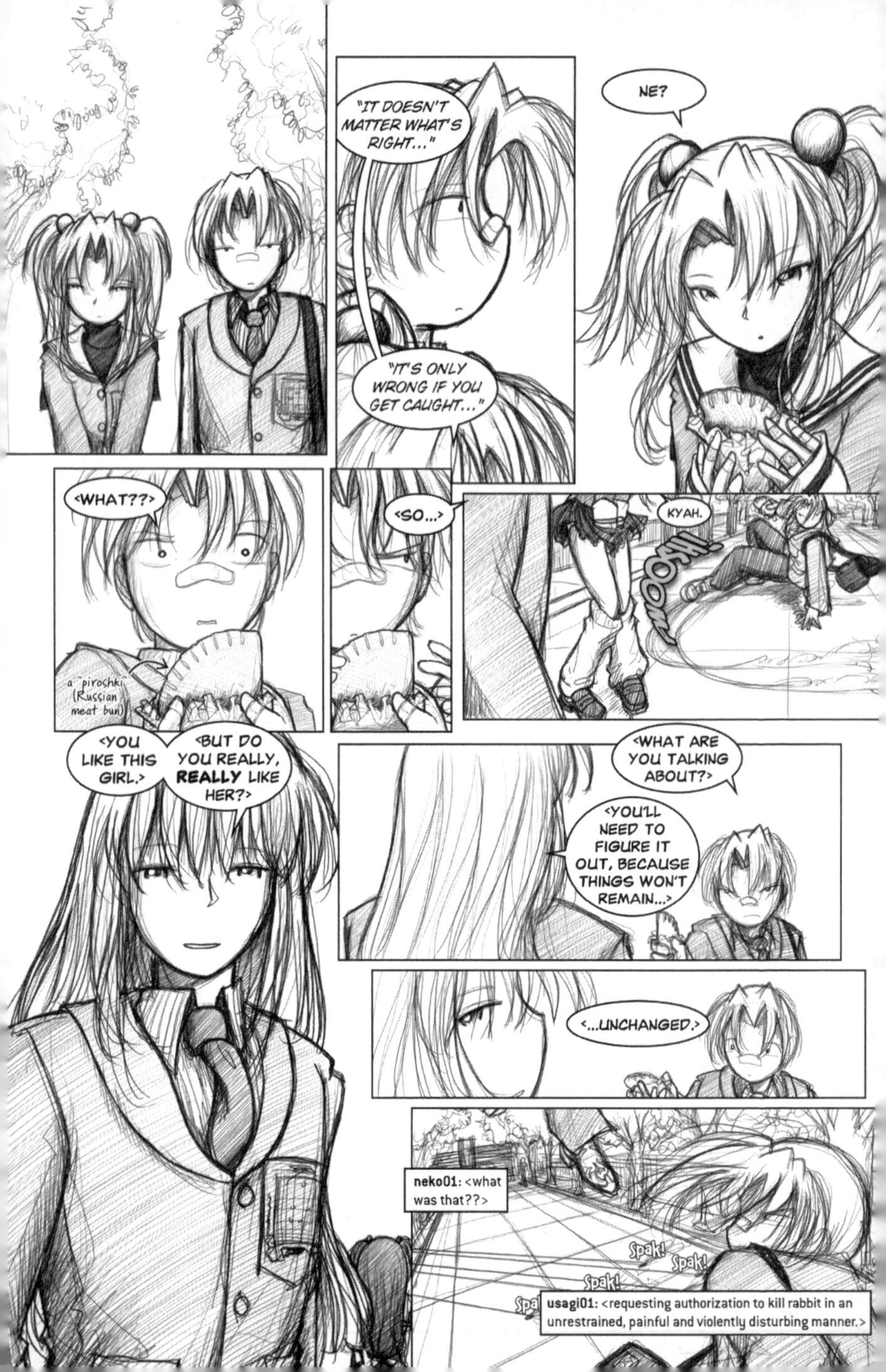
"IT DOESN'T MATTER WHAT'S RIGHT..."
"IT'S ONLY WRONG IF YOU GET CAUGHT..."
NE?
<WHAT??>
a "piroshki" (Russian meat bun)
<SO...>
KYAH.
WHOOM!!
<YOU LIKE THIS GIRL.>
<BUT DO YOU REALLY, **REALLY** LIKE HER?>
<WHAT ARE YOU TALKING ABOUT?>
<YOU'LL NEED TO FIGURE IT OUT, BECAUSE THINGS WON'T REMAIN...>
<...UNCHANGED.>
neko01: <what was that??>
Spak! Spak! Spak!
usagi01: <requesting authorization to kill rabbit in an unrestrained, painful and violently disturbing manner.>

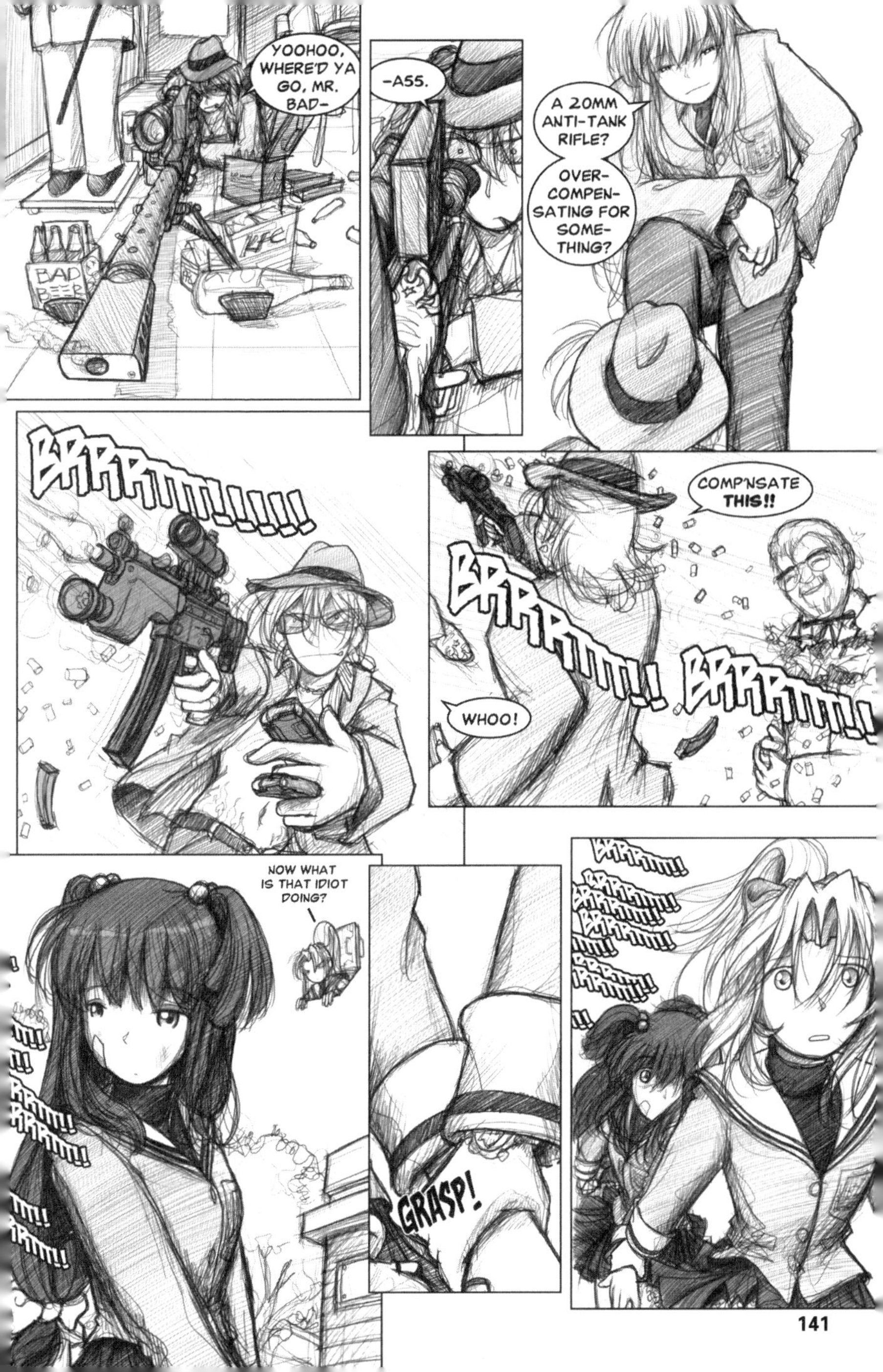
YOOHOO, WHERE'D YA GO, MR. BAD-
-ASS.
A 20MM ANTI-TANK RIFLE?
OVER-COMPEN-SATING FOR SOME-THING?
BRRRTTT!!!!!!
COMP'NSATE **THIS!!**
BRRRTTT!!
BRRRTTT!!
WHOO!
NOW WHAT IS THAT IDIOT DOING?
GRASP!

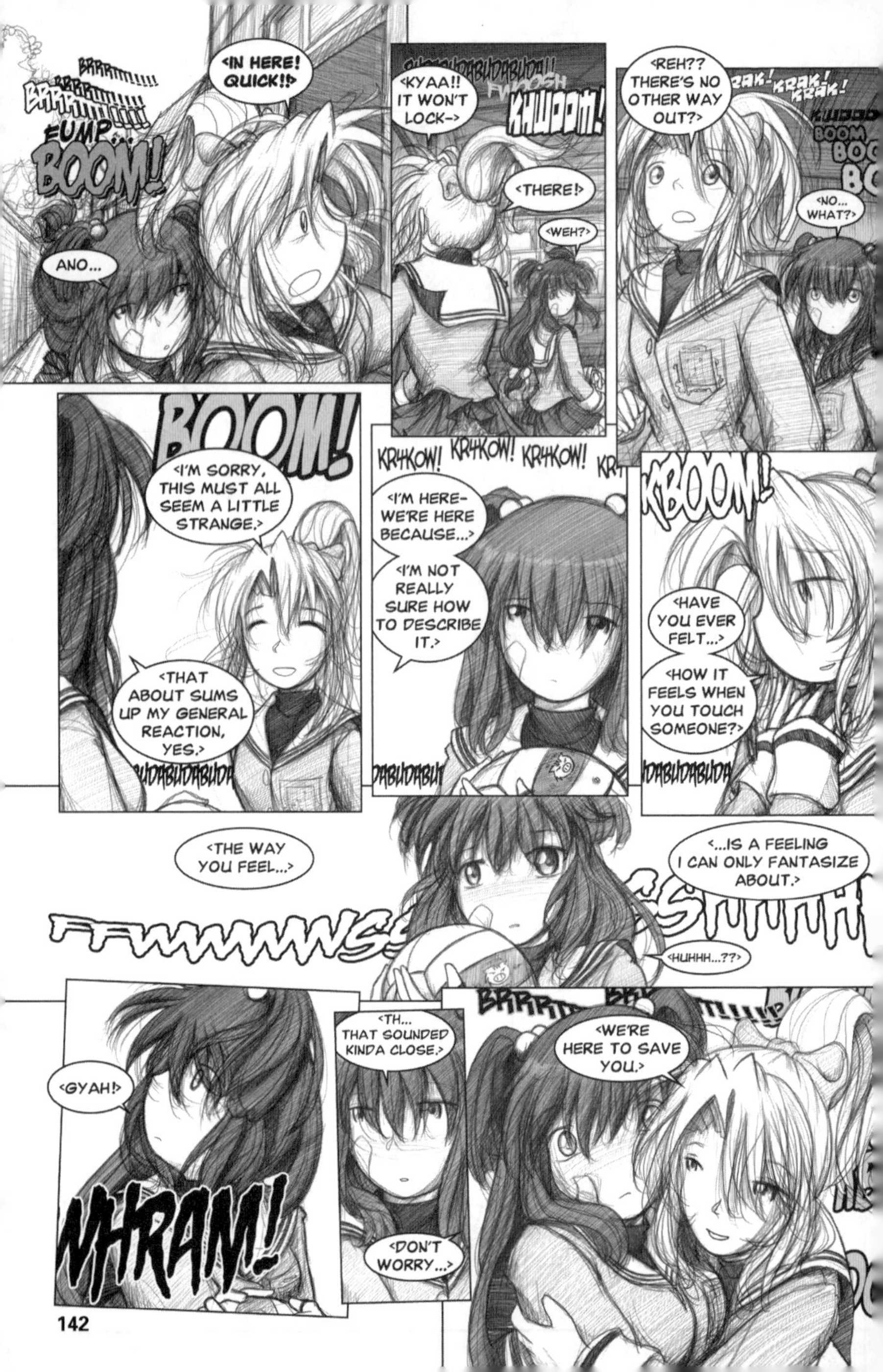
BRRRTTT!!!!!
FUMP...
BOOM!!
<IN HERE! QUICK!!>
ANO...
FWOOSH
KHUOOM!
<KYAA!! IT WON'T LOCK->
<THERE!>
<WEH?>
<REH?? THERE'S NO OTHER WAY OUT?>
KRAK! KRAK! KRAK!
BOOM
<NO... WHAT?>
BOOM!
<I'M SORRY, THIS MUST ALL SEEM A LITTLE STRANGE.>
<THAT ABOUT SUMS UP MY GENERAL REACTION, YES.>
BUDABUDABUDA
KR4KOW! KR4KOW! KR4KOW!
<I'M HERE- WE'RE HERE BECAUSE...>
<I'M NOT REALLY SURE HOW TO DESCRIBE IT.>
DABUDABU
KBOOM!
<HAVE YOU EVER FELT...>
<HOW IT FEELS WHEN YOU TOUCH SOMEONE?>
DABUDABUDA
<THE WAY YOU FEEL...>
<...IS A FEELING I CAN ONLY FANTASIZE ABOUT.>
<HUHHH...??>
<GYAH!>
WHRAM!
<TH... THAT SOUNDED KINDA CLOSE.>
<DON'T WORRY...>
<WE'RE HERE TO SAVE YOU.>

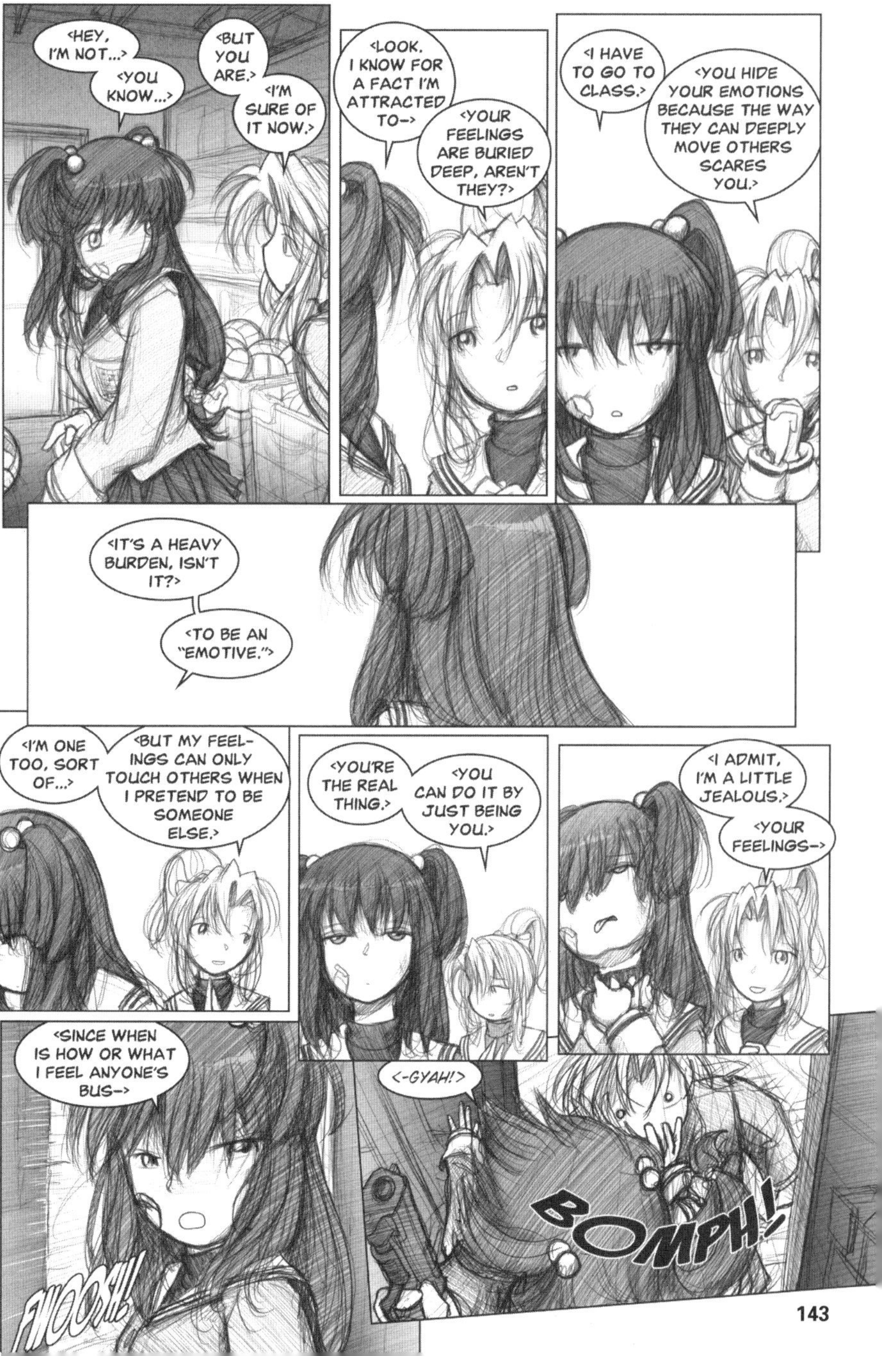
<HEY, I'M NOT...>
<YOU KNOW...>
<BUT YOU ARE.>
<I'M SURE OF IT NOW.>
<LOOK. I KNOW FOR A FACT I'M ATTRACTED TO–>
<YOUR FEELINGS ARE BURIED DEEP, AREN'T THEY?>
<I HAVE TO GO TO CLASS.>
<YOU HIDE YOUR EMOTIONS BECAUSE THE WAY THEY CAN DEEPLY MOVE OTHERS SCARES YOU.>
<IT'S A HEAVY BURDEN, ISN'T IT?>
<TO BE AN "EMOTIVE.">
<I'M ONE TOO, SORT OF...>
<BUT MY FEELINGS CAN ONLY TOUCH OTHERS WHEN I PRETEND TO BE SOMEONE ELSE.>
<YOU'RE THE REAL THING.>
<YOU CAN DO IT BY JUST BEING YOU.>
<I ADMIT, I'M A LITTLE JEALOUS.>
<YOUR FEELINGS–>
<SINCE WHEN IS HOW OR WHAT I FEEL ANYONE'S BUS–>
<-GYAH!>
BOMPH!

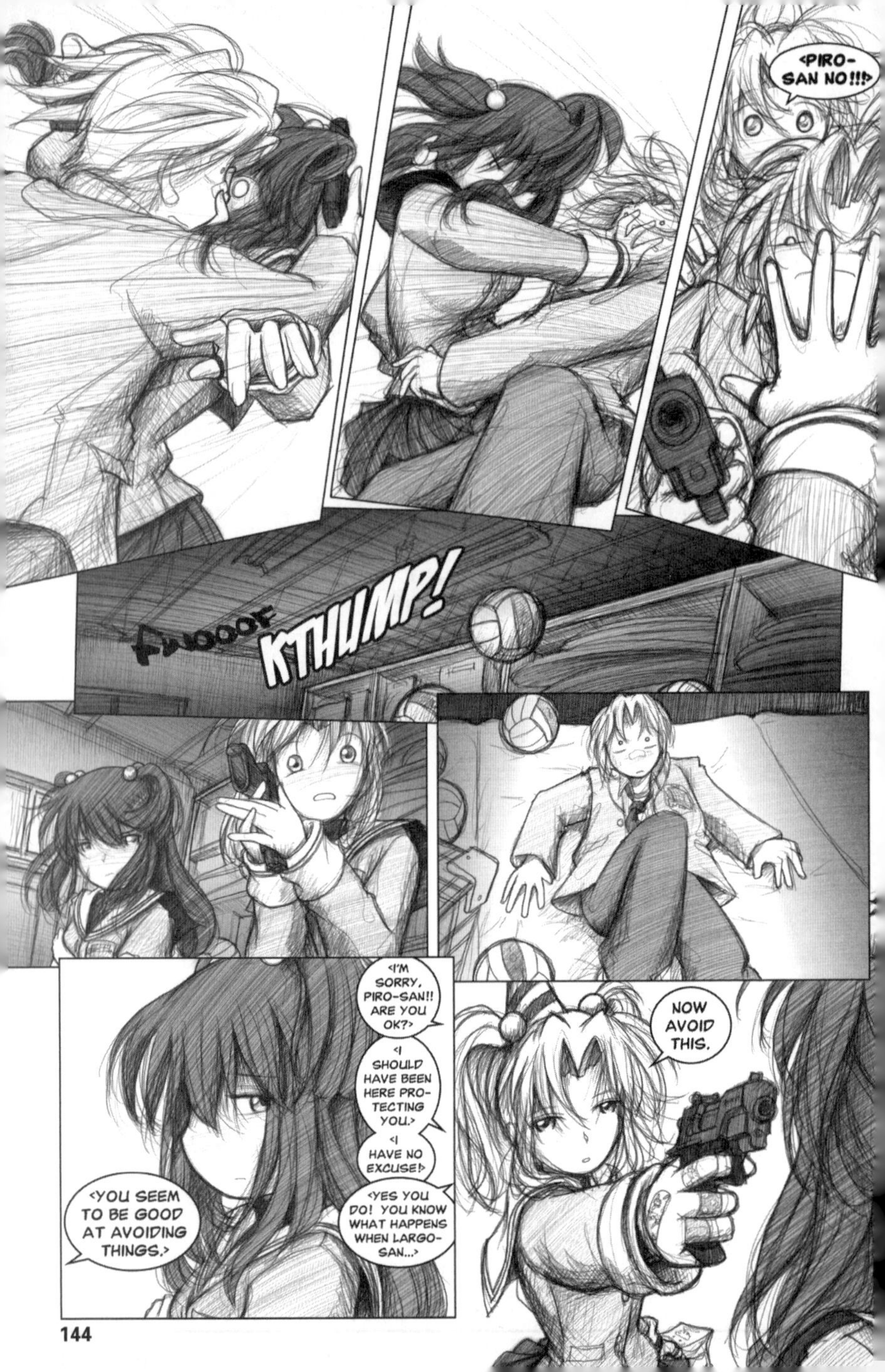

<PIRO-SAN NO!!!>
FWOOOF
KTHUMP!
<I'M SORRY, PIRO-SAN!! ARE YOU OK?>
<I SHOULD HAVE BEEN HERE PROTECTING YOU.>
<I HAVE NO EXCUSE!>
<YES YOU DO! YOU KNOW WHAT HAPPENS WHEN LARGO-SAN...>
<YOU SEEM TO BE GOOD AT AVOIDING THINGS.>
NOW AVOID THIS.

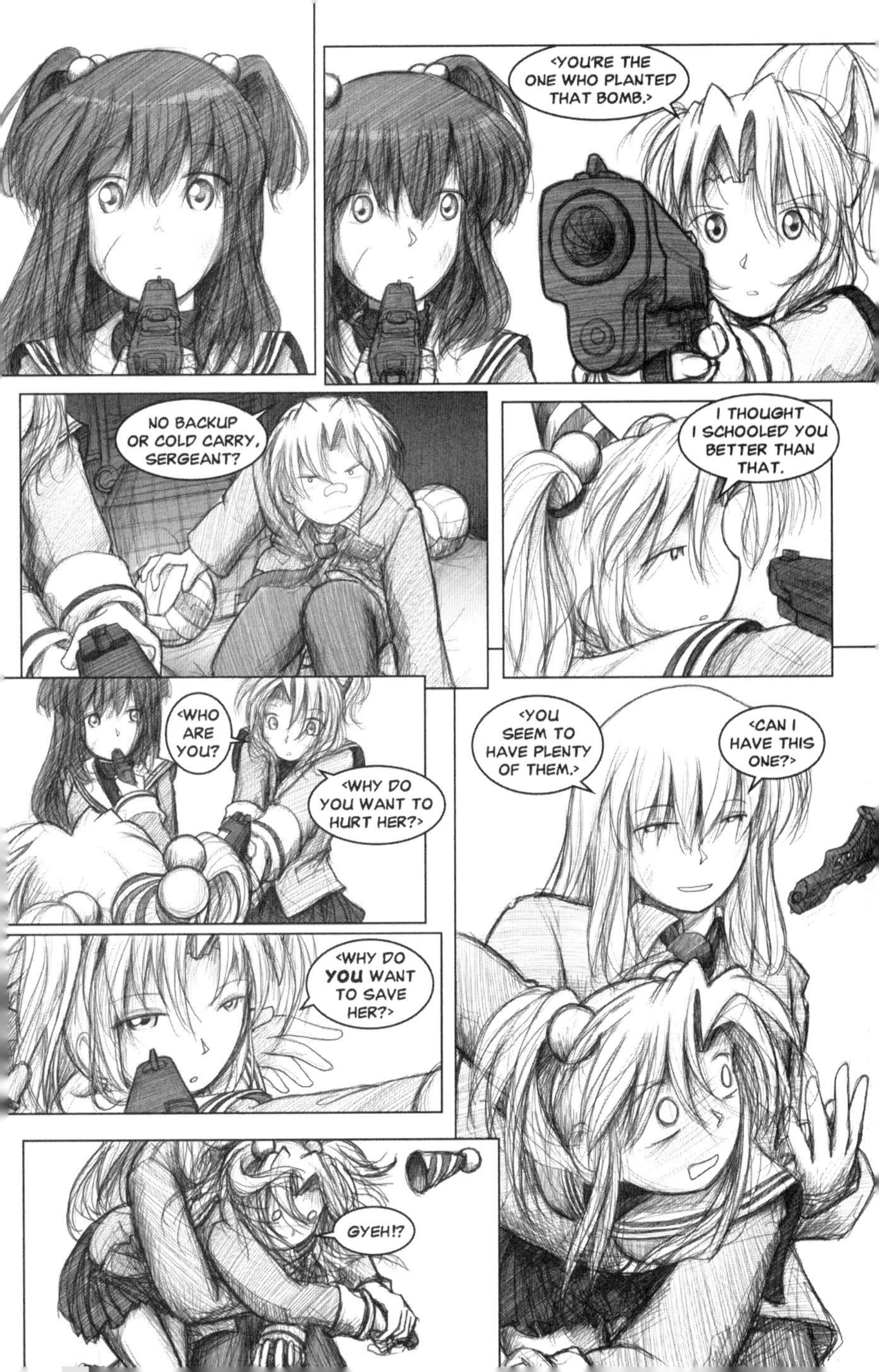
<YOU'RE THE ONE WHO PLANTED THAT BOMB.>
NO BACKUP OR COLD CARRY, SERGEANT?
I THOUGHT I SCHOOLED YOU BETTER THAN THAT.
<WHO ARE YOU?
<WHY DO YOU WANT TO HURT HER?>
<WHY DO **YOU** WANT TO SAVE HER?>
GYEH!?
<YOU SEEM TO HAVE PLENTY OF THEM.>
<CAN I HAVE THIS ONE?>

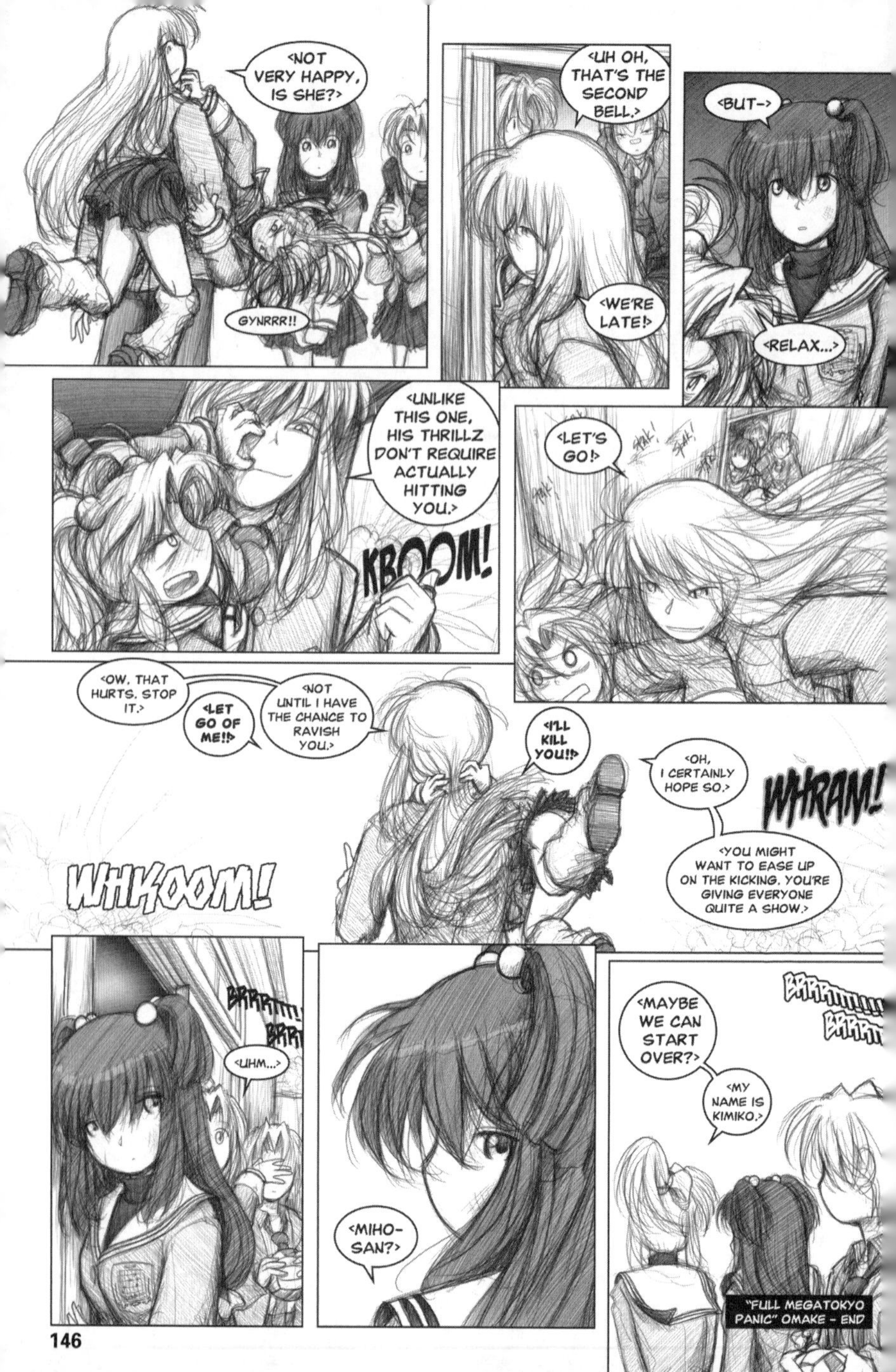
<NOT VERY HAPPY, IS SHE?>
GYNRRR!!
<UH OH, THAT'S THE SECOND BELL.>
<WE'RE LATE!>
<BUT->
<RELAX...>
<UNLIKE THIS ONE, HIS THRILLZ DON'T REQUIRE ACTUALLY HITTING YOU.>
KBOOM!
<LET'S GO!>
<OW. THAT HURTS. STOP IT.>
<NOT UNTIL I HAVE THE CHANCE TO RAVISH YOU.>
<LET GO OF ME!!>
<I'LL KILL YOU!!>
<OH, I CERTAINLY HOPE SO.>
WHRAM!
<YOU MIGHT WANT TO EASE UP ON THE KICKING. YOU'RE GIVING EVERYONE QUITE A SHOW.>
WHKOOM!
<UHM...>
<MIHO-SAN?>
<MAYBE WE CAN START OVER?>
<MY NAME IS KIMIKO.>
"FULL MEGATOKYO PANIC" OMAKE - END

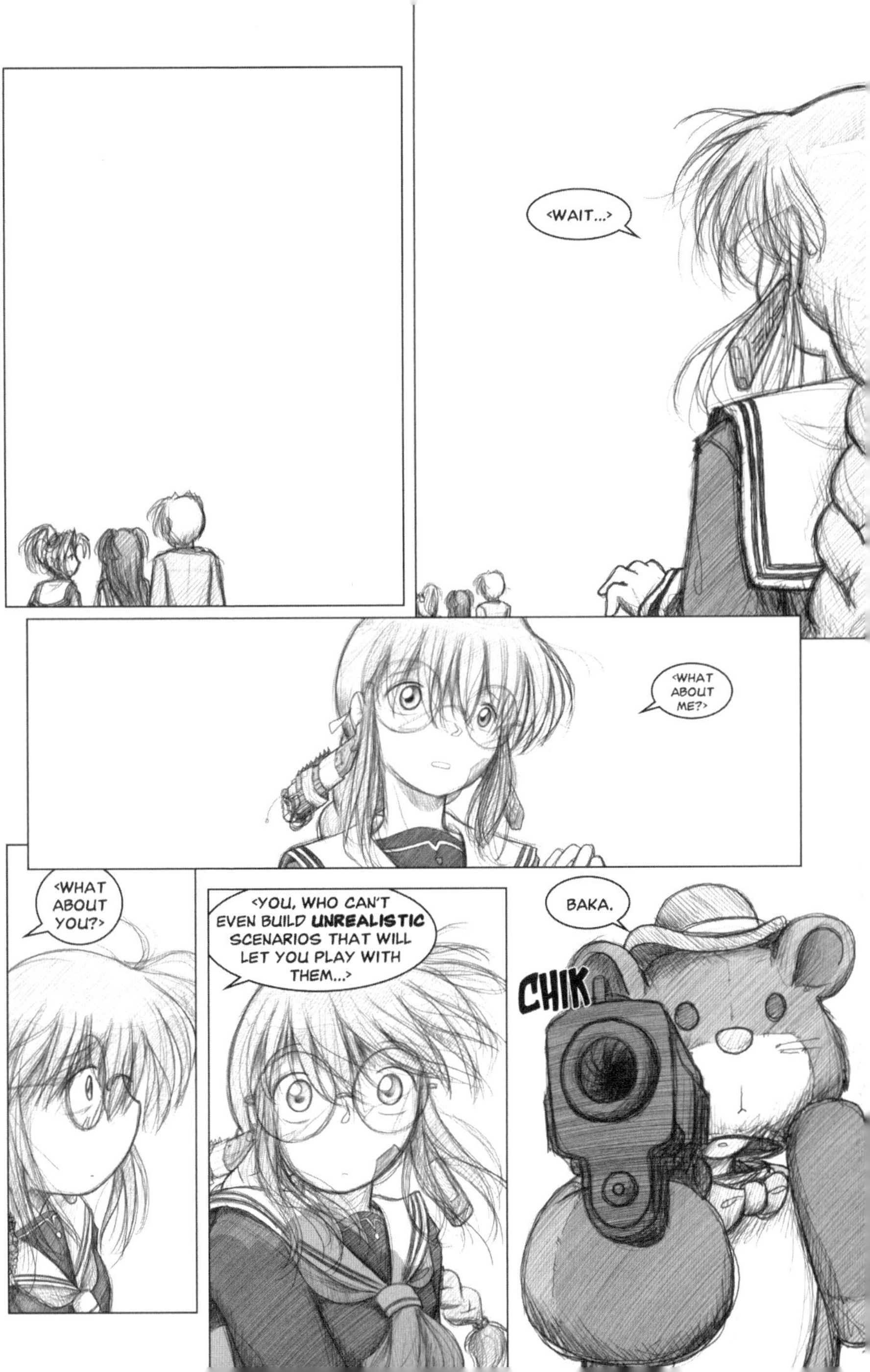

<WAIT...>
<WHAT ABOUT ME?>
<WHAT ABOUT YOU?>
<YOU, WHO CAN'T EVEN BUILD **UNREALISTIC** SCENARIOS THAT WILL LET YOU PLAY WITH THEM...>
BAKA.
CHIK

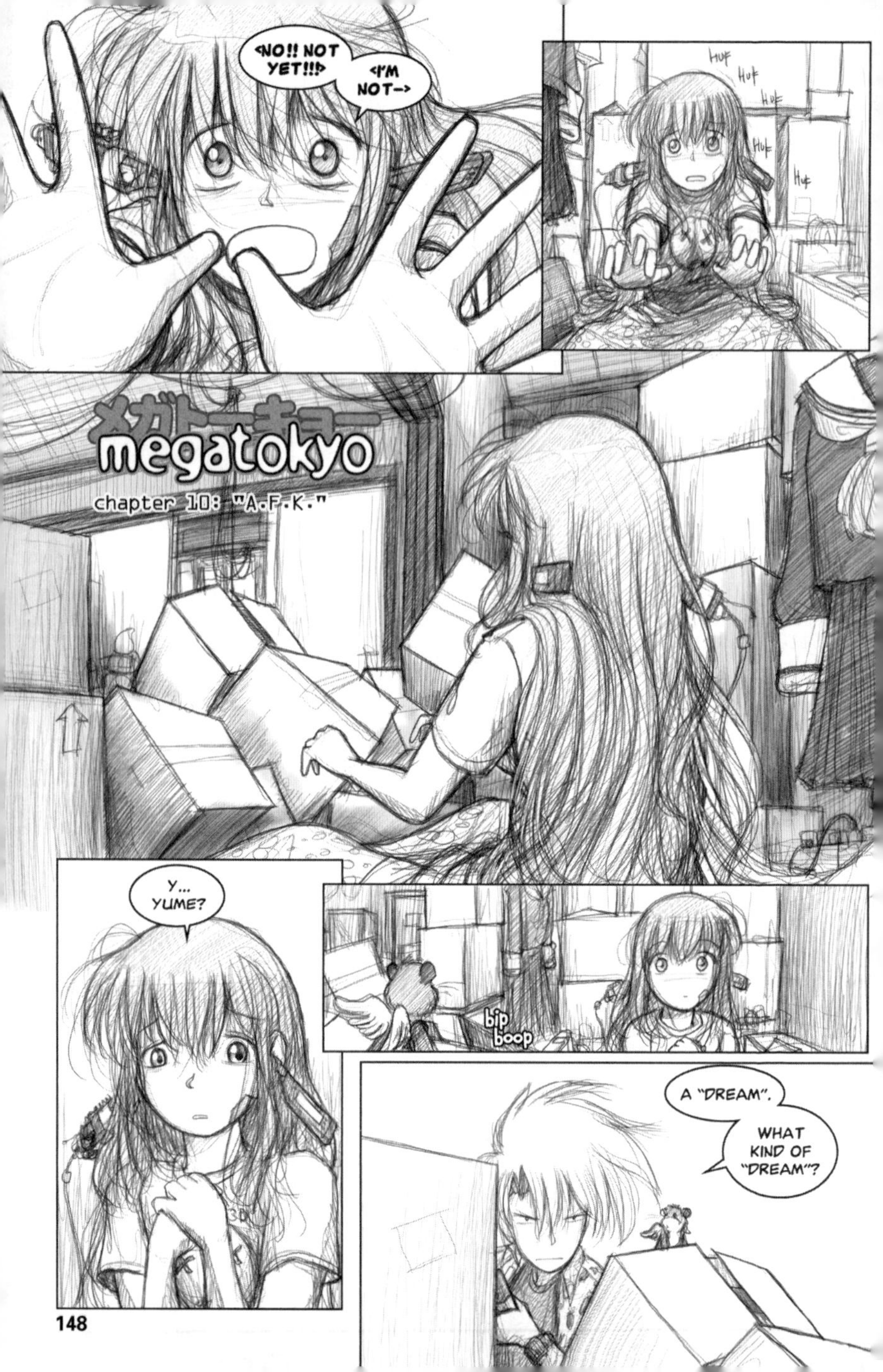
<NO!! NOT YET!!!>
<I'M NOT-->
HUF
HUF
HUF
HUF
HUF
メガトーキョー
megatokyo
chapter 10: "A.F.K."
Y... YUME?
bip
boop
A "DREAM".
WHAT KIND OF "DREAM"?

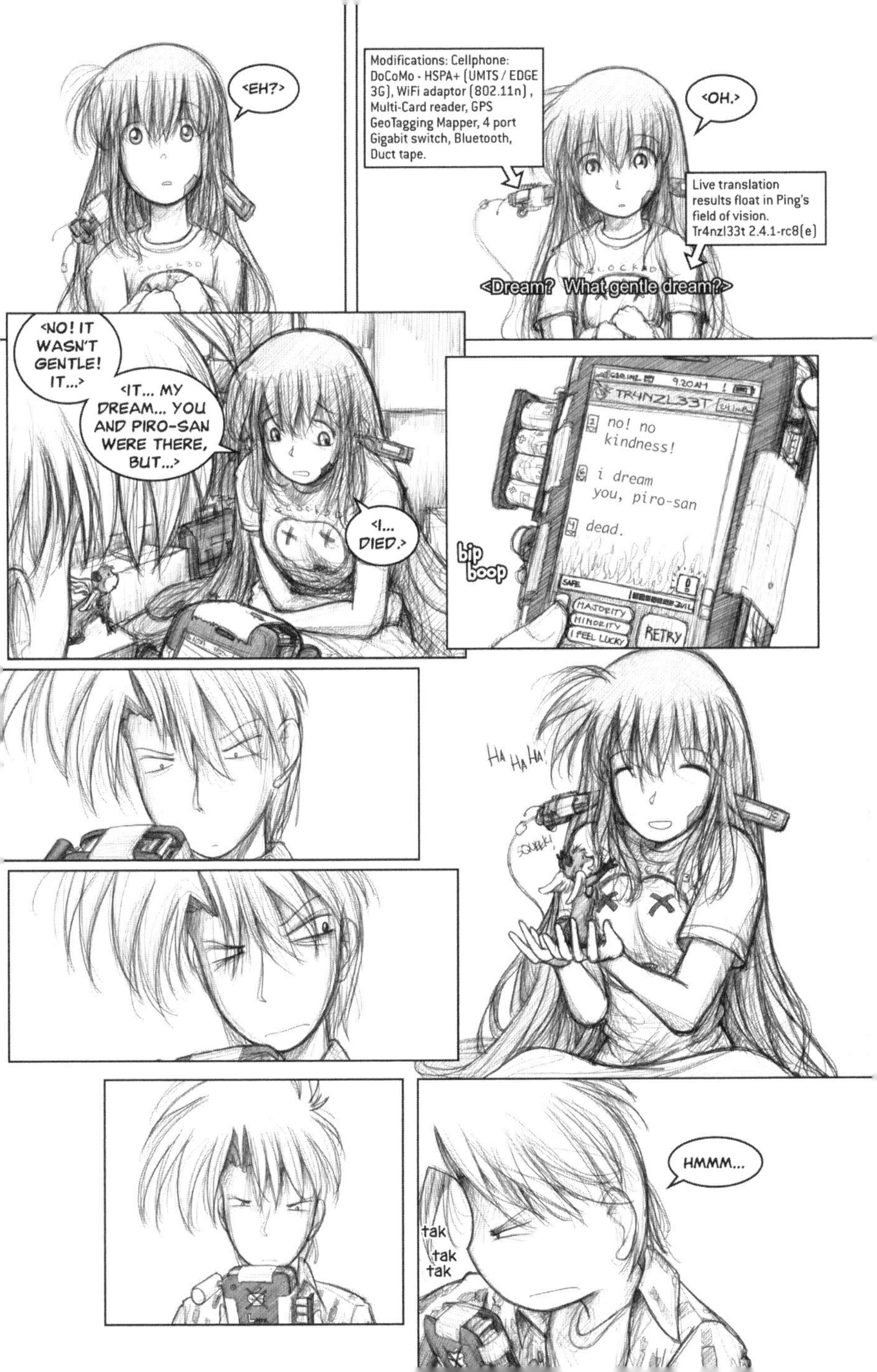
<EH?>
Modifications: Cellphone: DoCoMo - HSPA+ (UMTS / EDGE 3G), WiFi adaptor (802.11n), Multi-Card reader, GPS GeoTagging Mapper, 4 port Gigabit switch, Bluetooth, Duct tape.
<OH.>
Live translation results float in Ping's field of vision. Tr4nzl33t 2.4.1-rc8(e)
<Dream? What gentle dream?>
<NO! IT WASN'T GENTLE! IT...>
<IT... MY DREAM... YOU AND PIRO-SAN WERE THERE, BUT...>
<I... DIED.>
TR4NZL33T
no! no kindness!
i dream you, piro-san
dead.
MAJORITY
MINORITY
I FEEL LUCKY
RETRY
bip boop
HA HA HA
HMMM...
tak tak tak

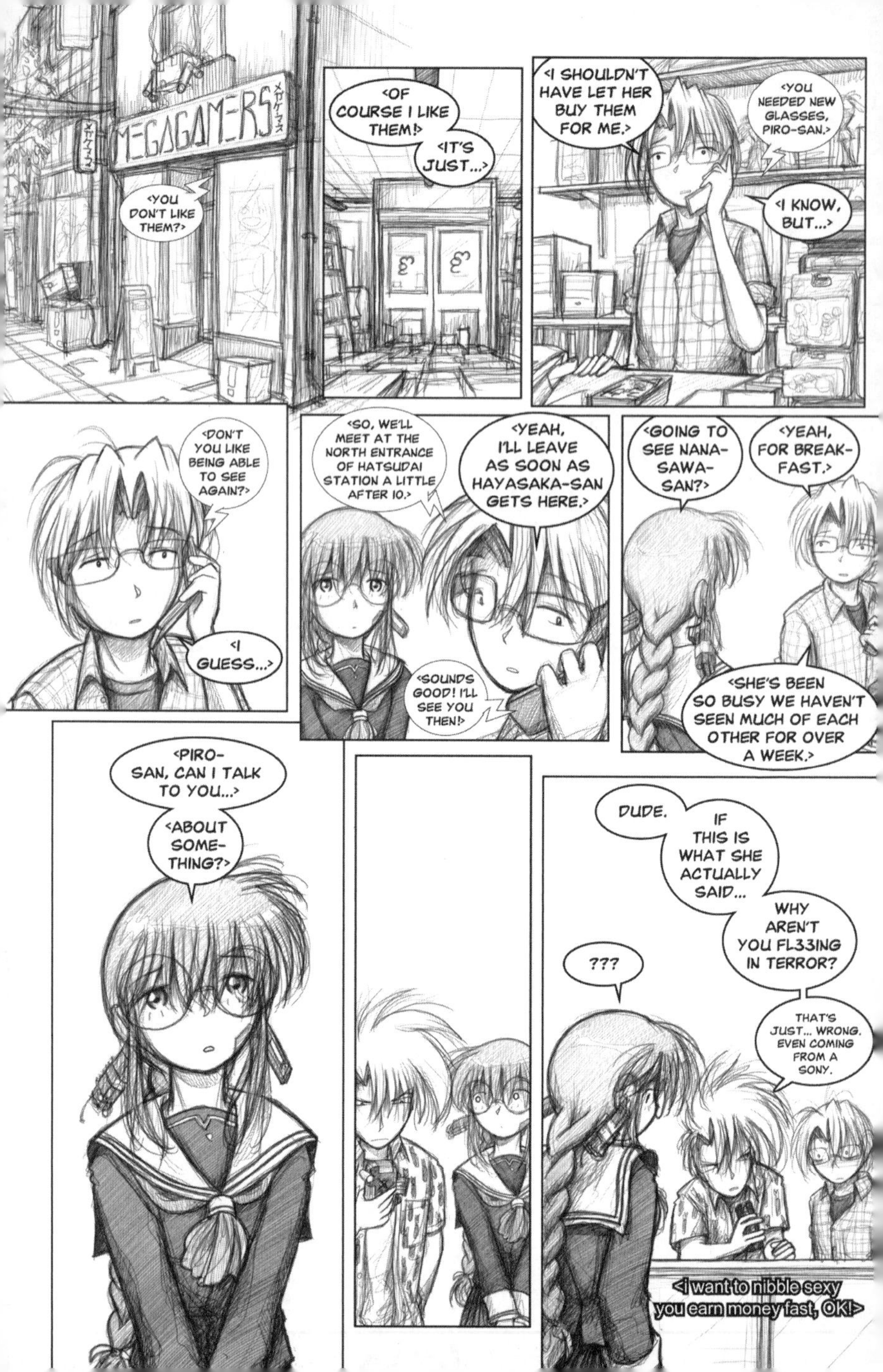
MEGAGAMERS
<YOU DON'T LIKE THEM?>
<OF COURSE I LIKE THEM!>
<IT'S JUST...>
<I SHOULDN'T HAVE LET HER BUY THEM FOR ME.>
<YOU NEEDED NEW GLASSES, PIRO-SAN.>
<I KNOW, BUT...>
<DON'T YOU LIKE BEING ABLE TO SEE AGAIN?>
<I GUESS...>
<SO, WE'LL MEET AT THE NORTH ENTRANCE OF HATSUDAI STATION A LITTLE AFTER 10.>
<YEAH, I'LL LEAVE AS SOON AS HAYASAKA-SAN GETS HERE.>
<SOUNDS GOOD! I'LL SEE YOU THEN!>
<GOING TO SEE NANA-SAWA-SAN?>
<YEAH, FOR BREAK-FAST.>
<SHE'S BEEN SO BUSY WE HAVEN'T SEEN MUCH OF EACH OTHER FOR OVER A WEEK.>
<PIRO-SAN, CAN I TALK TO YOU...>
<ABOUT SOME-THING?>
DUDE.
IF THIS IS WHAT SHE ACTUALLY SAID...
WHY AREN'T YOU FL33ING IN TERROR?
???
THAT'S JUST... WRONG. EVEN COMING FROM A SONY.
<i want to nibble sexy you earn money fast, OK!>

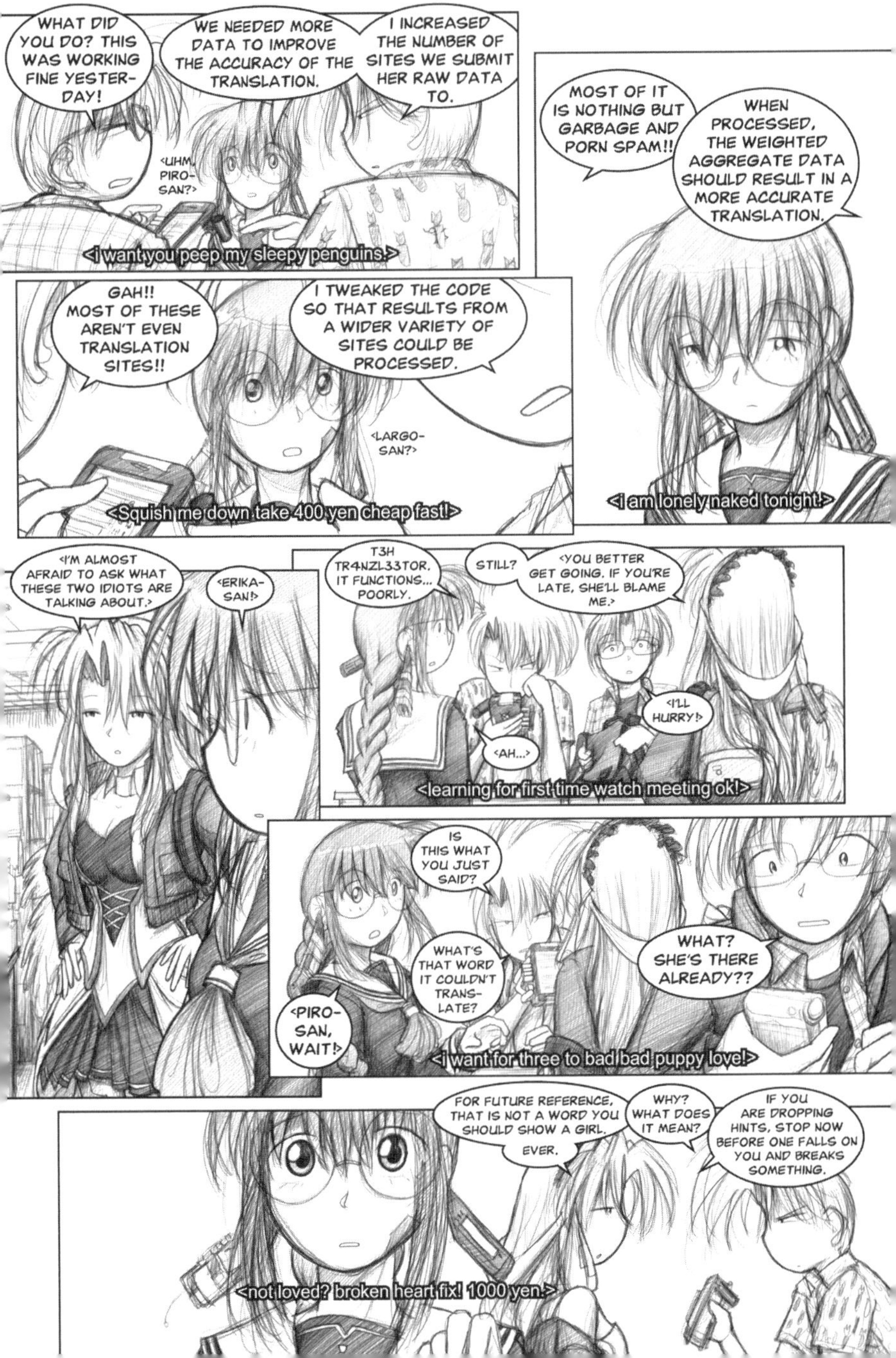
WHAT DID YOU DO? THIS WAS WORKING FINE YESTER-DAY!
WE NEEDED MORE DATA TO IMPROVE THE ACCURACY OF THE TRANSLATION.
I INCREASED THE NUMBER OF SITES WE SUBMIT HER RAW DATA TO.
<UHM, PIRO-SAN?>
<i want you peep my sleepy penguins.>
GAH!! MOST OF THESE AREN'T EVEN TRANSLATION SITES!!
I TWEAKED THE CODE SO THAT RESULTS FROM A WIDER VARIETY OF SITES COULD BE PROCESSED.
<LARGO-SAN?>
<Squish me down take 400 yen cheap fast!>
MOST OF IT IS NOTHING BUT GARBAGE AND PORN SPAM!!
WHEN PROCESSED, THE WEIGHTED AGGREGATE DATA SHOULD RESULT IN A MORE ACCURATE TRANSLATION.
<i am lonely naked tonight.>
<I'M ALMOST AFRAID TO ASK WHAT THESE TWO IDIOTS ARE TALKING ABOUT.>
<ERIKA-SAN!>
T3H TR4NZL33TOR. IT FUNCTIONS... POORLY.
STILL?
<YOU BETTER GET GOING. IF YOU'RE LATE, SHE'LL BLAME ME.>
<I'LL HURRY!>
<AH...>
<learning for first time watch meeting ok!>
IS THIS WHAT YOU JUST SAID?
WHAT'S THAT WORD IT COULDN'T TRANS-LATE?
WHAT? SHE'S THERE ALREADY??
<PIRO-SAN, WAIT!>
<i want for three to bad bad puppy love!>
FOR FUTURE REFERENCE, THAT IS NOT A WORD YOU SHOULD SHOW A GIRL.
EVER.
WHY? WHAT DOES IT MEAN?
IF YOU ARE DROPPING HINTS, STOP NOW BEFORE ONE FALLS ON YOU AND BREAKS SOMETHING.
<not loved? broken heart fix! 1000 yen.>

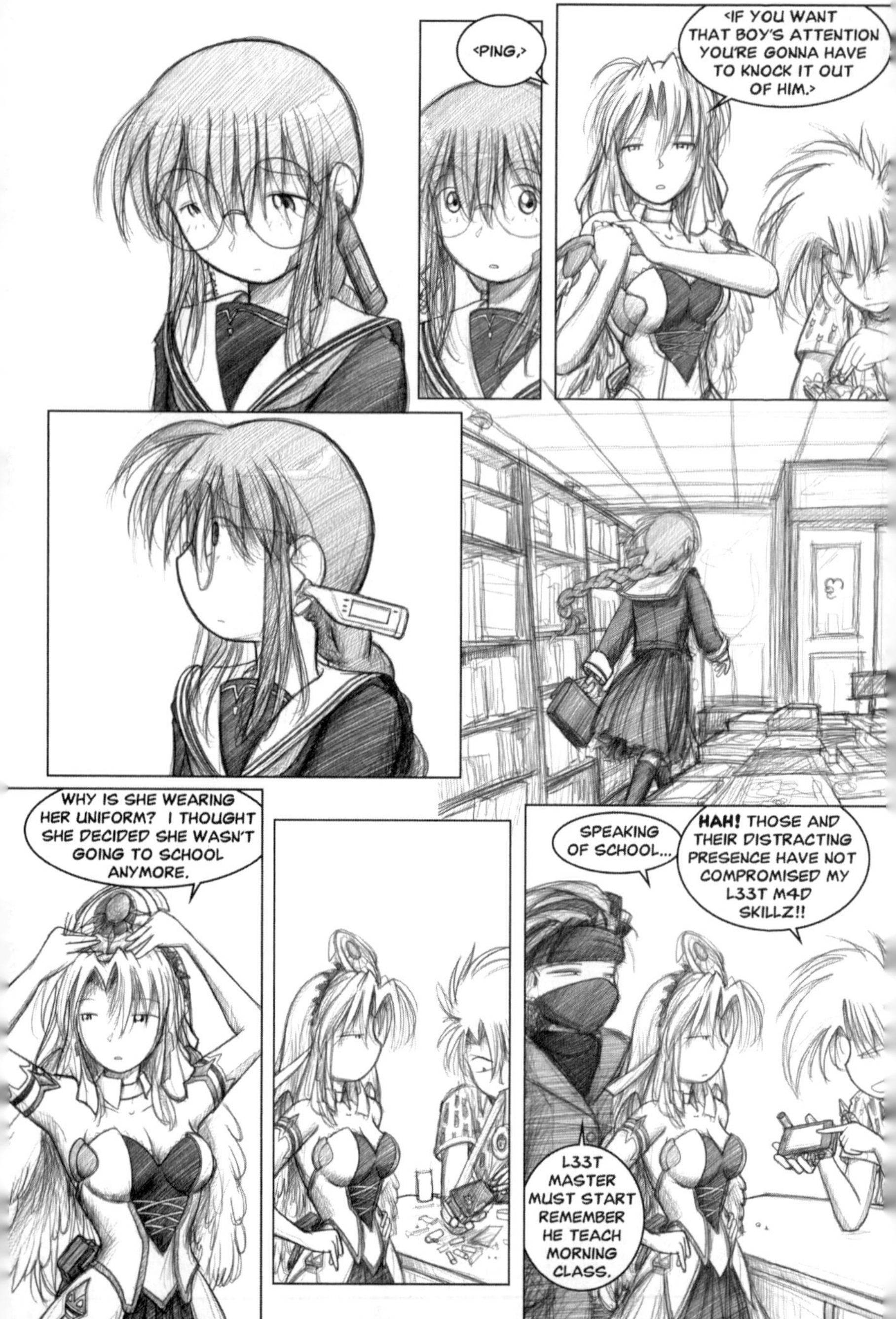
<PING,>
<IF YOU WANT THAT BOY'S ATTENTION YOU'RE GONNA HAVE TO KNOCK IT OUT OF HIM.>
WHY IS SHE WEARING HER UNIFORM? I THOUGHT SHE DECIDED SHE WASN'T GOING TO SCHOOL ANYMORE.
SPEAKING OF SCHOOL...
HAH! THOSE AND THEIR DISTRACTING PRESENCE HAVE NOT COMPROMISED MY L33T M4D SKILLZ!!
L33T MASTER MUST START REMEMBER HE TEACH MORNING CLASS.

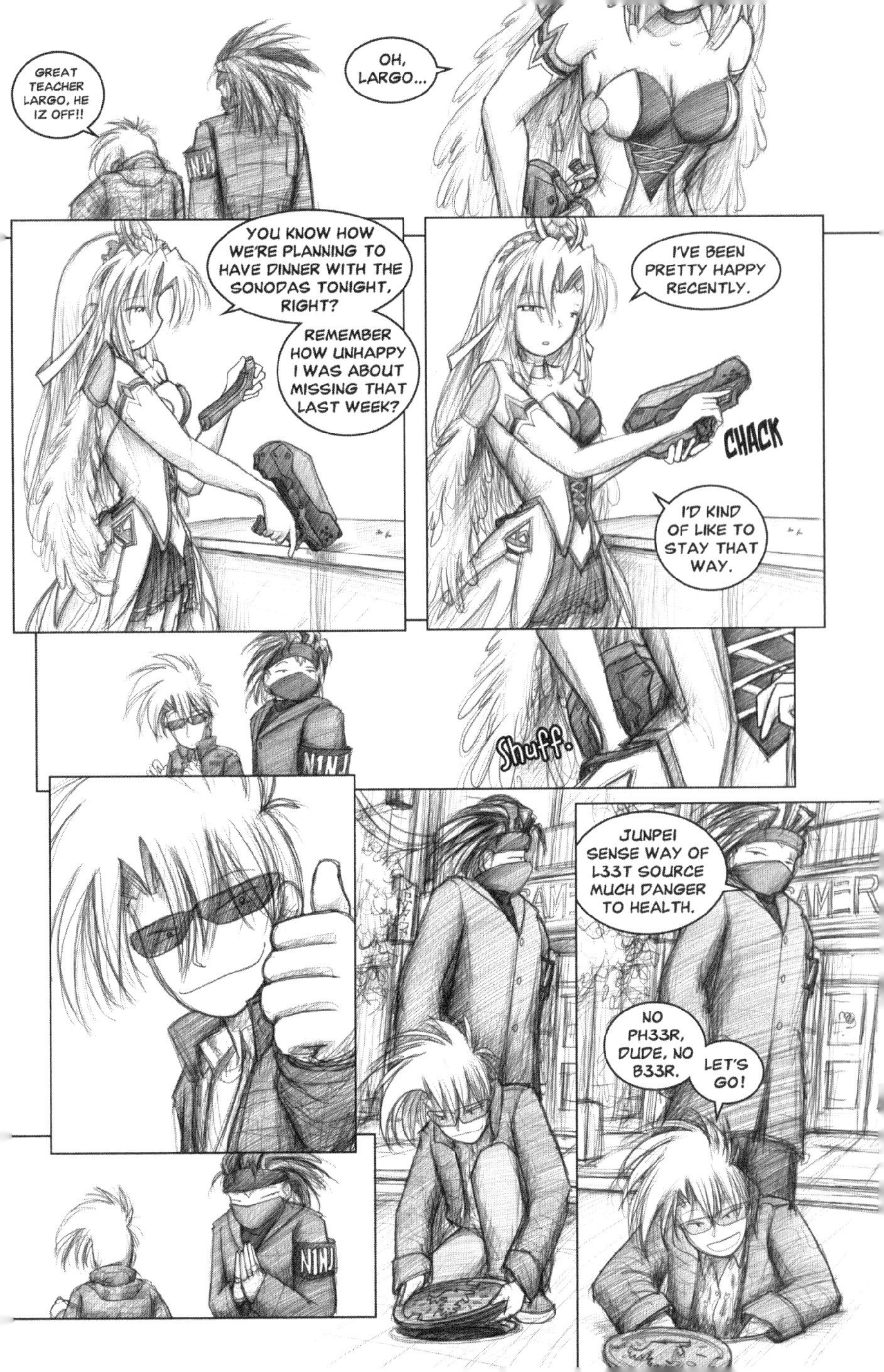
GREAT TEACHER LARGO, HE IZ OFF!!
OH, LARGO...
YOU KNOW HOW WE'RE PLANNING TO HAVE DINNER WITH THE SONODAS TONIGHT, RIGHT?
REMEMBER HOW UNHAPPY I WAS ABOUT MISSING THAT LAST WEEK?
I'VE BEEN PRETTY HAPPY RECENTLY.
CHACK
I'D KIND OF LIKE TO STAY THAT WAY.
Shuff.
JUNPEI SENSE WAY OF L33T SOURCE MUCH DANGER TO HEALTH.
NO PH33R, DUDE, NO B33R.
LET'S GO!

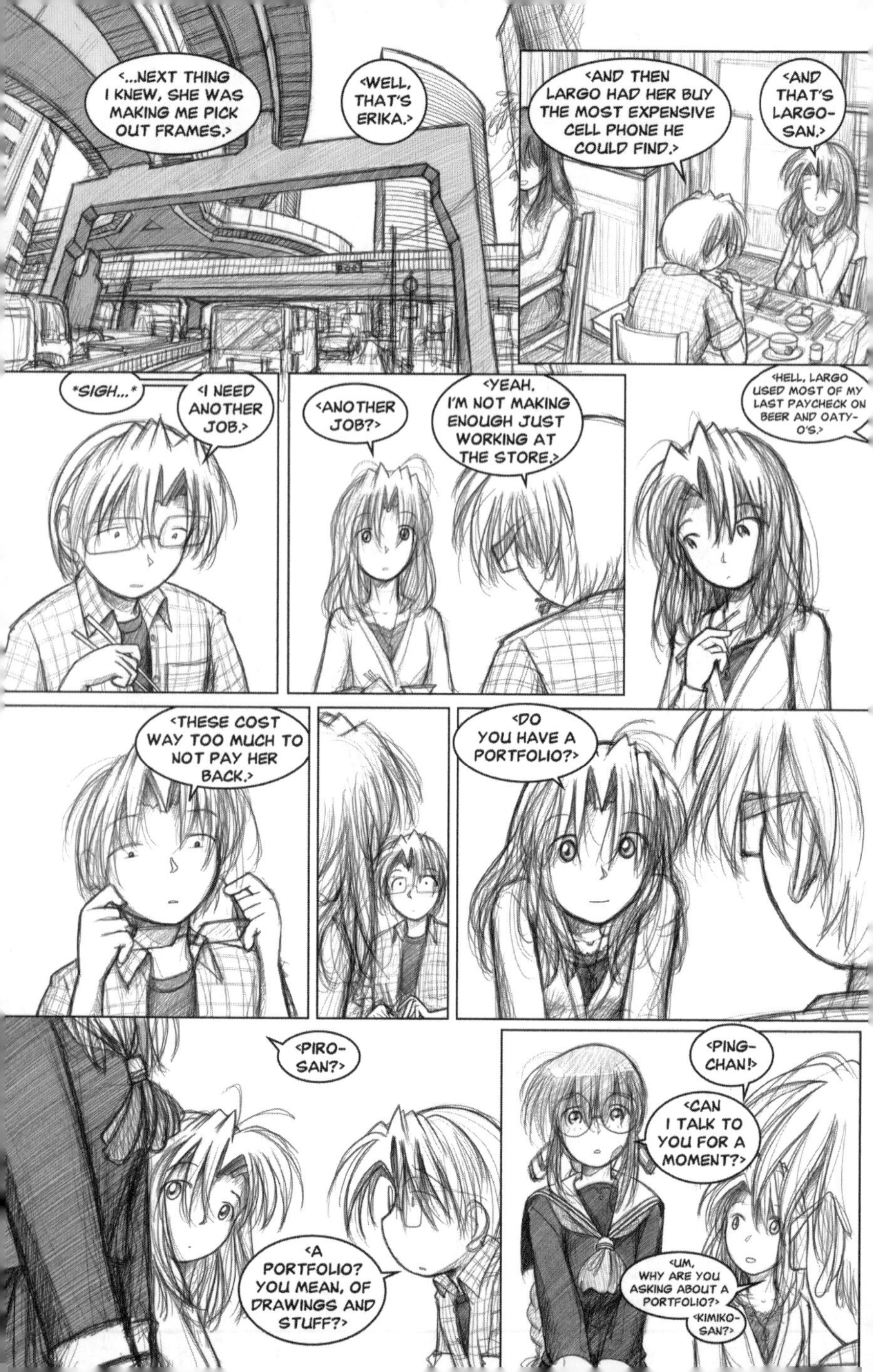
<...NEXT THING I KNEW, SHE WAS MAKING ME PICK OUT FRAMES.>
<WELL, THAT'S ERIKA.>
<AND THEN LARGO HAD HER BUY THE MOST EXPENSIVE CELL PHONE HE COULD FIND.>
<AND THAT'S LARGO-SAN.>
SIGH...
<I NEED ANOTHER JOB.>
<ANOTHER JOB?>
<YEAH. I'M NOT MAKING ENOUGH JUST WORKING AT THE STORE.>
<HELL, LARGO USED MOST OF MY LAST PAYCHECK ON BEER AND OATY-O'S.>
<THESE COST WAY TOO MUCH TO NOT PAY HER BACK.>
<DO YOU HAVE A PORTFOLIO?>
<PIRO-SAN?>
<A PORTFOLIO? YOU MEAN, OF DRAWINGS AND STUFF?>
<PING-CHAN!>
<CAN I TALK TO YOU FOR A MOMENT?>
<UM, WHY ARE YOU ASKING ABOUT A PORTFOLIO?>
<KIMIKO-SAN?>

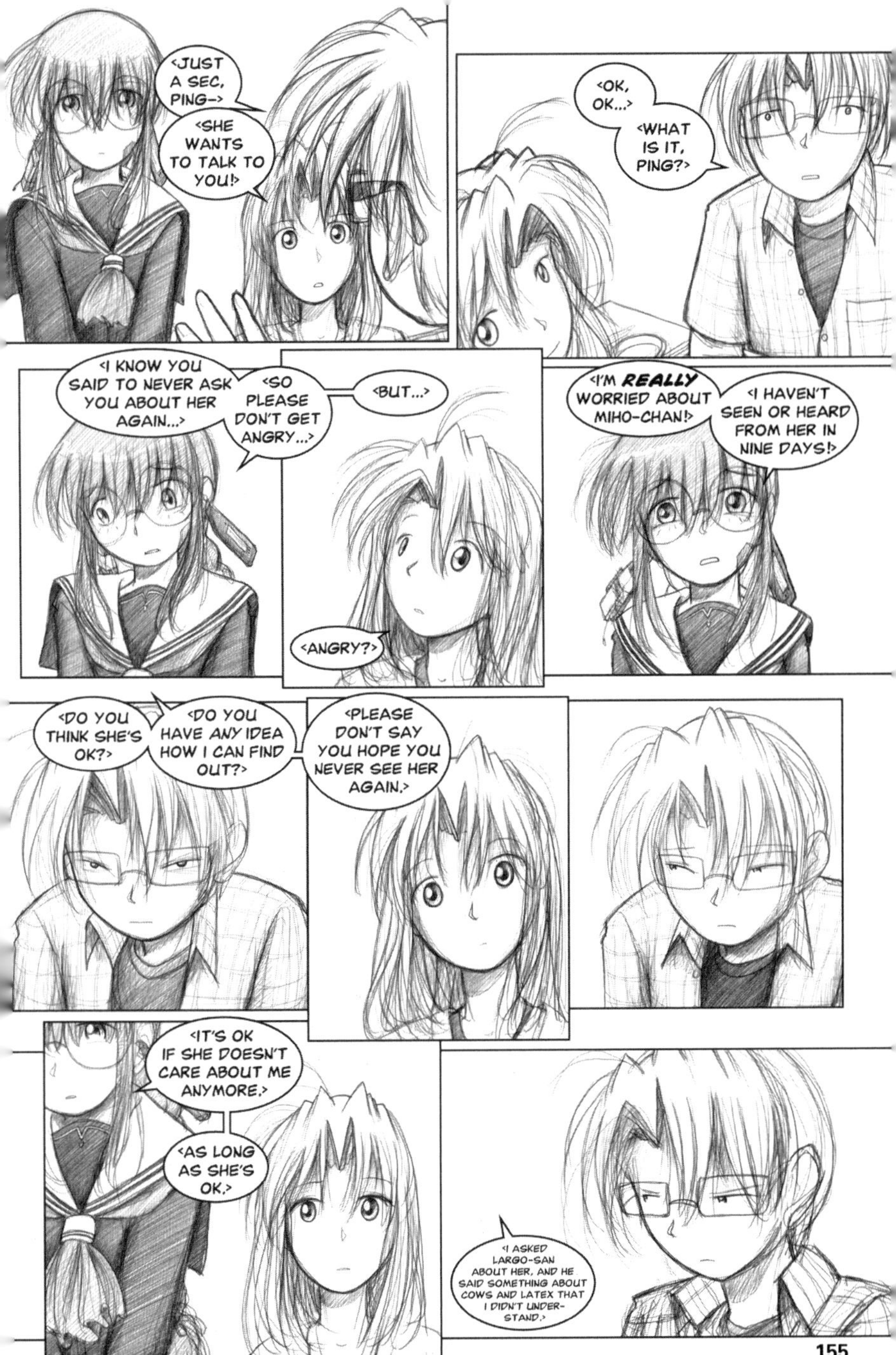
<JUST A SEC, PING–>
<SHE WANTS TO TALK TO YOU!>
<OK, OK...>
<WHAT IS IT, PING?>
<I KNOW YOU SAID TO NEVER ASK YOU ABOUT HER AGAIN...>
<SO PLEASE DON'T GET ANGRY...>
<BUT...>
<ANGRY?>
<I'M **REALLY** WORRIED ABOUT MIHO-CHAN!>
<I HAVEN'T SEEN OR HEARD FROM HER IN NINE DAYS!>
<DO YOU THINK SHE'S OK?>
<DO YOU HAVE *ANY* IDEA HOW I CAN FIND OUT?>
<PLEASE DON'T SAY YOU HOPE YOU NEVER SEE HER AGAIN.>
<IT'S OK IF SHE DOESN'T CARE ABOUT ME ANYMORE.>
<AS LONG AS SHE'S OK.>
<I ASKED LARGO-SAN ABOUT HER, AND HE SAID SOMETHING ABOUT COWS AND LATEX THAT I DIDN'T UNDER-STAND.>

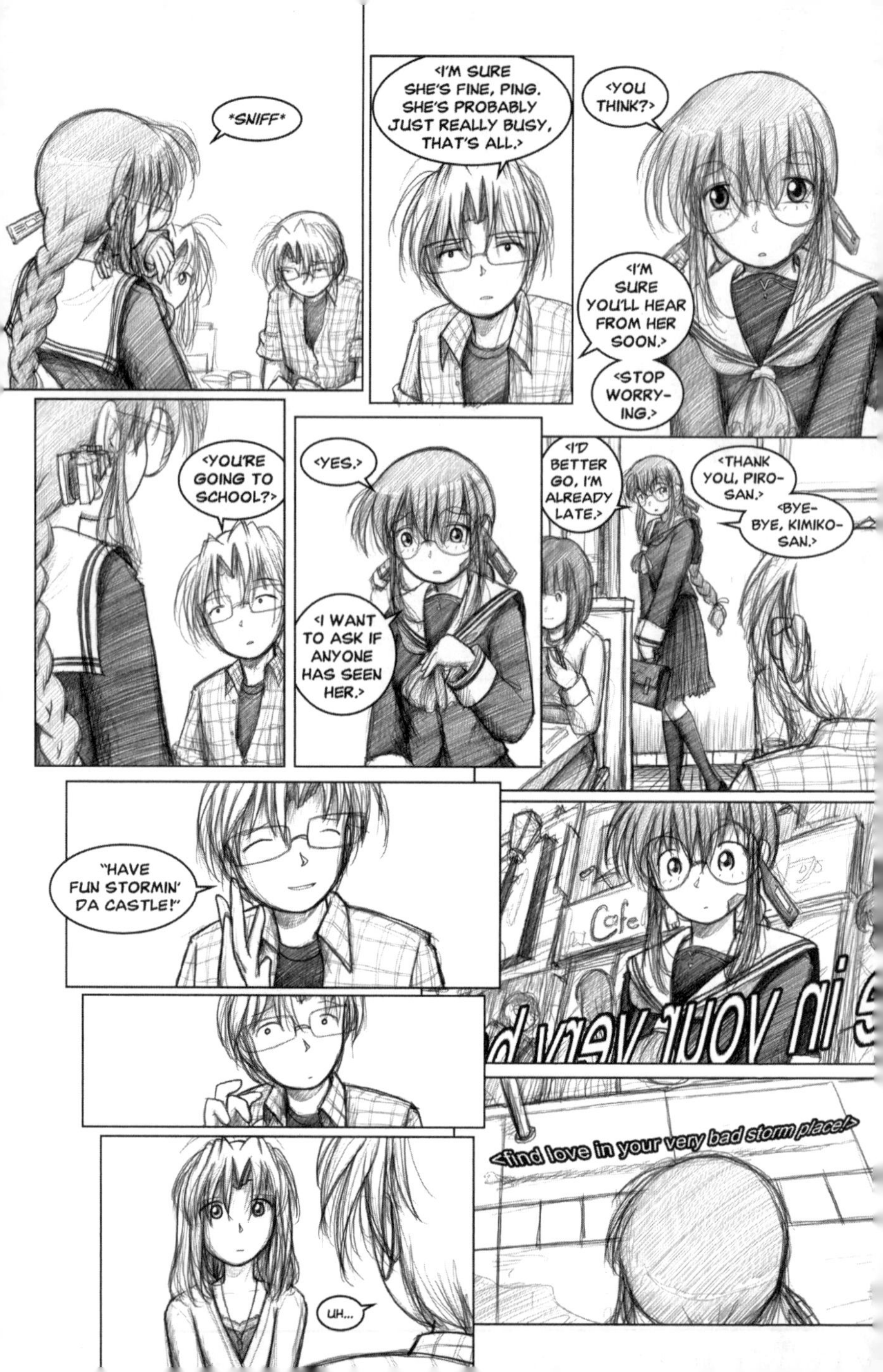
SNIFF
<I'M SURE SHE'S FINE, PING. SHE'S PROBABLY JUST REALLY BUSY, THAT'S ALL.>
<YOU THINK?>
<I'M SURE YOU'LL HEAR FROM HER SOON.>
<STOP WORRY-ING.>
<YOU'RE GOING TO SCHOOL?>
<YES.>
<I WANT TO ASK IF ANYONE HAS SEEN HER.>
<I'D BETTER GO, I'M ALREADY LATE.>
<THANK YOU, PIRO-SAN.>
<BYE-BYE, KIMIKO-SAN.>
"HAVE FUN STORMIN' DA CASTLE!"
UH...
Cafe
<find love in your very bad storm place!>

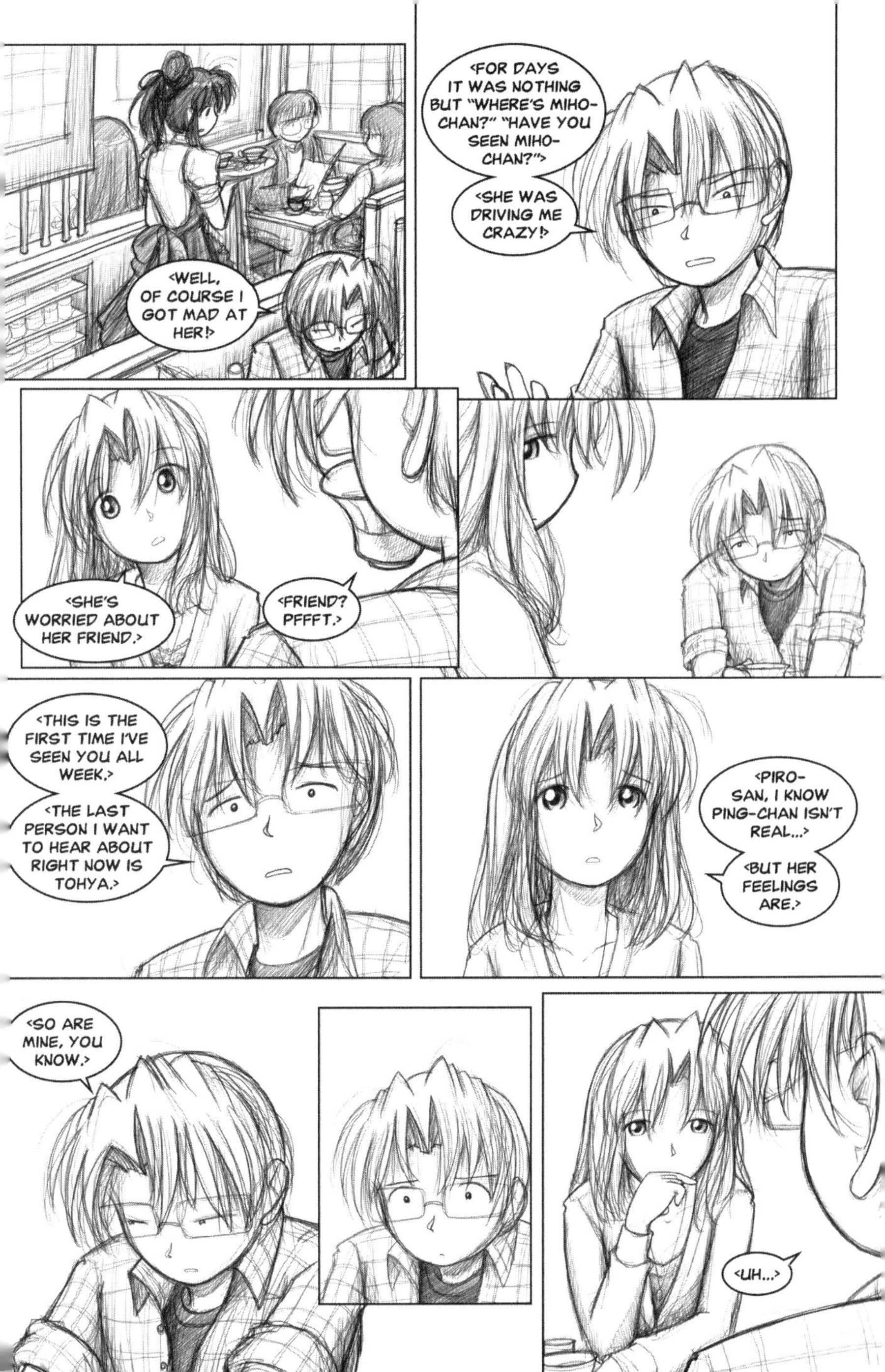
<WELL, OF COURSE I GOT MAD AT HER!>
<FOR DAYS IT WAS NOTHING BUT "WHERE'S MIHO-CHAN?" "HAVE YOU SEEN MIHO-CHAN?">
<SHE WAS DRIVING ME CRAZY!>
<SHE'S WORRIED ABOUT HER FRIEND.>
<FRIEND? PFFFT.>
<THIS IS THE FIRST TIME I'VE SEEN YOU ALL WEEK.>
<THE LAST PERSON I WANT TO HEAR ABOUT RIGHT NOW IS TOHYA.>
<PIRO-SAN, I KNOW PING-CHAN ISN'T REAL...>
<BUT HER FEELINGS ARE.>
<SO ARE MINE, YOU KNOW.>
<UH...>

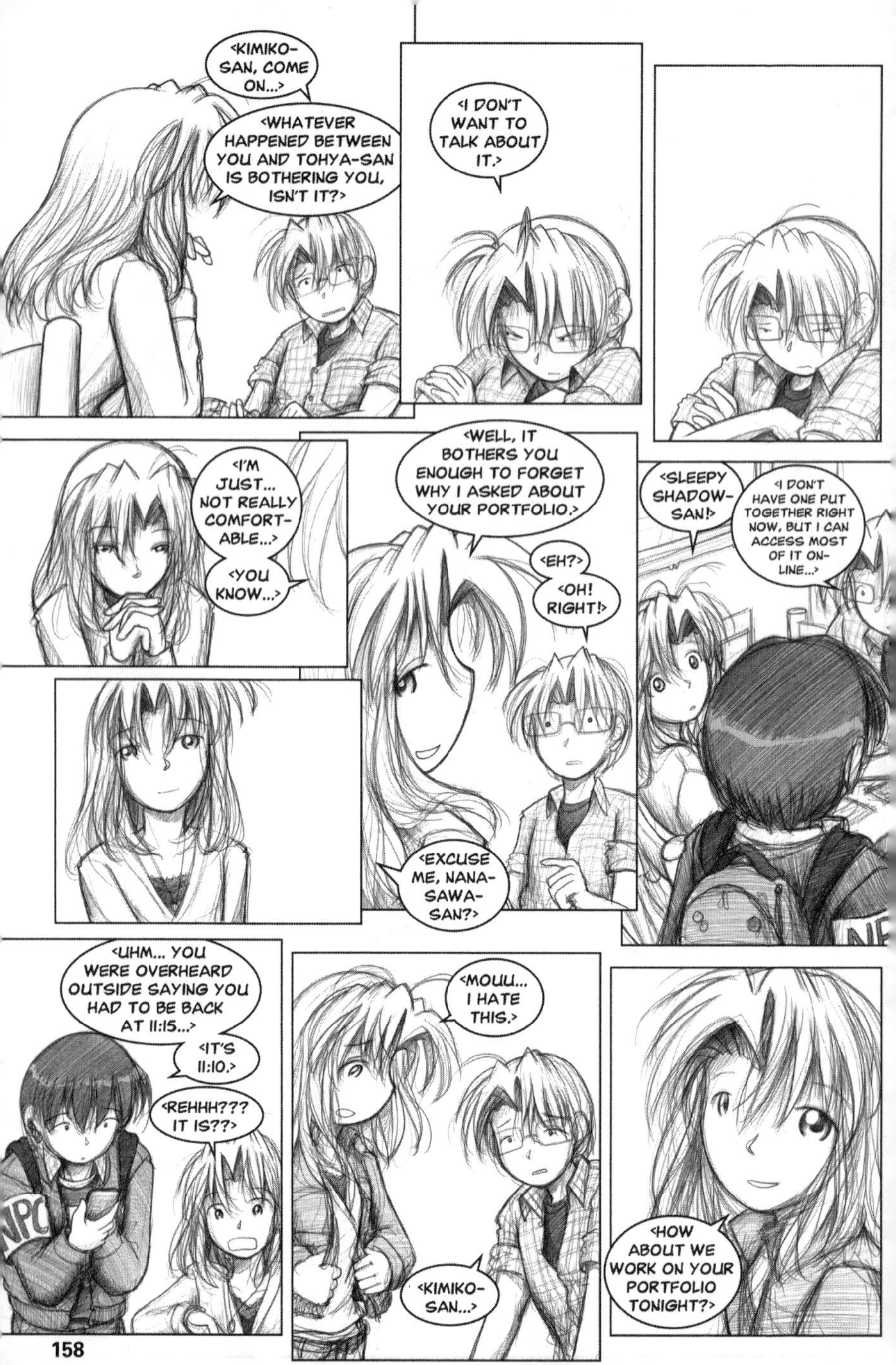
<KIMIKO-SAN, COME ON...>
<WHATEVER HAPPENED BETWEEN YOU AND TOHYA-SAN IS BOTHERING YOU, ISN'T IT?>
<I DON'T WANT TO TALK ABOUT IT.>
<I'M JUST... NOT REALLY COMFORT-ABLE...>
<YOU KNOW...>
<WELL, IT BOTHERS YOU ENOUGH TO FORGET WHY I ASKED ABOUT YOUR PORTFOLIO.>
<EH?>
<OH! RIGHT!>
<EXCUSE ME, NANA-SAWA-SAN?>
<SLEEPY SHADOW-SAN!>
<I DON'T HAVE ONE PUT TOGETHER RIGHT NOW, BUT I CAN ACCESS MOST OF IT ON-LINE...>
<UHM... YOU WERE OVERHEARD OUTSIDE SAYING YOU HAD TO BE BACK AT 11:15...>
<IT'S 11:10.>
<REHHH??? IT IS??>
<MOUU... I HATE THIS.>
<KIMIKO-SAN...>
<HOW ABOUT WE WORK ON YOUR PORTFOLIO TONIGHT?>

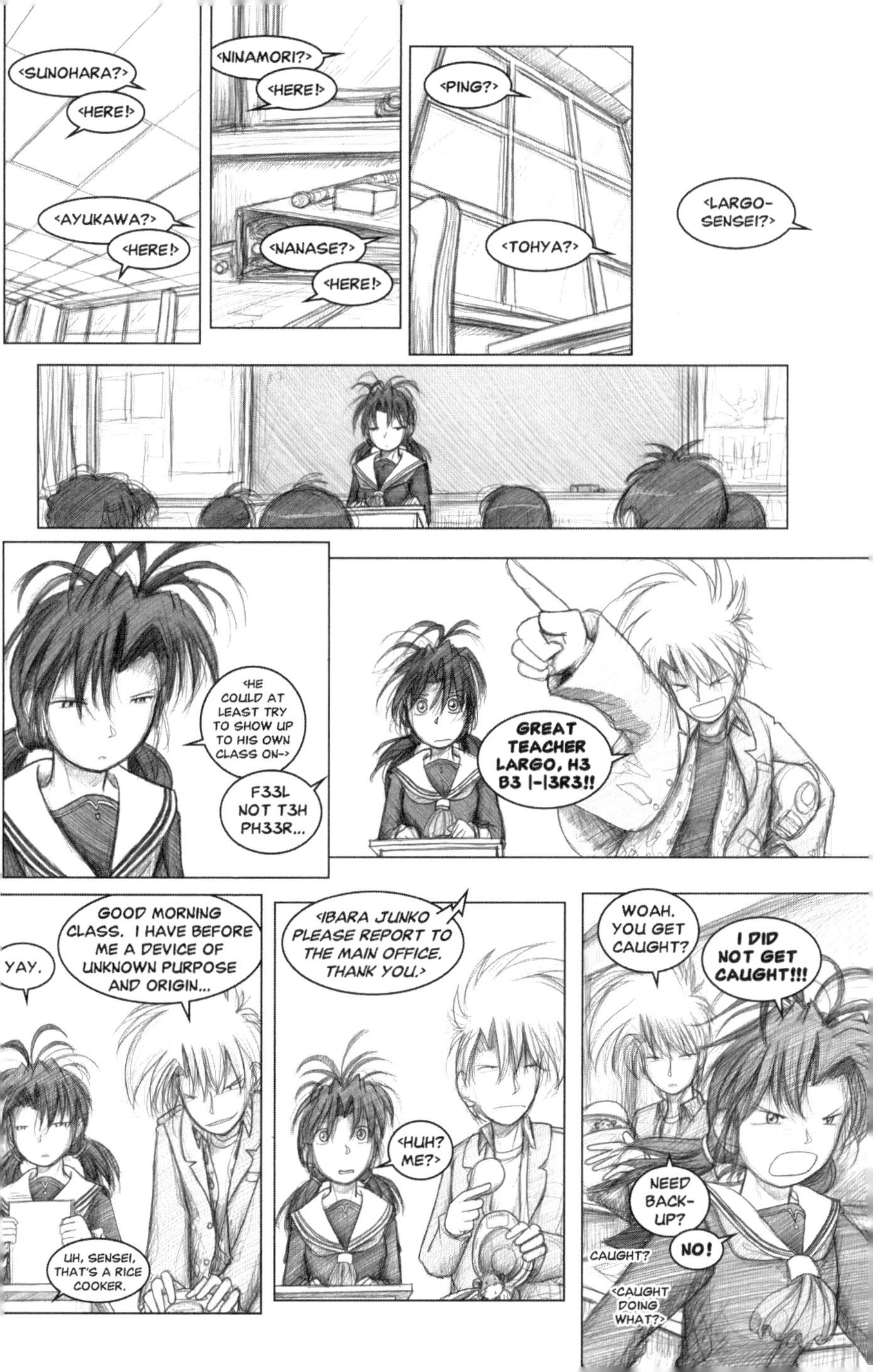
<SUNOHARA?>
<HERE!>
<AYUKAWA?>
<HERE!>
<NINAMORI?>
<HERE!>
<NANASE?>
<HERE!>
<PING?>
<TOHYA?>
<LARGO-SENSEI?>
<HE COULD AT LEAST TRY TO SHOW UP TO HIS OWN CLASS ON->
F33L NOT T3H PH33R...
GREAT TEACHER LARGO, H3 B3 |-|3R3!!
GOOD MORNING CLASS. I HAVE BEFORE ME A DEVICE OF UNKNOWN PURPOSE AND ORIGIN...
YAY.
UH, SENSEI, THAT'S A RICE COOKER.
<IBARA JUNKO PLEASE REPORT TO THE MAIN OFFICE. THANK YOU.>
<HUH? ME?>
WOAH. YOU GET CAUGHT?
I DID NOT GET CAUGHT!!!
NEED BACK-UP?
NO!
CAUGHT?
<CAUGHT DOING WHAT?>

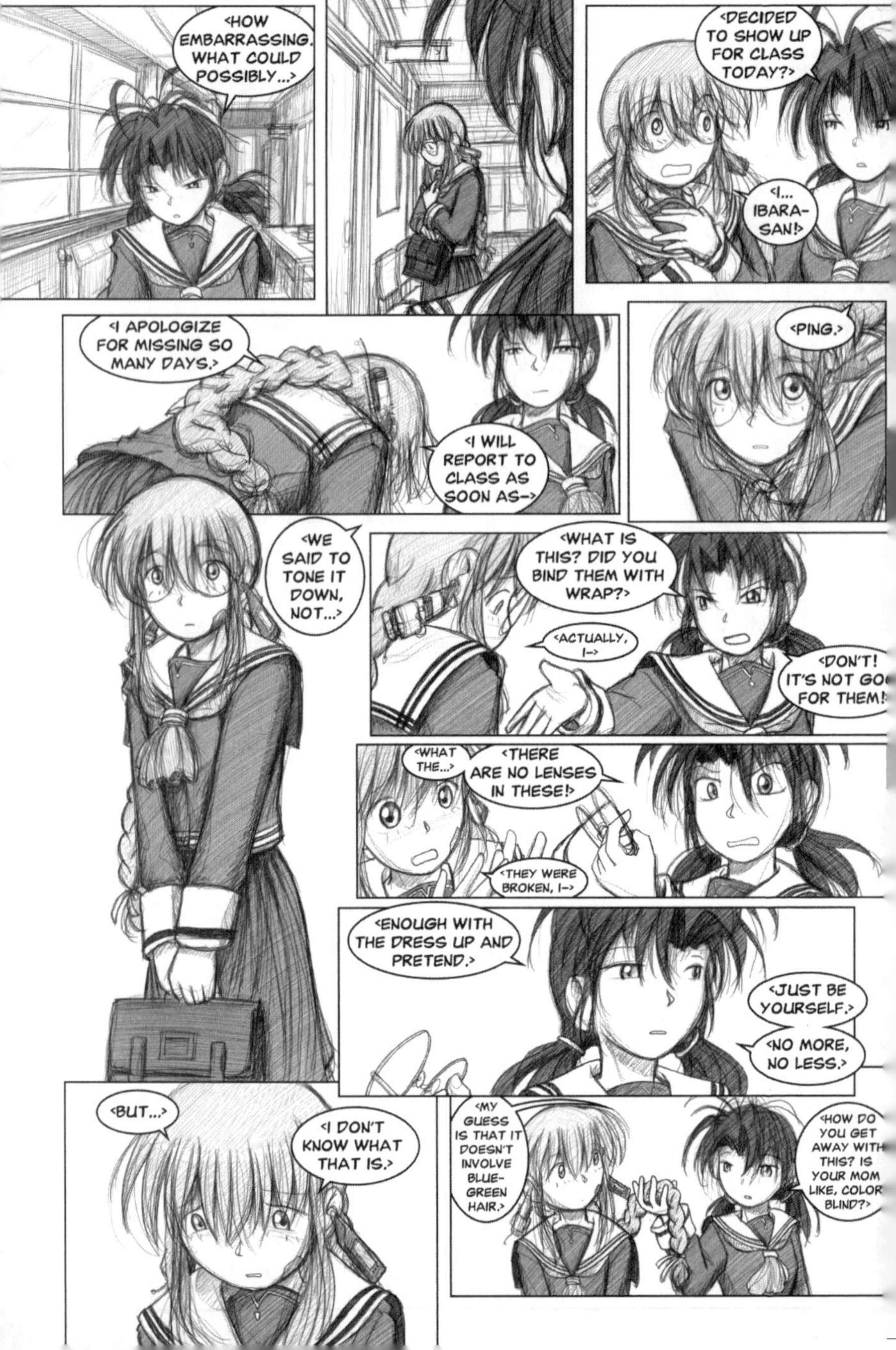
<HOW EMBARRASSING. WHAT COULD POSSIBLY...>
<DECIDED TO SHOW UP FOR CLASS TODAY?>
<I... IBARA-SAN!>
<I APOLOGIZE FOR MISSING SO MANY DAYS.>
<I WILL REPORT TO CLASS AS SOON AS->
<PING.>
<WE SAID TO TONE IT DOWN, NOT...>
<WHAT IS THIS? DID YOU BIND THEM WITH WRAP?>
<ACTUALLY, I->
<DON'T! IT'S NOT GOO FOR THEM!>
<WHAT THE...>
<THERE ARE NO LENSES IN THESE!>
<THEY WERE BROKEN, I->
<ENOUGH WITH THE DRESS UP AND PRETEND.>
<JUST BE YOURSELF.>
<NO MORE, NO LESS.>
<BUT...>
<I DON'T KNOW WHAT THAT IS.>
<MY GUESS IS THAT IT DOESN'T INVOLVE BLUE-GREEN HAIR.>
<HOW DO YOU GET AWAY WITH THIS? IS YOUR MOM LIKE, COLOR BLIND?>

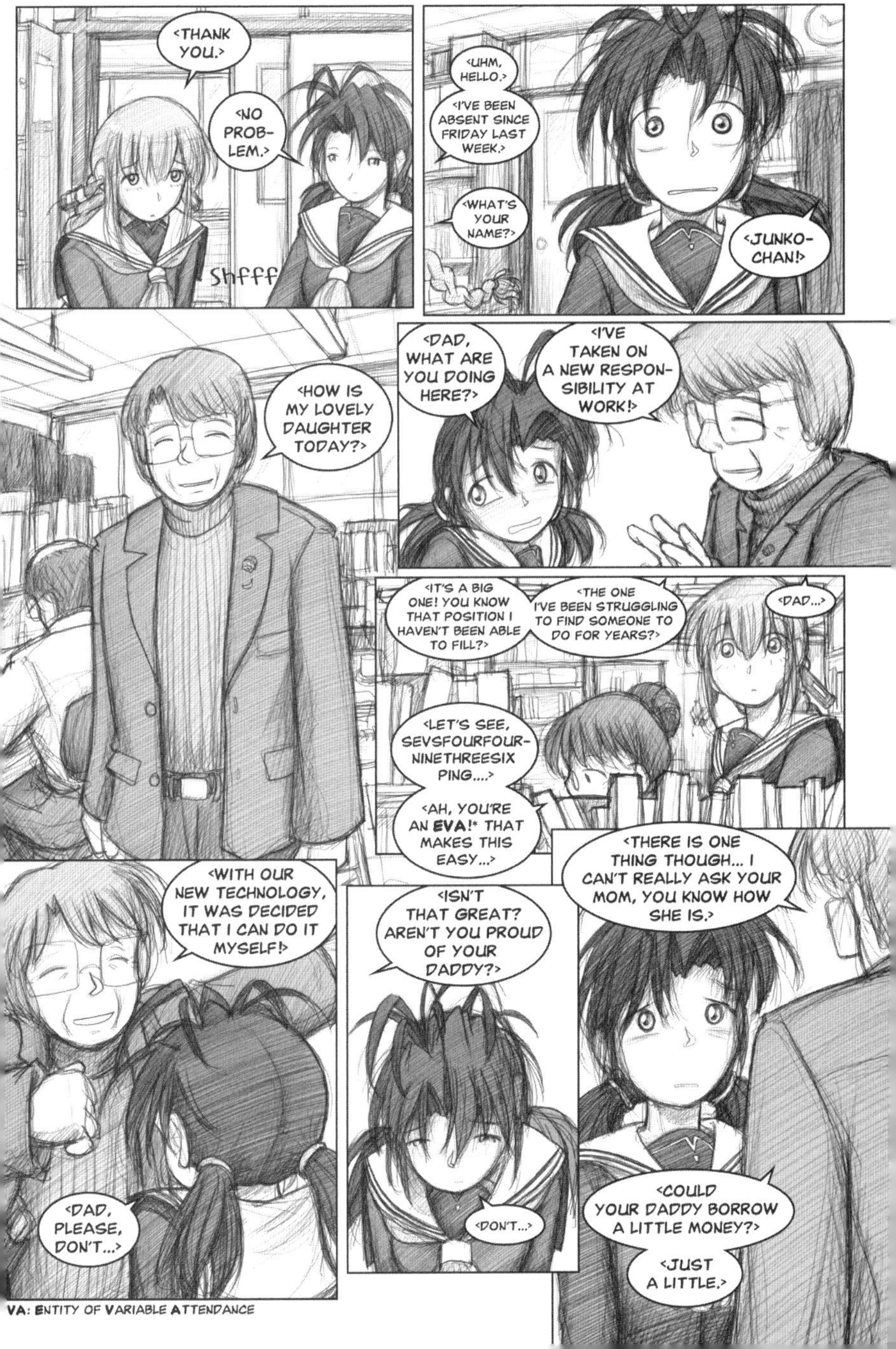
<THANK YOU.>
<NO PROB-LEM.>
Shfff
<UHM, HELLO.>
<I'VE BEEN ABSENT SINCE FRIDAY LAST WEEK.>
<WHAT'S YOUR NAME?>
<JUNKO-CHAN!>
<HOW IS MY LOVELY DAUGHTER TODAY?>
<DAD, WHAT ARE YOU DOING HERE?>
<I'VE TAKEN ON A NEW RESPON-SIBILITY AT WORK!>
<IT'S A BIG ONE! YOU KNOW THAT POSITION I HAVEN'T BEEN ABLE TO FILL?>
<THE ONE I'VE BEEN STRUGGLING TO FIND SOMEONE TO DO FOR YEARS?>
<DAD...>
<LET'S SEE, SEVSFOURFOUR-NINETHREESIX PING....>
<AH, YOU'RE AN EVA!* THAT MAKES THIS EASY...>
<WITH OUR NEW TECHNOLOGY, IT WAS DECIDED THAT I CAN DO IT MYSELF!>
<DAD, PLEASE, DON'T...>
<ISN'T THAT GREAT? AREN'T YOU PROUD OF YOUR DADDY?>
<DON'T...>
<THERE IS ONE THING THOUGH... I CAN'T REALLY ASK YOUR MOM, YOU KNOW HOW SHE IS.>
<COULD YOUR DADDY BORROW A LITTLE MONEY?>
<JUST A LITTLE.>

VA: ENTITY OF VARIABLE ATTENDANCE

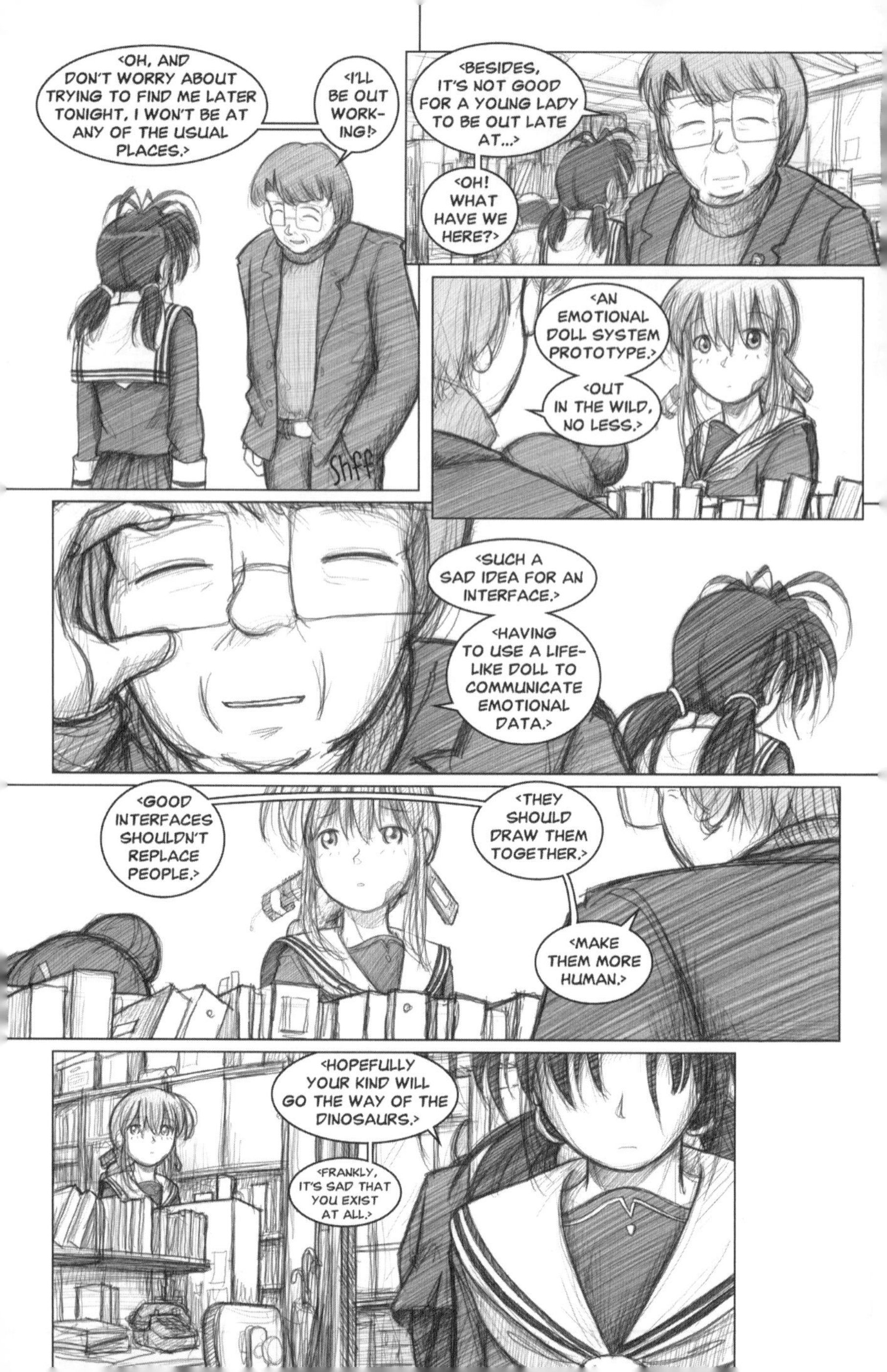
<OH, AND DON'T WORRY ABOUT TRYING TO FIND ME LATER TONIGHT, I WON'T BE AT ANY OF THE USUAL PLACES.>
<I'LL BE OUT WORKING!>
Shff
<BESIDES, IT'S NOT GOOD FOR A YOUNG LADY TO BE OUT LATE AT...>
<OH! WHAT HAVE WE HERE?>
<AN EMOTIONAL DOLL SYSTEM PROTOTYPE.>
<OUT IN THE WILD, NO LESS.>
<SUCH A SAD IDEA FOR AN INTERFACE.>
<HAVING TO USE A LIFE-LIKE DOLL TO COMMUNICATE EMOTIONAL DATA.>
<GOOD INTERFACES SHOULDN'T REPLACE PEOPLE.>
<THEY SHOULD DRAW THEM TOGETHER.>
<MAKE THEM MORE HUMAN.>
<HOPEFULLY YOUR KIND WILL GO THE WAY OF THE DINOSAURS.>
<FRANKLY, IT'S SAD THAT YOU EXIST AT ALL.>

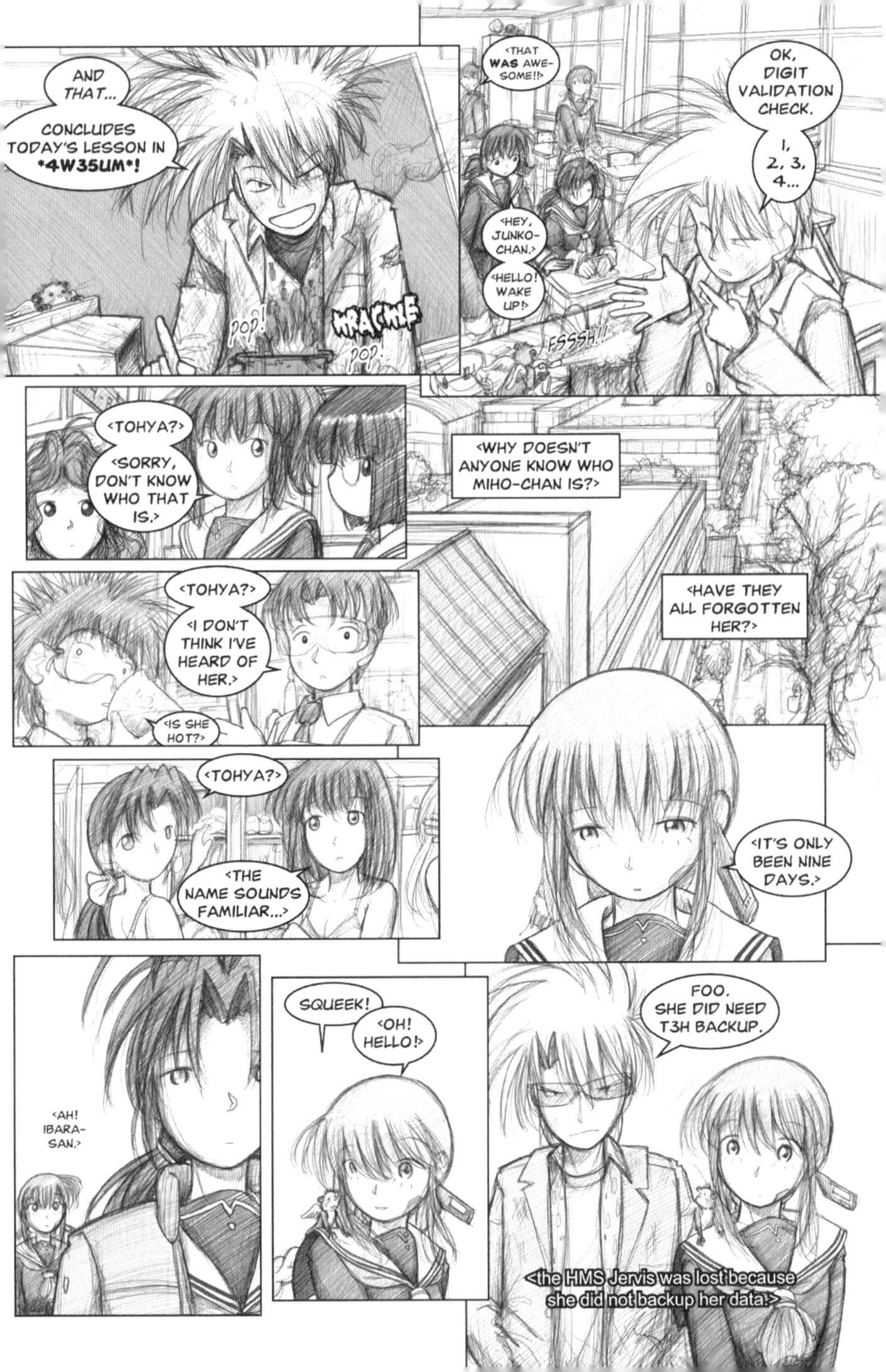
AND THAT...
CONCLUDES TODAY'S LESSON IN *4W35UM*!
pop!
WRACKLE
pop!
<THAT WAS AWE-SOME!!>
OK, DIGIT VALIDATION CHECK.
1, 2, 3, 4...
<HEY, JUNKO-CHAN.>
<HELLO! WAKE UP!>
FSSSH!!
<TOHYA?>
<SORRY, DON'T KNOW WHO THAT IS.>
<TOHYA?>
<I DON'T THINK I'VE HEARD OF HER.>
<IS SHE HOT?>
<TOHYA?>
<THE NAME SOUNDS FAMILIAR...>
<WHY DOESN'T ANYONE KNOW WHO MIHO-CHAN IS?>
<HAVE THEY ALL FORGOTTEN HER?>
<IT'S ONLY BEEN NINE DAYS.>
<AH! IBARA-SAN.>
SQUEEK!
<OH! HELLO!>
FOO. SHE DID NEED T3H BACKUP.
<the HMS Jervis was lost because she did not backup her data.>

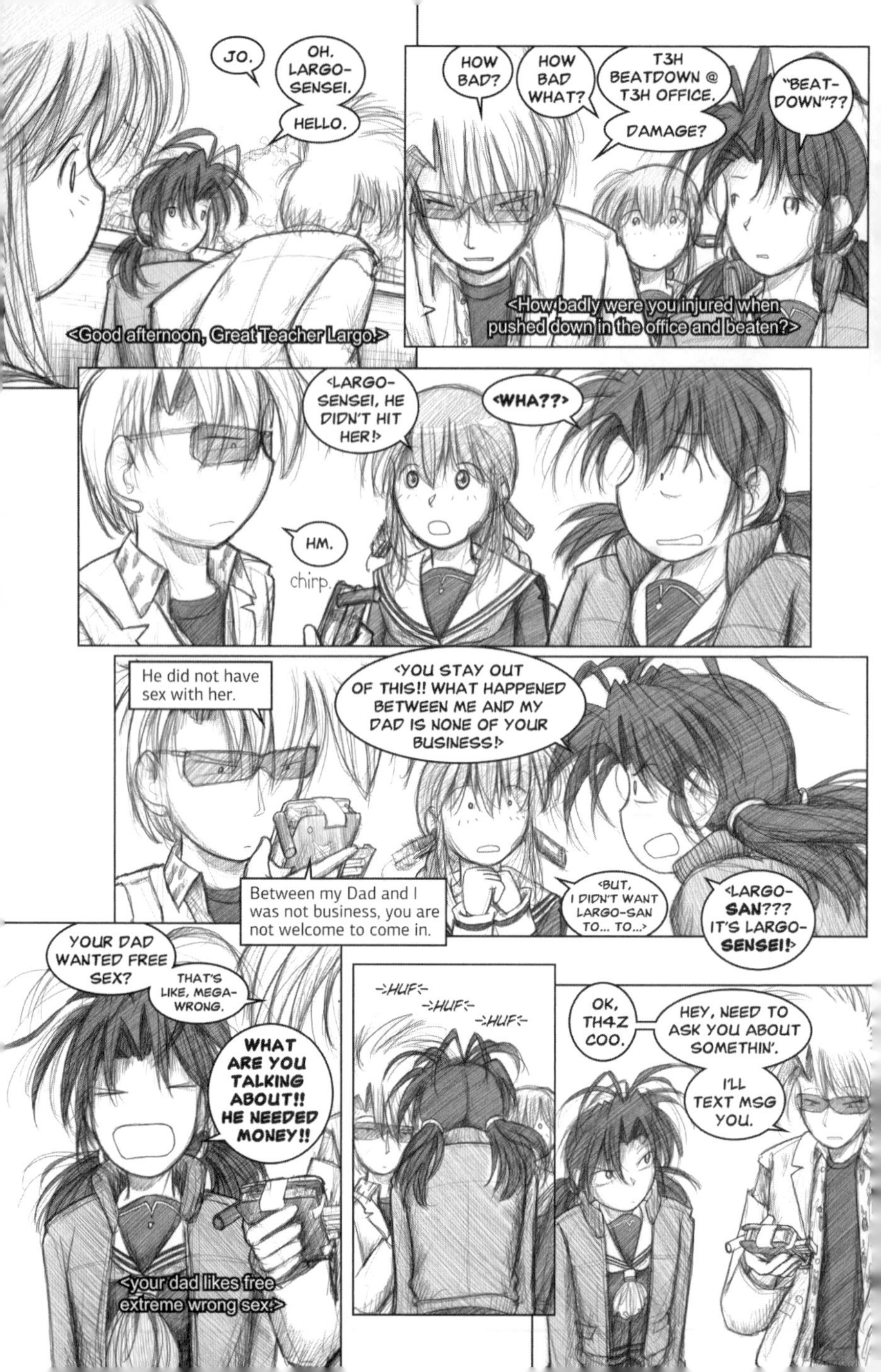
JO.
OH. LARGO-SENSEI.
HELLO.
<Good afternoon, Great Teacher Largo.>
HOW BAD?
HOW BAD WHAT?
T3H BEATDOWN @ T3H OFFICE.
DAMAGE?
"BEAT-DOWN"??
<How badly were you injured when pushed down in the office and beaten?>
<LARGO-SENSEI, HE DIDN'T HIT HER!>
<WHA??>
HM.
chirp.
He did not have sex with her.
<YOU STAY OUT OF THIS!! WHAT HAPPENED BETWEEN ME AND MY DAD IS NONE OF YOUR BUSINESS!>
Between my Dad and I was not business, you are not welcome to come in.
<BUT, I DIDN'T WANT LARGO-SAN TO... TO...>
<LARGO-SAN??? IT'S LARGO-SENSEI!>
YOUR DAD WANTED FREE SEX?
THAT'S LIKE, MEGA-WRONG.
WHAT ARE YOU TALKING ABOUT!! HE NEEDED MONEY!!
<your dad likes free extreme wrong sex.>
HUF
HUF
HUF
OK, TH4Z COO.
HEY, NEED TO ASK YOU ABOUT SOMETHIN'.
I'LL TEXT MSG YOU.

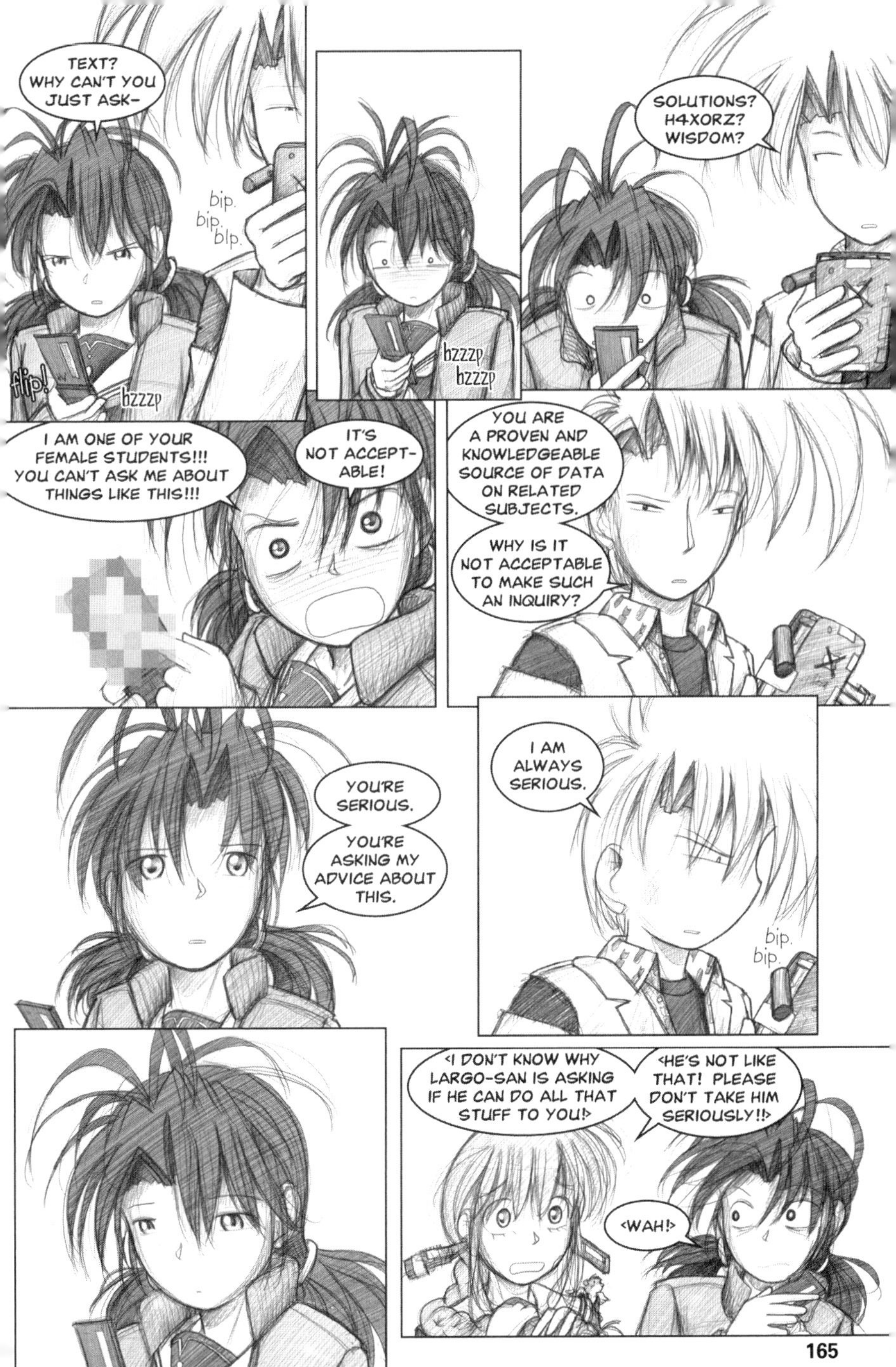

TEXT? WHY CAN'T YOU JUST ASK-
bip. bip. blip.
flip!
bzzzp
bzzzp bzzzp
SOLUTIONS? H4XORZ? WISDOM?
I AM ONE OF YOUR FEMALE STUDENTS!!! YOU CAN'T ASK ME ABOUT THINGS LIKE THIS!!!
IT'S NOT ACCEPT-ABLE!
YOU ARE A PROVEN AND KNOWLEDGEABLE SOURCE OF DATA ON RELATED SUBJECTS.
WHY IS IT NOT ACCEPTABLE TO MAKE SUCH AN INQUIRY?
YOU'RE SERIOUS.
YOU'RE ASKING MY ADVICE ABOUT THIS.
I AM ALWAYS SERIOUS.
bip. bip.
<I DON'T KNOW WHY LARGO-SAN IS ASKING IF HE CAN DO ALL THAT STUFF TO YOU!>
<HE'S NOT LIKE THAT! PLEASE DON'T TAKE HIM SERIOUSLY!!>
<WAH!>

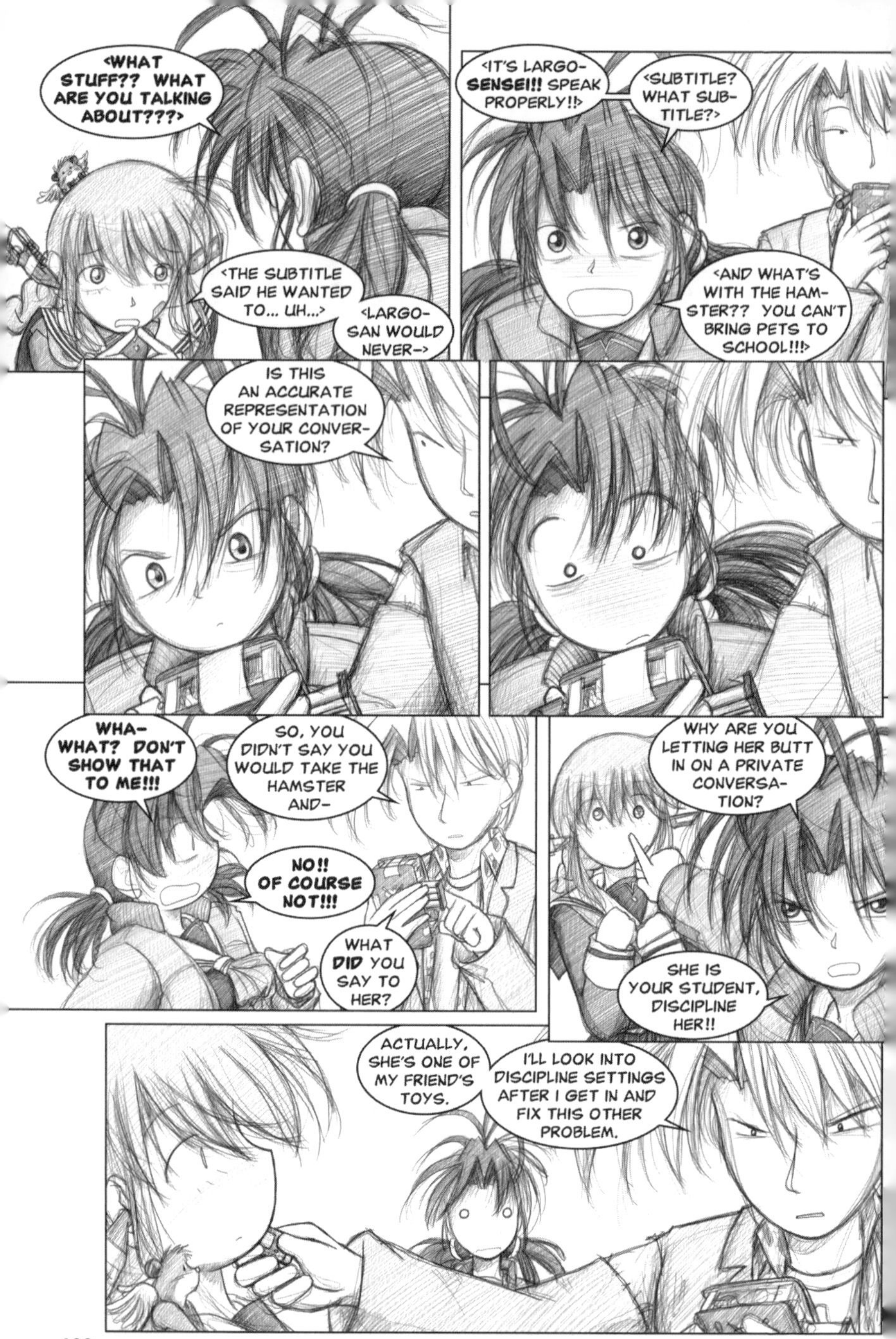
<WHAT STUFF?? WHAT ARE YOU TALKING ABOUT???>
<THE SUBTITLE SAID HE WANTED TO... UH...>
<LARGO-SAN WOULD NEVER->
<IT'S LARGO-**SENSEI!!!** SPEAK PROPERLY!!>
<SUBTITLE? WHAT SUB-TITLE?>
<AND WHAT'S WITH THE HAM-STER?? YOU CAN'T BRING PETS TO SCHOOL!!!>
IS THIS AN ACCURATE REPRESENTATION OF YOUR CONVER-SATION?
WHA-WHAT? DON'T SHOW THAT TO ME!!!
SO, YOU DIDN'T SAY YOU WOULD TAKE THE HAMSTER AND-
NO!! OF COURSE NOT!!!
WHAT **DID** YOU SAY TO HER?
WHY ARE YOU LETTING HER BUTT IN ON A PRIVATE CONVERSA-TION?
SHE IS YOUR STUDENT, DISCIPLINE HER!!
ACTUALLY, SHE'S ONE OF MY FRIEND'S TOYS.
I'LL LOOK INTO DISCIPLINE SETTINGS AFTER I GET IN AND FIX THIS OTHER PROBLEM.

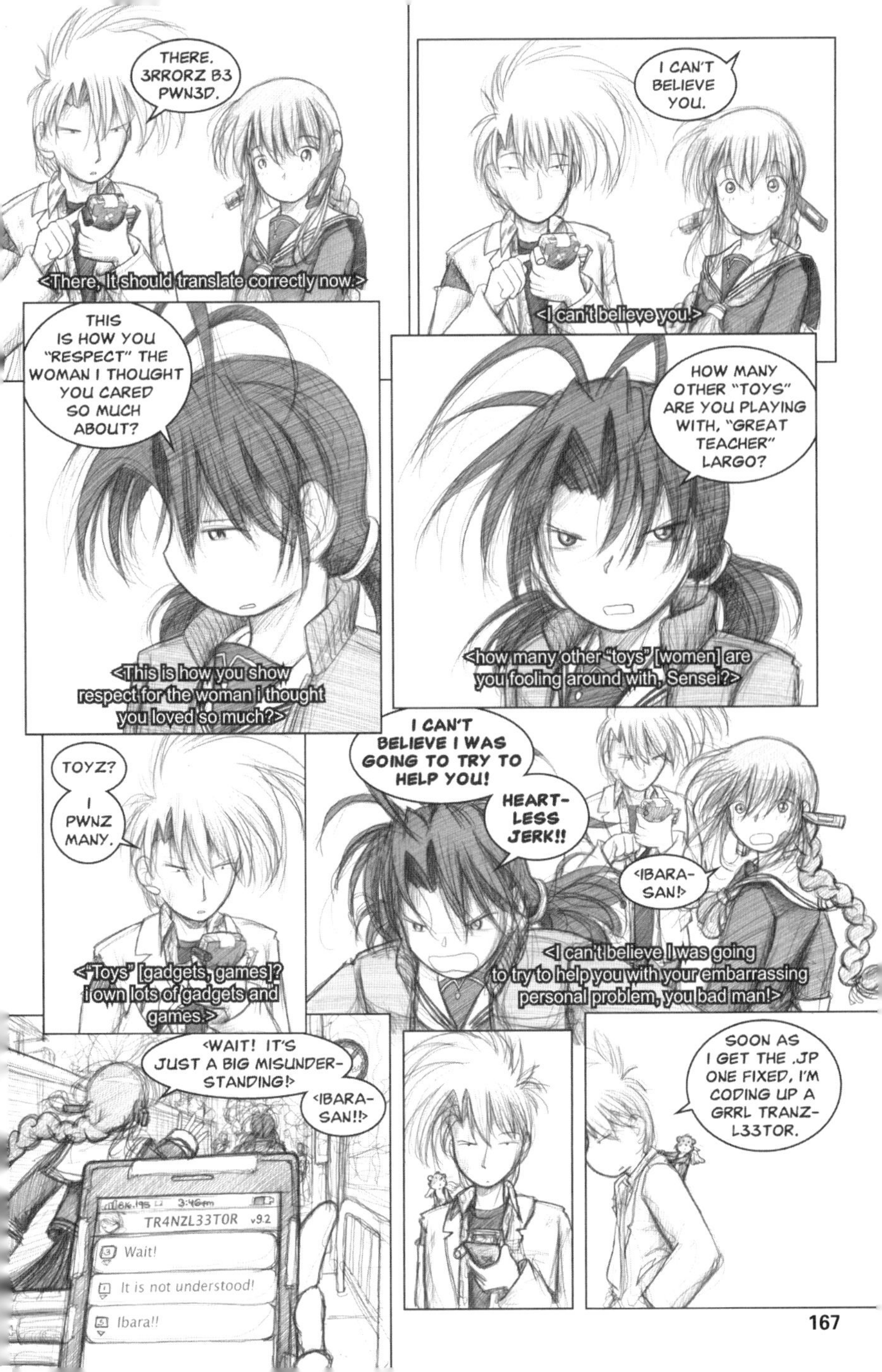
THERE. 3RRORZ B3 PWN3D.
<There, It should translate correctly now.>
I CAN'T BELIEVE YOU.
<I can't believe you.>
THIS IS HOW YOU "RESPECT" THE WOMAN I THOUGHT YOU CARED SO MUCH ABOUT?
<This is how you show respect for the woman i thought you loved so much?>
HOW MANY OTHER "TOYS" ARE YOU PLAYING WITH, "GREAT TEACHER" LARGO?
<how many other "toys" [women] are you fooling around with, Sensei?>
TOYZ?
I PWNZ MANY.
<"Toys" [gadgets, games]? i own lots of gadgets and games.>
I CAN'T BELIEVE I WAS GOING TO TRY TO HELP YOU!
HEART-LESS JERK!!
<IBARA-SAN!>
<I can't believe I was going to try to help you with your embarrassing personal problem, you bad man!>
<WAIT! IT'S JUST A BIG MISUNDER-STANDING!>
<IBARA-SAN!!>
3:46pm
TR4NZL33TOR v9.2
Wait!
It is not understood!
Ibara!!
SOON AS I GET THE .JP ONE FIXED, I'M CODING UP A GRRL TRANZ-L33TOR.

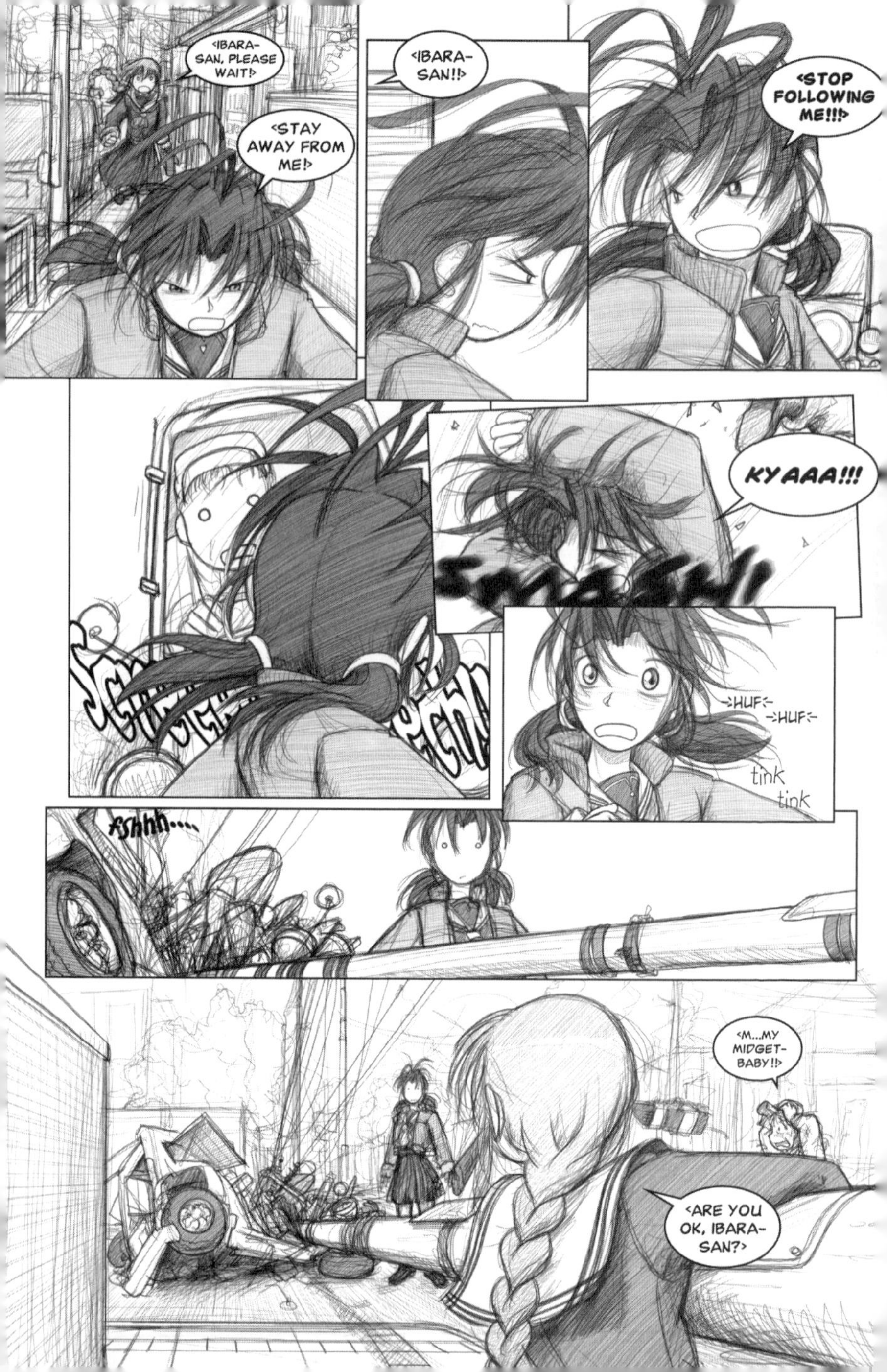

<IBARA-SAN, PLEASE WAIT!>
<STAY AWAY FROM ME!>
<IBARA-SAN!!>
<STOP FOLLOWING ME!!!>
KYAAA!!!
SMASH!
HUF HUF
tink tink
fshhh....
<M...MY MIDGET-BABY!!>
<ARE YOU OK, IBARA-SAN?>

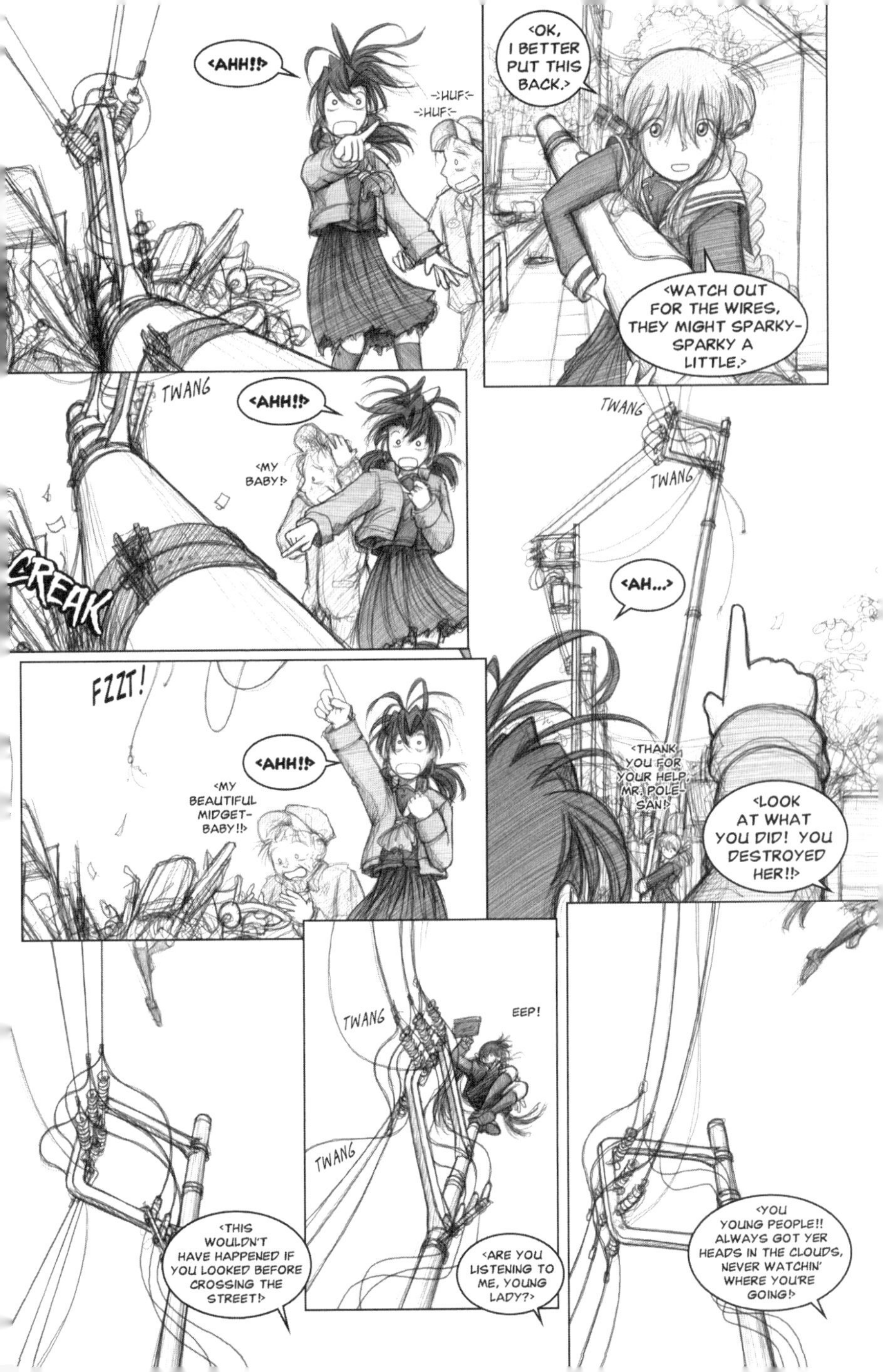
<AHH!!>
HUF
HUF
<OK, I BETTER PUT THIS BACK.>
<WATCH OUT FOR THE WIRES, THEY MIGHT SPARKY-SPARKY A LITTLE.>
TWANG
<AHH!!>
<MY BABY!>
CREAK
FZZT!
<AHH!!>
<MY BEAUTIFUL MIDGET-BABY!!>
TWANG
TWANG
<AH...>
<THANK YOU FOR YOUR HELP, MR. POLE-SAN!>
<LOOK AT WHAT YOU DID! YOU DESTROYED HER!!>
<THIS WOULDN'T HAVE HAPPENED IF YOU LOOKED BEFORE CROSSING THE STREET!>
TWANG
EEP!
TWANG
<ARE YOU LISTENING TO ME, YOUNG LADY?>
<YOU YOUNG PEOPLE!! ALWAYS GOT YER HEADS IN THE CLOUDS, NEVER WATCHIN' WHERE YOU'RE GOING!>

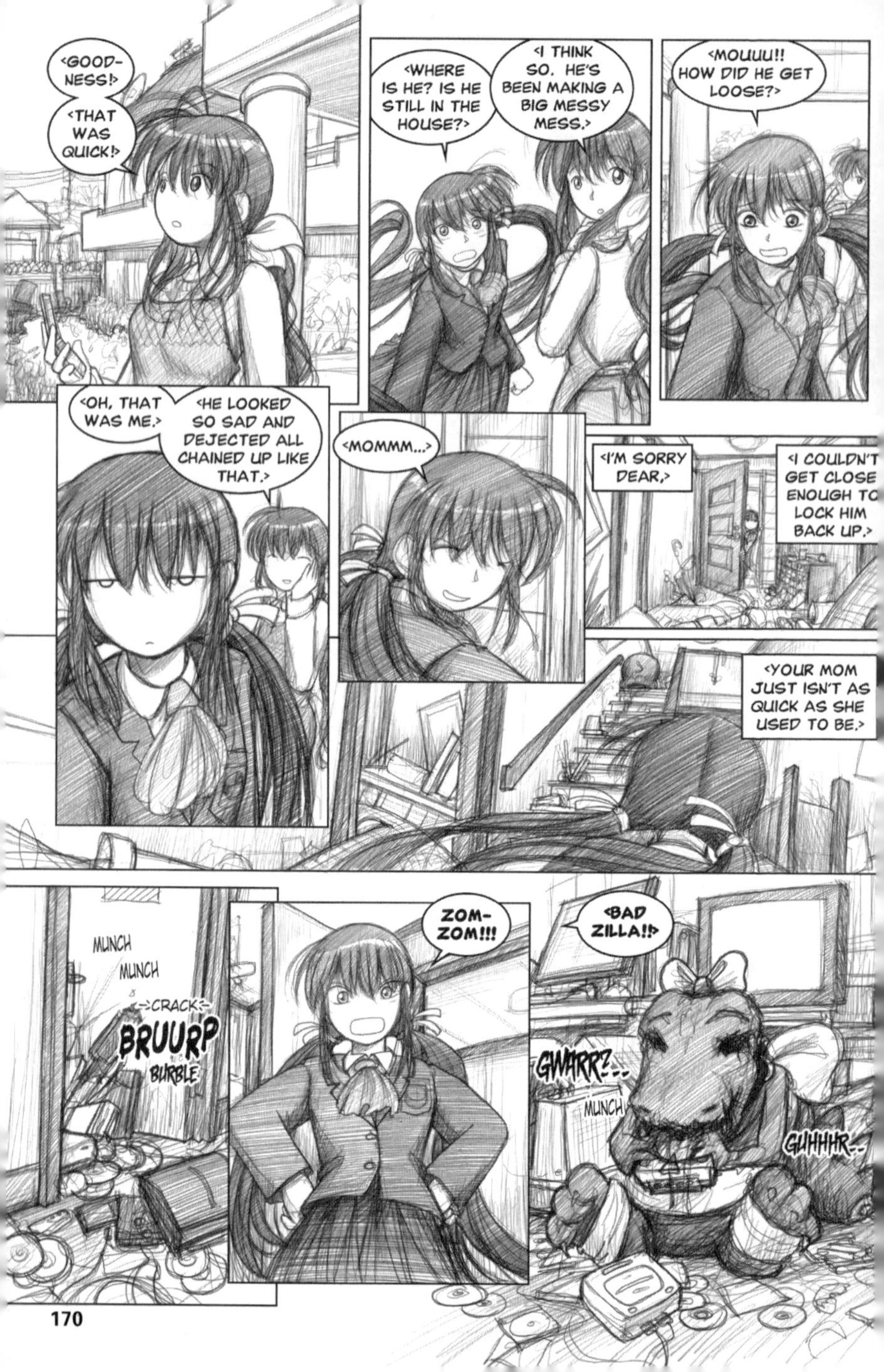
<GOOD-NESS!>
<THAT WAS QUICK!>
<WHERE IS HE? IS HE STILL IN THE HOUSE?>
<I THINK SO. HE'S BEEN MAKING A BIG MESSY MESS.>
<MOUUU!! HOW DID HE GET LOOSE?>
<OH, THAT WAS ME.>
<HE LOOKED SO SAD AND DEJECTED ALL CHAINED UP LIKE THAT.>
<MOMMM...>
<I'M SORRY DEAR,>
<I COULDN'T GET CLOSE ENOUGH TO LOCK HIM BACK UP.>
<YOUR MOM JUST ISN'T AS QUICK AS SHE USED TO BE.>
MUNCH
MUNCH
CRACK
BRUURP
BURBLE
ZOM-ZOM!!!
<BAD ZILLA!>
GWARR?...
MUNCH
GUHHHR...

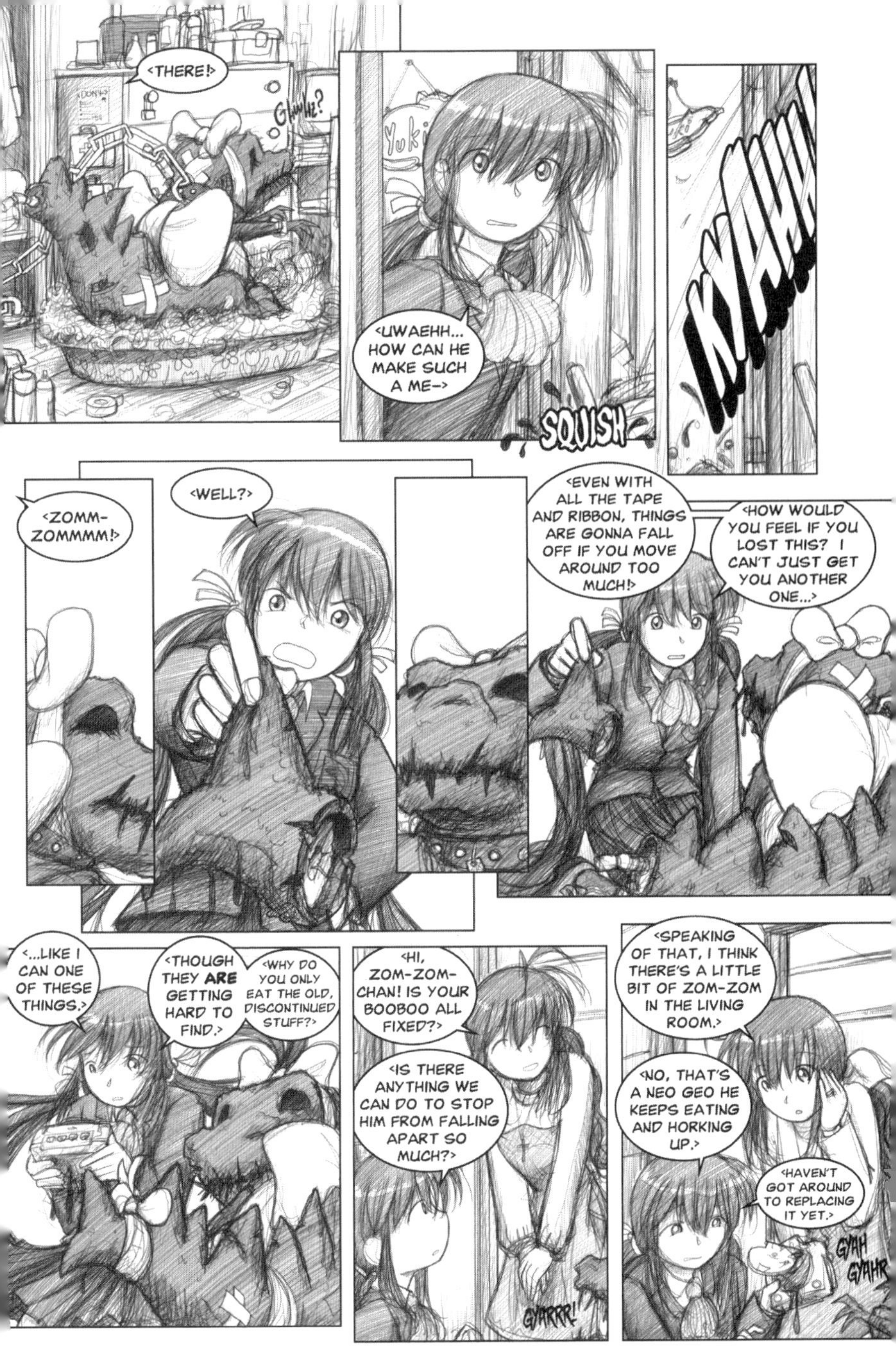
<THERE!>
Yuki
<UWAEHH... HOW CAN HE MAKE SUCH A ME->
SQUISH
KYAHH
<ZOMM-ZOMMMM!>
<WELL?>
<EVEN WITH ALL THE TAPE AND RIBBON, THINGS ARE GONNA FALL OFF IF YOU MOVE AROUND TOO MUCH!>
<HOW WOULD YOU FEEL IF YOU LOST THIS? I CAN'T JUST GET YOU ANOTHER ONE...>
<...LIKE I CAN ONE OF THESE THINGS.>
<THOUGH THEY **ARE** GETTING HARD TO FIND.>
<WHY DO YOU ONLY EAT THE OLD, DISCONTINUED STUFF?>
<HI, ZOM-ZOM-CHAN! IS YOUR BOOBOO ALL FIXED?>
<IS THERE ANYTHING WE CAN DO TO STOP HIM FROM FALLING APART SO MUCH?>
GYARRR!
<SPEAKING OF THAT, I THINK THERE'S A LITTLE BIT OF ZOM-ZOM IN THE LIVING ROOM.>
<NO, THAT'S A NEO GEO HE KEEPS EATING AND HORKING UP.>
<HAVEN'T GOT AROUND TO REPLACING IT YET.>
GYAH GYAHR

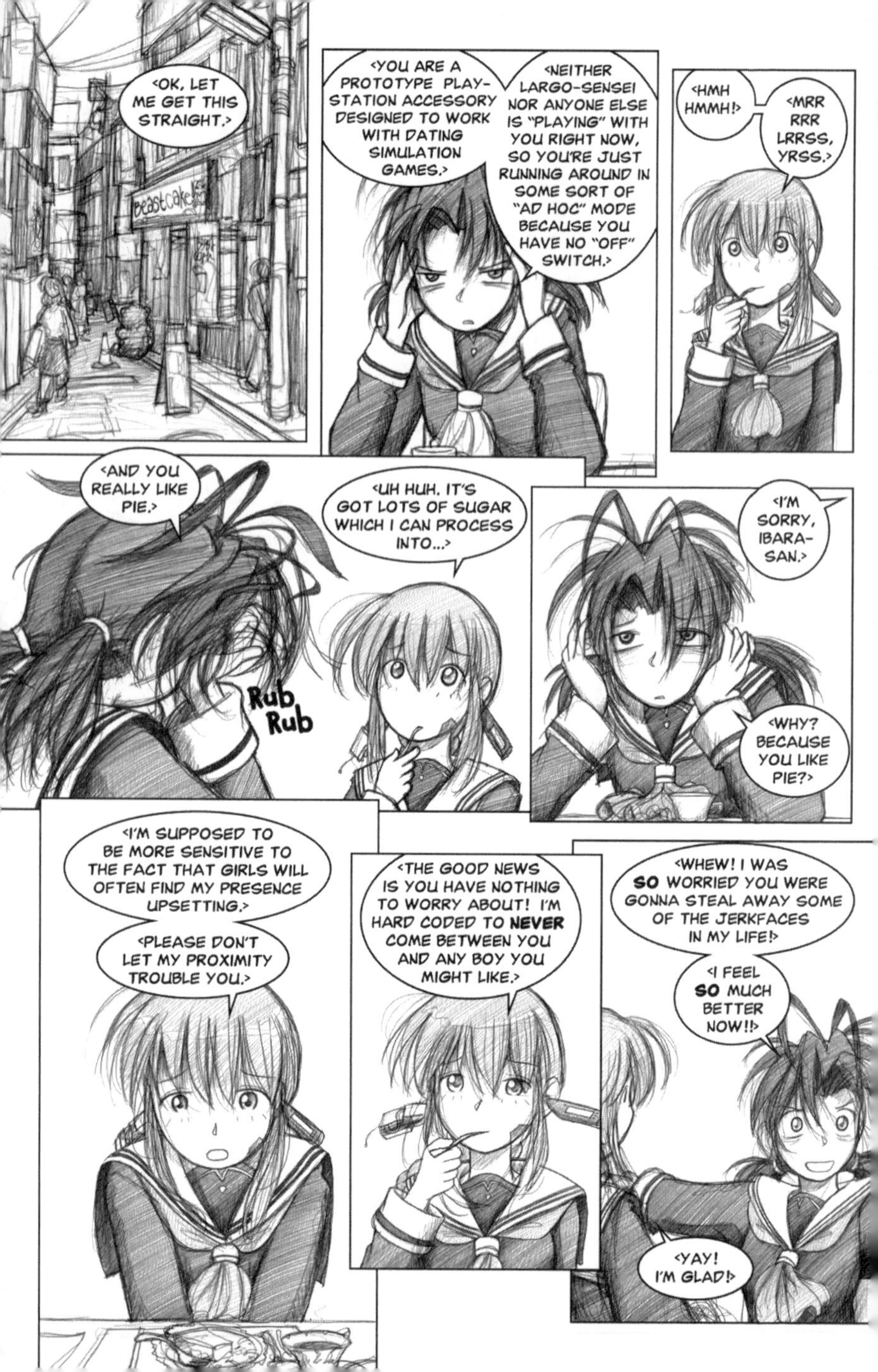
<OK, LET ME GET THIS STRAIGHT.>
beastcake
<YOU ARE A PROTOTYPE PLAY-STATION ACCESSORY DESIGNED TO WORK WITH DATING SIMULATION GAMES.>
<NEITHER LARGO-SENSEI NOR ANYONE ELSE IS "PLAYING" WITH YOU RIGHT NOW, SO YOU'RE JUST RUNNING AROUND IN SOME SORT OF "AD HOC" MODE BECAUSE YOU HAVE NO "OFF" SWITCH.>
<HMH HMMH!>
<MRR RRR LRRSS, YRSS.>
<AND YOU REALLY LIKE PIE.>
Rub Rub
<UH HUH. IT'S GOT LOTS OF SUGAR WHICH I CAN PROCESS INTO...>
<I'M SORRY, IBARA-SAN.>
<WHY? BECAUSE YOU LIKE PIE?>
<I'M SUPPOSED TO BE MORE SENSITIVE TO THE FACT THAT GIRLS WILL OFTEN FIND MY PRESENCE UPSETTING.>
<PLEASE DON'T LET MY PROXIMITY TROUBLE YOU.>
<THE GOOD NEWS IS YOU HAVE NOTHING TO WORRY ABOUT! I'M HARD CODED TO NEVER COME BETWEEN YOU AND ANY BOY YOU MIGHT LIKE.>
<WHEW! I WAS SO WORRIED YOU WERE GONNA STEAL AWAY SOME OF THE JERKFACES IN MY LIFE!>
<I FEEL SO MUCH BETTER NOW!!>
<YAY! I'M GLAD!>

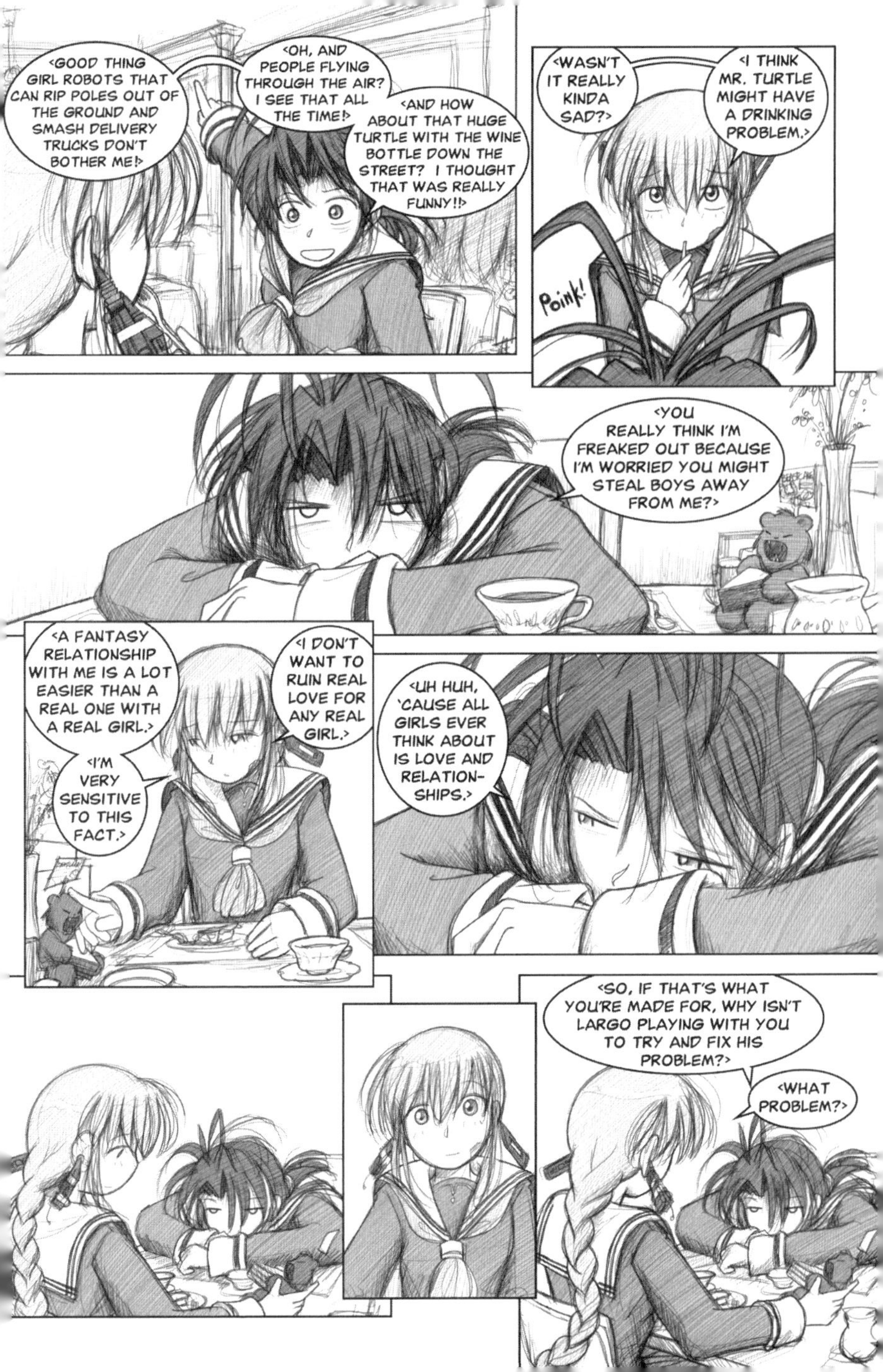
<GOOD THING GIRL ROBOTS THAT CAN RIP POLES OUT OF THE GROUND AND SMASH DELIVERY TRUCKS DON'T BOTHER ME!>
<OH, AND PEOPLE FLYING THROUGH THE AIR? I SEE THAT ALL THE TIME!>
<AND HOW ABOUT THAT HUGE TURTLE WITH THE WINE BOTTLE DOWN THE STREET? I THOUGHT THAT WAS REALLY FUNNY!!>
<WASN'T IT REALLY KINDA SAD?>
<I THINK MR. TURTLE MIGHT HAVE A DRINKING PROBLEM.>
POINK!
<YOU REALLY THINK I'M FREAKED OUT BECAUSE I'M WORRIED YOU MIGHT STEAL BOYS AWAY FROM ME?>
<A FANTASY RELATIONSHIP WITH ME IS A LOT EASIER THAN A REAL ONE WITH A REAL GIRL.>
<I DON'T WANT TO RUIN REAL LOVE FOR ANY REAL GIRL.>
<I'M VERY SENSITIVE TO THIS FACT.>
<UH HUH, 'CAUSE ALL GIRLS EVER THINK ABOUT IS LOVE AND RELATION-SHIPS.>
<SO, IF THAT'S WHAT YOU'RE MADE FOR, WHY ISN'T LARGO PLAYING WITH YOU TO TRY AND FIX HIS PROBLEM?>
<WHAT PROBLEM?>

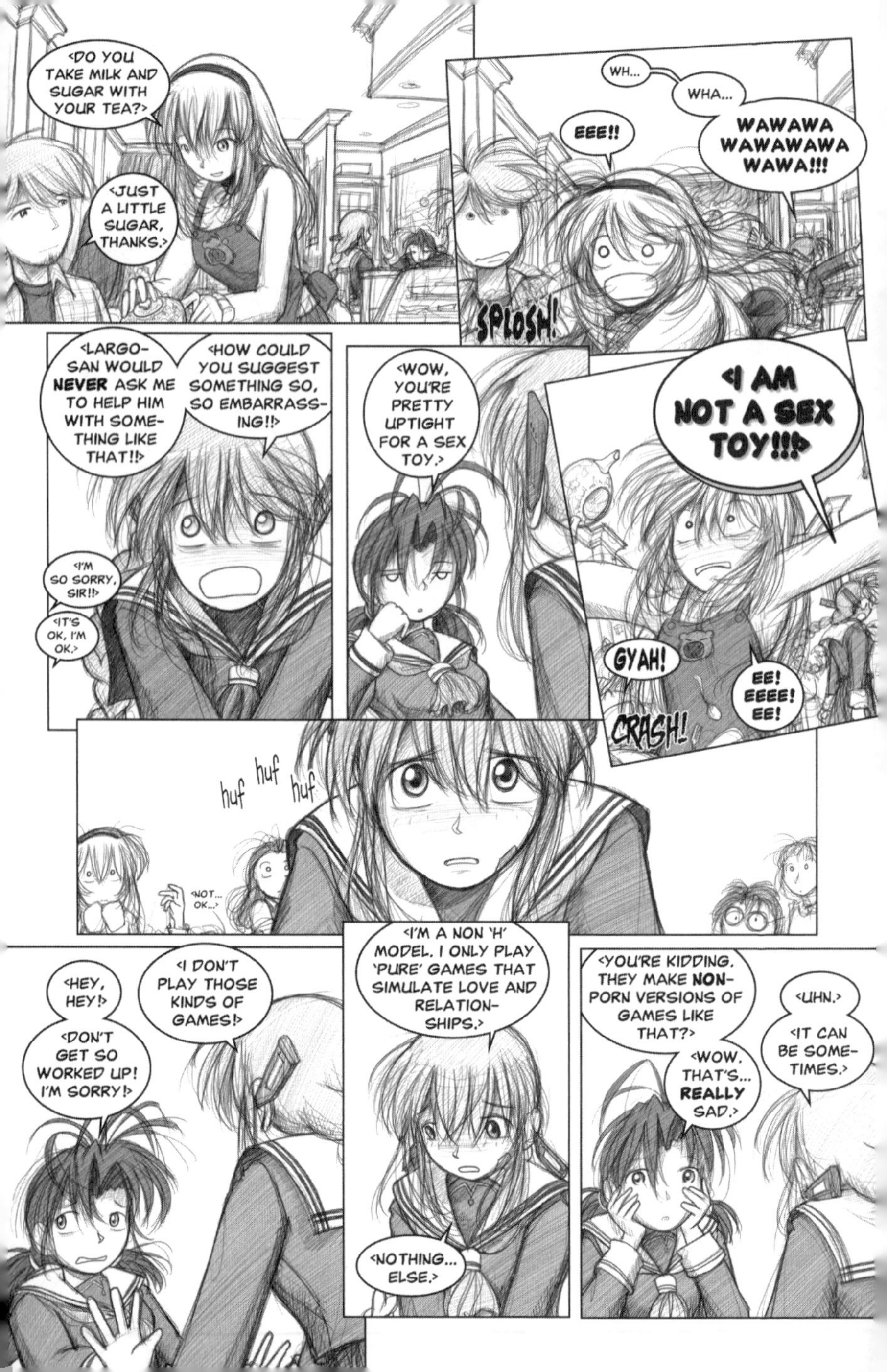
<DO YOU TAKE MILK AND SUGAR WITH YOUR TEA?>
<JUST A LITTLE SUGAR, THANKS.>
WH...
WHA...
EEE!!
WAWAWA WAWAWAWA WAWA!!!
SPLOSH!
<LARGO-SAN WOULD NEVER ASK ME TO HELP HIM WITH SOMETHING LIKE THAT!!>
<HOW COULD YOU SUGGEST SOMETHING SO, SO EMBARRASSING!!>
<I'M SO SORRY, SIR!!>
<IT'S OK, I'M OK.>
<WOW, YOU'RE PRETTY UPTIGHT FOR A SEX TOY.>
<I AM NOT A SEX TOY!!!>
GYAH!
CRASH!
EE! EEEE! EE!
huf huf huf
<NOT... OK...>
<HEY, HEY!>
<I DON'T PLAY THOSE KINDS OF GAMES!>
<DON'T GET SO WORKED UP! I'M SORRY!>
<I'M A NON 'H' MODEL. I ONLY PLAY 'PURE' GAMES THAT SIMULATE LOVE AND RELATIONSHIPS.>
<NOTHING... ELSE.>
<YOU'RE KIDDING. THEY MAKE NON-PORN VERSIONS OF GAMES LIKE THAT?>
<WOW. THAT'S... REALLY SAD.>
<UHN.>
<IT CAN BE SOMETIMES.>

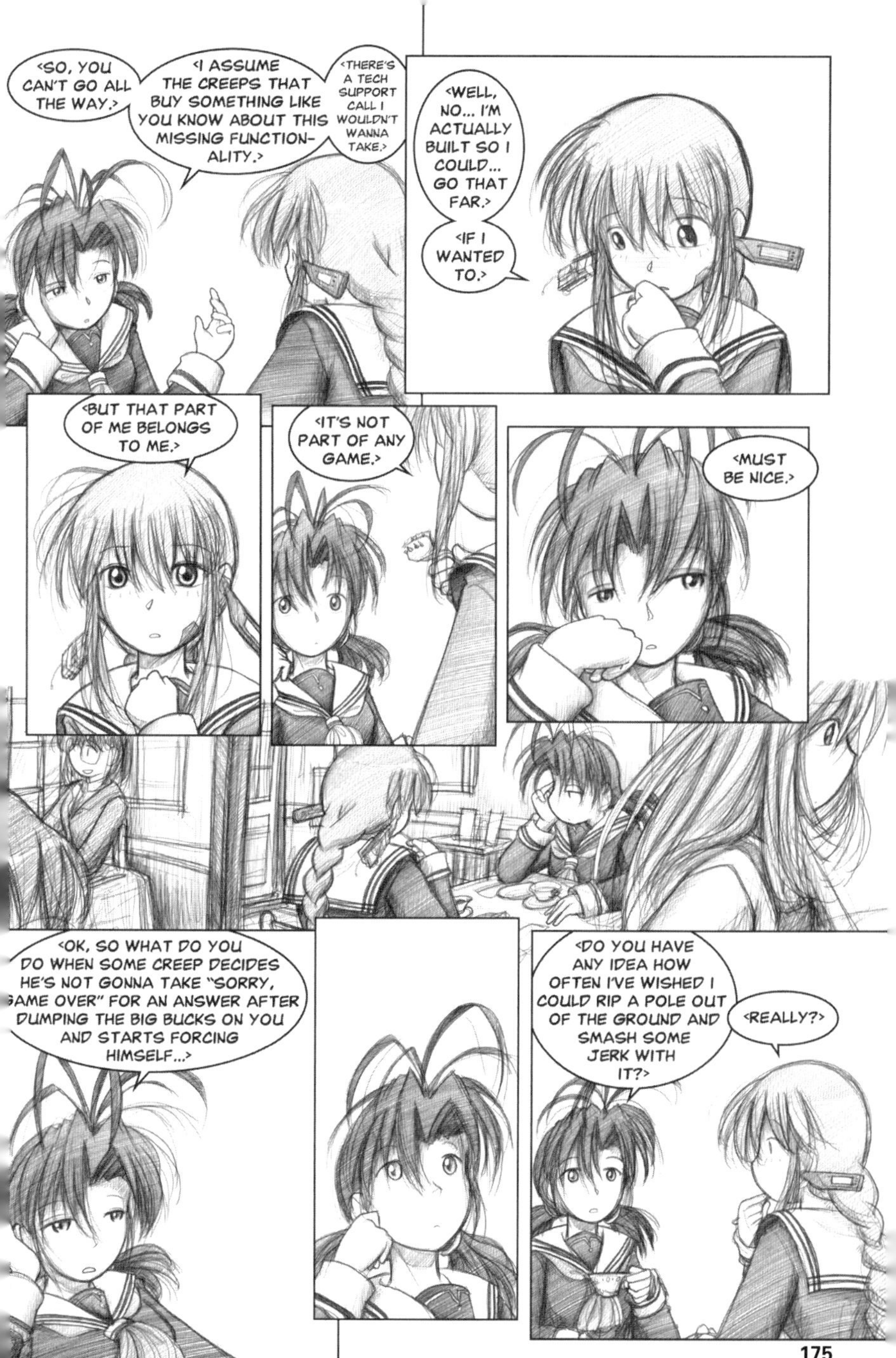

<SO, YOU CAN'T GO ALL THE WAY.>
<I ASSUME THE CREEPS THAT BUY SOMETHING LIKE YOU KNOW ABOUT THIS MISSING FUNCTION-ALITY.>
<THERE'S A TECH SUPPORT CALL I WOULDN'T WANNA TAKE.>
<WELL, NO... I'M ACTUALLY BUILT SO I COULD... GO THAT FAR.>
<IF I WANTED TO.>
<BUT THAT PART OF ME BELONGS TO ME.>
<IT'S NOT PART OF ANY GAME.>
<MUST BE NICE.>
<OK, SO WHAT DO YOU DO WHEN SOME CREEP DECIDES HE'S NOT GONNA TAKE "SORRY, GAME OVER" FOR AN ANSWER AFTER DUMPING THE BIG BUCKS ON YOU AND STARTS FORCING HIMSELF...>
<DO YOU HAVE ANY IDEA HOW OFTEN I'VE WISHED I COULD RIP A POLE OUT OF THE GROUND AND SMASH SOME JERK WITH IT?>
<REALLY?>

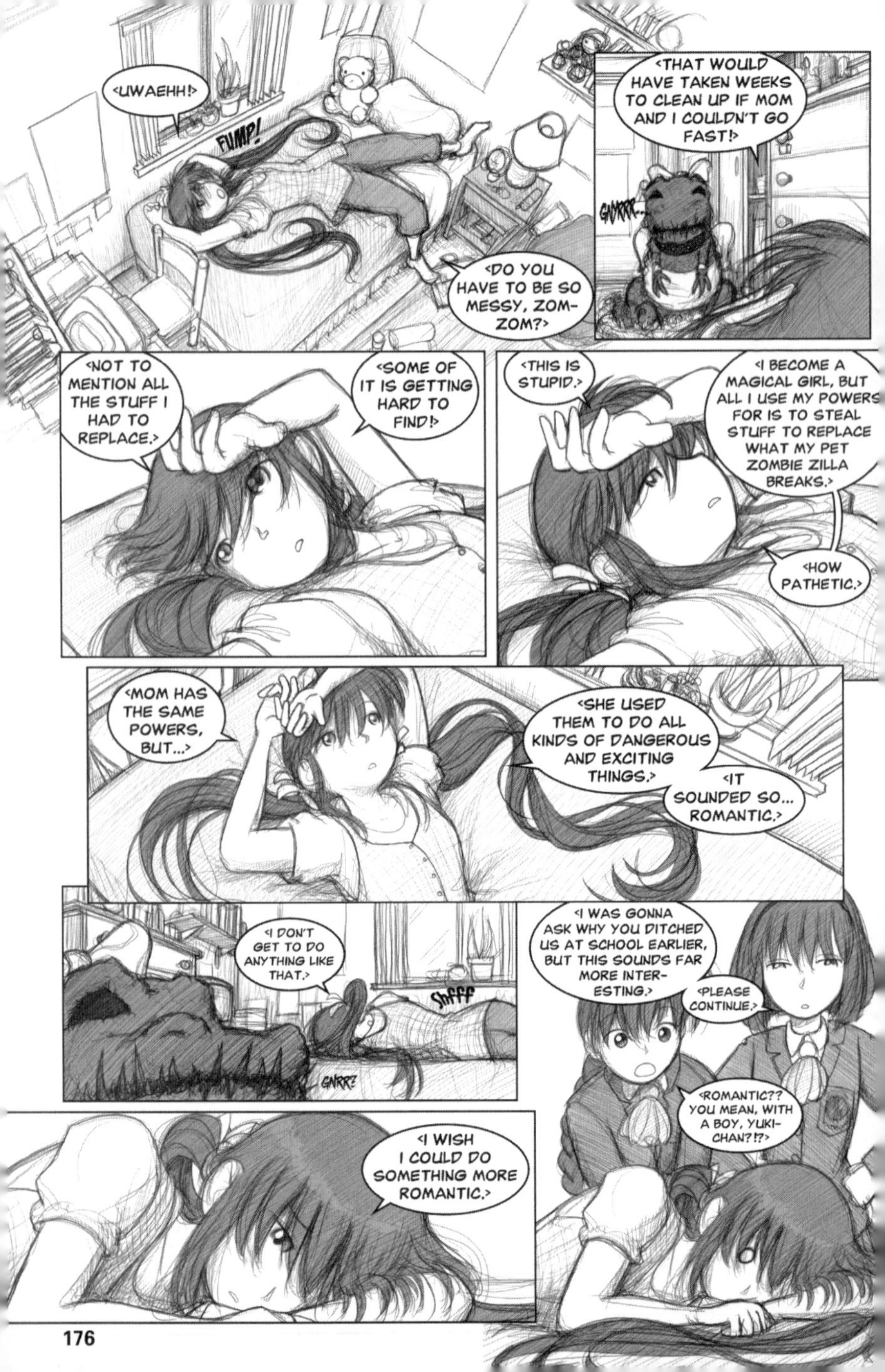

<UWAEHH!>
FUMP!
<DO YOU HAVE TO BE SO MESSY, ZOM-ZOM?>
<THAT WOULD HAVE TAKEN WEEKS TO CLEAN UP IF MOM AND I COULDN'T GO FAST!>
GNRRR...
<NOT TO MENTION ALL THE STUFF I HAD TO REPLACE.>
<SOME OF IT IS GETTING HARD TO FIND!>
<THIS IS STUPID.>
<I BECOME A MAGICAL GIRL, BUT ALL I USE MY POWERS FOR IS TO STEAL STUFF TO REPLACE WHAT MY PET ZOMBIE ZILLA BREAKS.>
<HOW PATHETIC.>
<MOM HAS THE SAME POWERS, BUT...>
<SHE USED THEM TO DO ALL KINDS OF DANGEROUS AND EXCITING THINGS.>
<IT SOUNDED SO... ROMANTIC.>
<I DON'T GET TO DO ANYTHING LIKE THAT.>
Shfff
GNRR?
<I WISH I COULD DO SOMETHING MORE ROMANTIC.>
<I WAS GONNA ASK WHY YOU DITCHED US AT SCHOOL EARLIER, BUT THIS SOUNDS FAR MORE INTER-ESTING.>
<PLEASE CONTINUE.>
<ROMANTIC?? YOU MEAN, WITH A BOY, YUKI-CHAN?!?>

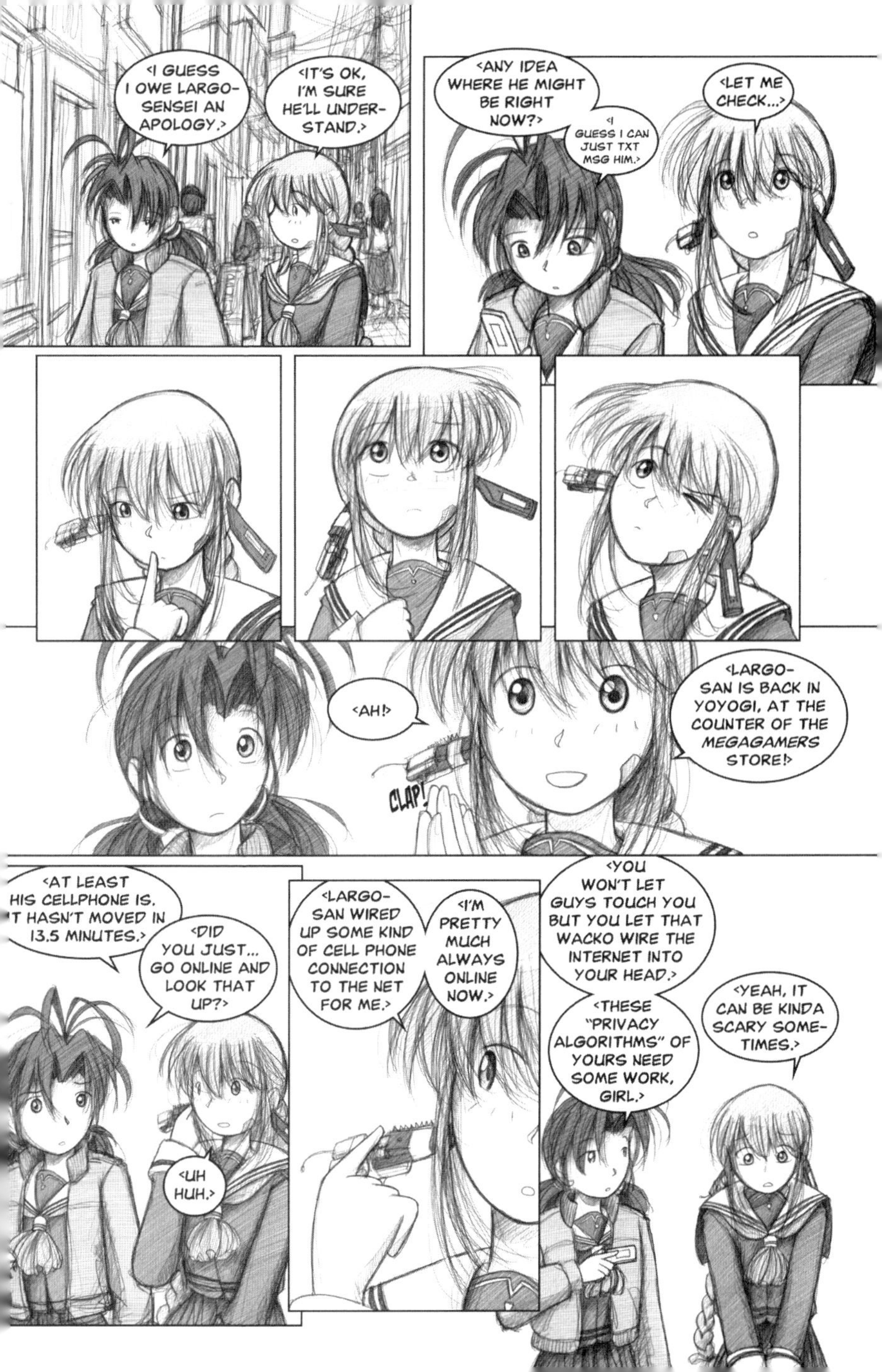
<I GUESS I OWE LARGO-SENSEI AN APOLOGY.>
<IT'S OK, I'M SURE HE'LL UNDERSTAND.>
<ANY IDEA WHERE HE MIGHT BE RIGHT NOW?>
<I GUESS I CAN JUST TXT MSG HIM.>
<LET ME CHECK...>
<AH!>
CLAP!
<LARGO-SAN IS BACK IN YOYOGI, AT THE COUNTER OF THE *MEGAGAMERS* STORE!>
<AT LEAST HIS CELLPHONE IS. IT HASN'T MOVED IN 13.5 MINUTES.>
<DID YOU JUST... GO ONLINE AND LOOK THAT UP?>
<UH HUH.>
<LARGO-SAN WIRED UP SOME KIND OF CELL PHONE CONNECTION TO THE NET FOR ME.>
<I'M PRETTY MUCH ALWAYS ONLINE NOW.>
<YOU WON'T LET GUYS TOUCH YOU BUT YOU LET THAT WACKO WIRE THE INTERNET INTO YOUR HEAD.>
<THESE "PRIVACY ALGORITHMS" OF YOURS NEED SOME WORK, GIRL.>
<YEAH, IT CAN BE KINDA SCARY SOMETIMES.>

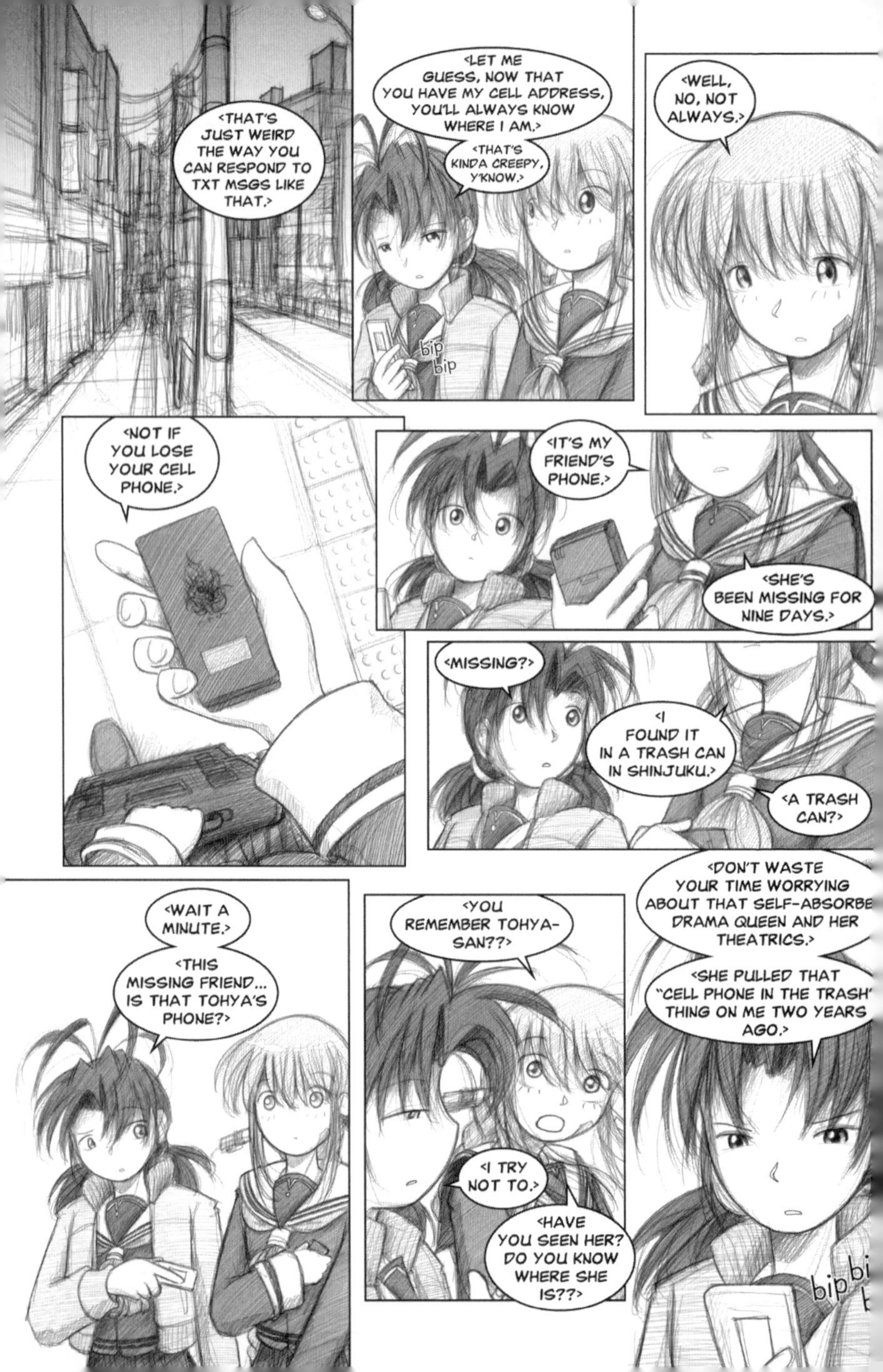
<THAT'S JUST WEIRD THE WAY YOU CAN RESPOND TO TXT MSGS LIKE THAT.>
<LET ME GUESS, NOW THAT YOU HAVE MY CELL ADDRESS, YOU'LL ALWAYS KNOW WHERE I AM.>
<THAT'S KINDA CREEPY, Y'KNOW.>
bip bip
<WELL, NO, NOT ALWAYS.>
<NOT IF YOU LOSE YOUR CELL PHONE.>
<IT'S MY FRIEND'S PHONE.>
<SHE'S BEEN MISSING FOR NINE DAYS.>
<MISSING?>
<I FOUND IT IN A TRASH CAN IN SHINJUKU.>
<A TRASH CAN?>
<WAIT A MINUTE.>
<THIS MISSING FRIEND... IS THAT TOHYA'S PHONE?>
<YOU REMEMBER TOHYA-SAN??>
<I TRY NOT TO.>
<HAVE YOU SEEN HER? DO YOU KNOW WHERE SHE IS??>
<DON'T WASTE YOUR TIME WORRYING ABOUT THAT SELF-ABSORBE DRAMA QUEEN AND HER THEATRICS.>
<SHE PULLED THAT "CELL PHONE IN THE TRASH" THING ON ME TWO YEARS AGO.>
bip

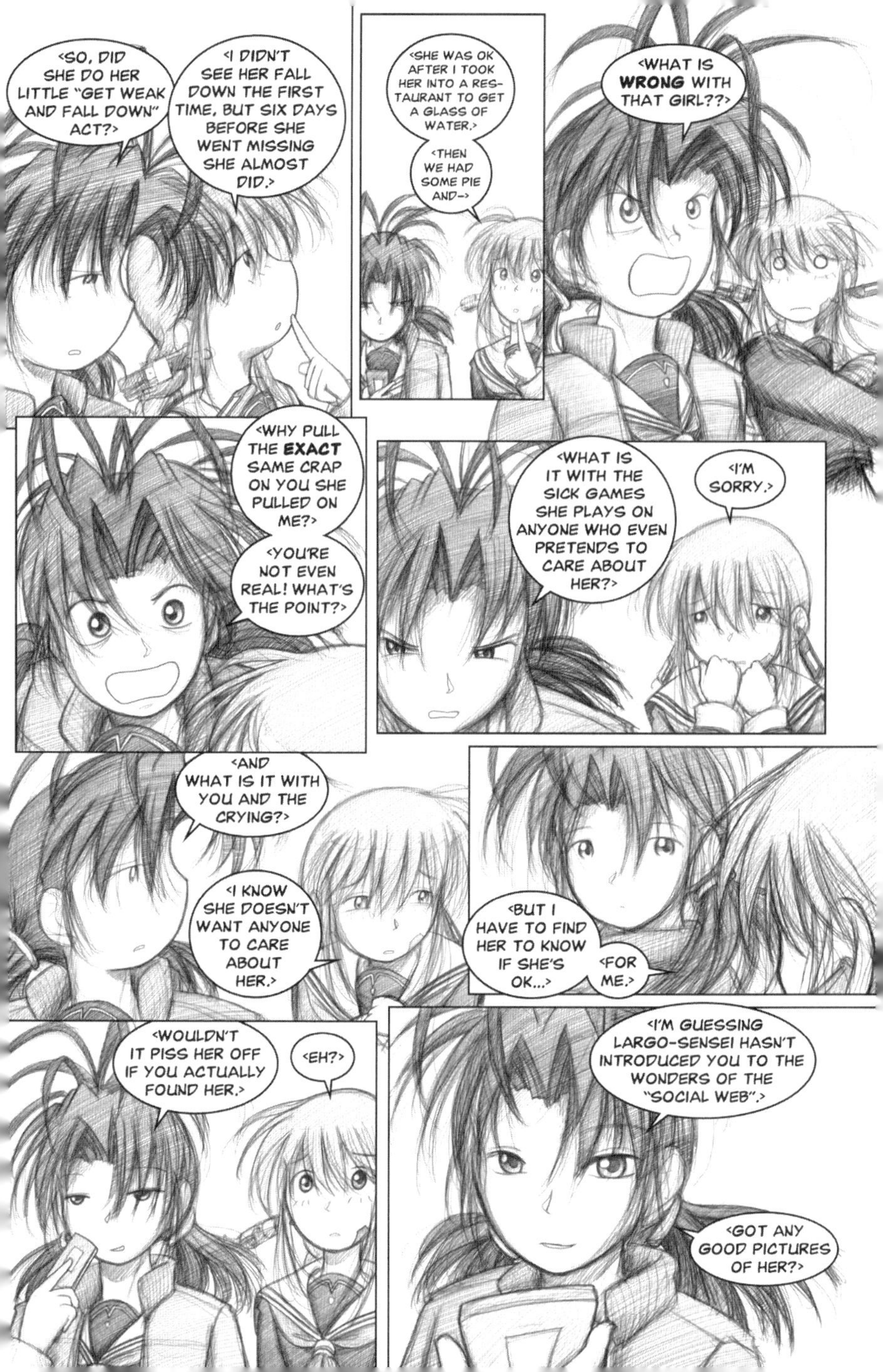

<SO, DID SHE DO HER LITTLE "GET WEAK AND FALL DOWN" ACT?>
<I DIDN'T SEE HER FALL DOWN THE FIRST TIME, BUT SIX DAYS BEFORE SHE WENT MISSING SHE ALMOST DID.>
<SHE WAS OK AFTER I TOOK HER INTO A RES-TAURANT TO GET A GLASS OF WATER.>
<THEN WE HAD SOME PIE AND–>
<WHAT IS **WRONG** WITH THAT GIRL??>
<WHY PULL THE **EXACT** SAME CRAP ON YOU SHE PULLED ON ME?>
<YOU'RE NOT EVEN REAL! WHAT'S THE POINT?>
<WHAT IS IT WITH THE SICK GAMES SHE PLAYS ON ANYONE WHO EVEN PRETENDS TO CARE ABOUT HER?>
<I'M SORRY.>
<AND WHAT IS IT WITH YOU AND THE CRYING?>
<I KNOW SHE DOESN'T WANT ANYONE TO CARE ABOUT HER.>
<BUT I HAVE TO FIND HER TO KNOW IF SHE'S OK...>
<FOR ME.>
<WOULDN'T IT PISS HER OFF IF YOU ACTUALLY FOUND HER.>
<EH?>
<I'M GUESSING LARGO-SENSEI HASN'T INTRODUCED YOU TO THE WONDERS OF THE "SOCIAL WEB".>
<GOT ANY GOOD PICTURES OF HER?>

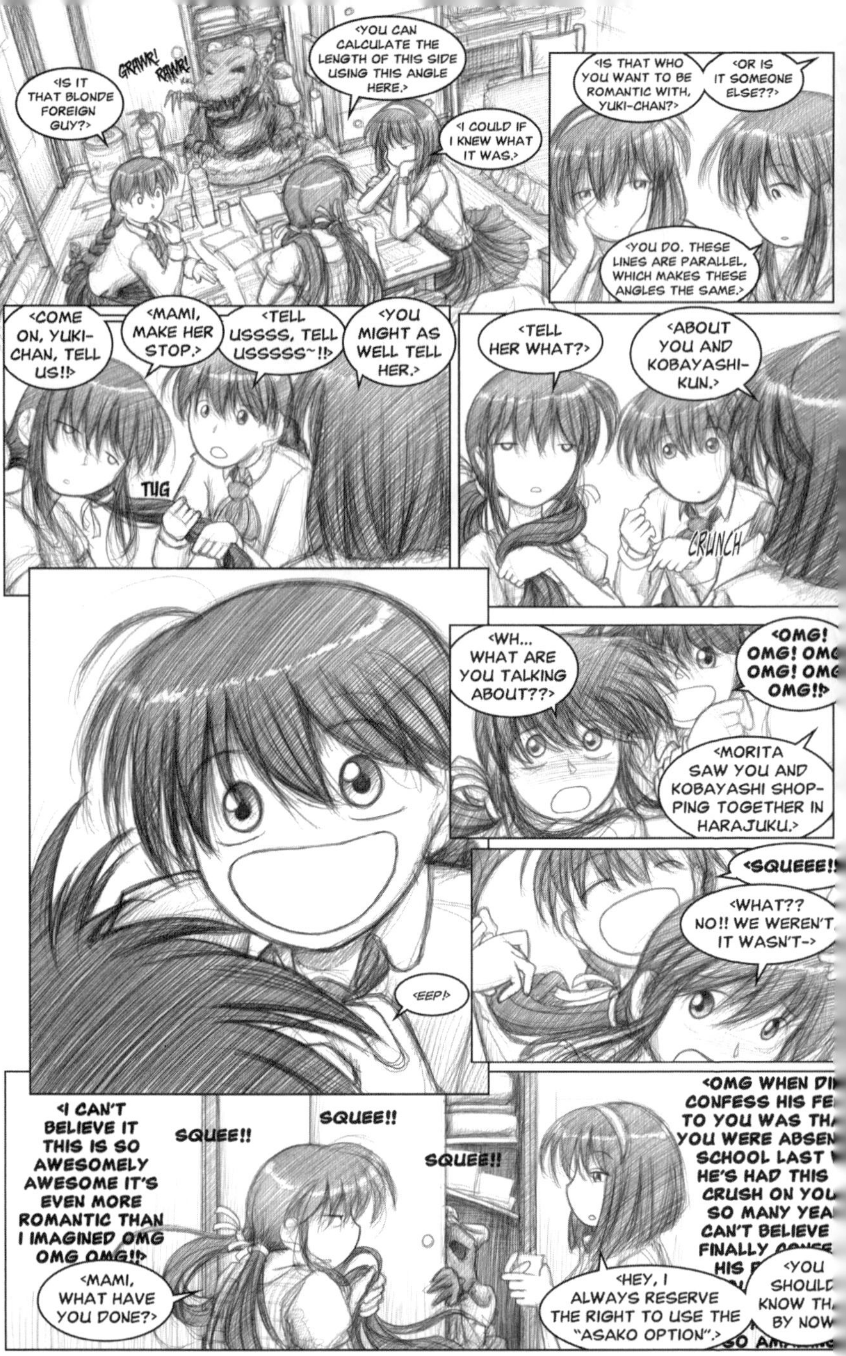

<IS IT THAT BLONDE FOREIGN GUY?>
GRAWR! RAWR!
<YOU CAN CALCULATE THE LENGTH OF THIS SIDE USING THIS ANGLE HERE.>
<I COULD IF I KNEW WHAT IT WAS.>
<IS THAT WHO YOU WANT TO BE ROMANTIC WITH, YUKI-CHAN?>
<OR IS IT SOMEONE ELSE??>
<YOU DO. THESE LINES ARE PARALLEL, WHICH MAKES THESE ANGLES THE SAME.>
<COME ON, YUKI-CHAN, TELL US!!>
<MAMI, MAKE HER STOP.>
<TELL USSSS, TELL USSSSS~!!>
<YOU MIGHT AS WELL TELL HER.>
TUG
<TELL HER WHAT?>
<ABOUT YOU AND KOBAYASHI-KUN.>
CRUNCH
<EEP!>
<WH... WHAT ARE YOU TALKING ABOUT??>
<OMG! OMG! OMG OMG! OMG OMG!!>
<MORITA SAW YOU AND KOBAYASHI SHOP-PING TOGETHER IN HARAJUKU.>
<SQUEEE!!
<WHAT?? NO!! WE WEREN'T IT WASN'T->
<I CAN'T BELIEVE IT THIS IS SO AWESOMELY AWESOME IT'S EVEN MORE ROMANTIC THAN I IMAGINED OMG OMG OMG!!>
SQUEE!!
SQUEE!!
SQUEE!!
<MAMI, WHAT HAVE YOU DONE?>
<OMG WHEN DI
CONFESS HIS FE
TO YOU WAS TH
YOU WERE ABSEN
SCHOOL LAST
HE'S HAD THIS
CRUSH ON YOU
SO MANY YEA
CAN'T BELIEVE
FINALLY
<HEY, I ALWAYS RESERVE THE RIGHT TO USE THE "ASAKO OPTION".>
<YOU SHOULD KNOW THA BY NOW

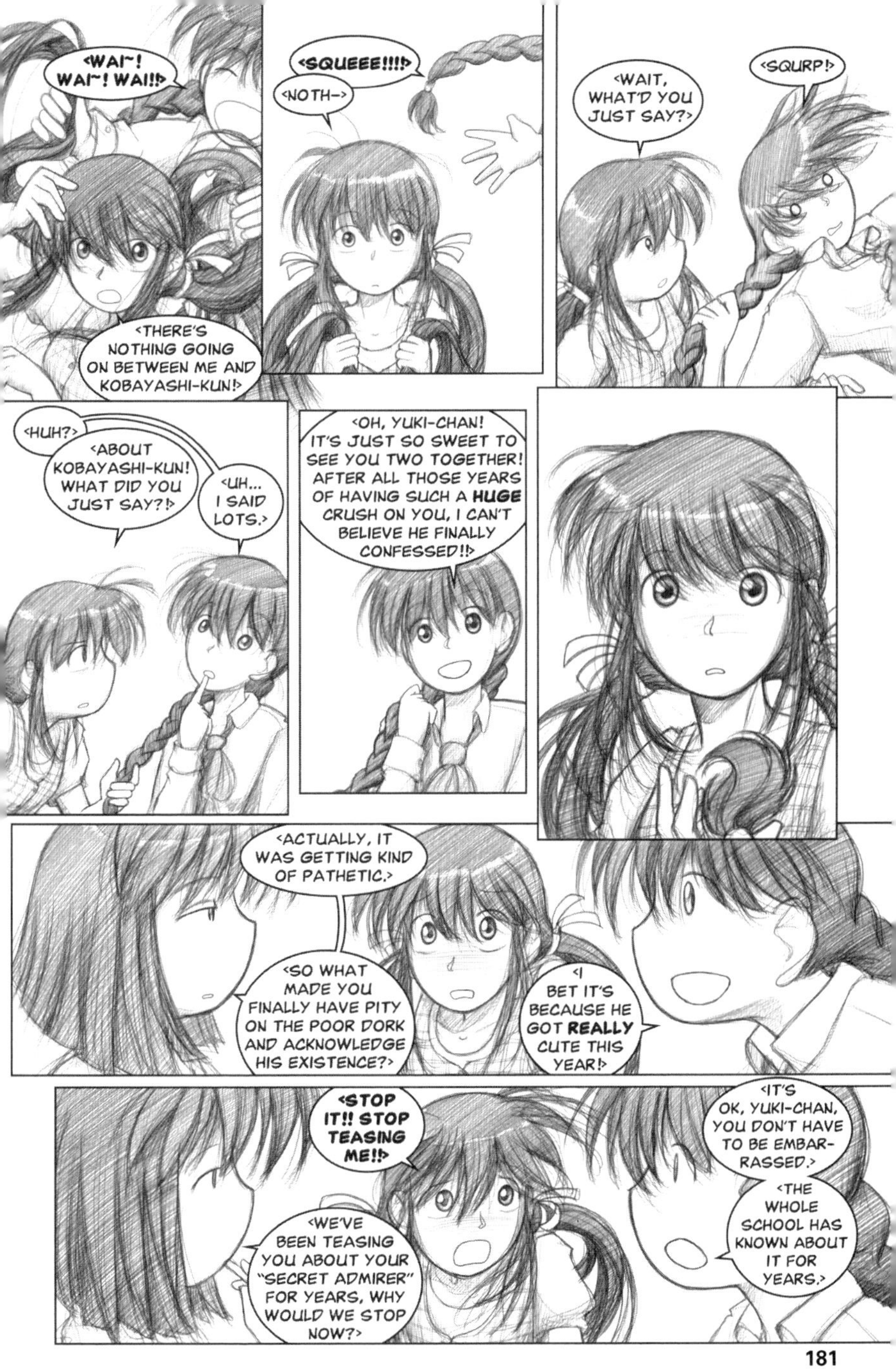
<WAI~! WAI~! WAI!!>
<THERE'S NOTHING GOING ON BETWEEN ME AND KOBAYASHI-KUN!>
<SQUEEE!!!!>
<NOTH–>
<WAIT, WHAT'D YOU JUST SAY?>
<SQURP!>
<HUH?>
<ABOUT KOBAYASHI-KUN! WHAT DID YOU JUST SAY?!>
<UH... I SAID LOTS.>
<OH, YUKI-CHAN! IT'S JUST SO SWEET TO SEE YOU TWO TOGETHER! AFTER ALL THOSE YEARS OF HAVING SUCH A **HUGE** CRUSH ON YOU, I CAN'T BELIEVE HE FINALLY CONFESSED!!>
<ACTUALLY, IT WAS GETTING KIND OF PATHETIC.>
<SO WHAT MADE YOU FINALLY HAVE PITY ON THE POOR DORK AND ACKNOWLEDGE HIS EXISTENCE?>
<I BET IT'S BECAUSE HE GOT **REALLY** CUTE THIS YEAR!>
<STOP IT!! STOP TEASING ME!!>
<WE'VE BEEN TEASING YOU ABOUT YOUR "SECRET ADMIRER" FOR YEARS, WHY WOULD WE STOP NOW?>
<IT'S OK, YUKI-CHAN, YOU DON'T HAVE TO BE EMBAR-RASSED.>
<THE WHOLE SCHOOL HAS KNOWN ABOUT IT FOR YEARS.>

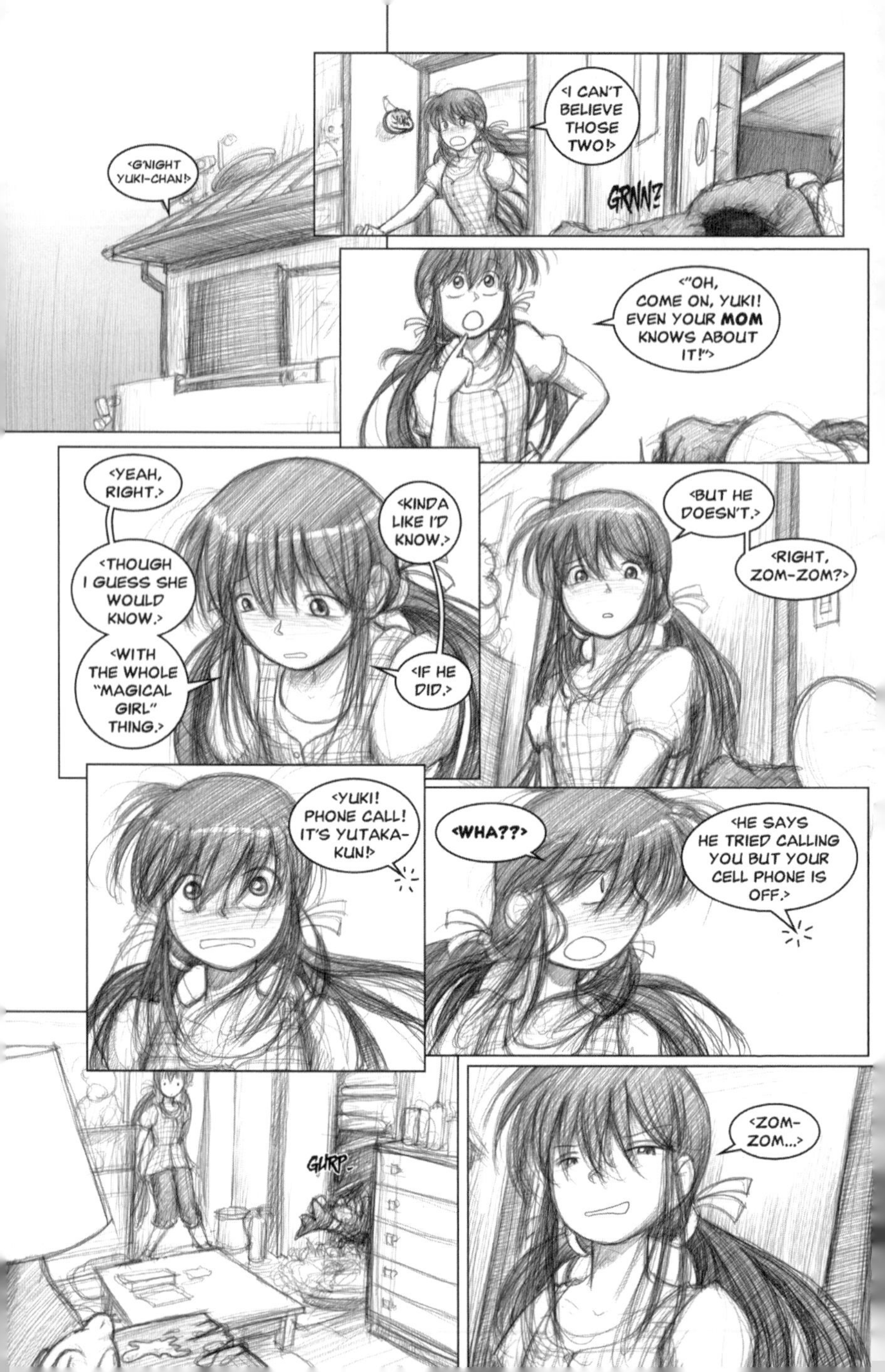
<G'NIGHT YUKI-CHAN!>
<I CAN'T BELIEVE THOSE TWO!>
GRNN?
<"OH, COME ON, YUKI! EVEN YOUR **MOM** KNOWS ABOUT IT!">
<YEAH, RIGHT.>
<KINDA LIKE I'D KNOW.>
<THOUGH I GUESS SHE WOULD KNOW.>
<WITH THE WHOLE "MAGICAL GIRL" THING.>
<IF HE DID.>
<BUT HE DOESN'T.>
<RIGHT, ZOM-ZOM?>
<YUKI! PHONE CALL! IT'S YUTAKA-KUN!>
<WHA??>
<HE SAYS HE TRIED CALLING YOU BUT YOUR CELL PHONE IS OFF.>
GURP
<ZOM-ZOM...>

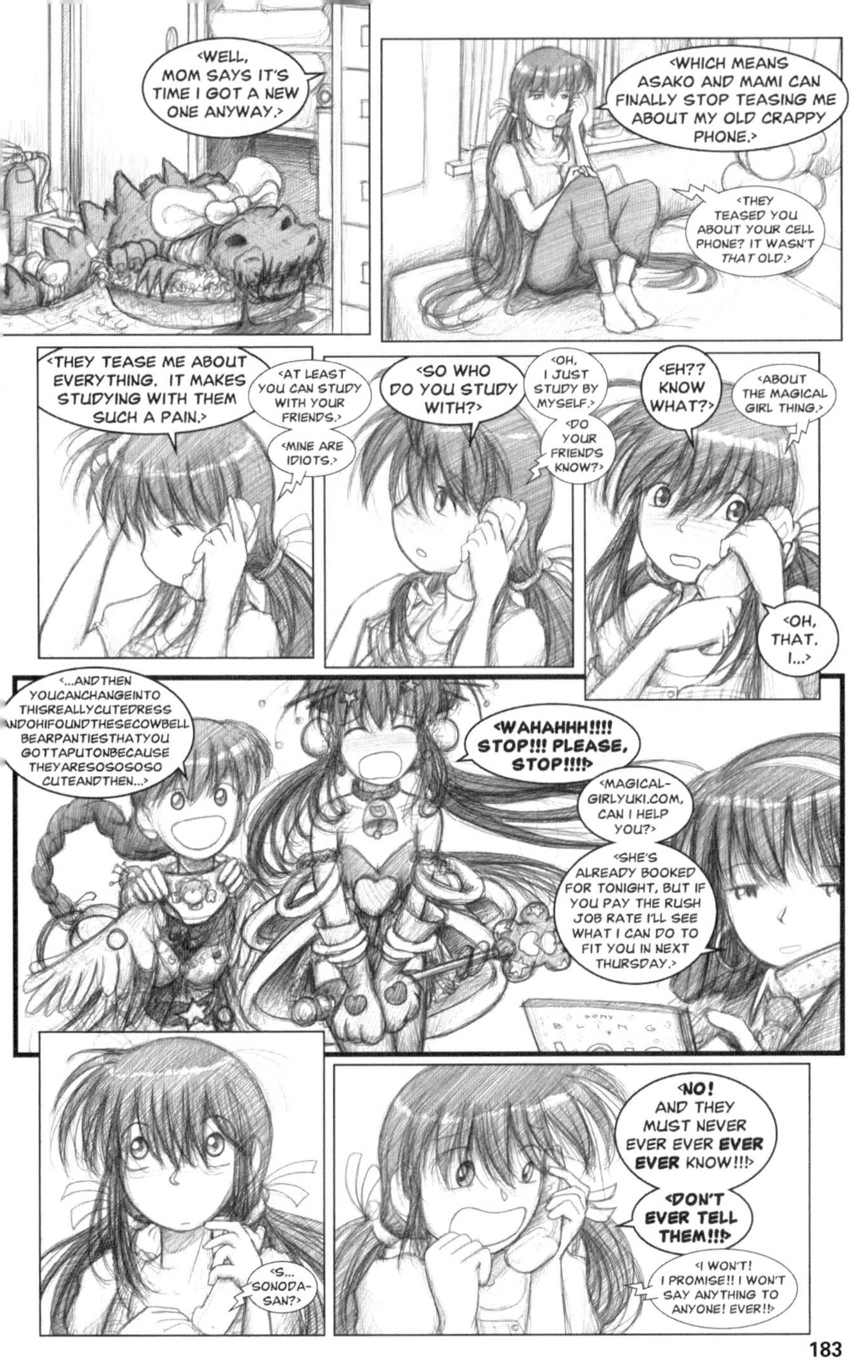
<WELL, MOM SAYS IT'S TIME I GOT A NEW ONE ANYWAY.>
<WHICH MEANS ASAKO AND MAMI CAN FINALLY STOP TEASING ME ABOUT MY OLD CRAPPY PHONE.>
<THEY TEASED YOU ABOUT YOUR CELL PHONE? IT WASN'T *THAT* OLD.>
<THEY TEASE ME ABOUT EVERYTHING. IT MAKES STUDYING WITH THEM SUCH A PAIN.>
<AT LEAST YOU CAN STUDY WITH YOUR FRIENDS.>
<MINE ARE IDIOTS.>
<SO WHO DO YOU STUDY WITH?>
<OH, I JUST STUDY BY MYSELF.>
<DO YOUR FRIENDS KNOW?>
<EH?? KNOW WHAT?>
<ABOUT THE MAGICAL GIRL THING.>
<OH, THAT. I...>
<...ANDTHEN YOUCANCHANGEINTO THISREALLYCUTEDRESS ANDOHIFOUNDTHESECOWBELL BEARPANTIESTHATYOU GOTTAPUTONBECAUSE THEYARESOSOSOSO CUTEANDTHEN...>
<WAHAHHH!!!! STOP!!! PLEASE, STOP!!!!>
<MAGICAL-GIRLYUKI.COM, CAN I HELP YOU?>
<SHE'S ALREADY BOOKED FOR TONIGHT, BUT IF YOU PAY THE RUSH JOB RATE I'LL SEE WHAT I CAN DO TO FIT YOU IN NEXT THURSDAY.>
<S... SONODA-SAN?>
<**NO!** AND THEY MUST NEVER EVER EVER **EVER EVER** KNOW!!!>
<DON'T EVER TELL THEM!!!>
<I WON'T! I PROMISE!! I WON'T SAY ANYTHING TO ANYONE! EVER!!>

‹I PROMISE!›

‹I MEAN IT! I WON'T SAY A WORD!!›

‹I BELIEVE YOU.›

‹SO...›

‹UHM...›

‹OH! THE REASON I CALLED?›

‹UWEH?›

‹REMEMBER WHEN WE TRIED TO FIND TOHYA'S HOUSE THE OTHER DAY?›

‹OH, YEAH.›

‹I CAN'T BELIEVE SHE GAVE THE SCHOOL A FAKE ADDRESS.›

‹IT'S NOT FAKE. YOU CAN SEE IT ON THE SATELLITE MAPS.›

‹I DON'T KNOW HOW, BUT WE WALKED RIGHT PAST IT SEVERAL TIMES.›

‹WE DID?›

‹YEAH, IT'S RIGHT AROUND THE CORNER FROM THE DAIRY MART WHERE THAT GUY THOUGHT SHE WORKED AT SOME CLUB IN HARAJUKU.›

‹BUT HE WAS THE ONLY PERSON WE TALKED TO WHO REMEMBERED HER.›

‹NO ONE IN HARAJUKU HAD EVER HEARD OF HER.›

‹WELL, WE HAVEN'T ASKED EVERYBODY.›

‹I'VE BEEN THINKING THAT WE MIGHT HAVE BETTER LUCK IF WE HAD SOME PICTURES OF HER, SO I DID SOME POKING AROUND TO SEE WHAT I COULD FIND.›

‹Y'KNOW... I DON'T THINK TOHYA HAS EVER POSTED ANYTHING ONLINE, ANYWHERE.›

‹MY BROTHER IS REALLY GOOD WITH THIS KINDA STUFF, AND HE SAYS IT'S SPOOKY, LIKE SHE DOESN'T EVEN EXIST AT ALL.›

‹AT LEAST ONLINE SHE DOESN'T.›

‹THAT'S WEIRD. SO NO PICTURES?›

‹WELL, NO...?›

‹...AT LEAST NOT UNTIL ABOUT AN HOUR AGO WHEN SOMEONE POSTED ENOUGH PICTURES AND VIDEO OF TOHYA TO BUILD A SHRINE.›

‹LOOKS LIKE WE AREN'T THE ONLY ONES LOOKING FOR HER.›

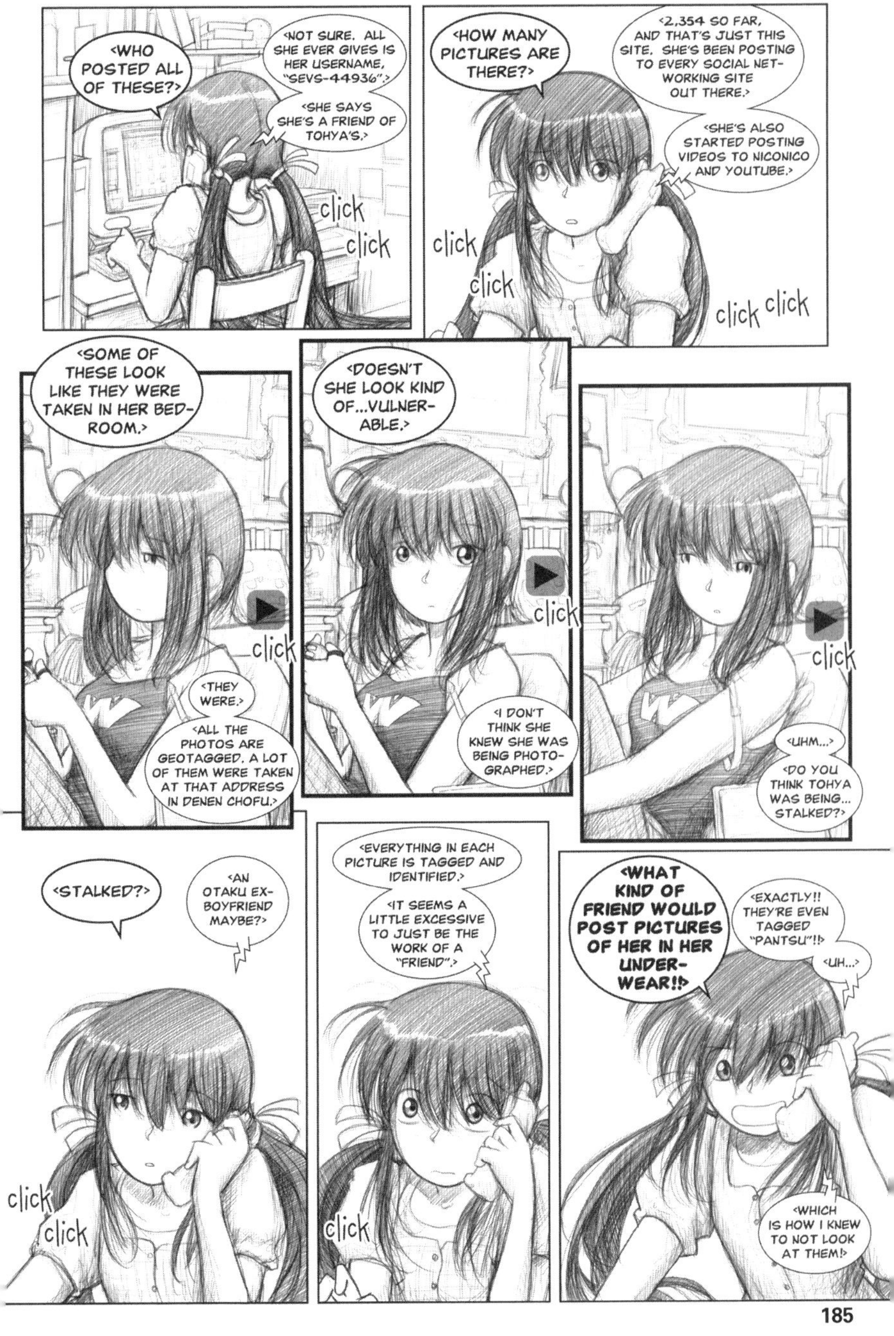
<WHO POSTED ALL OF THESE?>
<NOT SURE. ALL SHE EVER GIVES IS HER USERNAME, "SEVS-44936".>
<SHE SAYS SHE'S A FRIEND OF TOHYA'S.>
click
click
<HOW MANY PICTURES ARE THERE?>
<2,354 SO FAR, AND THAT'S JUST THIS SITE. SHE'S BEEN POSTING TO EVERY SOCIAL NET-WORKING SITE OUT THERE.>
<SHE'S ALSO STARTED POSTING VIDEOS TO NICONICO AND YOUTUBE.>
click
click
click click
<SOME OF THESE LOOK LIKE THEY WERE TAKEN IN HER BED-ROOM.>
click
<THEY WERE.>
<ALL THE PHOTOS ARE GEOTAGGED. A LOT OF THEM WERE TAKEN AT THAT ADDRESS IN DENEN CHOFU.>
<DOESN'T SHE LOOK KIND OF...VULNER-ABLE.>
click
<I DON'T THINK SHE KNEW SHE WAS BEING PHOTO-GRAPHED.>
click
<UHM...>
<DO YOU THINK TOHYA WAS BEING... STALKED?>
<STALKED?>
<AN OTAKU EX-BOYFRIEND MAYBE?>
click
click
<EVERYTHING IN EACH PICTURE IS TAGGED AND IDENTIFIED.>
<IT SEEMS A LITTLE EXCESSIVE TO JUST BE THE WORK OF A "FRIEND".>
click
<WHAT KIND OF FRIEND WOULD POST PICTURES OF HER IN HER UNDER-WEAR!!>
<EXACTLY!! THEY'RE EVEN TAGGED "PANTSU"!!>
<UH...>
<WHICH IS HOW I KNEW TO NOT LOOK AT THEM!>

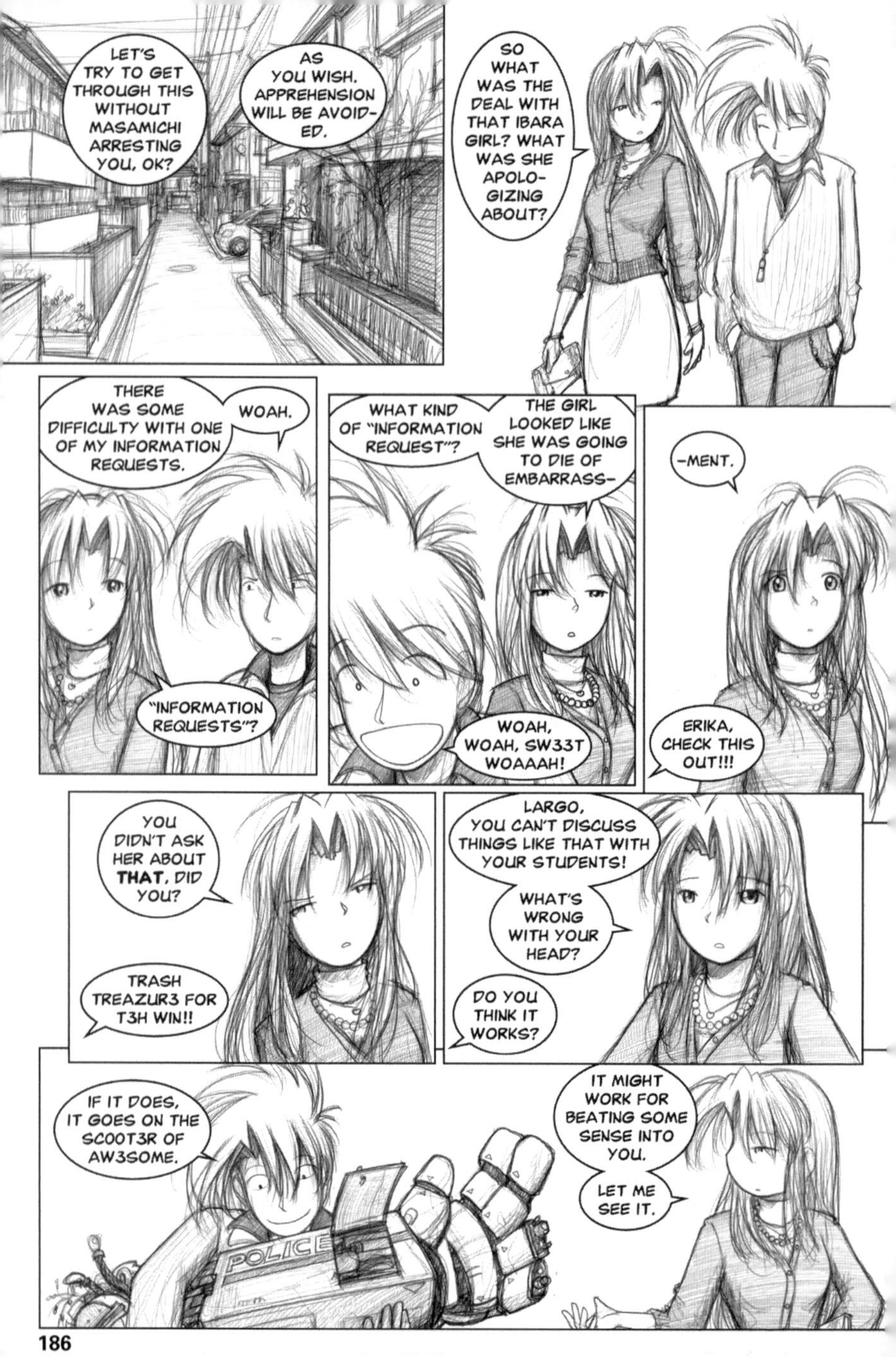
LET'S TRY TO GET THROUGH THIS WITHOUT MASAMICHI ARRESTING YOU, OK?
AS YOU WISH. APPREHENSION WILL BE AVOID-ED.
SO WHAT WAS THE DEAL WITH THAT IBARA GIRL? WHAT WAS SHE APOLO-GIZING ABOUT?
THERE WAS SOME DIFFICULTY WITH ONE OF MY INFORMATION REQUESTS.
WOAH.
"INFORMATION REQUESTS"?
WHAT KIND OF "INFORMATION REQUEST"?
THE GIRL LOOKED LIKE SHE WAS GOING TO DIE OF EMBARRASS-
WOAH, WOAH, SW33T WOAAAH!
-MENT.
ERIKA, CHECK THIS OUT!!!
YOU DIDN'T ASK HER ABOUT **THAT**, DID YOU?
TRASH TREAZUR3 FOR T3H WIN!!
LARGO, YOU CAN'T DISCUSS THINGS LIKE THAT WITH YOUR STUDENTS!
WHAT'S WRONG WITH YOUR HEAD?
DO YOU THINK IT WORKS?
IF IT DOES, IT GOES ON THE SCOOT3R OF AW3SOME.
POLICE
IT MIGHT WORK FOR BEATING SOME SENSE INTO YOU.
LET ME SEE IT.

‹YUUJI, I DON'T THINK THAT'S SOMETHING SHE WANTS TO TALK ABOUT.›

‹IT'S OK. I DON'T MIND.›

‹THERE IS ONE THING I DON'T MISS ABOUT BEING AN IDOL.›

‹MY ENTIRE LIFE ISN'T ON DISPLAY ANY-MORE.›

tak tak tak

‹OF COURSE, IT WASN'T MY "REAL" LIFE THAT PEOPLE SAW.›

‹IT WASN'T?›

‹NO, MY "LIFE" BECAME PART OF THE PERFORMANCE. IT WAS VERY STRESS-FUL.›

tak tak tak

‹I GUESS THAT'S WHY IT ALL BLEW UP IN MY FACE IN THE END.›

LARGO, DON'T DO THAT.

THE BURNER WANTS TO BURN!

NO, IT WANTS TO KEEP THE POT WARM. LEAVE IT ALONE.

(GIGGLE) ‹LARGO-SAN, YOU ARE SO FUNNY!›

FWOOSHH!

tak tak tak

‹IT WOULD HAVE BEEN BETTER IF YOU HAD JUST BEEN YOURSELF FROM THE START.›

‹I'D HAVE BEEN A LOT LESS POPULAR AND NEVER BECOME AN IDOL IF I HAD.›

‹SO MAYBE YOU'RE RIGHT.›

SQUIRCH!

SO, WHERE DO YOU KEEP YOUR GUNS?

LARGO...

SMALL ARMS OR THE BIG STUFF?

<DEAR...>

T3H AW3SOM3 STUFF.

SQUUUCH!

BUNKER OUT BACK. I'LL SHOW YOU AFTER DINNER.

<SO MUCH FOR ENDING THE EVENING WITHOUT HIM GETTING ARRESTED.>

YOU GOT ONE OF THESE?

THREE OF 'EM.

HOW ABOUT THESE?

SURE.

blip!

<OH, MY!>

<WHAT A BIG CELL PHONE YOU HAVE, LARGO-SAN!>

<YOU'RE KIDDING. YOU WANT TO COMPLIMENT HIM ABOUT HIS CELL PHONE?>

SHE LIKES YOUR CELL PHONE.

<YUKI'S WAS EATEN BY HER PET ZOMBIE ZILLA.>

YUKI'S WAS EATEN BY HER PET "ZOMBIE ZILLA."

<WAIT, HER WHAT?>

<ZOM-ZOM-CHAN IS KINDA STINKY BUT HE'S SO CUTE!>

189

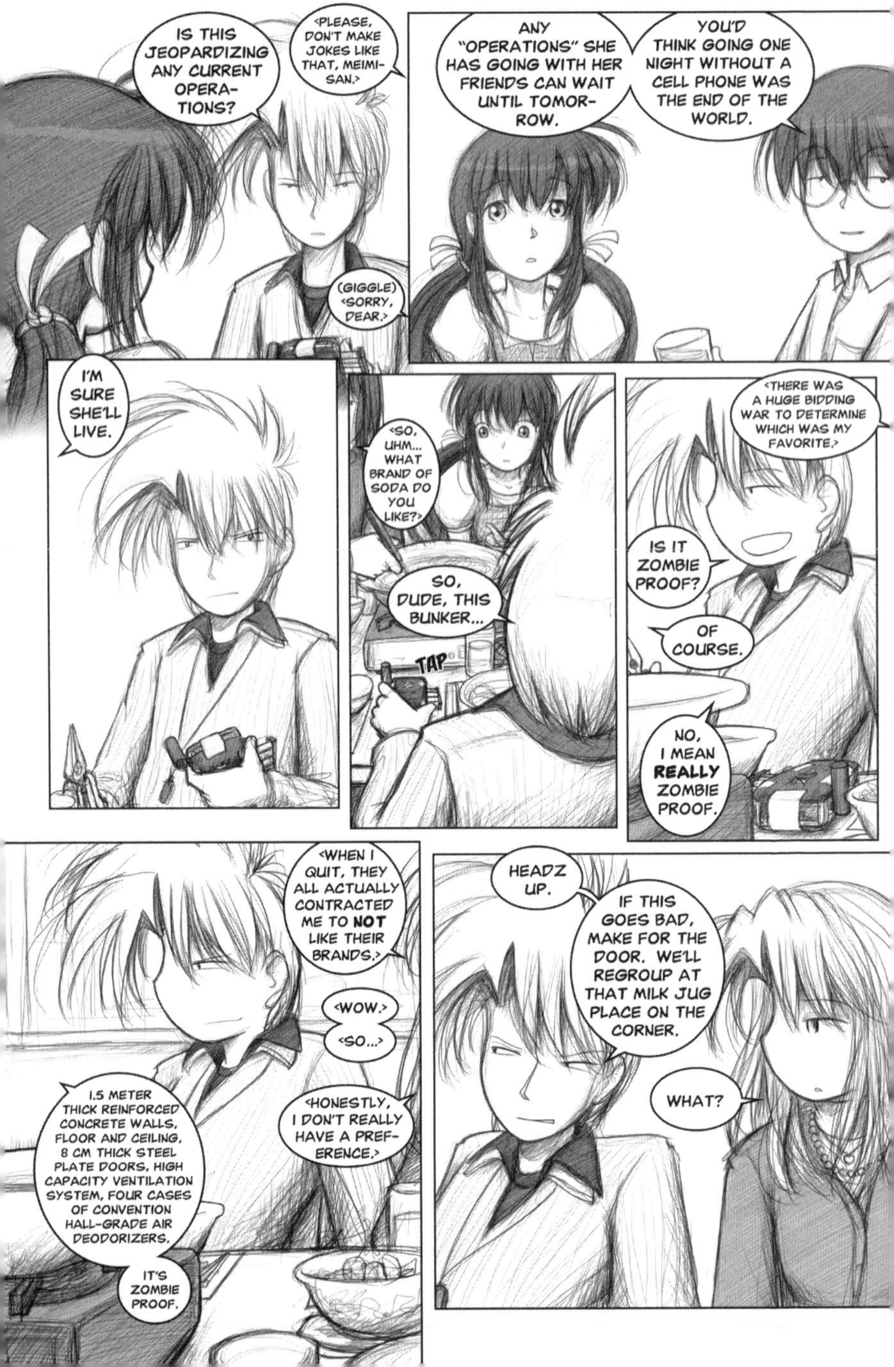
IS THIS JEOPARDIZING ANY CURRENT OPERATIONS?
<PLEASE, DON'T MAKE JOKES LIKE THAT, MEIMI-SAN.>
(GIGGLE) <SORRY, DEAR.>
ANY "OPERATIONS" SHE HAS GOING WITH HER FRIENDS CAN WAIT UNTIL TOMORROW.
YOU'D THINK GOING ONE NIGHT WITHOUT A CELL PHONE WAS THE END OF THE WORLD.
I'M SURE SHE'LL LIVE.
<SO, UHM... WHAT BRAND OF SODA DO YOU LIKE?>
SO, DUDE, THIS BUNKER...
TAP
<THERE WAS A HUGE BIDDING WAR TO DETERMINE WHICH WAS MY FAVORITE.>
IS IT ZOMBIE PROOF?
OF COURSE.
NO, I MEAN **REALLY** ZOMBIE PROOF.
<WHEN I QUIT, THEY ALL ACTUALLY CONTRACTED ME TO **NOT** LIKE THEIR BRANDS.>
<WOW.>
<SO...>
1.5 METER THICK REINFORCED CONCRETE WALLS, FLOOR AND CEILING, 8 CM THICK STEEL PLATE DOORS, HIGH CAPACITY VENTILATION SYSTEM, FOUR CASES OF CONVENTION HALL-GRADE AIR DEODORIZERS.
<HONESTLY, I DON'T REALLY HAVE A PREFERENCE.>
IT'S ZOMBIE PROOF.
HEADZ UP.
IF THIS GOES BAD, MAKE FOR THE DOOR. WE'LL REGROUP AT THAT MILK JUG PLACE ON THE CORNER.
WHAT?

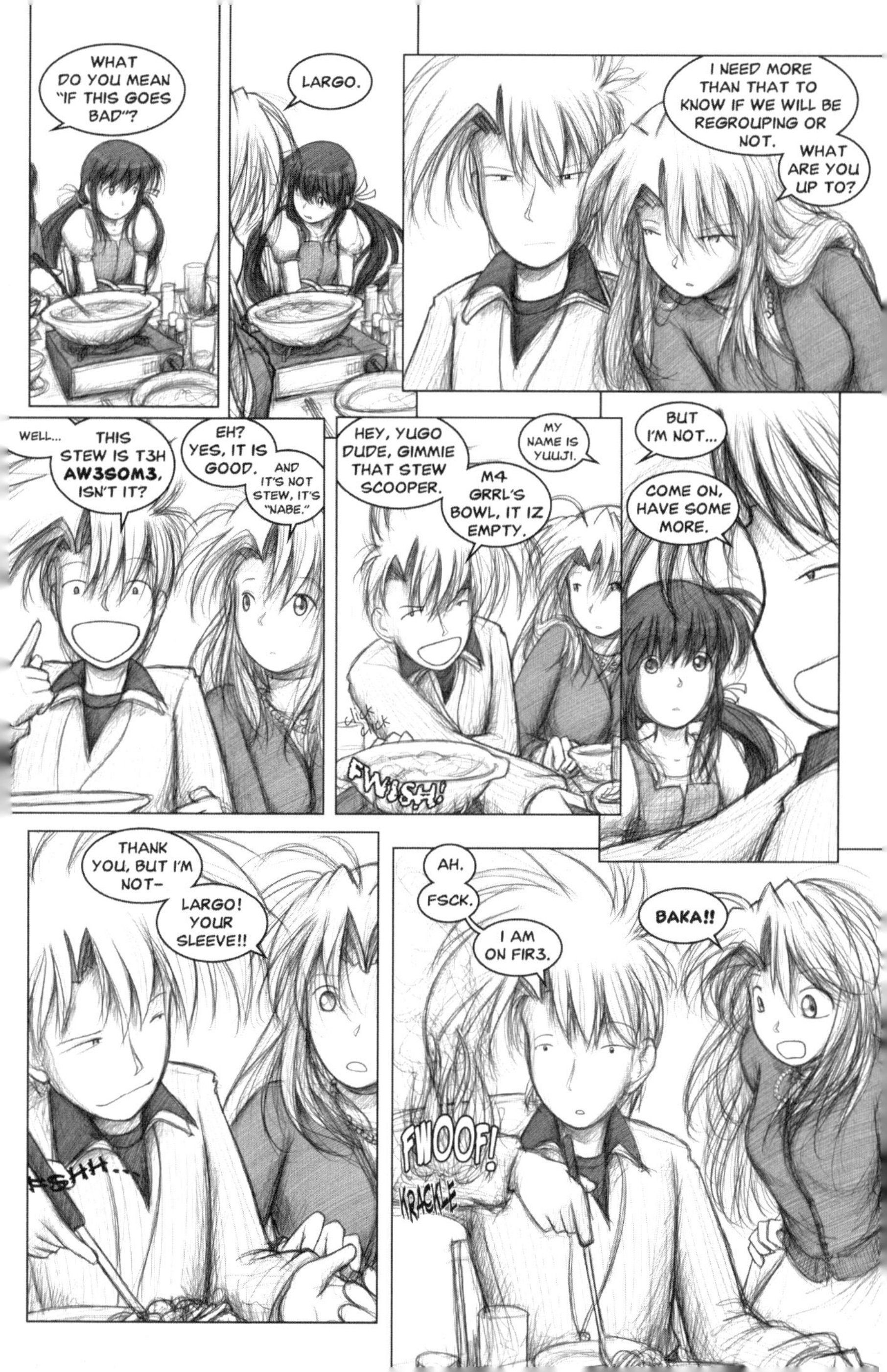

WHAT DO YOU MEAN "IF THIS GOES BAD"?
LARGO.
I NEED MORE THAN THAT TO KNOW IF WE WILL BE REGROUPING OR NOT.
WHAT ARE YOU UP TO?
WELL...
THIS STEW IS T3H **AW3SOM3,** ISN'T IT?
EH? YES, IT IS GOOD.
AND IT'S NOT STEW, IT'S "NABE."
HEY, YUGO DUDE, GIMMIE THAT STEW SCOOPER.
MY NAME IS YUUJI.
M4 GRRL'S BOWL, IT IZ EMPTY.
click click
FWISH!
BUT I'M NOT...
COME ON, HAVE SOME MORE.
THANK YOU, BUT I'M NOT-
LARGO! YOUR SLEEVE!!
FSHH...
AH.
FSCK.
I AM ON FIR3.
BAKA!!
FWOOF!
KRACKLE

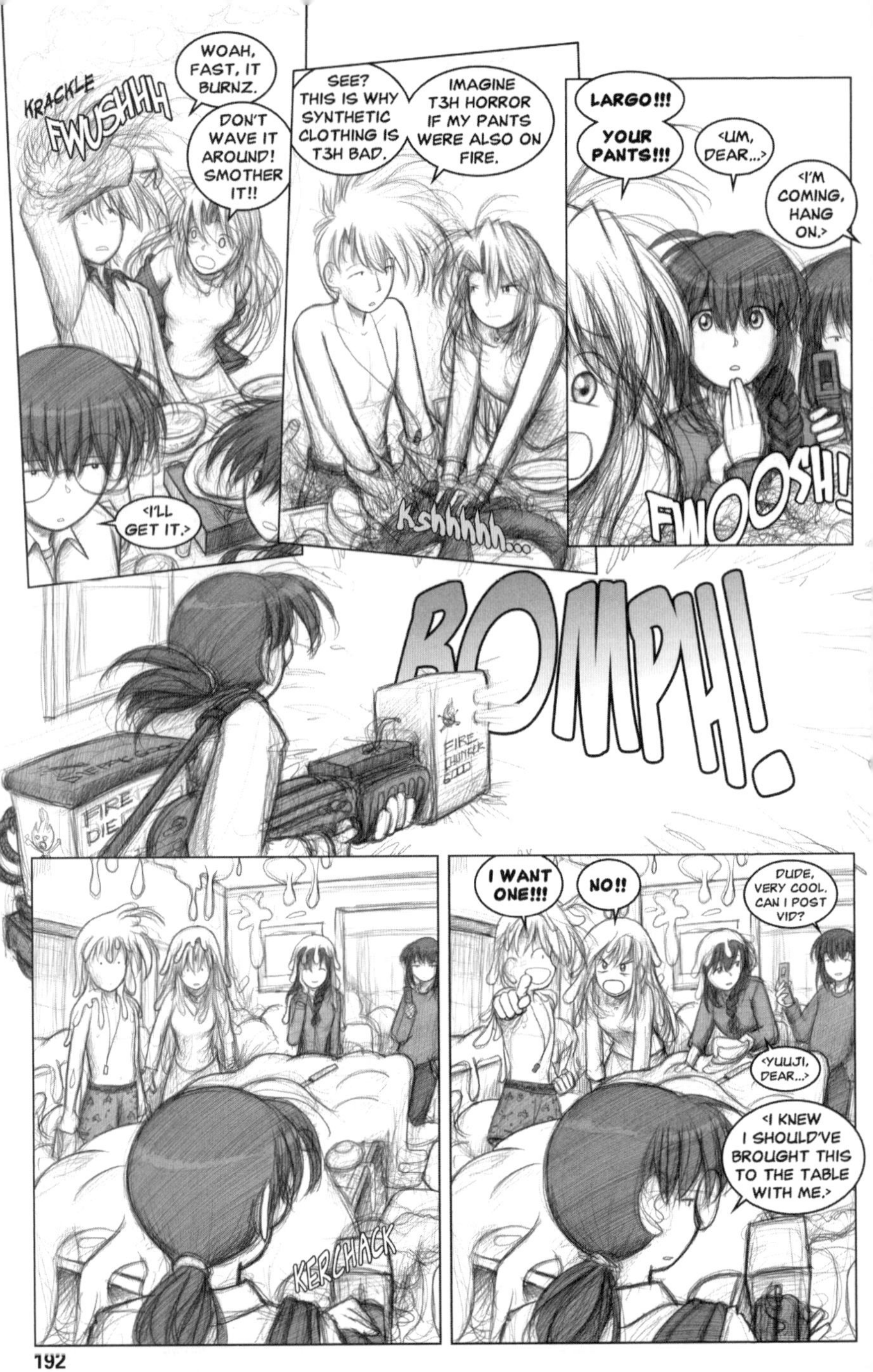
KRACKLE
FWUSHHH
WOAH, FAST, IT BURNZ.
DON'T WAVE IT AROUND! SMOTHER IT!!
<I'LL GET IT.>
SEE? THIS IS WHY SYNTHETIC CLOTHING IS T3H BAD.
IMAGINE T3H HORROR IF MY PANTS WERE ALSO ON FIRE.
Kshhhhh...
LARGO!!!
YOUR PANTS!!!
<UM, DEAR...>
<I'M COMING, HANG ON.>
FWOOSH!
BOMPH!
KERCHACK
I WANT ONE!!!
NO!!
DUDE, VERY COOL. CAN I POST VID?
<YUUJI, DEAR...>
<I KNEW I SHOULD'VE BROUGHT THIS TO THE TABLE WITH ME.>

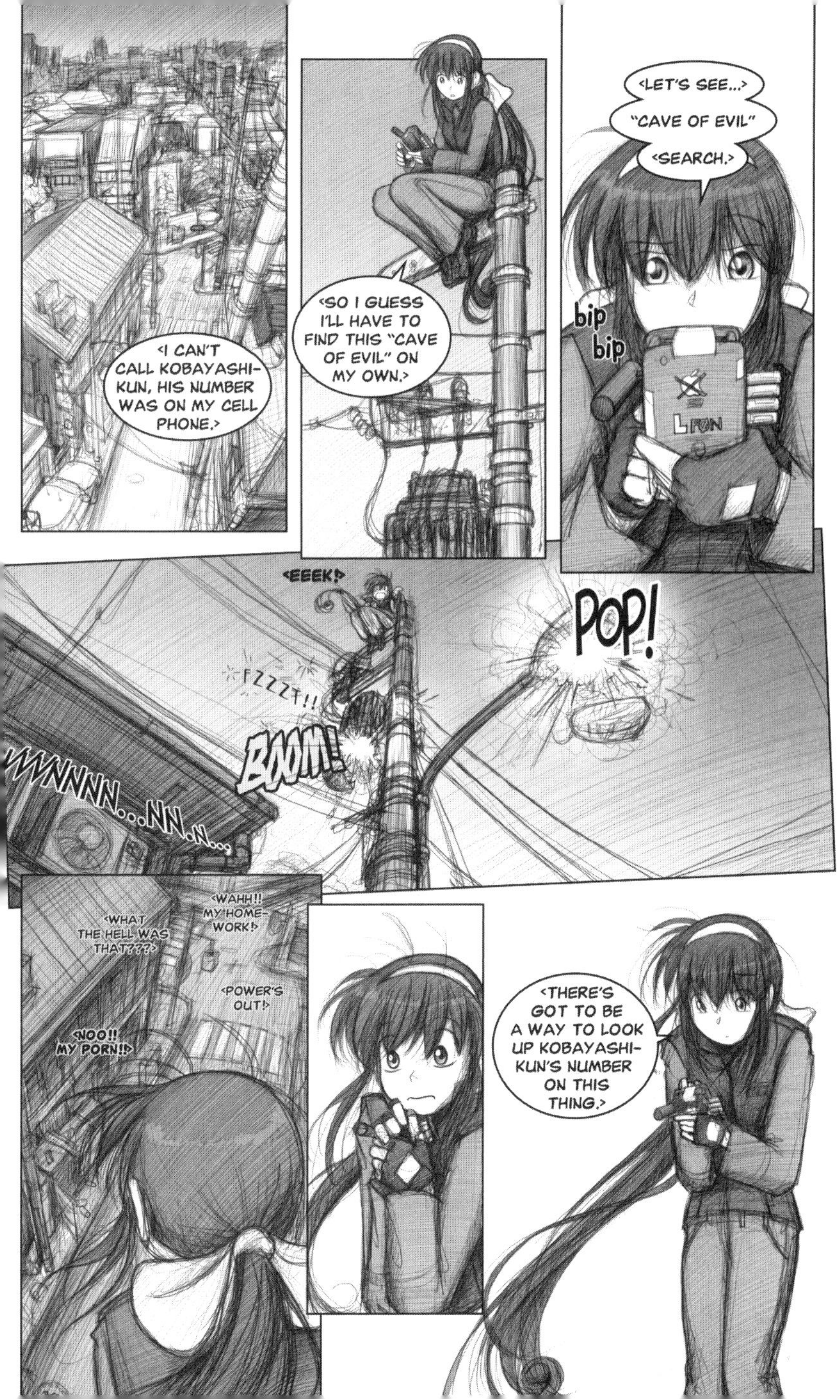
<I CAN'T CALL KOBAYASHI-KUN, HIS NUMBER WAS ON MY CELL PHONE.>
<SO I GUESS I'LL HAVE TO FIND THIS "CAVE OF EVIL" ON MY OWN.>
<LET'S SEE...>
"CAVE OF EVIL"
<SEARCH.>
bip
bip
<EEEK!>
FZZZT!!
BOOM!
POP!
NNNNN...NN.N...
<WHAT THE HELL WAS THAT???>
<WAHH!! MY HOME-WORK!>
<POWER'S OUT!>
<NOO!! MY PORN!!>
<THERE'S GOT TO BE A WAY TO LOOK UP KOBAYASHI-KUN'S NUMBER ON THIS THING.>

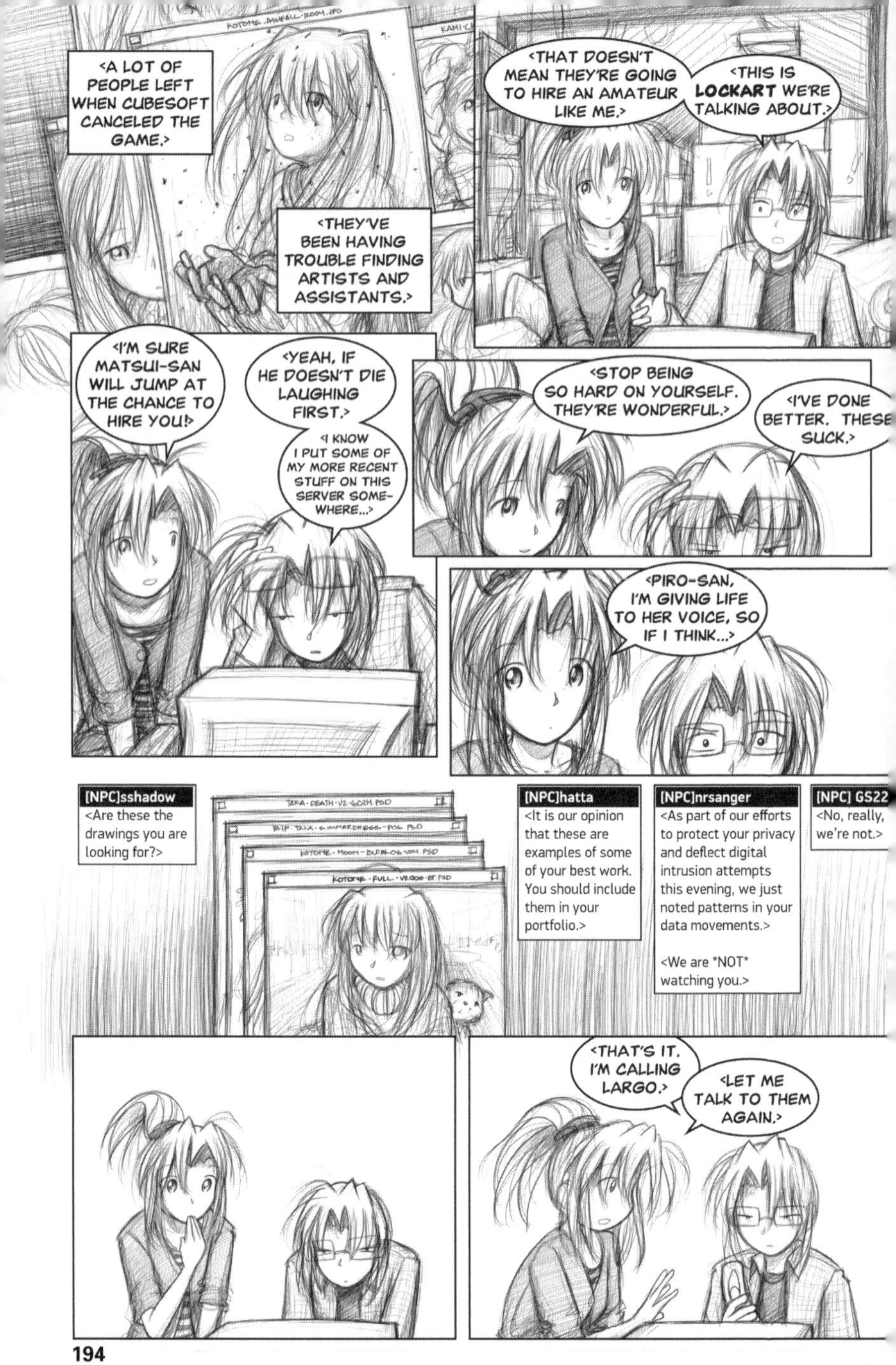

KOTOME_RAINFALL_ROOM.JPG
<A LOT OF PEOPLE LEFT WHEN CUBESOFT CANCELED THE GAME.>
<THEY'VE BEEN HAVING TROUBLE FINDING ARTISTS AND ASSISTANTS.>
<THAT DOESN'T MEAN THEY'RE GOING TO HIRE AN AMATEUR LIKE ME.>
<THIS IS **LOCKART** WE'RE TALKING ABOUT.>
<I'M SURE MATSUI-SAN WILL JUMP AT THE CHANCE TO HIRE YOU!>
<YEAH, IF HE DOESN'T DIE LAUGHING FIRST.>
<I KNOW I PUT SOME OF MY MORE RECENT STUFF ON THIS SERVER SOME-WHERE...>
<STOP BEING SO HARD ON YOURSELF. THEY'RE WONDERFUL.>
<I'VE DONE BETTER. THESE SUCK.>
<PIRO-SAN, I'M GIVING LIFE TO HER VOICE, SO IF I THINK...>
[NPC]sshadow
<Are these the drawings you are looking for?>
[NPC]hatta
<It is our opinion that these are examples of some of your best work. You should include them in your portfolio.>
[NPC]nrsanger
<As part of our efforts to protect your privacy and deflect digital intrusion attempts this evening, we just noted patterns in your data movements.>
<We are *NOT* watching you.>
[NPC] GS22
<No, really, we're not.>
<THAT'S IT. I'M CALLING LARGO.>
<LET ME TALK TO THEM AGAIN.>

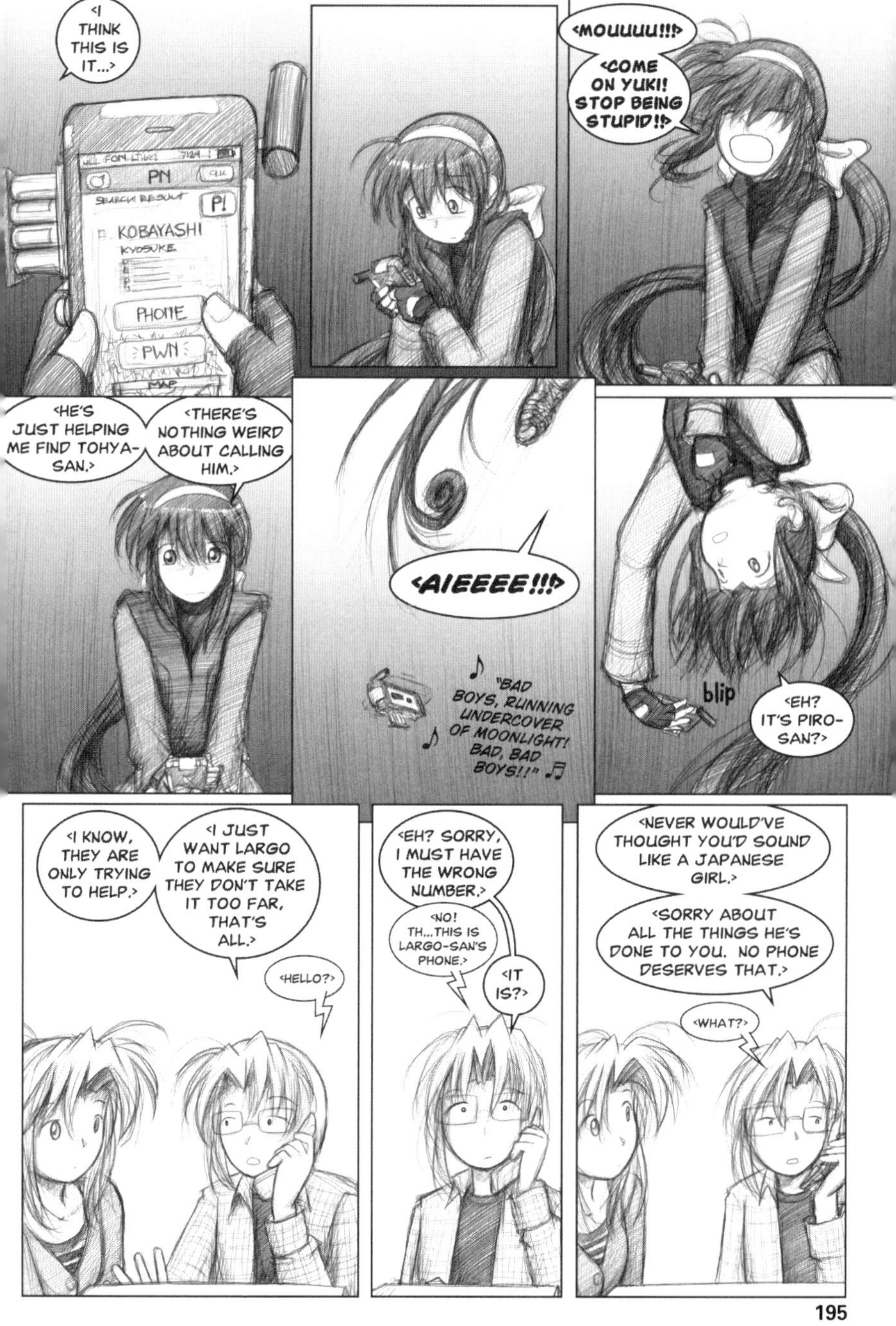
<I THINK THIS IS IT...>
PN
SEARCH RESULT
P!
KOBAYASHI
KYOSUKE
PHONE
PWN
MAP
<MOUUUU!!!>
<COME ON YUKI! STOP BEING STUPID!!>
<HE'S JUST HELPING ME FIND TOHYA-SAN.>
<THERE'S NOTHING WEIRD ABOUT CALLING HIM.>
<AIEEEE!!!>
"BAD BOYS, RUNNING UNDERCOVER OF MOONLIGHT! BAD, BAD BOYS!!"
blip
<EH? IT'S PIRO-SAN?>
<I KNOW, THEY ARE ONLY TRYING TO HELP.>
<I JUST WANT LARGO TO MAKE SURE THEY DON'T TAKE IT TOO FAR, THAT'S ALL.>
<HELLO?>
<EH? SORRY, I MUST HAVE THE WRONG NUMBER.>
<NO! TH...THIS IS LARGO-SAN'S PHONE.>
<IT IS?>
<NEVER WOULD'VE THOUGHT YOU'D SOUND LIKE A JAPANESE GIRL.>
<SORRY ABOUT ALL THE THINGS HE'S DONE TO YOU. NO PHONE DESERVES THAT.>
<WHAT?>

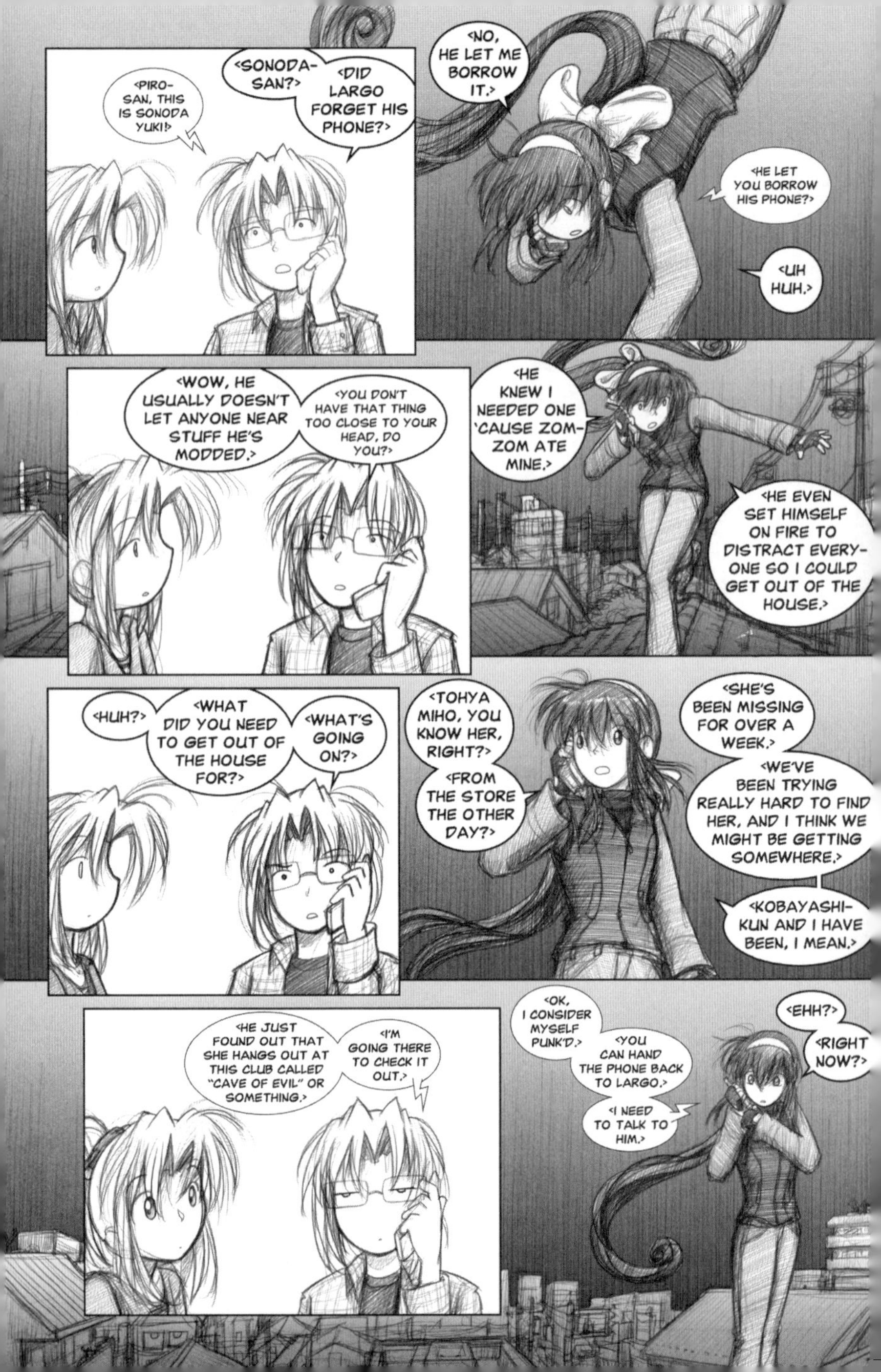
<PIRO-SAN, THIS IS SONODA YUKI!>
<SONODA-SAN?>
<DID LARGO FORGET HIS PHONE?>
<NO, HE LET ME BORROW IT.>
<HE LET YOU BORROW HIS PHONE?>
<UH HUH.>
<WOW, HE USUALLY DOESN'T LET ANYONE NEAR STUFF HE'S MODDED.>
<YOU DON'T HAVE THAT THING TOO CLOSE TO YOUR HEAD, DO YOU?>
<HE KNEW I NEEDED ONE 'CAUSE ZOM-ZOM ATE MINE.>
<HE EVEN SET HIMSELF ON FIRE TO DISTRACT EVERY-ONE SO I COULD GET OUT OF THE HOUSE.>
<HUH?>
<WHAT DID YOU NEED TO GET OUT OF THE HOUSE FOR?>
<WHAT'S GOING ON?>
<TOHYA MIHO, YOU KNOW HER, RIGHT?>
<FROM THE STORE THE OTHER DAY?>
<SHE'S BEEN MISSING FOR OVER A WEEK.>
<WE'VE BEEN TRYING REALLY HARD TO FIND HER, AND I THINK WE MIGHT BE GETTING SOMEWHERE.>
<KOBAYASHI-KUN AND I HAVE BEEN, I MEAN.>
<HE JUST FOUND OUT THAT SHE HANGS OUT AT THIS CLUB CALLED "CAVE OF EVIL" OR SOMETHING.>
<I'M GOING THERE TO CHECK IT OUT.>
<OK, I CONSIDER MYSELF PUNK'D.>
<YOU CAN HAND THE PHONE BACK TO LARGO.>
<I NEED TO TALK TO HIM.>
<EHH?>
<RIGHT NOW?>

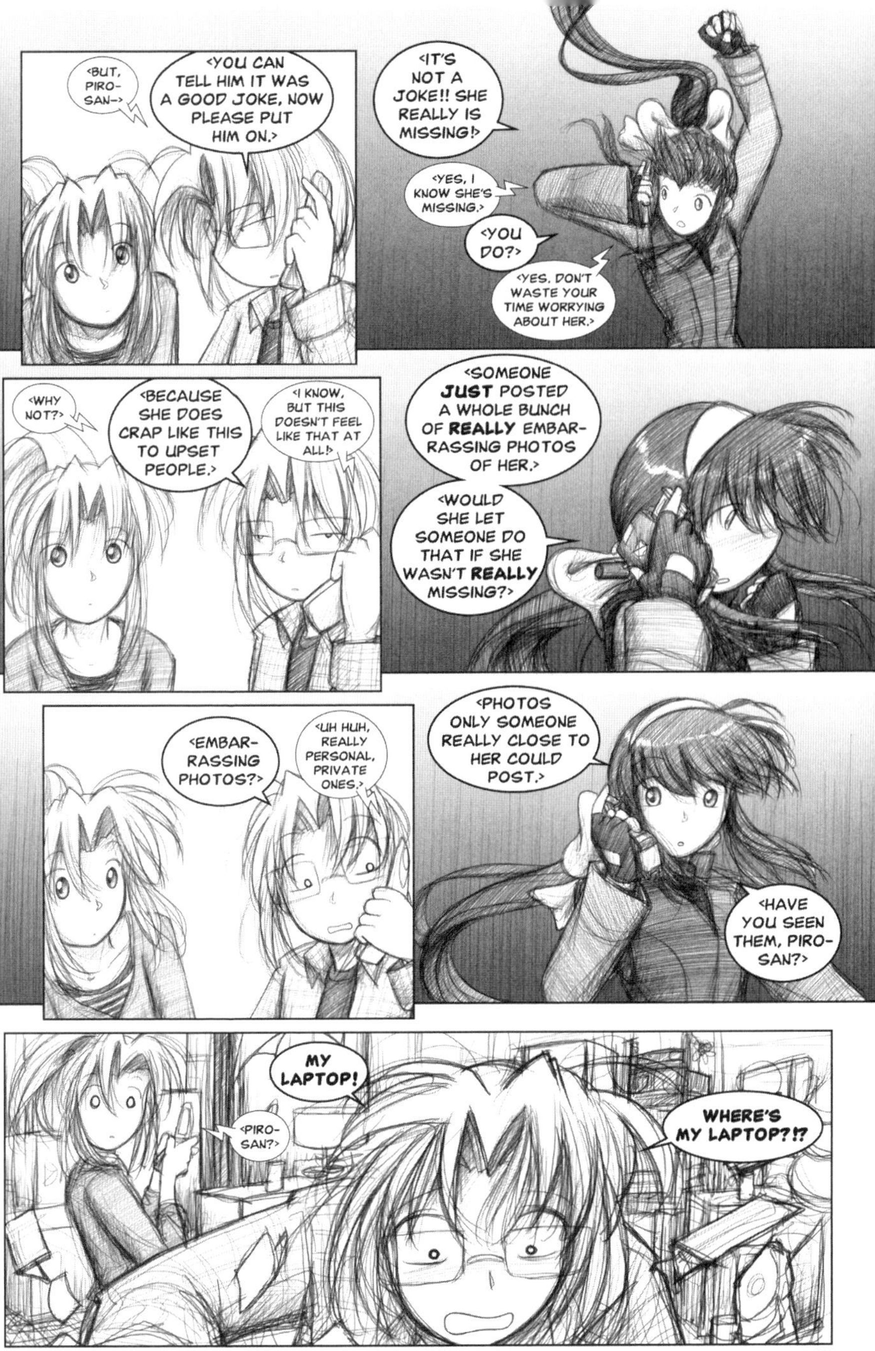
<BUT, PIRO-SAN—>
<YOU CAN TELL HIM IT WAS A GOOD JOKE, NOW PLEASE PUT HIM ON.>
<IT'S NOT A JOKE!! SHE REALLY IS MISSING!>
<YES, I KNOW SHE'S MISSING.>
<YOU DO?>
<YES. DON'T WASTE YOUR TIME WORRYING ABOUT HER.>
<WHY NOT?>
<BECAUSE SHE DOES CRAP LIKE THIS TO UPSET PEOPLE.>
<I KNOW, BUT THIS DOESN'T FEEL LIKE THAT AT ALL!>
<SOMEONE **JUST** POSTED A WHOLE BUNCH OF **REALLY** EMBARRASSING PHOTOS OF HER.>
<WOULD SHE LET SOMEONE DO THAT IF SHE WASN'T **REALLY** MISSING?>
<EMBARRASSING PHOTOS?>
<UH HUH, REALLY PERSONAL, PRIVATE ONES.>
<PHOTOS ONLY SOMEONE REALLY CLOSE TO HER COULD POST.>
<HAVE YOU SEEN THEM, PIRO-SAN?>
MY LAPTOP!
<PIRO-SAN?>
WHERE'S MY LAPTOP?!?

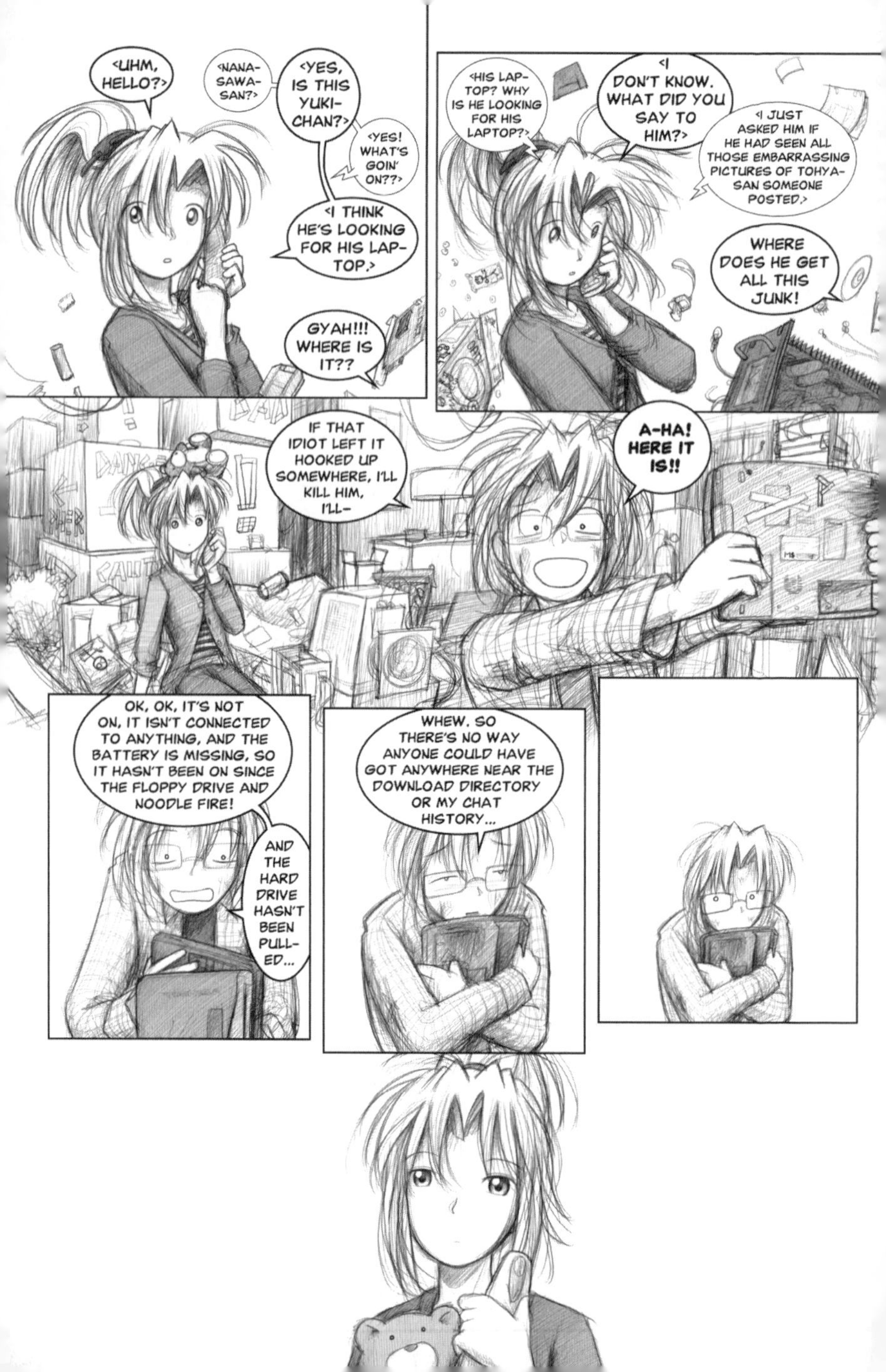
<UHM, HELLO?>
<NANA-SAWA-SAN?>
<YES, IS THIS YUKI-CHAN?>
<YES! WHAT'S GOIN' ON??>
<I THINK HE'S LOOKING FOR HIS LAP-TOP.>
GYAH!!! WHERE IS IT??
<HIS LAP-TOP? WHY IS HE LOOKING FOR HIS LAPTOP?>
<I DON'T KNOW. WHAT DID YOU SAY TO HIM?>
<I JUST ASKED HIM IF HE HAD SEEN ALL THOSE EMBARRASSING PICTURES OF TOHYA-SAN SOMEONE POSTED.>
WHERE DOES HE GET ALL THIS JUNK!
IF THAT IDIOT LEFT IT HOOKED UP SOMEWHERE, I'LL KILL HIM, I'LL-
A-HA! HERE IT IS!!
OK, OK, IT'S NOT ON, IT ISN'T CONNECTED TO ANYTHING, AND THE BATTERY IS MISSING, SO IT HASN'T BEEN ON SINCE THE FLOPPY DRIVE AND NOODLE FIRE!
AND THE HARD DRIVE HASN'T BEEN PULL-ED...
WHEW. SO THERE'S NO WAY ANYONE COULD HAVE GOT ANYWHERE NEAR THE DOWNLOAD DIRECTORY OR MY CHAT HISTORY...

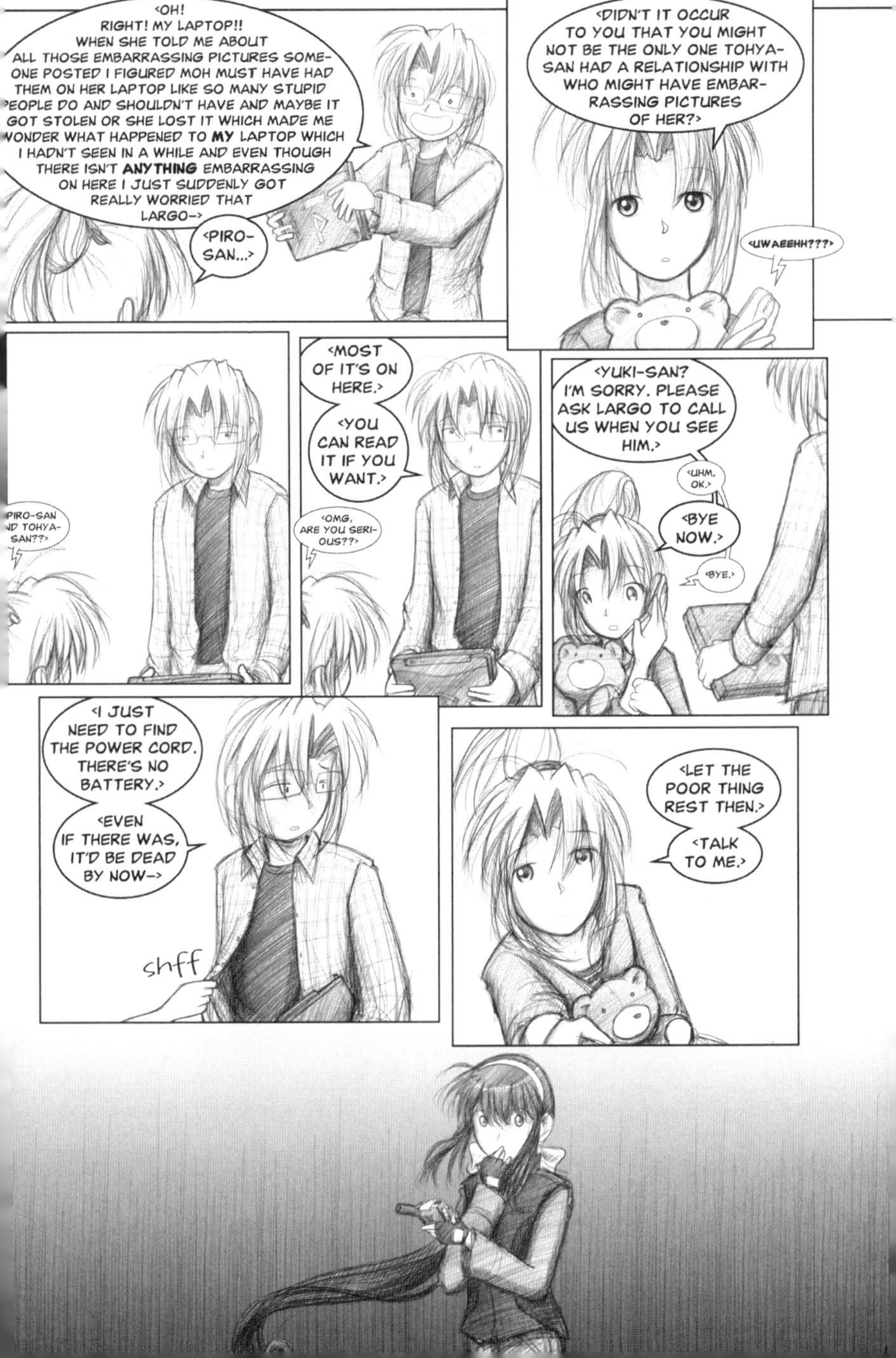

<OH! RIGHT! MY LAPTOP!! WHEN SHE TOLD ME ABOUT ALL THOSE EMBARRASSING PICTURES SOME-ONE POSTED I FIGURED MOH MUST HAVE HAD THEM ON HER LAPTOP LIKE SO MANY STUPID PEOPLE DO AND SHOULDN'T HAVE AND MAYBE IT GOT STOLEN OR SHE LOST IT WHICH MADE ME WONDER WHAT HAPPENED TO **MY** LAPTOP WHICH I HADN'T SEEN IN A WHILE AND EVEN THOUGH THERE ISN'T **ANYTHING** EMBARRASSING ON HERE I JUST SUDDENLY GOT REALLY WORRIED THAT LARGO–>
<PIRO-SAN...>
<DIDN'T IT OCCUR TO YOU THAT YOU MIGHT NOT BE THE ONLY ONE TOHYA-SAN HAD A RELATIONSHIP WITH WHO MIGHT HAVE EMBARRASSING PICTURES OF HER?>
<UWAEEHH???>
PIRO-SAN ND TOHYA-SAN??>
<MOST OF IT'S ON HERE.>
<YOU CAN READ IT IF YOU WANT.>
<OMG, ARE YOU SERIOUS??>
<YUKI-SAN? I'M SORRY. PLEASE ASK LARGO TO CALL US WHEN YOU SEE HIM.>
<UHM, OK.>
<BYE NOW.>
<BYE.>
<I JUST NEED TO FIND THE POWER CORD. THERE'S NO BATTERY.>
<EVEN IF THERE WAS, IT'D BE DEAD BY NOW–>
shff
<LET THE POOR THING REST THEN.>
<TALK TO ME.>

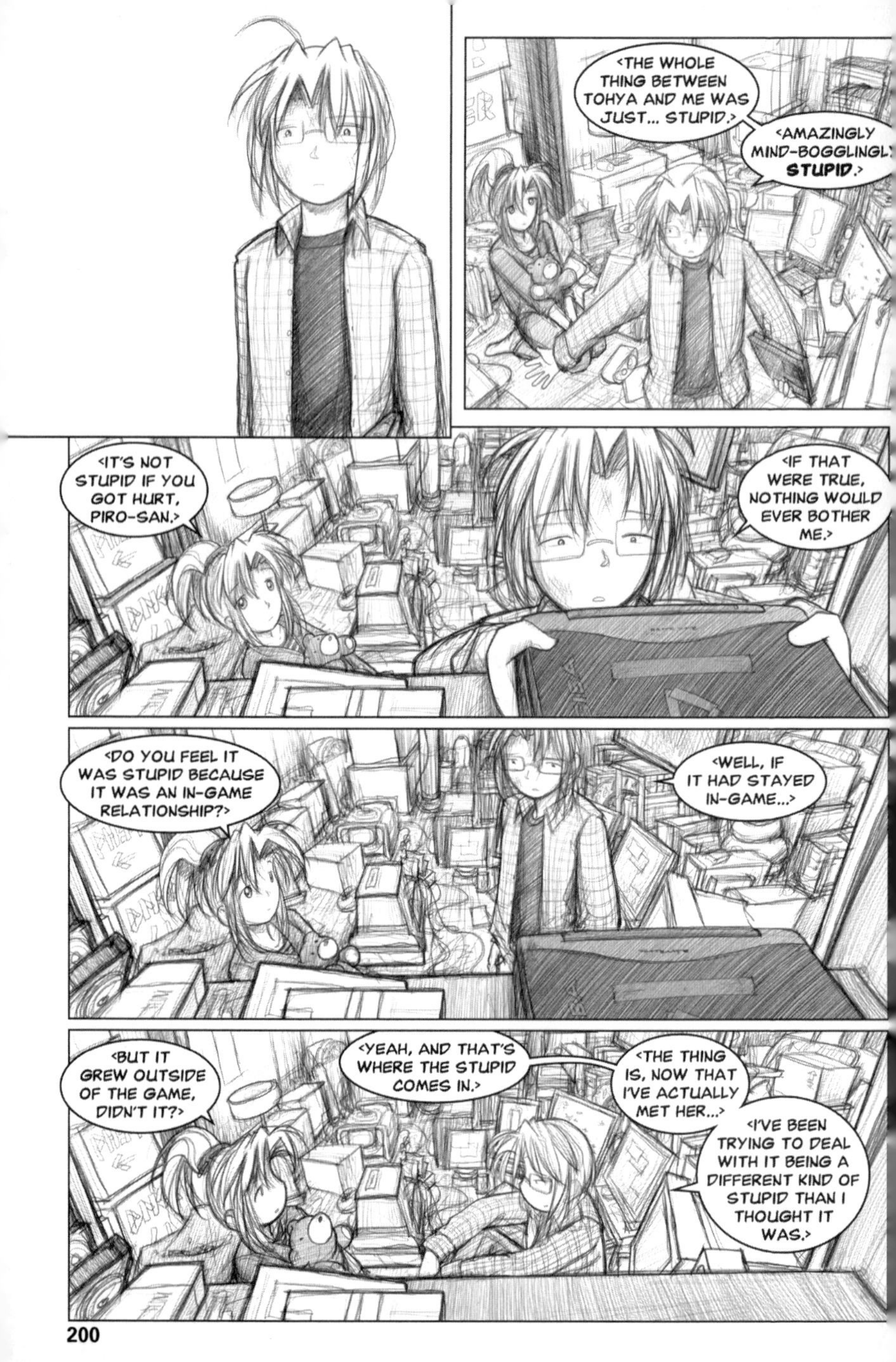
<THE WHOLE THING BETWEEN TOHYA AND ME WAS JUST... STUPID.>
<AMAZINGLY MIND-BOGGLINGLY **STUPID**.>
<IT'S NOT STUPID IF YOU GOT HURT, PIRO-SAN.>
<IF THAT WERE TRUE, NOTHING WOULD EVER BOTHER ME.>
<DO YOU FEEL IT WAS STUPID BECAUSE IT WAS AN IN-GAME RELATIONSHIP?>
<WELL, IF IT HAD STAYED IN-GAME...>
<BUT IT GREW OUTSIDE OF THE GAME, DIDN'T IT?>
<YEAH, AND THAT'S WHERE THE STUPID COMES IN.>
<THE THING IS, NOW THAT I'VE ACTUALLY MET HER...>
<I'VE BEEN TRYING TO DEAL WITH IT BEING A DIFFERENT KIND OF STUPID THAN I THOUGHT IT WAS.>

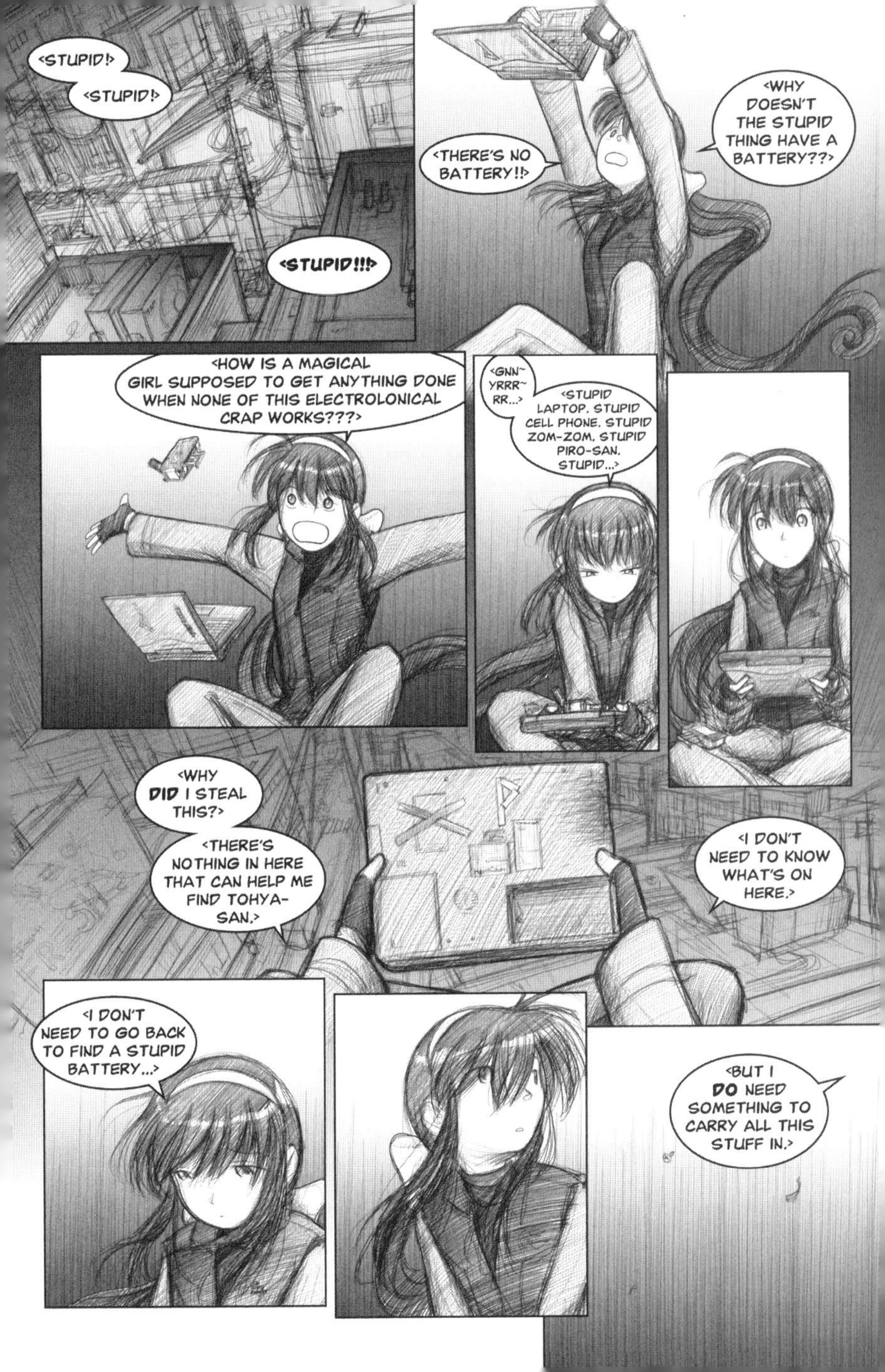
<STUPID!>
<STUPID!>
<STUPID!!!>
<THERE'S NO BATTERY!!>
<WHY DOESN'T THE STUPID THING HAVE A BATTERY??>
<HOW IS A MAGICAL GIRL SUPPOSED TO GET ANYTHING DONE WHEN NONE OF THIS ELECTROLONICAL CRAP WORKS???>
<GNN~ YRRR~ RR...>
<STUPID LAPTOP. STUPID CELL PHONE. STUPID ZOM-ZOM. STUPID PIRO-SAN. STUPID...>
<WHY **DID** I STEAL THIS?>
<THERE'S NOTHING IN HERE THAT CAN HELP ME FIND TOHYA-SAN.>
<I DON'T NEED TO KNOW WHAT'S ON HERE.>
<I DON'T NEED TO GO BACK TO FIND A STUPID BATTERY...>
<BUT I **DO** NEED SOMETHING TO CARRY ALL THIS STUFF IN.>

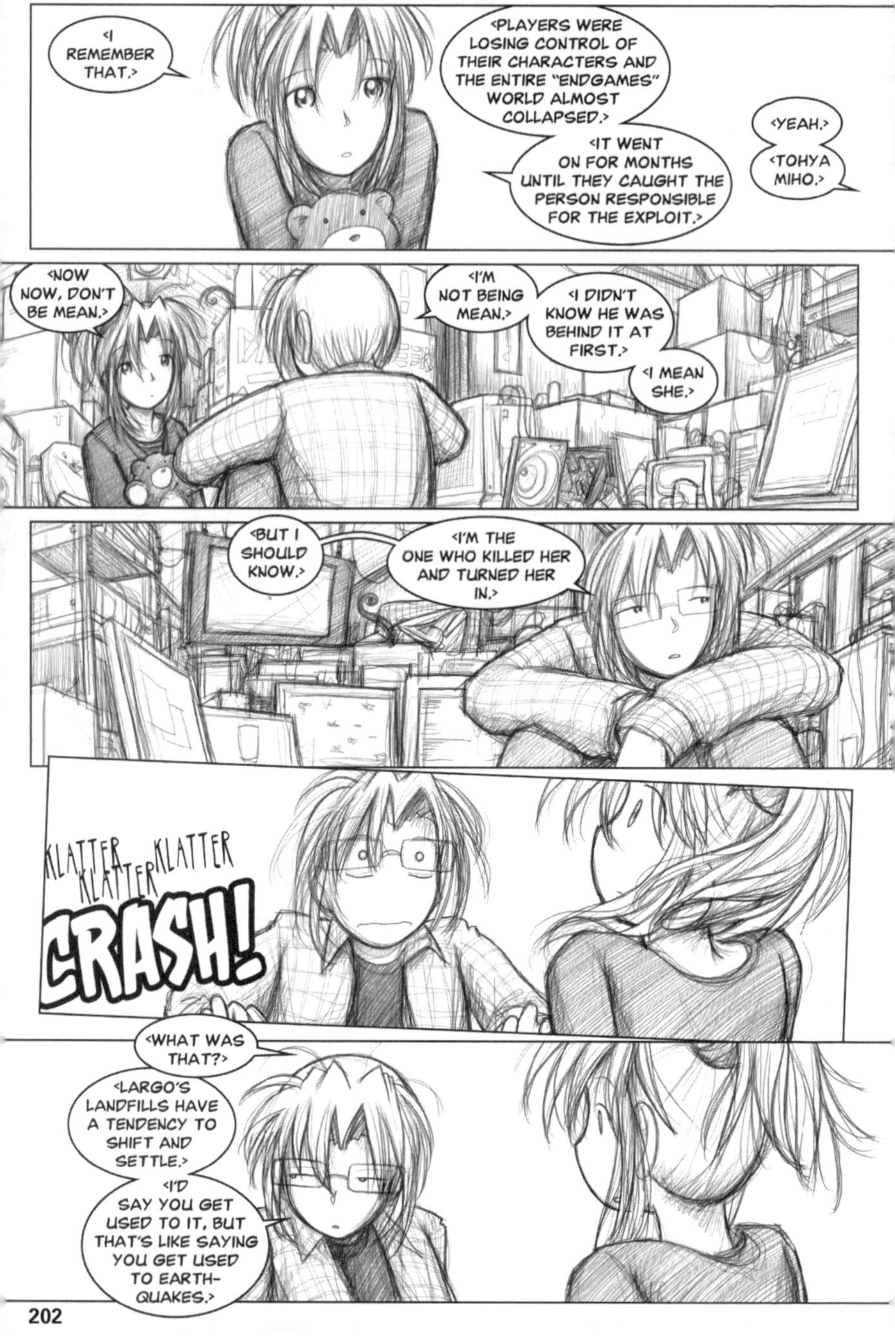

<I REMEMBER THAT.>
<PLAYERS WERE LOSING CONTROL OF THEIR CHARACTERS AND THE ENTIRE "ENDGAMES" WORLD ALMOST COLLAPSED.>
<IT WENT ON FOR MONTHS UNTIL THEY CAUGHT THE PERSON RESPONSIBLE FOR THE EXPLOIT.>
<YEAH.>
<TOHYA MIHO.>
<NOW NOW, DON'T BE MEAN.>
<I'M NOT BEING MEAN.>
<I DIDN'T KNOW HE WAS BEHIND IT AT FIRST.>
<I MEAN SHE.>
<BUT I SHOULD KNOW.>
<I'M THE ONE WHO KILLED HER AND TURNED HER IN.>
KLATTER KLATTER KLATTER
CRASH!
<WHAT WAS THAT?>
<LARGO'S LANDFILLS HAVE A TENDENCY TO SHIFT AND SETTLE.>
<I'D SAY YOU GET USED TO IT, BUT THAT'S LIKE SAYING YOU GET USED TO EARTH-QUAKES.>

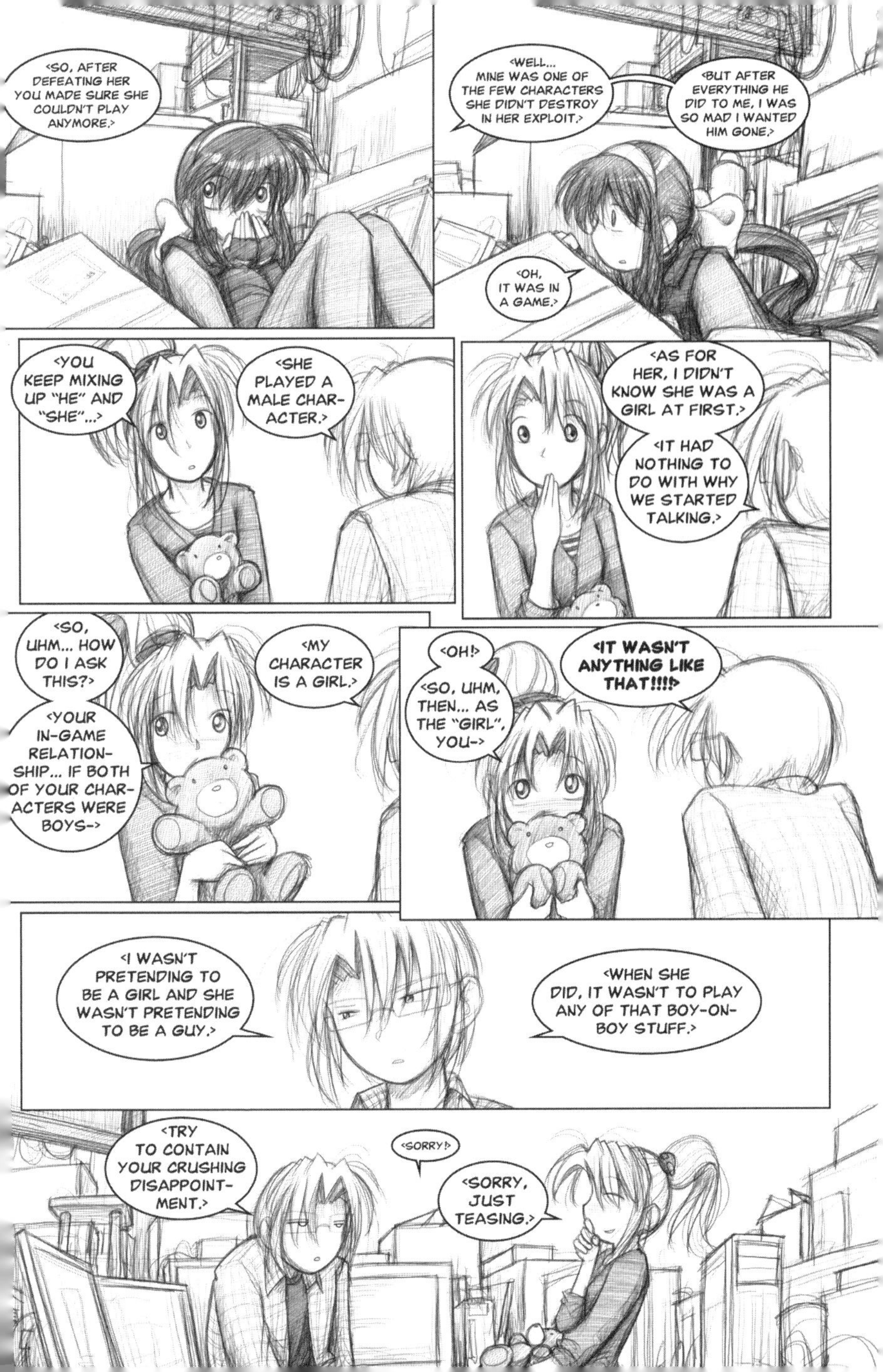

<SO, AFTER DEFEATING HER YOU MADE SURE SHE COULDN'T PLAY ANYMORE.>
<WELL... MINE WAS ONE OF THE FEW CHARACTERS SHE DIDN'T DESTROY IN HER EXPLOIT.>
<BUT AFTER EVERYTHING HE DID TO ME, I WAS SO MAD I WANTED HIM GONE.>
<OH, IT WAS IN A GAME.>
<YOU KEEP MIXING UP "HE" AND "SHE"...>
<SHE PLAYED A MALE CHARACTER.>
<AS FOR HER, I DIDN'T KNOW SHE WAS A GIRL AT FIRST.>
<IT HAD NOTHING TO DO WITH WHY WE STARTED TALKING.>
<SO, UHM... HOW DO I ASK THIS?>
<YOUR IN-GAME RELATIONSHIP... IF BOTH OF YOUR CHARACTERS WERE BOYS->
<MY CHARACTER IS A GIRL.>
<OH!>
<SO, UHM, THEN... AS THE "GIRL", YOU->
<IT WASN'T ANYTHING LIKE THAT!!!!>
<I WASN'T PRETENDING TO BE A GIRL AND SHE WASN'T PRETENDING TO BE A GUY.>
<WHEN SHE DID, IT WASN'T TO PLAY ANY OF THAT BOY-ON-BOY STUFF.>
<TRY TO CONTAIN YOUR CRUSHING DISAPPOINTMENT.>
<SORRY!>
<SORRY, JUST TEASING.>

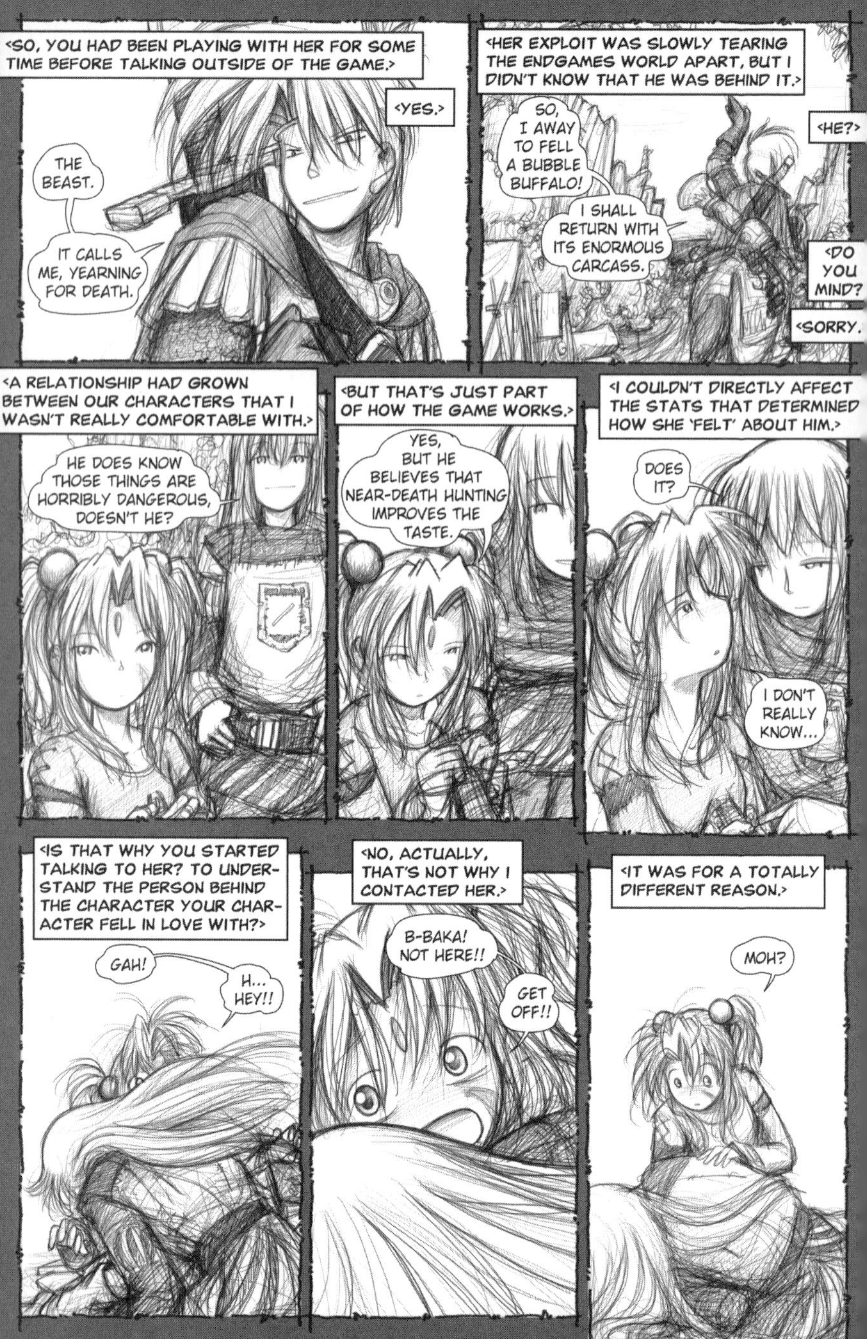
<SO, YOU HAD BEEN PLAYING WITH HER FOR SOME TIME BEFORE TALKING OUTSIDE OF THE GAME.>
<YES.>
THE BEAST.
IT CALLS ME, YEARNING FOR DEATH.
<HER EXPLOIT WAS SLOWLY TEARING THE ENDGAMES WORLD APART, BUT I DIDN'T KNOW THAT HE WAS BEHIND IT.>
SO, I AWAY TO FELL A BUBBLE BUFFALO!
I SHALL RETURN WITH ITS ENORMOUS CARCASS.
<HE?>
<DO YOU MIND?>
<SORRY.>
<A RELATIONSHIP HAD GROWN BETWEEN OUR CHARACTERS THAT I WASN'T REALLY COMFORTABLE WITH.>
HE DOES KNOW THOSE THINGS ARE HORRIBLY DANGEROUS, DOESN'T HE?
<BUT THAT'S JUST PART OF HOW THE GAME WORKS.>
YES, BUT HE BELIEVES THAT NEAR-DEATH HUNTING IMPROVES THE TASTE.
<I COULDN'T DIRECTLY AFFECT THE STATS THAT DETERMINED HOW SHE 'FELT' ABOUT HIM.>
DOES IT?
I DON'T REALLY KNOW...
<IS THAT WHY YOU STARTED TALKING TO HER? TO UNDERSTAND THE PERSON BEHIND THE CHARACTER YOUR CHARACTER FELL IN LOVE WITH?>
GAH!
H... HEY!!
<NO, ACTUALLY, THAT'S NOT WHY I CONTACTED HER.>
B-BAKA! NOT HERE!!
GET OFF!!
<IT WAS FOR A TOTALLY DIFFERENT REASON.>
MOH?

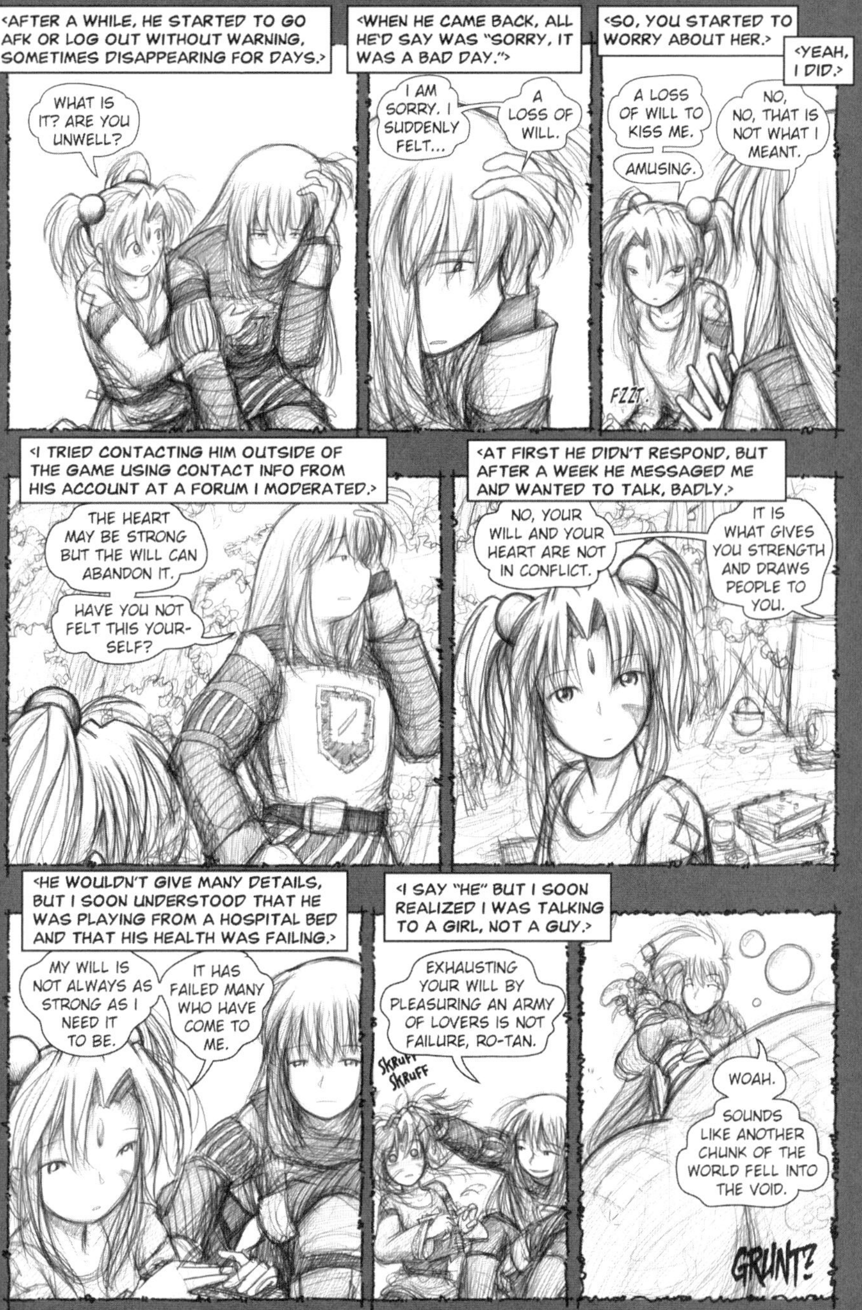

<AFTER A WHILE, HE STARTED TO GO AFK OR LOG OUT WITHOUT WARNING, SOMETIMES DISAPPEARING FOR DAYS.>
WHAT IS IT? ARE YOU UNWELL?
<WHEN HE CAME BACK, ALL HE'D SAY WAS "SORRY, IT WAS A BAD DAY.">
I AM SORRY. I SUDDENLY FELT...
A LOSS OF WILL.
<SO, YOU STARTED TO WORRY ABOUT HER.>
<YEAH, I DID.>
A LOSS OF WILL TO KISS ME.
AMUSING.
NO, NO, THAT IS NOT WHAT I MEANT.
FZZT.
<I TRIED CONTACTING HIM OUTSIDE OF THE GAME USING CONTACT INFO FROM HIS ACCOUNT AT A FORUM I MODERATED.>
THE HEART MAY BE STRONG BUT THE WILL CAN ABANDON IT.
HAVE YOU NOT FELT THIS YOURSELF?
<AT FIRST HE DIDN'T RESPOND, BUT AFTER A WEEK HE MESSAGED ME AND WANTED TO TALK, BADLY.>
NO, YOUR WILL AND YOUR HEART ARE NOT IN CONFLICT.
IT IS WHAT GIVES YOU STRENGTH AND DRAWS PEOPLE TO YOU.
<HE WOULDN'T GIVE MANY DETAILS, BUT I SOON UNDERSTOOD THAT HE WAS PLAYING FROM A HOSPITAL BED AND THAT HIS HEALTH WAS FAILING.>
MY WILL IS NOT ALWAYS AS STRONG AS I NEED IT TO BE.
IT HAS FAILED MANY WHO HAVE COME TO ME.
<I SAY "HE" BUT I SOON REALIZED I WAS TALKING TO A GIRL, NOT A GUY.>
EXHAUSTING YOUR WILL BY PLEASURING AN ARMY OF LOVERS IS NOT FAILURE, RO-TAN.
SKRUFF SKRUFF
WOAH.
SOUNDS LIKE ANOTHER CHUNK OF THE WORLD FELL INTO THE VOID.
GRUNT?

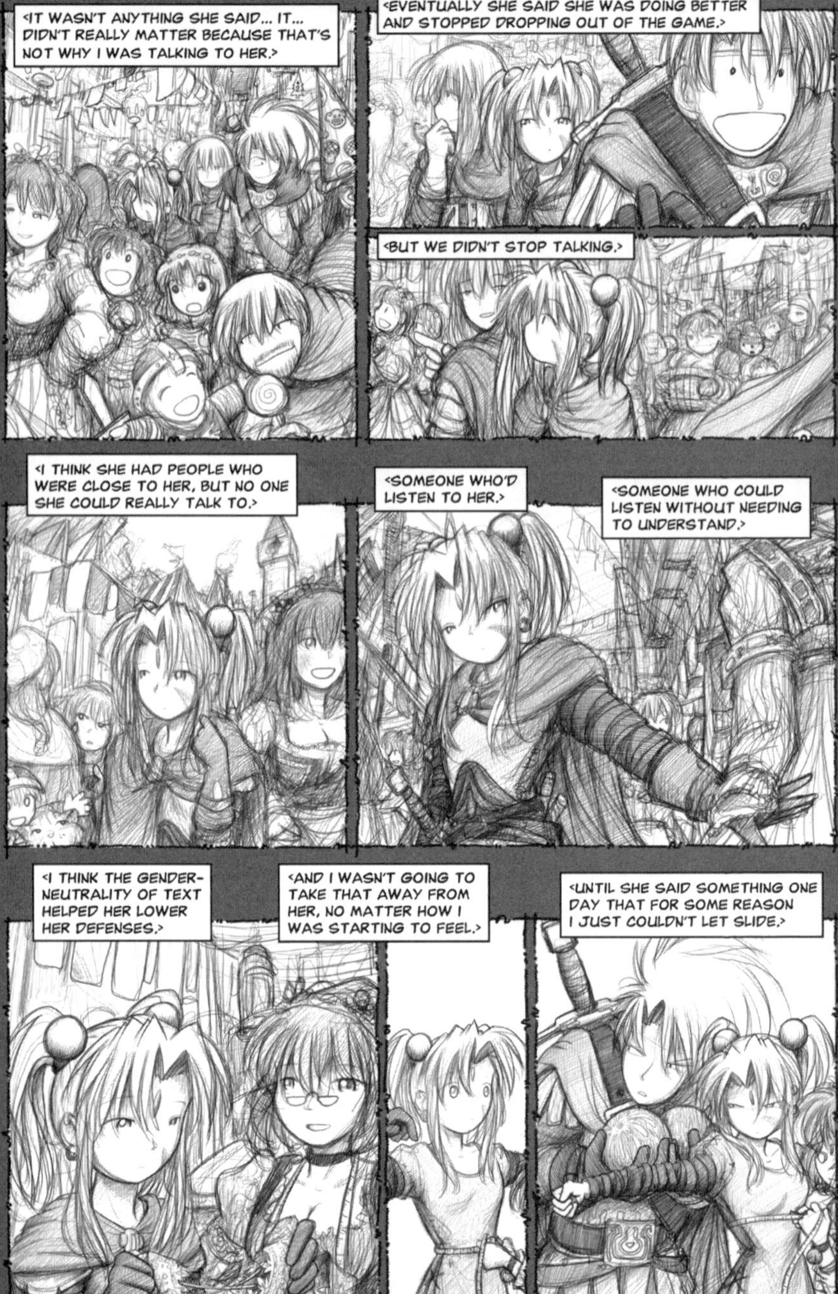
<IT WASN'T ANYTHING SHE SAID... IT... DIDN'T REALLY MATTER BECAUSE THAT'S NOT WHY I WAS TALKING TO HER.>
<EVENTUALLY SHE SAID SHE WAS DOING BETTER AND STOPPED DROPPING OUT OF THE GAME.>
<BUT WE DIDN'T STOP TALKING.>
<I THINK SHE HAD PEOPLE WHO WERE CLOSE TO HER, BUT NO ONE SHE COULD REALLY TALK TO.>
<SOMEONE WHO'D LISTEN TO HER.>
<SOMEONE WHO COULD LISTEN WITHOUT NEEDING TO UNDERSTAND.>
<I THINK THE GENDER-NEUTRALITY OF TEXT HELPED HER LOWER HER DEFENSES.>
<AND I WASN'T GOING TO TAKE THAT AWAY FROM HER, NO MATTER HOW I WAS STARTING TO FEEL.>
<UNTIL SHE SAID SOMETHING ONE DAY THAT FOR SOME REASON I JUST COULDN'T LET SLIDE.>

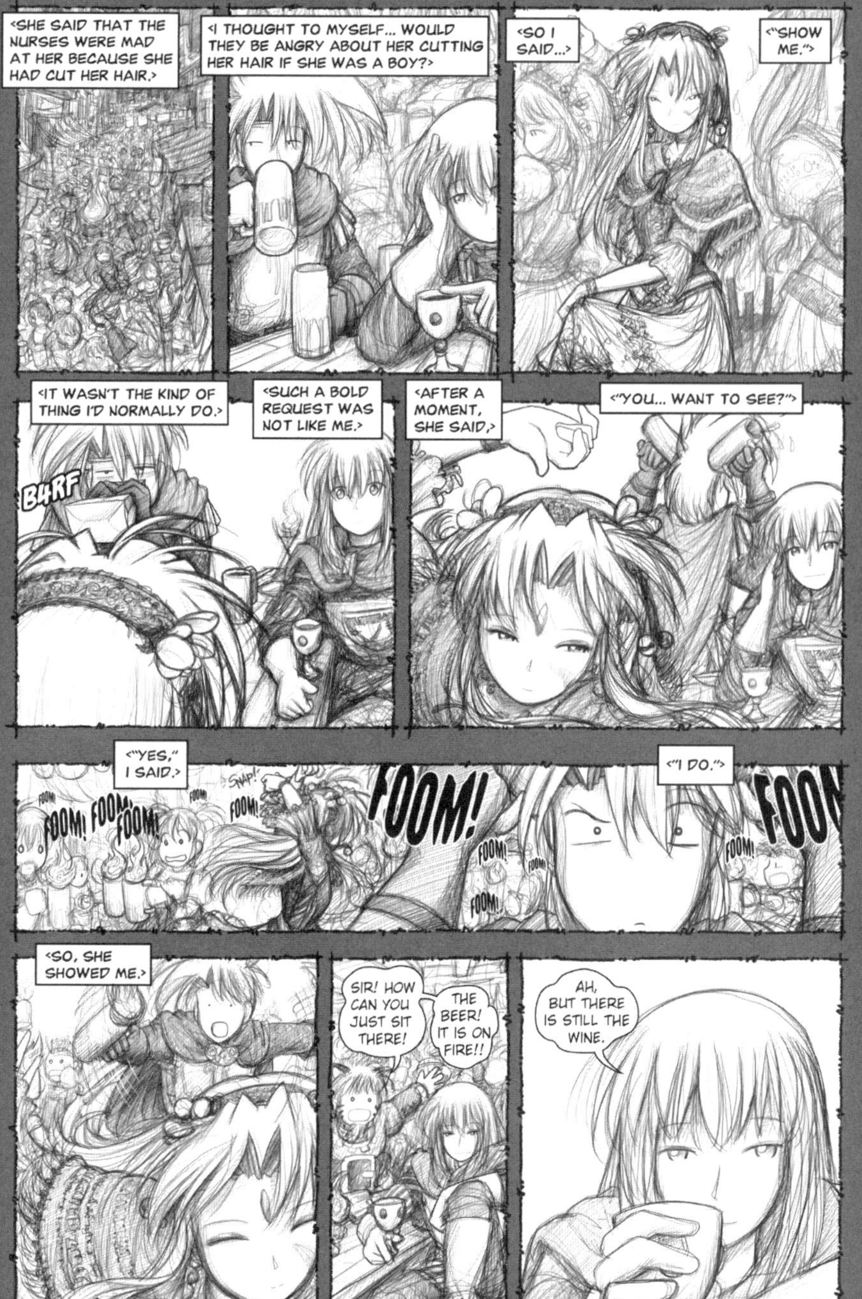
<SHE SAID THAT THE NURSES WERE MAD AT HER BECAUSE SHE HAD CUT HER HAIR.>
<I THOUGHT TO MYSELF... WOULD THEY BE ANGRY ABOUT HER CUTTING HER HAIR IF SHE WAS A BOY?>
<SO I SAID...>
<"SHOW ME.">
<IT WASN'T THE KIND OF THING I'D NORMALLY DO.>
B4RF
<SUCH A BOLD REQUEST WAS NOT LIKE ME.>
<AFTER A MOMENT, SHE SAID,>
<"YOU... WANT TO SEE?">
<"YES," I SAID.>
FOOM! FOOM! FOOM! FOOM!
FOOM!
SNAP!
FOOM!
FOOM!
FOOM!
FOOM!
FOOM!
<"I DO.">
FOOM!
FOOM
<SO, SHE SHOWED ME.>
SIR! HOW CAN YOU JUST SIT THERE!
THE BEER! IT IS ON FIRE!!
AH, BUT THERE IS STILL THE WINE.

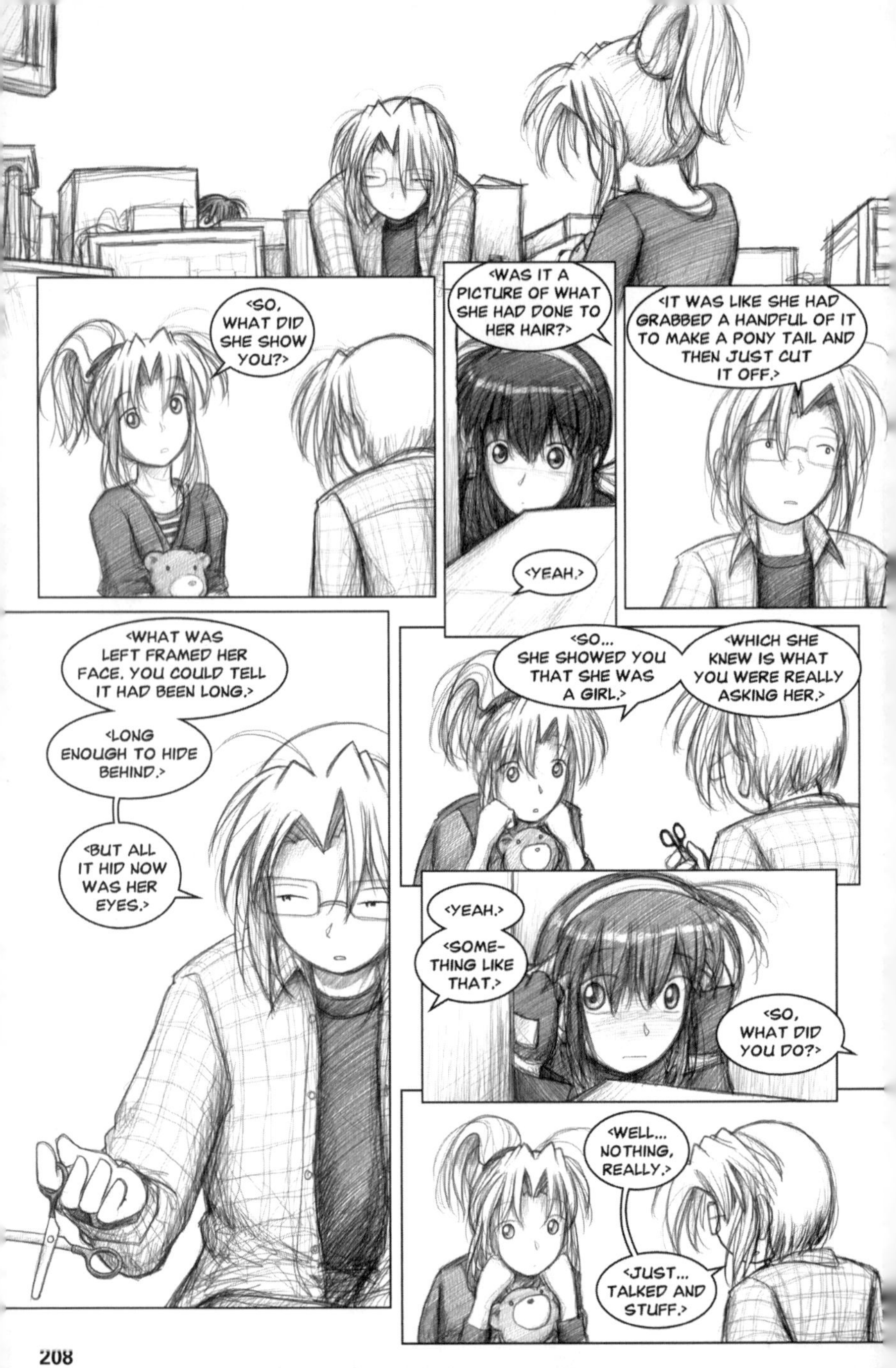
<SO, WHAT DID SHE SHOW YOU?>
<WAS IT A PICTURE OF WHAT SHE HAD DONE TO HER HAIR?>
<YEAH.>
<IT WAS LIKE SHE HAD GRABBED A HANDFUL OF IT TO MAKE A PONY TAIL AND THEN JUST CUT IT OFF.>
<WHAT WAS LEFT FRAMED HER FACE. YOU COULD TELL IT HAD BEEN LONG.>
<LONG ENOUGH TO HIDE BEHIND.>
<BUT ALL IT HID NOW WAS HER EYES.>
<SO... SHE SHOWED YOU THAT SHE WAS A GIRL.>
<WHICH SHE KNEW IS WHAT YOU WERE REALLY ASKING HER.>
<YEAH.>
<SOME-THING LIKE THAT.>
<SO, WHAT DID YOU DO?>
<WELL... NOTHING, REALLY.>
<JUST... TALKED AND STUFF.>

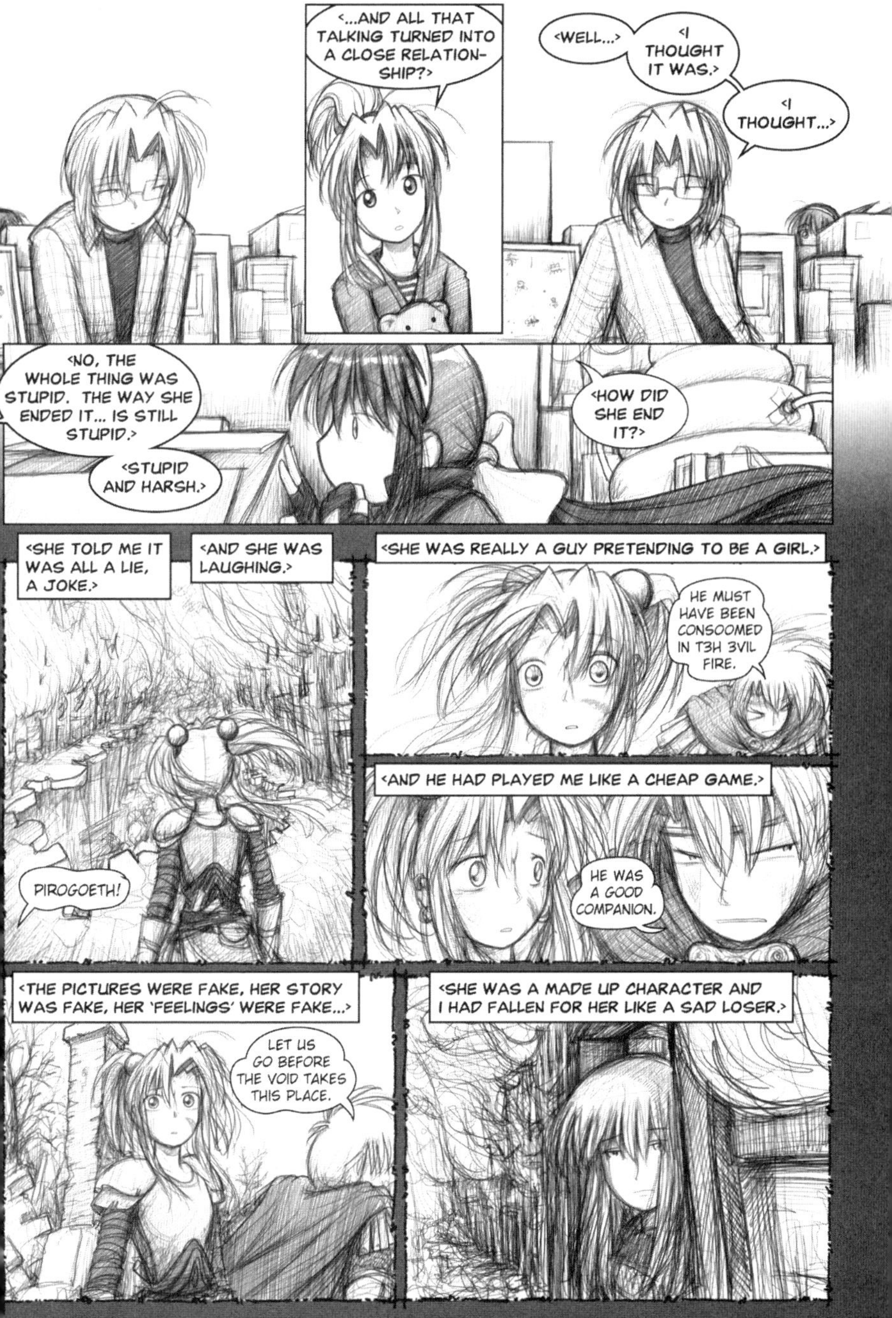

<...AND ALL THAT TALKING TURNED INTO A CLOSE RELATION-SHIP?>
<WELL...>
<I THOUGHT IT WAS.>
<I THOUGHT...>
<NO, THE WHOLE THING WAS STUPID. THE WAY SHE ENDED IT... IS STILL STUPID.>
<STUPID AND HARSH.>
<HOW DID SHE END IT?>
<SHE TOLD ME IT WAS ALL A LIE, A JOKE.>
<AND SHE WAS LAUGHING.>
PIROGOETH!
<SHE WAS REALLY A GUY PRETENDING TO BE A GIRL.>
HE MUST HAVE BEEN CONSOOMED IN T3H 3VIL FIRE.
<AND HE HAD PLAYED ME LIKE A CHEAP GAME.>
HE WAS A GOOD COMPANION.
<THE PICTURES WERE FAKE, HER STORY WAS FAKE, HER 'FEELINGS' WERE FAKE...>
LET US GO BEFORE THE VOID TAKES THIS PLACE.
<SHE WAS A MADE UP CHARACTER AND I HAD FALLEN FOR HER LIKE A SAD LOSER.>

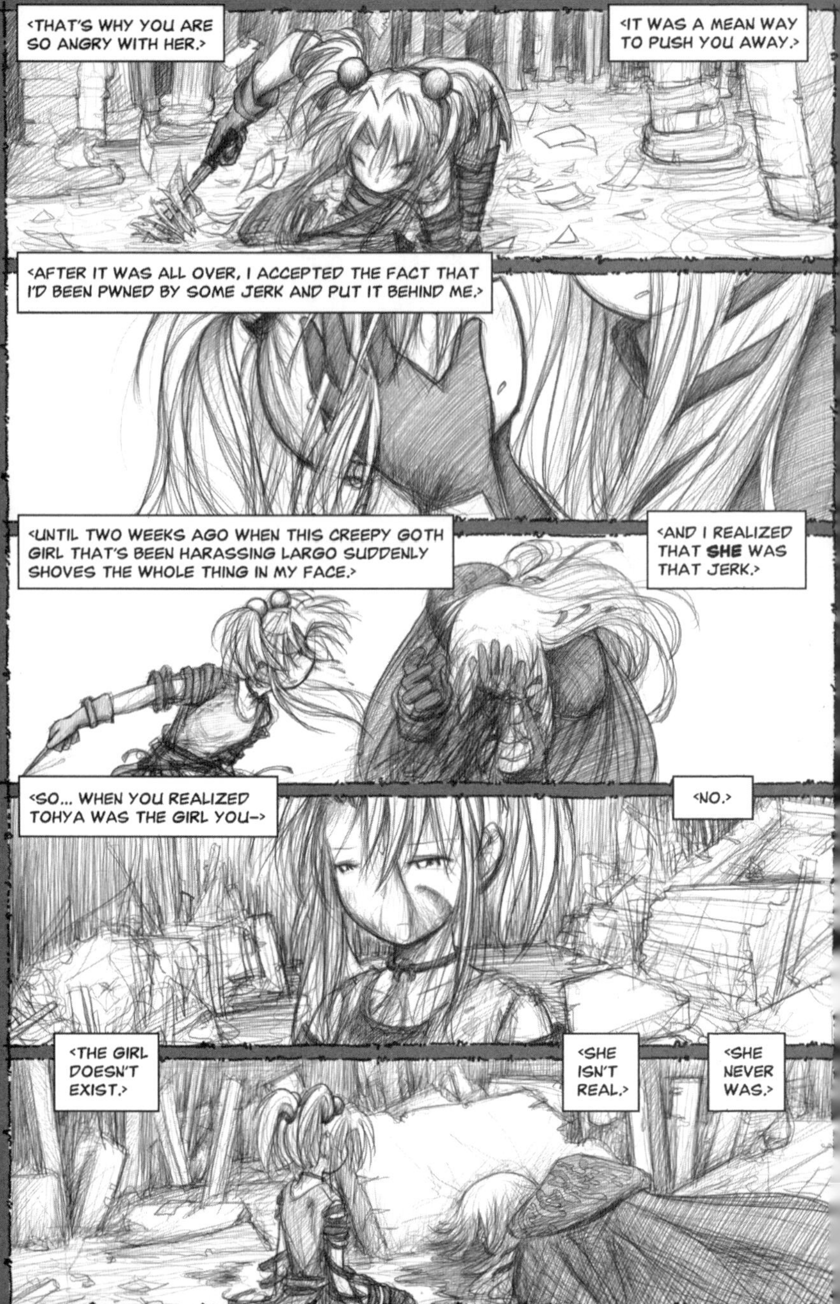
<THAT'S WHY YOU ARE SO ANGRY WITH HER.>
<IT WAS A MEAN WAY TO PUSH YOU AWAY.>
<AFTER IT WAS ALL OVER, I ACCEPTED THE FACT THAT I'D BEEN PWNED BY SOME JERK AND PUT IT BEHIND ME.>
<UNTIL TWO WEEKS AGO WHEN THIS CREEPY GOTH GIRL THAT'S BEEN HARASSING LARGO SUDDENLY SHOVES THE WHOLE THING IN MY FACE.>
<AND I REALIZED THAT **SHE** WAS THAT JERK.>
<SO... WHEN YOU REALIZED TOHYA WAS THE GIRL YOU-->
<NO.>
<THE GIRL DOESN'T EXIST.>
<SHE ISN'T REAL.>
<SHE NEVER WAS.>

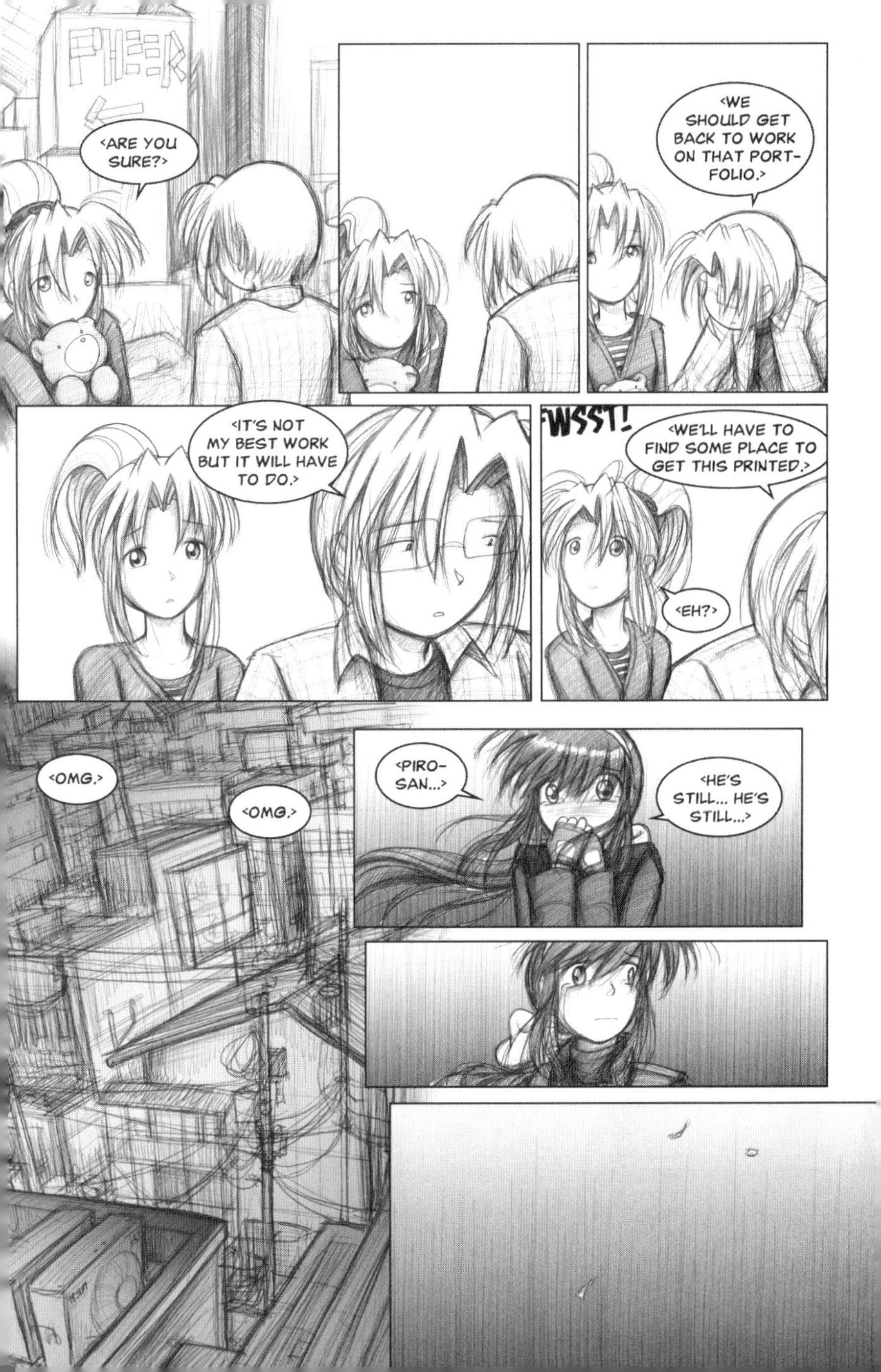
<ARE YOU SURE?>
<WE SHOULD GET BACK TO WORK ON THAT PORT-FOLIO.>
<IT'S NOT MY BEST WORK BUT IT WILL HAVE TO DO.>
FWSST!
<WE'LL HAVE TO FIND SOME PLACE TO GET THIS PRINTED.>
<EH?>
<OMG.>
<OMG.>
<PIRO-SAN...>
<HE'S STILL... HE'S STILL...>

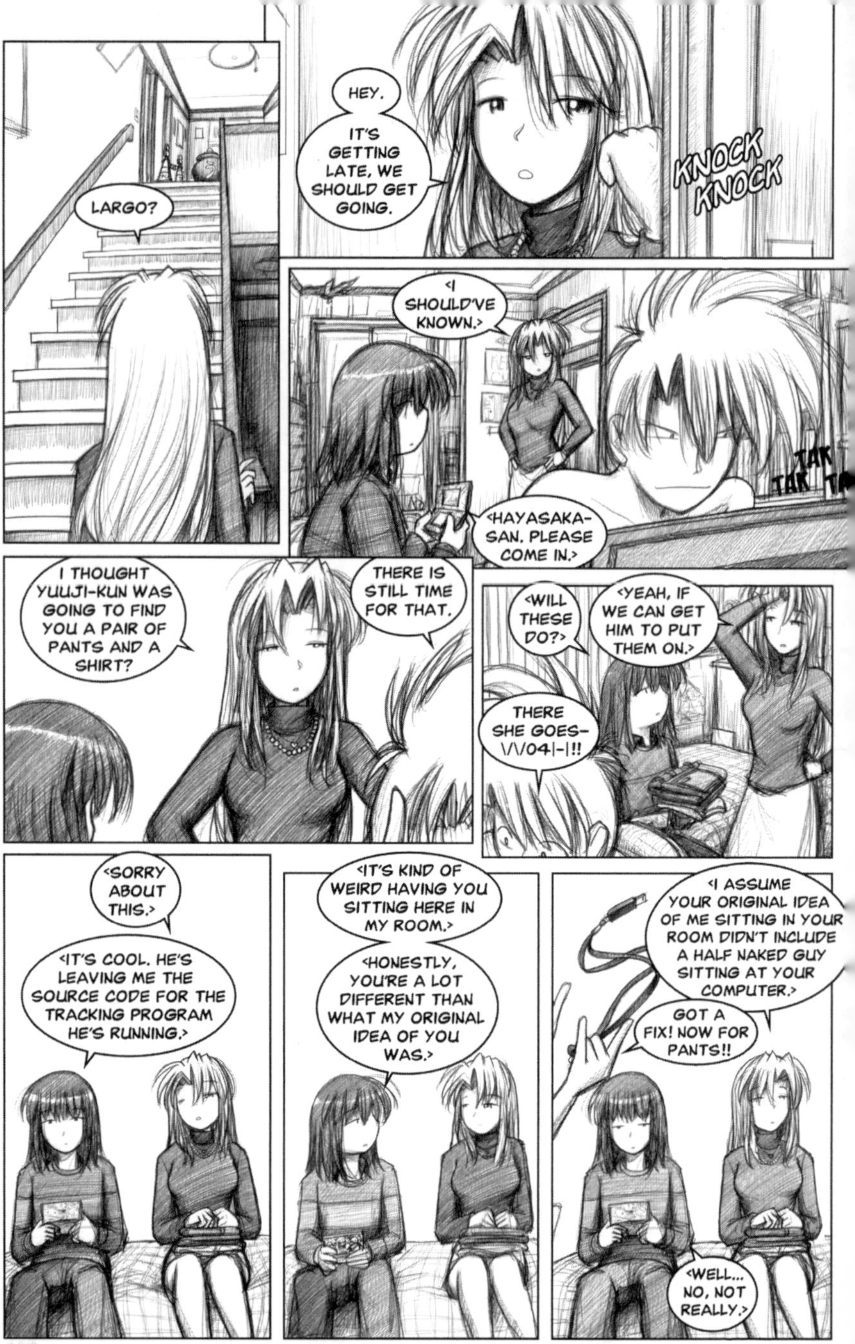
LARGO?
HEY.
IT'S GETTING LATE, WE SHOULD GET GOING.
KNOCK KNOCK
<I SHOULD'VE KNOWN.>
TAK TAK TA
<HAYASAKA-SAN. PLEASE COME IN.>
I THOUGHT YUUJI-KUN WAS GOING TO FIND YOU A PAIR OF PANTS AND A SHIRT?
THERE IS STILL TIME FOR THAT.
<WILL THESE DO?>
<YEAH, IF WE CAN GET HIM TO PUT THEM ON.>
THERE SHE GOES- \/\/04|-|!!
<SORRY ABOUT THIS.>
<IT'S COOL. HE'S LEAVING ME THE SOURCE CODE FOR THE TRACKING PROGRAM HE'S RUNNING.>
<IT'S KIND OF WEIRD HAVING YOU SITTING HERE IN MY ROOM.>
<HONESTLY, YOU'RE A LOT DIFFERENT THAN WHAT MY ORIGINAL IDEA OF YOU WAS.>
<I ASSUME YOUR ORIGINAL IDEA OF ME SITTING IN YOUR ROOM DIDN'T INCLUDE A HALF NAKED GUY SITTING AT YOUR COMPUTER.>
GOT A FIX! NOW FOR PANTS!!
<WELL... NO, NOT REALLY.>

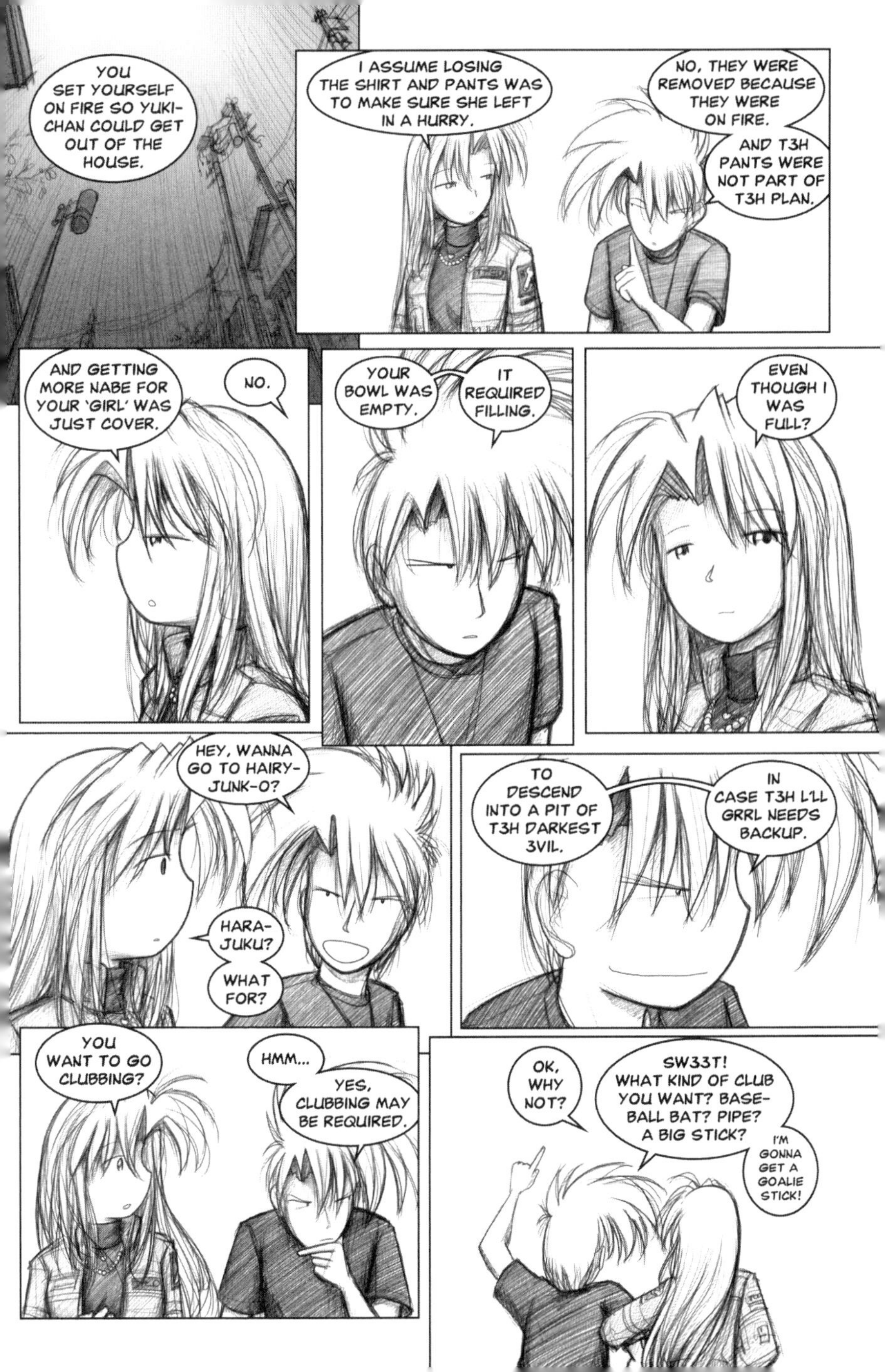

YOU SET YOURSELF ON FIRE SO YUKI-CHAN COULD GET OUT OF THE HOUSE.
I ASSUME LOSING THE SHIRT AND PANTS WAS TO MAKE SURE SHE LEFT IN A HURRY.
NO, THEY WERE REMOVED BECAUSE THEY WERE ON FIRE.
AND T3H PANTS WERE NOT PART OF T3H PLAN.
AND GETTING MORE NABE FOR YOUR 'GIRL' WAS JUST COVER.
NO.
YOUR BOWL WAS EMPTY.
IT REQUIRED FILLING.
EVEN THOUGH I WAS FULL?
HEY, WANNA GO TO HAIRY-JUNK-O?
HARA-JUKU?
WHAT FOR?
TO DESCEND INTO A PIT OF T3H DARKEST 3VIL.
IN CASE T3H L'LL GRRL NEEDS BACKUP.
YOU WANT TO GO CLUBBING?
HMM...
YES, CLUBBING MAY BE REQUIRED.
OK, WHY NOT?
SW33T! WHAT KIND OF CLUB YOU WANT? BASE-BALL BAT? PIPE? A BIG STICK?
I'M GONNA GET A GOALIE STICK!

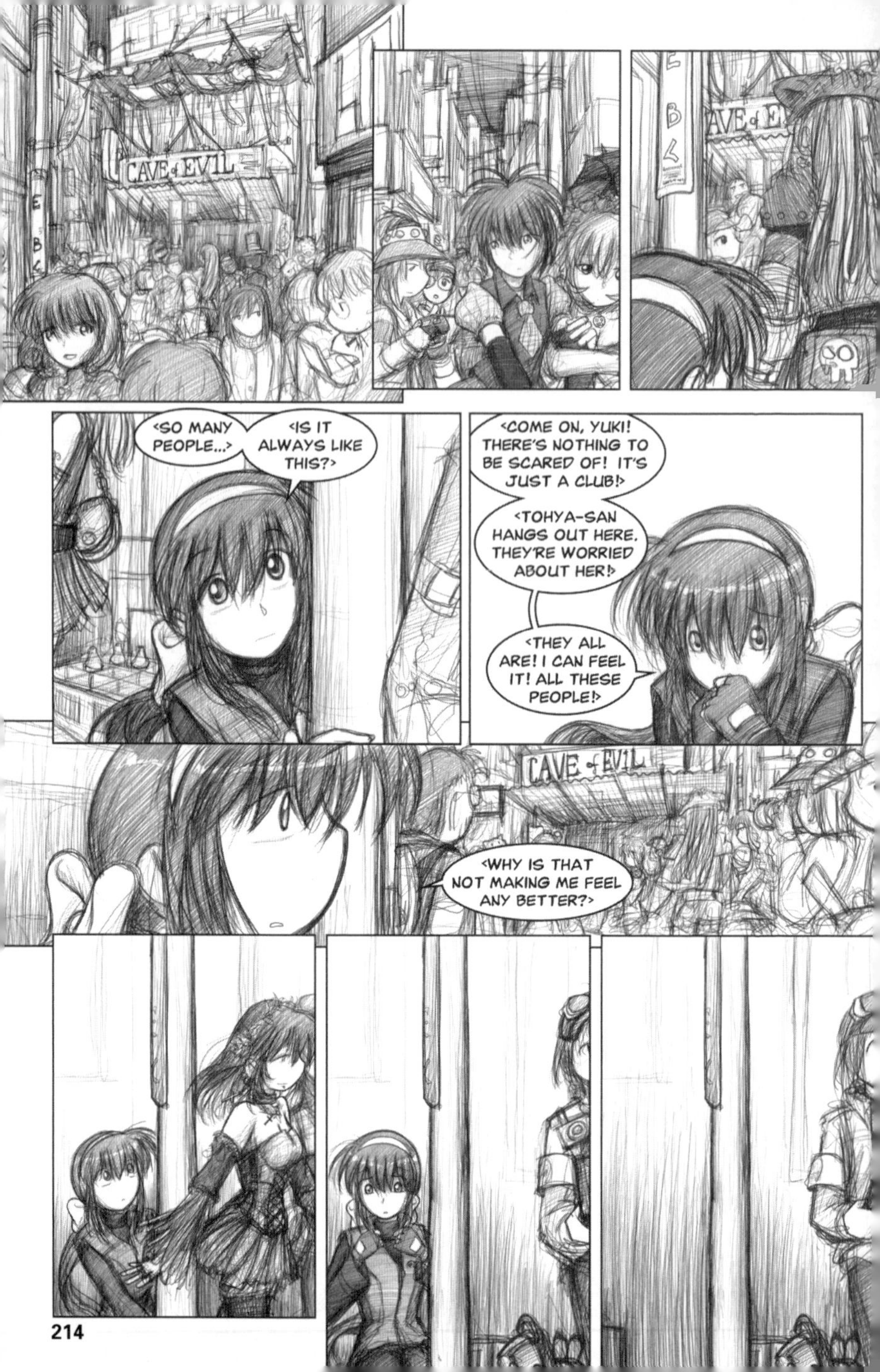
CAVE of EVIL
<SO MANY PEOPLE...>
<IS IT ALWAYS LIKE THIS?>
<COME ON, YUKI! THERE'S NOTHING TO BE SCARED OF! IT'S JUST A CLUB!>
<TOHYA-SAN HANGS OUT HERE. THEY'RE WORRIED ABOUT HER!>
<THEY ALL ARE! I CAN FEEL IT! ALL THESE PEOPLE!>
CAVE of EVIL
<WHY IS THAT NOT MAKING ME FEEL ANY BETTER?>

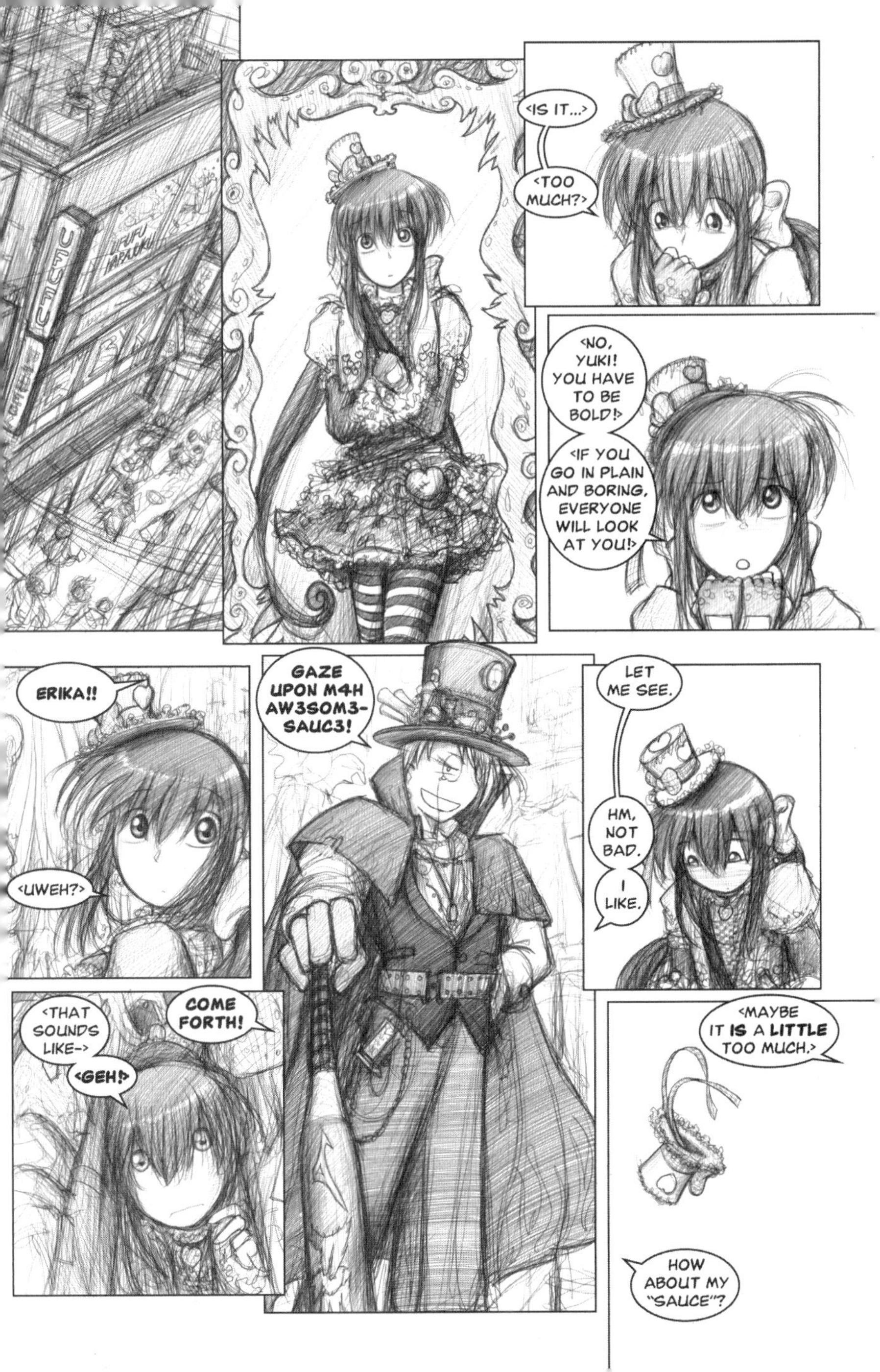
UFUFU
<IS IT...>
<TOO MUCH?>
<NO, YUKI! YOU HAVE TO BE BOLD!>
<IF YOU GO IN PLAIN AND BORING, EVERYONE WILL LOOK AT YOU!>
ERIKA!!
<UWEH?>
<THAT SOUNDS LIKE->
COME FORTH!
<GEH!>
GAZE UPON M4H AW3SOM3-SAUC3!
LET ME SEE.
HM, NOT BAD.
I LIKE.
<MAYBE IT IS A LITTLE TOO MUCH.>
HOW ABOUT MY "SAUCE"?

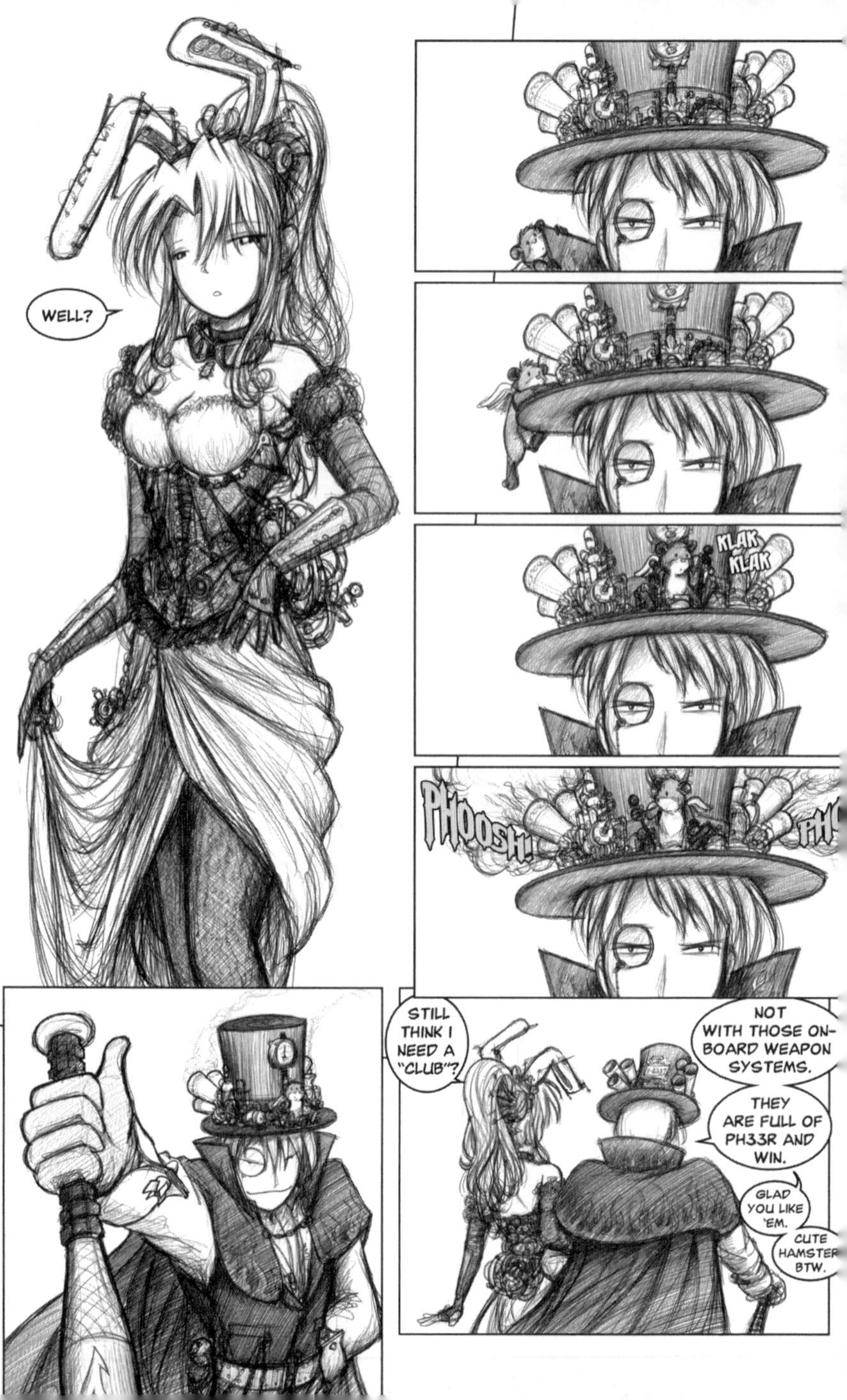
WELL?
KLAK KLAK
PHOOSH!
STILL THINK I NEED A "CLUB"?
NOT WITH THOSE ON-BOARD WEAPON SYSTEMS.
THEY ARE FULL OF PH33R AND WIN.
GLAD YOU LIKE 'EM.
CUTE HAMSTER BTW.

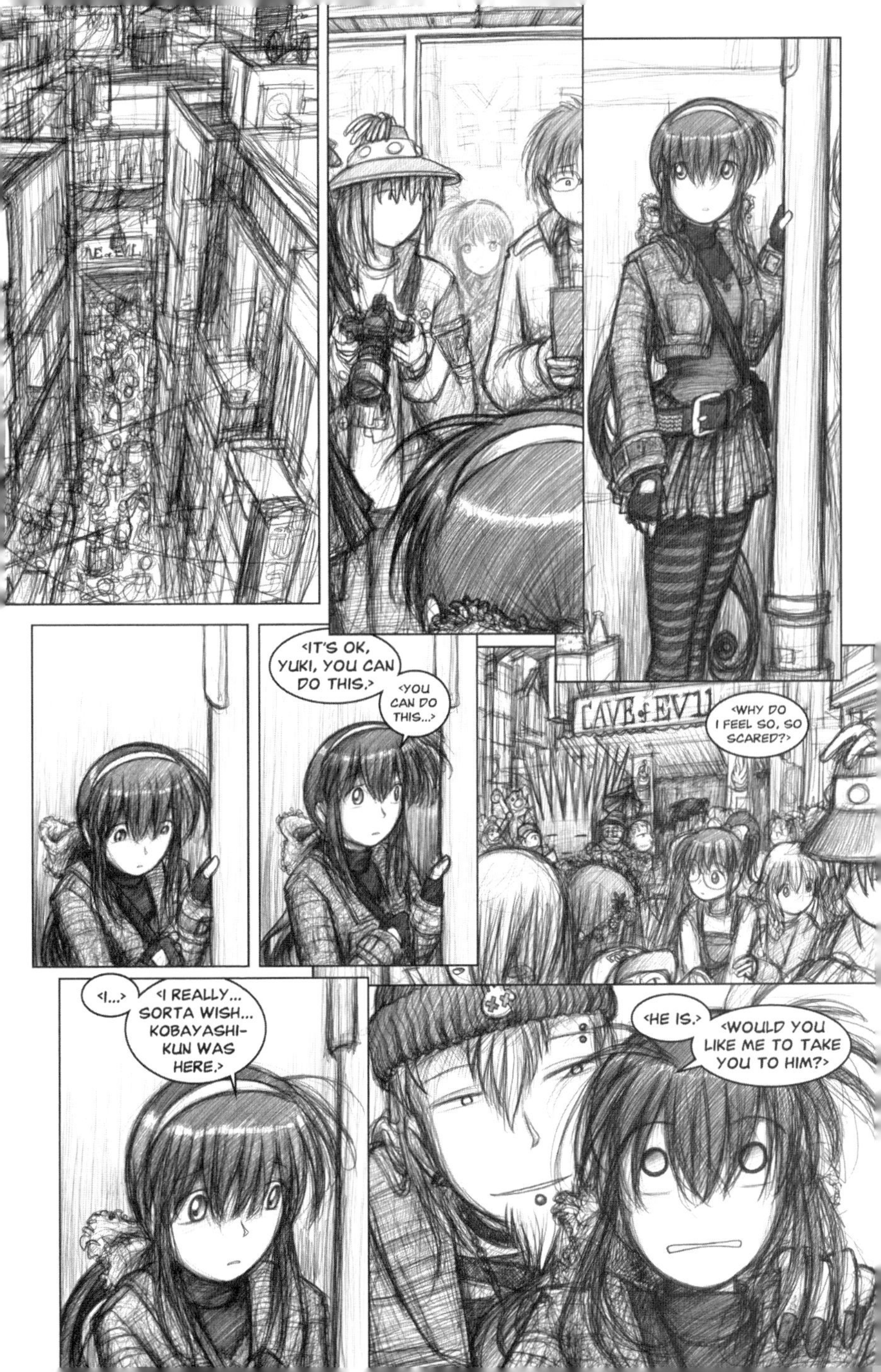
<IT'S OK, YUKI, YOU CAN DO THIS.>
<YOU CAN DO THIS...>
CAVE of EVIL
<WHY DO I FEEL SO, SO SCARED?>
<I...>
<I REALLY... SORTA WISH... KOBAYASHI-KUN WAS HERE.>
<HE IS.>
<WOULD YOU LIKE ME TO TAKE YOU TO HIM?>

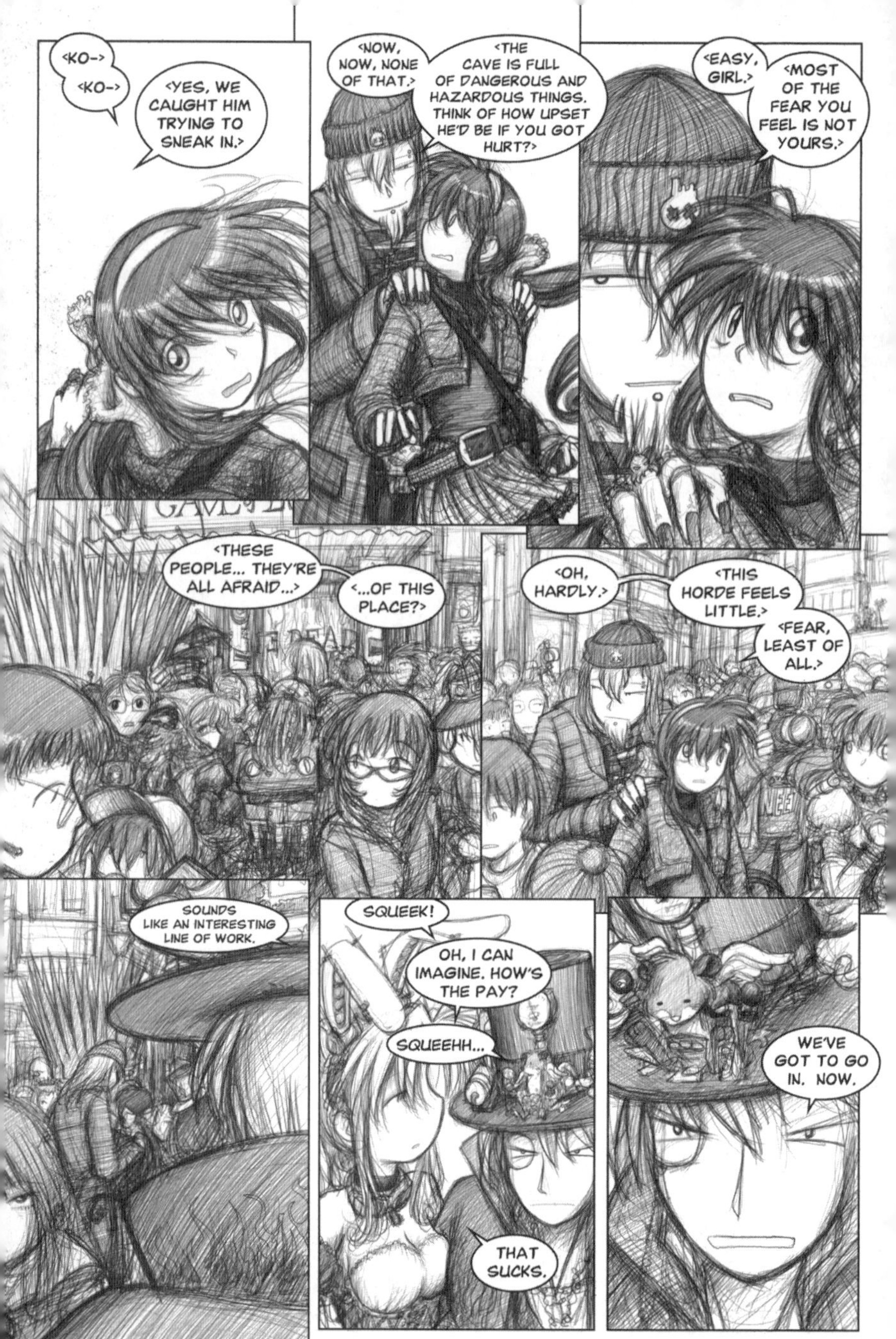
<KO->
<KO->
<YES, WE CAUGHT HIM TRYING TO SNEAK IN.>
<NOW, NOW, NONE OF THAT.>
<THE CAVE IS FULL OF DANGEROUS AND HAZARDOUS THINGS. THINK OF HOW UPSET HE'D BE IF YOU GOT HURT?>
<EASY, GIRL.>
<MOST OF THE FEAR YOU FEEL IS NOT YOURS.>
<THESE PEOPLE... THEY'RE ALL AFRAID...>
<...OF THIS PLACE?>
<OH, HARDLY.>
<THIS HORDE FEELS LITTLE.>
<FEAR, LEAST OF ALL.>
SOUNDS LIKE AN INTERESTING LINE OF WORK.
SQUEEK!
OH, I CAN IMAGINE. HOW'S THE PAY?
SQUEEHH...
THAT SUCKS.
WE'VE GOT TO GO IN. NOW.

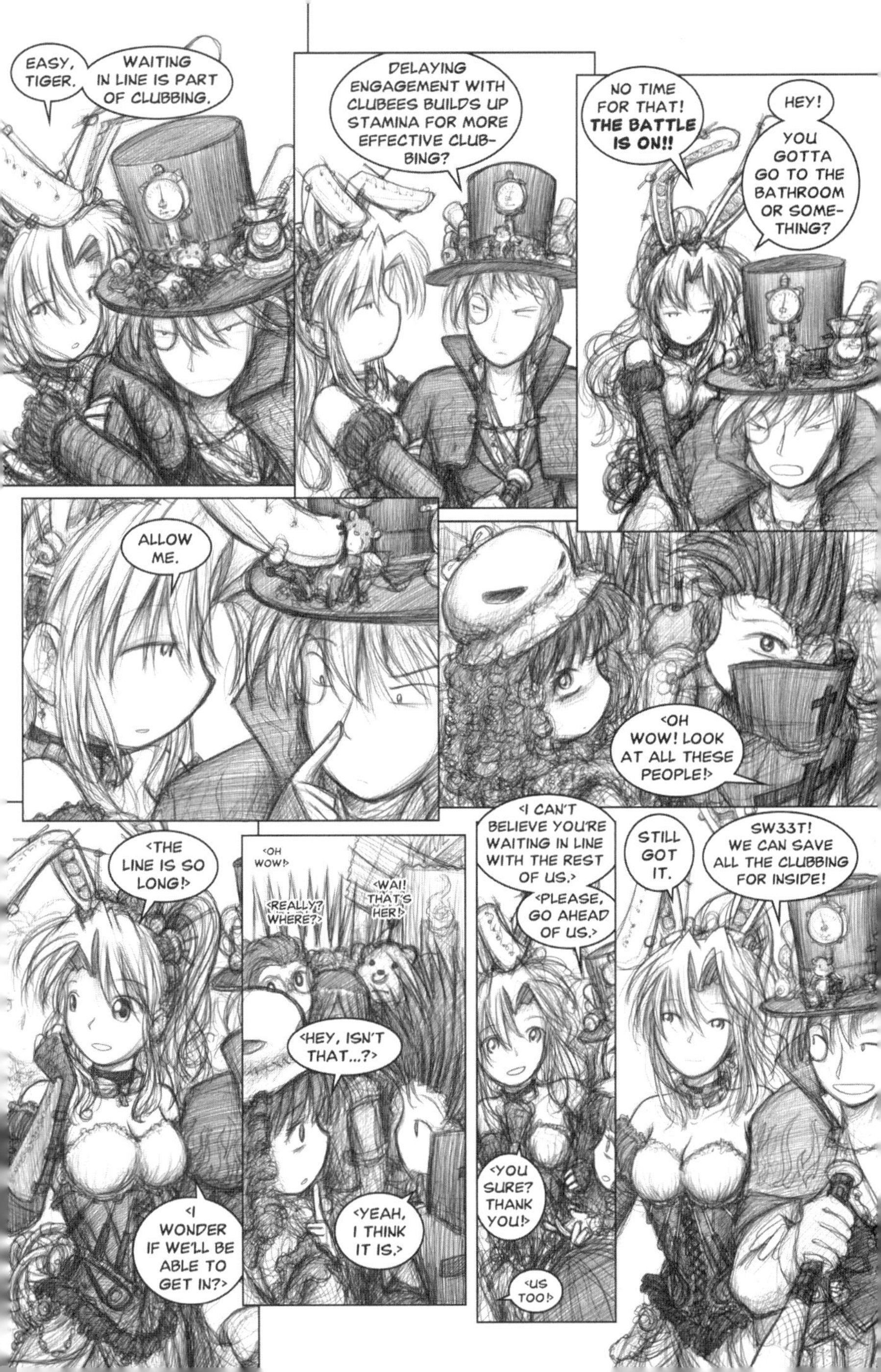
EASY, TIGER.
WAITING IN LINE IS PART OF CLUBBING.
DELAYING ENGAGEMENT WITH CLUBEES BUILDS UP STAMINA FOR MORE EFFECTIVE CLUB-BING?
NO TIME FOR THAT! **THE BATTLE IS ON!!**
HEY!
YOU GOTTA GO TO THE BATHROOM OR SOME-THING?
ALLOW ME.
<OH WOW! LOOK AT ALL THESE PEOPLE!>
<THE LINE IS SO LONG!>
<I WONDER IF WE'LL BE ABLE TO GET IN?>
<OH WOW!>
<REALLY? WHERE?>
<WAI! THAT'S HER!>
<HEY, ISN'T THAT...?>
<YEAH, I THINK IT IS.>
<I CAN'T BELIEVE YOU'RE WAITING IN LINE WITH THE REST OF US.>
<PLEASE, GO AHEAD OF US.>
<YOU SURE? THANK YOU!>
<US TOO!>
STILL GOT IT.
SW33T! WE CAN SAVE ALL THE CLUBBING FOR INSIDE!

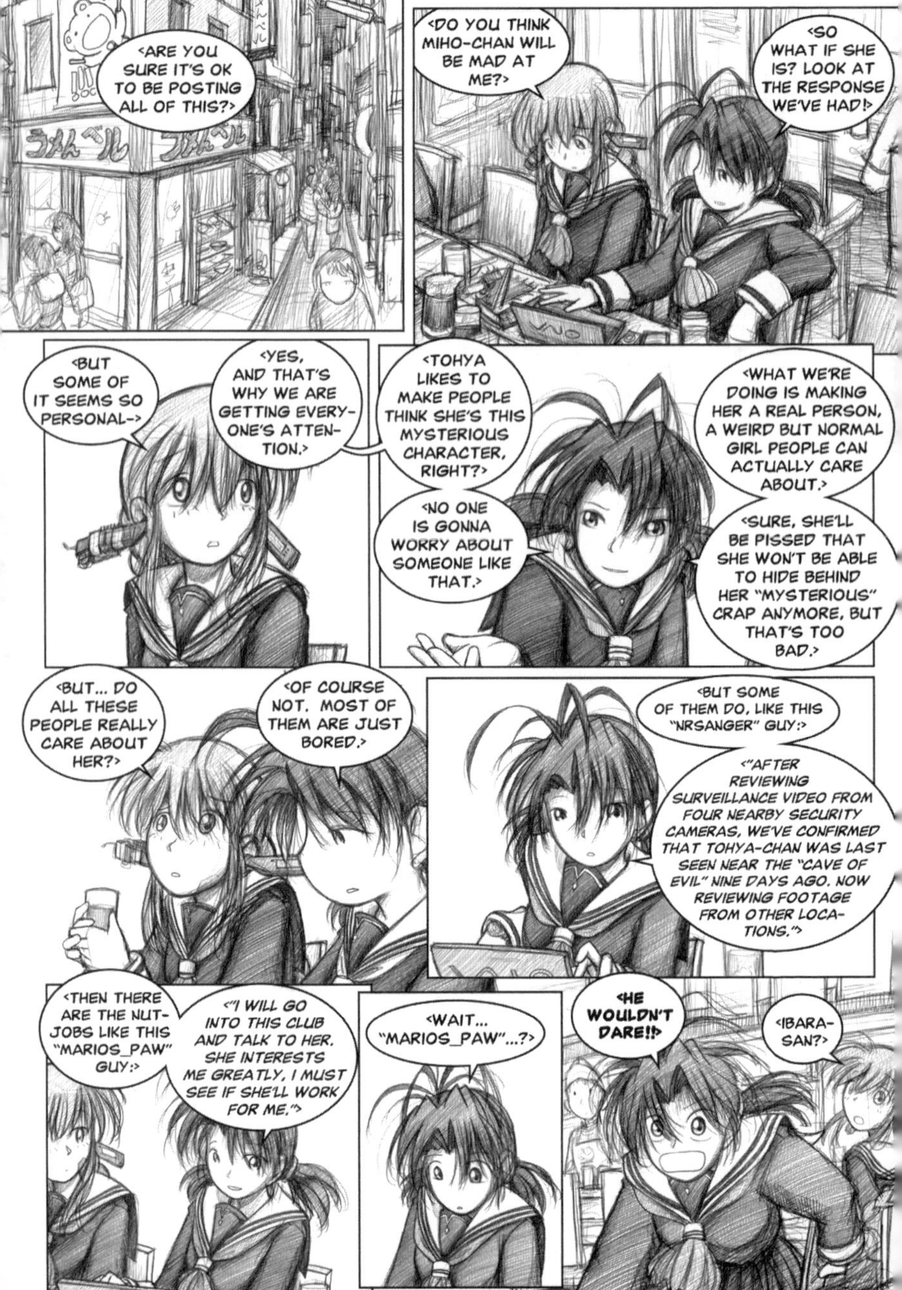
<ARE YOU SURE IT'S OK TO BE POSTING ALL OF THIS?>
<DO YOU THINK MIHO-CHAN WILL BE MAD AT ME?>
<SO WHAT IF SHE IS? LOOK AT THE RESPONSE WE'VE HAD!>
<BUT SOME OF IT SEEMS SO PERSONAL->
<YES, AND THAT'S WHY WE ARE GETTING EVERY-ONE'S ATTEN-TION.>
<TOHYA LIKES TO MAKE PEOPLE THINK SHE'S THIS MYSTERIOUS CHARACTER, RIGHT?>
<NO ONE IS GONNA WORRY ABOUT SOMEONE LIKE THAT.>
<WHAT WE'RE DOING IS MAKING HER A REAL PERSON, A WEIRD BUT NORMAL GIRL PEOPLE CAN ACTUALLY CARE ABOUT.>
<SURE, SHE'LL BE PISSED THAT SHE WON'T BE ABLE TO HIDE BEHIND HER "MYSTERIOUS" CRAP ANYMORE, BUT THAT'S TOO BAD.>
<BUT... DO ALL THESE PEOPLE REALLY CARE ABOUT HER?>
<OF COURSE NOT. MOST OF THEM ARE JUST BORED.>
<BUT SOME OF THEM DO, LIKE THIS "NRSANGER" GUY:>
<"AFTER REVIEWING SURVEILLANCE VIDEO FROM FOUR NEARBY SECURITY CAMERAS, WE'VE CONFIRMED THAT TOHYA-CHAN WAS LAST SEEN NEAR THE "CAVE OF EVIL" NINE DAYS AGO. NOW REVIEWING FOOTAGE FROM OTHER LOCA-TIONS.">
<THEN THERE ARE THE NUT-JOBS LIKE THIS "MARIOS_PAW" GUY:>
<"I WILL GO INTO THIS CLUB AND TALK TO HER. SHE INTERESTS ME GREATLY, I MUST SEE IF SHE'LL WORK FOR ME.">
<WAIT... "MARIOS_PAW"...?>
<HE WOULDN'T DARE!!>
<IBARA-SAN?>

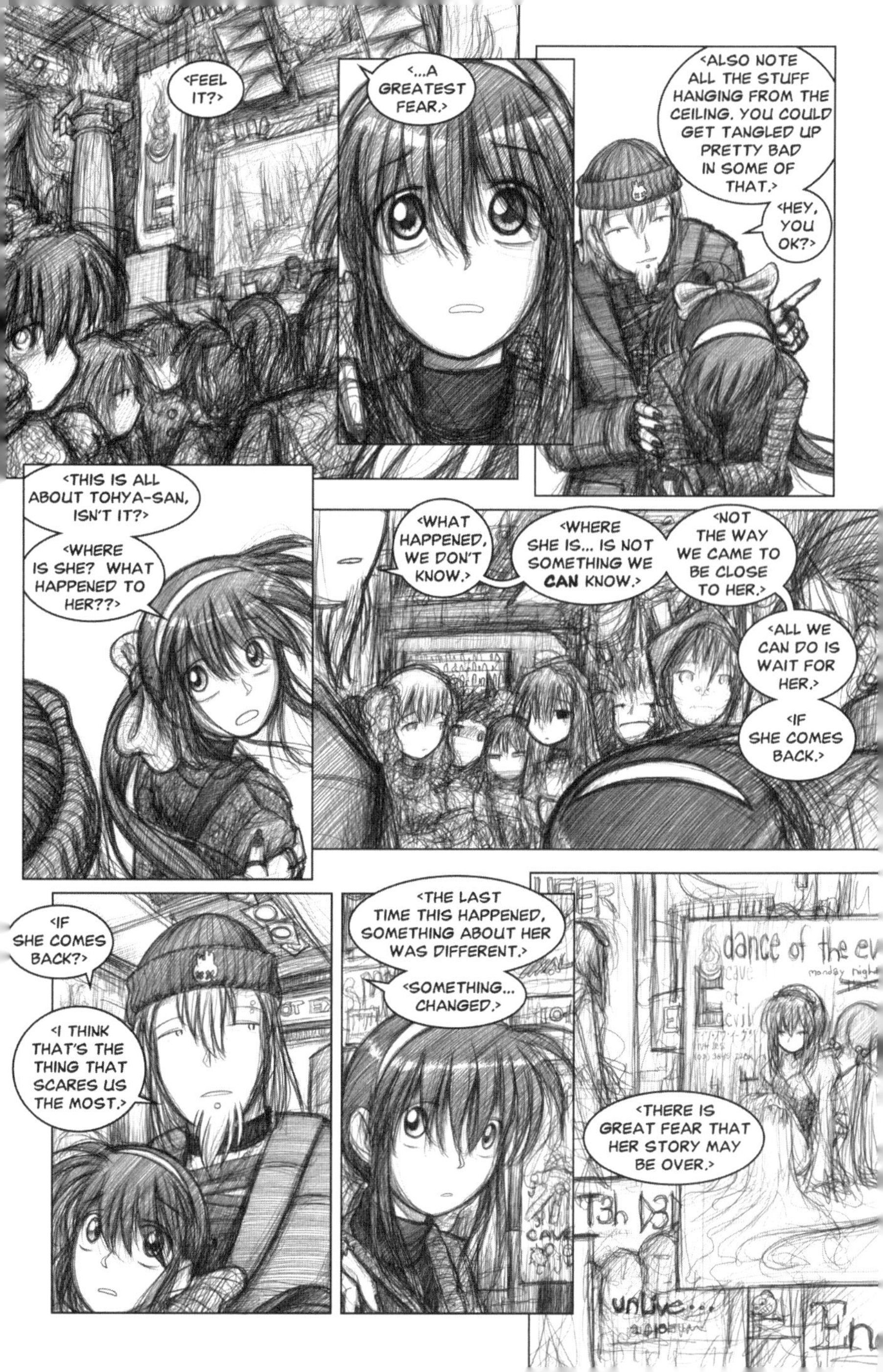

<FEEL IT?>
<...A GREATEST FEAR.>
<ALSO NOTE ALL THE STUFF HANGING FROM THE CEILING. YOU COULD GET TANGLED UP PRETTY BAD IN SOME OF THAT.>
<HEY, YOU OK?>
<THIS IS ALL ABOUT TOHYA-SAN, ISN'T IT?>
<WHERE IS SHE? WHAT HAPPENED TO HER??>
<WHAT HAPPENED, WE DON'T KNOW.>
<WHERE SHE IS... IS NOT SOMETHING WE **CAN** KNOW.>
<NOT THE WAY WE CAME TO BE CLOSE TO HER.>
<ALL WE CAN DO IS WAIT FOR HER.>
<IF SHE COMES BACK.>
<IF SHE COMES BACK?>
<I THINK THAT'S THE THING THAT SCARES US THE MOST.>
<THE LAST TIME THIS HAPPENED, SOMETHING ABOUT HER WAS DIFFERENT.>
<SOMETHING... CHANGED.>
dance of the ev
monday night
cave of evil
<THERE IS GREAT FEAR THAT HER STORY MAY BE OVER.>
T3h D8
unLive...

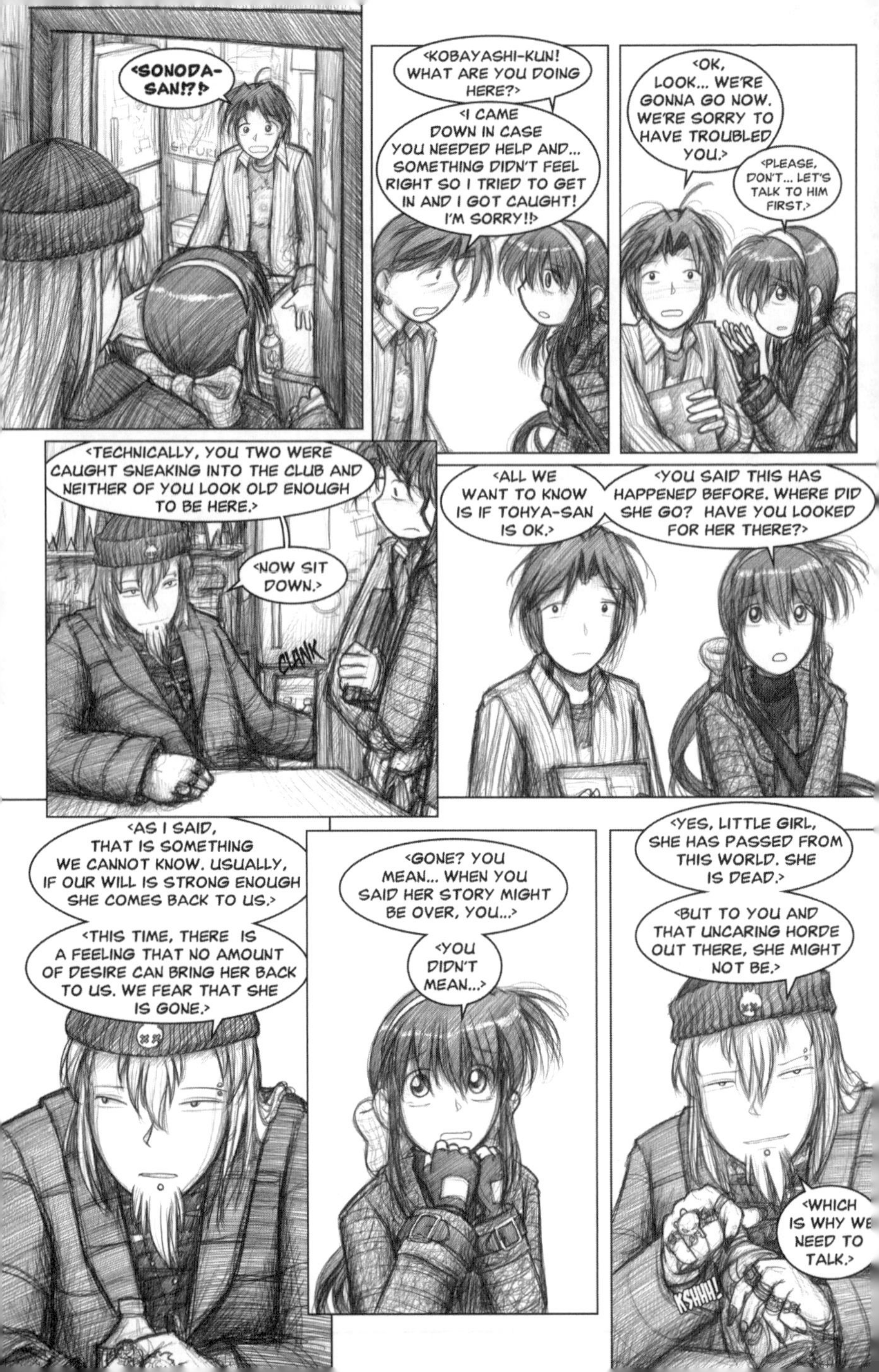

<SONODA-SAN!?!>
<KOBAYASHI-KUN! WHAT ARE YOU DOING HERE?>
<I CAME DOWN IN CASE YOU NEEDED HELP AND... SOMETHING DIDN'T FEEL RIGHT SO I TRIED TO GET IN AND I GOT CAUGHT! I'M SORRY!!>
<OK, LOOK... WE'RE GONNA GO NOW. WE'RE SORRY TO HAVE TROUBLED YOU.>
<PLEASE, DON'T... LET'S TALK TO HIM FIRST.>
<TECHNICALLY, YOU TWO WERE CAUGHT SNEAKING INTO THE CLUB AND NEITHER OF YOU LOOK OLD ENOUGH TO BE HERE.>
<NOW SIT DOWN.>
CLANK
<ALL WE WANT TO KNOW IS IF TOHYA-SAN IS OK.>
<YOU SAID THIS HAS HAPPENED BEFORE. WHERE DID SHE GO? HAVE YOU LOOKED FOR HER THERE?>
<AS I SAID, THAT IS SOMETHING WE CANNOT KNOW. USUALLY, IF OUR WILL IS STRONG ENOUGH SHE COMES BACK TO US.>
<THIS TIME, THERE IS A FEELING THAT NO AMOUNT OF DESIRE CAN BRING HER BACK TO US. WE FEAR THAT SHE IS GONE.>
<GONE? YOU MEAN... WHEN YOU SAID HER STORY MIGHT BE OVER, YOU...>
<YOU DIDN'T MEAN...>
<YES, LITTLE GIRL, SHE HAS PASSED FROM THIS WORLD. SHE IS DEAD.>
<BUT TO YOU AND THAT UNCARING HORDE OUT THERE, SHE MIGHT NOT BE.>
<WHICH IS WHY WE NEED TO TALK.>
KSHHH!

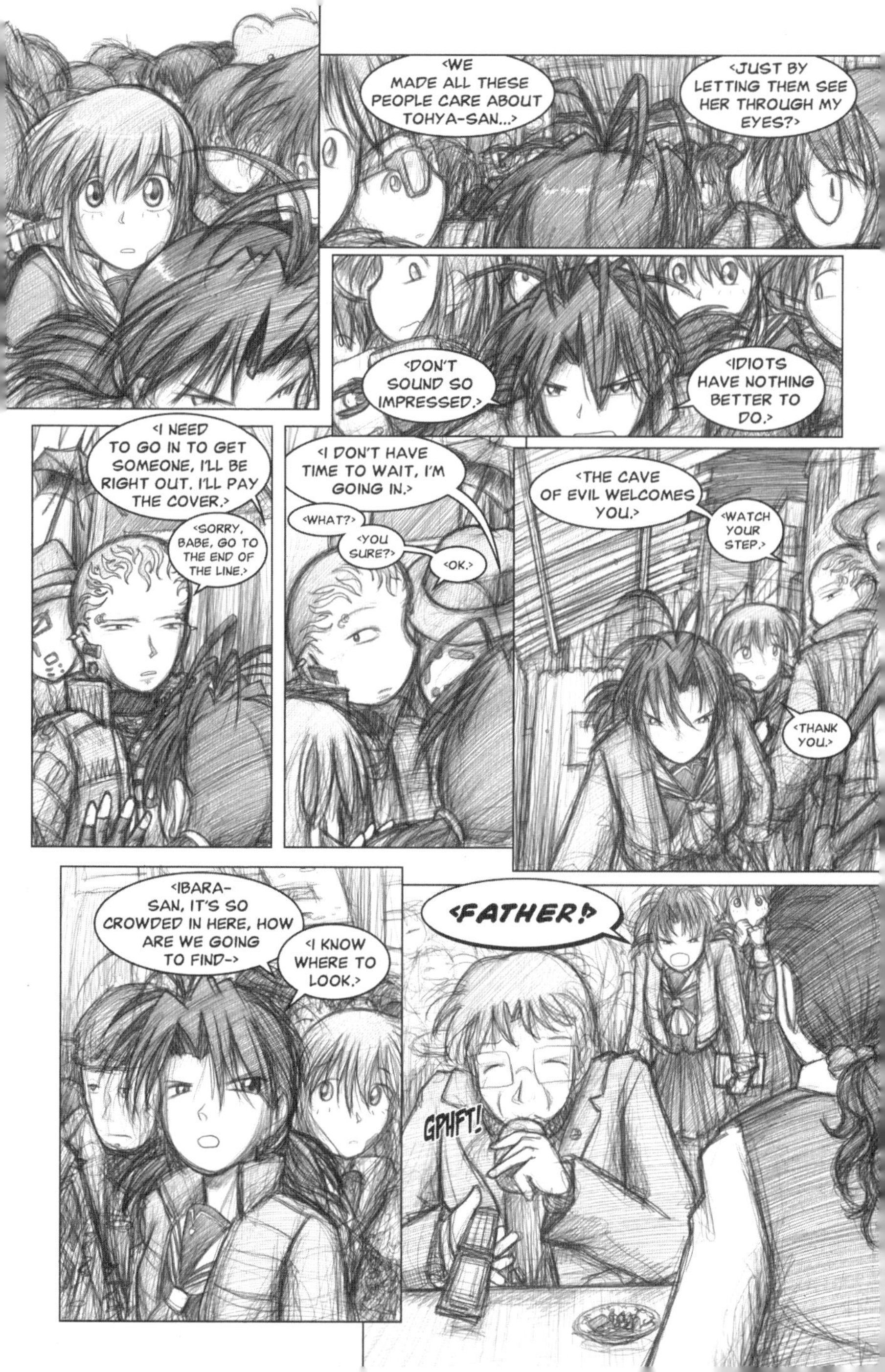
<WE MADE ALL THESE PEOPLE CARE ABOUT TOHYA-SAN...>
<JUST BY LETTING THEM SEE HER THROUGH MY EYES?>
<DON'T SOUND SO IMPRESSED.>
<IDIOTS HAVE NOTHING BETTER TO DO.>
<I NEED TO GO IN TO GET SOMEONE, I'LL BE RIGHT OUT. I'LL PAY THE COVER.>
<SORRY, BABE, GO TO THE END OF THE LINE.>
<I DON'T HAVE TIME TO WAIT, I'M GOING IN.>
<WHAT?>
<YOU SURE?>
<OK.>
<THE CAVE OF EVIL WELCOMES YOU.>
<WATCH YOUR STEP.>
<THANK YOU.>
<IBARA-SAN, IT'S SO CROWDED IN HERE, HOW ARE WE GOING TO FIND->
<I KNOW WHERE TO LOOK.>
<FATHER!>
GPHFT!

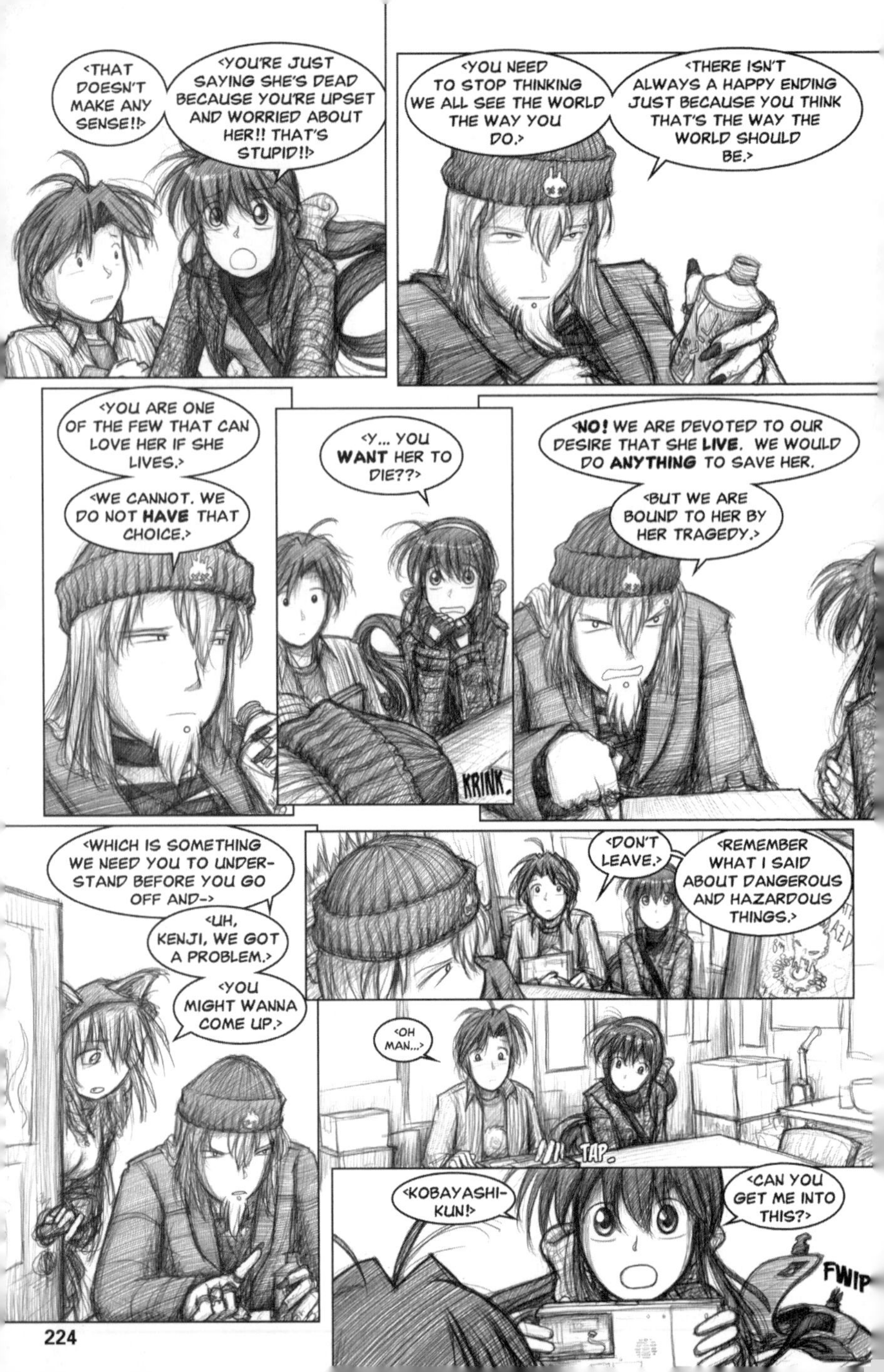

<THAT DOESN'T MAKE ANY SENSE!!>
<YOU'RE JUST SAYING SHE'S DEAD BECAUSE YOU'RE UPSET AND WORRIED ABOUT HER!! THAT'S STUPID!!>
<YOU NEED TO STOP THINKING WE ALL SEE THE WORLD THE WAY YOU DO.>
<THERE ISN'T ALWAYS A HAPPY ENDING JUST BECAUSE YOU THINK THAT'S THE WAY THE WORLD SHOULD BE.>
<YOU ARE ONE OF THE FEW THAT CAN LOVE HER IF SHE LIVES.>
<WE CANNOT. WE DO NOT HAVE THAT CHOICE.>
<Y... YOU WANT HER TO DIE??>
KRINK.
<NO! WE ARE DEVOTED TO OUR DESIRE THAT SHE LIVE. WE WOULD DO ANYTHING TO SAVE HER.
<BUT WE ARE BOUND TO HER BY HER TRAGEDY.>
<WHICH IS SOMETHING WE NEED YOU TO UNDERSTAND BEFORE YOU GO OFF AND->
<UH, KENJI, WE GOT A PROBLEM.>
<YOU MIGHT WANNA COME UP.>
<DON'T LEAVE.>
<REMEMBER WHAT I SAID ABOUT DANGEROUS AND HAZARDOUS THINGS.>
<OH MAN...>
TAP.
<KOBAYASHI-KUN!>
<CAN YOU GET ME INTO THIS?>
FWIP

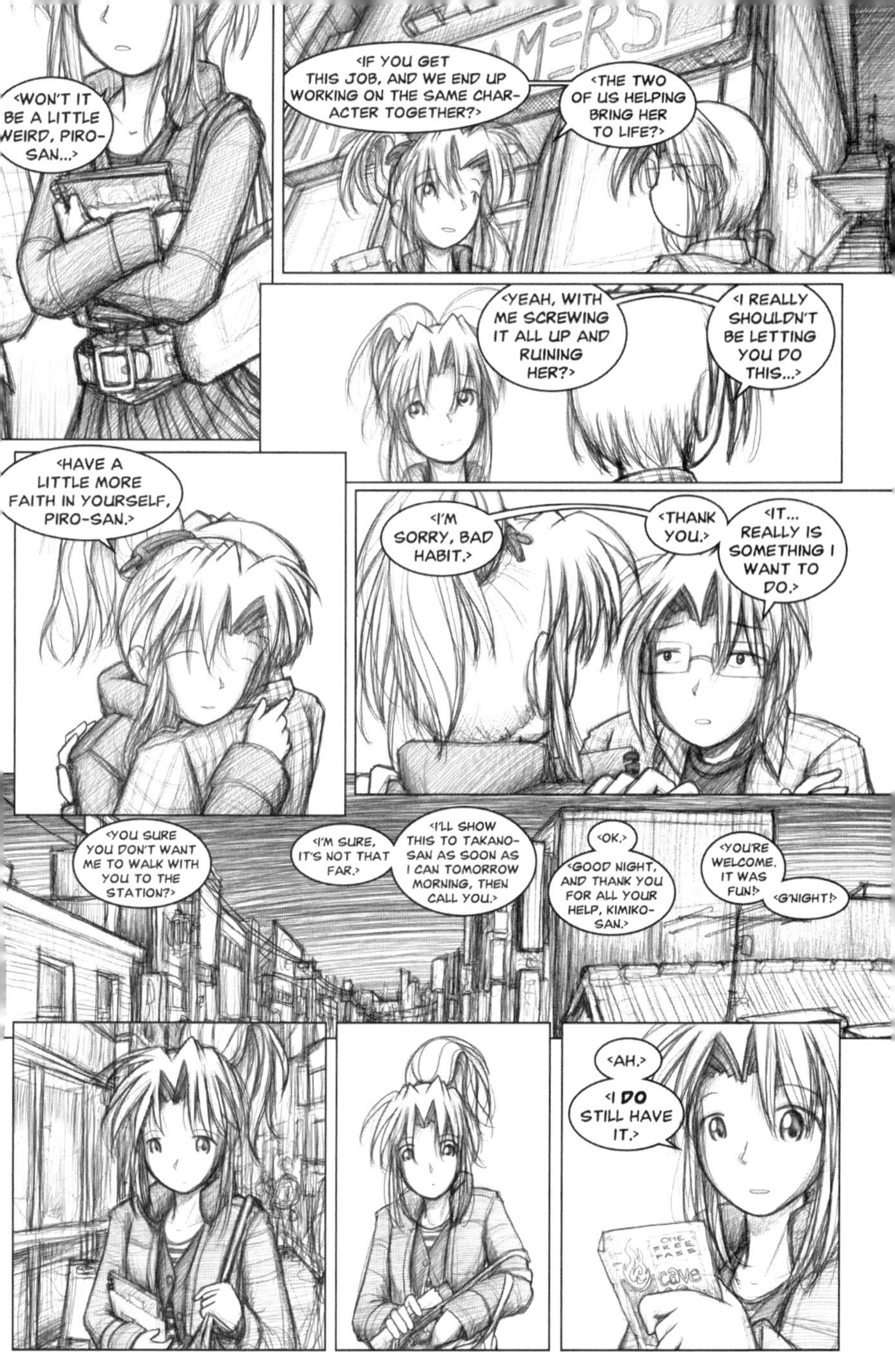
<WON'T IT BE A LITTLE WEIRD, PIRO-SAN...>
<IF YOU GET THIS JOB, AND WE END UP WORKING ON THE SAME CHARACTER TOGETHER?>
<THE TWO OF US HELPING BRING HER TO LIFE?>
<YEAH, WITH ME SCREWING IT ALL UP AND RUINING HER?>
<I REALLY SHOULDN'T BE LETTING YOU DO THIS...>
<HAVE A LITTLE MORE FAITH IN YOURSELF, PIRO-SAN.>
<I'M SORRY, BAD HABIT.>
<THANK YOU.>
<IT... REALLY IS SOMETHING I WANT TO DO.>
<YOU SURE YOU DON'T WANT ME TO WALK WITH YOU TO THE STATION?>
<I'M SURE, IT'S NOT THAT FAR.>
<I'LL SHOW THIS TO TAKANO-SAN AS SOON AS I CAN TOMORROW MORNING, THEN CALL YOU.>
<OK.>
<GOOD NIGHT, AND THANK YOU FOR ALL YOUR HELP, KIMIKO-SAN.>
<YOU'RE WELCOME. IT WAS FUN!>
<G'NIGHT!>
<AH.>
<I **DO** STILL HAVE IT.>
ONE FREE PASS
cave

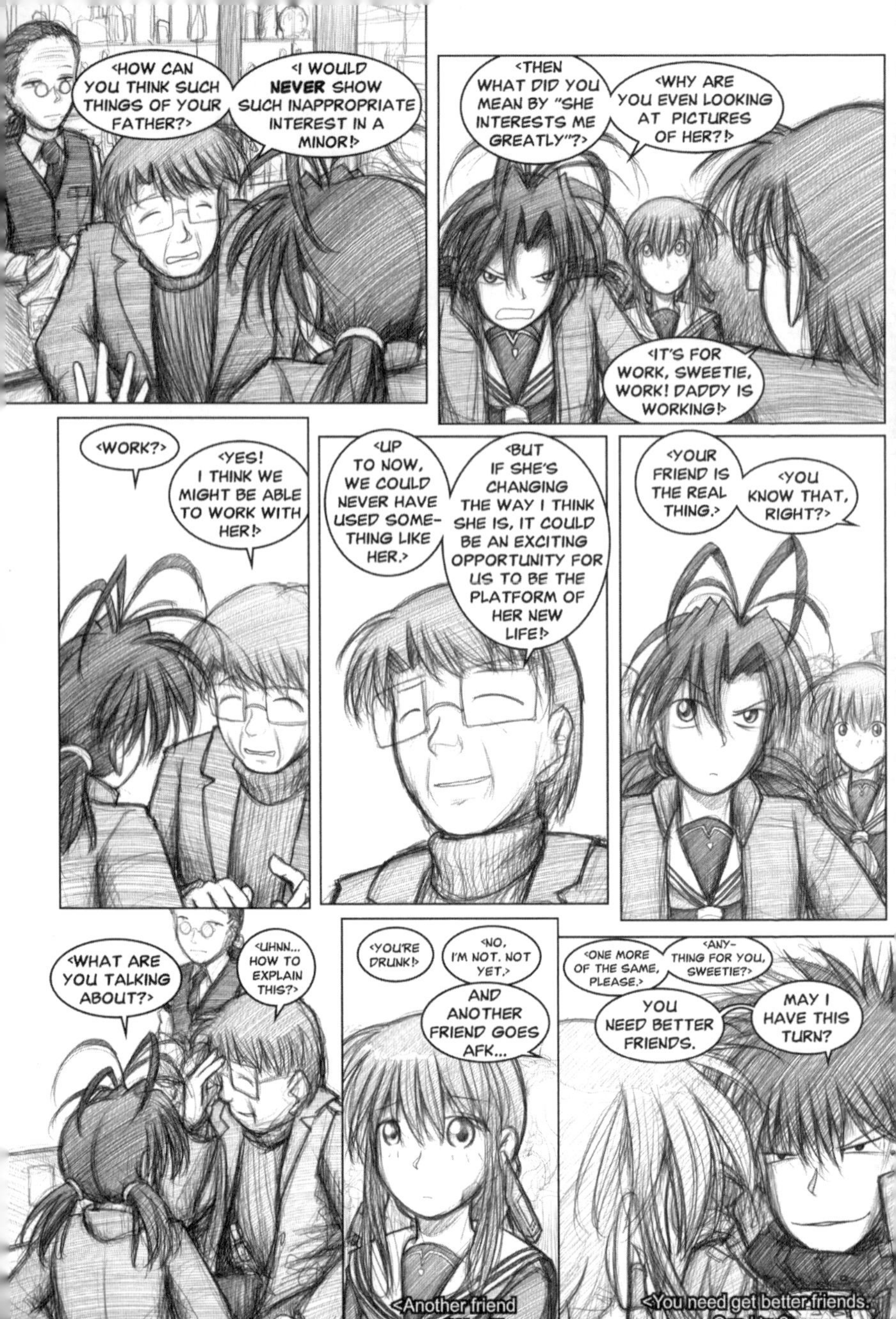
<HOW CAN YOU THINK SUCH THINGS OF YOUR FATHER?>
<I WOULD **NEVER** SHOW SUCH INAPPROPRIATE INTEREST IN A MINOR!>
<THEN WHAT DID YOU MEAN BY "SHE INTERESTS ME GREATLY"?>
<WHY ARE YOU EVEN LOOKING AT PICTURES OF HER?!>
<IT'S FOR WORK, SWEETIE, WORK! DADDY IS WORKING!>
<WORK?>
<YES! I THINK WE MIGHT BE ABLE TO WORK WITH HER!>
<UP TO NOW, WE COULD NEVER HAVE USED SOME-THING LIKE HER.>
<BUT IF SHE'S CHANGING THE WAY I THINK SHE IS, IT COULD BE AN EXCITING OPPORTUNITY FOR US TO BE THE PLATFORM OF HER NEW LIFE!>
<YOUR FRIEND IS THE REAL THING.>
<YOU KNOW THAT, RIGHT?>
<WHAT ARE YOU TALKING ABOUT?>
<UHNN... HOW TO EXPLAIN THIS?>
<YOU'RE DRUNK!>
<NO, I'M NOT. NOT YET.>
AND ANOTHER FRIEND GOES AFK...
<Another friend goes "Woof!">
<ONE MORE OF THE SAME, PLEASE.>
<ANY-THING FOR YOU, SWEETIE?>
YOU NEED BETTER FRIENDS.
MAY I HAVE THIS TURN?
<You need get better friends. Can i try?>

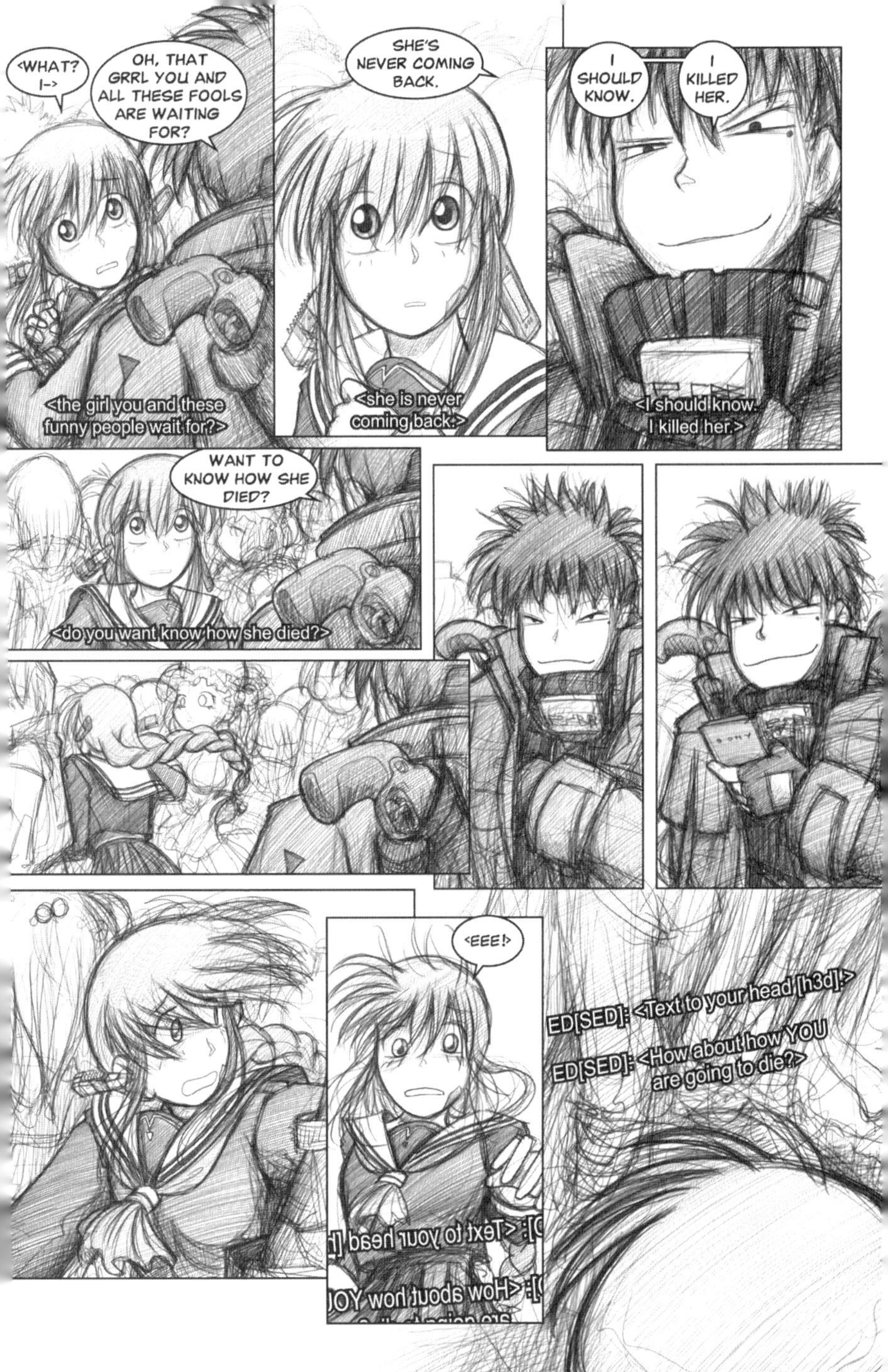
<WHAT? I->
OH, THAT GRRL YOU AND ALL THESE FOOLS ARE WAITING FOR?
<the girl you and these funny people wait for?>
SHE'S NEVER COMING BACK.
<she is never coming back.>
I SHOULD KNOW.
I KILLED HER.
<I should know. I killed her.>
WANT TO KNOW HOW SHE DIED?
<do you want know how she died?>
<EEE!>
ED[SED]: <Text to your head [h3d].>
ED[SED]: <How about how YOU are going to die?>

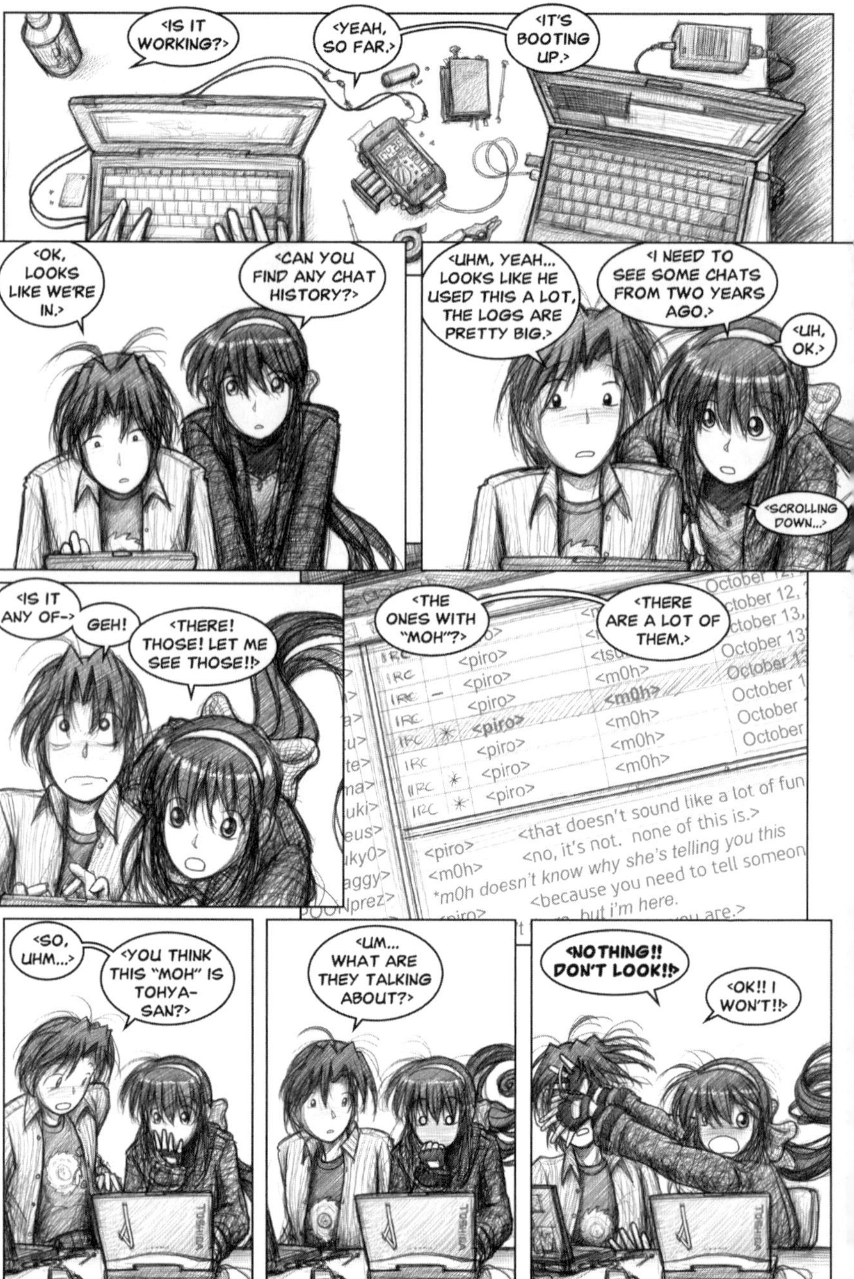
<IS IT WORKING?>
<YEAH, SO FAR.>
<IT'S BOOTING UP.>
<OK, LOOKS LIKE WE'RE IN.>
<CAN YOU FIND ANY CHAT HISTORY?>
<UHM, YEAH... LOOKS LIKE HE USED THIS A LOT, THE LOGS ARE PRETTY BIG.>
<I NEED TO SEE SOME CHATS FROM TWO YEARS AGO.>
<UH, OK.>
<SCROLLING DOWN...>
<IS IT ANY OF->
GEH!
<THERE! THOSE! LET ME SEE THOSE!!>
<THE ONES WITH "MOH"?>
<THERE ARE A LOT OF THEM.>
<piro> <that doesn't sound like a lot of fun
<m0h> <no, it's not. none of this is.>
*m0h doesn't know why she's telling you this
<because you need to tell someon
but i'm here.
<SO, UHM...>
<YOU THINK THIS "MOH" IS TOHYA-SAN?>
<UM... WHAT ARE THEY TALKING ABOUT?>
<NOTHING!! DON'T LOOK!!>
<OK!! I WON'T!!>

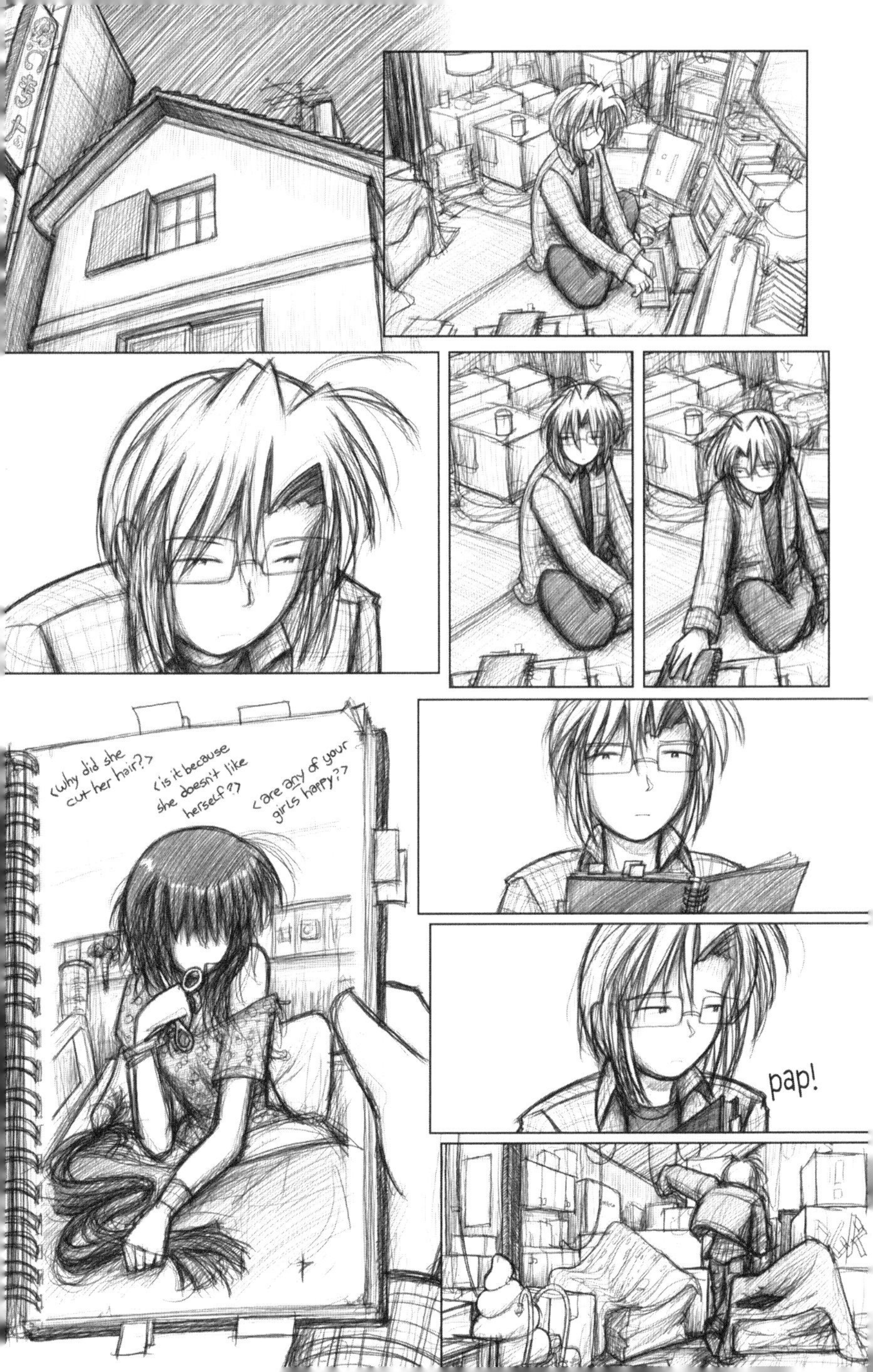
<why did she cut her hair?>
<is it because she doesn't like herself?>
<are any of your girls happy?>
pap!

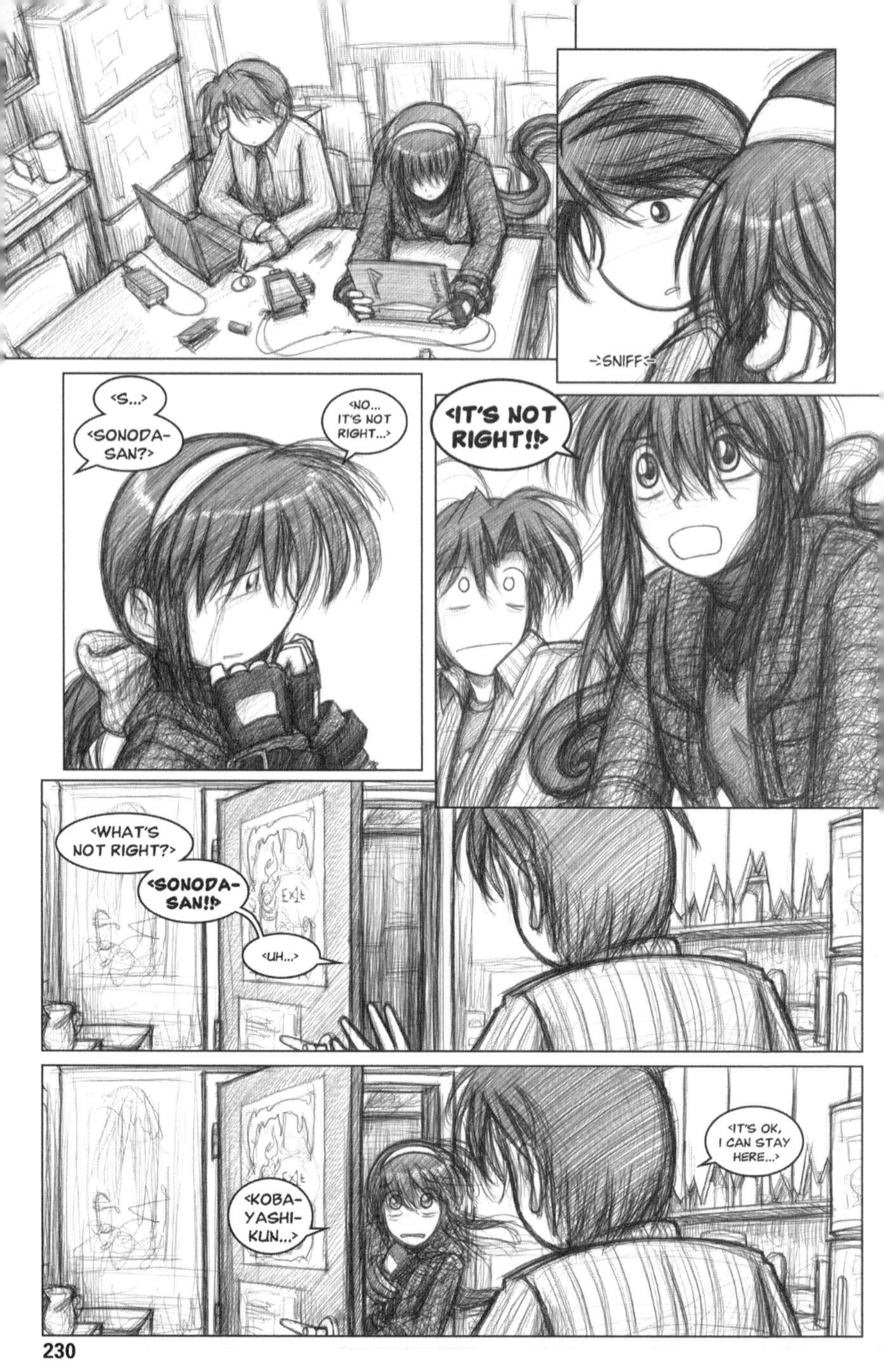

-SNIFF-
<S...>
<SONODA-SAN?>
<NO... IT'S NOT RIGHT...>
<IT'S NOT RIGHT!!>
<WHAT'S NOT RIGHT?>
<SONODA-SAN!!>
<UH...>
<KOBA-YASHI-KUN...>
<IT'S OK, I CAN STAY HERE...>

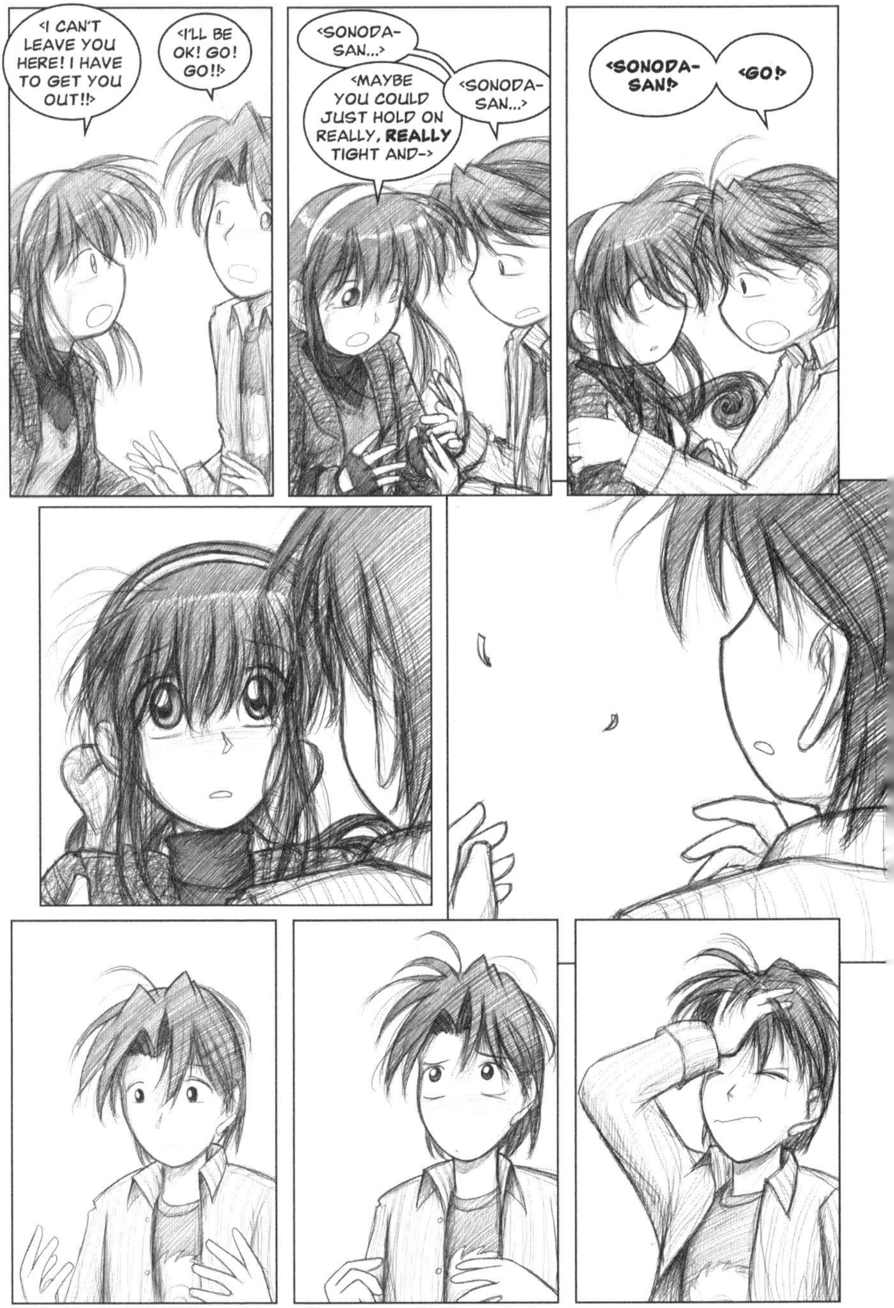
<I CAN'T LEAVE YOU HERE! I HAVE TO GET YOU OUT!!>
<I'LL BE OK! GO! GO!!>
<SONODA-SAN...>
<MAYBE YOU COULD JUST HOLD ON REALLY, **REALLY** TIGHT AND->
<SONODA-SAN...>
<SONODA-SAN!>
<GO!>

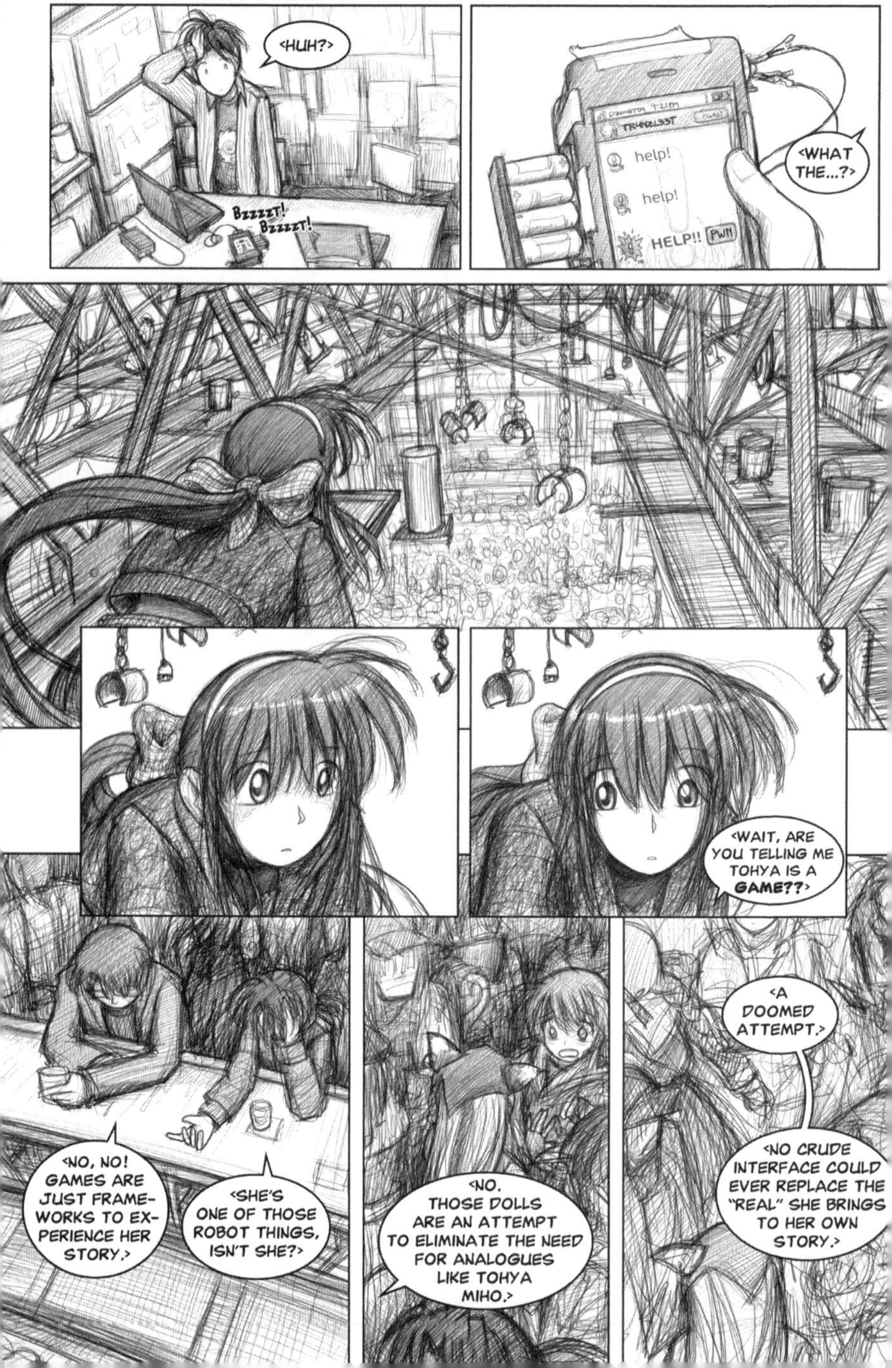
<HUH?>
Bzzzzt!
Bzzzzt!
help!
help!
HELP!!
PWN
<WHAT THE...?>
<WAIT, ARE YOU TELLING ME TOHYA IS A **GAME??**>
<NO, NO! GAMES ARE JUST FRAME-WORKS TO EX-PERIENCE HER STORY.>
<SHE'S ONE OF THOSE ROBOT THINGS, ISN'T SHE?>
<NO. THOSE DOLLS ARE AN ATTEMPT TO ELIMINATE THE NEED FOR ANALOGUES LIKE TOHYA MIHO.>
<A DOOMED ATTEMPT.>
<NO CRUDE INTERFACE COULD EVER REPLACE THE "REAL" SHE BRINGS TO HER OWN STORY.>

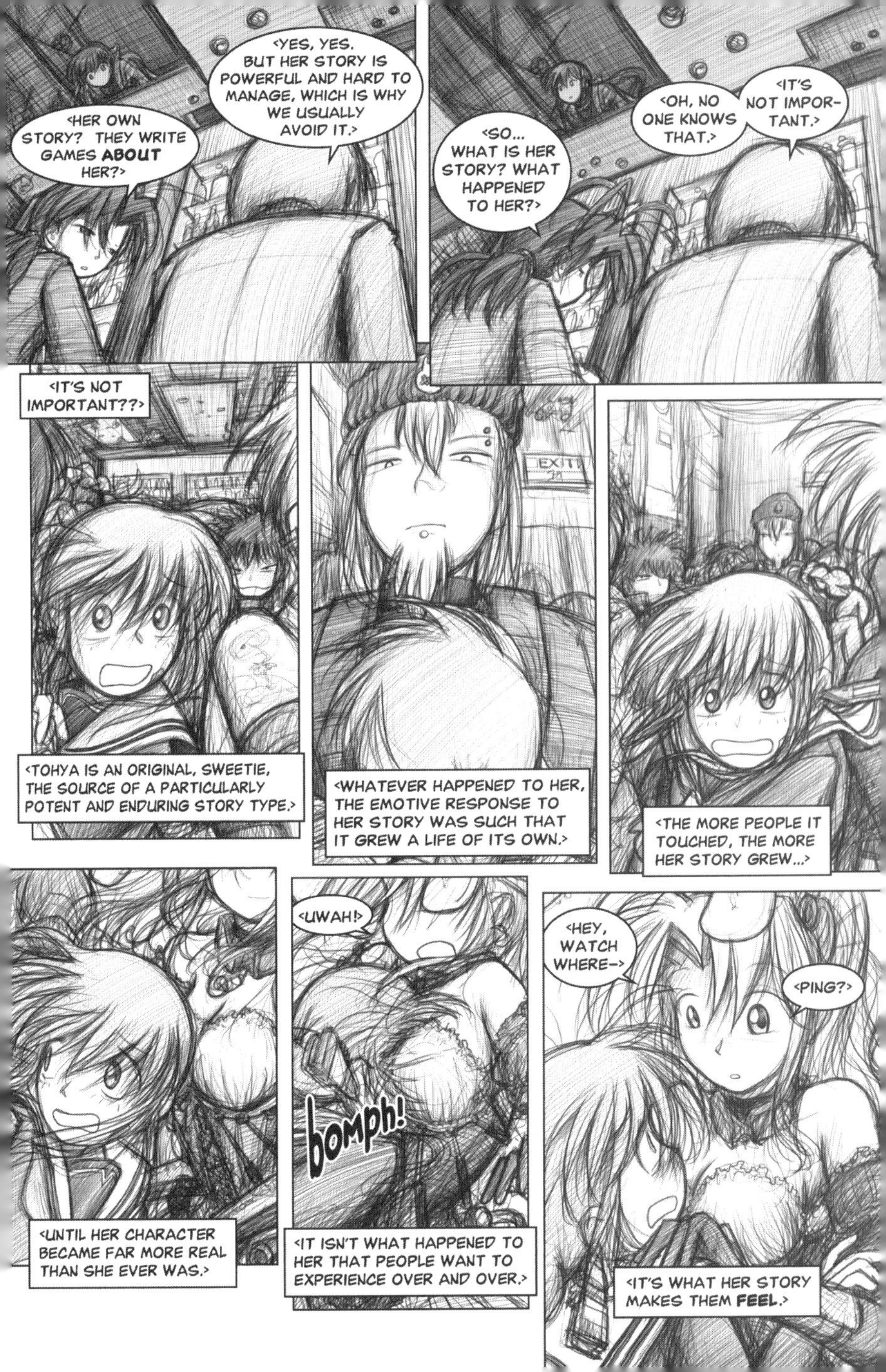
<HER OWN STORY? THEY WRITE GAMES **ABOUT** HER?>
<YES, YES. BUT HER STORY IS POWERFUL AND HARD TO MANAGE, WHICH IS WHY WE USUALLY AVOID IT.>
<SO... WHAT IS HER STORY? WHAT HAPPENED TO HER?>
<OH, NO ONE KNOWS THAT.>
<IT'S NOT IMPORTANT.>
<IT'S NOT IMPORTANT??>
<TOHYA IS AN ORIGINAL, SWEETIE, THE SOURCE OF A PARTICULARLY POTENT AND ENDURING STORY TYPE.>
EXIT
<WHATEVER HAPPENED TO HER, THE EMOTIVE RESPONSE TO HER STORY WAS SUCH THAT IT GREW A LIFE OF ITS OWN.>
<THE MORE PEOPLE IT TOUCHED, THE MORE HER STORY GREW...>
<UNTIL HER CHARACTER BECAME FAR MORE REAL THAN SHE EVER WAS.>
<UWAH!>
bomph!
<IT ISN'T WHAT HAPPENED TO HER THAT PEOPLE WANT TO EXPERIENCE OVER AND OVER.>
<HEY, WATCH WHERE–>
<PING?>
<IT'S WHAT HER STORY MAKES THEM **FEEL**.>

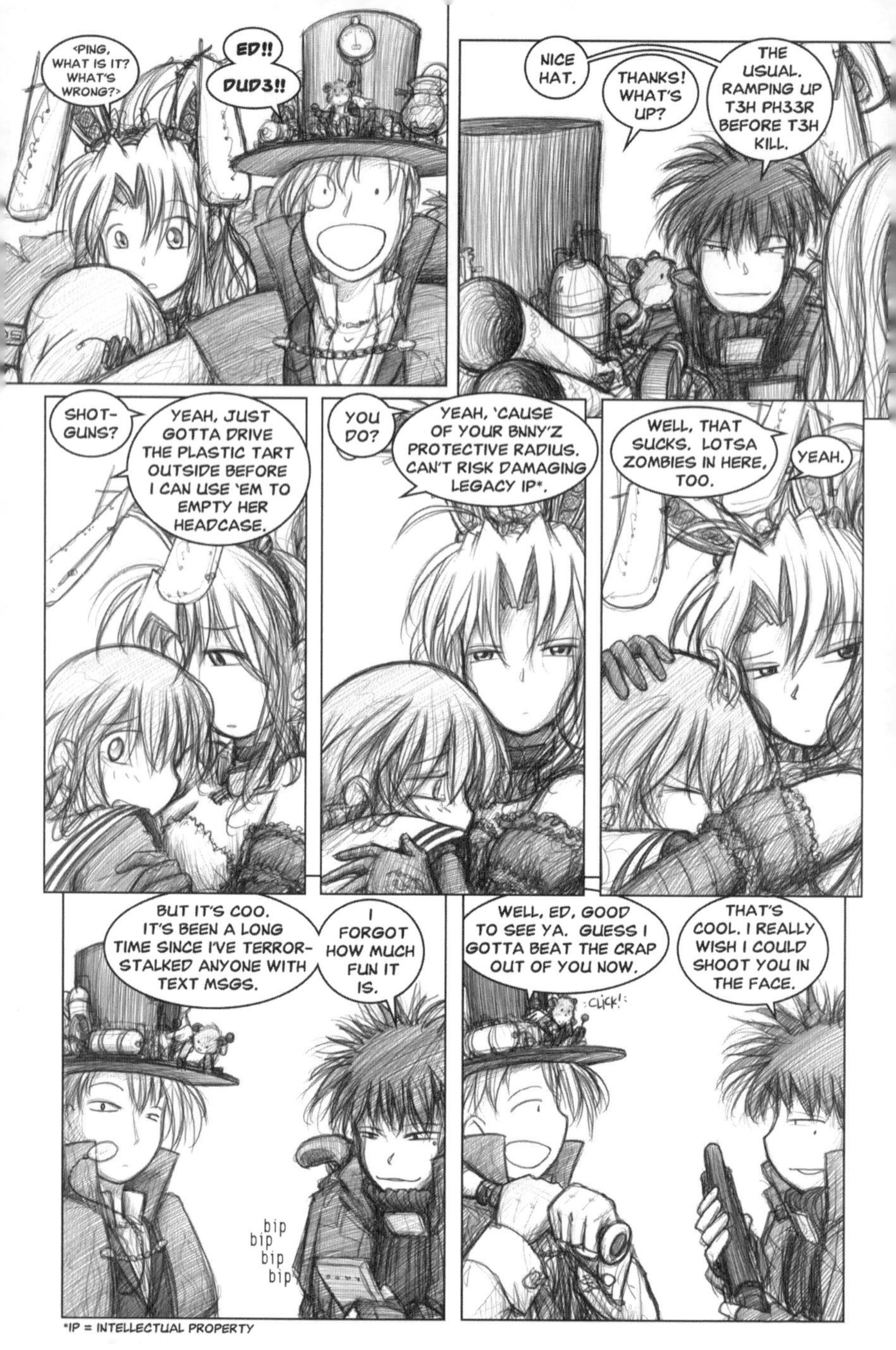

<PING, WHAT IS IT? WHAT'S WRONG?>
ED!!
DUD3!!
NICE HAT.
THANKS! WHAT'S UP?
THE USUAL. RAMPING UP T3H PH33R BEFORE T3H KILL.
SHOT-GUNS?
YEAH, JUST GOTTA DRIVE THE PLASTIC TART OUTSIDE BEFORE I CAN USE 'EM TO EMPTY HER HEADCASE.
YOU DO?
YEAH, 'CAUSE OF YOUR BNNY'Z PROTECTIVE RADIUS. CAN'T RISK DAMAGING LEGACY IP*.
WELL, THAT SUCKS. LOTSA ZOMBIES IN HERE, TOO.
YEAH.
BUT IT'S COO. IT'S BEEN A LONG TIME SINCE I'VE TERROR-STALKED ANYONE WITH TEXT MSGS.
I FORGOT HOW MUCH FUN IT IS.
bip bip bip bip
WELL, ED, GOOD TO SEE YA. GUESS I GOTTA BEAT THE CRAP OUT OF YOU NOW.
CLICK!
THAT'S COOL. I REALLY WISH I COULD SHOOT YOU IN THE FACE.

*IP = INTELLECTUAL PROPERTY

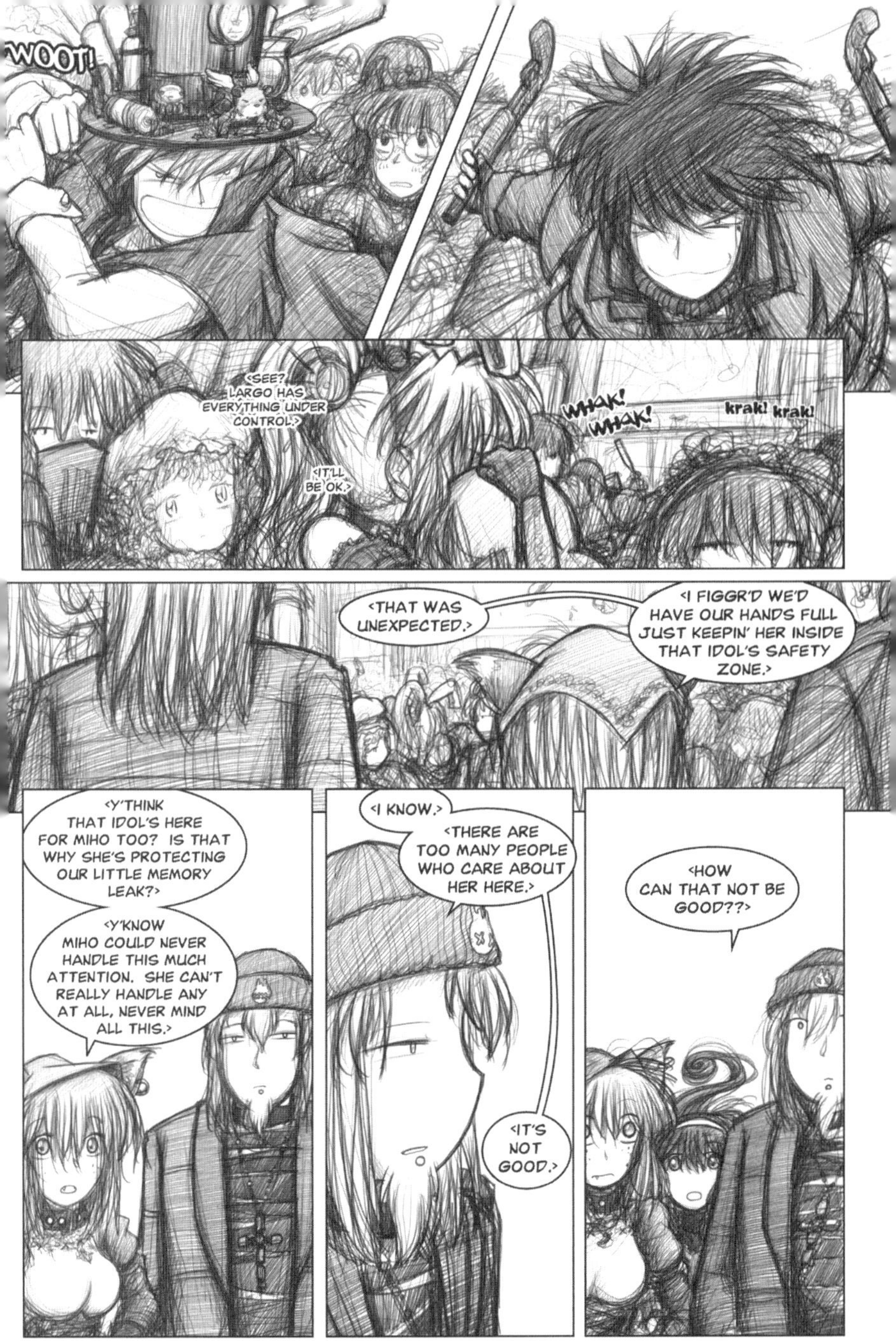
WOOT!
<SEE? LARGO HAS EVERYTHING UNDER CONTROL.>
<IT'LL BE OK.>
WHAK! WHAK!
krak! krak!
<THAT WAS UNEXPECTED.>
<I FIGGR'D WE'D HAVE OUR HANDS FULL JUST KEEPIN' HER INSIDE THAT IDOL'S SAFETY ZONE.>
<Y'THINK THAT IDOL'S HERE FOR MIHO TOO? IS THAT WHY SHE'S PROTECTING OUR LITTLE MEMORY LEAK?>
<Y'KNOW MIHO COULD NEVER HANDLE THIS MUCH ATTENTION. SHE CAN'T REALLY HANDLE ANY AT ALL, NEVER MIND ALL THIS.>
<I KNOW.>
<THERE ARE TOO MANY PEOPLE WHO CARE ABOUT HER HERE.>
<IT'S NOT GOOD.>
<HOW CAN THAT NOT BE GOOD??>

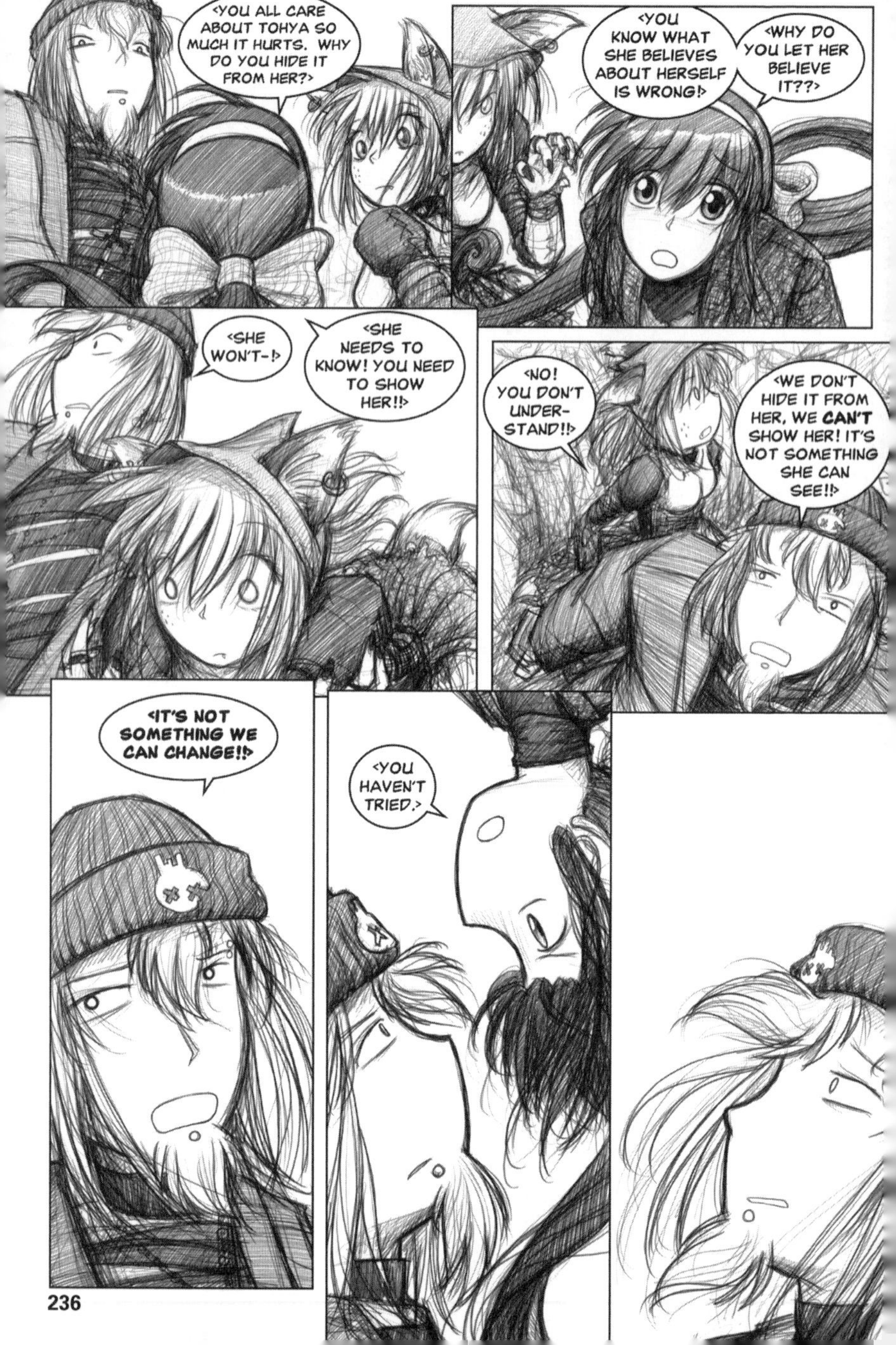
<YOU ALL CARE ABOUT TOHYA SO MUCH IT HURTS. WHY DO YOU HIDE IT FROM HER?>
<YOU KNOW WHAT SHE BELIEVES ABOUT HERSELF IS WRONG!>
<WHY DO YOU LET HER BELIEVE IT??>
<SHE WON'T-!>
<SHE NEEDS TO KNOW! YOU NEED TO SHOW HER!!>
<NO! YOU DON'T UNDER-STAND!!>
<WE DON'T HIDE IT FROM HER, WE **CAN'T** SHOW HER! IT'S NOT SOMETHING SHE CAN SEE!!>
<IT'S NOT SOMETHING WE CAN CHANGE!!>
<YOU HAVEN'T TRIED.>

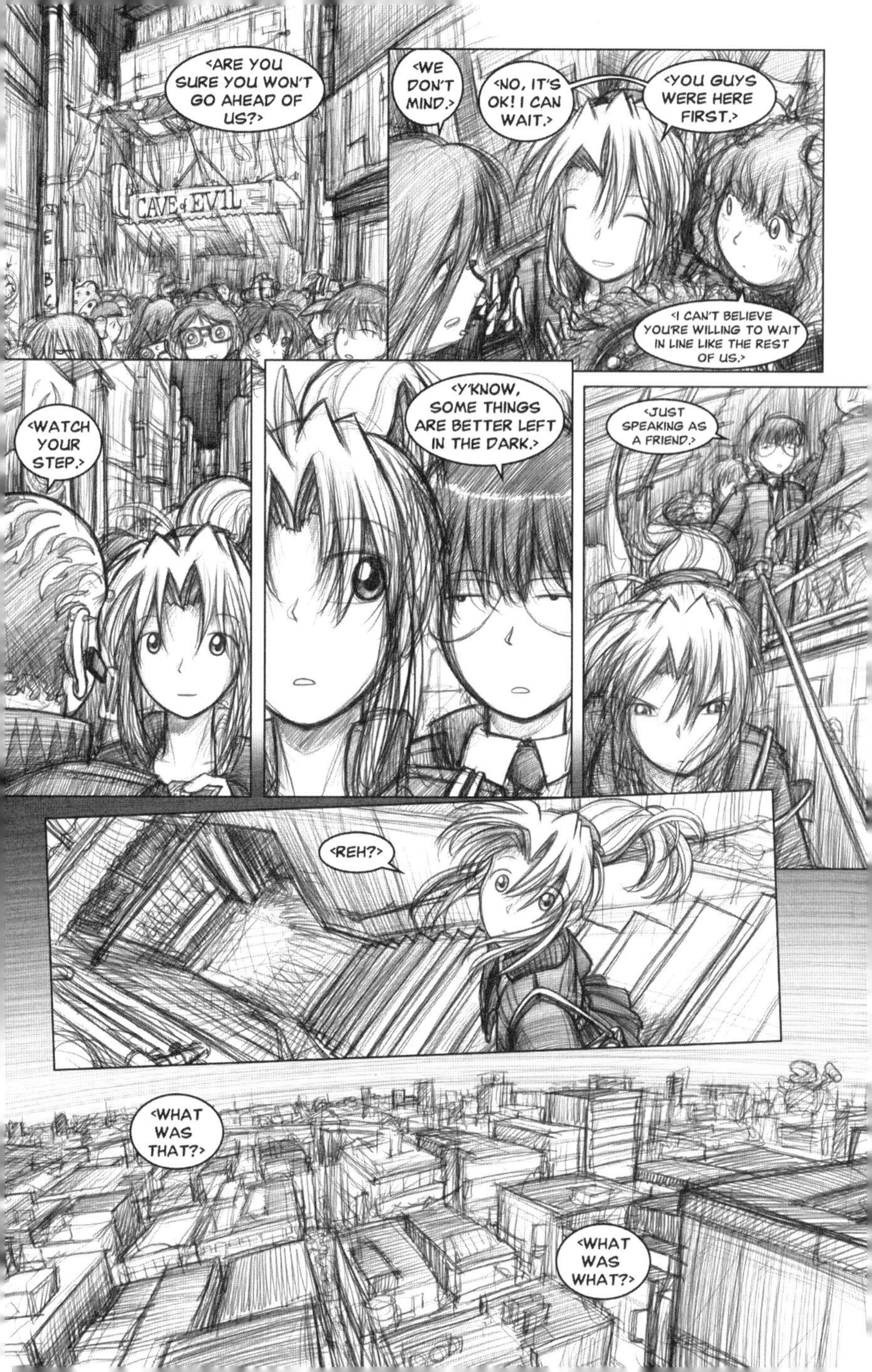
<ARE YOU SURE YOU WON'T GO AHEAD OF US?>
CAVE of EVIL
<WE DON'T MIND.>
<NO, IT'S OK! I CAN WAIT.>
<YOU GUYS WERE HERE FIRST.>
<I CAN'T BELIEVE YOU'RE WILLING TO WAIT IN LINE LIKE THE REST OF US.>
<WATCH YOUR STEP.>
<Y'KNOW, SOME THINGS ARE BETTER LEFT IN THE DARK.>
<JUST SPEAKING AS A FRIEND.>
<REH?>
<WHAT WAS THAT?>
<WHAT WAS WHAT?>

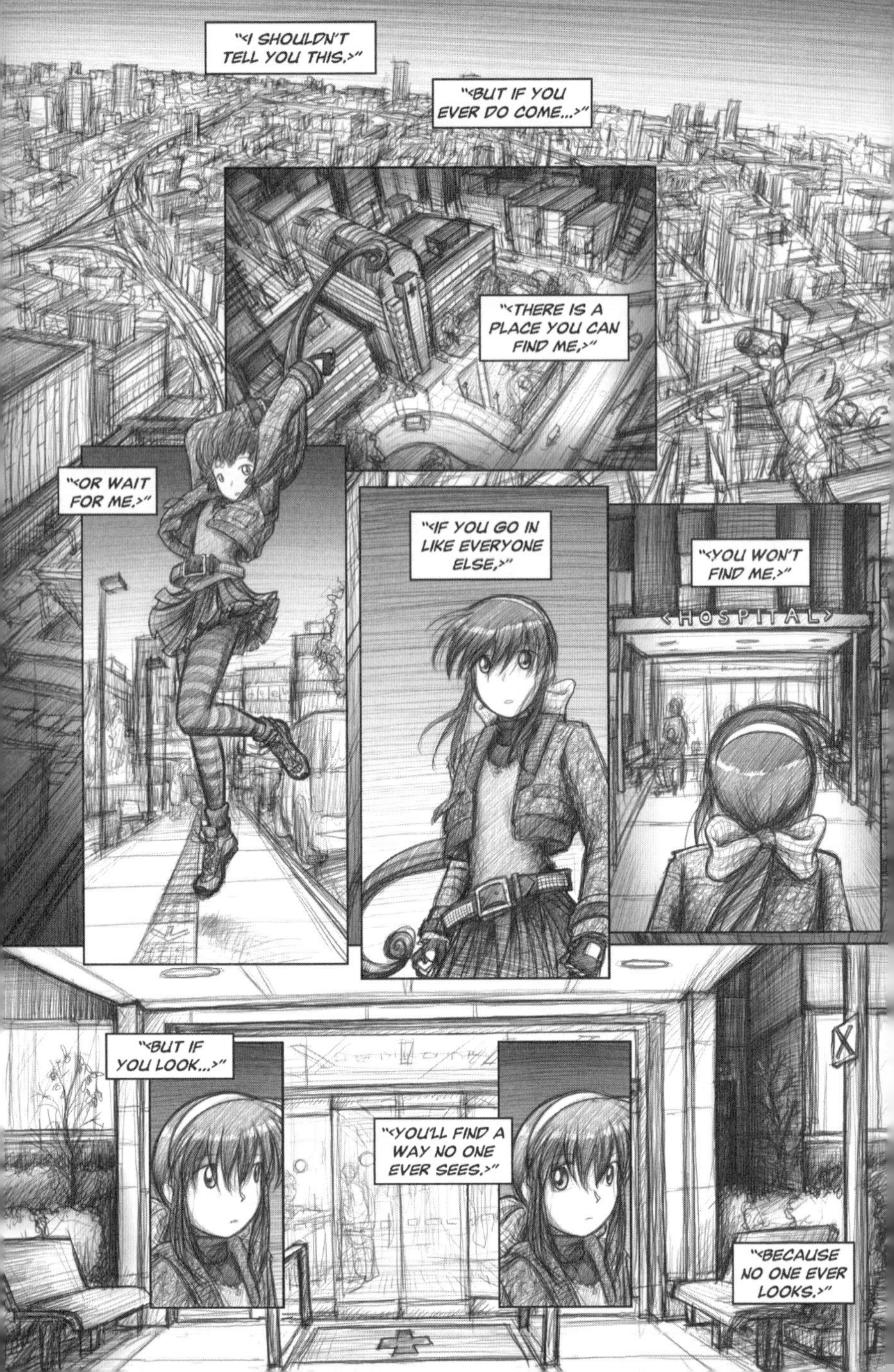
“<I SHOULDN'T TELL YOU THIS.>”
“<BUT IF YOU EVER DO COME...>”
“<THERE IS A PLACE YOU CAN FIND ME,>”
“<OR WAIT FOR ME.>”
“<IF YOU GO IN LIKE EVERYONE ELSE,>”
“<YOU WON'T FIND ME.>”
<HOSPITAL>
“<BUT IF YOU LOOK...>”
“<YOU'LL FIND A WAY NO ONE EVER SEES.>”
“<BECAUSE NO ONE EVER LOOKS.>”

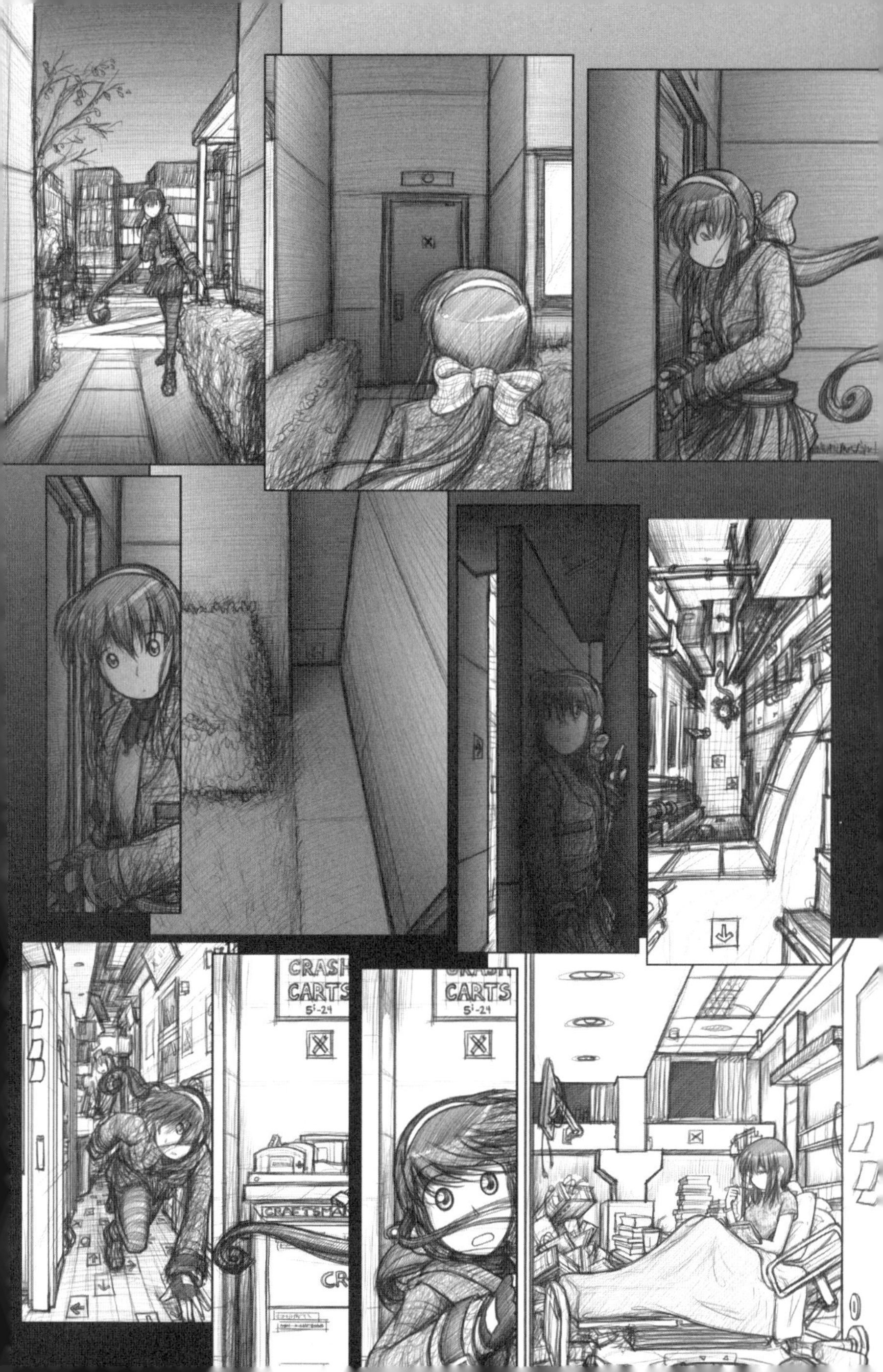
CRASH
CARTS
5i-24
CARTS
5i-24

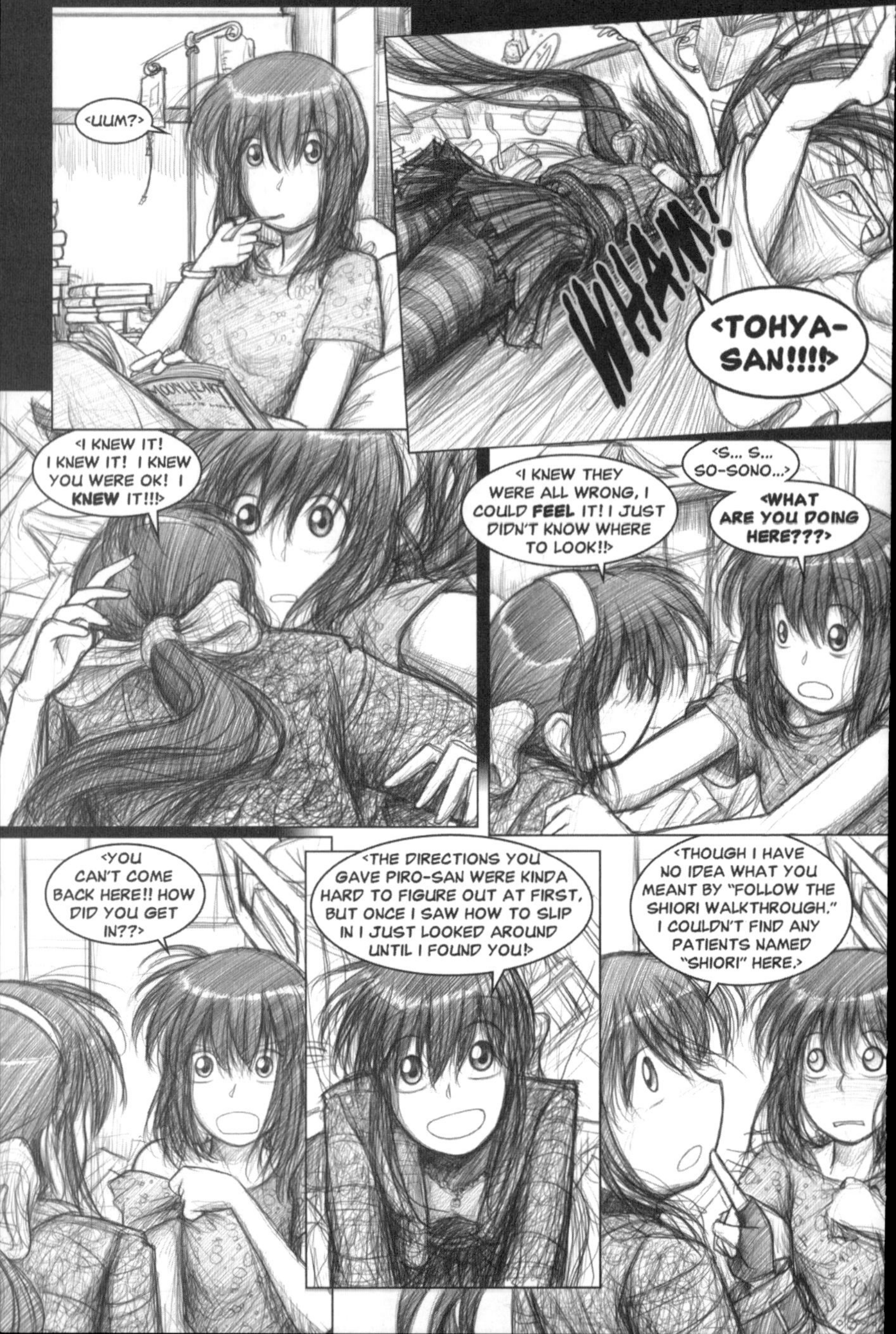
<UUM?>
WHAM!
<TOHYA-SAN!!!!>
<I KNEW IT! I KNEW IT! I KNEW YOU WERE OK! I **KNEW** IT!!!>
<I KNEW THEY WERE ALL WRONG, I COULD **FEEL** IT! I JUST DIDN'T KNOW WHERE TO LOOK!!>
<S... S... SO-SONO...>
<WHAT ARE YOU DOING HERE???>
<YOU CAN'T COME BACK HERE!! HOW DID YOU GET IN??>
<THE DIRECTIONS YOU GAVE PIRO-SAN WERE KINDA HARD TO FIGURE OUT AT FIRST, BUT ONCE I SAW HOW TO SLIP IN I JUST LOOKED AROUND UNTIL I FOUND YOU!>
<THOUGH I HAVE NO IDEA WHAT YOU MEANT BY "FOLLOW THE SHIORI WALKTHROUGH." I COULDN'T FIND ANY PATIENTS NAMED "SHIORI" HERE.>

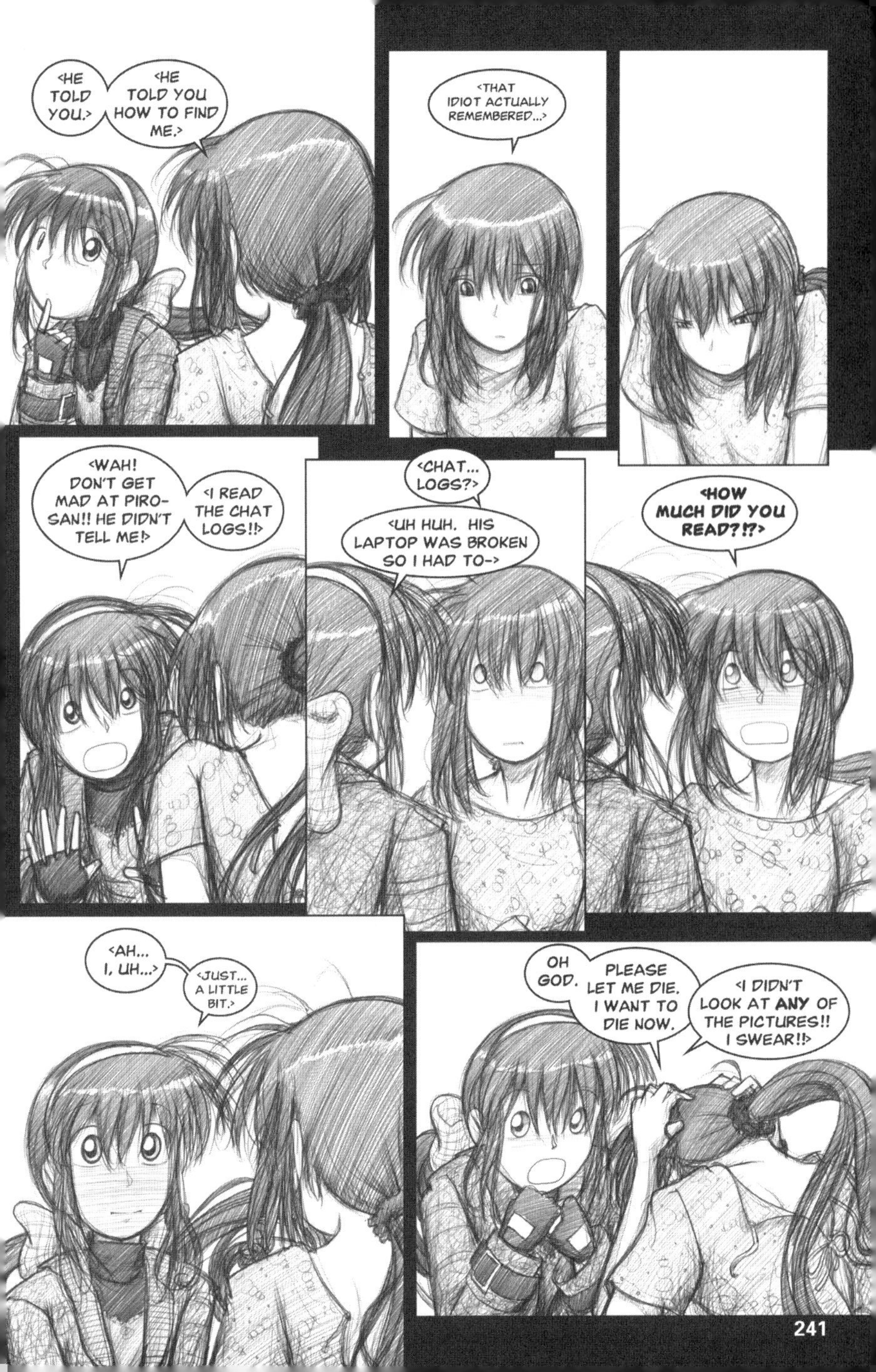

<HE TOLD YOU.>
<HE TOLD YOU HOW TO FIND ME.>
<THAT IDIOT ACTUALLY REMEMBERED...>
<WAH! DON'T GET MAD AT PIRO-SAN!! HE DIDN'T TELL ME!>
<I READ THE CHAT LOGS!!>
<CHAT... LOGS?>
<UH HUH. HIS LAPTOP WAS BROKEN SO I HAD TO->
<HOW MUCH DID YOU READ?!?>
<AH... I, UH...>
<JUST... A LITTLE BIT.>
OH GOD.
PLEASE LET ME DIE. I WANT TO DIE NOW.
<I DIDN'T LOOK AT ANY OF THE PICTURES!! I SWEAR!!>

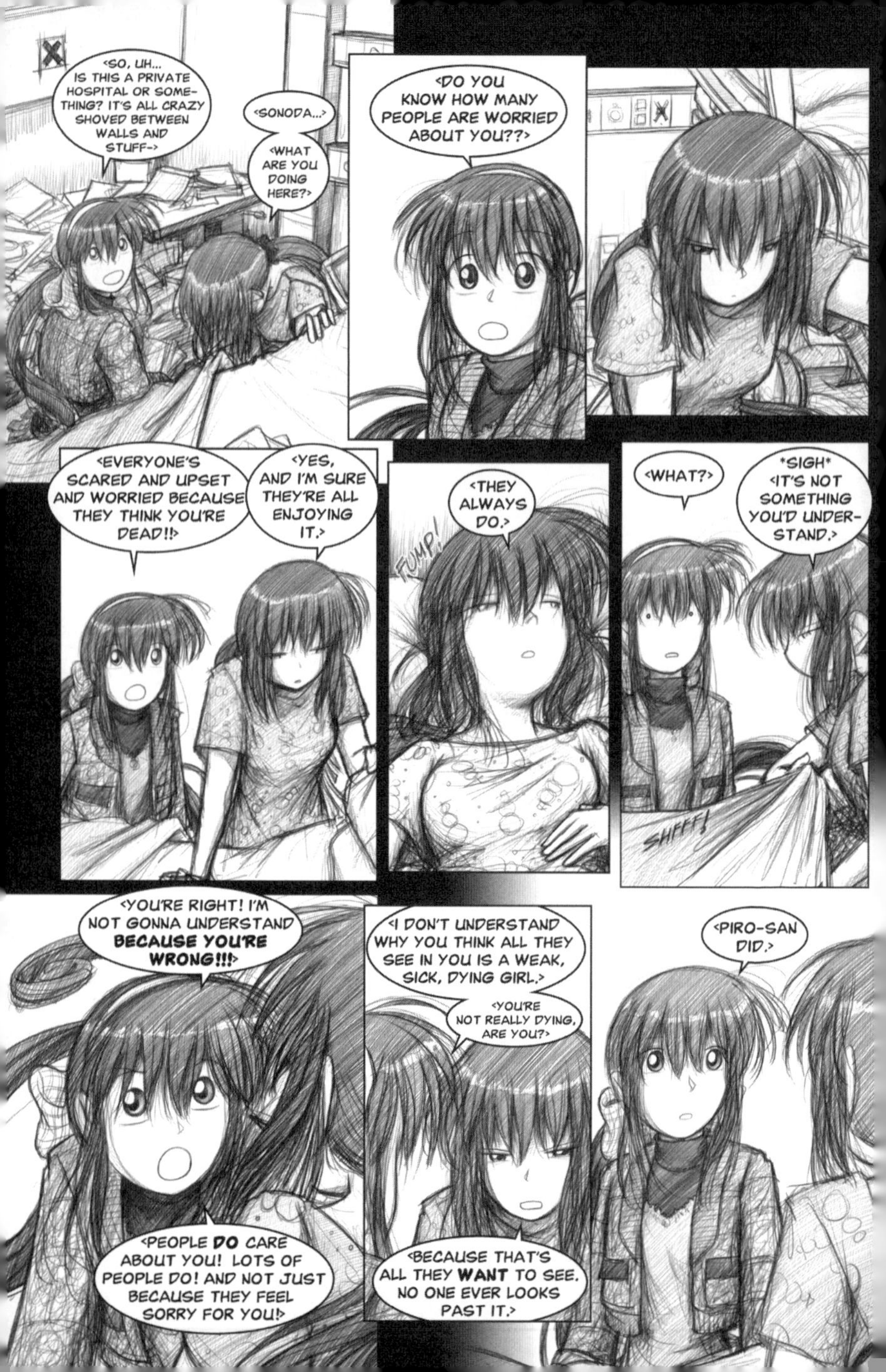
<SO, UH... IS THIS A PRIVATE HOSPITAL OR SOME-THING? IT'S ALL CRAZY SHOVED BETWEEN WALLS AND STUFF->
<SONODA...>
<WHAT ARE YOU DOING HERE?>
<DO YOU KNOW HOW MANY PEOPLE ARE WORRIED ABOUT YOU??>
<EVERYONE'S SCARED AND UPSET AND WORRIED BECAUSE THEY THINK YOU'RE DEAD!!>
<YES, AND I'M SURE THEY'RE ALL ENJOYING IT.>
FUMP!
<THEY ALWAYS DO.>
<WHAT?>
SIGH <IT'S NOT SOMETHING YOU'D UNDER-STAND.>
SHFFF!
<YOU'RE RIGHT! I'M NOT GONNA UNDERSTAND **BECAUSE YOU'RE WRONG!!!**>
<PEOPLE **DO** CARE ABOUT YOU! LOTS OF PEOPLE DO! AND NOT JUST BECAUSE THEY FEEL SORRY FOR YOU!>
<I DON'T UNDERSTAND WHY YOU THINK ALL THEY SEE IN YOU IS A WEAK, SICK, DYING GIRL.>
<YOU'RE NOT REALLY DYING, ARE YOU?>
<BECAUSE THAT'S ALL THEY **WANT** TO SEE. NO ONE EVER LOOKS PAST IT.>
<PIRO-SAN DID.>

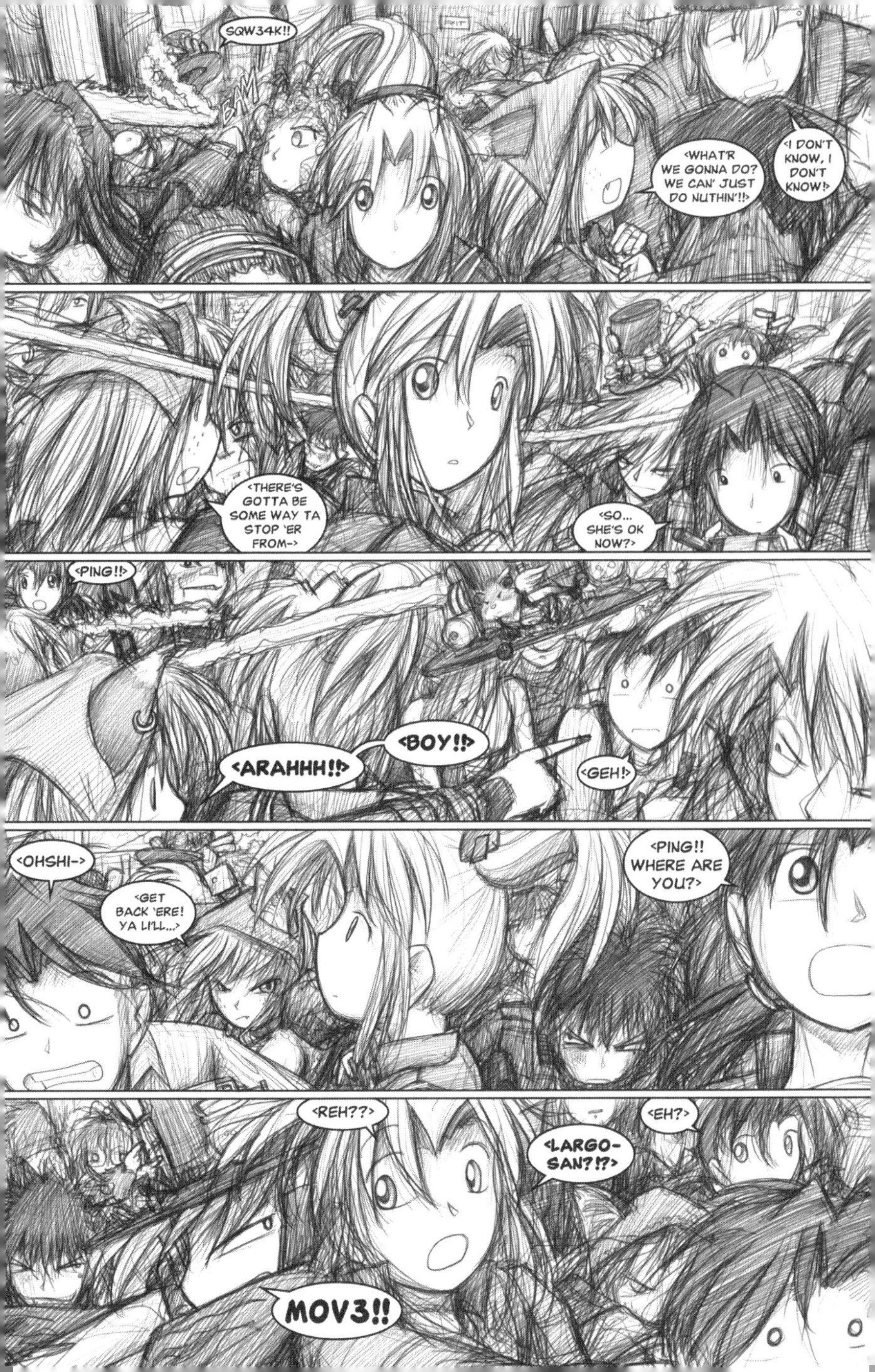
SQW34K!!
BAM
<WHAT'R WE GONNA DO? WE CAN' JUST DO NUTHIN'!!>
<I DON'T KNOW, I DON'T KNOW!>
<THERE'S GOTTA BE SOME WAY TA STOP 'ER FROM->
<SO... SHE'S OK NOW?>
<PING!!>
<BOY!!>
<ARAHHH!!>
<GEH!>
<OHSHI->
<GET BACK 'ERE! YA LI'LL...>
<PING!! WHERE ARE YOU?>
<REH??>
<EH?>
<LARGO-SAN?!?>
MOV3!!

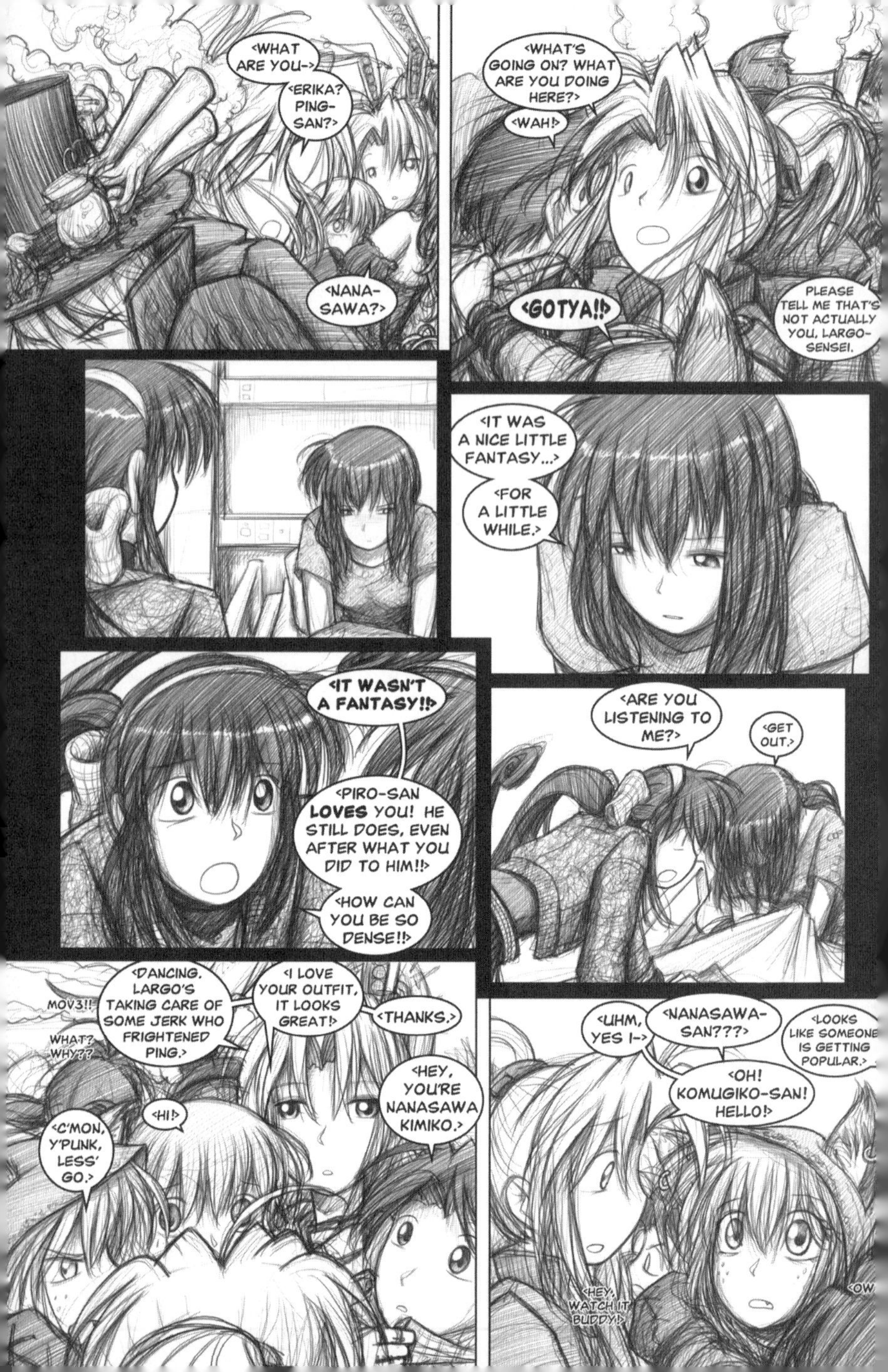

<WHAT ARE YOU->
<ERIKA? PING-SAN?>
<NANA-SAWA?>
<WHAT'S GOING ON? WHAT ARE YOU DOING HERE?>
<WAH!>
<GOTYA!!>
PLEASE TELL ME THAT'S NOT ACTUALLY YOU, LARGO-SENSEI.
<IT WAS A NICE LITTLE FANTASY...>
<FOR A LITTLE WHILE.>
<IT WASN'T A FANTASY!!>
<PIRO-SAN LOVES YOU! HE STILL DOES, EVEN AFTER WHAT YOU DID TO HIM!!>
<HOW CAN YOU BE SO DENSE!!>
<ARE YOU LISTENING TO ME?>
<GET OUT.>
MOV3!!
WHAT? WHY??
<DANCING. LARGO'S TAKING CARE OF SOME JERK WHO FRIGHTENED PING.>
<I LOVE YOUR OUTFIT, IT LOOKS GREAT!>
<THANKS.>
<HI!>
<HEY, YOU'RE NANASAWA KIMIKO.>
<C'MON, Y'PUNK, LESS' GO.>
<UHM, YES I->
<NANASAWA-SAN???>
<LOOKS LIKE SOMEONE IS GETTING POPULAR.>
<OH! KOMUGIKO-SAN! HELLO!>
<HEY, WATCH IT BUDDY!>
<OW

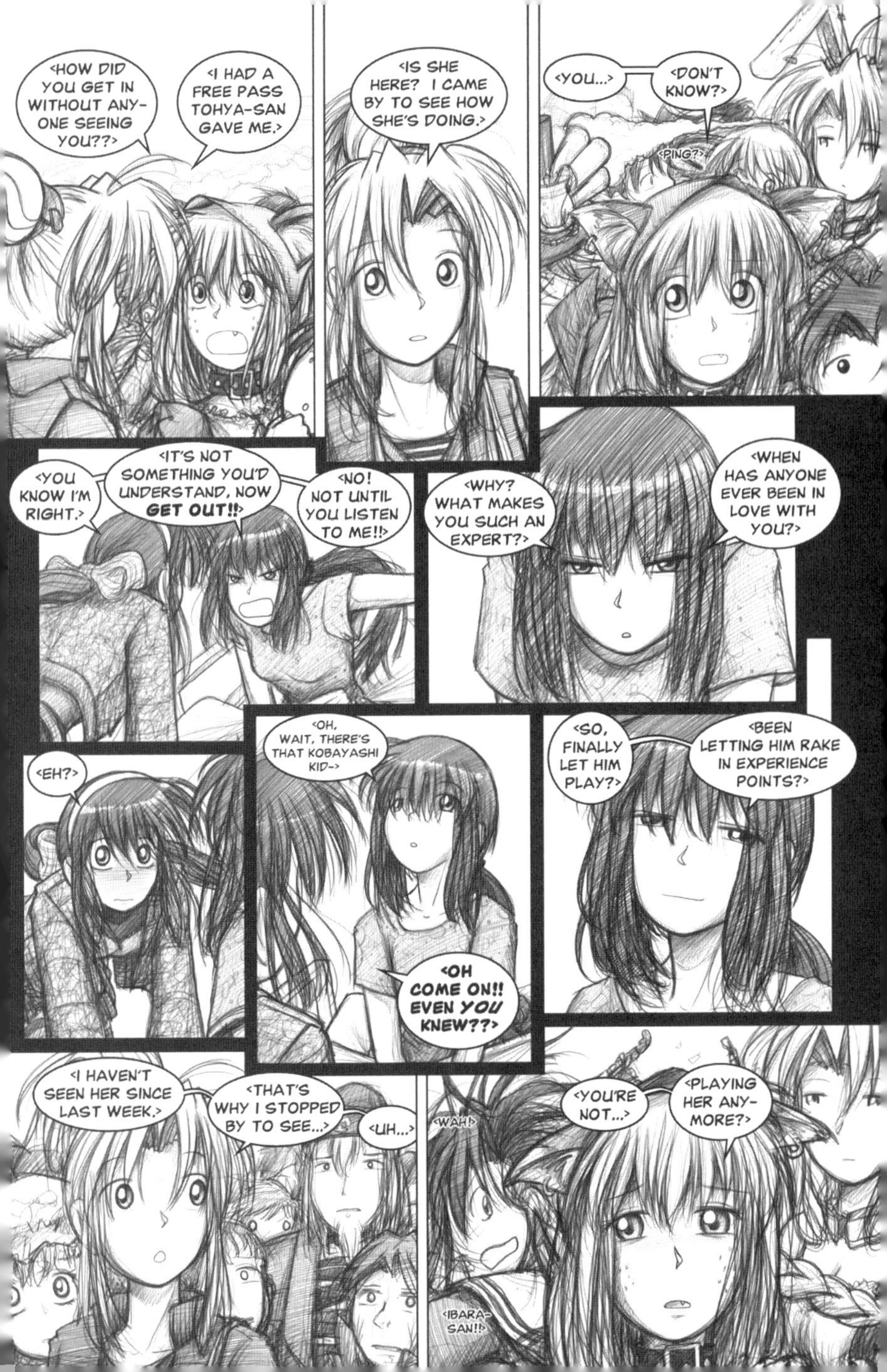
<HOW DID YOU GET IN WITHOUT ANYONE SEEING YOU??>
<I HAD A FREE PASS TOHYA-SAN GAVE ME.>
<IS SHE HERE? I CAME BY TO SEE HOW SHE'S DOING.>
<YOU...>
<DON'T KNOW?>
<PING?>
<YOU KNOW I'M RIGHT.>
<IT'S NOT SOMETHING YOU'D UNDERSTAND, NOW **GET OUT!!**>
<NO! NOT UNTIL YOU LISTEN TO ME!!>
<WHY? WHAT MAKES YOU SUCH AN EXPERT?>
<WHEN HAS ANYONE EVER BEEN IN LOVE WITH YOU?>
<EH?>
<OH, WAIT, THERE'S THAT KOBAYASHI KID->
<OH COME ON!! EVEN *YOU* KNEW??>
<SO, FINALLY LET HIM PLAY?>
<BEEN LETTING HIM RAKE IN EXPERIENCE POINTS?>
<I HAVEN'T SEEN HER SINCE LAST WEEK.>
<THAT'S WHY I STOPPED BY TO SEE...>
<UH...>
<WAH!>
<YOU'RE NOT...>
<PLAYING HER ANYMORE?>
<IBARA-SAN!!>

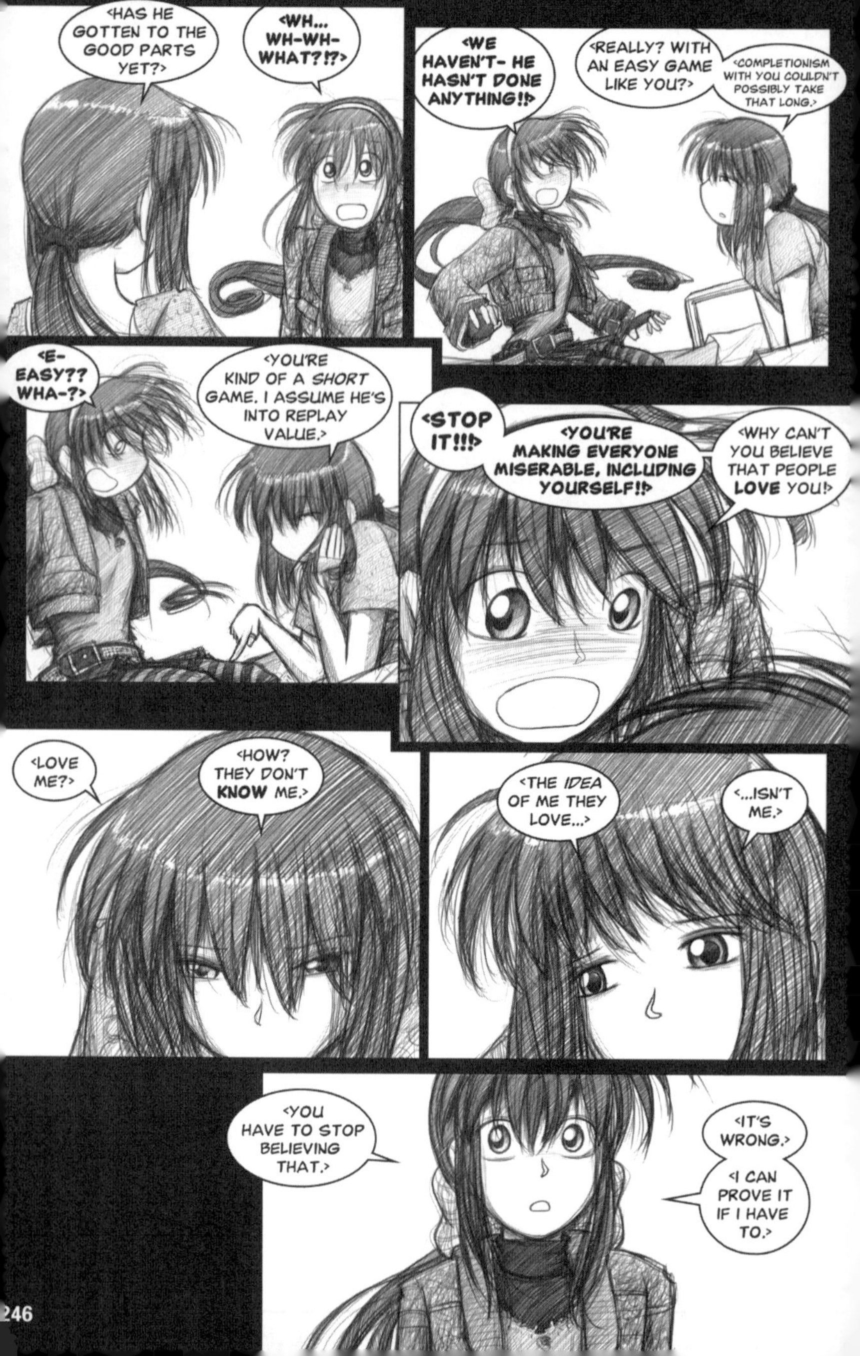
<HAS HE GOTTEN TO THE GOOD PARTS YET?>
<WH... WH-WH-WHAT?!?>
<WE HAVEN'T- HE HASN'T DONE ANYTHING!!>
<REALLY? WITH AN EASY GAME LIKE YOU?>
<COMPLETIONISM WITH YOU COULDN'T POSSIBLY TAKE THAT LONG.>
<E- EASY?? WHA-?>
<YOU'RE KIND OF A *SHORT* GAME. I ASSUME HE'S INTO REPLAY VALUE.>
<STOP IT!!!>
<YOU'RE MAKING EVERYONE MISERABLE, INCLUDING YOURSELF!!>
<WHY CAN'T YOU BELIEVE THAT PEOPLE **LOVE** YOU!>
<LOVE ME?>
<HOW? THEY DON'T **KNOW** ME.>
<THE *IDEA* OF ME THEY LOVE...>
<...ISN'T ME.>
<YOU HAVE TO STOP BELIEVING THAT.>
<IT'S WRONG.>
<I CAN PROVE IT IF I HAVE TO.>

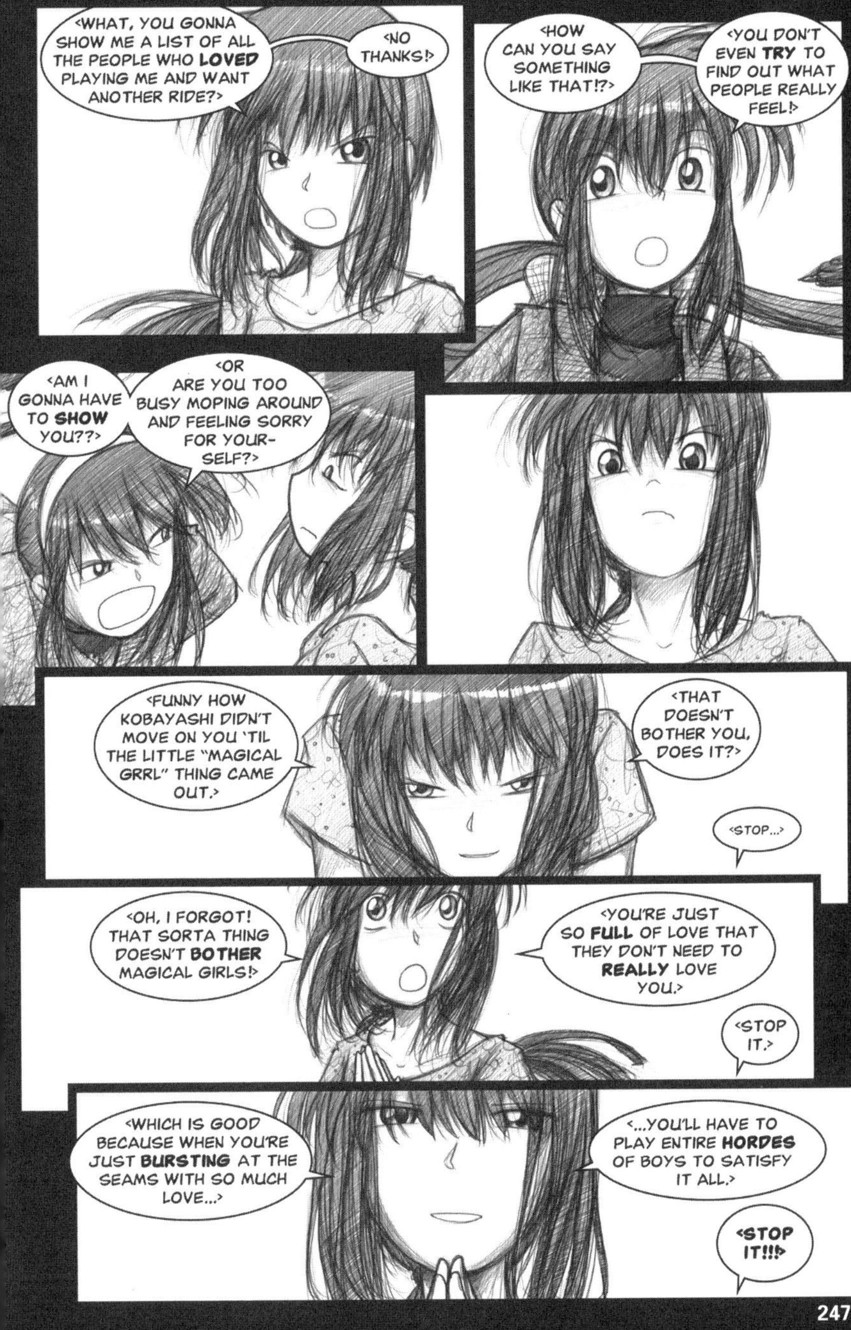
<WHAT, YOU GONNA SHOW ME A LIST OF ALL THE PEOPLE WHO **LOVED** PLAYING ME AND WANT ANOTHER RIDE?>
<NO THANKS!>
<HOW CAN YOU SAY SOMETHING LIKE THAT!?>
<YOU DON'T EVEN **TRY** TO FIND OUT WHAT PEOPLE REALLY FEEL!>
<AM I GONNA HAVE TO **SHOW** YOU??>
<OR ARE YOU TOO BUSY MOPING AROUND AND FEELING SORRY FOR YOUR-SELF?>
<FUNNY HOW KOBAYASHI DIDN'T MOVE ON YOU 'TIL THE LITTLE "MAGICAL GRRL" THING CAME OUT.>
<THAT DOESN'T BOTHER YOU, DOES IT?>
<STOP...>
<OH, I FORGOT! THAT SORTA THING DOESN'T **BOTHER** MAGICAL GIRLS!>
<YOU'RE JUST SO **FULL** OF LOVE THAT THEY DON'T NEED TO **REALLY** LOVE YOU.>
<STOP IT.>
<WHICH IS GOOD BECAUSE WHEN YOU'RE JUST **BURSTING** AT THE SEAMS WITH SO MUCH LOVE...>
<...YOU'LL HAVE TO PLAY ENTIRE **HORDES** OF BOYS TO SATISFY IT ALL.>
<STOP IT!!!>

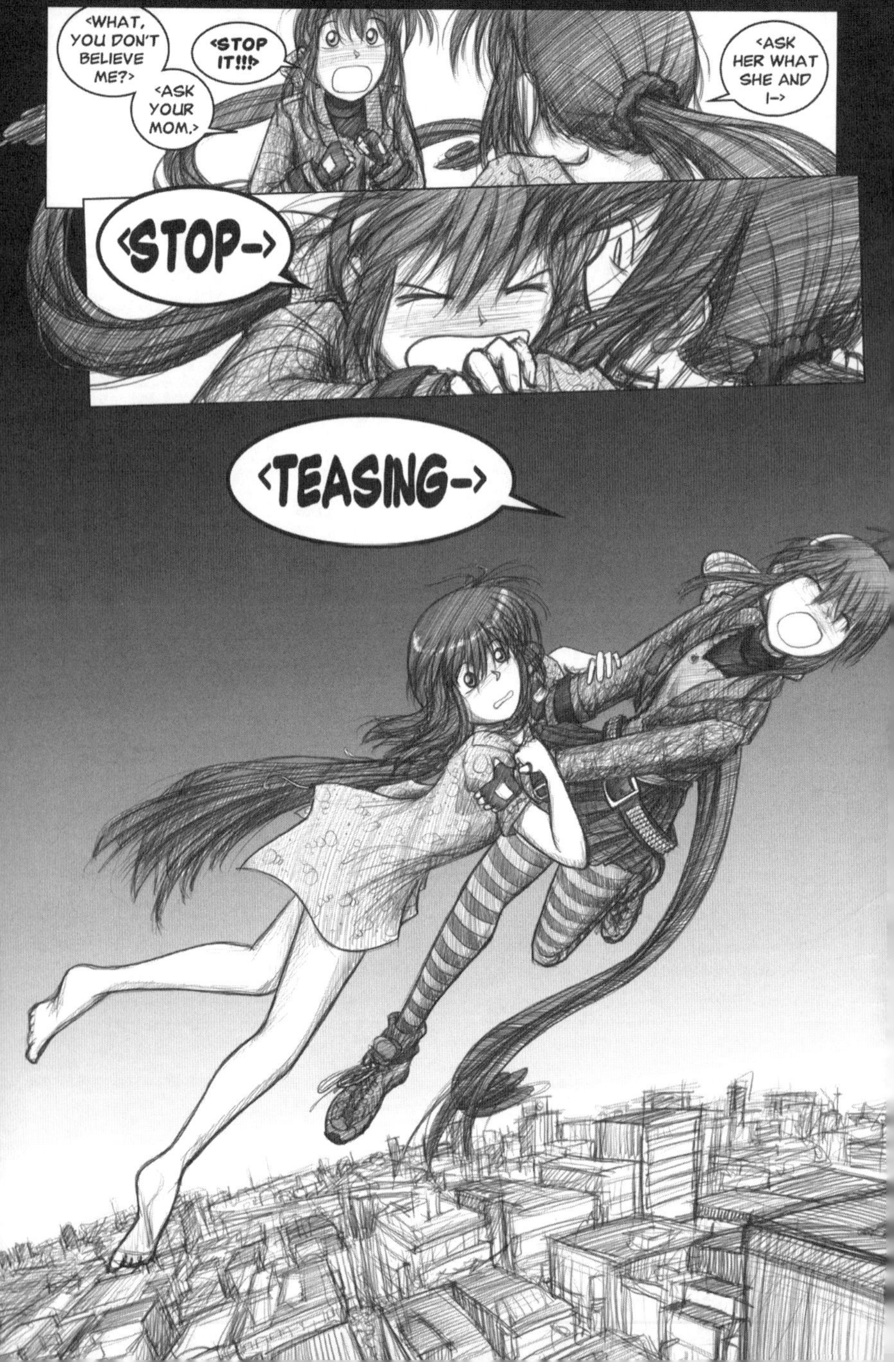
<WHAT, YOU DON'T BELIEVE ME?>
<ASK YOUR MOM.>
<STOP IT!!!>
<ASK HER WHAT SHE AND I->
<STOP->
<TEASING->

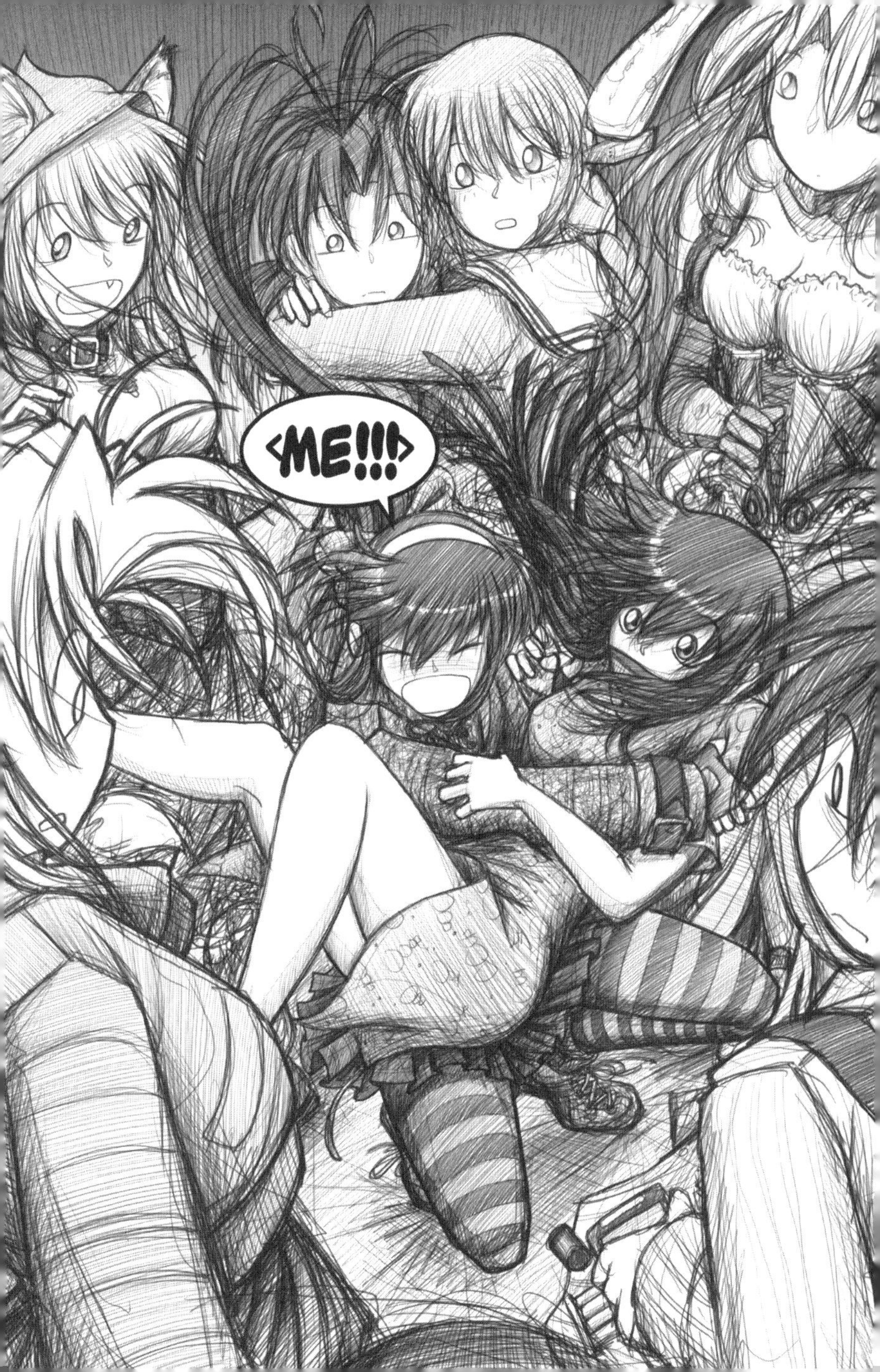
<ME!!!>

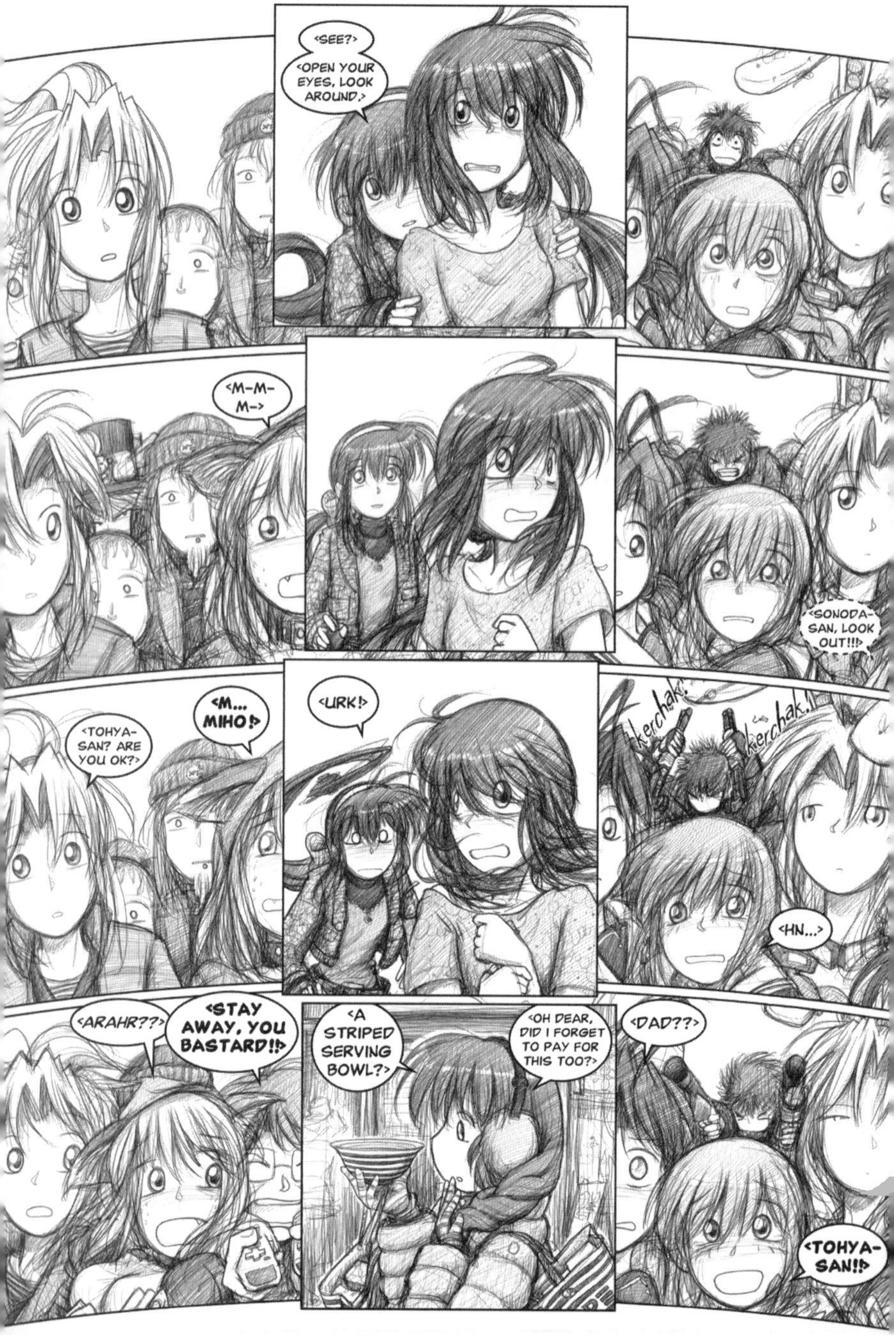
<SEE?>
<OPEN YOUR EYES, LOOK AROUND.>
<M-M-M->
<SONODA-SAN, LOOK OUT!!!>
<TOHYA-SAN? ARE YOU OK?>
<M... MIHO!>
<URK!>
kerchak!
kerchak!
<HN...>
<ARAHR??>
<STAY AWAY, YOU BASTARD!!>
<A STRIPED SERVING BOWL?>
<OH DEAR, DID I FORGET TO PAY FOR THIS TOO?>
<DAD??>
<TOHYA-SAN!!>

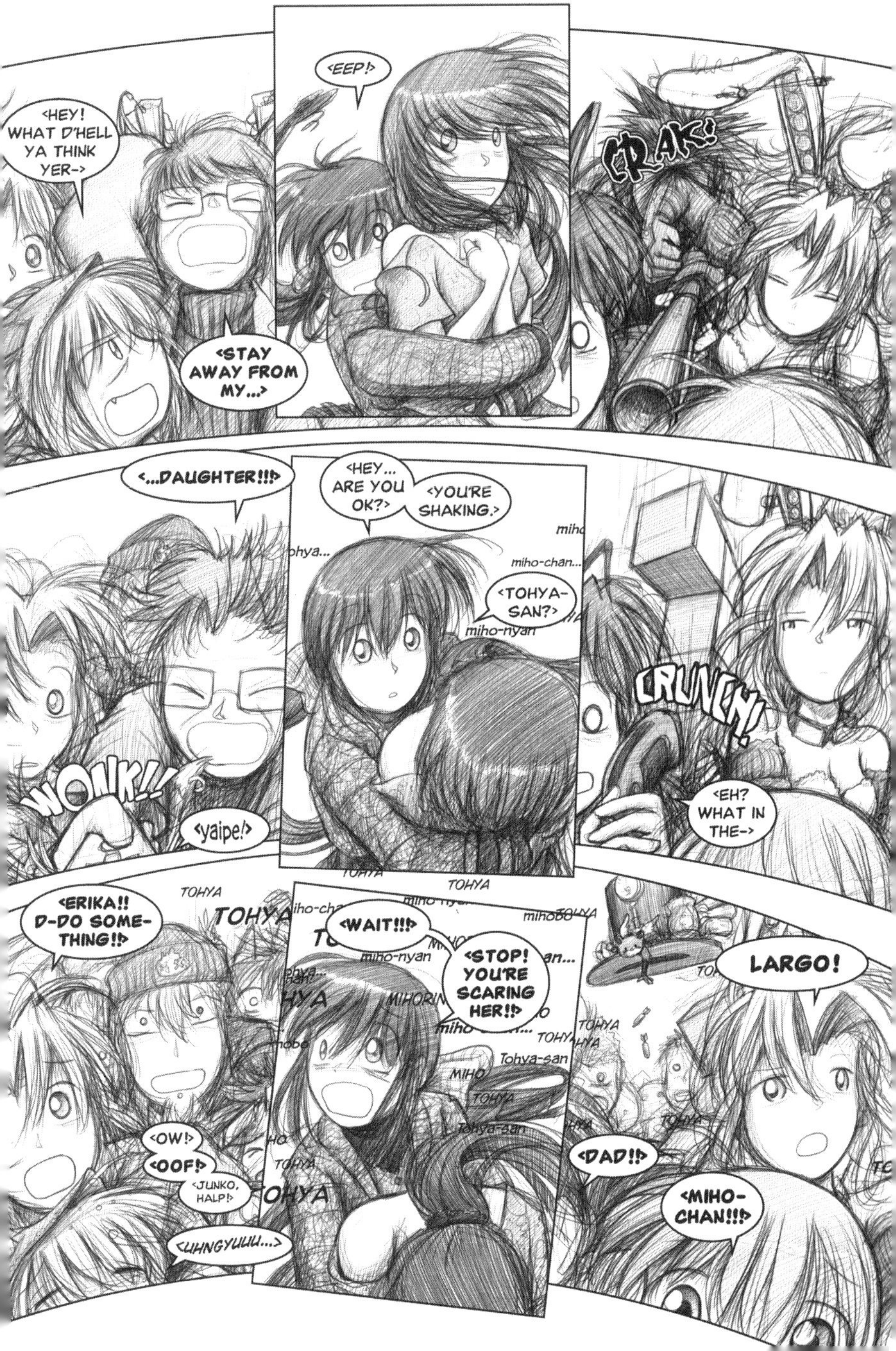

<HEY! WHAT D'HELL YA THINK YER->
<STAY AWAY FROM MY...>
<EEP!>
CRAK!
<...DAUGHTER!!!>
WONK!!
<yaipe!>
<HEY... ARE YOU OK?>
<YOU'RE SHAKING.>
tohya...
miho-chan...
<TOHYA-SAN?>
miho-nyan
CRUNCH!
<EH? WHAT IN THE->
<ERIKA!! D-DO SOME-THING!!>
TOHYA
TOHYA
<OW!>
<OOF!>
<JUNKO, HALP!>
<UHNGYUUU...>
<WAIT!!!>
<STOP! YOU'RE SCARING HER!!>
miho-nyan
MIHORIN
Tohya-san
TOHYA
LARGO!
<DAD!!>
<MIHO-CHAN!!!>

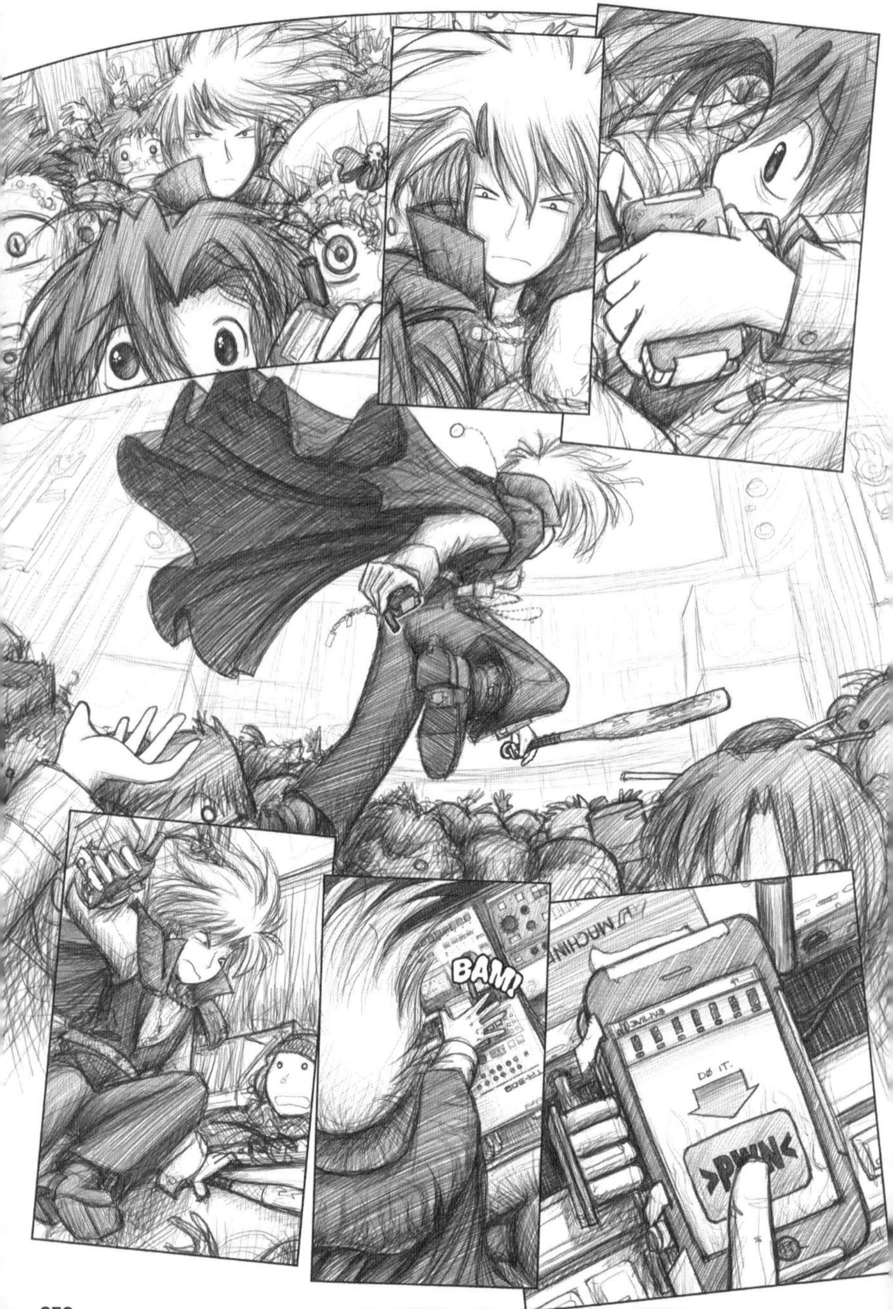
BAM!
DØ IT.
>PWN<

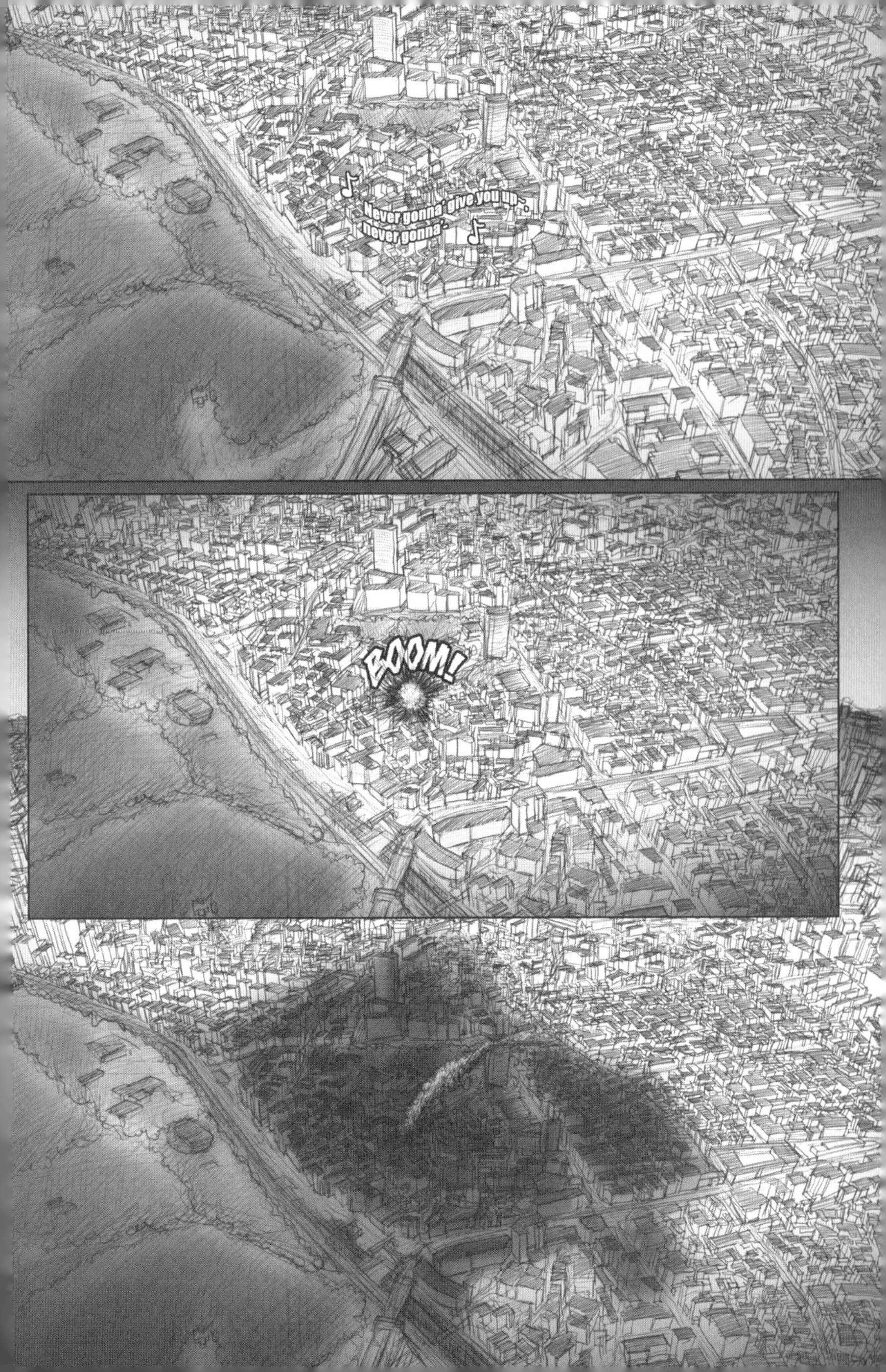
♪ Never gonna' give you up~, never gonna'~ ♪
BOOM!

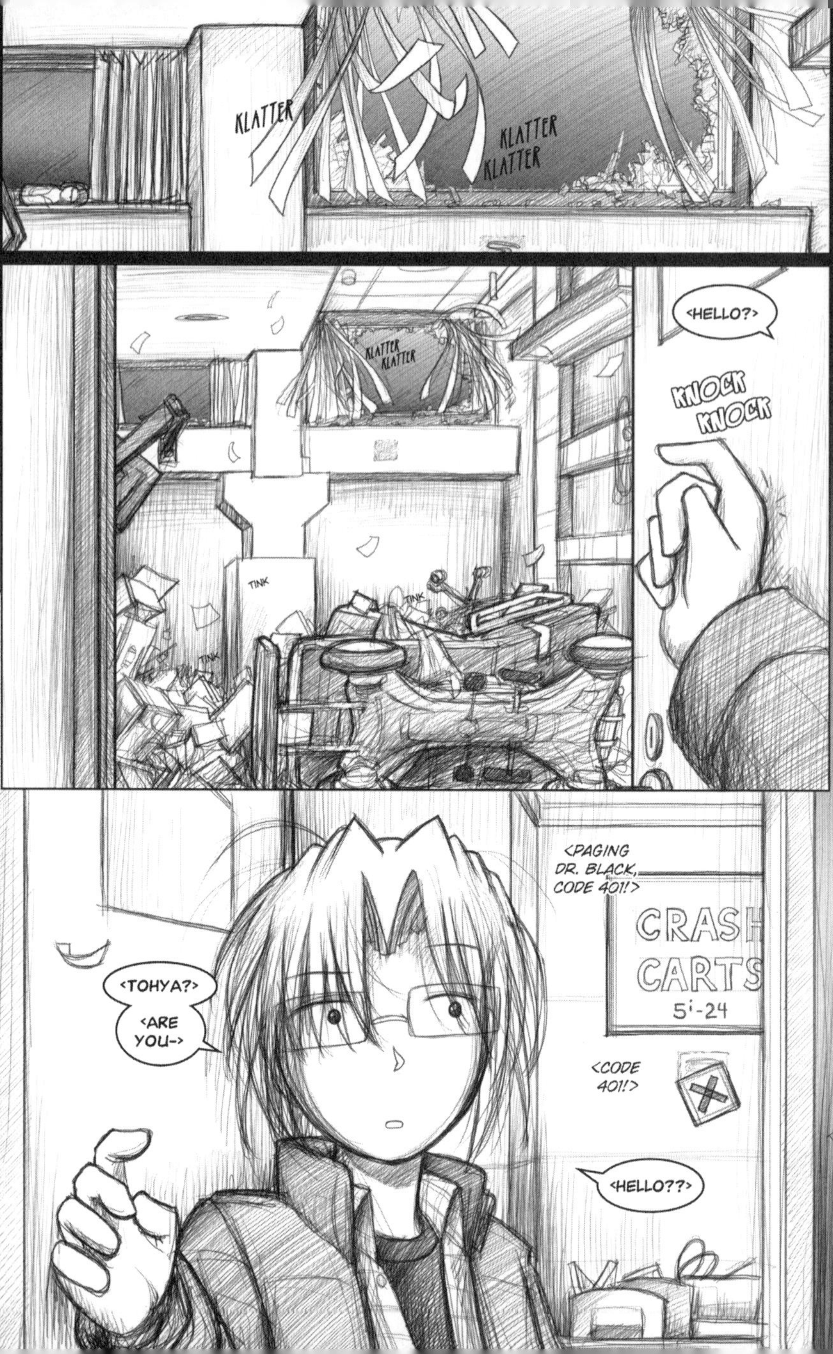

KLATTER
KLATTER
KLATTER
KLATTER
KLATTER
TINK
TINK
TINK
<HELLO?>
KNOCK
KNOCK
<PAGING DR. BLACK, CODE 401!>
CRASH
CARTS
5i-24
<TOHYA?>
<ARE YOU->
<CODE 401!>
<HELLO??>

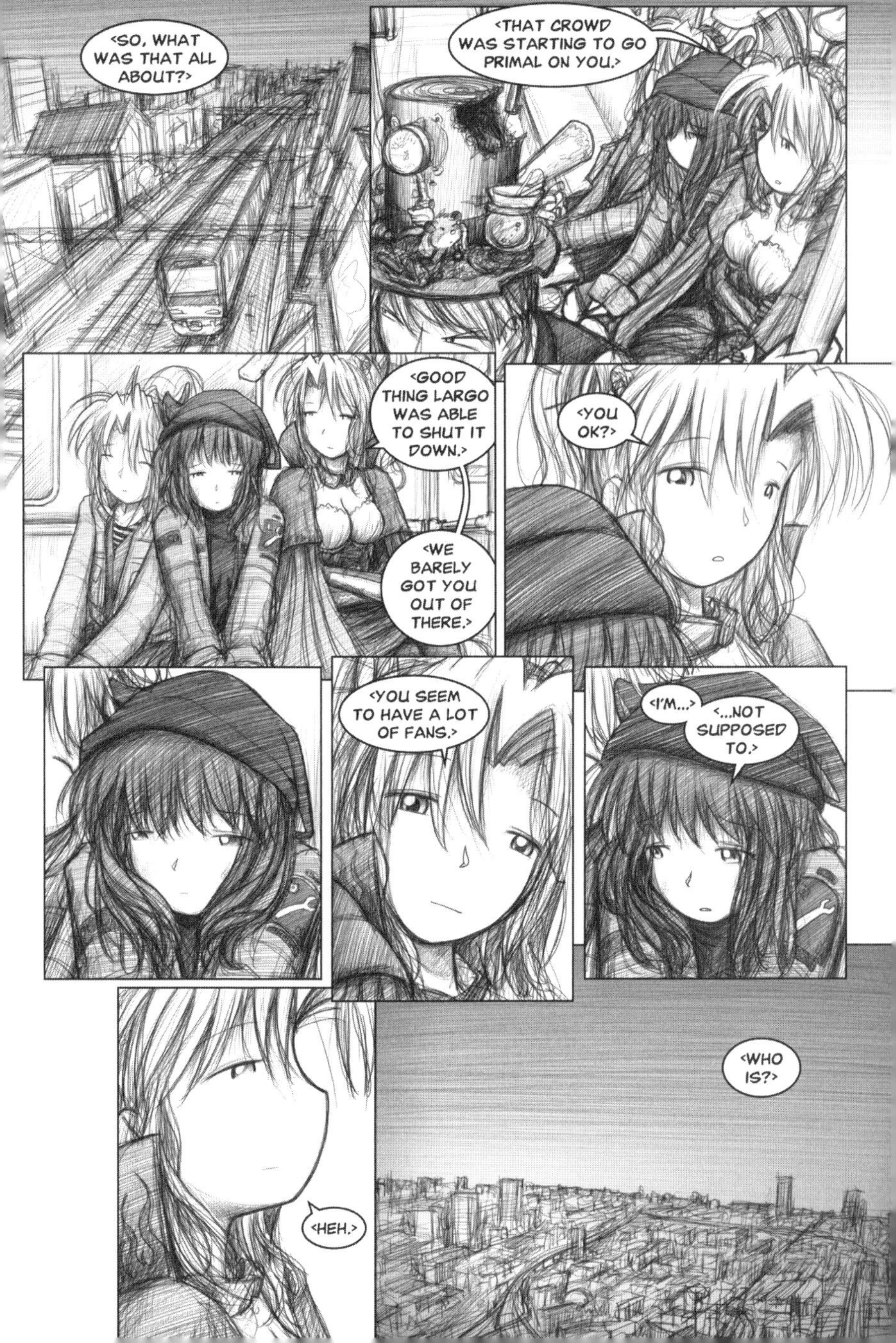
<SO, WHAT WAS THAT ALL ABOUT?>
<THAT CROWD WAS STARTING TO GO PRIMAL ON YOU.>
<GOOD THING LARGO WAS ABLE TO SHUT IT DOWN.>
<WE BARELY GOT YOU OUT OF THERE.>
<YOU OK?>
<YOU SEEM TO HAVE A LOT OF FANS.>
<I'M...>
<...NOT SUPPOSED TO.>
<HEH.>
<WHO IS?>

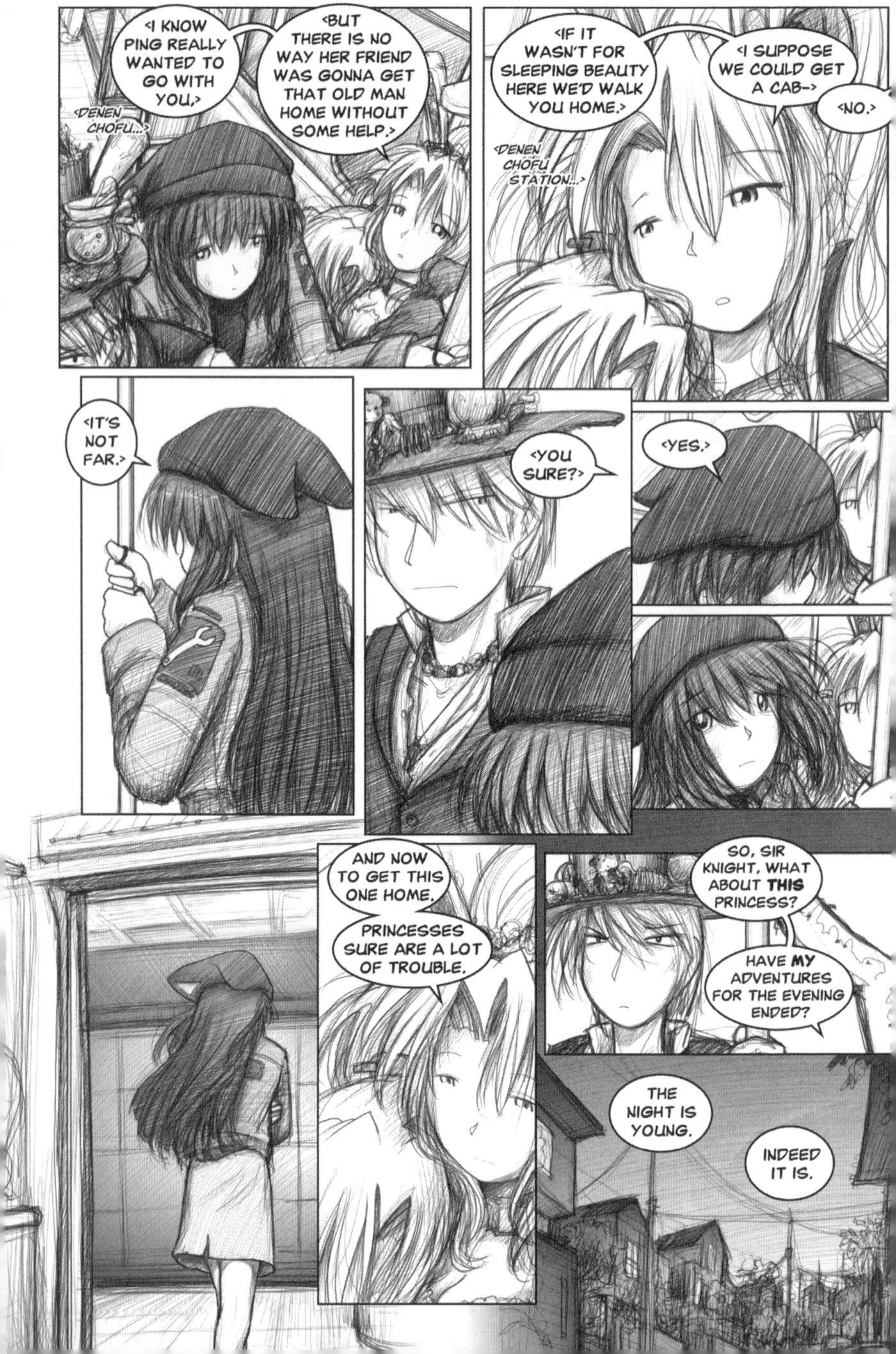
<I KNOW PING REALLY WANTED TO GO WITH YOU,>
<BUT THERE IS NO WAY HER FRIEND WAS GONNA GET THAT OLD MAN HOME WITHOUT SOME HELP.>
<DENEN CHOFU...>
<IF IT WASN'T FOR SLEEPING BEAUTY HERE WE'D WALK YOU HOME.>
<I SUPPOSE WE COULD GET A CAB–>
<NO.>
<DENEN CHOFU STATION...>
<IT'S NOT FAR.>
<YOU SURE?>
<YES.>
AND NOW TO GET THIS ONE HOME.
PRINCESSES SURE ARE A LOT OF TROUBLE.
SO, SIR KNIGHT, WHAT ABOUT **THIS** PRINCESS?
HAVE **MY** ADVENTURES FOR THE EVENING ENDED?
THE NIGHT IS YOUNG.
INDEED IT IS.

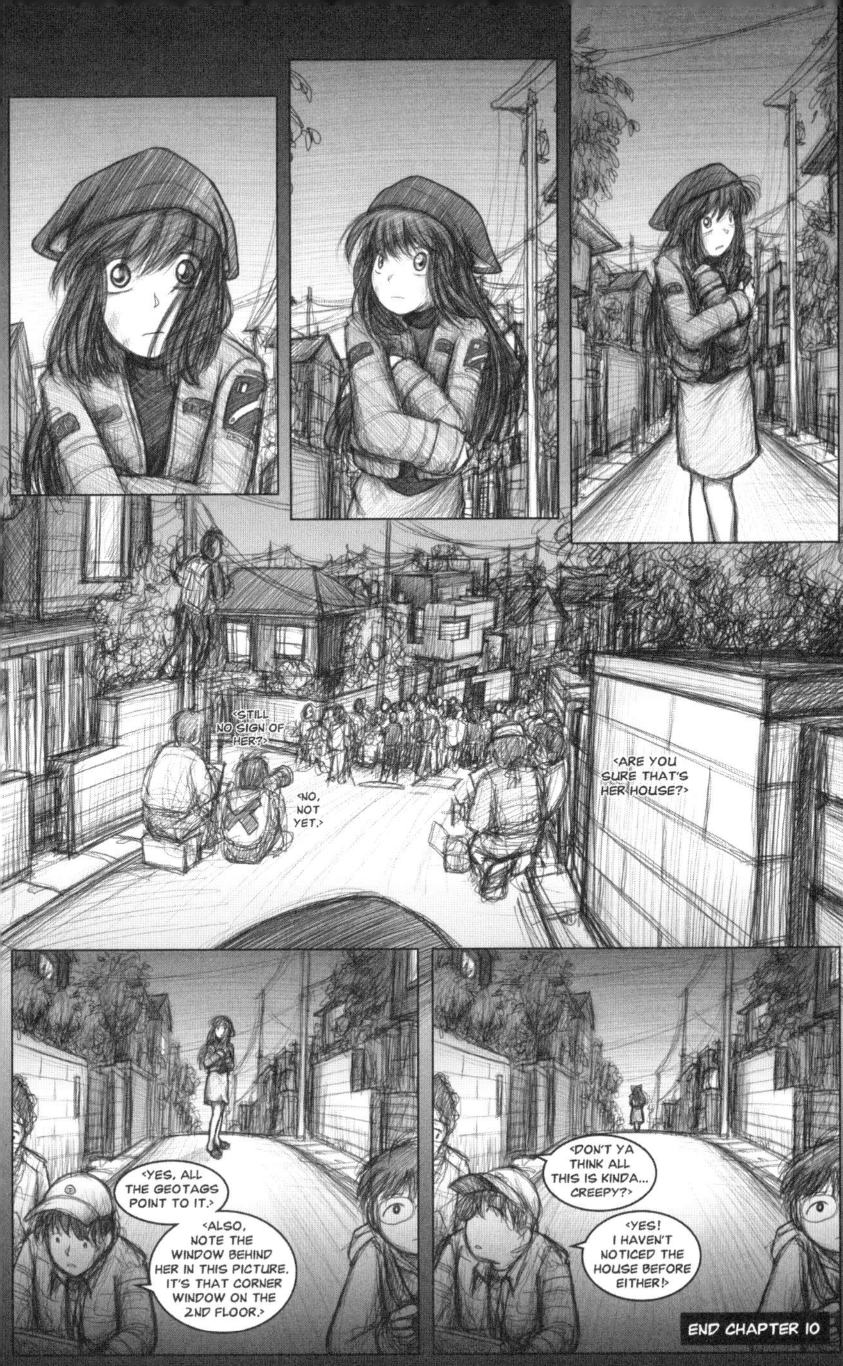
<STILL NO SIGN OF HER?>
<NO, NOT YET.>
<ARE YOU SURE THAT'S HER HOUSE?>
<YES, ALL THE GEOTAGS POINT TO IT.>
<ALSO, NOTE THE WINDOW BEHIND HER IN THIS PICTURE. IT'S THAT CORNER WINDOW ON THE 2ND FLOOR.>
<DON'T YA THINK ALL THIS IS KINDA... CREEPY?>
<YES! I HAVEN'T NOTICED THE HOUSE BEFORE EITHER!>
END CHAPTER 10

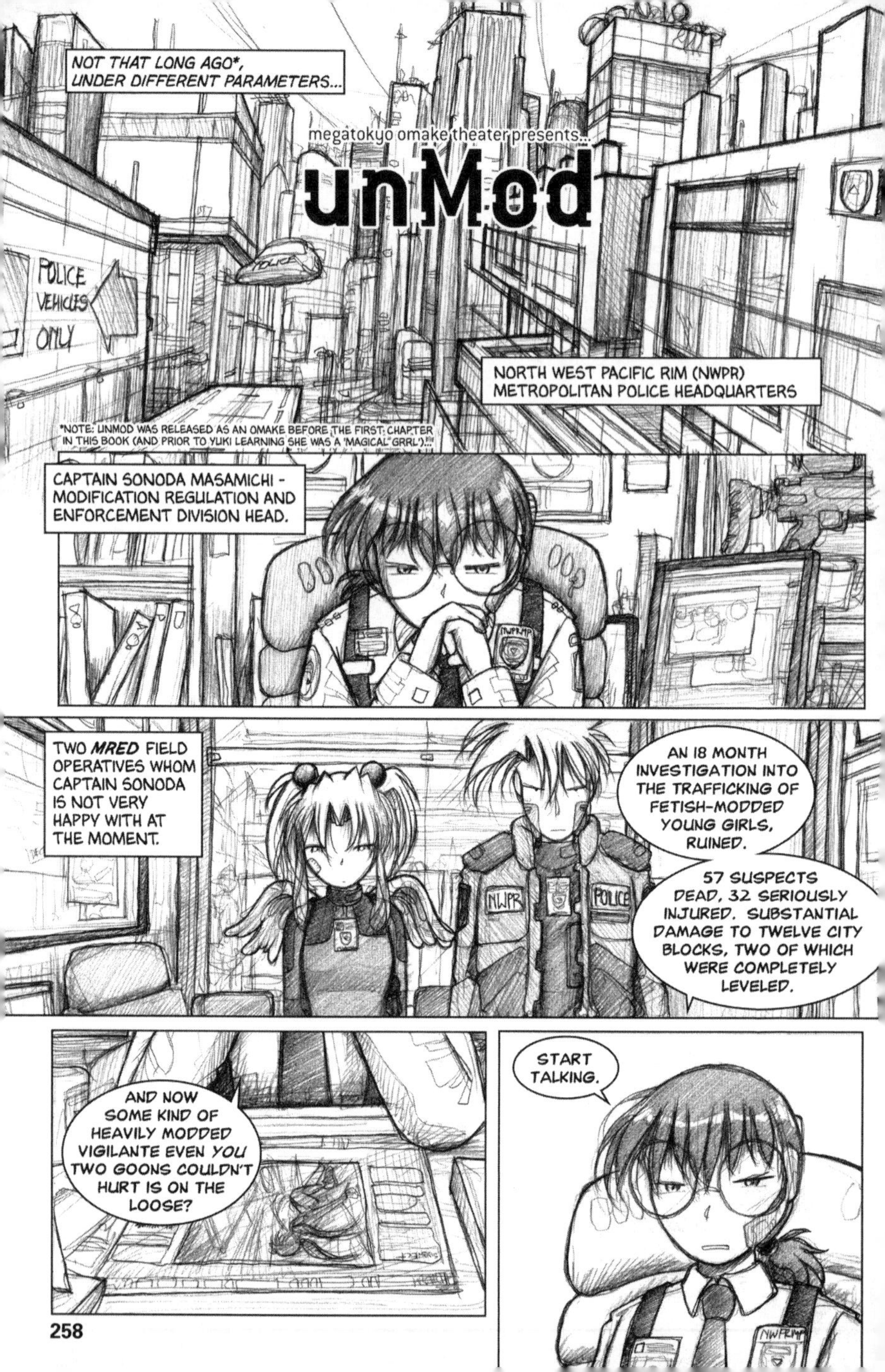
NOT THAT LONG AGO*, UNDER DIFFERENT PARAMETERS...
megatokyo omake theater presents...
unMod
POLICE
POLICE VEHICLES ONLY
NORTH WEST PACIFIC RIM (NWPR) METROPOLITAN POLICE HEADQUARTERS
*NOTE: UNMOD WAS RELEASED AS AN OMAKE BEFORE THE FIRST CHAPTER IN THIS BOOK (AND PRIOR TO YUKI LEARNING SHE WAS A 'MAGICAL GRRL')...
CAPTAIN SONODA MASAMICHI - MODIFICATION REGULATION AND ENFORCEMENT DIVISION HEAD.
NWPRMP
TWO *MRED* FIELD OPERATIVES WHOM CAPTAIN SONODA IS NOT VERY HAPPY WITH AT THE MOMENT.
NWPR
POLICE
AN 18 MONTH INVESTIGATION INTO THE TRAFFICKING OF FETISH-MODDED YOUNG GIRLS, RUINED.
57 SUSPECTS DEAD, 32 SERIOUSLY INJURED. SUBSTANTIAL DAMAGE TO TWELVE CITY BLOCKS, TWO OF WHICH WERE COMPLETELY LEVELED.
AND NOW SOME KIND OF HEAVILY MODDED VIGILANTE EVEN *YOU* TWO GOONS COULDN'T HURT IS ON THE LOOSE?
START TALKING.
NWPRMP

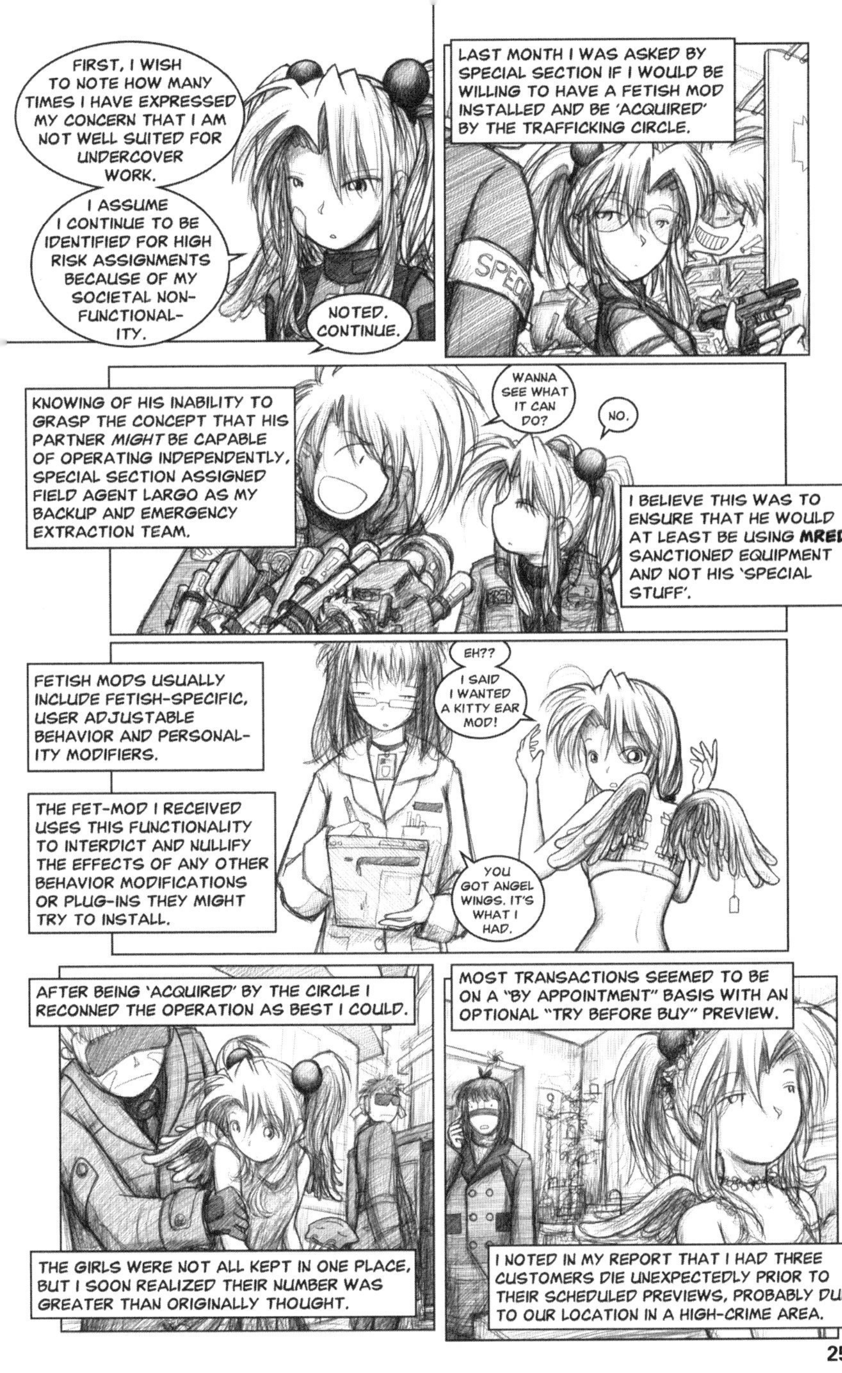
FIRST, I WISH TO NOTE HOW MANY TIMES I HAVE EXPRESSED MY CONCERN THAT I AM NOT WELL SUITED FOR UNDERCOVER WORK.
I ASSUME I CONTINUE TO BE IDENTIFIED FOR HIGH RISK ASSIGNMENTS BECAUSE OF MY SOCIETAL NON-FUNCTIONAL-ITY.
NOTED. CONTINUE.
LAST MONTH I WAS ASKED BY SPECIAL SECTION IF I WOULD BE WILLING TO HAVE A FETISH MOD INSTALLED AND BE 'ACQUIRED' BY THE TRAFFICKING CIRCLE.
KNOWING OF HIS INABILITY TO GRASP THE CONCEPT THAT HIS PARTNER *MIGHT* BE CAPABLE OF OPERATING INDEPENDENTLY, SPECIAL SECTION ASSIGNED FIELD AGENT LARGO AS MY BACKUP AND EMERGENCY EXTRACTION TEAM.
WANNA SEE WHAT IT CAN DO?
NO.
I BELIEVE THIS WAS TO ENSURE THAT HE WOULD AT LEAST BE USING **MRED** SANCTIONED EQUIPMENT AND NOT HIS 'SPECIAL STUFF'.
FETISH MODS USUALLY INCLUDE FETISH-SPECIFIC, USER ADJUSTABLE BEHAVIOR AND PERSONAL-ITY MODIFIERS.
THE FET-MOD I RECEIVED USES THIS FUNCTIONALITY TO INTERDICT AND NULLIFY THE EFFECTS OF ANY OTHER BEHAVIOR MODIFICATIONS OR PLUG-INS THEY MIGHT TRY TO INSTALL.
EH??
I SAID I WANTED A KITTY EAR MOD!
YOU GOT ANGEL WINGS. IT'S WHAT I HAD.
AFTER BEING 'ACQUIRED' BY THE CIRCLE I RECONNED THE OPERATION AS BEST I COULD.
THE GIRLS WERE NOT ALL KEPT IN ONE PLACE, BUT I SOON REALIZED THEIR NUMBER WAS GREATER THAN ORIGINALLY THOUGHT.
MOST TRANSACTIONS SEEMED TO BE ON A "BY APPOINTMENT" BASIS WITH AN OPTIONAL "TRY BEFORE BUY" PREVIEW.
I NOTED IN MY REPORT THAT I HAD THREE CUSTOMERS DIE UNEXPECTEDLY PRIOR TO THEIR SCHEDULED PREVIEWS, PROBABLY DUE TO OUR LOCATION IN A HIGH-CRIME AREA.

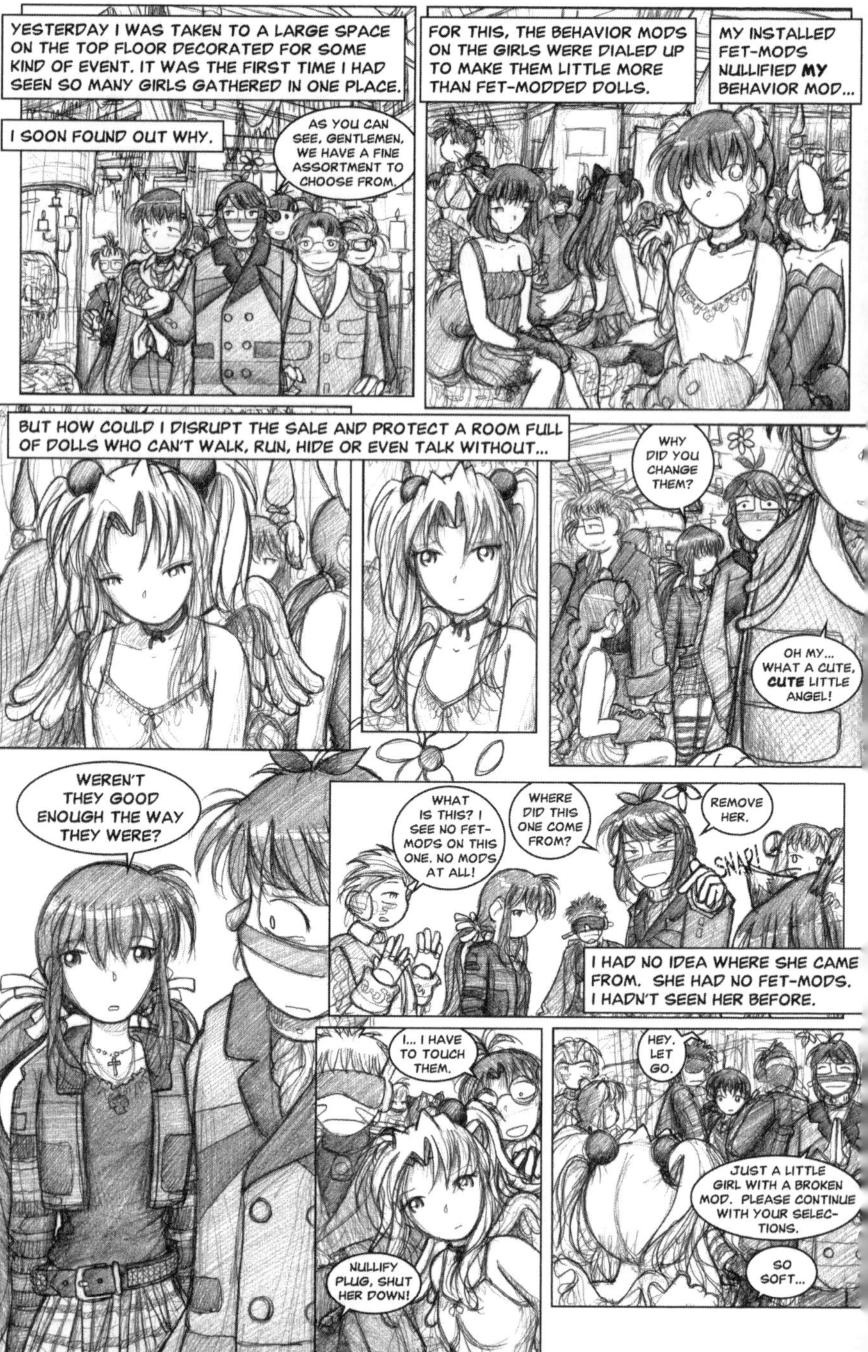
YESTERDAY I WAS TAKEN TO A LARGE SPACE ON THE TOP FLOOR DECORATED FOR SOME KIND OF EVENT. IT WAS THE FIRST TIME I HAD SEEN SO MANY GIRLS GATHERED IN ONE PLACE.
I SOON FOUND OUT WHY.
AS YOU CAN SEE, GENTLEMEN, WE HAVE A FINE ASSORTMENT TO CHOOSE FROM.
FOR THIS, THE BEHAVIOR MODS ON THE GIRLS WERE DIALED UP TO MAKE THEM LITTLE MORE THAN FET-MODDED DOLLS.
MY INSTALLED FET-MODS NULLIFIED **MY** BEHAVIOR MOD...
BUT HOW COULD I DISRUPT THE SALE AND PROTECT A ROOM FULL OF DOLLS WHO CAN'T WALK, RUN, HIDE OR EVEN TALK WITHOUT...
WHY DID YOU CHANGE THEM?
OH MY... WHAT A CUTE, **CUTE** LITTLE ANGEL!
WEREN'T THEY GOOD ENOUGH THE WAY THEY WERE?
WHAT IS THIS? I SEE NO FET-MODS ON THIS ONE. NO MODS AT ALL!
WHERE DID THIS ONE COME FROM?
REMOVE HER.
SNAP!
I HAD NO IDEA WHERE SHE CAME FROM. SHE HAD NO FET-MODS. I HADN'T SEEN HER BEFORE.
I... I HAVE TO TOUCH THEM.
NULLIFY PLUG, SHUT HER DOWN!
HEY. LET GO.
JUST A LITTLE GIRL WITH A BROKEN MOD. PLEASE CONTINUE WITH YOUR SELECTIONS.
SO SOFT...

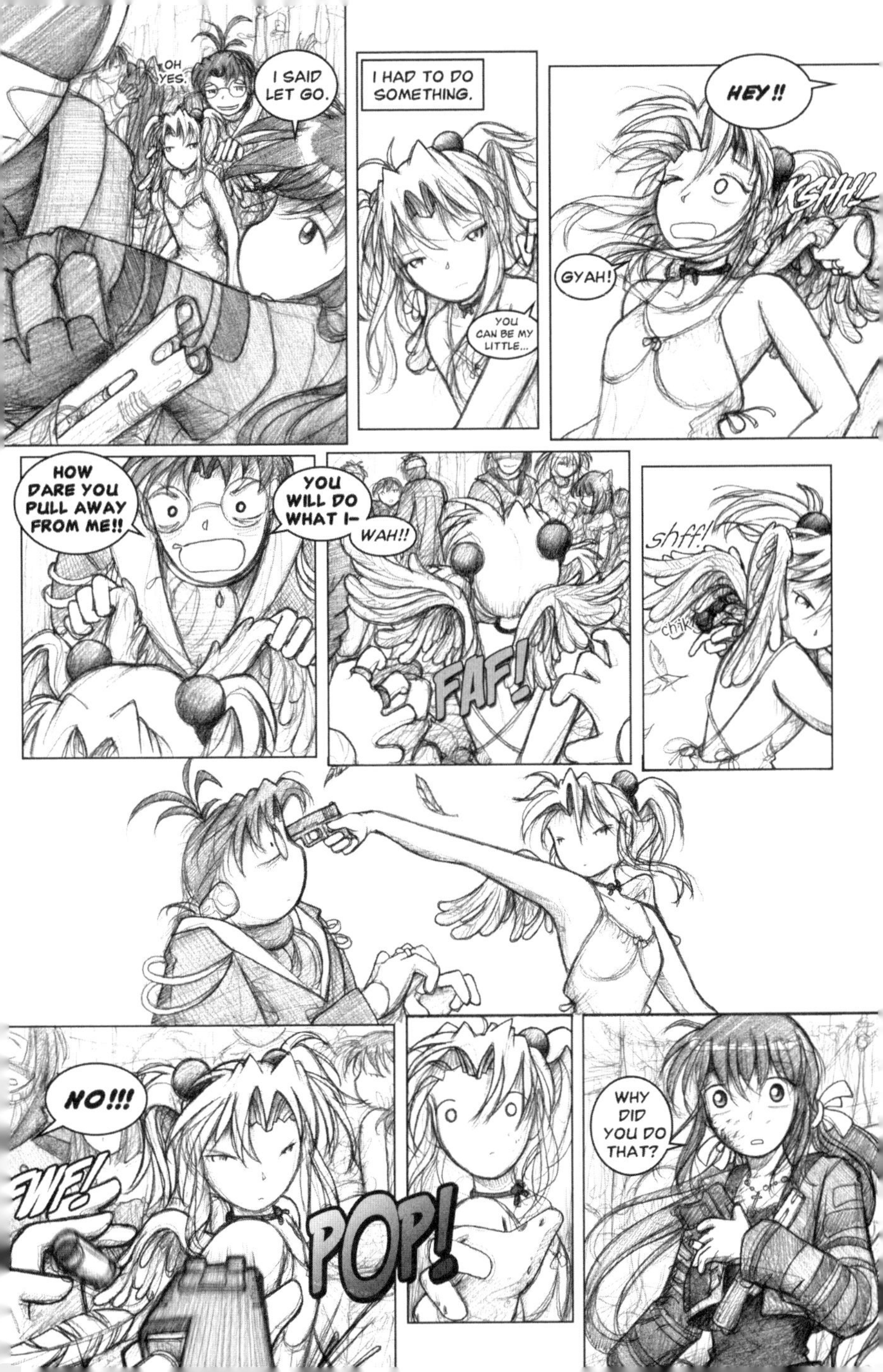
OH YES.
I SAID LET GO.
I HAD TO DO SOMETHING.
YOU CAN BE MY LITTLE...
HEY!!
KSHH!
GYAH!
HOW DARE YOU PULL AWAY FROM ME!!
YOU WILL DO WHAT I-
WAH!!
FAF!
shff!
NO!!!
FWF!
POP!
WHY DID YOU DO THAT?

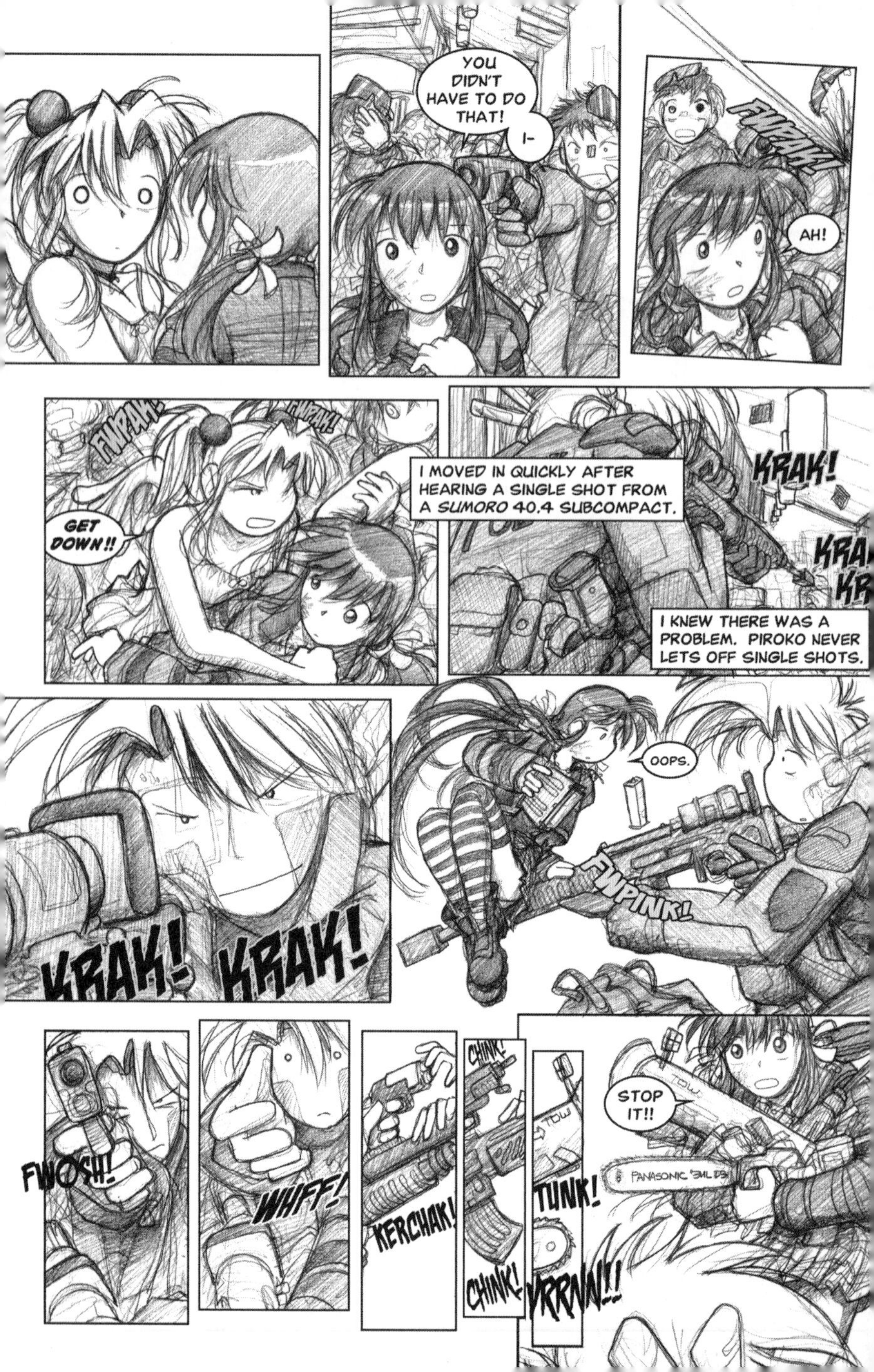
YOU DIDN'T HAVE TO DO THAT!
I-
FWPAK!
AH!
FWPAK!
FWPAK!
GET DOWN!!
I MOVED IN QUICKLY AFTER HEARING A SINGLE SHOT FROM A *SUMORO 40.4* SUBCOMPACT.
KRAK!
I KNEW THERE WAS A PROBLEM. PIROKO NEVER LETS OFF SINGLE SHOTS.
KRAK! KRAK!
OOPS.
FWPINK!
FWOSH!
WHIFF!
KERCHAK!
CHINK!
CHINK!
TUNK!
VRRNN!!
STOP IT!!

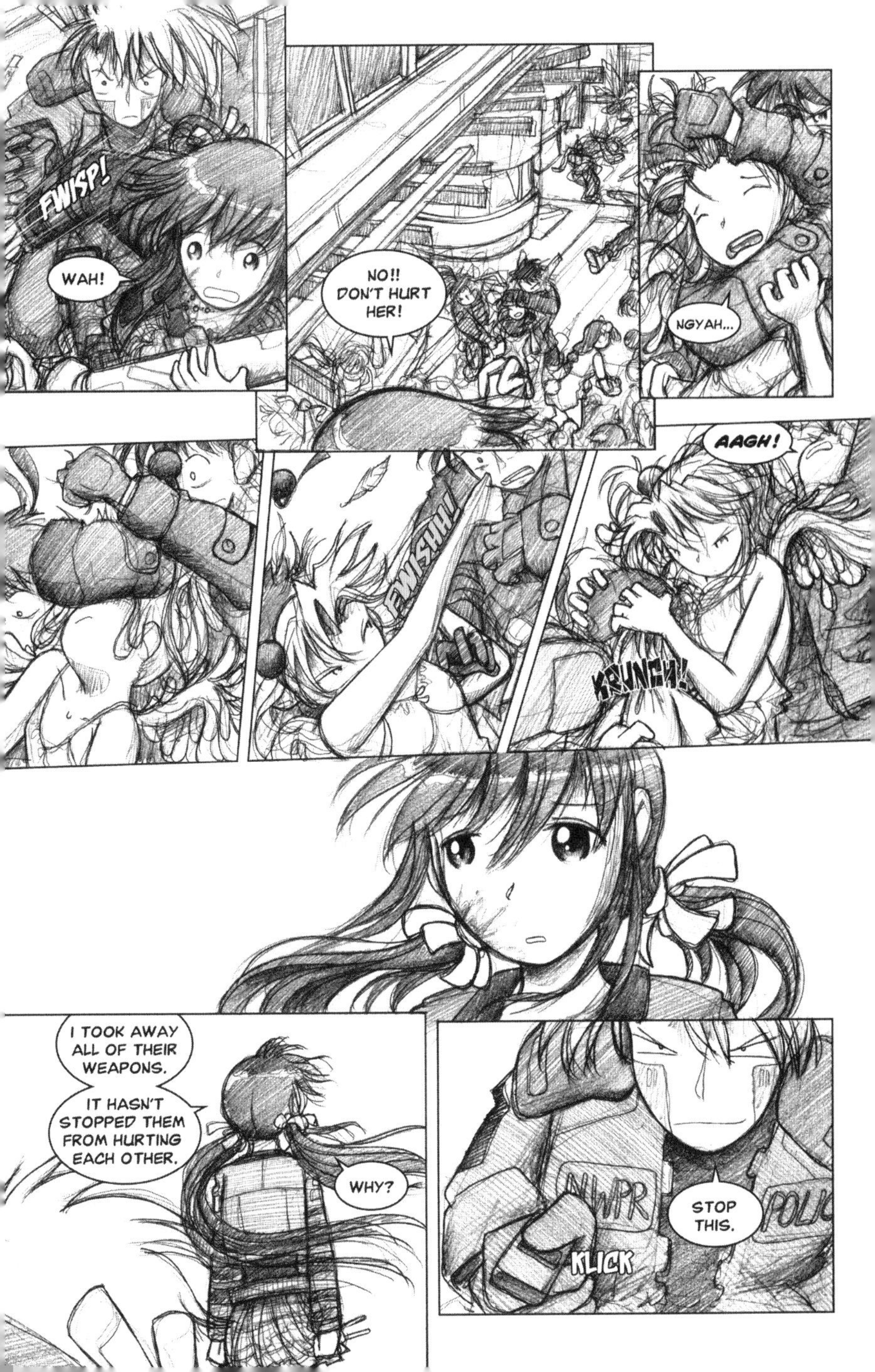
FWISP!
WAH!
NO!! DON'T HURT HER!
NGYAH...
FWISHH!
AAGH!
KRUNCH!
I TOOK AWAY ALL OF THEIR WEAPONS.
IT HASN'T STOPPED THEM FROM HURTING EACH OTHER.
WHY?
NWPR
POLIC
STOP THIS.
KLICK

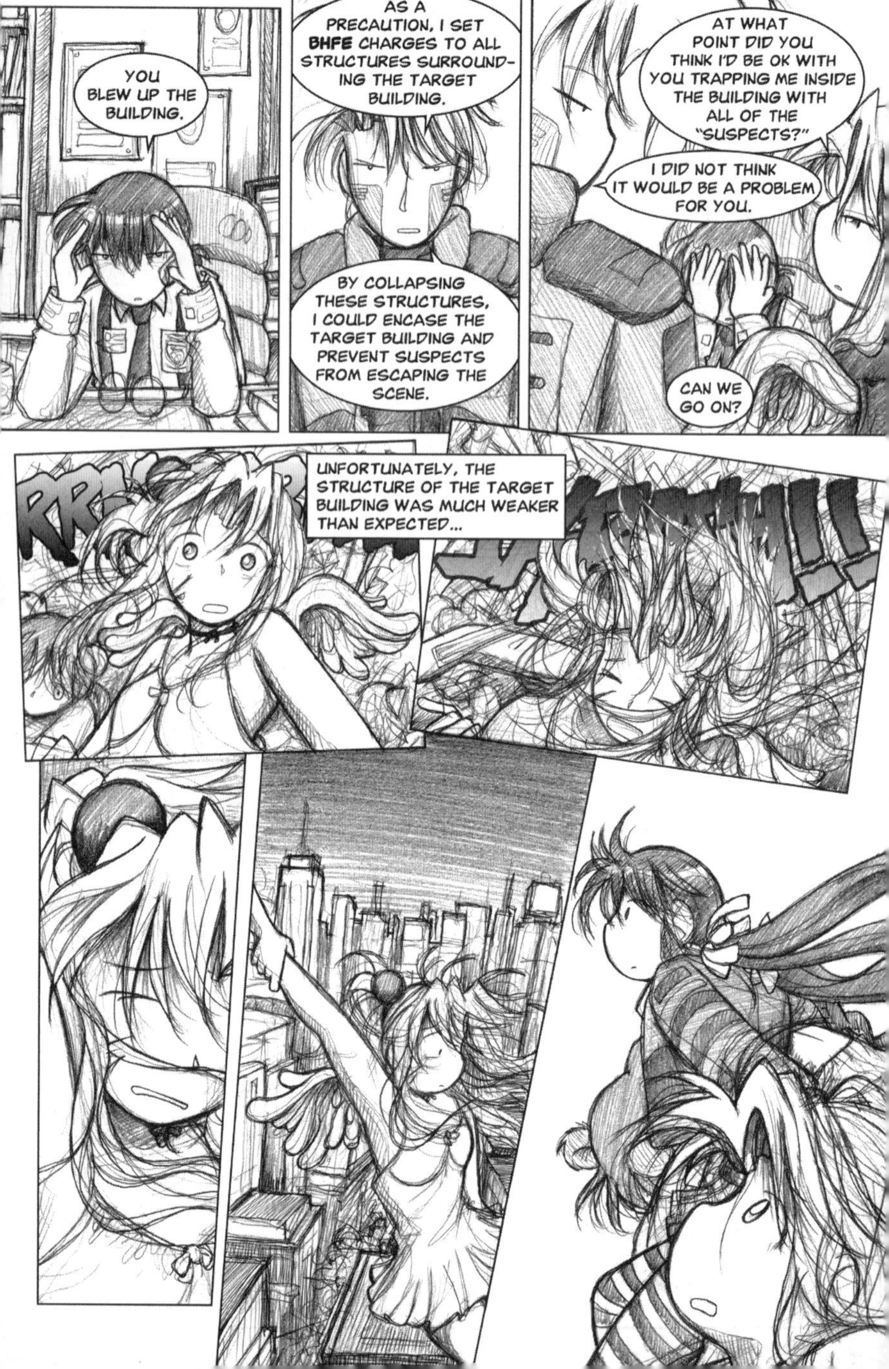
YOU BLEW UP THE BUILDING.
AS A PRECAUTION, I SET BHFE CHARGES TO ALL STRUCTURES SURROUNDING THE TARGET BUILDING.
BY COLLAPSING THESE STRUCTURES, I COULD ENCASE THE TARGET BUILDING AND PREVENT SUSPECTS FROM ESCAPING THE SCENE.
AT WHAT POINT DID YOU THINK I'D BE OK WITH YOU TRAPPING ME INSIDE THE BUILDING WITH ALL OF THE "SUSPECTS?"
I DID NOT THINK IT WOULD BE A PROBLEM FOR YOU.
CAN WE GO ON?
UNFORTUNATELY, THE STRUCTURE OF THE TARGET BUILDING WAS MUCH WEAKER THAN EXPECTED...

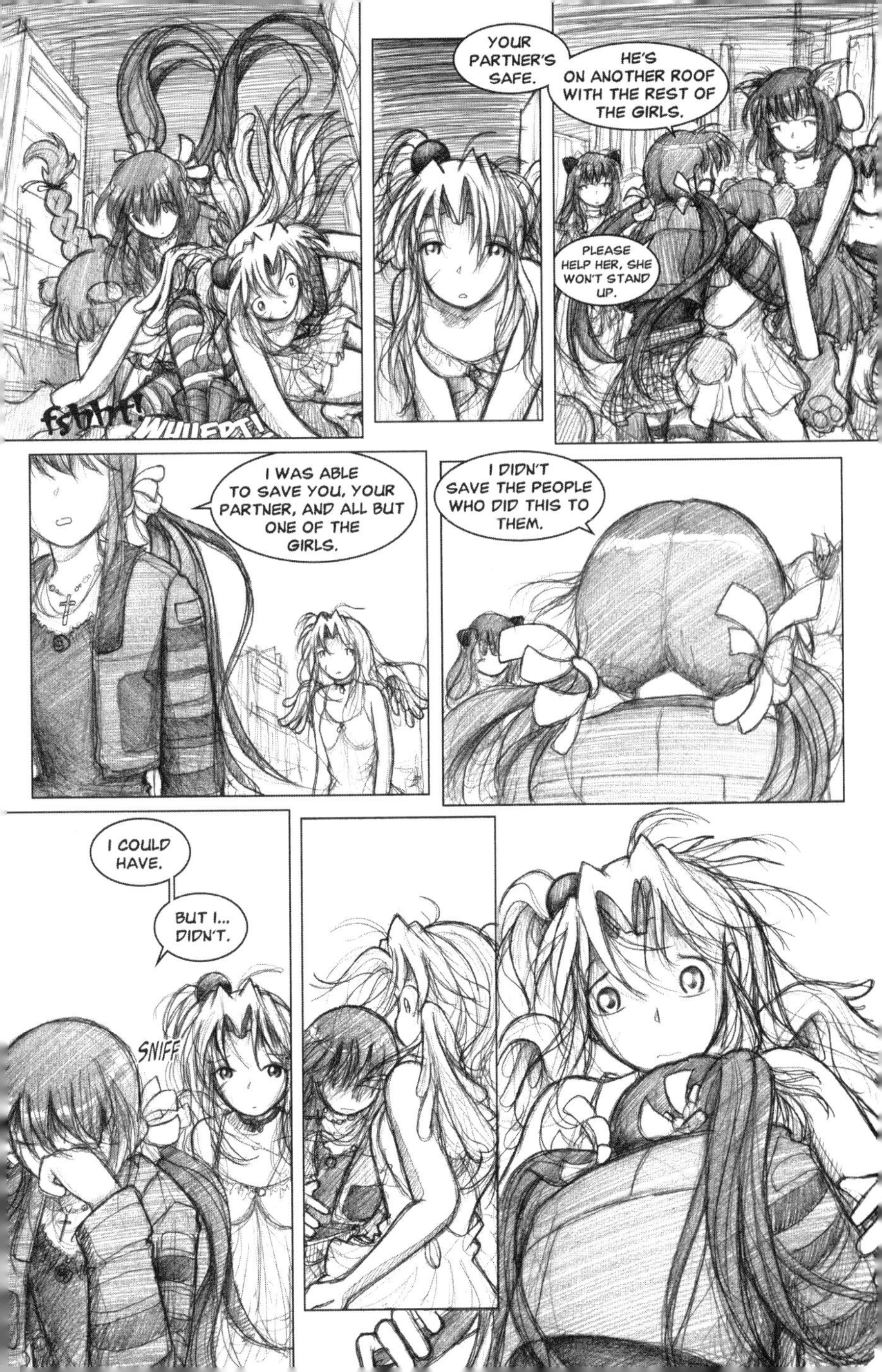
fsblrt!
YOUR PARTNER'S SAFE.
HE'S ON ANOTHER ROOF WITH THE REST OF THE GIRLS.
PLEASE HELP HER, SHE WON'T STAND UP.
I WAS ABLE TO SAVE YOU, YOUR PARTNER, AND ALL BUT ONE OF THE GIRLS.
I DIDN'T SAVE THE PEOPLE WHO DID THIS TO THEM.
I COULD HAVE.
BUT I... DIDN'T.
SNIFF

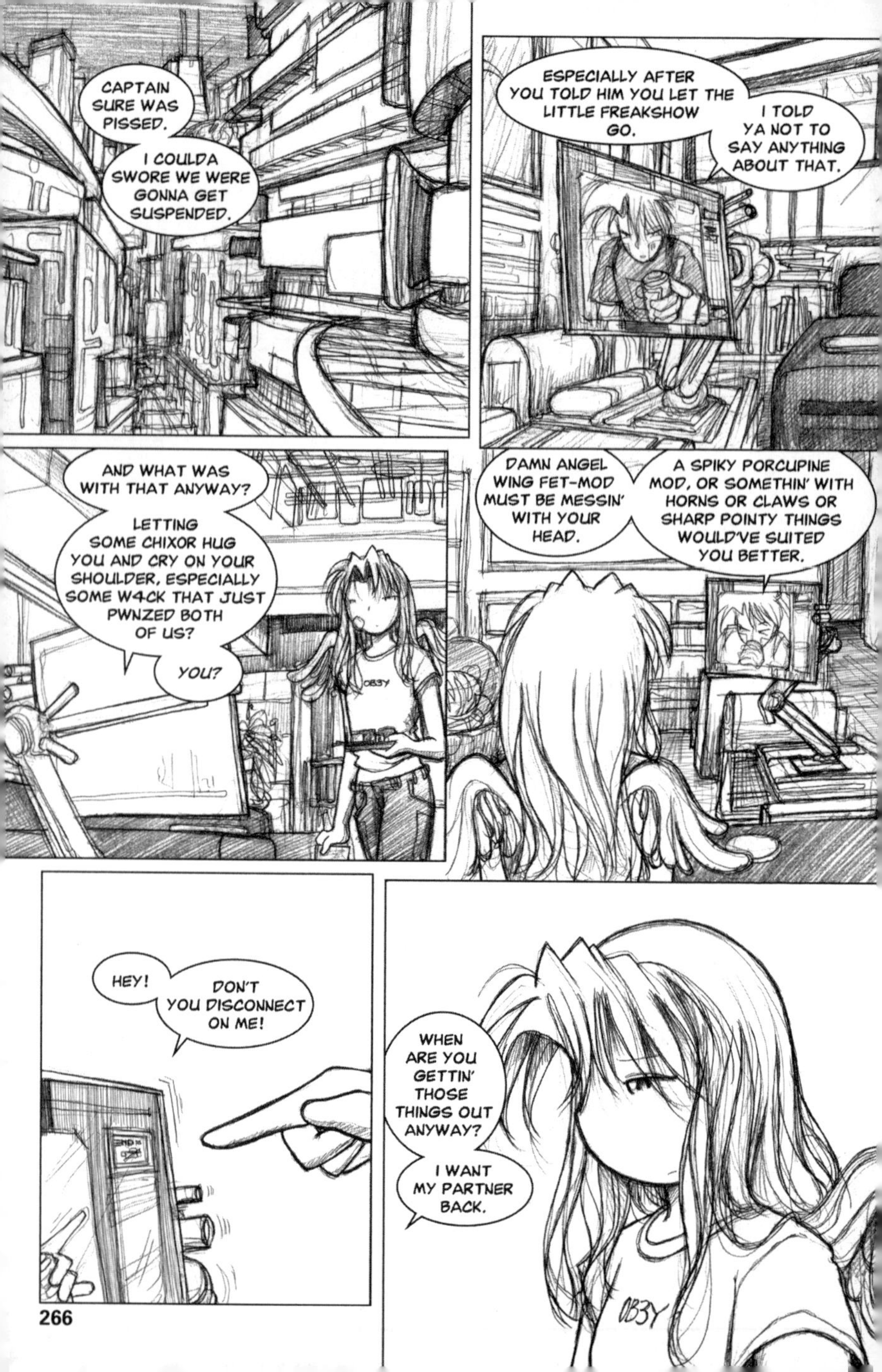
CAPTAIN SURE WAS PISSED.
I COULDA SWORE WE WERE GONNA GET SUSPENDED.
ESPECIALLY AFTER YOU TOLD HIM YOU LET THE LITTLE FREAKSHOW GO.
I TOLD YA NOT TO SAY ANYTHING ABOUT THAT.
AND WHAT WAS WITH THAT ANYWAY?
LETTING SOME CHIXOR HUG YOU AND CRY ON YOUR SHOULDER, ESPECIALLY SOME W4CK THAT JUST PWNZED BOTH OF US?
YOU?
OB3Y
DAMN ANGEL WING FET-MOD MUST BE MESSIN' WITH YOUR HEAD.
A SPIKY PORCUPINE MOD, OR SOMETHIN' WITH HORNS OR CLAWS OR SHARP POINTY THINGS WOULD'VE SUITED YOU BETTER.
HEY!
DON'T YOU DISCONNECT ON ME!
WHEN ARE YOU GETTIN' THOSE THINGS OUT ANYWAY?
I WANT MY PARTNER BACK.
OB3Y

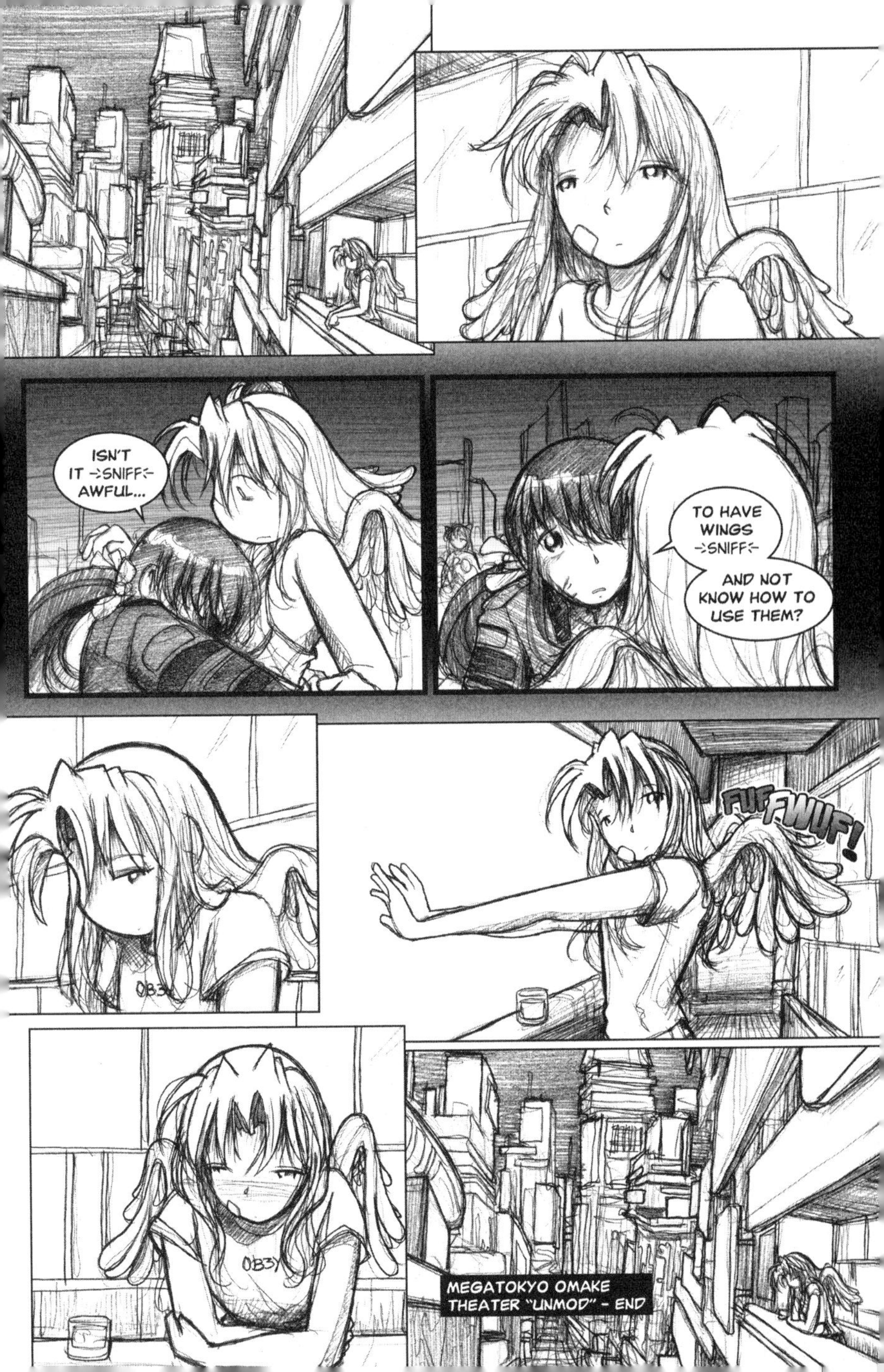
ISN'T IT -SNIFF- AWFUL...
TO HAVE WINGS -SNIFF-
AND NOT KNOW HOW TO USE THEM?
OB3Y
FUFFWUF!
OB3Y
MEGATOKYO OMAKE THEATER "UNMOD" - END

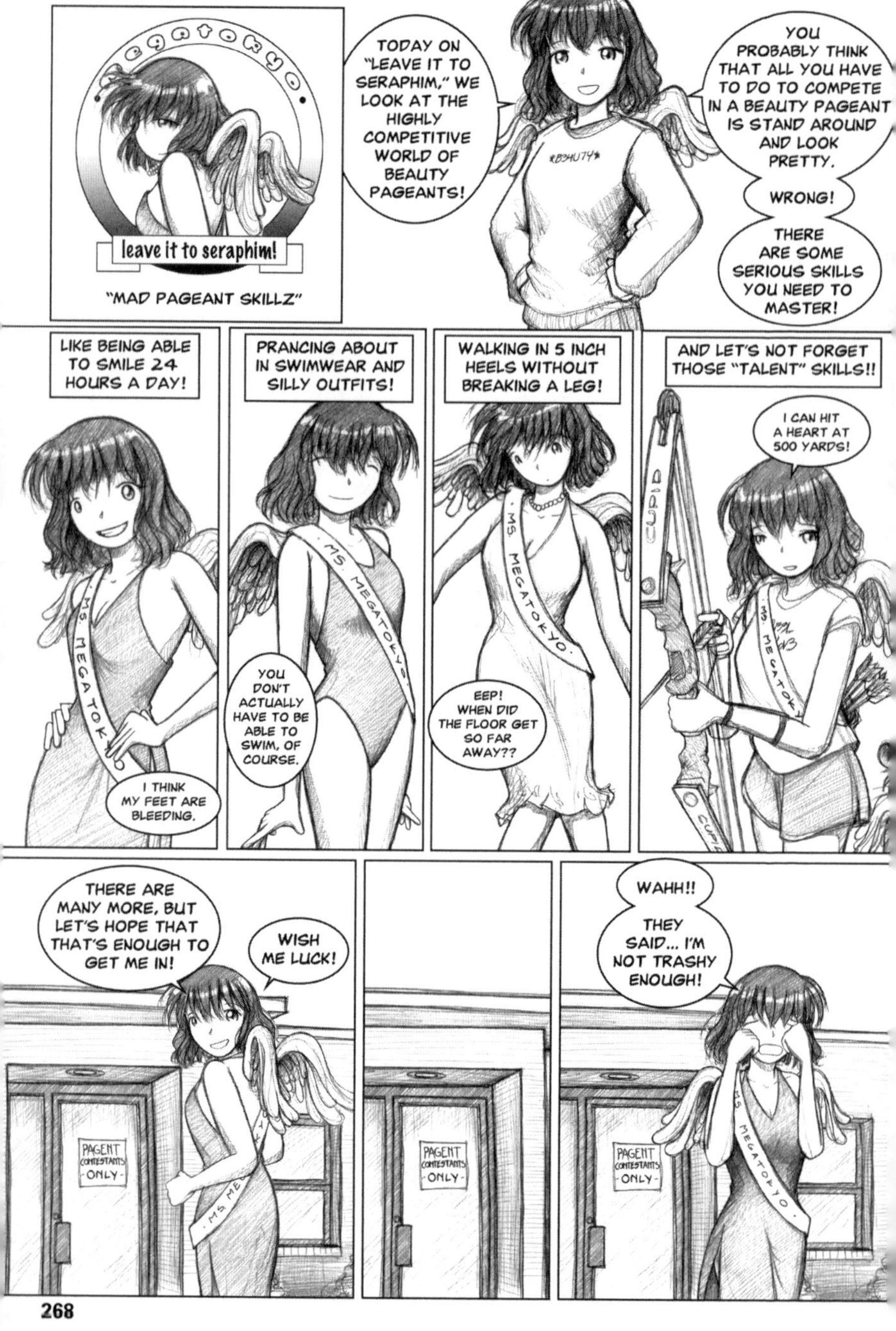
megatokyo
leave it to seraphim!
"MAD PAGEANT SKILLZ"
TODAY ON "LEAVE IT TO SERAPHIM," WE LOOK AT THE HIGHLY COMPETITIVE WORLD OF BEAUTY PAGEANTS!
YOU PROBABLY THINK THAT ALL YOU HAVE TO DO TO COMPETE IN A BEAUTY PAGEANT IS STAND AROUND AND LOOK PRETTY.
WRONG!
THERE ARE SOME SERIOUS SKILLS YOU NEED TO MASTER!
LIKE BEING ABLE TO SMILE 24 HOURS A DAY!
I THINK MY FEET ARE BLEEDING.
PRANCING ABOUT IN SWIMWEAR AND SILLY OUTFITS!
MS. MEGATOKYO
YOU DON'T ACTUALLY HAVE TO BE ABLE TO SWIM, OF COURSE.
WALKING IN 5 INCH HEELS WITHOUT BREAKING A LEG!
MS. MEGATOKYO
EEP! WHEN DID THE FLOOR GET SO FAR AWAY??
AND LET'S NOT FORGET THOSE "TALENT" SKILLS!!
I CAN HIT A HEART AT 500 YARDS!
CUPID
THERE ARE MANY MORE, BUT LET'S HOPE THAT THAT'S ENOUGH TO GET ME IN!
WISH ME LUCK!
PAGENT CONTESTANTS -ONLY-
PAGENT CONTESTANTS -ONLY-
WAHH!!
THEY SAID... I'M NOT TRASHY ENOUGH!
PAGENT CONTESTANTS -ONLY-
MS. MEGATOKYO

Megatokyo - Volume 6 index

This book contains strips from Chapter 9, Chapter 10 and includes extra material produced between March 2007 and March 2010. For more information and more comics, visit www.megatokyo.com

Page No.	Strip Title	Date	Online Strip ID
93	quite the character	2008-02-18	1089
94	we need no command	2008-02-20	1090
95	suddenly really grouchy	2008-02-22	1091
96	not good	2008-02-25	1092
97	bad 3nd	2008-02-29	1093
98	what else?	2008-03-04	1094
99	i fsck'd up	2008-03-05	1095
100	that idol priestess thing	2008-03-07	1096
101	never been very convincing	2008-03-10	1097
102	we got him	2008-03-13	1098
103	Piro Protagonist	2008-03-15	1099
104	player one wins	2008-03-17	1100
105	what's wrong with j00?	2008-03-19	1101
106	mocking concern	2008-03-21	1102
107	a good lover	2008-03-27	1104
108	thinking	2008-03-29	1105
109	heavi3z	2008-03-31	1106
110	what is she doing?	2008-04-02	1107
111	potentially catastrophic grade	2008-04-08	1108
112	panic permits	2008-04-10	1109
113	how many?	2008-04-15	1110
114	no cure	2008-04-16	1111
115	a new kind of monster	2008-04-21	1112
116	my favorite episode	2008-04-23	1113
117	end of the world	2008-04-28	1114
118	I think it's time	2008-04-30	1115
119	about to get worse	2008-05-02	1116
120	should we?	2008-05-05	1117
121	not what we wanted	2008-05-07	1118
122	a rare thing these days	2008-05-11	1119
123	i wanted	2008-05-16	1121
124	falling back into character	2008-05-19	1122
125	bye bye	2008-05-21	1123
126	sad little dead grrl	2008-05-23	1124
127	(2 page spread)	~	~
128	something very sad	2008-05-26	1125

Meanwhile...The Real Ping

Page No.	Strip Title	Date	Online Strip ID
129	I feel so fake	05/30/07	1006
130	Not Working -&- not working at all	06/01/07	1007[08]
131	afraid -&- is that bad?	06/06/07	1009[10]
132	real brains -&- it real	06/11/07	1011[12]
133	really real -&- overdoing it	06/15/07	1013[14]
134	DDD (Dead Dom Day)	~	(new)

"Full Megatokyo Panic" Omake

Page No.	Strip Title	Date	Online Strip ID
135	Full Megatokyo Panic - Clan'd War3z	2008-05-28	1126
136	FMP: evidence	2008-06-02	1127
137	FMP: Chain Combo	2008-06-05	1128
138	FMP: target	2008-06-13	1130
139	FMP: suspicious activity	2008-06-16	1131
140	FMP: right	2008-06-19	1132
141	FMP: overcompensation	2008-06-23	1134
142	FMP: Blush Response	2008-06-26	1135
143	FMP: emotive	2008-06-30	1136
144	FMP: avoidance	2008-07-02	1137
145	FMP: cold carry	2008-07-04	1138
146	FMP: hitting	2008-07-09	1139
147	unrealistic scenario	2008-07-11	1140

Chapter 10 - "A.F.K."

Page No.	Strip Title	Date	Online Strip ID
148	Chapter 10: A.F.K.	2008-07-14	1141
149	I dream you	2008-07-16	1142
150	being able to see	2008-07-24	1144
151	weighted aggregate	2008-08-07	1148
152	distracting presence	2008-08-11	1149
153	been really happy	2008-08-18	1150
154	way too much	2008-08-25	1151
155	really worried	2008-08-27	1152
156	your very bad storm place	2008-09-03	1153
157	debugging	2008-09-06	1154
158	space & time	2008-09-16	1156
159	role call	2008-09-19	1157
160	no more, no less.	2008-09-22	1158
161	just a little	2008-09-26	1159
162	such a sad idea for an interface	2008-09-29	1160
163	9 days	2008-10-06	1162
164	none of your business	2008-10-13	1163
165	solutions? h4xorz? wisdom?	2008-10-17	1164
166	accurate representation	2008-10-21	1165
167	grrl transl33tor	2008-10-27	1167
168	Are you ok, Ibara-san?	2008-10-31	1168
169	Look both ways	2008-11-09	1169
170	Bad Zilla!	2008-11-14	1170
171	another one	2008-11-18	1171
172	ad hoc mode	2008-11-21	1172
173	real love	2008-11-24	1173
174	nothing else	2008-11-26	1174
175	not part of any game	2008-12-10	1175
176	romantic	2008-12-22	1176
177	let me check	2009-01-05	1178
178	my friend's phone	2009-01-09	1179
179	The exact same crap	2009-01-14	1180
180	the Asako Option	2009-01-20	1181
181	public admirer	2009-01-23	1182

Page No.	Strip Title	Date	Online Strip ID
182	but he doesn't	2009-01-28	1183
183	Magical Grrl Potential Future Visualization Attack!	2009-02-04	1185
184	it's spooky	2009-02-10	1187
185	pantsutagging	2009-02-14	1188
186	information requests	2009-03-04	1190
187	trouble	2009-03-07	1191
188	less hope this time	2009-03-12	1193
189	t3h aw3som3 stuff	2009-03-23	1195
190	the end of the world	2009-03-25	1196
191	have some more	2009-03-29	1197
192	imagine t3h horror	2009-04-06	1198
193	search results	2009-04-13	1199
194	patterns in your data movements	2009-04-17	1200
195	nothing weird	2009-04-20	1201
196	punk'd	2009-04-24	1202
197	personal, private ones	2009-04-27	1203
198	the only secure computer is...	2009-05-01	1204
199	let the poor thing rest	2009-05-06	1205
200	a different kind of stupid	2009-05-11	1206
201	stupid battery	2009-05-15	1207
202	shift and settle	2009-05-20	1208
203	how do i ask this?	2009-05-26	1209
204	near-death hunting	2009-05-29	1210
205	a loss of will	2009-06-02	1211
206	The gender neutrality of text	2009-06-09	1212
207	there is still the wine	2009-06-16	1213
208	long enough to hide behind	2009-06-19	1214
209	stupid and harsh	2009-06-24	1215
210	she never was	2009-06-27	1216
211	not my best work	2009-06-30	1217
212	my original idea	2009-07-07	1218
213	clubbing may be required	2009-07-11	1219
214	not making me feel better	2009-07-15	1220
215	too much	2009-07-20	1221
216	onboard weapon systems	2009-07-26	1222
217	wish you were here	2009-07-31	1223
218	Dangerous and Hazardous Things	2009-08-07	1224
219	still got it	2009-08-20	1226
220	she interests me greatly	2009-08-13	1225
221	a greatest fear	2009-08-25	1227
222	she has passed from this world	2009-09-02	1228
223	watch your step	2009-09-08	1229
224	there isn't always a happy ending	2009-09-12	1230
225	something i want to do	2009-09-16	1231
226	inappropriate interest	2009-09-22	1232
227	txt 2 j00r h3d	2009-09-30	1234
228	don't look	2009-10-08	1235
229	are any of your girls happy?	2009-10-13	1236
230	it's not right!	2009-10-17	1237
231	you could just hold on really, really tight	2009-10-20	1238
232	frameworks	2009-10-28	1239
233	the source	2009-11-07	1240
234	t3h ph33r before t3h kill	2009-11-11	1241
235	memory leak	2009-11-18	1242
236	not something we can change	2009-11-23	1243
237	some things are better left in the dark	2009-12-07	1245
238	glitching	2009-12-16	1247
239	noclip	2010-01-01	1248
240	walkthrough	2010-01-05	1249
241	what has been logged cannot be unlogged	2010-01-09	1250
242	not something you'd understand	2010-01-15	1251
243	eye of the perception vortex	2010-01-21	1252
244	shedding density	2010-01-26	1253
245	experience points	2010-02-03	1254
246	replay value	2010-02-09	1255
247	bursting at the seams	2010-02-17	1256
248	breech explosion	2010-02-20	1257
249	bak	2010-02-28	1258
250	DDOS	2010-03-05	1259
251	Haptic feedback	2010-03-13	1260
252	G4M3.0VR	2010-03-20	1261
253	Rickb00ted	2010-03-30	1262
254	Code 401	2010-04-18	1264
255	primal	2010-04-21	1265
256	princesses sure are a lot of trouble	2010-04-25	1266
257	kimochi warui	2010-04-29	1267
	"unMod" Omake		
258	[Omake : unMod] 01 - start talking	2007-03-08	973
259	[Omake : unMod] 01.5 - scheduled previews	2010-05-04	1268
260	[Omake : unMod] 02 - weren't they good enough?	2007-03-12	974
261	[Omake : unMod] 03 - why did you do that?	2007-03-15	975
262	[Omake : unMod] 04 - stop it!	2007-03-17	976
263	[Omake : unMod] 05 - stop this!	2007-03-19	977
264	[Omake : unMod] 06 - weaker than expected	2007-03-21	978
265	[Omake : unMod] 07 - i could have...	2007-03-23	979
266	[Omake : unMod] 08 - sharp pointy things	2007-03-26	980
267	[Omake : unMod] 09 - ignorance of flight	2007-03-28	981
	One Shot Episodes		
268	Seraphim Check - L33t Pageant Skillz	2007-04-09	986

▶STOP!◀

This is the back of the book!

What? Y'think this book is gonna make more sense backwards or someth'n? It's English y'goof, so turn 'er over and read 'er right.

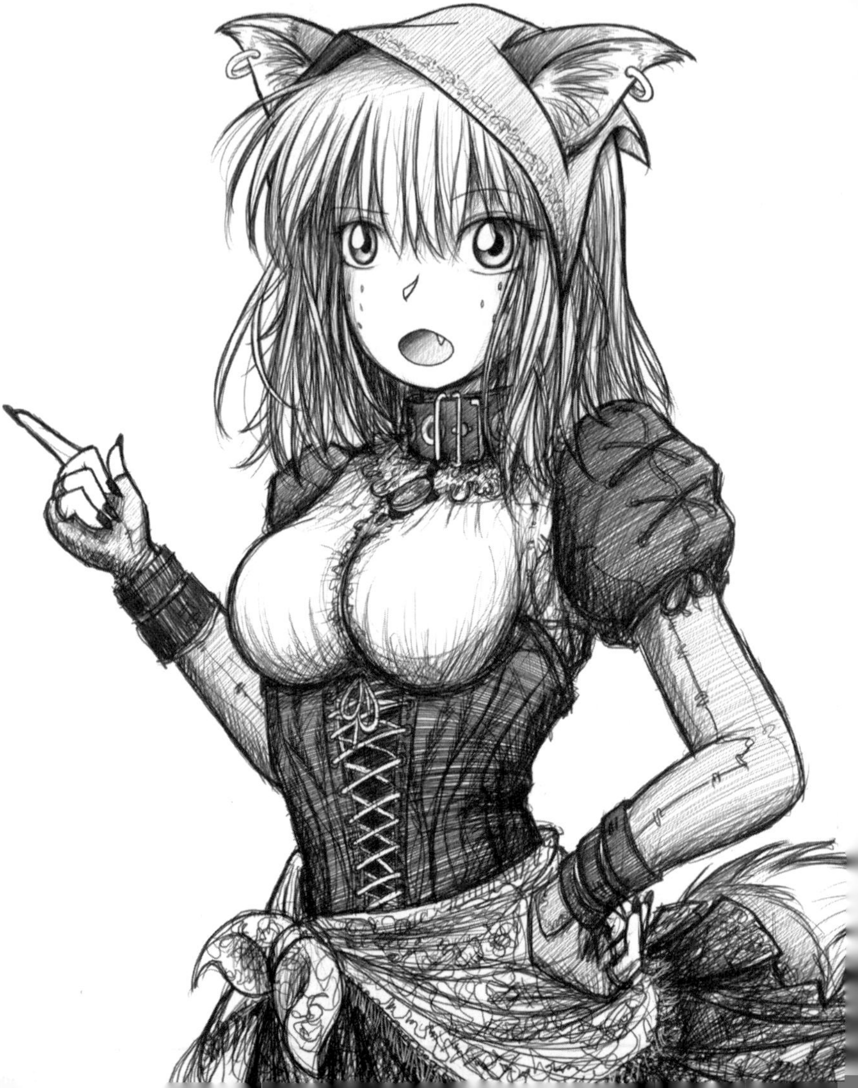